P9-CIU-519

Cat Owner's Home
VETERINARY
Handbook

COUNTY LIBRARY DISCARD TILLAMOOK, ORE.

This book is not intended as a substitute for the medical advice of veterinarians. Readers should regularly consult a veterinarian in matters relating to their cat's health, and particularly with respect to any symptoms that may require medical attention.

In writing this book, we have described the signs and symptoms that will lead you to a preliminary idea of what is happening with your cat, so you can weigh the severity of the problem. Knowing when to call your veterinarian is very important. Delays can be dangerous.

At the same time, we have sought to provide guidance for the acute or emergency situations that you must handle on your own until you can get your cat to a veterinarian. Life-saving procedures such as artificial respiration and heart massage, and what to do in the event of poisonings, obstetrical problems, and other emergencies, are explained step by step.

But a veterinary handbook is not a substitute for professional care. Advice from a book can never be as helpful or as safe as actual medical advice. No text can replace the interview and the hands-on examination that enable a veterinarian to make a speedy and accurate diagnosis.

However, the knowledge provided in this book will enable you to more effectively cooperate and better understand your interactions with your veterinarian. You'll be more alert to the signs of health problems and better able to describe them. You'll know more about basic care for your cat, and you'll be prepared in an emergency. Together, you and your veterinarian make a great health team for your cat!

Cat Owner's Home
VETERINARY
Handbook

Third Edition

Debra M. Eldredge, DVM
Delbert G. Carlson, DVM
Liisa D. Carlson, DVM
James M. Giffin, MD

Edited by Beth Adelman

Wiley Publishing, Inc.

Copyright © 2008 by Delbert Carlson, DVM, and James M. Giffin, MD. All rights reserved.

Howell Book House
Published by Wiley Publishing, Inc., Hoboken, New Jersey

No part of this publication may be reproduced, stored in a retrieval system or transmitted in any form or by any means, electronic, mechanical, photocopying, recording, scanning or otherwise, except as permitted under Sections 107 or 108 of the 1976 United States Copyright Act, without either the prior written permission of the Publisher, or authorization through payment of the appropriate per-copy fee to the Copyright Clearance Center, 222 Rosewood Drive, Danvers, MA 01923, (978) 750-8400, fax (978) 646-8600, or on the web at www.copyright.com. Requests to the Publisher for permission should be addressed to the Legal Department, Wiley Publishing, Inc., 10475 Crosspoint Blvd., Indianapolis, IN 46256, (317) 572-3447, fax (317) 572-4355, or online at http://www.wiley.com/go/permissions.

Wiley, the Wiley Publishing logo, Howell Book House, and related trademarks are trademarks or registered trademarks of John Wiley & Sons, Inc. and/or its affiliates. All other trademarks are the property of their respective owners. Wiley Publishing, Inc. is not associated with any product or vendor mentioned in this book.

The publisher and the author make no representations or warranties with respect to the accuracy or completeness of the contents of this work and specifically disclaim all warranties, including without limitation warranties of fitness for a particular purpose. No warranty may be created or extended by sales or promotional materials. The advice and strategies contained herein may not be suitable for every situation. This work is sold with the understanding that the publisher is not engaged in rendering legal, accounting, or other professional services. If professional assistance is required, the services of a competent professional person should be sought. Neither the publisher nor the author shall be liable for damages arising here from. The fact that an organization or Website is referred to in this work as a citation and/or a potential source of further information does not mean that the author or the publisher endorses the information the organization or Website may provide or recommendations it may make. Further, readers should be aware that Internet Websites listed in this work may have changed or disappeared between when this work was written and when it is read.

For general information on our other products and services or to obtain technical support, please contact our Customer Care Department within the U.S. at (800) 762-2974, outside the U.S. at (317) 572-3993 or fax (317) 572-4002.

Wiley also publishes its books in a variety of electronic formats. Some content that appears in print may not be available in electronic books. For more information about Wiley products, please visit our web site at www.wiley.com.

Library of Congress Cataloging-in-Publication Data:
Cat owner's home veterinary handbook / Debra M. Eldredge ... [et al.] ; edited by Beth Adelman. — 3rd ed.
    p. cm.
    Rev. ed. of: Cat owner's home veterinary handbook / Delbert G. Carlson, James M. Giffin. 2nd ed. ©1995.
    Includes index.
    ISBN-13: 978-0-470-09530-0
    ISBN-10: 0-470-09530-X
    1. Cats—Diseases—Handbooks, manuals, etc. I. Eldredge, Debra. II. Adelman, Beth. III. Carlson, Delbert G. Cat owner's home veterinary handbook.
    SF985.C29 2007
    636.8'089—dc22
                            2007035470

Printed in the United States of America

10 9 8 7 6 5 4 3

Third Edition

Cover design by José Almaguer
Wiley Bicentennial Logo: Richard J. Pacifico
Book production by Wiley Publishing, Inc. Composition Services

The smallest feline is a masterpiece.
—Leonardo da Vinci

FINDING IT QUICKLY

A special **Index of Signs and Symptoms** is on the inside of the front cover for fast referral. Consult this index if your cat exhibits any unexplained behavior. It will help you identify the problem.

The detailed **Contents** outlines the organs and body systems that are the sites of disease. If you can locate the problem anatomically, look here first.

The general **Index** begins on page 596 and gives you a comprehensive guide to the book's medical information. Where a page number is in bold, it indicates more detailed coverage of the subject.

Cross-references note pertinent supplementary information.

A **Glossary** on page 576 defines medical terms used to best explain the subject or condition. Many of these words are now being used commonly among veterinarians and their clients. Glossary terms will usually be found in italics in the text. (Italics may also be used for emphasis.)

In memory of James R. Richards, DVM, director of the Cornell University Feline Health Center, president of the American Association of Feline Practitioners, director of the Dr. Louis J. Camuti Memorial Feline Consultation and Diagnostic Service, co-chair of the Vaccine-Associated Feline Sarcoma Task Force, author, educator, communicator, and a man who worked endlessly for better feline health and care.

He treated everyone as a personal friend and a respected colleague. He understood the importance of communicating what we know. Although he was much in the public eye, it was never about him and always about the cats. He inspired everyone who knew him. He was a friend of everyone who was a friend of cats.

There are some people whose passing makes even the angels weep.

July 19, 1948–April 24, 2007

ACKNOWLEDGMENTS

This book has been a team effort and a labor of love. Editor Beth Adelman has cracked the whip, but gently, and virtually coauthored this rewrite. Researcher Marcella Durand found obscure facts and neat photos. Technical editor Dr. Lorraine Jarboe added from her vast store of cat knowledge. Sophomore student Valerie Toukatly added artwork, as did the incomparable Wendy Christensen. Chris Stambaugh saved us with her technical expertise. Thanks to Roxanne Cerda, who pushed and prodded me into doing this. And thanks to my family, who have all dodged around piles of cat veterinary articles, books, and brochures throughout the house.

A special thanks to all the cats of my life—most especially my beloved Sam, who graced my life for 22 years. From my first cat, Fredericka the Freeloader, to my current orange guy, Firecracker (born on the Fourth of July), my cats have provided me with endless hours of entertainment and company. All of these cats—client cats, shelter cats, cats of friends, stray cats—have added to my enjoyment of life. Special love to Venus de Milo, my classic three-legged black beauty; Jenny, the feline ballerina and opera star; Tiger, who thought she was a dog; and C2, who loved me despite the fact that I was her veterinarian. Sharing space with another species is not always easy, but with a cat it is always interesting!

—*Debra M. Eldredge, DVM*

CONTENTS

INTRODUCTION

Cat Owner's Home Veterinary Handbook has been a familiar title on my bookshelf for more than two decades. It's the book I turn to, time and again, for definitive answers on feline health. My own cats have pawed at, sat on, and nibbled the corners of many of its pages.

I've owned both editions of this book, replacing my old one in 1995 with the latest volume. But I have been surprised to learn that many cat breeders, and several of my journalist colleagues, have both editions, going all the way back to 1983, because they just can't bear to part with them. I have participated in quite a few feline e-mail group discussions that include the phrase, "According to *Cat Owner's Home Vet . . .*" This is an old book with a long legacy—but also a new one that has been completely revamped and greatly expanded.

That's because in the past decade, much of what we know about feline medicine has changed. At one time, many veterinary treatments for cats were based on research that had been done on dogs. It was assumed cats were very similar—just small dogs, really—and would respond to similar treatments and medications.

In fact, nothing could be further from the truth. We now know that cats and dogs are as different, biologically speaking, as cats and people. And the research in veterinary medicine is finally catching up. Accordingly, this book is much longer than its predecessor (because we know so much more!) and has undergone some major changes.

You'll find the latest information here on vaccine protocols, flea, tick, and heartworm preventives, reading cat food labels, nutrition, joint supplements, treatments for cancer and kidney disease, and treatments for diabetes. Newly recognized heart, muscle, and dental diseases are discussed, as are new ways of understanding feline lower urinary tract disease, hip dysplasia, feline calicirvirus, and many other conditions. New drugs and surgical techniques are explained. Controversial subjects, such as vaccine-associated sarcoma and declawing, are covered. There are spectacular new anatomical drawings. And the entire section on feline behavior has been rewritten, based on new findings.

When the second edition was published in 1995, therapies using supplements, nutraceuticals, and holistic modalities such as acupuncture were largely untested. Now, for illnesses where holistic treatments have proven to be beneficial, they are listed under the *Treatments* section.

According to a 2006 study by Veterinary Pet Insurance Co., the top ten feline medical conditions for which their policyholders filed claims were:

1. Urinary tract infections
2. Stomach upsets
3. Kidney disease
4. Skin allergies
5. Respiratory infections
6. Diabetes
7. Ear infections
8. Colitis
9. Eye infections
10. Wound infections

You will also find all of those common feline health problems here—covered completely and comprehensively. And, whatever troubles your cat, you will find it described clearly and have a variety of treatment options to discuss with your veterinarian.

As an editor, it's always an honor to work on a book that is already a classic and will continue to be one. But editors are a rather compulsive breed, and I tend to look at every book I own very critically. I have spent more than a decade wishing I could make some changes in this one. At last, I have my chance. In this edition, you'll find an extensive glossary. The cross-references are easier to use, the index is expanded, there's a list of tables (and more of them!), there are more appendices, and overall, when you come home with your cat from the veterinarian's office full of questions, it's easier to find what you are looking for.

Beth Adelman
Editor

EMERGENCIES

Emergency care is just that—care applied to a potentially serious condition as soon as possible while you are trying to reach your veterinarian. One of the cardinal rules in dealing with any emergency is for *you* to remain calm. If you panic, you won't be thinking clearly and you will panic your cat. Take a deep breath, quietly reassure your cat, and then do what is necessary. Don't hesitate to ask for help and remember that your cat is relying on you.

Home Emergency Medical Kit

Container for equipment	Tweezers
Penlight	Scissors
Blanket	Grooming clippers
Rectal thermometer	Needle-nose pliers
Surgical gloves	K-Y lubricant or petroleum jelly
Cotton balls	Rubbing alcohol
Cotton swabs	Betadine or similar antiseptic scrub
Gauze pads (1 inch, 2.5 cm, square)	Hydrogen peroxide
Gauze roll (1 or 2 inches, 2.5 or 5 cm, wide)	Topical antibiotic ointment
Ace bandage (1 or 2 inches, 2.5 or 5 cm, wide)	Sterile saline eyewash
Surgical adhesive tape (½ or 1 inch, 1.5 or 2.5 cm, wide)	List of emergency phone numbers:
Syringe (plastic) without a needle	Your veterinarian's office
	24-hour emergency clinic
Compressed activated charcoal tables (5 grams each)	ASPCA Animal Poison Control Center (888) 426-4435

Handling and Restraint

Any cat, no matter how docile he may be, has the potential to bite when he is severely injured, frightened, or in pain. It is important to recognize this and take proper precautions to keep from being bitten. It is therefore wise to always have control of a cat's head.

There are several effective ways to handle and restrain a cat. Your choice will depend on whether the individual animal is tranquil and cooperative or frightened and aggressive. Remember that cats have five sets of weapons—one mouth and four feet. They are extremely skilled in using these weapons, and will not hesitate to do so.

PICKING UP A CAT

As a general rule, it is advisable to reach down and pick up a cat from above. A face-to-face confrontation might provoke the cat into becoming uncooperative or aggressive.

Cooperative cats can be picked up by placing one hand around the cat beneath the chest and taking hold of the cat's front legs so they cross over each other, keeping your index finger between them for a secure grip. Pick up the cat and snuggle him close to your body, supporting his hind legs if necessary. Cradle his chin with your other hand.

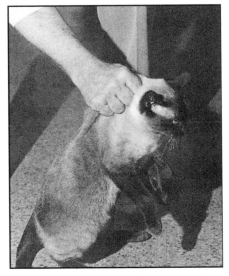

To pick up an apprehensive cat, reach down and grasp him by the scruff of the neck.

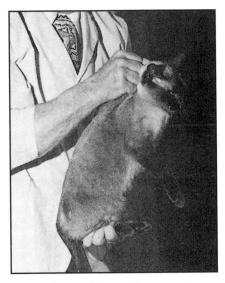

Secure the back feet with your other hand.

A leash and loop restraint for an aggressive cat. The cat is immobilized by drawing the leash taut.

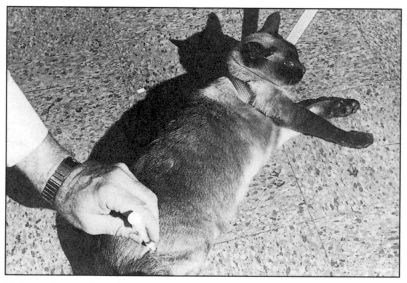

To keep the cat from being choked, the loop should include one front leg.

Apprehensive cats can be picked up by reaching down and lifting the cat by the scruff of his neck. Most cats under the age of 1 go limp—as they did when their mothers carried them as kittens. Older cats may not be as cooperative about scruffing. Support the cat's back feet and body with your other hand.

Frightened cats can be picked up by covering the animal with a towel. After a minute or two, as the cat becomes calmer, slide the rest of the towel underneath and lift the cat up as a bundle. This method works for aggressive cats as well, although you may want to wear thick leather gloves and use a thick blanket. It is a good idea to push a slip leash over the cat's head. This way, if he struggles and jumps out of your arms, at least he cannot completely escape.

Aggressive cats can be picked up by slipping a leash or a loop of rope over the cat's head and one front leg. Then lift the animal by the leash and set him down on a table or into a cat carrier or box. Do not attempt to lift the cat simply with a loop around his neck. This method should be used *only as a last resort* (when the method above doesn't work), because it is certain to agitate the cat further.

Another option is to use a small squeeze cage or squeeze box. The cat is lured into a special box that can be tightened gently around the body to allow for injections and a minimal physical exam. A fishing net can also be used to contain the cat, but beware of claws reaching through!

RESTRAINING FOR TREATMENT

When the cat is cooperative, routine procedures such as grooming, bathing, and medicating the cat are best carried out in quiet surroundings with a minimum of physical restraint. Approach the cat with confidence and handle him gently. If you are calm and go about this matter-of-factly, most cats handle moderate restraint and treatments reasonably well. Many can be coaxed into accepting the procedure and do not need to be restrained.

Cooperative cats can be lifted onto a smooth, raised surface, such as a tabletop or a high tier of a cat tree. The cat will be less secure—but still not frightened. Speak in a calm, soothing voice until the cat relaxes. Rubbing the ears and scratching the head will calm many cats. Place one hand around the front of the cat's chest to keep him from moving forward. Use your other hand to administer treatment.

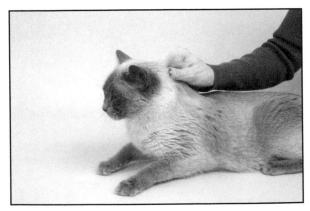

Some cats are quite cooperative while being held by the scruff of the neck. However, some cats will object strenuously.

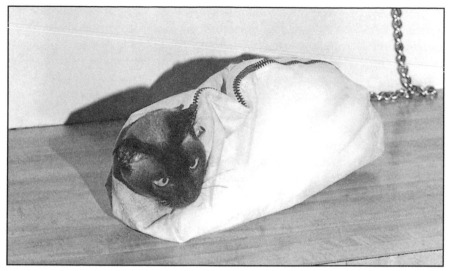

A cat bag restraint may be useful for treating the head, but some cats really hate getting into them.

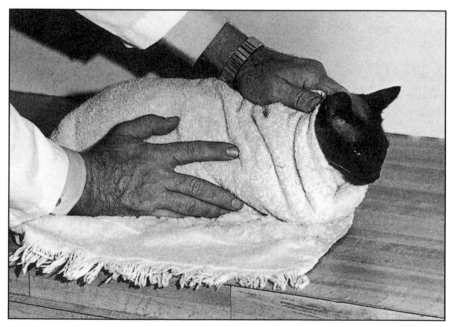

Simply wrapping the cat in a towel is often the easier solution. Some veterinary hospitals transport their cats around the hospital this way.

Uncooperative cats can be handled in several ways, depending on the degree of agitation. If the cat is cooperative enough to permit handling. Some cats respond with quiet to simply having the scruff held and gently tugged back and forth or holding the scruff and gently tapping on the head as a distraction. This is more likely to be true for cats under age 1. If this is not the case, hold the scruff and press firmly against the top of the table so that the cat stretches out. These actions will prevent you from being scratched by the cat's rear claws.

When help is available, have your assistant stand behind the cat and place both hands around the cat's neck or front legs while pressing their arms against the cat's sides. Wrapping a towel or blanket around the cat has a calming effect and is useful for short procedures such as giving medication. An assistant is required to steady the cat and hold the wraps in place.

A coat sleeve makes an excellent restraint. The cat will often scoot into it willingly. Hold the end of the sleeve securely around the cat's neck. Now you can treat the head or tail.

Cat bags are special bags made for restraining cats. You place the cat on the unzipped bag, then quickly zip it around his body up to his neck. Some veterinarians really like them. However, cat bags are widely disliked by cats, and they struggle about getting into it and may not be calm once inside. An easier solution may be to simply wrap the cat in a towel.

There are also muzzles made especially for cats. These have a cloth circle to enclose the muzzle and, usually, a snap lock strap to go behind the ears.

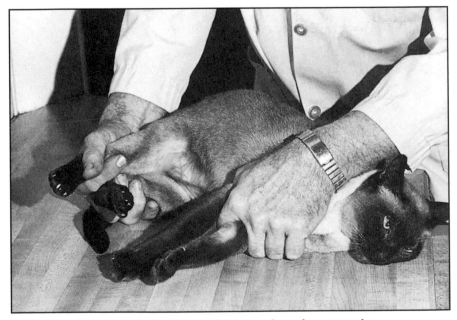

An assistant is required to restrain a cat this way for a short procedure.

When procedures take longer and the cat cannot be managed by the methods just described, lift the cat straight up from behind by the scruff of the neck with one hand and hold his rear paws together with the other. Press down firmly on the table so the cat is lying on his side with his body extended. Now have an assistant hold the front legs together in one hand and the back legs together in the other hand, as shown in the photo on page 6.

If you don't have an assistant, you may bind the front legs together with something soft, such as a bandana, taking two or three turns below the elbows and tying it off securely. Secure the rear legs by wrapping another bandana above the hocks. Calm the cat by covering his head with a towel or cloth. Do not leave a cat alone when restrained like this.

When properly restrained, cats usually settle down and accept the treatment. Once released, most soon forget the unpleasant experience. Some cats will turn and strike as soon as they are released, however, so be prepared.

If the cat is truly upset, consider sedation for any involved treatments he needs. The risks of sedation may be minimal in a healthy cat, compared to the stress of fighting him for treatment. There are also special restraint cages, usually used by veterinarians and humane societies to handle feral or extremely agitated cats. Ask your veterinarian about these.

RESTRAINING COLLARS

An Elizabethan collar, named for the high neck ruff popular during the reign of Queen Elizabeth I of England, is a useful device to keep a cat from scratching at the ears and biting at wounds and skin problems. Older models are made of hard plastic, but newer ones are softer and more flexible, making them less annoying for the cat. These collars can be purchased from pet supply stores and some veterinarians may loan them out with a deposit. Make sure the collar is not too tight around the cat's neck.

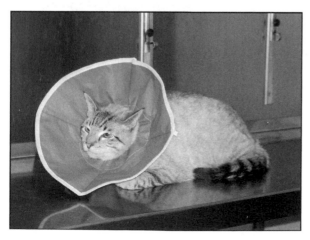

The newer Elizabethan collars are softer and less annoying for the cat than hard plastic models.

The BiteNot collar may be more comfortable for a cat than an Elizabethan collar.

A newer option is the BiteNot collar. This high-necked collar prevents a cat from turning his head to bite. As with an Elizabethan collar, good fit is important. The collar must be just as long as the cat's neck.

Another option is a neck collar, which is simply a wide collar made of flexible cardboard that is taped around the neck. The collar should be about 2 or 3 inches (5 or 8 cm) wide, so that the cat is comfortable, but cannot bend his head and neck all the way down. Be sure to pad the area around the neck to prevent sores and irritation.

Many cats cannot or will not drink water or eat while wearing any type of restraining collar. In that case, temporarily remove the collar several times each day and monitor the cat. Cats with restraining collars must be kept indoors.

TRANSPORTING AN INJURED CAT

No matter how docile by basic nature, *any cat in pain may scratch or bite*. Proper handling will prevent injuries. Furthermore, struggling can cause a weak or injured cat to tire quickly and can induce shock and collapse.

If you are able to handle the cat, pick him up as described in *Cooperative Cat* (page 2), then settle him over your hip so his rear claws project out behind you where they can do no harm. Press the inside of your elbow and forearm against the cat's side, holding him firmly against your body.

If the cat is frightened or in pain, take precautions to avoid injury. Lift the cat at once from behind by the nape of the neck, support his body underneath, and lower him into a cat carrier or a cloth bag such as a pillowcase. The material must not be airtight, or the cat will smother.

If you have a blanket or towel, throwing this over the cat and then scooping him up often works well. Make sure the cat can breathe. To transport the cat, lower him, towel and all, into a carrier or box. *Transport the cat to the veterinary hospital.*

A cat with a possible back injury should be carried on a piece of stiff cardboard or small wooden board or stretcher. Masking tape can be stretched over the cat to hold him on the stretcher or a blanket can be wrapped around the stretcher and cat to hold him securely.

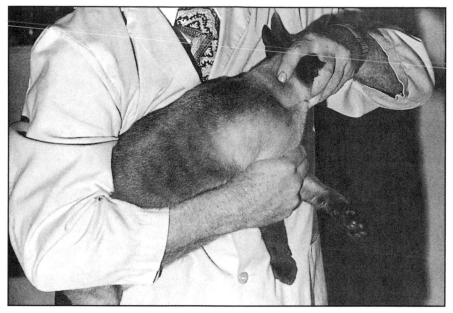

If you can safely handle the injured cat, hold him firmly against your body with his rear feet pressed out behind. Cover his eyes and ears with your other hand to help calm him.

This carrier loads from the top or the side. It's a lot easier to lower an uncooperative cat in from the top than it is to push him in from the side.

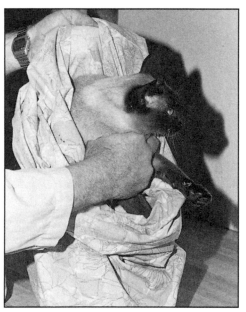

If you don't have a carrier, lift the cat as described in the text on page 8 and lower him into a sack or a pillowcase.

Artificial Respiration and Heart Massage

Artificial respiration is an emergency procedure used to exchange air in an unconscious cat who's not breathing. Heart massage is used when no heartbeat can be heard or felt. When heart massage is combined with artificial respiration, it is called *cardiopulmonary resuscitation (CPR)*. When a cat stops breathing, heart function soon also stops, and vice versa. It is therefore important to know both aspects of CPR. CPR can be performed by one person, but it is easier if two people are available. One does the breathing and the other does the heart massage.

The following emergencies may require artificial respiration or CPR:

Coma

Electric shock

Head injury

Metabolic problems

Obstructed airway (choking)

Poisoning

Prolonged seizure

Shock

Sudden death

Trauma

Before you begin any emergency aid, you need to determine how much help your cat needs and of what type. If your cat is awake and resists any of this treatment, he does not need it.

Artificial Respiration or CPR?

Is the cat breathing? Observe the rise and fall of the chest. Feel for air against your cheek.	If **YES,** pull out the tongue and clear the airway. You may need to clear the airway by gently opening the mouth and wiping with your finger to be sure nothing is stuck or collecting in the mouth or opening to the airway, such as vomit. Observe the cat. If **NO,** feel for a pulse.
Does the cat have a pulse? Feel for the femoral artery located in the groin. Or feel the chest carefully to detect a heartbeat. Put your hand under and around the cat's chest and compress very lightly to feel for a heartbeat.	If **YES,** start artificial respiration. If **NO,** start CPR.

ARTIFICIAL RESPIRATION

1. Lay the cat on a flat surface with his *right* side down.

2. Open his mouth and clear any secretions with a cloth or handkerchief. Check for a foreign body. If present, remove it if possible. If it is impossible to reach or dislodge, perform the *Heimlich Maneuver*, described on page 33.

3. Pull the tongue forward and close the mouth. Place your mouth over the cat's nose (but not the mouth). Blow gently into the cat's nostrils. The chest will expand. Remember, *gentle* blowing—you should not be blowing hard enough to inflate a balloon.

4. Release to let the air come back out. Excess air will escape through the cat's lips, preventing overinflation of the lungs and overdistension of the stomach.

5. If the chest does not rise and fall, blow more forcefully; or, if necessary, lightly seal the lips with your hand.

6. The rate is one breath every four to five seconds (12 to 15 per minute).

7. Continue until the cat breathes on his own, or as long as the heart continues to beat.

Artificial respiration. Blow gently into the cat's nostrils.

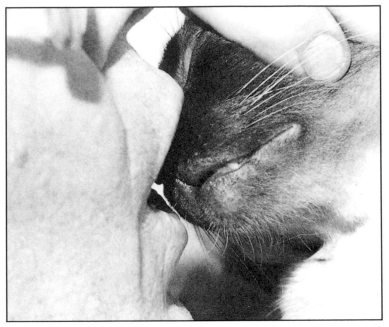

In this close view, you can see how leaving the mouth uncovered avoids the problem of overinflation.

CPR

CRP is a combination of artificial respiration and heart massage. If a cat needs heart massage, he also needs artificial respiration. On the other hand, if the cat resists your attempts to perform CPR, he probably does not need it!

1. Continue with mouth-to-nose breathing.
2. Prepare for heart massage. Place your fingers and thumb on either side of the cat's sternum or chest, behind his elbows.
3. Compress the chest firmly 6 times; administer a breath. Then repeat. Massage rate is 80 to 120 compressions per minute.
4. If possible, do not stop heart massage while administering a breath.
5. Pause every 2 minutes for 10 to 15 seconds to check for a pulse and spontaneous breathing.
6. Continue until the heart beats and the cat breathes on his own, or until no heartbeat is felt for 30 minutes.

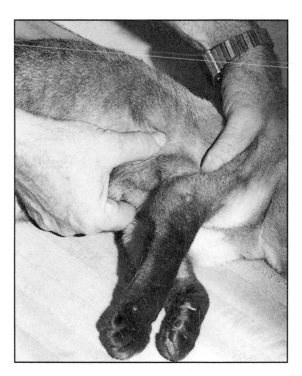

For heart massage, place the fingers and thumb on either side of the sternum behind the cat's elbows.

Shock

Shock is caused by insufficient blood flow and oxygen to meet the body's needs. Adequate blood flow requires effective heart pumping; open, intact blood vessels; and sufficient blood volume to maintain flow and pressure. Adequate oxygenation requires an open respiratory tract and enough energy to breathe. Any condition that adversely affects the circulatory or respiratory systems, making these things impossible, can cause shock.

The cardiovascular system of an animal in shock will try to compensate for inadequate oxygen and blood flow by increasing the heart and respiratory rates, constricting the skin's blood vessels, and maintaining fluid in the circulation by reducing urinary output. This requires additional energy at a time when the vital organs aren't getting enough oxygen to carry out normal activities. After a time, shock becomes self-perpetuating. Untreated, it results in death.

Common causes of shock are dehydration (often caused by prolonged vomiting and diarrhea), heat stroke, severe infections, poisoning, and uncontrolled bleeding. Falling from a height or being hit by a car are the most common causes of traumatic shock in cats.

Signs of early shock include panting, rapid heart rate, bounding pulse, and a bright red color to the mucous membranes of the lips, gums, and tongue. Many of these signs will be missed or considered mild—perhaps looked at as a cat who overexerted himself or is very excited. The later signs are when most owners notice and respond to their cat's condition. Signs of late shock (the ones seen most often) are pale skin and mucous membranes, a drop in body temperature, cold feet and legs, a slow respiratory rate, apathy and depression, unconsciousness, and a weak or absent pulse.

Treatment: First, evaluate. Is the cat breathing? Does he have a heartbeat? What is the extent of his injuries? Is the cat in shock? If so, proceed as follows:

1. If the cat is not breathing, proceed with *Artificial Respiration* (page 11).

2. If there is no heartbeat or pulse, administer *CPR* (page 12).

3. If the cat is unconscious, check to be sure the airway is open. Clear secretions from the mouth with your fingers. Pull out the tongue to keep the airway clear of secretions. Keep the head lower than the body.

4. Control bleeding (as described in *Wounds*, page 48).

5. To prevent further aggravating the shock:
   - Calm the cat, and speak soothingly.
   - Allow your cat to assume the most comfortable position. An animal will naturally adopt the one that causes the least pain. Do not force the cat to lie down—this may make breathing more difficult.
   - When possible, splint or support broken bones before moving the cat (see *Broken Bones*, page 16).
   - Wrap the cat in a blanket to provide warmth and to protect injured extremities. (How to handle and restrain an injured cat for transport to the veterinary hospital is discussed in *Handling and Restraint*, page 2.) Do not attempt to muzzle the cat, as this can impair breathing.

6. Head for the nearest veterinary hospital.

ANAPHYLACTIC SHOCK

Anaphylactic shock is an immediate, serious allergic reaction. It occurs when a cat is exposed to an *allergen* to which he has been sensitized. Sensitivity occurs through prior contact.

The most common drug allergen that causes anaphylactic shock is penicillin. The venom in the stings of bees and wasps can also occasionally produce anaphylactic shock. Some cats have been known to experience shock after a vaccination, although this is not common.

Anaphylactic shock causes signs and symptoms different from those described in the previous section on shock. Initially, there may be local signs at the point of contact, including pain, itching, swelling, and redness of the skin. With acute anaphylaxis, the allergic response becomes generalized, either immediately or over the course of several hours. Signs are agitation, diarrhea, vomiting, difficulty breathing, *stridor* (harsh breathing sounds) from a swollen larynx, weakness, and circulatory collapse. In untreated cases, coma and death follow.

Treatment: Emergency treatment of anaphylactic shock involves administering adrenaline (epinephrine), oxygen, antihistamines, IV fluids, and hydrocortisone—drugs that are not available at home. This is why it is best to have your veterinarian give vaccines—he or she has the drugs and equipment to treat allergic reactions in time.

A cat who has had an allergic reaction to a drug in the past should not be given that drug again. (Also see *Insect Stings*, page 43.)

Acute Painful Abdomen

An acute abdomen is an emergency that can lead to death unless treatment is started as soon as possible. The condition is characterized by the sudden onset of abdominal pain along with vomiting, retching, extreme restlessness and inability to find a comfortable position, purring, meowing, crying, grunting, and labored breathing. The abdomen is extremely painful when pressed. A characteristic position is sometimes seen in which the cat rests his chest against the floor with his rump up in the air. As the condition worsens, his pulse becomes weak and thready, his mucous membranes appear pale, and he goes into shock.

One of the following may be the cause:

- Urinary tract obstruction
- Blunt abdominal trauma (such as being kicked or hit by a car) with internal bleeding
- Rupture of the bladder
- Perforation of the stomach and/or intestines
- Poisoning
- Rupture of a pregnant uterus

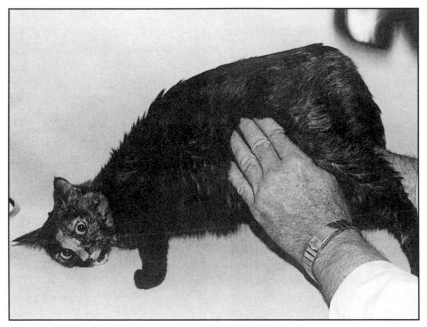

A painful abdomen indicates the need for immediate veterinary attention.

- Acute peritonitis
- Intestinal obstruction

A cat with an acute abdomen is critically ill and needs *immediate* veterinary attention.

Broken Bones

Most broken bones are caused by automobile accidents and falls. Falls from apartment windows are most common in warm weather, when a screen is left open or the weight of the cat pushing on it removes the screen. The bones most commonly broken are the femur, pelvis, and jaw. Fractures of the skull and spine occur less frequently. A rather common type of fracture occurs when a car runs over a cat's tail; it is discussed in *Spinal Cord Injuries* (page 343).

Fractures are classified by type and whether the injury involves a break in the skin. Young bones tend to crack and these are called greenstick fractures, whereas the bones of elderly cats are brittle and are more likely to break.

Complete breaks are classified as open or closed. In a closed fracture, the bone does not break through the skin. In an open fracture, the bone makes contact with the outside, either because of a deep laceration exposing it or because the point of the bone protrudes through the skin. Open fractures are associated with a high incidence of bone infection.

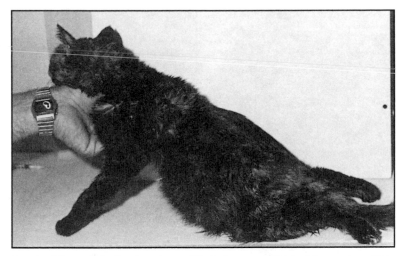

A cat with a pelvic fracture is unable to bear weight on his rear legs. This might be confused with a spinal cord injury or arterial thromboembolism.

Treatment: Many of these injuries are accompanied by shock, blood loss, and injuries to other organs. Controlling shock takes precedence over treating the fracture (see *Shock,* page 15). Cats with injury or pain should be handled gently, as described in *Handling and Restraint* (page 2). Take precautions to avoid a scratch or bite.

Fractures should be immobilized to prevent further injury as you transport the cat to a veterinary hospital. Splint the involved limb. A satisfactory splint is one that crosses the joint above and below the injury. When the fracture is below the knee or elbow, immobilize the limb by folding a magazine or piece of thick cardboard around the leg. A toilet paper cardboard roll is often the right size. Then wrap it with gauze, a necktie, or tape.

Limb fractures above the knee or elbow are immobilized by binding the leg to the body. Sometimes it is best to simply wrap the cat gently in a blanket or towel, with the injured leg close to his body. Then have someone hold the cat as still as possible while another person drives to the veterinary hospital.

If the bone is completely broken and the ends are displaced, your veterinarian will need to reduce the fracture and return the ends of the bones to their original position. Reduction is done by pulling on the limb to overcome the muscle spasm that caused the shortening. Obviously, this requires general anesthesia. Once reduced, the position of the bones must be maintained. In general, fractures above the knee or elbow are stabilized with pins and metallic plates, while those below are immobilized with splints and casts.

Displaced jaw fractures can cause malposition of the teeth. The jaw should be adjusted and the teeth wired together to maintain the correct position until healing is complete. Skull fractures may require surgery to elevate the depressed fragment. For more information, see *Head Injuries* (page 330).

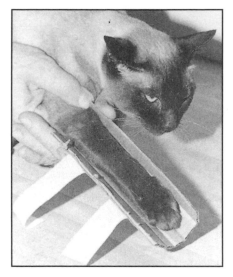
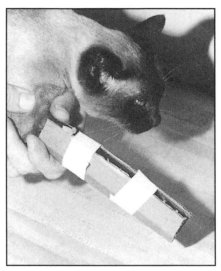

A piece of cardboard makes a good temporary splint.

Use it for fractures of the front leg below the elbow.

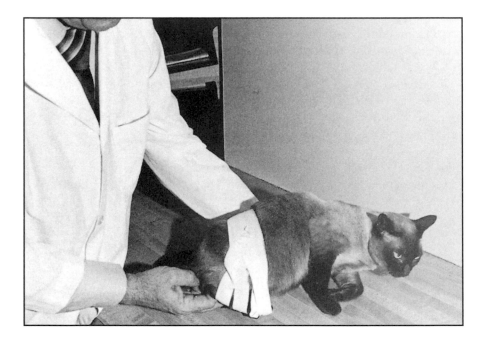

Fractures above the knee joint can be immobilized by taping the leg to the body.

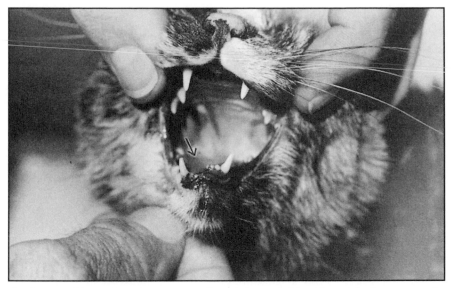

The fractured lower jaw shows separation of the two sides. These injuries commonly follow blows to the head.

Burns

Burns are caused by heat, chemicals, electric shocks, or radiation. Sunburn is an example of a radiation burn. It occurs on the ear flaps of cats with white coats or white noses (see *Sunburn*, page 211), and on the skin of white-coated cats who have been clipped down. A cat may be scalded by having hot liquid spilled on him or by being involved in some other household accident. A common type of burn occurs on the foot pads after walking on a hot surface such as a tin roof, stove top, or freshly tarred road.

The depth of injury depends on the length and intensity of exposure.

A **first-degree burn** causes the skin to become red, slightly swollen, and painful. You will see redness of the skin, occasionally blistering, perhaps slight swelling, and the burn area is tender. These superficial burns usually heal in about five to seven days.

A **second-degree burn** is deeper and there is blistering. These burns are extremely painful. These wounds may take up to 21 days to heal, or longer if the area gets infected.

A **third-degree burn** involves the full thickness of skin and extends into the subcutaneous fat. The skin appears white or leathery, the hair comes out easily when pulled, and pain is severe initially, but fades if nerve endings are destroyed. These burns penetrate the outer layers of the skin. Since nerve endings are usually destroyed, these burns are often not as painful as second-degree ones. If more than 20 percent of the body surface is deeply burned, the outlook is poor. Fluid loss is excessive. Shock can occur and infection is likely because skin defenses are gone.

Treatment: If your cat appears to be suffering from electrical shock, use a wooden implement to slide any power cords away from him before you touch him. Alternatively, unplug all cords or turn off the circuit breakers so that you won't get a shock too.

Most burns should receive veterinary attention. Fluid loss, shock, and possible infection can be life-threatening complications of all but minor burns. *Do not* put butter or any greasy ointment on the burns. Cover with damp gauze and head to your veterinarian.

For minor burns, apply cool compresses (not ice packs) to damaged areas for 30 minutes to relieve pain. Replace as the compress becomes warm. Clip away the hair and wash the area gently with a surgical soap. Blot dry. Apply Silvadene cream or triple antibiotic ointment. Protect the area from rubbing by wrapping it with a loose-fitting gauze dressing. This bandage should be changed at least once every day so the area can be cleaned and treated. Do not using a rubbing action on damaged skin.

Treat acid, alkali, gasoline, kerosene, and other chemical burns by flushing with large amounts of water for 10 minutes. Do not let your cat groom these substances off his coat. Wear gloves and bathe the cat with mild soap and water. Blot dry and apply antibiotic ointment. Bandage loosely. If you see signs of obvious burns, such as blistering, you need to contact your veterinarian. Along with burns, some of these substances can cause toxicity.

Cats should not be allowed to groom near burned areas of skin. It may be necessary to have the cat wear an Elizabethan collar or a BiteNot collar (see page 7) to prevent grooming. Alternatively, if the area is small, it can be bandaged to keep the cat from licking it. (Mouth burns from electric cords are discussed on page 235.)

Cold Exposure
HYPOTHERMIA (LOW BODY TEMPERATURE)

Prolonged exposure to cold results in a drop in body temperature. This is most likely to occur when a cat is wet. Hypothermia also occurs with shock, after a long period under anesthesia, and in newborn kittens. (How to warm a chilled kitten is discussed in *Warming a Chilled Kitten*, page 456.) Prolonged chilling burns up the available energy in the body and predisposes the cat to low blood sugar.

The signs of hypothermia are violent shivering followed by listlessness and lethargy, a rectal temperature below 97°F (36°C), and finally, collapse and coma. Hypothermic cats can withstand extended periods of cardiac arrest because the low body temperature lowers the metabolic rate. CPR may be successful in such cases.

Treatment: Wrap your cat in a blanket or coat and carry him into the house. If the cat is wet (having fallen into icy water or been out in cold rain), give him a warm bath. Rub vigorously with towels to dry the skin.

Warm a chilled cat by applying warm water packs, wrapped in towels, to the armpits, chest, and abdomen. The temperature of the pack should be about that of a baby's bottle—warm to the wrist. Take the cat's rectal temperature every 10 minutes. Continue to change the packs until the rectal temperature reaches 100°F (37.8°C). Do not warm the cat with a hair dryer, which may cause burns.

As the cat begins to move about, give him some honey or a few spoonfuls of a glucose solution—made by adding 4 teaspoons of sugar to a pint of warm water (7 g of sugar added to 500 ml of warm water). If your cat won't drink or lick it, dab a bit of honey or Karo syrup on his gums.

FROSTBITE

Frostbite is damage to the skin and underlying tissues caused by extreme cold. It often accompanies hypothermia. It most commonly involves the toes, ears, scrotum, and tail. (Frostbite of the ear flaps is discussed on page 211.) These areas are the most exposed and are only lightly protected by fur. At first, frostbitten skin is pale and white. With the return of circulation, it becomes red and swollen. Later it may peel. Eventually, it looks much like a burn, with a line of demarcation between live and dead tissue. The dead area will turn dark and become hardened and brittle. The actual extent of the damage may not be apparent for a week or more. The dead skin separates in one to three weeks.

Treatment: Warm frostbitten areas by immersing in warm (not hot) water for 20 minutes or until the tissue becomes flushed. *Never apply snow or ice.* Tissue damage is greatly increased if thawing is followed by refreezing. Do not rub or massage the affected parts, because the damaged tissue is easily destroyed. Your cat should be taken to the veterinarian for follow-up care. Topical or oral antibiotics may be prescribed.

As sensation returns to the cold areas, they may be painful. Do not let your cat excessively groom those areas or chew on them.

Dehydration

Dehydration occurs when your cat loses body fluids faster than he can replace them. Usually it involves loss of both water and *electrolytes* (which are minerals such as sodium, chloride, and potassium). If the cat is ill, dehydration may be due to an inadequate fluid intake. Fever increases the loss of water. This becomes significant if the cat does not drink enough to offset the loss. Other common causes of dehydration are prolonged vomiting and diarrhea.

One sign of dehydration is loss of skin elasticity. When the skin along the back is pinched up into a fold, it should spring smoothly back into place. In a dehydrated cat, the skin stays up in a ridge. Another sign is dryness of the mouth. The gums, which should be wet and glistening, are dry and tacky to the touch. The saliva is thick and tenacious. Late signs are sunken eyeballs and shock.

Treatment: A cat who is noticeably dehydrated should receive prompt veterinary attention. Treatment involves replacing fluids and preventing further losses.

In mild cases without vomiting, fluids can be given by mouth. Make sure fresh, clean water is always available for your cat to drink on his own. If the cat won't drink, give him an electrolyte solution by bottle or syringe into the cheek pouch (see page XX for advice on administering liquids to your cat). Balanced electrolyte solutions for treating dehydration in children are available at drugstores. Ringer's lactate, with 5 percent dextrose in water, and Pedialyte are both suitable for cats. These solutions should only be given orally. They are given at the rate of 2 to 4 milliliters per pound (.5 k) of body weight per hour, depending on the severity of the dehydration (or as directed by your veterinarian).

Many cats will need subcutaneous or intravenous fluids administered at the veterinary hospital. Secondary kidney failure can occur as a result of severe dehydration. (Treating dehydration in infant kittens is discussed in *Common Feeding Problems*, page 466.)

Drowning and Suffocation

Conditions that prevent oxygen from getting into the lungs and blood cause asphyxiation or suffocation. These include carbon monoxide poisoning, inhaling toxic fumes (smoke, gasoline, propane, refrigerants, solvents, and others), drowning, and smothering (which can happen when a cat is left too long in an airtight space). Other causes include foreign bodies in the airways and injuries to the chest that interfere with breathing.

A cat's collar can get snagged on a fence, and the cat can strangle while struggling to get free. Be sure to provide an elastic collar that can stretch and slip over your cat's head in an emergency, or a breakaway collar with a special quick-release clasp.

Cats are natural swimmers and can negotiate short distances well. However, they can't climb out of water if the sides are steep or over a ledge. They might drown in a swimming pool if a ramp exit is not provided or if they panic and can't find the ramp and swim to exhaustion. They can also drown in a pond if they break through ice and can't get out.

The symptoms of oxygen deprivation, also called *hypoxia*, are straining to breathe, gasping for breath (often with the head extended), extreme anxiety, and weakness progressing to loss of consciousness as the cat begins to succumb. The pupils begin to dilate. The tongue and mucous membranes turn blue, also called *cyanosis*, which is a sign of insufficient oxygen in the blood.

One exception to the blue color is carbon monoxide poisoning, in which the membranes are a bright red. Carbon monoxide poisoning can be seen in cats rescued from burning buildings, trapped in car trunks, or left in a closed garage with an engine running.

Treatment: The most important consideration is to provide your cat with fresh air to breathe. (Better yet, give oxygen if it is available.) If respiration is shallow or absent, immediately give artificial respiration (see page 11). Get the cat to the nearest veterinary hospital—ideally, with one person driving while another gives respiratory support.

Carbon monoxide poisoning is frequently associated with smoke inhalation and burns of the mouth and throat. Carbon monoxide binds with hemoglobin in the blood and blocks the delivery of oxygen to the tissues. Even though the cat is breathing deeply, oxygen transport will be compromised for several hours. Breathing a high concentration of oxygen helps to overcome these effects. A veterinarian will be able to provide this therapy using an oxygen mask, a nasal tube, or an oxygen cage.

If the cat has a *pneumothorax*, an open wound into the chest (which you can determine if you hear air sucking in and out as the cat breathes), seal off the chest by pinching the skin together over the wound. Maintain this seal with a bandage wrapped around the chest or a gauze pad held firmly against the chest wound while transporting the cat to the veterinarian. For drowning, first you want to remove as much water as possible from the lungs. Hold the cat upside down by placing your hands around his lower abdomen, and gently swing the cat back and forth for 30 seconds while supporting the head. Then position the cat on his right side with the head lower than the chest and begin artificial respiration (see page 11). If there is no pulse or discernible heartbeat, heart massage should be attempted (see CPR, page 12). Continue efforts to resuscitate until the cat breathes without assistance or until no heartbeat is felt for 30 minutes. Remember, cats who have been in cold water or cold temperatures can often be resuscitated even after a long time.

Once the immediate crisis is over, veterinary aid should be sought. Pneumonia from inhalation is a frequent complication.

Electric Shock

Electric shocks can be caused by chewing on power cords or coming in contact with downed wires. A shock can cause involuntary muscle contractions of the jaw that may prevent a cat from releasing the live wire. Lightning strikes are almost always fatal, and leave behind the telltale signs of singed hair and skin.

Cats who receive an electric shock may be burned, or the shock may cause an irregular heartbeat with signs of circulatory collapse. Electric current also damages the capillaries of the lungs and leads to *pulmonary edema*, which is the accumulation of fluid in the air sacs. The signs are straining to breathe, gasping for breath (often with the head extended), extreme anxiety, and weakness progressing to loss of consciousness as the cat begins to succumb. If the cat bit into a cord, you may see drooling, ulcers or burns on the lips, and coughing from lung damage.

Treatment: If your cat is found in contact with an electric cord or appliance, or downed wires, *do not touch the cat*. If possible, throw the circuit breaker or pull out the plug. Or use a wooden stick or broom handle to move the live cord away from the cat. If the cat is unconscious and is not breathing, administer artificial respiration (see page 11). Pulmonary edema must be treated by a veterinarian, and any cat with an electrical shock should be seen by a veterinarian.

Treat any burn as described in *Burns* (page 19). Mouth burns from electric cords are discussed on page 235.

Prevention: Try to move electric cords out of the way to minimize the chances of your cat playing with them. This is especially true with kittens. Try tacking the cords to the wall or enclosing them in plastic sleeves or lengths of hose.

Heat Stroke

Heat stroke is an emergency that requires immediate recognition and prompt treatment. Cats do not tolerate high temperatures as well as humans do. They sweat very minimally through their paws, and instead depend on rapid breathing to exchange warm air for cool air. Heat-stressed cats drool a great deal and lick themselves to spread the saliva on their coats, because the evaporation of saliva is an important additional cooling mechanism. But when air temperature is close to body temperature, cooling by evaporation is not an efficient process. Cats with airway disease also have difficulty with excess heat.

Common causes of overheating or heat stroke include

- Increased environmental temperature, such as being left in a car in hot weather or being confined to a crate without water
- Airway disease that interferes with heat dissipation through rapid breathing
- Heart or lung disease that interferes with efficient breathing
- Excessive heat production caused by high fever, seizures, or strenuous exercise

Heat stroke begins with rapid, frantic, noisy breathing. The tongue and mucous membranes are bright red, saliva is thick and tenacious, and the cat often vomits. His temperature, as measured with a rectal thermometer, rises, sometimes to over 106°F (41°C). The problem is usually evident by the appearance of the cat. The condition can be confirmed by taking the animal's temperature.

If heat stroke goes untreated, the cat becomes unsteady and staggers, has diarrhea that is often bloody, and becomes progressively weaker. His lips and mucous membranes become a pale blue or gray. Collapse, coma, and death ensue.

Treatment: *Emergency measures must begin at once.* Take the rectal temperature every 10 minutes. Mild cases respond by moving the cat to cooler surroundings, such as an air-conditioned building or car. If the cat's temperature is over 106°F (39.4°C) or if the cat becomes unsteady, apply wet, cold towels to the armpits and groin, as well as on the head, or immerse the cat's body (not the head) in cool water until the rectal temperature reaches 103°F. As an alternative, wet the cat down with a garden hose. Ice packs can be applied to the head and the groin area. Stop the cooling process and dry the cat when the temperature falls below 103°F. The thermoregulatory system is not functioning normally, and further cooling may produce hypothermia.

Any cat with suspected heat stroke should be seen by a veterinarian. Delayed and secondary problems can include kidney failure, cardiac arrhythmias, and seizures. Heat stroke can also be associated with swelling of the throat. This aggravates the problem. A cortisone injection from your veterinarian may be required to treat this.

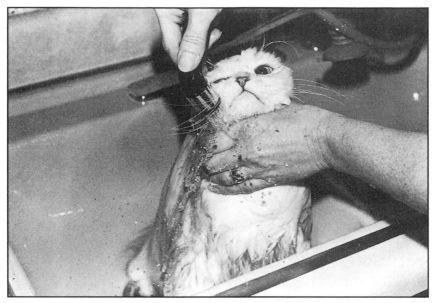

Heat stroke is an emergency. Cool the cat with a cool water spray or immerse him in a tub of cool water.

Prevention:

- Do not expose cats with airway disease or impaired breathing to prolonged heat.
- Do not leave a cat in a car with the windows closed, even if the car is parked in the shade.
- If traveling in a car, keep the cat in a well-ventilated cat carrier, or better yet, an open wire cage, so the car windows can be left open.
- Provide shade and cool water to cats who spend time outdoors in runs.
- Take extra precautions in hot, humid weather and with cats who have shortened faces and muzzles, such as Persians.

Poisoning

A poison is any substance that is harmful to the body. This includes manufactured products such as prescription drugs and cleaning solutions, and also natural herbs and other plants. Their innate curiosity may lead cats to lick or taste things that are poisonous. Fastidious grooming may cause a cat to lick poisonous products from his coat.

Animal baits are palatable poisons that encourage ingestion. This makes them an obvious choice for intentional poisoning. Cats may also be unintentionally poisoned by these products if they eat a rodent who has ingested poisoned bait. (Remember that even indoor cats may hunt and kill small prey animals—rodents, insects, or small reptiles.)

Most cases suspected of being malicious poisoning actually are not. Cats, by nature, are curious and have a tendency to explore out-of-the-way places such as wood piles, weed thickets, and storage areas. They also hunt small animals, often chasing them into confined spaces. These environments put cats into contact with insects, dead animals, and toxic plants. It also means that in many cases of suspected poisoning, the actual agent will be unknown. The great variety of potentially poisonous plants and shrubs makes identification difficult or impossible, unless you have direct knowledge that the cat has eaten a certain plant or product.

Many cases of poisoning occur in the home or in the garage. Potentially poisonous substances should be kept in secure containers and, ideally, in cupboards that close securely (remember that prying paws can open some cupboard doors). Poisonous houseplants can be removed and outdoor plants removed or fenced off from pets. Keep medications in childproof containers and inside secure cupboards.

The Top Ten Poisonings in Cats

According to the ASPCA Animal Poison Control Center, these are most common poisonings that occur among cats.

1. Permethrin insecticides designed for dogs; never use dog flea and tick products on cats!

2. Other topical insecticides; follow directions carefully.

3. Venlafaxine, a human antidepressant that goes by the brand name Effexor; apparently, cats are attracted to the capsules.

4. Glow jewelry and sticks; the liquid inside is mildly toxic.

5. Lilies; virtually all varieties of lilies can lead to kidney failure.

6. Liquid potpourri; cats may lick this or clean it off their paws after stepping in it.

7. Nonsteroidal anti-inflammatory drugs, including ibuprofen and aspirin.

8. Acetaminophen (Tylenol); even one tablet can be fatal.

9. Anticoagulant rodenticides; cats may eat these or may eat rodents who have the poison in their system.

10. Amphetamines; even very small amounts are serious.

GENERAL TREATMENT OF POISONING

If your cat ingests an unknown substance, it is important to determine whether that substance is a poison. Most products have labels that list their ingredients, but if the label doesn't tell you the composition and toxicity of the product, call the ASPCA Animal Poison Control Center at (888) 426-4435 for specific information. The Poison Control Center has a staff of licensed veterinarians and board-certified toxicologists on call 24 hours a day, every day of the year. You will be charged a consultation fee of $50 per case, which can be charged to most major credit cards. There is no charge for follow-up calls in critical cases. At your request, the center will also contact your veterinarian. You can also log onto www.aspca.org and click on "Animal Poison Control Center" for more information, including a list of toxic and nontoxic plants.

Other poison control hotlines include the Angell Animal Poison Control Hotline, operated by Angell Animal Medical Centers and the Massachusetts SPCA (877-226-4355, www.smspca.org) and the Animal Poison Hotline, operated by the North Shore Animal League and PROSAR International Animal Poison Center at (888) 232-8870.

In some cases, you can call the emergency room at your local hospital, which may be able to give you information about how to treat the poison. Specific antidotes are available for some poisons, but they cannot be administered unless the poison is known, or at least suspected by the circumstances. Some product labels have phone numbers you can call for safety information about their products.

When signs of poisoning develop, the most important consideration is to get your cat to the nearest emergency veterinary facility at once. If possible, find the poison and bring the container with you. This provides the emergency personnel with an immediate diagnosis and expedites treatment.

If the cat has ingested the substance recently, residual poison is often present in his stomach. An initial and most important step is to rid the cat's stomach of any remaining poison. The most effective way to empty the stomach is to pass a stomach tube, remove as much of the stomach contents as possible, and then wash the stomach out with large volumes of water. This must be done by your veterinarian.

In many cases, it is preferable to induce vomiting at the scene rather than proceed directly to the veterinary hospital. For example, if you see the cat swallow the poisonous substance, it is obviously best to make the cat vomit it right back up. Similarly, if the poison was ingested within two hours but it will take 30 minutes or longer to get to a veterinary facility, it is frequently advisable to induce vomiting at home. However,

DO NOT *induce vomiting*

- If the cat has already vomited
- If the cat is in a stupor, breathing with difficulty, or shows any sign of neurological involvement

- If the cat is unconscious or convulsing
- If the cat has swallowed an acid, alkali, cleaning solution, household chemical, or petroleum product
- If the cat has swallowed a sharp object that could lodge in the esophagus or perforate the stomach
- If the label on the product says, "Do not induce vomiting"

How to Induce Vomiting and Prevent Poison Absorption

Induce vomiting by giving the cat hydrogen peroxide. A 3 percent solution is most effective. Give 1 teaspoon (5 ml) hydrogen peroxide per 10 pounds (4.53 kg) body weight of the cat, with a limit of 3 teaspoons. If the cat doesn't vomit after the first dose, you may repeat every 10 minutes, up to three times, until the cat vomits. If possible, get your cat to walk around or shake him gently in your arms after giving the hydrogen peroxide. This often helps stimulate vomiting.

Once the poison has been cleared from the cat's stomach, give him activated charcoal to bind any remaining poison and prevent further absorption. The most effective and easily administered home oral charcoal product is compressed activated charcoal, which comes in 5-gram tablets (recommended for the home emergency medical kit, see page 1). The dose is one tablet per 10 pounds (4.5 kg) of body weight. Products that come in a liquid, or as a powder made into a slurry, are extremely difficult to administer at home with a syringe or medicine bottle. The slurry is dense and gooey, and few cats will swallow it voluntarily. (A few cats will eat the slurry mixed with food.) These products are best administered by stomach tube. This is routinely done by your veterinarian after flushing out the stomach.

If activated charcoal is not available, coat the intestines with milk and egg whites using ¼ cup (60 ml) egg whites and ¼ cup milk. Mix this and give the cat about 2 teaspoons (10 ml) by mouth. Administer into the cat's cheek pouch using a plastic syringe (see *How to Give Medications*, page 554), or add to food. If you use the syringe, drip the mixture in because you don't want the cat to aspirate it into his lungs, which can lead to aspiration pneumonia.

Intensive care in a veterinary hospital improves the survival rate for cats who have been poisoned. Intravenous fluids support circulation, treat shock, and protect the kidneys. A large urine output assists in eliminating the poison. Corticosteroids may be given for their anti-inflammatory effects. A cat in a coma may benefit from tracheal intubation and artificial ventilation during the acute phase of respiratory depression.

A cat who is beginning to show signs of nervous system involvement is in deep trouble. *Get your cat to a veterinarian as quickly as possible.* Try to bring a sample of vomitus or, better yet, the actual poison in the original container. Do not delay administering first aid. If the cat is convulsing, unconscious, or not breathing, administer CPR (page 12).

Seizures

Seizures caused by poisons are associated with prolonged periods of hypoxia and the potential for brain damage. Continuous or recurrent seizures are controlled with intravenous diazepam (Valium) or barbiturates, which must be administered by a veterinarian.

Seizures caused by strychnine and other central nervous system poisons may be mistaken for epilepsy. This could be a problem, because immediate veterinary attention is needed in cases of poisoning, but not for most epileptic seizures. Seizures caused by poisoning usually are continuous or recur within minutes. Between seizures the cat may exhibit tremors, lack of coordination, weakness, abdominal pain, and diarrhea. In contrast, most epileptic seizures are brief, seldom lasting more than two minutes, and are followed by a quiet period in which the cat appears dazed but otherwise normal.

See *Seizures* (page 339) for seizure care. Cats cannot swallow their tongues, so don't try to pull the tongue out while the cat is having a seizure or you risk a serious bite. Wrapping the cat in a towel or blanket may help keep him quiet and out of harm during the seizure.

Contact Poisons

If your cat has a poisonous substance on his skin or coat, flush the area with large amounts of lukewarm water for 30 minutes. Wearing gloves, give the cat a complete bath in *lukewarm*, not cold, water, as described on page 124. Even if the substance is not irritating the skin, it must be removed. Otherwise, the cat will likely lick it off and swallow it. Soak gasoline and oil stains with mineral or vegetable oil (do not use paint thinner or turpentine). Work in well. Then wash the cat with a mild soap. Rub in cornstarch or flour to absorb any residual oils, then brush it out.

DRUG POISONING

Unintentional overdose with veterinary medications and accidental ingestion of both human and veterinary pills are a common cause of poisoning in all pets. Veterinary products, in particular, are often flavored to encourage a pet to take them, and will be eagerly consumed if they are discovered. Curious cats are often attracted to dropped or rolling pills and may chase and try to eat them.

Many people give over-the-counter medications to their cats, without veterinary approval, to treat a variety of symptoms; they believe that what works for people works for cats. Unfortunately, this is not true. Cats are unusually sensitive to many medications. Drugs given to cats in human dosages are almost always toxic—and some human drugs cannot be given to cats in any amount.

Common pain relievers such as ibuprofen (Advil) and acetaminophen (Tylenol) are very toxic to cats. Cats do not have the necessary enzymes to detoxify and eliminate these drugs. Specifically, they are lacking the liver enzyme glucuronyl transferase. This enzyme breaks down drugs so they can be metabolized. Without it, ingesting certain drugs can lead to the accumulation of dangerous substances in the animal that are left behind when the drugs are metabolized. Symptoms develop quickly and include abdominal pain, salivation, vomiting, and weakness.

Other human drugs that produce a variety of toxic effects and are commonly involved in accidental poisonings include antidepressants, antihistamines, nonsteroidal pain relievers, sleeping pills, diet pills, heart pills, blood pressure pills, and vitamins.

Treatment: All instances of drug ingestion should be taken seriously. If you suspect your pet has swallowed any drug, immediately induce vomiting and coat the bowel as described on page 29. Call your veterinarian for further instructions. A specific antidote may be available for the drug in question. Also call a poison control center (see page 28).

Prevention: All medications should be safely stored in childproof containers and in closed cupboards. Always consult your veterinarian before administering any medication. Follow instructions exactly for frequency and dosage. *Never assume that a human drug is safe for pets!*

ANTIFREEZE

Poisoning by antifreeze that contains ethylene glycol is one of the most common small animal toxicities. Exposure typically occurs when antifreeze drips from the car radiator and is lapped up by the cat.

The poison primarily affects the brain and the kidneys. Signs of toxicity are dose-related, and occur within 30 minutes and up to 12 hours after ingestion. They include depression, vomiting, an uncoordinated "drunken" gait, and seizures. Coma and death can occur in a matter of hours. Cats who recover from acute intoxication frequently develop kidney failure one to three days later. Death is common.

Treatment: If you see or suspect that your pet has ingested even a small amount of antifreeze, immediately induce vomiting (see page 29) and take your cat to the veterinarian. If treatment will be delayed, administer activated charcoal (see page 29) to prevent further absorption of ethylene glycol. Cats should be placed on IV fluids and given ethanol therapy to prevent the metabolism of ethylene glycol. Intensive care in an animal hospital may prevent kidney failure. Some veterinary referral centers may offer dialysis as part of the cat's treatment.

Prevention: This common cause of pet and child poisoning can be prevented by keeping all antifreeze containers tightly closed and properly stored, preventing spills, and properly disposing of used antifreeze. A new generation of antifreeze products contains propylene glycol rather than ethylene glycol.

The U.S. Food and Drug Administration has labeled propylene glycol as "generally recognized as safe," which means it can be added to foods. However, that is in small amounts and only for people. Cats should not consume this either. Ingesting propylene glycol antifreeze can cause lack of coordination and, possibly, seizures, but is unlikely to be fatal.

RODENT POISONS

Common rat and mouse poisons include anticoagulants and hypercalcemic agents. Both can be deadly if your cat ingests them and, in some cases, if he eats a rodent who has these poisons in its system.

Anticoagulants

Anticoagulant rat and mouse poisons are the most commonly used household poisons. These products account for a large number of accidental poisonings in cats and dogs. Anticoagulants block the synthesis of vitamin K-dependent coagulation factors, which are essential for normal blood clotting.

Observable signs of poisoning do not occur until several days after ingestion. The cat may become weak and pale from blood loss, have nosebleeds, vomit blood, have rectal bleeding, develop *hematomas* and bruises beneath the skin, or have hemorrhages beneath the gums. The cat may be found dead from bleeding into the chest or abdomen.

There are two generations of anticoagulants, both in current use. The first-generation anticoagulants are cumulative poisons that require multiple feedings over several days to kill the rodent. These poisons contain the anticoagulants warfarin and hydroxycoumarin.

Second-generation anticoagulants contain bromadiolone and brodifacoum, poisons that are 50 to 200 times more toxic than warfarin and hydroxycoumarin. These products are more dangerous to pets and are capable of killing rodents after a single feeding. It is possible for a cat to be poisoned by eating a dead rodent with residual poison in its stomach.

Closely related to the second-generation anticoagulants are the long-acting anticoagulants of the indanedione class (pindone, diphacinone, diphenadione, and chlorphacinone), which are extremely toxic.

Treatment: Seek immediate veterinary help. If at all possible, bring in the product container so the veterinarian can identify the poison. This is important, because treatment depends on whether the poison was a first- or second-generation anticoagulant. With observed or suspected recent ingestion, induce vomiting (see page 29).

Treatment of spontaneous bleeding caused by all anticoagulants involves your veterinarian administering fresh whole blood or frozen plasma in amounts determined by the rate and volume of blood loss. Vitamin K_1 is a specific antidote. It is given by subcutaneous injection and repeated subcutaneously or orally as necessary until clotting time returns to normal. With first-generation anticoagulants, this often occurs within a week. With long-acting anticoagulants, treatment takes up to a month because of the length of time the poison remains in the cat's system.

Hypercalcemic Agents

Hypercalcemic agents are poisons that contain vitamin D (cholecalciferol) as their effective agent. Cholecalciferol poisons work by raising the calcium content in blood serum to toxic levels, eventually producing cardiac arrhythmias and death. They are becoming increasingly popular because rodents do not develop resistance to them. Cats who eat poisoned rodents may develop toxicity, but in most cases, the cat must eat the poison itself to become ill.

In cats, signs of hypercalcemia appear 18 to 36 hours after ingesting the poison. The signs include thirst and frequent urination, vomiting, generalized weakness, muscle twitching, seizures, and, finally, death. Among survivors, the effects of an elevated serum calcium may persist for weeks.

Treatment: If you suspect your cat has ingested one of these poisons within the past four hours, induce vomiting (see page 29) and notify your veterinarian. Veterinary treatment involves correcting the fluid and electrolyte imbalances and lowering calcium levels using diuretics, prednisone, oral phosphorus binders, and a low-calcium prescription diet. Calcitonin is a specific antidote, but it is difficult to obtain and has only short-term effects.

Bromethalin

This rodenticide acts on the central nervous system by causing *edema* in the cells of the brain and spinal cord. One of the first signs seen in cats is paralysis, including seizures or inability to urinate. Mild cases may show only *ataxia*.

Treatment: If caught soon after ingestion, induce vomiting (see page 29) and follow up with activated charcoal (page 29). Get the cat to your veterinarian. Steroids given by your veterinarian and gingko supplements may help, at least somewhat. Once symptoms have started it can be dangerous to give any oral treatments. If the cat survives, recovery may take weeks.

POISON BAITS

Animal baits containing strychnine, sodium fluoroacetate, phosphorus, zinc phosphide, and metaldehyde are used in rural areas to control gophers, coyotes, and other predators. They are also used in stables and barns to eliminate rodents. These baits are highly palatable and therefore may be ingested by a cat. Many are extremely toxic and kill in a matter of minutes. Fortunately, they are being used less frequently because of livestock losses, concerns about persistence in the environment, and their potential to poison pets and children.

Strychnine

Strychnine is used as a rat, mouse, and mole poison. It has also been a common coyote bait. Fortunately, the use of strychnine is decreasing. In concentrations greater than 0.5 percent, its use is restricted to certified exterminators. It is available to the public in concentrations of 0.3 percent or less. With better regulation and the use of lower concentrations, strychnine is becoming a less common cause of accidental poisoning.

It is available commercially as coated pellets dyed purple, red, or green. Signs of poisoning are so typical that the diagnosis can be made almost at once. Onset is sudden (less than two hours after ingestion). The first signs are agitation, excitability, and apprehension. They are followed rather quickly by intensely painful muscular seizures that last about 60 seconds, during which the cat throws his head back, can't breathe, and turns blue. The slightest stimulation, such as tapping the cat or clapping your hands, starts a seizure. This characteristic response is used to make the diagnosis. Other signs associated with nervous system involvement include tremors, champing, drooling, uncoordinated muscle spasms, collapse, and paddling the legs.

Seizures due to strychnine and other central nervous system toxins are sometimes misdiagnosed as epilepsy. This error can be a fatal mistake, because immediate veterinary attention is necessary to treat poisoning. Epileptic seizures usually last a few minutes and do not recur during the same episode. Signs always appear in a certain order, and each attack is the same. They are over before the cat can get to a veterinarian. Usually, they are not considered emergencies (see *Seizures*, page 339).

Treatment: If your cat is showing the first signs of poisoning and hasn't vomited, induce vomiting as discussed on page 29. Do not induce vomiting if the cat exhibits signs of labored breathing or has started having seizures.

With signs of central nervous system involvement, do not delay to induce vomiting. It is important to avoid loud noises or unnecessary handling that might trigger a seizure. Cover your cat with a coat or blanket and immediately go to the nearest veterinary clinic. Further treatment involves your veterinarian administering intravenous diazepam (Valium) or barbiturates to control seizures. The cat is then placed in a dark, quiet room and disturbed as little as possible.

Sodium Fluoroacetate

Sodium fluoroacetate (compound 1080/1081), a very potent rat and gopher poison, is mixed with cereal, bran, and other rodent feeds. It is so potent that cats and dogs can be poisoned just by eating a dead rodent. Its use is restricted to licensed pest control operators and it is used infrequently in the United States, but it might be found in old barns.

The onset of signs is sudden and begins with vomiting, followed by agitation, straining to urinate or defecate, a staggering gait, atypical fits or true convulsions, and then collapse. Seizures are not triggered by external stimuli, as are those of strychnine poisoning.

Treatment: Immediately after the cat ingests the poison, induce vomiting (see page 29). Care and handling is the same as for strychnine poisoning (page 34).

Arsenic

Arsenic has been combined with metaldehyde in slug and snail baits and may appear in ant poisons, weed killers, wood preservatives, and insecticides. Its use is on the decline. Arsenic is also a common impurity found in many chemicals. Death can occur quickly after ingestion, before there is time to observe the symptoms. In more protracted cases the signs include thirst, drooling, vomiting, staggering, intense abdominal pain, cramps, diarrhea, paralysis, and death. The breath of the cat will have a strong odor of garlic.

Treatment: Induce vomiting (see page 29). Go to your veterinarian to start intravenous fluid therapy to flush the kidneys. A chelating agent to bind the arsenic, called dimercaprol, may be used, but it has side effects. British anti-Lewisite (BAL) is a specific antidote.

Metaldehyde

This poison, often combined with arsenic, is used commonly in rat, snail, and slug baits. It may also be a component of solid fuel for camp stoves. The signs of toxicity are excitation, drooling and slobbering, uncoordinated gait, muscle tremors, and weakness that leads to inability to stand within a few hours after ingestion. The tremors are not triggered by external stimuli.

Treatment: Immediately after the cat ingests the poison, induce vomiting (see page 29). The care and handling are similar as described for strychnine poisoning (page 34). Death may occur days later from liver failure.

Phosphorus

This chemical is present in rat and roach poisons, fireworks, flares, matches, and matchboxes. A poisoned cat may have a garlic odor to his breath. The first signs of intoxication are vomiting and diarrhea. They may be followed by a symptom-free interval, then by recurrent vomiting, cramps, pain in the abdomen, convulsions, and coma.

Treatment: Induce vomiting (see page 29) when you suspect the cat has ingested a product or poison that contains phosphorus. Do not coat the bowel with milk or egg whites, as this can actually promote absorption. Take your cat to the nearest veterinary facility. There is no specific antidote.

Zinc Phosphide

This substance is found in rat poisons and grain fumigant. Intoxication causes central nervous system depression, labored breathing, vomiting (often with blood), weakness, convulsions, and death. Cats who eat rodents or birds poisoned by zinc phosphide may show signs of toxicity.

Treatment: There is no specific antidote. Treat as you would for strychnine poisoning (see page 34). A stomach *lavage* must be done at a veterinary clinic. The stomach should be lavaged with 5 percent sodium bicarbonate, which raises the gastric pH and delays the formation of gas.

INSECTICIDES

There are dozens of products sold at hardware, home repair, and agricultural stores to kill ants, termites, wasps, garden pests, and other insects. Most of them contain organophosphates and carbamates as their active ingredients. With the development of pyrethrin insecticides that are equally effective but much less toxic, organophosphates and carbamates are being used less frequently.

Organophosphates and Carbamates

The organophosphates include chlorpyrifos, diazinon, phosmet, fenthion cythioate, and tetrachlorvinphos. The two most common carbamates in pet products are carbaryl and propoxur. Most cases of organophosphate or carbamate poisoning occur because the cat ingested a poison bait or was treated with flea products made for dogs. Exposure to high concentrations of chemicals in sprays and dusts is also possible. Organophosphates are especially toxic to cats.

Signs of toxicity include hyperexcitability, excessive salivation and drooling, frequent urination, diarrhea, muscle twitching, weakness, staggering, collapse, and coma. Death is by respiratory failure.

Treatment: If you suspect your cat has ingested an insecticide poison, immediately induce vomiting (see page 29) and notify your veterinarian. With any sign of toxicity, the first priority is to get your cat to the veterinarian as quickly as possible.

The specific antidote your veterinarian will administer for organophosphate poisoning (*not* carbamate poisoning) is 2-PAM (pralidoxime chloride). Atropine is given for both organophosphate and carbamate poisoning to control excessive salivation, vomiting, frequent urination and defecation, and to reverse a slow heart rate. Seizures are controlled with diazepam (Valium) or barbiturates.

In the event of skin exposure, give the cat a bath with soapy water and rinse thoroughly to remove residual insecticide.

Chlorinated Hydrocarbons

These compounds, of which the prototype is DDT, are added to sprays and dusts to control plant pests. Their use has been curtailed because of persistent toxicity in the environment. Only lindane and methoxychlor are currently approved for use around livestock. Chlorinated hydrocarbons are readily inhaled and easily absorbed through the skin. Toxicity can occur from repeated exposure or a single excessive exposure. These compounds are extremely toxic to cats.

Signs of toxicity appear rapidly. The signs include hyperexcitability with twitching of the face, followed by muscle tremors that begin at the head and progress back to involve the neck, shoulder, trunk, and rear legs. Seizures and convulsions are followed by respiratory paralysis and death.

Treatment: There is no specific antidote. The cat should be thoroughly bathed. Treatment at a veterinary hospital includes supporting life functions, removing ingested poison from the stomach by gastric lavage and/or activated charcoal, and controlling seizures.

Pyrethrins and Pyrethroids

These compounds are incorporated into many insecticidal shampoos, sprays, dusts, dips, foggers, and sprays. Pyrethrins and the synthetic pyrethroids are much safer to use on and around dogs (and humans) than are other insecticides, and they are being used more widely. However, *only* the pyrethrins are safe for cats. In addition, many over-the-counter topical flea products have concentrated pyrethrins as their active ingredient. Cats may be affected by that high level of pyrethrins.

The synthetic pyrethroids are *not* safe for use in cats. Common chemicals in this class include permethrin, allethrin, fenvalerate, resmethrin, and sumethrin. Some cats have been poisoned by simply curling up and sleeping with a dog who has one of the topical permethrin products on him or by licking or grooming a dog with those products on his coat.

Signs of toxicity include drooling, depression, muscle tremors, staggering, vomiting, and rapid, labored breathing. Simultaneous exposure to organophosphates increases the toxicity of pyrethroids. Hyperthermia (high body temperature) may be noted.

Treatment: Induce vomiting (see page 29) within two hours of ingestion. Call your veterinarian for further instructions. Do not induce vomiting if the product contains a petroleum distillate. With signs of toxicity, proceed immediately to the veterinary clinic.

For topical exposure, remove residual insecticide by bathing the cat in *lukewarm* water (bathing in hot or cold water may actually increase the rate of absorption or cause hypothermia, which increases toxicity) and Dawn dishwashing soap or feline shampoo to strip out the chemicals. (*Do not* use flea shampoo.) Rinse very thoroughly. After bathing, keep the cat warm.

If signs of hyperthermia are evident, you must attempt to cool the cat down (see *Heat Stroke*, page 24). This is more common with permethrin toxicity.

Methocarbamol may be administered by your veterinarian to control tremors; diazepam is not usually effective. Fluid therapy is recommended to thoroughly flush the kidneys.

Prevention: Most cases of poisoning occur because flea control products are not applied properly. Follow all instructions carefully. *Only use products approved for cats on cats. Never use a product made for dogs on a cat.*

Petroleum Products

Gasoline, kerosene, turpentine, and similar volatile liquids can cause pneumonia if they are aspirated (enter the lungs) or inhaled. The signs of toxicity include vomiting, difficulty breathing, tremors, convulsions, and coma. Death is by respiratory failure. Ingesting these compounds will cause gastrointestinal upset and may burn the mouth and esophagus, and may cause liver or kidney failure.

Treatment: *Do not induce vomiting.* Flush the mouth thoroughly to remove any traces of residue. Be prepared to administer artificial respiration (see page 11). Activated charcoal may be recommended by your veterinarian, or stomach lavage may be used to remove as much as possible of the ingested products.

These products can be very irritating to the skin, so remove them as quickly as possible. Bathe the cat using warm, soapy water. For tar in the coat, see page 127.

Lead

Lead is found in insecticides and previously served as a base for many commercial paints. Intoxication occurs mainly in kittens and young cats who chew on substances that have been coated with a lead paint. Other sources of lead are linoleum, fishing weights, batteries, and plumbing materials. Lead poisoning can occur in older cats if they ingest an insecticide containing lead. A chronic form does occur with repeated low-level exposure.

Acute poisoning begins with abdominal pain and vomiting. In the chronic form, a variety of central nervous system signs are possible. They include fits, uncoordinated gait, excitation, attacks of hysteria, weakness, stupor, and blindness. These are also signs of encephalitis (see page 334).

Treatment: Immediately after ingestion, induce vomiting. Seek immediate medical attention. Specific antidotes are available from your veterinarian, who can also do blood tests to determine the lead levels.

CORROSIVE HOUSEHOLD PRODUCTS

Corrosive and caustic chemicals (acids and alkalis) are found in household cleaners, dishwasher detergents, toilet bowl cleaners, drain decloggers, and commercial solvents. When ingested, they cause burns of the mouth, esophagus, and stomach. Severe cases are associated with acute perforation of the esophagus and stomach. Later, strictures of these organs may develop from tissue damage and scarring. Even simply walking through a phenolic disinfectant solution, such as Lysol, can be dangerous for cats, especially if they lick their feet to clean them.

Treatment: *Do not induce vomiting!* Vomiting will simply double the tissue damage. Rinse out your cat's mouth—under a running faucet, if possible, or with a hose. Contact your veterinarian following any exposures to these products.

The practice of giving an acid to neutralize an alkali, and vice versa, is no longer recommended because it causes heat injury to the lining of the stomach.

If these products get on the cat's skin, prevent him from licking or grooming and flush the area thoroughly for at least 10 to 30 minutes with running water.

GARBAGE AND FOOD POISONS

Cats are more particular than dogs about what they eat. Nevertheless, they do sometimes scavenge and come into contact with carrion (rotting flesh or meat), decomposing foods, animal manure, and other noxious substances (some of which are listed in *Diarrhea*, page 228). Cats are more sensitive than dogs to food poisoning and exhibit effects at lower levels of exposure. This is partly due to their smaller size and the lack of the liver enzyme glucuronyl transferase.

Signs of poisoning usually begin with vomiting and pain in the abdomen. In severe cases, they are followed two to six hours later by a diarrhea that is often bloody. Shock may occur—particularly if the problem is complicated by bacterial infection. Mild cases recover in one to two days.

Treatment: *Seek immediate veterinary attention* for signs of dehydration, toxicity, and shock. In mild cases, coat the bowel as described in *How to Induce Vomiting and Prevent Poison Absorption* (page 29).

Dangerous Foods

Along with food poisoning from spoiled foods, cats lack the enzymes to properly digest some foods. Two of these are onions and garlic. Cats can be exposed to onion from the onion powder in some baby foods or by chewing on *Allium* species plants. Garlic may be a component of some natural flea repellant products. Signs are intestinal upset and possibly anemia as toxins build up that destroy red blood cells. Treatment may include antioxidants, oxygen therapy, and even blood transfusions for severe cases.

Chocolate and coffee can be toxic to cats, due to the stimulants they contain—theobromine and caffeine, respectively. Signs include excitability, weakness, rapid breathing, and even death. Induce vomiting (see page 29). Activated charcoal (see page 29) may also be helpful. The cat may need fluid therapy at a veterinary clinic to flush the system.

Grapes, raisins, and macadamia nuts are all foods that have been found to be toxic in dogs. It can be assumed they are not good for cats, although luckily, cats seem to avoid these products. Xylitol, an artificial sweetener found in sugar-free baked goods and gums, is another food that is toxic to dogs and can be assumed to be toxic in cats.

POISONOUS PLANTS

With some types of vegetation, only certain parts of the plant are toxic. With others, the whole plant is poisonous. Ingestion causes a wide range of symptoms. They include mouth irritation, drooling, vomiting, diarrhea, hallucinations, seizures, coma, and death. Other plant substances cause skin rash. Some toxic plants have specific pharmacological actions, and are used in making medicines. The signs they cause vary widely.

Tables of toxic plants, shrubs, and trees are included on pages 41 to 43 for reference. This list is a collection of common toxic plants. It is not a list of all poisonous plants. If you're not sure about a plant, ask your veterinarian or the local plant nursery. The ASPCA also has a list of poisonous plants on its web site (www.aspca.org). Your local Cooperative Extension is often a good source of information about poisonous plants.

TOAD AND SALAMANDER POISONING

In North America there are two species of poisonous toad (*Bufo*). The Colorado River toad is found in the Southwest and Hawaii. The marine toad is found in Florida. There is one species of poisonous salamander, the California newt, found in California.

All toads, even nontoxic ones, have a bad taste. Cats who mouth them slobber, spit, and drool. The marine toad is highly poisonous, causing death in as little as 15 minutes.

Symptoms in cats depend on the toxicity of the toad or salamander and the amount of poison absorbed. They vary from slobbering to convulsions, blindness, and death.

Treatment: Flush out your cat's mouth (use a garden hose if necessary) and induce vomiting, as described on page 29. Be prepared to administer CPR (see page 12). Take your cat to the veterinarian. Be prepared to describe the toad or salamander in as much detail as you can. Cats with salamander poisoning usually recover quickly.

Indoor Plants with Toxic Effects

Houseplants that cause a skin reaction after contact with the skin or mouth

Chrysanthemum	Poinsettia
Creeping fig	Weeping fig

Irritating plants, some of which contain oxalic acid, which causes mouth swelling, difficulty swallowing, respiratory problems, and gastrointestinal upsets

Arrowhead vine	Marble queen
Boston ivy	Mother-in-law plant
Caladium	Neththyis
Calla or arum lily	Parlor ivy
Dumbcane (dieffenbachia)	Pothos or devil's lily
Elephant's ear	Peace lily
Emerald duke	Red princess
Heart leaf (philodendron)	Saddle leaf (philodendron)
Jack-in-the-pulpit	Split leaf (philodendron)
Majesty	Tuberous begonia
Malanga	

Plants that contain a wide variety of poisons—most cause vomiting, an acutely painful abdomen, and cramps; some cause tremors, heart and respiratory problems, and/or kidney problems, which are difficult for owners to interpret

Amaryllis	Jerusalem cherry
Asparagus fern	Nightshade
Azalea	Pot mum
Bird-of-paradise	Ripple ivy
Creeping Charlie	Spider mum
Crown of thorns	Sprengeri fern
Elephant's ear	Umbrella plant
Ivy species	

continued

Outdoor Plants with Toxic Effects

Outdoor plants that can cause vomiting and diarrhea

Bittersweet woody	Indian tobacco
Castor bean	Indian turnip
Crocus	Larkspur woody
Daffodil	Poke weed
Delphinium	Skunk cabbage
Foxglove	Soapberry
Ground cherry	Tulip
Hyacinth	Wisteria

Trees and shrubs that may cause vomiting, painful abdomen, and diarrhea

American yew	Horse chestnut
Apricot	Japanese plum
Almond	Mock orange
Azalea (rhododendron)	Monkey pod
Balsam pear	Peach
Bird-of-paradise bush	Privet
Buckeye	Rain tree
Cherry	Western black locust yew
English holly	Wild cherry
English yew	

Outdoor plants with varied toxic effects

Angel's trumpet	Mescal bean
Buttercup	Moonseed
Day lily	Mushrooms
Dologeton	Nightshades
Dutchman's breeches	Pigweed
Jasmine	Poison hemlock
Jimsonweed	Rhubarb
Locoweed	Spinach
Lupine	Sunburned potatoes

Outdoor Plants with Toxic Effects	
May apple	Tomato vine
Matrimony vine	Water hemlock
Tiger lily	
Hallucinogens	
Locoweed	Periwinkle
Marijuana	Peyote
Morning glory	Poppies
Nutmeg	
Outdoor plants that cause convulsions	
Chinaberry	Nux vomica
Coriaria	Water hemlock
Moonweed	

Insect Stings, Spiders, and Scorpions

Because cats are predators and are curious by nature, they tend to be at risk from small poisonous creatures. The stings of bees, wasps, yellow jackets, and ants cause painful swelling at the site of the sting. Cats tend to get stung about the face and on the paws. Swelling may include the face and neck, or be localized to the area of the sting. If a cat is stung many times, he could go into shock as the result of absorbed toxins. Rarely, a hypersensitivity reaction (anaphylactic shock) can occur if the cat was exposed in the past (see page 13).

The stings of black widow and brown recluse spiders and tarantulas are toxic to animals. The first sign is sharp pain at the sting site. Later, the cat may develop excitability, chills, fever, and labored breathing. Shock and seizures may occur, with early paralysis from black widow bites. Most cats will die. There is antivenin if it can be obtained from your veterinarian in time. Brown recluse spider bites cause two syndromes. One is a cutaneous form with a localized blister and pain. Eventually, a bull's-eye lesion may be noted. Over a week or two, the involved skin will die and ulcerate, leaving a wound that may take months to heal. The second, visceral form is accompanied by fever, painful joints, and possibly vomiting and seizures. Cats may develop blood disorders and kidney failure. This form is much rarer and is often fatal.

Tarantula bites are usually not serious, but the barbed hairs they drop can be irritating to skin and mucous membranes.

The stings of centipedes and scorpions cause a local reaction and, at times, severe illness. These bites heal slowly. Poisonous scorpions are found only in southern Arizona (two species). A young kitten or small cat is at greater risk due to his small size.

TREATING STINGS AND BITES

1. Identify the insect or animal, if possible.
2. Remove an embedded stinger with tweezers, or scrape it out with a credit card. (Only bees leave their stingers behind.)
3. Make a paste of baking soda and apply it directly to the sting.
4. Apply ice packs to relieve swelling and pain.
5. Apply Calamine lotion and Cortaid to relieve itching if needed, but cover the area with a loose bandage so the cat will not lick off the medication.

If the cat exhibits signs of generalized toxicity or anaphylaxis (restlessness, agitation, face scratching, drooling, vomiting, diarrhea, difficulty breathing, collapse, or seizures), transport him immediately to the nearest veterinary facility. If your cat is known to have reactions to bee stings, ask your veterinarian about keeping an EpiPen kit available and what dose to use for your cat. The EpiPen kits are special prepackaged kits of injectable epinephrine for counteracting anaphylactic shock. Epinephrine has a short expiration date, so check frequently to be sure your kit is not outdated.

Snake and Lizard Bites

Poisonous and nonpoisonous snakes are widely distributed throughout North America. Cats may come into contact with snakes while hunting or out of curiosity. In general, bites of nonpoisonous snakes do not cause swelling or pain. They show teeth marks in the shape of a horseshoe (no fang marks).

Ninety percent of snake bites in cats involve the head and legs. Body bites from poisonous snakes usually are lethal.

In the United States there are four poisonous varieties: cottonmouths (also called water moccasins), rattlesnakes, copperheads, and coral snakes. The diagnosis of poison snake bite is made by the appearance of the bite, the behavior of the animal bitten, and identification of the species of snake. (Kill it first, if possible.)

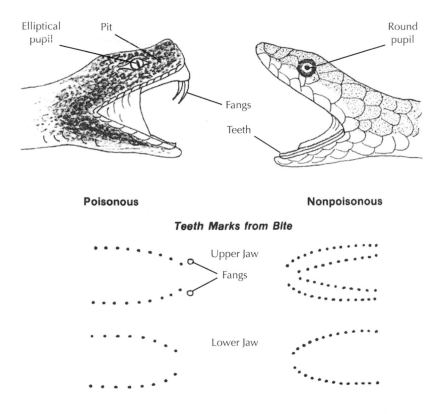

Poisonous   **Nonpoisonous**

Teeth Marks from Bite

Upper Jaw

Fangs

Lower Jaw

Except for the coral snake, all poisonous species in North America are pit vipers. Note the elliptical pupil, the pit below the eye, the large fangs, and the characteristic bite.

PIT VIPERS (RATTLESNAKES, COTTONMOUTHS, AND COPPERHEADS)

You can identify these species by their large size (4 to 8 feet, 1.2 to 2.4 m long), triangular heads, pits below and between the eyes, elliptical pupils, rough scales, and the presence of retractable fangs in the upper jaw.

The bite: You may see one or two bleeding puncture wounds in the skin; these are fang marks. You may have to search the haircoat and skin carefully at first to find the punctures. Signs of local reaction appear quickly and include sudden severe swelling, redness, and hemorrhages in the skin. The pain is immediate and severe.

Note that 25 percent of poisonous snake bites lack venom and thus do not produce a local reaction. While absence of local swelling and pain is a good sign, it does not guarantee the cat won't become sick. Severe venom poisoning has been known to occur without a local reaction.

The cat's behavior: Signs of envenomation may take several hours to appear because of variables such as time of the year, species of the snake, toxicity of the venom, amount injected, location of the bite, and size and health of the cat. The amount of venom injected bears no relationship to the size of the snake. The first signs are extreme restlessness, panting, drooling, and weakness. These are followed by diarrhea, depressed breathing, collapse, sometimes seizures, shock, and death in severe cases.

Coral Snakes

Identify this snake by its rather small size (less than 3 feet, .9 m long), small head with black nose, and brightly colored alternating bands (red, yellow and black) fully encircling the body. The fangs in the upper jaw are not retractable.

The bite: There is less severe redness and swelling at the site of the bite, but the pain may range from mild to excruciating, depending on whether venom was injected. Look for the fang marks.

The cat's behavior: Coral snake venom is a neurotoxin, meaning it affects the nerves and causes weakness and paralysis. Signs include vomiting, diarrhea, urinary incontinence, paralysis, convulsions, and coma. Some cats will survive.

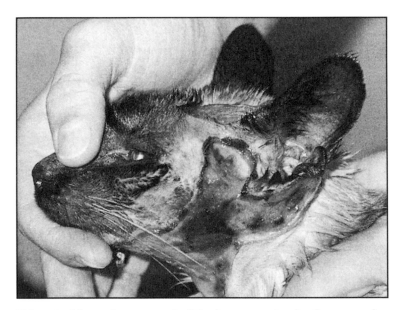

This cat with a poisonous snake bite shows an extensive face wound after loss of devitalized tissue.

LIZARDS

Two species of poisonous lizard are found in the United States, both in south-western states. They are the Gila monster and the Mexican bearded lizard. The bite of these lizards could potentially be fatal to a cat. If the lizard has a firm hold on the cat, pry open the lizard's jaws with pliers and remove the cat from the lizard.

TREATING SNAKE AND LIZARD BITES

First identify the snake or lizard and look at the bite. If the animal is not poisonous, clean and dress the wound as described in the section on *Wounds* (below). If it appears the cat has been bitten by a poisonous snake or lizard and if you are within 30 minutes of a veterinary hospital, *proceed at once to the veterinary hospital*. If you are unable to get help within 30 minutes, follow these steps, then go to the nearest veterinarian.

- *Keep the cat quiet.* Venom spreads rapidly if the cat is active. Excitement, exercise, and struggling increase the rate of absorption. Carry the cat.
- If the bite is on the leg, apply a constricting bandage (a handkerchief or a strip of cloth) between the bite and the cat's heart. You should be able to get a finger beneath the bandage; loosen the bandage for five minutes every hour.
- Do not wash the wound, because this will increase venom absorption.
- Do not apply ice, because this does not slow absorption and can damage tissue.
- Do not make cuts over the wound and/or attempt to suck out the venom. This is never successful and you could absorb venom.

Proceed to the veterinary hospital. Veterinary treatment involves respiratory and circulatory support, antihistamines, intravenous fluids, and species-specific antivenin. The earlier the antivenin is given, the better the results. Because signs of envenomation are often delayed, all cats who have been bitten by a poisonous snake or lizard—even those who don't show signs—should be hospitalized and observed for 24 hours.

Wounds

The two most important goals in treating wounds are to stop the bleeding and to prevent infection. Wounds are painful, so be prepared to restrain the cat before treating the wound (see *Handling and Restraint*, page 2).

CONTROLLING BLEEDING

Bleeding may be arterial (bright red blood will spurt out) or venous (dark red blood will ooze out), or sometimes both. Do not wipe a wound that has stopped bleeding, as this will dislodge the clot. Similarly, don't pour hydrogen peroxide on a fresh wound. Peroxide dissolves clots and starts a fresh round of bleeding. It may also damage the tissues and delay healing.

The two methods used to control bleeding in an emergency situation are a pressure dressing and a tourniquet.

Pressure Dressing

The most effective and safest method for controlling bleeding is to apply pressure directly to the wound. Take several sterile gauze squares (or, in an emergency, use any clean cloth such as a thickly folded pad of clothing) and place it over the wound. Apply direct pressure for 5 to 10 minutes. Leave the dressing in place and bandage snugly. If material for bandaging is not available, hold the pack in place until help arrives.

Watch for signs of swelling of the limb below the pressure pack (see *Foot and Leg Bandages*, page 52). This indicates impaired circulation. If you see these signs, the bandage must be loosened or removed. Consider adding more bulk to the pack and apply a second bandage over the first. Transport the cat to a veterinary hospital.

Tourniquet

Tourniquets can be used on the extremities and tail to control arterial bleeding that can't be controlled with a pressure pack. *Tourniquets should never be used if bleeding can be controlled by direct pressure.* Always place the tourniquet *above* the wound (between the wound and the heart).

A suitable tourniquet can be made from a piece of cloth, belt, or length of gauze. Loop the tourniquet around the limb, then tighten it by hand or with a stick inserted beneath the loop. Twist the loop until the bleeding stops.

If you see the end of the artery, you might attempt to pick it up with a pair of tweezers and tie it off with a piece of cotton thread. When possible, this should be left to a trained practitioner.

A tourniquet should be loosened every 10 minutes to prevent tissue hypoxia and to check for persistent bleeding. If bleeding has stopped, apply a pressure bandage as described in the previous section. If bleeding continues, let the blood flow for 30 seconds and then retighten the tourniquet for another 10 minutes.

PUNCTURE WOUNDS

Puncture wounds are caused by bites and pointed objects. Animal bites, in particular, are heavily contaminated with bacteria. There may be bleeding. There may also be bruising, particularly if the cat was picked up in the teeth of a bigger animal and shaken. Puncture wounds are often concealed by the cat's coat and may easily be overlooked until an abscess develops a few days later.

Treating a puncture wound requires a veterinarian. It involves surgically enlarging the skin opening to provide drainage, after which the area is irrigated with a dilute antiseptic surgical solution. These wounds should not be closed. With all animal bites, keep in mind the possibility of rabies. If your cat is bitten by an animal of unknown vaccination status or a wild animal, a rabies booster may be recommended.

Bites from other cats very often lead to abscesses. Antibiotics are frequently prescribed for bite wounds and wounds that are heavily contaminated, such as puncture wounds.

TREATING WOUNDS

Nearly all animal wounds are contaminated with dirt and bacteria. Proper care and handling will reduce the risk of tetanus and prevent many infections. Before handling a wound, make sure your hands and instruments are clean.

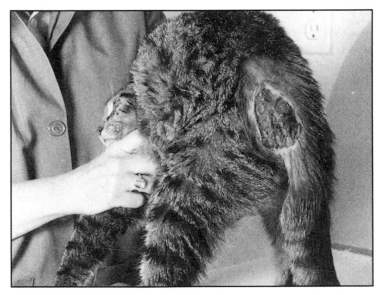

An infected wound near the base of the tail from a cat fight. Because of the bacteria in cats' mouths, bites from other cats often lead to infection and abscess.

The five steps in wound care are as follows:

1. Skin preparation
2. Wound irrigation
3. Debridement
4. Wound closure
5. Bandaging

Skin Preparation

Remove the original pressure dressing and cleanse the area around the wound with a surgical scrub solution. The most commonly used solutions are Betadine (povidone-iodine) and Nolvasan (chlorhexidine diacetate). Both products are extremely irritating to exposed tissue in the concentrations provided in the stock solutions (Betadine 10 percent, chlorhexidine 2 percent), so be very careful that the solution does not get in the wound while scrubbing the skin around it. Dilute the solution to a weak tea color for Betadine or a pale blue color for Nolvasan.

After the scrub, start at the edges of the wound and clip the cat's coat back far enough to prevent any long hairs from getting into the wound.

Three-percent hydrogen peroxide, often recommended as a wound cleanser, has little value as an antiseptic and is extremely toxic to tissues. Do not use it on a wound, as it can damage tissues and delay healing.

Wound Irrigation

The purpose of irrigation is to remove dirt and bacteria. The gentlest and most effective method of wound cleansing is by *lavage*, which involves irrigating the wound with large amounts of fluid until the tissues are clean and glistening. Do not vigorously cleanse the wound using a brush or gauze pad because this causes bleeding and traumatizes the exposed tissue.

Tap water is an acceptable and convenient irrigating solution. Tap water has a negligible bacterial count and is known to cause less tissue reaction than sterile or distilled water.

If possible, add chlorhexidine solution or Betadine solution to the tap water for antibacterial activity. Chlorhexidine has the greater residual antiseptic effect, but either antiseptic solution (not soap solutions) is satisfactory when correctly diluted. To dilute chlorhexidine, add 25 ml of the 2 percent stock solution to 2 quarts (2 l) of water, making a 0.05 percent irrigating solution. To dilute Betadine, add 10 ml of the 10 percent stock solution to 2 quarts (2 l) of water to make a 0.2 percent irrigating solution.

The effectiveness of the irrigation is related to the volume and pressure of the fluid used. A bulb syringe is a low-pressure system. It is least effective and requires more fluid to achieve satisfactory irrigation. A large plastic syringe removes a moderate amount of dirt and bacteria. A home Waterpik unit (used by people to clean their teeth) or a commercial lavage unit that provides a high-pressure stream of fluid is the most effective.

A garden hose with a pressure nozzle for the initial lavage, or a kitchen sink spray unit, followed by one of the methods just described to deliver the antiseptic, is a good alternative. You want to flush and clean the wound, not force dirt deeper into the tissues. Angle your flow of liquid to accomplish that and let the fluid pool to bring debris to the surface.

Debridement

Debridement means removing dying tissue and any remaining foreign matter using tissue forceps (tweezers) and scissors or a scalpel. Debridement requires experience to determine the difference between normal and devitalized tissue, and instruments to control bleeding and close the wound. Accordingly, wounds that require debridement and closure should be treated by a veterinarian.

Wound Closure

Fresh lacerations on the lips, face, eyelids, and ears are best sutured or stapled to prevent infection, minimize scarring, and speed recovery. Lacerations longer than half an inch (1.25 cm) on the body and extremities probably should be closed, but small lacerations may not need to be. The exception is small V-shaped lacerations, which almost always heal best if sutured.

Wounds contaminated by dirt and debris are quite likely to become infected if they are closed at the time of injury. These wounds should be left open or sutured around a drain that can be used for through and through irrigation. Similarly, wounds older than 12 hours should not be closed without drainage. Suturing or stapling should be avoided if the wound appears to be infected (is red, swollen, or has a surface discharge).

Your veterinarian may decide to close a wound that has been left open for several days and has developed a bed of clean tissue. Wounds that are clean after several days are resistant to infection and usually can be closed without negative consequences. Suturing such a wound is called delayed primary closure.

The length of time sutures or staples should remain in place depends on the wound's location and other characteristics. Most sutures and staples can be removed after 10 to 14 days.

Bandaging

Bandaging protects the wound from dirt and contaminants. It also restricts movement, compresses skin flaps, eliminates pockets of serum, keeps the edges of the wound from pulling apart, and prevents the cat from biting and licking at the wound. Bandaging is most effective for wounds to the extremities. Dressings over draining or infected wounds must be changed once or twice a day. The bandage should be bulky enough to absorb the drainage without soaking through.

Bandages are more difficult to apply to cats than to dogs and, once applied, are more difficult to keep in place. Cats who do not tolerate bandages and continually remove them may be helped by mild sedation. As an alternative, an Elizabethan collar or a BiteNot collar may be helpful. Wounds about the head and those draining pus are best left open to help drainage and ease of treatment.

When a cat claws and macerates a wound or continually scratches at a skin condition, treatment can be facilitated by bandaging his back feet or securing baby socks over the paws, and clipping his nails.

Bandaging is made much easier when a cat is gently but firmly restrained, as discussed on page 2. The bandaging equipment you will need is listed in the *Home Emergency and Medical Kit* (page 1).

Foot and Leg Bandages

To bandage a foot, place several sterile gauze pads over the wound. Pull apart a cotton ball and insert small bits between the cat's toes. Hold in place with adhesive tape looped around the bottom of the foot and back across the top until the foot is snugly wrapped.

For leg wounds, begin by wrapping the foot as just described. Then cover the wound with several sterile gauze pads and hold in place with strips of adhesive tape. On top, pad the entire leg with plenty of cotton so the dressing won't become too tight and interfere with circulation. Wrap the leg first with roll gauze, firmly but not too tightly, then wrap the leg with elastic tape or bandage, as shown in the photographs on page 53. Your veterinarian or a veterinary technician can show you the best way to bandage an individual wound.

Veterinary wraps, such as VetWrap, work well, but you need practice to have the right amount of tension so you don't cut off circulation. Flex the knee and foot several times to be sure the bandage is not too tight and that there is good movement at the joints.

Wrap the tape around the leg at the top, but do not overlap it because you want the tape to stick to the cat's hair. This technique keeps the dressing from sliding up and down, which often happens when only a roll gauze bandage is used without tape at the top. When a dressing is to be left in place for some time, check every few hours to be sure the foot is not swelling. Over the next few hours, check the toes for coolness and observe the feet for swelling. Swelling of the leg below a bandage will be seen in the toes. When the toes are swollen, the nails are spread apart instead of being side by side. If this swelling is not treated by removing the bandage, the foot becomes cold and loses feeling. If there is any question about the sensation or circulation to the

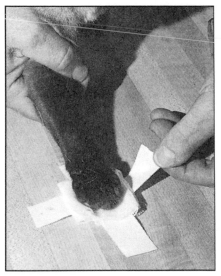

To apply a foot bandage, start by covering the injured area with several layers of gauze.

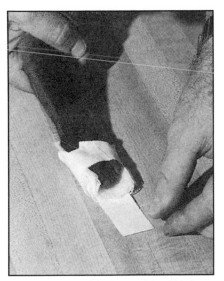

Hold the gauze in place with adhesive tape looped around the bottom of the foot and back across the top.

foot, loosen the dressing. Cats will frequently attempt to lick, bite or remove dressings that are too tight and uncomfortable.

You may need to put a plastic baggie over the wound bandage when the cat goes to the litter box, to prevent litter from getting up inside the bandage. A cat with a bandage should not be allowed outside.

Bandages over clean, healing wounds can be changed every two days, but should be inspected three or four times a day for signs of constriction, limb swelling, slippage, drainage, or soiling. If there are signs of any of these problems, replace the bandage.

Wounds on the foot or leg may be covered with a splint as well as a bandage. The splint minimizes movement of the area and speeds healing.

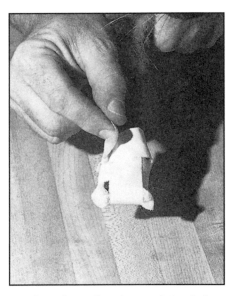

Tape loosely to allow for good circulation.

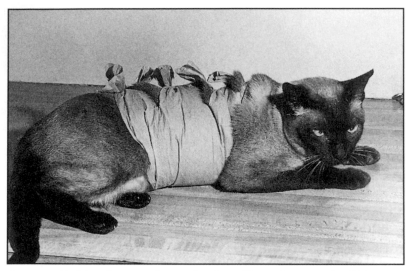

A many-tailed bandage may be used to keep kittens from nursing if the mother's breasts are infected.

Many-Tailed Bandage

This bandage is used to protect the skin of the abdomen, flanks, or back from scratching and biting and to hold dressings in place. It is made by taking a rectangular piece of linen and cutting the sides to make tails. Tie the tails together over the back to hold the bandage in place.

Ear Bandage

These dressings are difficult to apply. Most ear injuries can be left open. To protect the ears from scratching, use an Elizabethan or a BiteNot collar.

Eye Bandage

Your veterinarian may prescribe an eye bandage as part of the treatment of an eye ailment. Place a sterile gauze square over the affected eye and hold it in place by taping around the head with 1-inch-wide (25-mm) adhesive. Be careful not to wind the tape too tight. Apply the dressing so that the ears are free.

You may need to change the dressing from time to time to apply medication to the eye. Many cats will need to wear an Elizabethan or a BiteNot collar to prevent them from removing the bandage.

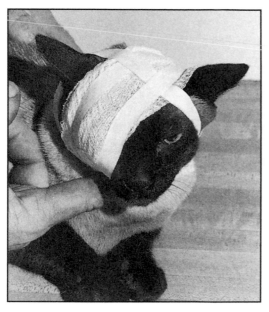

To make an eye bandage, wrap a gauze roll around the eye. A pad may be placed beneath the gauze. Secure with tape. The ears should be free.

HOME WOUND CARE

Small, open wounds can be treated at home without sutures or staples. Medicate the area twice a day with a topical antibiotic ointment such as triple antibiotic. The wound can be left open or covered with a dressing. Make sure the cat is not licking or chewing at the wound. You may need to use a wound covering such as a sock, or put an Elizabethan or a BiteNot collar on the cat.

Infected wounds that are draining pus require the application of moist sterile compresses. A number of topical antiseptics are effective in treating superficial wound infections. They include chlorhexidine, Betadine (diluted as described in *Wound Irrigation*, page 50), Furacin (both the topical cream and the 0.2 percent solution), 1 percent Silvadene cream, and topical antibiotics containing bacitracin, neomycin, and polymyxin B (triple antibiotic). Apply the topical antibiotic directly to the wound or place it on a gauze pad and dab the wound.

Change the dressing once or twice a day to facilitate pus drainage. Again, try to keep the cat from licking or grooming off the medication. Distracting the cat with play or food may give the medication time to be absorbed.

2

GASTROINTESTINAL PARASITES

Most cats will suffer from internal parasites at some time in their lives. Kittens can be infected through nursing. Cats who go outside, especially if they hunt, are also prone to picking up parasites. Even cats who live completely indoors may be exposed from a new cat joining the family or by catching a mouse that snuck into the house. Mosquitoes and fleas inside your home can also carry parasites.

The ideal parasite lives in its host without causing serious health problems. However, once parasite populations reach a certain size, clinical signs of illness become evident in the animal in which they live. If worms are causing a problem, there is often some change in the appearance of the cat's stool, which may include the passage of mucus or blood. There is also a decline in the cat's general health. You may note decreased appetite, loss of weight, sometimes protrusion of the third eyelid, diarrhea, and anemia.

Ascarids (roundworms), tapeworms, and hookworms are the most common intestinal parasites in cats. Healthy adult cats develop a certain degree of immunity to parasites, which helps keep any populations down. This varies with the individual parasite, though. For example, some parasites, such as tapeworms, return time after time. It is probable that cats, like dogs, develop a resistance to certain intestinal parasites whose larvae migrate in the animal's tissues (such as ascarids and hookworms), although this has not been proven in cats. Tapeworms have no migratory phase and thus cause little buildup of immunity.

Resistance to ascarids also appears to be age-related. Kittens and young cats show less resistance and, in consequence, may experience a heavy infestation. This can lead to marked debility or even death. Cats over 6 months of age are less likely to show significant clinical signs.

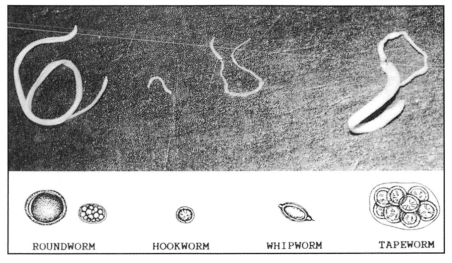

ROUNDWORM   HOOKWORM   WHIPWORM   TAPEWORM

Common adult feline worms, showing the relative size and appearance of adult worms and eggs. (There are two species of roundworm eggs.)

Immunosuppressive drugs, such as cortisone and some chemotherapy drugs, have been shown to activate large numbers of hookworm larvae lying dormant in an animal's tissues. Stressful events, such as trauma, surgery, severe disease, or emotional upsets, can also activate dormant larvae. This leads to the appearance of eggs in the stool.

During lactation, dormant ascarid larvae are activated and appear in the queen's milk. Therefore, a heavy parasite problem might develop in the litter even when the mother was effectively dewormed. This can happen because none of the deworming agents are completely effective against larvae that are encysted in the tissue.

Deworming Your Cat

Although some deworming medications are effective against more than one species of worms, there is no medication that is effective against them all. Accordingly, for a medication to be safe and effective, a precise diagnosis is required. It is also important that the medication be given precisely as directed. Natural side effects, such as diarrhea and vomiting, must be distinguished from toxic reactions. All dewormers are poisons—ideally, they are more poisonous to the parasites than they are to the hosts. For these reasons, it is advisable to deworm your cat *only* under veterinary supervision.

Deworming Kittens

A very large proportion of kittens are infested with ascarids. Other worms may be present, too. It is advisable to have your veterinarian check your kitten's stool before treating her for ascarids. Otherwise, other worms and internal parasites, such as coccidia, may go undetected.

Worm infestations are particularly harmful in kittens who are subjected to overfeeding, chilling, close confinement, or a sudden change in diet. Stressful conditions such as these should be corrected before administering a deworming agent. Do not deworm a kitten with diarrhea or other signs of illness, unless your veterinarian has determined that the illness is caused by an intestinal parasite.

Kittens with ascarids should be dewormed at 2 to 3 weeks of age and again at 5 to 6 weeks (see *Ascarids*, page 60). If eggs or worms are still found in the stool, subsequent treatment should be given. Due to public health considerations, many veterinarians recommend deworming kittens with a safe dewormer every month until 6 months of age.

Deworming Adult Cats

Most veterinarians recommend that adult cats be dewormed only when there is specific evidence of an infestation. A microscopic stool examination is the most effective way of making an exact diagnosis and choosing the best deworming agent.

It is not advisable to deworm a cat who is suffering from some unexplained illness that is assumed to be caused by worms. *All dewormers are poison*— meant to poison the worm, but not the cat. Cats who are debilitated by another disease may be too weak to resist the toxic effects of the deworming agent.

Cats of all ages, particularly those who hunt and roam freely, can be subject to periodic heavy worm infestations. These cats should be checked once or twice a year. If parasites are identified, they should be treated. It is reasonable to deworm outdoor cats routinely for ascarids and tapeworms, even without a positive stool sample. Many anthelmintics are safe for repeated use. Tapeworms segments may be seen frequently, and when discovered, they should be treated. Cats with tapeworms may need to be treated as often as four or five times a year.

A queen should have her stool checked before breeding. If parasites are found, she should receive a thorough deworming. This will not protect her kittens from all worm infestations, but it will decrease the frequency and severity of any parasite infestation. It will also help to put her in the best condition for a healthy pregnancy.

Common Deworming Medications

Medication	Ascarids	Hookworms	Tapeworms	Comments
Epsiprantel	No effect	No effect	Good	
Fenbendazole	Good	Good	Good	Also treats giardia
Ivermectin	Fair	Good	No effect	Also prevents heartworm
Milbemycin oxime	Good	Good	No effect	Also prevents heartworm
Piperazine	Good	No effect	No effect	
Praziquantal	No effect	No effect	Good	
Praziquantel with pyrantel	Good	Good	Good	
Pyrantel pamoate	Good	Good	No effect	
Selamectin	Good	Good	No effect	Also prevents heartworm

HOW TO CONTROL WORMS

The life cycles of most worms are such that the possibility of reinfestation is great. To keep worms under control, you must destroy the eggs or larvae *before* they reinfest the cat. This means good sanitation and maintaining clean, dry quarters for your cat. It also means controlling intermediate hosts, such as fleas and rodents.

Cats should be kept as indoor pets, but some cats may live or go outside and others may have safe enclosures that are outside. For outside enclosures, cats should not be crowded together on shaded earth, which provides ideal conditions for seeding eggs and larvae. A watertight flooring surface, such as cement, is the easiest to keep clean. Hose it down daily and allow it to dry in the sun. Concrete surfaces can be disinfected with lime, salt, or borax (1 ounce per 10 square feet; 2 ml per .9 sq m). Remove stools from the cat pens daily. Lawns should be cut short and watered only when necessary. Stools elsewhere in the yard should be removed at least twice a week.

Fleas, lice, cockroaches, beetles, waterbugs, and rodents are intermediate hosts of tapeworms or ascarids. It is necessary to get rid of these pests to control reinfestation, as described in *Eliminating Fleas on the Premises* (page 139).

Stool and wet areas should be removed daily from the litter box. The litter box should be kept clean and dry and should be washed frequently with a solution of bleach and boiling water. Rinse thoroughly and dry completely before refilling with litter.

Many internal parasites spend the early stages of their life cycle in another animal and can only infect the cat and develop into adults when the cat preys on and eats this other animal. Accordingly, cats should not be allowed to roam and hunt. Be sure to thoroughly cook all fresh meat before feeding it to your cat.

Catteries that have continuous problems with worms often have other problems, too. These problems include skin, bowel, and respiratory difficulties. Steps should be taken to improve the management of the cattery, especially sanitation measures.

Ascarids (Roundworms)

Ascarids are the most common worm parasite in cats, occurring in a large percentage of kittens and in 25 to 75 percent of adults. There are two common species that infest the cat. Adult ascarids live in the stomach and intestines and can grow to 5 inches (13 cm) long. The eggs are protected by a hard shell. They are extremely hardy and can live for months or years in the soil. They become infective in three to four weeks after being passed out in stool.

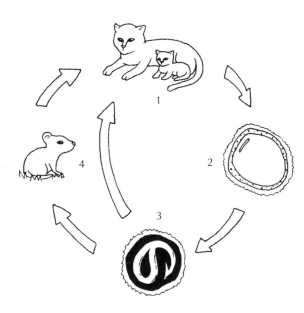

The cat passes eggs in her stool or larvae in her milk (1). The larvae infect her nursing kitten. Eggs from the stool (2) develop into larvae (3) and are eaten by rodents (4). The cat then eats the rodents while hunting. If the larvae pass through the kitten before maturing, the mother cat can also reinfest herself while grooming her kittens.

Life cycle of *Toxocara cati*

Cats acquire the disease by ingesting the eggs, perhaps through contact with soil containing the eggs, by them licking off their feet, or by eating a host animal, such as a beetle or rodent, which has acquired encysted larvae in its tissues. The larvae are then released in the cat's digestive tract.

Larvae of the common feline ascarid *Toxocara cati* are capable of migrating in tissues. Eggs, entering orally, hatch in the intestines. Larvae are carried to the lungs by the bloodstream. There, they become mobile and crawl up the trachea where they are then swallowed. This may cause bouts of coughing and gagging. They return to the intestines and develop into adults. This version of migration is most common in kittens.

In adult cats, only a few larvae return to the intestines. The others encyst in tissues and remain dormant. During lactation, these dormant larvae are released, reenter the circulation, and are transmitted to kittens in the mother's milk. When the queen is shedding larvae in her milk, she may not pass any eggs in her stool. Therefore, it makes sense to deworm both mother and kittens starting about 3 weeks of age, even if a fecal exam is negative.

Deworming the queen before or during pregnancy does not prevent all ascarid infestation of kittens after birth, but it will decrease the frequency and severity. Medications do not eliminate encysted larvae.

The second most common feline ascarid is *Toxascaris leonina*. This ascarid is not passed via the milk into nursing kittens but can be acquired by ingesting the eggs or by eating infected rodents.

Ascarids usually do not produce a heavy infestation in adult cats, but may do so among cats who do a lot of hunting. In kittens, a heavy infestation can result in severe illness or even death. Such kittens appear thin and have a pot-bellied look. They sometimes cough or vomit, have diarrhea, are anemic, and may develop pneumonia as the worms migrate from the blood vessels to the air sacs of the lungs. Worms may be found in the vomitus or the stool. Typically, they look like white earthworms or strands of spaghetti that are alive and moving.

Treatment: Pyrantel pamoate is a safe, effective choice and can be used in nursing kittens. Kittens should be dewormed by 3 weeks of age to prevent contamination of their quarters by ascarid eggs. A second course should be given two to three weeks later to kill any adult worms that were in the larval stage at the first deworming. Subsequent courses are indicated if eggs or worms are found in the stool. Many veterinarians suggest deworming kittens monthly until 6 months of age.

Pyrantel pamoate dewormers can be obtained from your veterinarian. You do not have to fast your cat before using this medication. Be sure to follow the directions of the manufacturer about dosage. Milbemycin, ivermectin, and selamectin are also very effective dewormers, but they are generally used in older kittens and adult cats.

Public health considerations: Ascarids can cause a disease in humans called visceral larva migrans. This is considered to be a serious public health problem and is one of the top *zoonotic* diseases. Most cases are caused by the canine ascarid, *Toxocara canis*, but *Toxocara cati* also can produce this disease. Some cases are reported each year, usually from areas with a mild climate. Children are most frequently affected, and often have a history of eating dirt. Outdoor sandboxes should be covered when not in use to prevent cats from using them as litter boxes, and gloves should be worn when gardening.

When a human eats an ascarid egg, larvae develop as in the cat. However, because humans are not a definitive host, the larvae do not progress to adult ascarids. Instead, they migrate in the tissues and wander aimlessly, causing fever, anemia, liver enlargement, pneumonia, and other ill effects. In children, the migrating larvae may enter the eye, leading to a disease called ocular larva migrans and potentially causing the loss of that eye. The disease runs its course in about a year. It is best prevented by controlling infestation in dogs and cats through periodic deworming and good sanitation.

Hookworms

Hookworms are small, thin worms about ¼ to ½ inches (.6 to 1.3 cm) long. They fasten to the wall of the small intestines and draw blood from the host. There are four species of hookworms that afflict the cat. Hookworms are not as common in cats as they are in dogs. They are most prevalent in areas that have high temperature and humidity (for example, in the southern United States), where conditions are favorable for the rapid development and spread of larvae.

A cat acquires the disease by ingesting infected larvae in soil or feces or by direct penetration of the skin (usually the pads of the feet). In rare cases, a cat may acquire the parasite by eating mice that host the larvae. The immature worms migrate through the lungs to the intestines, where they become adults. In about two weeks, the cat begins to pass eggs in her feces. The eggs incubate in the soil. Depending on conditions, larvae can become infective within two to five days after being passed.

The typical signs of hookworm infestation are diarrhea, anemia, weight loss, and progressive weakness. With a heavy infestation, stools may be bloody, wine-dark or tarry-black, but this is uncommon. A hookworm infestation can be fatal in very young kittens. The diagnosis is made by finding the eggs in the feces.

Newborn kittens do not acquire the infection *in utero* but might via the milk of the queen. Chronic infestation is a more common problem in adult cats than it is in kittens.

Many cats who recover from the disease become carriers via cysts in the tissue. During periods of stress or some other illness, a new outbreak can occur as the larvae are released.

Treatment: Pyrantel pamoate and selamectin have become the deworming medications of choice because of their safety and effectiveness. Milbemycin and ivermectin are also very effective dewormers but are generally used only in older kittens and adult cats. Two treatments are given two weeks apart. The stool should be checked to determine the effectiveness of treatment.

Kittens with acute signs and symptoms require intensive veterinary management. To prevent reinfestation, see *How to Control Worms*, page 59.

Public health considerations: A disease in humans called cutaneous larvae migrans (creeping eruption) is caused by hookworm species. Larvae present in the soil penetrate the skin and travel through the body. It causes lumps, streaks beneath the skin, and itching. The condition is self-limiting.

Tapeworms

Tapeworms are the most common internal parasite in adult cats. They live in the small intestines, and vary in length from less than 1 inch (25 mm) to several feet (1 foot is .3 meters). The scolex (head) of the parasite fastens itself to

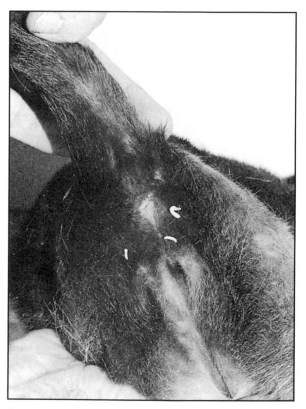

the wall of the gut using hooks and suckers. The body is composed of segments that contain egg packets. To eliminate tapeworm infection, the head must be destroyed. Otherwise, the worm will regenerate.

The body segments containing the eggs are passed in the feces. These are called proglottids. Fresh moist segments are capable of moving. They are about .25 inches (6.3 mm) long. Occasionally, you might see them in the fur about your cat's anus or in her stool. When dry, they resemble grains of rice.

There are two common tapeworm species found in cats; both are

Tapeworm segments can sometimes be found crawling in the fur around the anus of an infested cat.

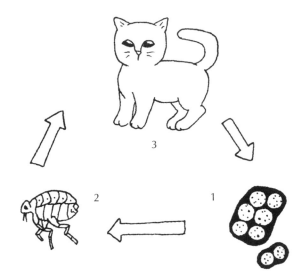

Segments pass in the stool and around the cat's rectum (1). The segments or individual egg packets are eaten by fleas (2). The cat then ingests fleas while grooming (3).

Life cycle of *Dipylidium caninum*

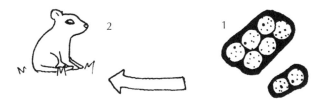

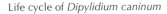

Segments pass in the stool and around the cat's rectum (1). The segments or individual egg packets are eaten by rodents (2). The cat then ingests the rodent while hunting (3).

Life cycle of *Taenia taeniaeformis*

transmitted by an intermediate host. *Dipylidium caninum* is acquired from fleas or lice that harbor immature tapeworms in their intestines. These insects acquire the parasite by eating tapeworm eggs. The cat must bite or swallow the insect to become infested. The tapeworm *Taenia taeniaformis* is acquired by eating rodents, uncooked meat, raw freshwater fish, or discarded animal parts.

Dibothriocephalus latus and *Spirometra mansonoides* are two uncommon tapeworms cats might acquire from eating uncooked freshwater fish or a water snake. *Spirometra mansonoides* is seen primarily in outdoor cats along the Gulf Coast region. *Dibothriocephalus latus* might be seen in the Gulf Coast region or around the Great Lakes. *Echinococcus* tapeworms are rarely found in cats.

Treatment: Praziquantal is one of the most effective medications for both common species of cat tapeworm. Other suitable treatments are fenbendazole and espirantal. Use under veterinary guidance. Deworming must be combined with control of fleas and lice (see A *Suggested Flea-control Program*, page 138), in the case of *Dipylidium caninum*, and by preventing roaming and hunting in the case of other tapeworms.

Public health considerations: A child could acquire a tapeworm if they accidentally swallowed an infected flea. Except for this unusual circumstance, cat tapeworms do not present a hazard to human health.

Other Worm Parasites

All the parasites in this section occur rarely in cats. Heartworms are discussed in chapter 11 (see page 326). Eye worms occur among cats living on the West Coast of the United States. They are discussed in chapter 5 (see page 192). Pinworms, which are a common cause of concern to families with children, are not acquired or spread by cats.

TRICHINOSIS

Trichinosis is acquired by ingesting uncooked pork that contains the encysted larvae of *Trichina spiralis*. It is estimated that 15 percent of the people living in the United States have, at some time, acquired trichinosis, although only a few clinical cases are reported each year. The incidence is probably somewhat higher in cats and dogs. Signs include muscle pain, headaches, and joint pain.

Prevent this disease by keeping your cat from roaming, particularly if you live in a rural area. Cook all fresh meat (your own *and* your cat's).

Treatment: This involves using the drug mebendazole, under the supervision of your veterinarian.

STRONGYLOIDES

There are two primary species of this parasite: *Strongyloides cati*, which is mainly found in subtropical climates and may be seen in the southern United States; and *Strongyloides stercoralis*, which is actually a human parasite but can be passed to cats (and then back again.) These are not common parasites. Signs of infestation include diarrhea with blood and mucus.

Treatment: The treatment is ivermectin or thiabendazole.

WHIPWORMS

These are slender parasites, 2 to 3 inches (50 to 76 mm) long that live in the cecum (the first part of the large intestine). Since they are thicker at one end, they have the appearance of a whip. Whipworms are usually found incidentally and are not known to cause disease in cats.

Treatment: No treatment is necessary.

FLUKES

Flukes are flatworms ranging in size from a few millimeters up to an inch or more in length. There are several species that colonize different parts of the cat's body, including the lung, liver, and small intestines. Gastrointestinal flukes are acquired by eating infected raw fish and small prey such as snails, frogs, and crayfish. It is suspected that the fluke parasite *Alaria marcianae* could also be passed to kittens of infected queens through the mother's milk.

Signs of fluke infestation vary and are often minimal. Infection should be prevented by cooking fish and restricting your cat's hunting opportunities.

Treatment: Professional diagnosis and treatment are required. Drug treatment is difficult and is not always successful.

STOMACH WORMS

These parasites are most likely to affect cats living in the southwestern United States. There are primarily two species of stomach worms that affect cats. The infection is acquired by eating beetles, cockroaches, crickets, lizards, or hedgehogs that have ingested eggs from the soil, in the case of *Physaloptera praeputialis*, or by contact with vomitus from an infected cat in the case of *Ollulanus tricuspis*.

Recurrent vomiting is the most common sign. Veterinary diagnosis is necessary to distinguish stomach worms from other causes of vomiting and to determine the specific species causing the infection. Eggs are not usually found in the feces, but worms may be detected by gastric *lavage* or by checking the vomitus. Prevent this disease by keeping your cat from roaming and hunting.

Treatment: The most effective dewormers are tetramisole for *Ollulanus* species and ivermectin or levamisole for *Physlaoptera*.

Protozoal Parasites

Protozoa are single-celled animals that are not visible to the naked eye but are easily seen under a microscope. They are usually carried by and live in water. A fresh stool specimen is required to identify the adult parasite or its cysts (called oocysts), because these disease agents are not usually identified by the standard fecal flotation techniques.

Giardiasis

This disease is caused by a protozoan of the *Giardia* species. Cats have their own species-specific version of *Giardia*. Cats acquire the infection by drinking water from streams and other sources that are contaminated with infective cysts.

Most infections in adult cats are subclinical. Young cats and kittens can develop a diarrhea syndrome characterized by the passage of large volumes of foul-smelling, watery stools. The diarrhea maybe acute or chronic, intermittent or persistent, and may be accompanied by weight loss.

Diagnosis is made by finding the protozoan or its characteristics cysts in saline smears of fresh stool. Smears from rectal swabs are satisfactory. A negative smear does not exclude giardia, as cysts are shed only intermittently. Three negative fecal smears collected at least two days apart should be obtained before the diagnosis is excluded. Serology tests (*ELISA* and *IFA*) are now available.

Cats do not seem to develop an immunity to giardiasis, so prevention includes cleaning up areas of stagnant water where the protozoa may flourish and/or keeping cats away from those areas. The indoor environment should be thoroughly cleaned as well.

Treatment: Giardiasis responds well to Flagyl (metronidazole). Because Flagyl causes developmental malformations in the fetus, it should not be administered to pregnant queens. Metronidazole also prevents bacterial overgrowth and may influence existing immune disorders in the intestines. Other effective drugs are available, such as febendazole. There is now a vaccine available for giardiasis, but it is rarely recommended because the disease is usually mild and responds well to treatment.

Toxoplasmosis

This disease is caused by the protozoan *Toxoplasma gondii*. Cats are likely to acquire the infection by consuming infected birds or rodents or, rarely, by ingesting oocysts in contaminated soil. Cats are the primary host for this obligate intracellular parasite (a parasite that can only exist inside the living cell of another organism), but it can infect other warm-blooded animals.

Evidence strongly suggests that cats (and people) can also get the disease from eating raw or undercooked pork, beef, mutton, or veal or unpasteurized dairy products that contains toxoplasma organisms. In cats, the oocysts develop in the intestines and are passed out in the feces, so the feces of infected cats present another source of infection. These infective oocysts are only passed for a very short time after initial exposure. Cats and humans can transmit toxoplasma *in utero* to their unborn offspring.

Feline intestinal toxoplasmosis is usually asymptomatic. When symptomatic, it affects the brain, spinal cord, eyes, lymphatic system, and lungs. The most common signs are loss of appetite, lethargy, cough, and rapid breathing. Visual and neurological signs may be evident. Other signs are fever, weight loss, diarrhea, and swelling of the abdomen. Lymph nodes may enlarge. Kittens may exhibit encephalitis, liver insufficiency, or pneumonia. Prenatal infection may be responsible for abortion, stillbirths, and unexplained perinatal deaths, including the fading kitten syndrome. Many cats that show clinical signs are concurrently infected with feline immunodeficiency virus (FIV) or feline leukemia virus (FeLV).

The finding of *T. gondii* oocysts in the cat's stool indicates the cat is currently infective to other cats and people. Serologic tests (including *ELISA*) will show whether a cat has ever been exposed. A positive test in a healthy cat signifies that the cat has acquired active immunity and is therefore not a source of human contamination.

To prevent this parasite, cats should not be fed raw meat or allowed to hunt. They also should not be given unpasteurized dairy products. If you have an indoor cat who eats only cat food, she's not likely to ever be infected.

Treatment: Antibiotics such as clindamycin are available to treat active infection and prevent the intestinal phase of oocyst shedding.

Public health considerations: About half the human adult population shows serological evidence of having been exposed in the past. Men and women with protective antibodies probably will be immune to infection. However, the disease is a particular hazard when a pregnant woman without prior immunity is exposed to it. Immunocompromised people are also at risk.

Toxoplasmosis infection in a pregnant woman can result in abortion, stillbirth, and birth of babies with central nervous system infection. Cats are the only animals who pass on the infectious stage of this parasite through their feces, and this has given rise to the incorrect assumption that pregnant women should not have cats. If you are pregnant, *it is not necessary to get rid of your cat!* The majority of human cases—by a wide margin—come from eating raw or undercooked meat, particularly lamb or pork. Unpasteurized dairy products can also be a source of infection. Wash fresh vegetables carefully, because oocysts can also cling to bits of soil. And wear gloves while gardening to avoid contact with infected soil.

It is important to understand the mode of transmission from cats to understand how minimal the risk is. Even a cat with an active toxoplasmosis infection is only capable of passing it on for seven to ten days *of her entire life*, when there's an acute infection. It takes anywhere from one to three days for oocysts shed in the feces to become infectious—which means the litter box would have to sit unscooped for one to three days before the infection could be passed on. Then, to become infected from cat feces, a person would have to touch the feces and then touch an opening in their body.

Pregnant women can be tested to determine if they have had prior exposure, in which case they have acquired immunity and there is no risk. They can also take precautions to avoid contact with fecal material from cats by wearing gloves when gardening and cleaning the litter box.

Prevent the disease in your cat by keeping the cat from roaming and hunting. Wear disposable plastic gloves when handling the cat's litter. Remove stools every day from the litter box. Dispose of the litter carefully so that others will not come into contact with it. Clean and disinfect litter boxes often using boiling water and a diluted bleach solution. Cover children's sandboxes when not in use to keep them from being used as a litter box by stray cats.

Cook all fresh meat, both yours and your cat's, maintaining a temperature of at least 150°F (65.5°C, medium well). Wash your hands with soap and water after handling raw meat. Clean all kitchen surfaces that have been in contact with raw meat.

COCCIDIOSIS

Coccidiosis usually targets young kittens shortly after weaning, although adult cats can be affected. The disease is highly contagious. Immunity following recovery from infection is short-lived. Cats who recover often become carriers and shed adult oocysts in their feces.

There are several species of coccidia. Only *Cystoisospora* (formerly known as *Isospora*) *felis* is directly transmitted by fecal contamination from cat to cat. Other species use birds and animals as intermediate transport hosts. These species complete their life cycle when the transport host is eaten by the cat. Kittens acquire Cystoisospora felis from mothers who are carriers.

Five to seven days after ingesting the oocysts, infective cysts appear in the feces. Much of the life cycle takes place in the cells lining the small intestines. Diarrhea is the most common sign of infection. The feces are mucuslike and tinged with blood. In severe cases, a bloody diarrhea may develop. These cases are complicated by weakness, dehydration, and anemia.

Coccidia can be found in the stools of kittens without causing problems, until some stress factor, such as overcrowding, malnutrition, weaning problems, an outbreak of ascarids, or shipping reduces their resistance. Normal fecal flotations will pick up these parasites.

Treatment: Offer a bland diet and encourage fluid intake. A severely dehydrated or anemic cat may need to be hospitalized for fluid replacement or blood transfusion. Kittens are more likely to require intensive care than adult cats.

Supportive treatment is important, since in most cases the acute phase of the illness lasts about ten days and the cat then recovers. Sulfonamides and nitrofurazone are the antibiotics of choice.

Known carriers should be isolated and treated. Cat quarters and runs should be washed daily with disinfectants and boiling water to destroy infective oocysts.

TRICHOMONIASIS

Trichomoniasis is caused by the protozoan *Tritrichomonas foetus*. In cats, *T. foetus* infects and colonizes the large intestines, and causes chronic, recurrent diarrhea, sometimes tinged with blood or *mucus*. Infection is most commonly seen in kittens and cats from catteries, where, presumably, the organism is spread among cats by close contact. There has been no evidence of spread from other species. Diagnosis is by fecal examination.

Treatment: Treatment with the various antiprotozoal drugs is usually unsuccessful. Most cats will slowly overcome the infection on their own. However, this can take nine months or more. It appears that most infected cats continue to shed low levels of the organism in their feces for many months after the diarrhea has resolved.

3

INFECTIOUS DISEASES

Infectious diseases are caused by bacteria, viruses, protozoa, or fungi that invade the body of a susceptible host and cause an illness. These infectious agents are collectively known as *pathogens*.

Infectious diseases are often transmitted from one cat to another by contact with infected feces, urine, *mucus*, or other bodily secretions, or by inhaling pathogen-laden droplets in the air. A few are transmitted via the genital tract when cats mate. Others are acquired by contact with spores in the soil that get into the body through the respiratory tract or a break in the skin.

Although pathogens exist everywhere in the environment, only a few cause infection. Fewer still are contagious. Many infectious diseases are species-specific. For example, a cat cannot catch a disease that is specific to a horse, and vice versa. Other infectious diseases are not species-specific, so they are capable of causing disease in many animals, including humans. In instances where a disease is *zoonotic*, public health considerations will be discussed here.

Many infectious agents are able to survive for long periods outside the host animal. This knowledge is important in determining how to contain the spread of infection. For many diseases, the best way to prevent them is by vaccination. Immunity and vaccinations are discussed at the end of this chapter.

Bacterial Diseases

Bacteria are single-celled microorganisms that cause disease. Some bacterial diseases are discussed in the chapters on the body system they primarily affect.

SALMONELLA

This disease is caused by a type of bacteria that produces gastrointestinal infection in susceptible animals. It tends to affect kittens housed in crowded, unsanitary surroundings and cats whose natural resistance has been weakened by a viral infection, malnutrition, or other stress. Salmonella remain alive for many months or years in soil and manure. In cats, the disease is acquired by consuming raw or commercially contaminated foods, by licking animal manure off their feet or coats, or by making oral contact with surfaces that have been contaminated by the diarrhea of an infected cat. This bacterial infection is a risk for cats fed a raw diet, unless excellent food-handling hygiene is practiced at all times.

Signs of infection include high fever, vomiting and diarrhea (in 90 percent of cases), dehydration, and weakness. The stool may be bloody and foul smelling. Dehydration develops when vomiting and diarrhea are prolonged. Bacteria in the bloodstream can cause abscesses in the liver, kidneys, uterus, and lungs. Conjunctivitis will be seen in some cats. The acute illness, which lasts four to ten days, may be followed by a chronic diarrhea that persists for more than a month. Death will occur in about half of cases. Abortions have been reported.

Cats (and dogs) often are asymptomatic carriers. Bacteria shed in their feces can, under appropriate conditions, produce active infection in domestic animals and humans.

Diagnosis is made by identifying salmonella bacteria in stool cultures (carrier state) or in the blood, feces, and infected tissues of cats suffering acute infection.

Treatment: Mild, uncomplicated cases respond to correction of the dehydration, vomiting, and diarrhea. Antibiotics (chloramphenicol, amoxicillin, the quinolone class of antibiotics, and sulfa drugs) are reserved for severely ill cats. Antibiotics can *favor* the growth of drug-resistant salmonella species. When antibiotics are used, it is best to administer them via injection and not orally. This will minimize the chances of the cat developing resistant strains of this bacteria.

Intravenous fluids will be needed for severely ill cats. Even cats with mild cases of this type of infectious diarrhea may need subcutaneous fluids and replacement of electrolytes.

Prevention: Prevent the disease by housing cats in roomy, sanitary conditions where they can be well cared for and properly fed.

Public health considerations: Since this is a disease that can spread to people, excellent hygiene must be practiced when handling feces and cleaning litter boxes.

Campylobacteriosis

Campylobacteriosis is a disease that produces acute infectious diarrhea in kittens. It also occurs in catteries and shelter cats—most of whom are in poor condition and are suffering from other intestinal infections.

The bacterium is acquired by contact with contaminated food, water, uncooked poultry or beef, or animal feces. *Campylobacter* species can survive for up to five weeks in water or unpasteurized milk.

The incubation period for disease is one to seven days. Signs of acute infection include vomiting and watery diarrhea that contains *mucus* and sometimes blood. The disease usually runs its course in 5 to 15 days, but may be followed by chronic diarrhea in which bacteria is shed in the feces.

Treatment: Treat mild diarrhea as described in *Diarrhea*, page 278. Keep the cat warm, dry, and in a stress-free environment. More severely affected cats will require veterinary management with intravenous fluids to correct dehydration. Antibiotics may be advisable. Erythromycin and ciprofloxacin are the current drugs of choice.

Public health considerations: Campylobacteriosis is a common cause of diarrhea in humans. Most human cases arise from contact with newly acquired kittens and puppies who are suffering from diarrhea. Parents should be aware that kittens with diarrhea may harbor *zoonotic* pathogens. Good hygiene is essential, especially for young children and people who are immunocompromised.

Clostridium perfringens

This is a spore-forming bacteria that produces a toxin. Because it forms spores that become airborne, this bacteria is more resistant to cleaning and environmental influences. The toxin causes an acute, watery diarrhea. Mucus and blood may be present, and the cat may be seen straining in the litter box.

Treatment: Tylosin, ampicillin, and metronidazole are antibiotics that may be used in treatment, but equally importantly, the cat's hydration must be maintained. Antibiotics may be needed for weeks in severe cases.

Tetanus

This disease is caused by *Clostridium tetani* bacteria. It occurs in all warm-blooded animals. It is rare in cats because they possess a high natural immunity. Tetanus bacteria are found in soil contaminated by horse and cow manure. They are also present in the intestinal tract of most animals, where it does not cause disease. Bacteria enter the skin via an open wound such as a bite or puncture. A rusty nail is a classic example. But any cut or injury that penetrates the full thickness of the skin can act as a point of entry.

Symptoms appear 2 to 14 days after initial injury. Tetanus bacteria grow best in tissues where the oxygen level is low (anaerobic conditions). The ideal environment is a deep wound that has sealed over or one in which there is devitalized tissue that is heavily contaminated with filth.

The bacteria make a neurotoxin that affects the nervous system. Signs of disease are due to this neurotoxin. In cats, tetanus is often a localized disease, with stiffness and rigidity in one leg—usually one with an obvious wound. This may spread to the other legs. In cats with generalized tetanus, signs include spastic contractions and rigid extension of the legs, difficulty opening the mouth and swallowing, and retraction of the lips and eyeballs. The tail sometimes stands straight out. Muscle spasms are triggered by almost anything that stimulates the cat. Death is caused by dehydration, exhaustion, and difficulty breathing.

Treatment: Fatalities from tetanus may sometimes be avoided by prompt, early veterinary care. Tetanus antitoxins, antibiotics, sedatives, intravenous fluids, and care of the wound alter the course for the better. Recovery can take four to six weeks, during which time the cat needs to be maintained in a dark, quiet environment to minimize stimulation.

Prevention: The disease can be prevented by prompt attention to skin wounds (see *Wounds*, page 47).

HELICOBACTER

Helicobacter pylori is the bacteria associated with gastric ulcers in humans. In cats, this bacteria may cause vomiting, diarrhea, and abdominal pain. Chronic, low-grade vomiting may be the most common sign, but many cats have this bacteria without any clinical signs.

A gastric *biopsy*, often done via *endoscopy*, is the best way to definitively diagnose this problem.

Treatment: Treatment involves famotidine (Pepcid) to help decrease stomach acid, and an antibiotic such as amoxicillin or metronidazole.

Public health considerations: While no direct connection has been made between human and feline cases, there are *Helicobacter* species that do occur in both.

TULAREMIA

Tularemia is an uncommon disease in cats caused by the bacteria *Francisella tularensis*. It occurs naturally in wild animals, especially rodents and rabbits. Cats (and dogs) usually acquire the disease from the bite of a blood-sucking tick or flea that has fed on an infected host. Direct contact with an infected wild animal or carcass is another route of infection, especially if the cat is allowed outdoors and hunts.

Cats with tularemia exhibit weight loss, fever, apathy and depression, lymph node enlargement, and signs of pneumonia. Oral ulcers may be noted. There may be an ulcerated skin sore at the sight of the insect bite. Some cats will have a discharge from the eyes and the nose and may even have a rash on the skin—most easily seen in the groin area.

Treatment: Antibiotics are the treatment of choice. Tetracycline, chloramphenicol, streptomycin, and gentamicin are effective. A long course of treatment may be necessary, and relapses can occur.

Prevention: Eliminating fleas and other insect parasites reduces the likelihood of infection (see A *Suggested Flea-Control Program*, page 138), as does preventing your cat from roaming and hunting. Wear rubber gloves and use strict hygienic precautions when handling cats with draining wounds. Surgical removal of the ulcerated skin lesion may be helpful.

Public health considerations: Infected cats can transmit the disease to humans through bites and scratches or by contact with draining skin ulcers. Tularemia is an occupational hazard for those who handle rabbit meat and pelts. This bacteria can survive even in frozen rabbit meat. Great care must be taken if cats are fed rabbit meat, especially from wild rabbits.

PLAGUE

Plague (bubonic plague) is a devastating disease caused by the bacteria *Yersinia pestis*. About 13 cases occur in humans in the United States each year, with some evidence that the disease is on the increase. Ninety percent of human cases occur in New Mexico, Arizona, and California. New Mexico accounts for 50 percent of reported cases annually. This disease is of concern because of potential cat-to-human transmission.

In nature, plague is perpetuated as fleas move from one rodent to another. Squirrels and prairie dogs are frequently infected. Cats, dogs, wild carnivores, and humans are accidental hosts. Cats and other carnivores acquire the disease by mouth contact with infected rodents or by the bite of infected fleas. Cats are highly susceptible to the disease, although in 50 percent of cases, the infection is mild or unapparent. The death rate in cats with severe illness is 30 to 50 percent.

Signs of severe illness in cats appear shortly after exposure. They include high fever, loss of appetite, apathy and depression, dehydration, mouth ulcers, coughing, and difficulty breathing. Large swellings (*bubos*, hence the name bubonic plague) involve the lymph nodes, especially those beneath the jaw. These swellings form abscesses that drain infective material. This is the most common form. Plague can also show up as a *septicemic* disease in the bloodstream or pneumonic plague in the lungs. In that case, cats may spread the disease by coughing out infected air droplets.

Diagnosis is established by chest X-ray, blood and tissue cultures, gram stains, and serial antibody *titers* to Y. *pestis*.

Treatment: Great care must be taken by all people involved in the care of a plague-infected cat. Strict hygienic and isolation precautions under professional guidance are required. Hospitalization and veterinary management are imperative. Because the disease can be rapidly fatal, treatment is started before the diagnosis is confirmed by a laboratory. Y. *pestis* is susceptible to a number of antibiotics, including streptomycin, gentamicin, doxycycline, tetracycline, and chloramphenicol (but not penicillins). Antibiotics may need to be given for weeks.

Prevention: Control of fleas is of prime importance (see A *Suggested Flea-Control Program*, page 138). Exposure to plague can be minimized by preventing cats from roaming and hunting. This restriction is especially important in plague-endemic areas.

Public health considerations: The most common mode of transmission to humans is the bite of an infected flea. Cats (and dogs) may transport the flea from plague-infected wildlife. Sick cats may transmit the bacteria through bites or scratches. Cats with pneumonia may transmit the disease through droplet formation from sneezing and coughing. Handling an infected cat may result in transmission through breaks in your own skin or contact with mucous membranes. Fleas and external parasites are also a danger to personnel treating the cat, and should be rapidly extinguished by appropriate insecticide treatment.

All individuals who have handled, contacted, or participated in the care of a plague-infected animal should contact a physician immediately; prophylactic antibiotics may be required.

TUBERCULOSIS

This rare disease in cats is caused by the tubercle bacillus (*Mycobacterium*). There are three strains of bacilli that produce disease in humans, but only the bovine type (M. *bovis*) and the avian type (M. *avian*) infect cats. Cats are resistant to infection by the human type (M. *tuberculosis*). Avian tuberculosis is not common.

Tuberculosis in cats is usually acquired by ingesting infected cow's milk or by eating contaminated uncooked beef. Even though there has been a steady decline in tuberculosis with pasteurization of milk and elimination of this disease from dairy herds, it has not been completely wiped out.

Feline tuberculosis (M. *bovis*) is primarily a gastrointestinal problem. Common signs include low-grade fever with chronic wasting and loss of condition despite good care and feeding. Abscesses form in the intestinal lymph nodes and liver. Lung infection may also occur. Occasionally, an open wound becomes infected, leading to skin involvement with draining sinuses and a discharge containing bacteria.

Respiratory tuberculosis causes rapid labored breathing, shortness of breath, and production of bloody sputum.

The finding of tubercle bacilli in the feces, in sputum, or in drainage from a wound makes the diagnosis. Special stains are needed when looking at samples on a slide under a microscope. A chest X-ray may be suggestive. The tuberculin skin test is not reliable in cats. A new blood test for nitric oxide may be useful for cats suspected of having tuberculosis.

Treatment: Treatment, which involves antituberculous drugs, is difficult and prolonged.

Public health considerations: Humans can also become infected from *M. bovis*. Therefore, the hazard to human health often makes euthanasia of an infected cat the wisest choice.

BORDETELLA

Bordetella bronchiseptica is a cause of upper respiratory infection in cats. This bacteria is present in normal, healthy cats as well, so it seems to be a problem secondary to viral upper respiratory infections. Rarely, pneumonia will develop.

This illness is more severe in young cats and in shelters or situations with crowding, poor ventilation, and stress. Clinical signs include lethargy, fever, anorexia, coughing, sneezing, discharges from the eyes and nose, and swollen lymph nodes under the chin. Difficulty breathing suggests pneumonia.

Treatment: Supportive care is important, with antibiotics if needed. (See chapter 10 for more information.) An intranasal vaccine is available.

FELINE PNEUMONITIS (FELINE CHLAMYDIOSIS)

At one time, *Chlamydophila felis* (formerly called *Chlamydia psittaci*) was thought to be a major cause of feline respiratory disease. However, current research has shown that this bacteria-like organism can cause conjunctivitis and a relatively mild, persistent upper respiratory disease called feline pneumonitis. The primary clinical sign is conjunctivitis with a discharge that will change from *serous* to *purulent*. This is most often seen in kittens up to 3 months of age. A respiratory form of the disease is sometimes seen as well, usually secondary to a viral upper respiratory infection.

Treatment: Tetracycline drugs are used, including ophthalmic preparations. There is a vaccine, but it is not generally recommended because of the high incidence of adverse reactions and the relative infrequency of chlamydial infection in North America.

Feline chlamydiosis is a common cause of conjunctivitis in kittens. Typically, their eyelids are pasted shut.

FELINE MYCOPLASMAL INFECTION

Mycoplasma felis may cause an upper respiratory infection with conjunctivitis and a nasal discharge. This may be bilateral, or just on one side. The infection may resolve spontaneously in two to four weeks. This infection may occur secondary to a viral upper respiratory infection.

Treatment: Tetracyclines, including ophthalmic preparations, can be used for treatment if the illness does not resolve on its own.

FELINE INFECTIOUS ANEMIAS

Cytauxzoon felis and *Mycoplasma haemophilus* (previously known as *Hemobartonella felis*) are two infectious causes of anemia in cats. See chapter 11 for information on these diseases.

Feline Upper Respiratory Diseases				
Signs	Herpesvirus	Calicivirus	Bordetella	Mycoplasma
Length of illness	2 to 4 weeks	1 to 2 weeks	1 to 2 weeks	2 to 4 weeks
Nasal	Sneezing, discharge	Discharge	Cough, sneezing	Discharge
Eyes	Conjunctivitis, corneal ulcers	Discharge	Discharge	Conjunctivitis
Mouth	Drooling	Ulcers, chronic gingivitis	None	None
Fever	Yes	Sometimes	Mild	Yes
Pneumonia	Rare	Common	Sometimes	Rare
Lethargy	Severe	Mild	Mild	Mild
Unusual signs	None	Lameness	Enlarged lymph nodes	Nasal discharge may be unilateral

Viral Diseases
FELINE VIRAL RESPIRATORY DISEASE COMPLEX

Feline viral respiratory diseases are highly contagious, often serious illnesses of cats that can spread rapidly through a multicat home, a cattery, or a shelter. They are one of the most common infectious disease problems a cat owner is likely to encounter. Although few adult cats die of upper respiratory disease, the death rate among young kittens approaches 50 percent.

Although these diseases are highly contagious among cats, they cannot be transmitted to humans. Cats also cannot catch our colds. This is because the viruses that attack cats do not affect humans, and vice versa.

Recently, it has been recognized that two major viral groups are responsible for the majority of clinical upper respiratory infections in cats (80 to 90 percent). The first is the herpesvirus group, which includes feline viral rhinotracheitis (FVR). The second is the calicivirus group, which includes feline caliciviral disease.

Other viral agents, especially those of the reovirus group, cause feline viral respiratory illness. They account for a minority of cases.

There are two distinct stages in the feline viral respiratory disease complex. The acute stage is followed by the chronic carrier state.

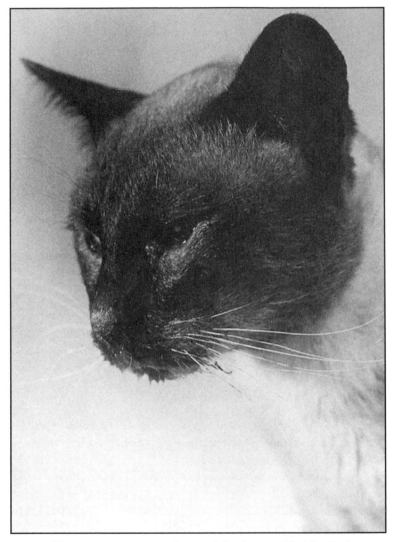

A cat with an acute upper respiratory infection, typified by discharge from the eyes, nose, and mouth.

Acute Viral Respiratory Infection

There is considerable variation in the severity of illness. Some cats have mild symptoms, while in others the disease is rapidly progressive and sometimes fatal.

The disease is transmitted from cat to cat by direct contact with infected discharge from the eyes, nose, mouth; by contaminated litter boxes, water bowls, and human hands; and rarely, by airborne droplets. The virus is stable outside the host for as short as 24 hours or as long as 10 days, depending on conditions.

Regardless of which virus is responsible for the infection, the initial signs are similar. The infected organism can be identified only by viral or *serologic*

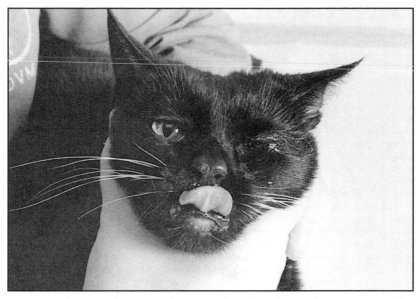

Upper respiratory infection with a severely inflamed eye, characteristic of the herpesvirus.

tests. These tests are not always available quickly enough to be of use in planning treatment.

Clinical signs appear 2 to 17 days after exposure and reach maximum severity 10 days later. Illness begins with severe bouts of sneezing lasting one to two days. This is followed by conjunctivitis and watery discharge from the eyes and nose, which may suggest a cold or flu. By the third to fifth day, a cat exhibits fever, apathy, and loss of appetite. The eye and/or nasal discharge becomes *mucoid* or *purulent*. Cats with obstructed nasal passages breathe with their mouths open.

Further signs depend on the particular respiratory virus in question. A cat with herpesvirus develops a spastic cough. If the surface of the eye is severely inflamed, the cat may develop keratitis or corneal ulcerations.

In a cat with calicivirus, you may see ulceration of the mucous membranes of the mouth (stomatitis). This is particularly disabling, because the cat loses his taste for food and refuses to eat and drink. Drooling is common. Shortness of breath and viral pneumonia can occur. Secondary bacterial infection, dehydration, starvation, and rapid weight loss are all complications that can lead to death.

A diagnosis can be suspected from the clinical signs. It can be confirmed by isolating the virus from the throat or by specific *serologic* blood tests. Because these diseases are highly contagious, these tests are most important when the disease involves a cattery, a shelter, or a multicat household.

Treatment: Cats suspected of having acute viral respiratory infection should be strictly isolated for three to four weeks so as not to infect others. It

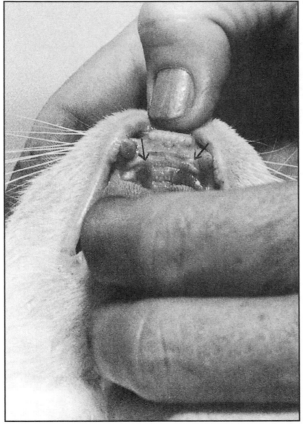

The ulcers on the roof of the cat's mouth are caused by the calicivirus.

is important to disinfect any bedding, bowls, cages, or other items the sick cat has come into contact with by washing them thoroughly with a dilute solution of bleach and water. Human caretakers should change their clothing, wear disposable shoe covers, and wash their hands frequently.

For the patient, rest and proper humidification of the atmosphere are important. Confine your cat in a warm room and use a home vaporizer. A cool steam vaporizer offers some advantage over a warm vaporizer because it is less likely to cause additional breathing problems. At the very minimum, keeping the cat in the bathroom while you shower will help.

Because dehydration and anorexia seriously weaken a cat, it is important to encourage eating and drinking. Feed highly palatable foods with a strong smell, such as tuna-flavored foods or strained baby food (make sure it doesn't contain onion powder), diluted with water. Supplemental fluids can be given using a syringe (see *How to Give Medications*, page 556). Once the cat begins to eat and drink again, the worst danger is past.

Clean secretions from the eyes, nose, and mouth with moist cotton balls as often as needed.

Shrink swollen nasal membranes by administering Afrin Children's Strength Nose Drops (.025 percent; see *Over-the-Counter Drugs for Home Veterinary Use*, page 561, for dosage). Administer just one drop to one nostril the first day. The next day, put one drop in the other nostril. The medicine is absorbed and works on both nasal passages. Continue to alternate between nostrils. Administer cautiously to prevent rebound congestion and excessive drying out of the mucous membranes. Use the decongestant for no more than five days.

If the cat becomes dehydrated, refuses to eat, loses weight, or does not respond to home care, *seek prompt veterinary help.*

Antibiotics are important to manage moderate to severe respiratory infections by treating secondary bacterial infections when present. Antibiotics are not needed or recommended for mild upper respiratory infections. Amoxicillin-clavulanate and doxycycline are good choices. Antibiotics must be prescribed by a veterinarian. L-Lysine is an amino acid that may help clear the infection if it is related to herpesvirus.

Chronic Carrier State

Almost all the cats who have been infected with FVR will become chronic carriers. FVR lives and multiplies in the cells lining the throat. During periods of stress (such as illness, anesthesia, surgery, lactation, medication with steroids, or even emotional stresses), the cat's immunity breaks down and the virus is shed in mouth secretions. At this time, the cat may exhibit signs of a mild upper respiratory illness.

Calicivirus can be shed continuously, and 80 percent of cats who have had calicivirus will continue to be chronic carriers. Cats infected with calicivirus therefore present an especially serious hazard to other cats living on the premises. Periodic outbreaks are likely to occur.

Prevention: Separating virus-positive cats from a breeding colony or household is difficult. Several months of segregation and testing are required. Cats who are newly entering a household or cattery present a further potential source of infection. Such cats should be placed in strict isolation for 10 to 14 days and observed for signs of infection. A cat admitted as a boarder should be housed in separate quarters and handled and fed separately from the other cats. All cats should be routinely tested for feline leukemia and feline immunodeficiency virus. Well-ventilated surroundings and ample living space to avoid crowding are important in good cattery management, as are strict hygiene and frequent disinfection of dishes and living areas.

The most effective step by far is to vaccinate all cats, but even then, control is not 100 percent. Vaccination will not eliminate the chronic carrier states. For more information on these vaccines, see *Feline Viral Respiratory Disease Complex*, page 108.

VIRULENT SYSTEMIC FELINE CALICIVIRUS

A new mutation of the calicivirus has been identified in various outbreaks in cats. The first outbreak was in California, but outbreaks have since been identified across the United States. The calicivirus in these cases seems to have mutated to a more virulent form, and is therefore now known as virulent systemic feline calicivirus (VS-FCV).

The virus may be shed in feces, sloughed skin and hair, and nasal, ocular, and oral secretions. Asymptomatic and mildly affected cats may transmit the fatal disease to other cats; therefore, all exposed cats should be considered a potential infectious risk. This virus is very contagious and easily spread by both direct contact and on clothes, dishes, bedding, and other objects. Strict hygiene is required to stop the spread in outbreaks.

Along with respiratory signs, cats will show a high fever, *edema* of the face and limbs, and ulceration and hair loss on the face, feet, and pinnas. There may also be other signs seen with more typical feline upper respiratory diseases, including nasal and ocular discharge, oral ulceration, anorexia, and depression.

A secondary immune response is believed to be responsible for the organ damage that accompanies these signs, and leads to a 60 percent fatality rate. The mortality rate is higher in adults than it is in kittens.

Although this syndrome remains uncommon, occasional outbreaks and clusters of cases have been documented throughout the United States. So far, this has occurred in cats of all ages, including those vaccinated for the common calicivirus as well as nonvaccinates. No other species is known to be affected by this strain of calicivirus. There is no known risk to human health.

Treatment: For affected cats, treatment consists of supportive care, along with drug therapy using steroids and interferon. Bovine lactoferrin may be useful. The efficacy of these treatments is not yet known.

Prevention: Isolate all cats suspected of being infected. VS-FCV can survive up to four weeks in the environment and is resistant to some disinfectants, but a bleach solution (diluted with water at 1:32) has been used to effectively contain previous outbreaks. All surfaces should be thoroughly cleaned and disinfected. Do not introduce any new cats for at least four weeks.

A new vaccine from Fort Dodge Animal Health, called CaliciVax, has recently been licensed for control (see page 108).

FELINE PANLEUKOPENIA

Feline panleukopenia, also called feline infectious enteritis, is a leading cause of death in kittens. It has been called feline distemper, but it bears no relation to the virus that causes distemper in dogs. There may, however, be crossover infectivity between cats and the newer forms of parvovirus isolated in dogs.

Panleukopenia virus is present wherever there are susceptible animals. Mink, ferrets, raccoons, and wild cats all serve as a reservoir. The virus is highly contagious. It is spread by direct contact with infected animals or their secretions. Contaminated food dishes, bedding, litter boxes, and the clothes or hands of people who have treated an infected cat are other routes of exposure.

The panleukopenia virus has a special affinity for attacking white blood cells. The reduction of circulating white cells (leukopenia) gives the disease its name. Signs of acute illness appear two to ten days after exposure. Early signs include loss of appetite, severe apathy, and fever up to 105°F (40.5°C). The cat often vomits repeatedly and brings up frothy, yellow-stained bile. The cat may be seen crouching in pain, his head hanging a few inches over the surface of the water bowl. If he is able to drink, he immediately vomits. With pain in the abdomen, the cat cries plaintively.

Diarrhea may appear early in the course of the disease, but frequently comes on later. The stools are yellow or blood-streaked. In young kittens (and some older cats), the onset can be so sudden that death occurs before the owner realizes the cat is ill. It may seem as if the cat was poisoned.

Panleukopenia can be transmitted to kittens both before and shortly after birth. In such cases, the mortality rate is 90 percent. Kittens recovering from neonatal infection may have cerebellar brain damage and exhibit a wobbly, jerky, uncoordinated gait that is noted when they first begin to walk. Secondary bacterial infections are common. The bacterial infection, rather than the virus itself, may be the cause of death.

A white blood cell count confirms the diagnosis. In-office tests for canine parvovirus will also detect feline panleukopenia virus, which is a member of the parvovirus family.

Cats who survive are solidly immune to reinfection but can shed the virus for several weeks. Along with asymptomatic carriers, this leads to repeated exposure in a population of cats. The repeated exposure helps to boost immunity among cats who have already acquired protective antibodies, by continuing to stimulate their immune systems.

Treatment: Detecting panleukopenia early in the course of the illness is of prime importance, because intensive treatment must be started at once to save the cat's life. It is better to consult your veterinarian on a false alarm than to wait until the cat is desperately ill. Supportive measures include fluid replacement, antibiotics, maintaining nutrition, and, occasionally, blood transfusions.

Prevention: The panleukopenia virus is hardy. It can survive in carpets, cracks and furnishings for more than a year. It is resistant to ordinary household disinfectants but can be destroyed using a bleach solution (diluted with water at 1:32).

Most cats are exposed to panleukopenia sometime during their life. Vaccination is the most effective way to prevent serious infection (see page 107).

FELINE INFECTIOUS PERITONITIS

Feline enteric coronavirus (FeCV) is a common disease of wild and domestic cats that is caused by a member of the coronavirus group. The disease is spread from cat to cat, but requires close and continuous contact with infective secretions. The incubation period is two to three weeks or longer, but 75 percent of cats exposed experience no apparent infection. Among those who do, a mild respiratory infection, with a runny nose or eye discharge, is the most common sign.

Cats who recover from mild infection can become asymptomatic carriers. Most cats who have been infected in this way are not immune to future infections with the coronavirus. It is estimated that 30 to 40 percent of all cats are positive for antibodies to FeCV, with that rising to 80 to 90 percent in catteries.

Fewer than 1 percent of all exposed cats will develop the secondary fatal disease known as feline infectious peritonitis (FIP). Why some cats develop FIP and others do not is not known for sure. It is believed that FIP is a mutation of the benign coronavirus and is therefore not contagious. The virus may change from benign to virulent weeks, months, or even years after the initial exposure to the coronavirus. Factors that seem to play a part in the change from benign to virulent are a genetic predisposition, exposure to chronic shedding of the virus, and living in a multicat environment, which could mean more stress.

Genetic susceptibility is *polygenic*. One study suggested that Persians and Birmans have an increased incidence, but other studies say Abyssinians, Bengals, Birmans, Himalayans, Ragdolls, and the Rex breeds are especially at risk. Pedigreed cats, in general, do seem to be at higher risk, but that may relate to the fact that they are often housed in catteries.

It is known that FIP tends to most often affect kittens, cats between 6 months and 2 years of age, and cats older than 14 years of age. Neonatal FIP has been implicated as a cause of fading kittens (see page 472). There is a higher rate of infection in catteries, where conditions are apt to be crowded and there is greater opportunity for continuous and prolonged exposure. Cats who are poorly nourished, run-down, or suffering from other illnesses, such as feline leukemia, are most susceptible. These factors may lower the cat's natural resistance to FIP.

Despite its name, FIP is not strictly a disease of the abdominal cavity. The virus acts on capillary blood vessels throughout the body—especially those of the abdomen, chest cavity, eyes, brain, internal organs, and lymph nodes. Damage to these minute blood vessels results in loss of fluid into tissues and body spaces. FIP tends to run a prolonged course. It may go on for weeks before signs are evident. The immune system of the infected cat plays a part in the disease. Cats have both cell-mediated and humoral (antibody) immunity. In cats with FIP, the system backfires and normal cells are targeted for destruction.

FIP occurs in two forms—wet and dry—both of which are invariably fatal.

Wet form early signs are nonspecific and mimic several other feline disorders. They include loss of appetite, weight loss, listlessness, and depression. The cat appears to be chronically ill. As fluid begins to accumulate in the body spaces, you may notice labored breathing from fluid in the chest or abdominal enlargement from fluid in the abdomen. Sudden death may occur from fluid in the heart sac. Other signs that accompany the wet form are fever up to 106°F (41°C), dehydration, anemia, vomiting, and diarrhea. Jaundice and dark urine are caused by liver failure.

Dry or disseminated form early signs are similar to those of the wet form, except fluid is not produced. The disseminated form is even more difficult to diagnose. It affects a variety of organs, including the eyes (15 percent of cases affect the eyes only), brain, liver, kidney, and pancreas. Sixty percent of dry form cases will show eye or brain involvement, or both.

At surgical exploration, which may be necessary to make the diagnosis, sticky mucus or strands of fibrous protein may be found on the surface of the liver, spleen, or intestines. Previously, 10 to 20 percent of cats with the dry form were also infected with the feline leukemia virus. With more testing and control of FeLV that number is down to less than 5 percent.

The diagnosis of FIP can be suspected based on typical clinical signs along with an abnormal blood count, liver function tests, and an abnormal serum protein pattern. Analysis of peritoneal (chest) fluid, if present, is helpful. *Serologic* blood tests to detect coronavirus antibodies are not always conclusive and can lead to false positive interpretations. So far, no tests are consistent in identifying *titers* due to the benign presence of the virus, the virulent virus, or vaccination antibodies. The only certain way to confirm the diagnosis is by organ biopsy. In the wet form, fluid aspirated from the chest or abdomen may be highly suggestive of the diagnosis.

Treatment: Unfortunately, once a cat develops signs of secondary disease (either the wet or dry form), he will die. The wet form is worse, with cats often dying within two months. Cats with the dry form may have up to a year of good quality life. The cat can be made more comfortable by using medications; life may be prolonged with chemotherapy drugs such as cyclophosphamide or immunosuppressive doses of cortisone. Interferon and vitamin supplementation, especially vitamin C, can be helpful. Some cats do well with low-dose aspirin to reduce inflammation. Pentoxifylline (Trental) is being used by some veterinarians to treat the damage to blood vessels.

Prevention: Physical and environmental stresses lower a cat's immunity and increase susceptibility to the virus, so it is important to maintain good nutrition, control parasites, treat health problems promptly, and groom regularly.

FIP presents its greatest hazard in multicat families, shelters, boarding establishments, and catteries. The dried virus can survive for weeks in the environment. Fortunately, the virus is easily killed by household disinfectants. A bleach

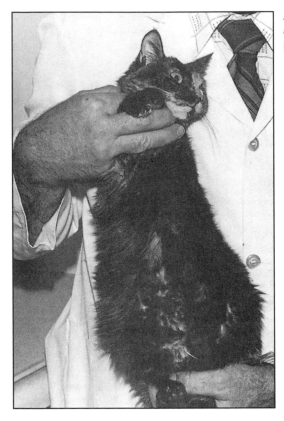

Abdominal enlargement in a cat with the wet form of feline infectious peritonitis.

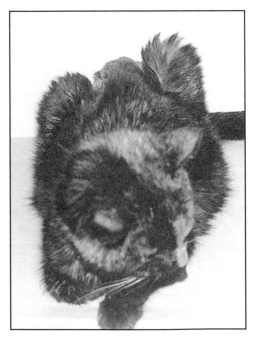

Note the extreme depression, muscular wasting, and prominence of the backbone in this cat with FIP.

solution (diluted with water at 1:32) is a good disinfectant. Disinfect cat quarters regularly. Provide a spacious enclosure for each cat and allow ample opportunity for exercise.

Routine FIP testing of all cats in a multicat household or cattery is often an exercise in frustration. Kittens can be tested for coronavirus antibody at 12 to 16 weeks.

A new cat arriving in the household can be isolated for two weeks and tested for FIP. No healthy cat should be removed due to a positive corona virus titer, however, because there is no way to tell if the virus is the benign or virulent form from a titer.

FIP is an active area of research in the feline community and there are special research funds that can always benefit from donations. (The Winn Feline Foundation has such as fund. See appendix D.) An intranasal modified live vaccine is now available (see page 111), but it is not currently recommended as part of the routine vaccination schedule because its effectiveness has not been proven.

FELINE LEUKEMIA VIRUS DISEASE COMPLEX

The feline leukemia virus (FeLV) is responsible for more cat diseases than any other infectious agent and is second only to trauma as the leading cause of death in household cats. It is the most important cause of cancer in cats (see chapter 19) and significantly contributes to the severity of other feline diseases. The virus is transmitted from one cat to another by infected saliva. Sharing water bowls or food dishes, cat-to-cat grooming, and cat bites can also spread the disease. The virus can be shed to a lesser extent in urine and feces. Kittens can acquire the virus *in utero* and through infected mother's milk.

The incidence of active infection varies. About 1 to 2 percent of healthy, free-roaming cats are infected. In multicat households and in catteries, the incidence may be higher, in some cases with 20 to 30 percent of cats showing the presence of FeLV virus in the blood. About 50 percent show neutralizing antibodies, indicating prior infection from which the cat has recovered. Ill feral or free-roaming urban cats may have an incidence as high as 40 percent.

Repeated or continuous exposure is necessary for transmission of the disease. For healthy adult cats, very prolonged exposure is required to develop infection. Kittens and young cats have less resistance. The virus does not appear in blood tests until a cat has been exposed for at least four weeks. After 20 weeks of exposure, 80 percent of cats are infected. In others, it may take up to a year. Environmental stresses, including illness, overcrowding, and poor sanitation, play a role in weakening a cat's resistance to the virus and make infection more likely.

The feline leukemia virus has three subgroups. A single cat may have one or more of these subgroups. Subgroup A is the most common, and this type is responsible for the immunosuppression that leaves FeLV-positive cats open to many infections. Subgroup B, when combined with subgroup A, is responsible for many of the FeLV-associated cancers. Subgroup C is the least common form and is responsible for severe anemias and bone marrow damage.

Feline oncovirus-associated cell membrane antigen (FOCMA) is a protein found on some feline cancer cells and is seen in both FeLV-positive and FeLV-negative cats. Cats who have antibodies to this protein are protected from certain cancers, such as lymphomas. However, they are not protective against FeLV infection or other FeLV-related diseases.

Signs of Illness

The initial illness lasts 2 to 16 weeks. Signs are nonspecific and include fever, apathy, and loss of appetite and weight. Other signs are vomiting and constipation or diarrhea. Some cats develop enlarged lymph nodes, anemia, and pale mucous membranes. Death at this stage is not common and signs may be so mild that they are missed.

Following exposure to the virus, there are four possible outcomes for cats:

1. About 30 percent of cats do not develop an infection at all—whether due to resistance or inadequate exposure is not known.

2. About 30 percent of cats develop a transient *viremia* with infectious virus present in their blood and saliva for less than 12 weeks. This stage is followed by the production of neutralizing antibodies that extinguish the disease. These cats are cured, cannot transmit the disease, have a normal life expectancy, and are at no increased risk of developing FeLV-related diseases.

3. About 30 percent of cats develop a persistent viremia with infectious virus present in their blood and saliva for more than 12 weeks. Persistently viremic cats do not mount an effective antiviral immune response and are susceptible to a number of diseases that are invariably fatal. About 50 percent die within six months and 80 percent succumb within three and a half years. These cats shed the virus while they are alive.

4. About 5 to 10 percent of cats develop a latent infection. These cats are able to produce virus-neutralizing antibodies that eliminate the virus from blood and saliva but do not extinguish the virus completely. The virus persists in the bone marrow and in T-cell lymphocytes. Over many months, the majority of latent-infected cats overcome and extinguish the virus, so the incidence of latent infection after three years is quite low. In latent-infected cats, the disease can become activated during

periods of stress or concurrent illness, leading to a recurrence of viremia. Cats who remain persistently latent are at increased risk for developing FeLV-associated diseases. Queens who have a latent infection may infect their kittens *in utero* or while nursing.

In cats with persistent viremia, the FeLV virus suppresses the cat's immunity, thereby allowing other diseases to develop. Diseases potentiated by the FeLV virus include feline infectious peritonitis, feline infectious anemia, feline viral respiratory disease complex, toxoplasmosis, chronic cystitis, periodontal disease, and opportunistic bacterial infections. The virus can also cause bone marrow suppression with anemia and spontaneous bleeding.

Maternally transmitted infection is responsible for some cases of reproductive failure, including repeated abortion, stillbirth, fetal reabsorption, and fading kitten syndrome.

About 30 percent of cats with persistent viremia develop a virus-related cancer months or years after exposure. Lymphosarcoma is the most common variety. One or more painless masses may be felt in the abdomen. There may be enlargement of lymph nodes in the groin, armpit, neck, or chest. The cancer may spread to the eyes, brain, skin, kidneys, and other organs, producing a variety of symptoms.

Leukemia is another malignant transformation. It is defined as rapid and uncontrolled growth of white blood cells. It may be accompanied by anemia and other changes in the blood-cell picture. It is much less common than lymphosarcoma.

Diagnosing FeLV

Currently, there are two tests available to detect FeLV infection.

1. The IFA test, performed by a reference laboratory, detects virus antigen in infected white blood cells. This indicates that the bone marrow is infected and there is a high probability that the cat is persistently viremic and is shedding the virus in his saliva, making him infective to other cats. About 97 percent of IFA-positive cats remain viremic for life and never extinguish the virus.

2. The *ELISA* test detects virus antigen in whole blood, serum, saliva, and tears. Blood is the recommended sample for testing. A rapid screening leukemia test kit is available for home and veterinary clinic use. The ELISA test is more likely to detect weak, early, or transient infections.

The common practice is to screen for FeLV using the ELISA test. If positive, the cat may have a transient viremia from which he will recover completely, or he may be in the early stages of a progressive infection. A positive ELISA test should be confirmed with an IFA test. A positive IFA test indicates that the cat is shedding virus and is capable of infecting others.

The ELISA test should be repeated in 8 to 12 weeks to see if the virus has been eliminated. The IFA test should also be repeated at this time because if the cat was in an early stage of infection, the IFA initially may not have been positive but may become so after 12 weeks.

Cats with latent infection test negative on both the ELISA and IFA tests. This is because the virus is absent in both serum and white cells. The only way to diagnose a latent infection is to remove a sample of the cat's bone marrow containing the dormant virus and grow the cells in culture.

Vaccination does not interfere with FeLV testing results.

Treating FeLV

Despite research, there is currently no effective treatment for FeLV. Cats who are healthy but FeLV-positive can live long, full lives in many cases. They need excellent care, including parasite control, a strictly indoor life, top-quality nutrition, regular grooming, and minimal stress.

Once ill, there are limited options. These include the drugs ImmunoRegulin, interferon, and acemannan.

Cancers produced by the FeLV virus cannot be cured and FeLV-positive cats with associated cancers have an average survival time of only six months, even with extensive treatment. Early diagnosis may allow successful relief, but not cure, in some individuals. Treatment includes antibiotics, vitamin-mineral supplements, transfusions, and anticancer drugs. Cats who respond to the medications may be made more comfortable and their lives may be prolonged. Unfortunately, there is no way to know in advance which cats are likely to respond. Such cats will continue to shed virus and thus present a hazard to the health of other cats with whom they come in contact.

Controlling and Preventing FeLV

Control depends first on accurate identification and removal of all virus-positive cats from multicat households, shelters, and catteries. Vaccination programs are secondary. FeLV vaccines are not as effective as some other vaccines, but do provide some protection (see page 109).

The following steps may prevent the spread of infection in a cattery, shelter, or isolated cat colony.

- Do not introduce new cats into the group without first testing them.
- IFA test all cats on the premises and repeat the test in three months. Remove all cats who test positive after each test. All positive cats should be isolated and retested after three months.
- All cats with two negative tests are considered free of active disease and not likely to transmit the disease to other cats. Retest annually.
- Do not allow new cats into the colony until they have been quarantined, tested twice (three months apart), and found to test negative.

- Toms and queens should be certified free of virus before being bred.
- Clean and disinfect the house, bowls, bedding, and cat quarters with ordinary household detergents or bleach solution. The FeLV virus is not hardy and is easily killed. Be sure to disinfect spots the cat might have soiled with urine, saliva, or feces.

There is no evidence that FeLV has ever caused an illness in humans. However, the virus does replicate in human tissue cells in the laboratory. In theory, children and patients with immune deficiency diseases could be at risk. As a sensible precaution, such individuals, and women who are pregnant or are considering becoming pregnant, are advised to avoid contact with virus-positive cats.

FELINE IMMUNODEFICIENCY VIRUS

The feline immunodeficiency virus (FIV), first discovered in a northern California cattery in 1986, is a major cause of chronic immunodeficiency in cats. FIV is a retrovirus belonging to the lentivirus family. It is related to the HIV virus in humans (the virus that causes AIDS). However, these two viruses are species-specific. *HIV does not produce disease in cats and FIV does not produce disease in humans.*

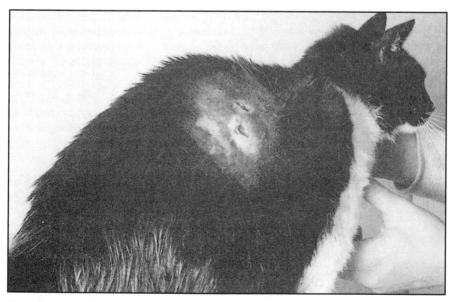

FIV infection is believed to be transmitted by cat bites, such as the one causing this infected wound.

Although its exact incidence has yet to be determined, FIV has been found in cats throughout the United States and is believed to affect 2 to 4 percent of cats in the general population. The incidence is highest in outdoor cats and in males 3 to 5 years of age. This suggests that cat bites, occurring during fights among toms, are a source of virus transmission, especially since the virus is shed in saliva.

Close or casual contact alone is not a major mode of transmission. There is no evidence that the disease is transmitted by mating. However, if a queen becomes infected while pregnant, she may pass the virus on to her unborn kittens.

Signs of Illness

Four to six weeks after FIV exposure, there is acute illness characterized by fever and swelling of the lymph nodes. The white cell count is below normal. The cat may have diarrhea, skin infections, and anemia. After the acute infection, there is a latent period from several months up to 12 years during which the cat appears to be healthy. Eventually, signs of a chronic immunodeficiency syndrome appear and progress slowly (again, over a period of months or years).

Cats with chronic FIV infection present with a variety of unexplained signs of ill health, including severe mouth and gum disease, long-standing diarrhea, loss of appetite and weight with emaciation, fever, recurrent upper respiratory infections with eye and nasal discharge, ear canal infections, and recurrent urinary tract infections. These signs are similar to those associated with other immunodeficiency disorders, such as feline leukemia, severe malnutrition, immunosuppressive drug therapy, and widespread cancer. About 50 percent will have chronic oral conditions and about 30 percent will have chronic upper respiratory infections. Ten to 20 percent will have diarrhea. Many will show neurological signs such as dementia. FIV-infected cats also are much more likely to develop lymphoma.

Diagnosing FIV

If antibodies to FIV are found in the cat's serum using an *ELISA* test, it can be assumed that the cat is persistently *viremic* and can be a source of infection to other cats, or has been vaccinated with the FIV vaccine. All ELISA-positive tests should be confirmed with another test, such as an IFA or Western blot immunoassay, performed at a reference laboratory. However, even these tests cannot distinguish vaccinated cats from infected cats. Research continues for a test that will distinguish between truly infected cats and cats who have been vaccinated.

There are two sets of circumstances in which these tests may have a false negative result. One is during the terminal stages of FIV when the cat is unable to produce detectable antibodies. The other is during the early stages when virus is present in the serum but antibodies have not yet been produced. In the latter case, the cat can be retested in two to three months.

False positive tests can occur in kittens who receive antibodies in the milk of an infected queen. Retest kittens 12 to 14 weeks later or after 6 months of age to determine if they are truly infected.

Treating FIV

There is currently no effective treatment for FIV virus infection. However, the massive effort to develop drugs to cure AIDS in humans involves FIV infection in cats as an animal research model. As this research progresses, it can be anticipated that effective treatment for cats may become available. Drugs used in the treatment of AIDS may provide benefit in individual cats. However, these drugs, especially AZT, are more toxic to cats than to humans. ImmunoRegulin, interferon, and acemannan have shown some benefits. Stampidine is an experimental drug that shows great promise.

It is important that the routine care of infected cats be of the highest quality: top-notch nutrition, parasite control, keeping them indoors, and minimizing stresses.

Preventing FIV

There is a vaccine available for FIV, but it is not generally recommended (see page 110). There have been problems with cats who have been vaccinated but are not truly infected testing positive for the virus. The most effective way of preventing the disease is to keep cats from roaming and fighting with infected strays. This will dramatically lower the likelihood of infection. Neutering males may reduce the incidence of fighting.

All cats in a multicat household should be tested. FIV-positive cats should be removed or isolated from contact with others. These cats should be retested using a Western blot test. Any new cat or kitten being added to your home should first be tested for FeLV and FIV.

RABIES

Rabies is a fatal disease that occurs in nearly all warm-blooded animals, although rarely in rodents. In the United States, vaccination programs for cats and other domestic animals have been remarkably effective. This has greatly reduced the risk of rabies in pets and their owners.

Ninety percent of cats with rabies are under 3 years old, and the majority are male. Rural cats are at the highest risk for rabies because of the potential for wildlife exposure.

The major wildlife reservoirs for rabies (with substantial overlap) are the skunk in the Midwest, Southwest, and California; raccoons in New England and the East; foxes in New York, neighboring eastern Canada, Alaska, and the Southwest; and coyotes and foxes in Texas. Bats, which are distributed widely, also carry rabies.

The main source of infection for humans outside the United States continues to be a bite from an infected dog or cat. In India, for example, a country that lacks an effective rabies control program, it is estimated that several thousand people die of rabies each year. Travelers to countries where rabies is endemic should be aware of the risk of animal bites.

The rabies virus, which is present in an infected animal's saliva, usually enters the body at the site of a bite. Saliva on an open wound or mucous membrane also constitutes exposure to rabies. The incubation period in cats can be 9 days to one year, but usually signs appear within 15 to 25 days of exposure. The virus travels to the brain along nerve networks. The more distant the bite is from the brain, the longer the period of incubation. The virus then travels back along the nerves to the mouth. Entry into the salivary glands occurs less than 10 days before symptoms appear—which means animals can be infectious before they show any signs of rabies (this is unusual but possible).

Signs and symptoms of rabies are due to inflammation of the brain, called encephalitis. During the prodromal (first) stage, which lasts one to three days, signs are quite subtle and consist of personality changes. Affectionate and sociable cats often become increasingly irritable or aggressive and may bite repeatedly at the site where the virus entered the body. Shy and less outgoing cats may become overly affectionate. Soon, affected animals become withdrawn and stare off into space. They avoid light and may hide and die without ever being discovered.

There are two characteristic forms of encephalitis: the furious form and the paralytic form. A rabid cat may show signs of one or both. The furious form, or the "mad dog" type of rabies, is the most common. It lasts two to four days. A rabid cat can actually be more dangerous than a rabid dog, springing up suddenly and attacking people about the face and neck. Soon the cat develops muscle twitching, tremors, staggering, hind leg incoordination, and violent convulsions.

The paralytic form, which occurs in 30 percent of cases, causes the swallowing muscles to become paralyzed. The cat drools, coughs, and paws at his mouth. As encephalitis progresses, the cat loses control of his rear legs, collapses, and is unable to get up. Death from respiratory arrest occurs in one to two days. Because of the rapid course of rabies, paralysis may be the only sign noted.

Any cat who is bitten by an animal who is not absolutely known to be free of rabies must be assumed to have been exposed to rabies, until proven otherwise. Immediately wash out the bite wound and any saliva on the coat, taking precautions for yourself by wearing gloves.

The National Association of State Public Health Veterinarians recommends that if the cat has previously been vaccinated against rabies, revaccinate immediately and observe the cat under strict confinement indoors at home for 45 days. If the cat has not been vaccinated, either euthanize the animal or confine him under strict quarantine without direct handling by humans or contact with other animals for six months. Vaccinate him one month before he is released (that is, at five months after the bite). If this seems harsh, keep in mind that it would not have been necessary if the pet had been vaccinated. Different states may have their own specific quarantine and vaccination regulations for cats who have been exposed to rabies.

Treatment: If you or your cat are bitten by any animal of unknown rabies status, it is extremely important to vigorously cleanse all wounds and scratches, washing them thoroughly with soap and water. Studies in animals have shown that prompt local wound cleansing greatly reduces the risk of rabies. The wound should not be sutured.

Prophylaxis in a previously vaccinated cat consists of a booster shot, which should be given as soon as possible after exposure. Vaccination is not effective once signs of rabies infection appear.

The introduction of inactivated vaccines grown in human diploid cell cultures has improved the effectiveness and safety of postexposure vaccination for humans. Assuming the human bite victim did not have a pre-exposure rabies immunization, both passive rabies immune globulin and human origin active diploid cell vaccine should be given.

There is no effective treatment for rabies. Be sure your pet is properly vaccinated. It is important that cats are vaccinated only under the supervision of a veterinarian. Furthermore, a veterinarian can provide legal proof of vaccination should the need arise.

Public health considerations: Do not pet, handle or give first aid to any animal suspected of having rabies. All bites of wild animals, whether provoked or not, must be regarded as having rabies potential. If your cat is bitten by a wild animal or a domestic animal whose rabies status is unknown, wear gloves when handling your pet to clean his wounds. The saliva from the animal that is in and around the bite wound can infect a person if it gets into a cut or onto a mucous membrane.

Preventive vaccinations are available for high-risk groups of humans, including veterinarians, animal handlers, cave explorers, and laboratory workers.

Early laboratory confirmation of rabies in an animal is essential so that exposed humans can receive rabies prophylaxis as quickly as possible. The animal must be euthanized and his head sent in a chilled (not frozen) state to a laboratory equipped to diagnose rabies. Rabies is confirmed by finding rabies virus or rabies antigen in the brain or salivary tissues of the suspected animal. If the animal cannot be captured and his rabies status can't be verified, you need to consult your physician, who may suggest prophylactic vaccinations.

Whenever you have physical contact with an animal who may conceivably be rabid, *immediately consult your physician and veterinarian*, and also notify the local health department. Biting cats who have been allowed outdoors and appear healthy should be confined indoors and kept under observation for 10 days. *This is true even if the cat is known to be vaccinated for rabies.*

Fungal Diseases

Fungi are a large family that includes mushrooms. They live in soil and organic material. Many types of fungi spread via airborne spores. Fungus spores, which resist heat and can live for long periods without water, gain entrance to the body through the respiratory tract or a break in the skin.

Fungal diseases can be divided into two categories. The first are fungi that affect only the skin or mucous membranes, such as ringworm and thrush. In the second category, the fungus is widespread and involves the liver, lungs, brain, and other organs, in which case the disease is systemic.

Systemic diseases are caused by fungi that live in soil and organic material. Spores, which resist heat and can live for long periods without water, gain entrance through the respiratory system or through the skin at the site of a puncture. Systemic fungal diseases tend to occur in chronically ill or poorly nourished cats. Prolonged treatment with steroids or antibiotics may change an animal's pattern of resistance and allow a fungus infection to develop. Some cases are associated with the immune-depressant effects of feline leukemia, feline panleukopenia, or feline immunodeficiency virus.

Fungal diseases are difficult to recognize and treat. X-rays, biopsies, fungal cultures, and serologic blood tests are used to make a diagnosis. Suspect a fungus when an unexplained infection fails to respond to a full course of antibiotics. Although many systemic fungal agents can both infect humans and cats, only *Sporotrichosis* has been shown to infect humans following direct exposure to infected cats.

CRYPTOCOCCOSIS

This disease, caused by the yeastlike fungus *Cryptococcus neoformans*, is the most common systemic fungal infection of cats. It tends to occur in young adult animals. It is acquired by inhaling spores found in soil heavily contaminated by bird droppings, especially those of pigeons. The likelihood of infection is increased if the cat has an immune deficiency. However, not all cats who develop cryptococcosis are immune depressed.

The most common forms of the disease are nasal, cutaneous, and neurologic cryptococcosis. In other forms nodules, which ulcerate and drain pus, occur beneath the skin of the body.

Nasal cryptococcosis occurs in 50 percent of cases. Signs include sneezing, snuffling, a mucoid to bloody discharge from one or both nostrils, coughing, and obstructed breathing. Flesh-colored polyplike growths may protrude from the nose. The infection may extend to the brain and cause fatal meningitis with neurological signs such as circling and seizures. Ocular damage, including blindness, may also be noted.

Cutaneous cryptococcosis, which occurs in 25 percent of cases, frequently produces a firm swelling over the bridge of the nose. The face and neck are other common sites.

Neurologic cryptococcosis can show a variety of signs, depending on where the infection is located. These include blindness, seizures, and vestibular signs, such as incoordination or a head tilt. The diagnosis can be made by fungus culture or tissue *biopsy*. Often, the organisms can be identified in a smear from the nasal discharge. A cryptococcus latex agglutination test is available.

Treatment: Oral antifungal drugs of the imidazole group, such as ketoconazole, are effective when started early in the course of the disease. Fluconazole and itraconazole are newer drugs that are far better tolerated by cats. These drugs are slow acting. Treatment is prolonged. If those drugs are not successful, amphotercin B or flucytosine can be tried, but they are medications of last resort because they have many serious side effects.

Prevention: Preventing cats from hunting is helpful in preventing this disease. There are no documented cases of transmission from cats to people.

HISTOPLASMOSIS

This disease is caused by a fungus found in the central United States near the Great Lakes, the Appalachian Mountains, Texas, and the valleys of the Mississippi, Ohio, and St. Lawrence Rivers. In these areas, the nitrogen-rich soil facilitates growth of the causative fungus (*Histoplasma capsulatum*).

In the majority of cats, histoplasmosis is an insidious disease with fever, loss of appetite, weakness, weight loss, and debilitation. The liver, respiratory system, eyes, and skin may be involved. Lameness may be noted.

Cats who hunt are at risk for this problem, but cases have been documented where spores blew in a window from pigeon nests on a building. Diagnosis is made by fungal culture, needle aspirate, or tissue biopsy.

Treatment: Successful treatment with antifungal drugs, such as itraconazole, depends on early diagnosis. Despite treatment, most cats die from this infection. Mild respiratory cases have the best prognosis.

SPOROTRICHOSIS

This uncommon skin infection is caused by fungus spores in the soil. These spores usually gain access through a break in the skin. Other routes of infection are by ingesting or inhaling spores. The disease is most common among male cats who prowl in thorny underbrush or sharp prairie grass. Most cases are reported in the northern and central portions of the United States, along river valleys and in coastal areas.

A nodule forms at the site of a skin wound, usually on the feet or legs, the face, or the base of the tail. The hair over the nodule falls out, leaving a moist, ulcerated surface. In some cases there is little surface reaction, but you may see several small firm nodules beneath the skin that appear to form a chain.

On rare occasions, the disease spreads internally to the liver and lungs. In these individuals the outlook for a cure is guarded. The diagnosis is made by removing a piece of tissue and examining it under a microscope, or more conclusively, by growing the fungus in culture. Fungal elements may also be noted in the exudates from wounds.

Treatment: The response to treatment is excellent when disease is limited to the skin and surrounding tissues. Potassium iodide was the agent of choice and is given orally. Cats must be carefully observed for any signs of iodide toxicity, however, such as vomiting, depression, twitching, and cardiac problems. Itraconazole is one of the newer antifungal drugs and is currently recommended. Amphotericin B is used to treat an internal infection, but only as a last resort. These drugs have toxic potential and require close veterinary management.

Public health considerations: Sporotrichosis has been known to infect humans who handle cats with infective drainage from nodules and ulcers. Wear rubber gloves and use strict hygienic precautions when handling cats with draining wounds. Cats can shed the organism both from the infected wounds and via their feces, so care must be taken when cleaning the litter box, as well.

ASPERGILLOSIS

This fungus is found in decaying vegetation and organic-rich soils. Aspergillosis has usually been reported in immunodeficient cats with concurrent feline panleukopenia. Nasal infection similar to that of cryptococcosis and systemic involvement like that of histoplasmosis have been described. Cats may show both pulmonary and intestinal signs.

Nasal discharge may show organisms. The nose may be quite painful and ulcerated. X-rays often show destruction of the bones and sinuses. Blood tests can help in diagnosis, including agar gel immunodiffusion (AGID) and ELISA tests.

Treatment: Early detection and treatment greatly increase the odds of success. Opening up the sinuses to provide direct topical treatment is the most successful treatment. Enilconazole has been used for treatment (even applied topically, much gets absorbed systemically), and the drug clotrimazole, which has been used in dogs, may work as well. Itraconazole can be tried.

BLASTOMYCOSIS

This disease is found along the Eastern seaboard, Great Lakes region, and Mississippi, Ohio, and St. Lawrence River valleys. The fungus has been isolated from cedar trees and pigeon droppings. Cats are more resistant to blastomycosis than are dogs and humans.

Most cases of blastomycosis in cats involve the respiratory system, skin, eyes, and brain. Respiratory signs are the most common and may involve coughing and labored breathing. Skin lesions in cats may involve large abscesses. The nose, face, and nail beds are common sites of such lesions. Nervous system involvement is not common in cats.

Diagnosis is established by biopsy of infected tissue or culture of infected drainage. Organisms may be identified in discharges. A variety of *serologic* tests are available.

Treatment: Itraconazole is the preferred medication and may be needed for as long as two months.

Public health considerations: The hazard to human health is minimal. However, humans have contracted blastomycosis from dog bites.

Protozoan Diseases

Protozoa are one-celled animals that are not visible to the naked eye but are easily seen under the microscope. They are usually found in water. A fresh stool specimen is required to identify the adult parasite or its cysts (called oocysts).

The life cycle of protozoans is complicated. Basically, infection results from the ingestion of the cyst form (oocyst). Cysts invade the lining of the bowel, where they mature into adult forms and are shed in the feces. Under favorable conditions they develop into the infective form.

The two most common protozoan diseases that affect cats are coccidiosis (see page 69) and toxoplasmosis (see page 67).

Rickettsial Diseases

Rickettsia are various disease-causing parasites (about the size of bacteria) that are carried by fleas, ticks, and lice. They live within cells. The majority are maintained in nature by a cycle that involves an insect vector, a permanent host, and an animal reservoir.

BARTONELLA (CAT SCRATCH DISEASE)

Once thought to be caused by a virus, the majority of cases are now believed to be caused by the rickettsial organism *Bartonella henselae*. This organism is present in infected fleas that then feed on the cat. Bartonella usually does not make cats sick. It does, however, affect about 22,000 people each year. It is included in this chapter because of its relationship to cats and the concern surrounding its diagnosis and treatment.

The majority of human cases occur in September through January. Patients, especially children and young adults, commonly present with enlarged, tender lymph nodes of several weeks duration and of unknown cause. These patients often undergo lymph node *biopsy* to rule out lymphoma, a condition unrelated to cat scratch disease.

The cat, usually an asymptomatic carrier of the infection, is able to transmit the disease to humans indirectly via infected flea feces under the cat's nails or in his mouth from grooming. In 90 percent of cases there is a history of a cat (usually a kitten) biting, licking, or scratching the human. This suggests the infective organism is carried in the cat's mouth and may be transferred to his claws when he grooms or scratches.

Three to 10 days after exposure, a raised red sore develops in the human at the site of transmittal. This occurs in about 50 percent of cases. There may be a red streak up the arm or leg. In all cases there is tender enlargement of lymph nodes in the armpit, neck, or groin. Enlargement of the lymph nodes may persist for two to five months.

Less than 5 percent of those infected develop generalized signs, such as low-grade fever, fatigue, headache, and loss of appetite. In rare cases, there is involvement of the spleen, brain, joints, eyes, lungs, and other organs. In immunosuppressed individuals, the disease can be life-threatening.

In cats, there are usually no signs, although cats with chronic inflammatory conditions such as gingivitis, stomatitis, or inflammatory bowel disease may also have bartonellosis.

Treatment: For humans, consult your physician and follow their recommendations for diagnostic tests and treatment.

If the cat seems to show clinical illness, he can be treated with doxycycline, amoxicillin-clavulanate, or azithromycin. A major effort should be aimed at flea control (see page 138).

Prevention: Wash all cat bites and scratches promptly. Do not allow cats to lick open wounds.

There is no way to know when a particular cat harbors the infection. If one family member becomes ill following a scratch, quarantine the cat for two to three weeks to prevent him from infecting others. As a precaution, sick children and immunodeficient individuals should avoid contact with cats under 1 year of age. Routine declawing of cats to prevent human illness is not recommended. Claws can be trimmed and cats should be discouraged from rough play. Again, the emphasis should be on flea control and on treating any cat who shows clinical illness.

Antibodies and Immunity

An animal who is immune to a specific pathogen has natural substances in his system called *antibodies* that attack and destroy that pathogen before it can cause disease. Antibodies are produced by the reticuloendothelial system, which is made up of white blood cells, lymph nodes, and special cells in the bone marrow, spleen, liver, and lungs. These special cells act along with antibodies and other substances in the blood to attack and destroy pathogens.

Antibodies are highly specific. They destroy only the type of pathogen that stimulated their production. When a cat becomes ill with an infectious disease, his immune system makes antibodies against that particular pathogen. These antibodies protect the cat against reinfection. The cat has now acquired active immunity. Active immunity is self-perpetuating; the cat continues to make antibodies long after the disease has gone away. Any time the cat is exposed to that particular pathogen, his immune system will produce more antibodies. The duration of active immunity varies, depending on the pathogen and the cat. Following natural exposure, active immunity often persists for life. In general, immunity to viruses lasts longer than immunity to bacteria.

Active immunity also can be induced by vaccination. The cat is exposed to heat-killed pathogens, live or attenuated (antigens that have been treated to make them less infectious) pathogens rendered incapable of causing disease, or toxins and pathogen products that will also stimulate a response by the cat's immune system. As with natural exposure, vaccination stimulates the production of antibodies that are specific for the particular pathogen in the vaccine. However, unlike natural exposure, the duration of protection may be limited. Accordingly, to maintain high levels of protection, booster vaccines are recommended. How frequently a cat will need boosters depends on the antigen used, the number of exposures to the pathogens, the cat's own immune response, and the type of vaccination used. Vaccination schedules need to be customized for each individual cat.

Another type of immunity is called passive. Passive immunity is passed from one animal to another. The classic example is the antibodies newborn kittens absorb from the *colostrum* of their mother. Kittens are best able to absorb antibodies from their mother's milk during the first 24 to 36 hours of life. The immunity persists only as long as the antibodies remain in the kittens' circulation. The duration of immunity depends on the concentration of antibodies in maternal milk when the kittens were born. Queens vaccinated just before they were bred have the highest antibody levels and are capable of protecting kittens for up to 16 weeks. However, some veterinarians believe this additional booster is unnecessary.

Kittens younger than 3 weeks old may be incapable of developing antibodies in response to vaccination because of physical immaturity or interference by passive maternally acquired antibodies. Maternal antibodies can bind the antigen in the vaccine and keep it from stimulating the immune system. These passive antibodies disappear at between 6 and 16 weeks of age. Therefore, when vaccinating very young kittens, the vaccine must be given more frequently to ensure that the vaccine will stimulate immunity as soon as maternal antibody levels decline and can no longer interfere with the vaccine.

Another source of passive immunity can occur with a transfusion of blood products with antibodies into a cat with a serious infection or immune problem. This is not done frequently, but can be a life-saver for some cats.

Vaccinations

There are several types of vaccines currently available for use in cats: modified live virus (MLV), inactivated or killed virus, and the newest recombinant technologies—live vectored, subunit, and DNA vaccines. Modified live virus vaccines are vaccines that contain virus that is alive and that will replicate when in a cat, but that has been modified so it shouldn't cause the actual disease. These vaccines tend to generate a quick and full immune response. Modified live vaccines are more effective and produce longer-lasting immunity than do killed vaccines.

Killed virus vaccines are vaccines with dead virus, which will not replicate in a cat, so they are incapable of causing disease. Instead, they rely on surface antigens, along with immunity stimulants called adjuvants, to stimulate an immune response.

Recombinant vaccines are among the newest products in the rapidly emerging biotechnology market. The technology relies on the ability to splice gene-size fragments of DNA from one organism (a virus or bacteria) and to deliver these fragments to another organism (the cat), where they stimulate the production of antibodies.

For the live vectored version, genes from a feline *antigen* may be put into a noninfectious virus. Antibodies are stimulated; there is no replication of the antigen. Subunit vaccines stimulate immunity to a part of the antigen of an infectious organism. These are set up to provide the most immunity for the least amount of antigen used. With DNA vaccines—currently experimental for cats—only a small amount of DNA from the infectious agent is used.

Thus, recombinant vaccines deliver specific antigen material on a cellular level without the risk of vaccination reactions associated with giving the entire disease-causing organism. This represents a truly new development. It is expected that recombinant vaccines will soon replace MLVs and whole killed vaccines for many, if not most, feline infectious diseases.

Results for recombinant vaccines indicate that immunity can last as long as with MLVs. With all types of vaccines, booster shots are necessary to maintain an adequate level of protection. The frequency of needed booster shots varies, depending on the disease involved, the individual vaccine, the cat's own immune system, and whether he has been exposed to the disease agent naturally.

Various technologies are available for giving vaccines to cats. Vaccines may be injected under the skin (subcutaneously, or SC) or into a muscle (intramuscularly, or IM). Drops may be put into the nose and/or eyes, and a new transdermal version of some vaccines is absorbed through the skin.

WHY VACCINES FAIL

Vaccines are highly effective in preventing certain infectious diseases in cats, but failures do occur. They can be due to improper handling and storage, incorrect administration, or inability of the cat to respond to the vaccine because of a run-down condition or concurrent illness that stresses his immune system. Giving too many vaccinations at the same time or too frequently can cause immune system overload and a failure to produce antibodies. If a cat is already infected, vaccinating him will not alter the course of the disease. Stretching out the vaccine by dividing a single dose between two cats is another reason a vaccine may not be effective.

Because each cat is an individual, proper handling and administration of the vaccine is important. Vaccinations should be given only by those familiar with the technique.

Vaccinations may not be successful in all cats. Run-down, malnourished, debilitated cats may not be capable of responding to a disease challenge by developing antibodies or building immunity. Such cats should not be vaccinated at that time, but should be vaccinated when they're in better health. Immunosuppressive drugs, such as cortisone and chemotherapy agents, depress the immune system and also prevent the body from making antibodies.

Between 6 and 16 weeks of age, there is a window of risk during which a kitten's passive antibodies (ingested from the mother's milk) are no longer fully protective, but may yet interfere with the vaccination process. For this reason, nursing kittens should not be vaccinated before 6 weeks of age and should not complete their vaccination series before 16 weeks of age.

Young kittens are highly susceptible to certain infectious diseases and should be vaccinated against them as soon as they are old enough to build an immunity. These diseases are panleukopenia, feline viral respiratory disease complex, possibly feline leukemia, and rabies. Vaccines against feline infectious peritonitis, ringworm, giardia, feline immunodeficiency virus, and feline pneumonitis (chlamydia infection) are available and may be indicated in special situations.

To be effective, vaccinations must be kept current (see *Vaccination Recommendations*, page 111).

Allergic reactions in cats tend to be vomiting, with or without diarrhea, difficulty breathing, and itching and hives. Collapse can follow if no action is taken. This is a good reason to have vaccinations done at the veterinary hospital, where care is readily available.

Cats who have had mild vaccine reactions may benefit from a prophylactic dose of an antihistamine or corticosteroid prior to the vaccination. The cat should remain at the veterinary hospital for a short time after vaccination to be sure there will be no reaction.

THE REVACCINATION DEBATE

A subject of much debate in the field of immunology is the timing of booster injections. Based on a growing body of evidence, recommendations for booster vaccinations have been changing. In general, viral vaccines tend to stimulate longer immunity than bacterial vaccines.

It is now believed that the protective response to vaccines for viruses probably persists for several years following a vaccination series and that booster shots can be given every three years instead of every year. This interval for booster shots may be extended even longer with the newer vaccines and updated research on the duration of immunity.

The best way to manage vaccinations is to work with your veterinarian to develop a customized vaccination schedule for your cat, based on your own cat's health and risk factors.

COMBINATION VACCINES

Many feline vaccines are combination or multivalent vaccines. This means a vaccine includes antigens for several diseases all in one injection. At one time, vaccines had as many as five disease antigens included in one injection. It is now believed that less is better—both because some vaccines simply aren't necessary for all cats and because you don't want to overwhelm a cat's immune system.

The most common combination vaccines currently are FVR, FCV, and FPL for rhinotracheitis (herpes), calicivirus, and feline panleukopenia. Most veterinarians use these minimal multivalent vaccines.

For cats who have had—or are at risk for—vaccine reactions, the core vaccines, such as calicivirus, rhinotracheitis, and panleukopenia, may be given separately and only boostered as indicated by titers. (Titers measure the immunity present in a cat's system, but more research is needed to determine exactly what minimum titer levels indicate a cat is safe from disease.)

CORE AND NONCORE VACCINES

The veterinary community has divided vaccines into two main categories, with a smaller third category. Core vaccines are vaccines that every cat should have at some time in his life. Noncore vaccines are vaccines that only some cats need, depending on factors such as geographic location and lifestyle. Other vaccines are also available but are generally not recommended for any cats.

VACCINE-ASSOCIATED FELINE SARCOMA

An association between vaccine administration and sarcoma development has been established in cats. Feline leukemia and rabies virus vaccines have more frequently been implicated in sarcoma development than have other vaccines. Both subcutaneous and intramuscular sites have been affected. See *Vaccine-Associated Feline Sarcoma*, page 530, for more information.

Due to concerns about adjuvants and inflammatory response leading to the cancers, the American Association of Feline Practitioners, together with other veterinary organizations, has established new guidelines for vaccinations. These guidelines include injection site recommendations that make it easier to track any problems that develop, and to treat any cancer that might develop. Recommended sites are right rear limb for rabies, left rear limb for feline leukemia, and right shoulder, off the midline, for any other subcutaneous vaccinations.

Available Vaccines

Young kittens are highly susceptible to certain infectious diseases and should be vaccinated against them as soon as they are old enough to build immunity. The American Association of Feline Practitioners has drawn up guidelines categorizing vaccines as core, noncore, or not recommended, and these categories will be indicated for all the vaccines described in this section. While these guidelines suggest that kittens as young as 6 weeks may be vaccinated, most veterinarians and breeders wait until 7 or 8 weeks of age. Also, vaccine recommendations state that many vaccines do not need boosters beyond 12 weeks of age, but veterinarians, particularly in endemic disease areas, may do a final kitten vaccine at about 16 weeks.

PANLEUKOPENIA (CORE)

The first panleukopenia (FPV) shot should be given at 6 to 8 weeks of age, before a kitten is placed in a new home where he may be exposed to other cats. If the kitten is at particular risk in an area where the disease has occurred, vaccination can be given at 6 weeks of age and then every three to four weeks until the kitten is 16 weeks old. Discuss this with your veterinarian.

After the initial kitten series, a booster given at 1 to 2 years of age may be sufficient in cats who mix with others, because exposure to the disease boosts immunity. A booster after one year is recommended, and then no more frequently than every three years.

Two types of injectable vaccines are available. One is a killed virus and one is a modified live strain. An intranasal vaccine is also available. The modified live virus vaccine is not recommended for pregnant cats or kittens younger than 4 weeks. Killed virus vaccines may be more appropriate in disease-free colonies because there is no risk of reversion to virulence.

Panleukopenia vaccine is often combined with the feline viral respiratory disease complex vaccines and given as a single injection.

FELINE VIRAL RESPIRATORY DISEASE COMPLEX (CORE)

Your veterinarian may recommend an injectable vaccine containing strains of the herpesvirus (FHV) and calicivirus (FCV). Usually, they are combined with panleukopenia vaccine and given at least twice as a single injection, with the last vaccination not before 16 weeks of age. Kittens may be vaccinated as early as 6 weeks of age.

Adolescent and adult cats should receive two initial doses, administered three to four weeks apart. In both kittens and adults, a booster after one year is recommended, and then every three years.

Although viral respiratory disease vaccines are highly effective, they do not prevent all cases of illness. The cat can be exposed to individual strains of virus that are not countered by the vaccine, or the infection can be so severe that it overcomes the cat's protection against it. When this happens, the resulting disease usually is milder than it would be in an unvaccinated cat. Vaccination will not prevent carrier states in cats who do become infected.

Vaccines for the respiratory viruses are available as injectable modified live virus, injectable killed virus, and modified live intranasal. The intranasal route may produce sneezing and nasal discharge. The killed virus vaccine is preferred for pregnant queens and in disease-free colonies because there is no risk of reversion to virulence.

Virulent Systemic Feline Calicivirus

A new vaccine, CaliciVax, was recently introduced to combat virulent systemic feline calicivirus. It is an adjuvanted killed virus. CaliciVax contains a VS-FCV strain, as well as the older strain of FCV. It is labeled for injection in healthy cats 8 to 10 weeks of age, with a second dose in three to four weeks and annual boosters thereafter. However, the risks of using an adjuvanted vaccine (see *Vaccine-Associated Feline Sarcoma*, page 530) may not be worth it, unless VS-FCV has been confirmed in your area.

This vaccine was introduced in 2007, after the most recent AAFP vaccination guidelines were issued. Its ultimate efficacy will be proved only with widespread, long-term use.

RABIES (CORE)

State and city statutes establish requirements for rabies vaccinations. All rabies vaccinations should be administered by a veterinarian, and in many states this is the law. A cat being shipped across some state lines must have a current rabies vaccination, and a certificate attesting to that fact must accompany the cat.

There are three types of rabies vaccines available: These include recombinant, nonadjuvanted canary pox vectored, and killed adjuvanted. All of them are injectable. In general, it is recommended that kittens receive a single dose of killed or recombinant rabies vaccine at 8 or 12 weeks of age, depending on the vaccine used. Adult cats with unknown vaccination history should also receive a single dose of killed or recombinant rabies vaccine. For the recombinant vaccines, boosters are recommended annually. For the killed rabies vaccines, a booster is required at one year, and thereafter, three years using a vaccine approved for three-year administration.

According to recommendations of the Vaccine-Associated Sarcoma Task Force, rabies vaccines are administered subcutaneously as distally as possible in the right rear limb.

FELINE LEUKEMIA VIRUS (NONCORE)

The development of a vaccine against retroviral infection is a long-awaited achievement in veterinary medicine. However, this vaccine is not 100 percent effective. It is possible that some cats vaccinated for FeLV may still become infected.

This vaccine is noncore because of its incomplete effectiveness and because indoor cats who have been tested before coming home should have minimal risk of acquiring FeLV and therefore should not need this vaccine. Kittens born to immune queens acquire protective antibodies in the *colostrum* of the queen. This protection begins to disappear at 6 to 12 weeks of age, after which kittens are susceptible.

Cats with access to the outdoors or who roam free may need this vaccine. However, since kittens are most susceptible to FeLV and may escape, some veterinarians recommend vaccinating kittens and giving a first booster at 1 year. If the cat is then firmly established as an indoor-only cat, no more boosters are needed.

Testing for FeLV is recommended before vaccination. Vaccination is not effective if the cat is positive and already infected. If the *ELISA* test is negative, vaccinate kittens at 8 to 12 weeks of age and again at 14 or 16 weeks. The first booster is given one year later.

To be effective, a full course of vaccination must be administered. This involves two vaccinations two to three weeks apart, a booster a year later, and then annual boosters, if needed.

Vaccines available include injectable adjuvanted killed virus, nonadjuvanted recombinant for transdermal use, and, in Europe, a nonadjuvanted recombinant for subcutaneous injection. According to recommendations of the Vaccine-Associated Sarcoma Task Force, FeLV vaccines are administered subcutaneously as distally as possible in the left rear limb.

FELINE IMMUNODEFICIENCY VIRUS (NONCORE)

The FIV vaccine is an inactivated, killed, injectable vaccine. Unfortunately, vaccination of FIV-negative cats causes the *serologic* tests that are currently available to read as positive. In addition, previous vaccination does not rule out infection, so the significance of a positive test result in a vaccinated cat cannot be assessed. There is concern that the subtype of virus used in the vaccine may not protect against the more common subtypes of the disease. Therefore, the risks and benefits of the use of this vaccine should be carefully discussed with your veterinarian.

CHLAMYDOPHILA FELIS (NONCORE)

Chlamydophila felis causes feline pneumonitis in cats. Immunity induced by vaccination is probably of short duration and the vaccine provides only incomplete protection. Vaccinated cats can still come down with pneumonitis but usually have a shorter, milder illness. The use of this vaccine could be considered for a cat entering a population of cats where infection is known to be endemic. However, the vaccine has been associated with adverse reactions in 3 percent of vaccinated cats.

BORDETELLA BRONCHISEPTICA (NONCORE)

This is a modified live intranasal vaccine. *Bordetella bronchiseptica* is primarily a problem of very young kittens, where it can cause severe lower respiratory tract disease. It appears to be uncommon in adult cats and pet cats in general, and should respond readily to antibiotics, so vaccination is generally not recommended.

FELINE INFECTIOUS PERITONITIS (NOT RECOMMENDED)

The FIP vaccine is an intranasal modified live virus product. The efficacy of this vaccine is controversial, and duration of immunity is short. Although exposure to feline coronaviruses in the cat population is high, the incidence of FIP is very low, especially in single-cat households. Most cats in cattery situations where FIP is a problem become infected with coronaviruses prior to 16 weeks of age, which is the age at which vaccination is first recommended.

GIARDIA LAMBLIA (NOT RECOMMENDED)

This is a killed, injectable vaccine. It is not recommended because the disease is easy to treat and because there is not enough evidence to support the role of the vaccine in preventing disease.

Vaccination Recommendations

This chart is based on the recommendations of the American Association of Feline Practitioners 2006 Vaccine Guidelines. An individual vaccine schedule should be customized for each cat. Booster recommendations are changing frequently, with longer intervals becoming more common.

	Kitten Vaccines	Boosters
CORE VACCINES *These vaccines are* *recommended for all cats*		
Rabies Required by law	1 dose at 2 to 4 months of age, depending on the vaccine	1 year later, then annually or every 3 years, as per vaccine labeling and as required by local law
Panleukopenia (FPV) Important for every cat	First given at 6 to 8 weeks of age, then every 3 to 4 weeks until 16 weeks of age	At 1 year following the last dose, then no more often than every 3 years
Feline Herpesvirus (FHV) Important for every cat	First given at 6 to 8 weeks of age, then every 3 to 4 weeks until 16 weeks of age	At 1 year following the last dose, then every 3 years
Feline Calicivirus (FCV) Important for every cat	First given at 6 to 8 weeks of age, then every 3 to 4 weeks until 16 weeks of age	At 1 year following the last dose, then no more often than every 3 years

continued

Vaccination Recommendations *(continued)*		
	Kitten Vaccines	**Boosters**
NONCORE VACCINES *Depending on individual* *circumstances, these* *vaccines may or may not* *be important for your cat*		
Feline Leukemia Virus (FeLV)	1 dose at 8 weeks of age, then 1 dose 3 to 4 weeks later	At 1 year following the last dose, then annually in cats with sustained risk
Feline Immunodeficiency Virus (FIV)	First given at 8 weeks of age, then 2 more doses at 2- to 3-week intervals	At 1 year following the last dose, then annually in cats with sustained risk
Bordetella bronchiseptica	1 dose at 8 weeks of age	Annually in cats with sustained risk
Chlamydophila felis	1 dose at 9 weeks of age then a second dose 3 to 4 weeks later	Annually in cats with sustained risk
NOT GENERALLY RECOMMENDED These vaccines are not recommended due to mild disease and/or inadequate efficacy		
Feline Infectious Peritonitis (FIP)		
Giardia lamblia		

Shelter Recommendations

For cats in high-risk situations such as shelters, the vaccination schedule may need to be adjusted. Kittens should get a feline panleukopenia vaccination as soon as they enter a shelter—even as early as 4 to 6 weeks of age. Boosters can be administered every two weeks until they are 16 weeks of age.

The same holds true for rhinotracheitis (herpes) and calicivirus vaccinations. Rabies should be given as early as possible (12 weeks of age, generally) and then a booster should be given at one year. For older cats, a rabies vaccine should be given as soon as they enter the shelter, unless they are under quarantine.

It is also recommended that all kittens and cats be tested for FeLV and FIV. Those who test positive should be isolated and retested, unless they are clinically ill.

THE SKIN AND COAT

The condition of a cat's skin and coat can often tell you a great deal about her general health and condition.

Unlike human skin, your cat's skin is thinner and more sensitive to injury. It is easily damaged by careless or rough handling, or with the wrong kind of grooming equipment. Because this skin is loosely applied to the underlying muscle, most bites and lacerations are rather superficial.

The skin serves many functions. Without an intact skin, moisture from the cat's tissues would quickly evaporate, draining her of body heat and water and leading to death from cold and dehydration. Skin is a barrier that keeps out bacteria and other foreign agents. Skin provides sensation to the surface of the body, gives form to the body, and insulates the cat against extreme heat and cold.

The outer layer is the epidermis. It is a scaly layer varying in thickness over different parts of the cat's body. It is thick and tough over the nose and foot pads, and thin and most susceptible to injury in the creases of the groin and beneath the front legs.

The dermis is the next layer inward. Its main function is to supply nourishment to the epidermis. It also gives rise to the skin appendages, which are hair follicles, sebaceous glands, sweat glands, and claws. They are epidermal cells that are modified to serve special functions.

The skin follicles produce three different types of hair. The first, called primary hair, is exemplified by long guardhair, which makes up the outer coat. Each guardhair grows from its own individual root. Tiny muscles connected to the roots of guardhairs enable the cat to fluff out her coat in cold weather, thus trapping warm air and providing better insulation. Secondary hair, or undercoat, is much more abundant. Its function is to provide added warmth and protection. Secondary hairs grow in groups from a single opening in the dermis. This type of hair can be further subdivided into awn hair and wool hair. Awn hair is the intermediate-length hairs in the coat, while the wool hair is also called down hair and consists of short, wooly fibers.

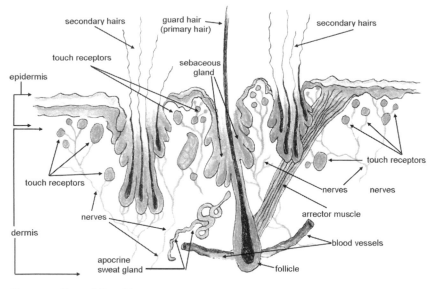

Cross-section of the skin.

Whiskers, eyebrows, chin hair, and carpal hair (found on the backs of the front legs) comprise the third type of hair, called tactile hair, which is especially modified to serve the sense of touch. The whiskers are long, thick, stiff hairs that can be fanned out, rotated forward, or swept back. Their roots are set deep in a cat's tissue. Richly supplied with nerve endings, whiskers give cats extraordinarily detailed information about air currents, air pressure, and anything they touch, supplementing the cat's keen senses of smell and hearing. They are important in sensing and investigating objects close to the cat. It is said that a cat's whiskers are the width of her body at the widest spot, so she can easily tell if she will fit through small spaces. This may not be true for overweight cats!

The function of the sebaceous glands is to secrete an oily substance called sebum, which coats and waterproofs the hair, giving the coat a healthy shine. The amount of oil produced is influenced by hormone levels in the blood. Large amounts of the female hormone estrogen reduce oil production, while small amounts of the male hormone androgen increase it.

Specialized apocrine sweat glands, found all over the body but particularly at the base of the tail, associated with the anal glands, and on the sides of the face, produce a milky fluid whose scent may be involved in sexual attraction. These glands may develop tumors in older cats, generally benign adenomas. Siamese cats may be predisposed to malignant adenocarcinomas. Surgery is the best treatment for these tumors.

In humans, the skin is well supplied with eccrine sweat glands; sweat on the surface of the skin helps regulate loss of heat from the body through evaporation. In the cat, eccrine sweat glands are found only on the foot pads. They secrete sweat when the cat is overheated, frightened, or excited, leaving damp footprints. A cat cools herself by panting and licking her fur. Cooling results from the evaporation of liquid.

Moisture at the tip of the nose is fluid secreted from the mucous membrane of the nostrils.

The front paws are equipped with five toe pads and five claws on each foot, plus two metacarpal pads that normally do not make contact with the ground. The back feet have four toe pads and four claws on each foot, plus a large metatarsal pad that does not make contact with the ground. The natural position of the claws is retracted beneath the skin folds; they can be extended when the cat flexes her flexor tendons.

The skin of the foot pads is rough to provide traction. It is also 75 times thicker than the skin on other parts of the cat's body. Yet it is remarkably sensitive to touch. A cat will extend one paw and gently feel an unfamiliar surface to test the size, texture, and distance from the cat's own body. Such tactile sensitivity is because of the numerous touch receptors located in the deeper layers of the cat's foot pads.

The cat's claws are composed of keratin, a fibrous protein, encased in a hard sheath (called the cuticle). Running through the center of each claw is the quick (seen as a pink line); it contains blood vessels, nerves, and the germinal cells that are responsible for nail growth. The claws grow continuously. Nails will shed the outer layer or sheath. Cats do this themselves by using a scratching post or scratching any rough surface. Claws should be trimmed regularly. This is especially important if they are not worn down by activity or scratching, because they can grow so long that they puncture the foot pads.

The Cat's Coat

The quality of a cat's coat is controlled by a number of factors, including hormone concentrations, nutrition, general health, parasite infestations, genetics, how well the cat grooms herself, and how often you brush her.

HAIR GROWTH

Cat hair grows in cycles. Each follicle has a period of rapid growth (the anagen phase), followed by slower growth and then a resting phase (the catagen phase). During the resting phase, mature hair remains in the follicles and eventually detaches at the base. When the cat sheds her coat (the telogen phase), a young hair pushes out the old hair and the cycle begins anew. Cat hair grows about one-third of an inch (8 mm) each month, on average.

There are hairless cat breeds, such as the Peterbald (who is born with some hair and loses it by about age 2) and the Sphynx (whose body is covered by a fine down and who may have hair on the nose, toes, and tail). Hairlessness in these cats is due to a genetic mutation, not a health problem.

Too much female hormone in the system can slow the growth of hair. Too little thyroid hormone often impairs the growth, texture, and luster of a cat's coat. Ill health, run-down condition, hormone imbalance, vitamin deficiency, or parasites on the cat or within the cat's system may cause the coat to be too thin and brittle. If you suspect your cat's coat is below par, you should see a veterinarian. A poor haircoat often reflects a *systemic* health problem.

Some breeds of cats naturally have a more abundant coat. The environment also has a definite influence on the thickness and abundance of the coat. Cats living outdoors in cold weather grow a heavy coat for insulation and protection. Some additional fat in the diet is desirable at this time, because fat supplies a more concentrated source of energy for coat growth. Fat also aids in the absorption of fat-soluble vitamins, provides essential fatty acids for healthy skin and coat, and improves the palatability of food. Commercial concentrated fatty acid supplements are available. When stools become soft, the cat's diet is too high in fat.

The average indoor cat will not need any fatty supplements. As a precaution, *do not* add fat supplements to the diet of *any* cat with pancreatitis, gallstones, or malabsorption syndrome. Excess fat supplements can interfere with the metabolization of vitamin E. Before making long-term adjustments in the diet's fat content, read chapter 18 and discuss such adjustments with your veterinarian. Always consult your veterinarian before adding any supplements. You do not want to upset a well-balanced diet.

SHEDDING

Some people believe seasonal temperature changes govern when a cat sheds. In fact, shedding is influenced more by changes in ambient light. The more exposure to natural light, the greater the shedding. This applies to both neutered and intact cats.

For cats who spend all their time outdoors, the longer hours of sunlight in late spring activate a shedding process that can last for weeks. Cats who go outdoors part of the day normally shed and grow a new coat at the beginning of summer. In fall, as the days grow shorter, the coat begins to thicken for winter. Indoor cats exposed to constant light may shed lightly and grow new coat year-round.

The tabby pattern is the most common coat pattern in the wild. The tiger is a striped tabby, the leopard is a spotted tabby, and the lion is a tabby agouti. It is also very common among domestic cats, such as this American Shorthair.

Most cats have a double coat made up of long, coarse, outer guardhairs and a soft, fine, woolly undercoat. The Devon and Cornish Rex breeds are exceptions. Rex cats have a single coat made of fine curly hair. The Selkirk Rex has a slightly longer, curly coat. These cats shed but less than a cat with a normal coat. This is a dominant mutation.

Wirehaired cats have a tightly crimped coat, including the whiskers. This is a dominant mutation. The coat is coarse and harsh to the touch.

When a cat with a double coat begins to shed, the undercoat is shed in a mosaic or patchy fashion, giving the cat a moth-eaten look. This is perfectly normal. Totally indoor cats may shed somewhat all year round and never go through this kind of extreme shed. When shedding begins, prevent skin irritation by removing as much dead hair as possible by daily brushing.

COAT COLOR CHANGES

In the pointed cat breeds—cats who are predominantly light with darker colors at the tips of the ears, tail, legs, and on the face—the appearance of these color points is temperature-dependent. These breeds include Siamese, Burmese, Balinese, and Himalayan. Areas where the body temperature is cooler have darker hair, while the main body, where the temperature is higher, has lighter hair.

Anything that changes the body temperature in a certain area may influence the haircoat color in these cats. For example, if a Siamese cat has to be clipped on her side, the hair may grow in dark since the temperature is cooler without the hair covering. Eventually, the darker hair will shed out and the next hair growth should be the normal color. Kittens of these breeds are usually born with a solid light color, and their points appear as they grow.

How to Avoid Coat and Skin Problems
GROOMING

The cat's tongue has a spiny surface that acts like a comb. As cats groom themselves, saliva wets the fur, and then cats lick themselves to take up the moisture, catching dirt and pulling out loose hair as they do. Mothers teach their kittens how to do this. When two cats live together, grooming often becomes a mutual activity.

Even though your cat keeps relatively clean, brush her regularly. The more hair you remove, the less can be licked off, swallowed, or shed. This helps to reduce the problem of hairballs, and also means less cat hair will be shed around your home. Frequent brushing also keeps the coat sleek and healthy, and free of parasites and other skin problems.

Kittens should be groomed in very short sessions every day, beginning shortly after they are weaned. This is good training. An adult cat unaccustomed to grooming can present a difficult problem when tangles and mats must be removed. Use a very soft bristle brush and keep the sessions short and happy.

How often to groom an adult cat depends on the thickness and length of her coat and the condition of her hair and skin. Shorthaired cats usually need less grooming, and once a week may be sufficient. Longhaired cats with thick coats—Persians, Himalayans, and Angoras, for example—should be combed every day to keep their coats from matting and tangling. As cats age, even shorthaired ones will need more frequent grooming, because older cats tend to groom less.

Longhaired cats need to be brushed every day to keep their coat from tangling and matting.

Groom a shorthaired cat once or twice a week to remove loose hair and to reduce the likelihood of hairballs.

A variety of grooming tools are described in the list that follows. What you'll need for your cat depends on the type of coat your cat has.

- **Comb.** A metal comb will last the lifetime of your cat. It should have smooth, round teeth designed to avoid trauma to the skin. You should have a narrow-toothed comb to remove dirt and fleas. A wide-toothed comb is best for grooming long hair, and for attending to the hair around the head and in other sensitive areas on all cats. You can buy a combination comb that has narrow teeth on one side and wide teeth on the other.

- **Brush.** Brushes with natural bristles produce less static electricity and broken hair than do nylon ones. A slicker brush (a rectangular bush with short, stiff wires) works well for most shorthaired cats. The wires feel like the spines on a cat's tongue and are excellent for removing dead hair. For Rex cats, an ultra short-bristled brush or a brush with rubber nubs is most desirable, because this breed is prone to excessive hair loss if brushed too vigorously.

- **Palm brush (hound glove).** This is used on shorthaired cats to remove dead hair and polish the coat. A piece of chamois leather or nylon stocking also works well. For a Sphynx cat, a damp washcloth may be adequate for most grooming needs.

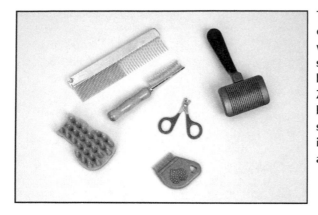

Top left is a combination comb with narrow and wide teeth; below it is a skip-tooth comb for long-haired cats; far left is a Zoom Groom rubber brush, center is a scissors-style nail clipper; bottom is a flea comb; far right is a slicker brush.

- **Scissors.** These may be needed to cut out mats (adequate grooming ensures that mats will never form). Buy a pair with a blunt tip or rounded bead on the end of each blade.
- **Nail clippers.** We prefer those that have two cutting edges—a scissor effect rather than a guillotine.
- **Grooming table.** This is really a luxury item, unless you are showing your cat. Some people prefer to hold their cat on their lap when they groom, but some cats just won't sit in a lap. And it is easier to work with the cat on an elevated surface. If the table is the correct height, you can work on your cat comfortably without having to bend. Any table should be solid with a nonslip surface. You can also use an ordinary table or any flat, sold surface, with a nonslip mat placed on top to prevent your cat from slipping.

How to Groom

Always try to avoid adding static to the coat, because this is very uncomfortable for cats. Dampening the brush first or misting it lightly with water will help. With a shorthaired cat, begin at the head and work toward the tail, drawing a narrow-toothed comb carefully through the coat. Gently roll the cat over to groom the belly and armpit areas. Then brush in the same direction with a bristle or slicker brush. Finally, using a palm brush or chamois cloth, polish the coat to give it a sheen.

With a longhaired cat, use a wide-toothed comb and begin near the head by brushing or combing toward the head and against the lay of the hair, to fluff out the coat. Work upward over the legs and sides of the chest, the back, flanks, and tail. Then use a brush in the same way. The coat around the neck is brushed up to form a frame for the face. Roll the cat over gently to comb out the belly and armpit areas. Then comb the hair back down along the body, unless you are fluffing the cat out for the show ring.

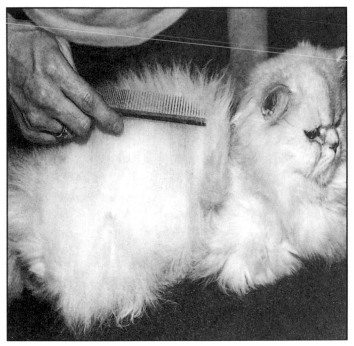

Longhaired cats are combed against the lay of the hair.

A discoloration at the base of the tail, which may be accompanied by loss of hair, is caused by overactivity of large oil-producing glands at the base of the tail. It is most common in unneutered males, but may occur in other cats (see *Stud Tail*, page 164).

Use special care to make sure any soft, woolly hair behind the ears and under the legs is completely combed out. These are two areas where mats (clumps of hair) form if neglected. Any mats should be removed. Mats that are not removed will continue to catch up more and more hair, pinching your cat's skin and causing pain and irritation.

There are commercial tangle remover liquids and sprays that may soften these mats and facilitate removal. To remove mats, first saturate the clumps of hair with such a product. This rehydrates the hair and closes the barbs. Then separate as much of the mat as you can with your fingers.

Some mats can be removed with the tip of a comb. In many cases, however, they will need to be cut out. Cutting into mats with scissors must be done with extreme care, because a cat's skin is not attached to the underlying muscle and tents up as the mat is pulled. Do not slide the scissors beneath the mat and attempt to remove it flush with the skin. You will almost certainly remove a piece of skin. When possible, slide a comb beneath the mat as a barrier between the scissors and the skin. Then hold the scissors *perpendicular* to the comb and carefully snip into the fur ball in narrow strips. Tease the mat out gently with your fingers. After the mat has been removed, comb out residual snarls.

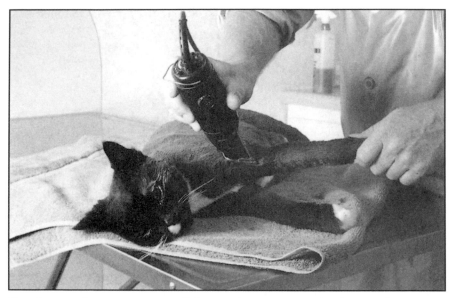

Shearing may become necessary if the coat becomes too matted to comb. Because removing mats can be painful, this cat has been tranquilized to facilitate clipping.

Cats with badly matted coats may need a whole body clipping done by a professional groomer or a veterinarian. Some owners of longhaired cats keep their cats in a short clip, especially in the warm weather.

Beyond the Brush

Your cat's ears should be inspected weekly. To remove dirt and debris, see *Basic Ear Care* (page 206). Routine inspection of the teeth will tell you if there is any buildup of tartar or calculus. To learn more about oral hygiene, see *Taking Care of Your Cat's Teeth* (page 244). Inspection of the anal sacs may disclose a buildup of secretions. To care for the anal sacs, see *Impacted Anal Sacs* (page 283).

A show cat may require special care and grooming. If you plan to show your cat, it is a good idea to ask her breeder to give you a demonstration.

TRIMMING THE CLAWS

Indoor cats should be trained to use a scratching post to keep their front claws worn down and to remove the older outer sheaths. In all likelihood, you'll still need to trim your indoor cat's claws. This is especially true of cats who are less active.

Outdoor cats do not need to have their claws trimmed. Activity keeps them worn down. In addition, they may be needed as defensive weapons.

Older or arthritic cats may not be able to groom their claws very well, so in those cases, you may need to trim the back nails. If you do not, the nails can actually grow around into the pads, which can be very painful. Cats with extra toes also often need weekly checks of their claws to be sure no nails are growing around and into the pads.

Cats should get used to having their paws handled and their nails trimmed while they are still kittens. Older cats who have not grown accustomed to the procedure might be difficult to manage. Positive reinforcement with play or treats after trimmings will help.

Nail clippers with two cutting edges are the most satisfactory. Place your cat on a firm, raised surface or in your lap. Lift up one front paw and gently squeeze one toe between your thumb and finger to extend the nail. Or, alternatively, push up on the bottom of the toe to extend the nail. Identify the pink part of the nail (the quick) that contains the nerves and blood vessels. Be sure to cut the clear part of the nail well beyond the pink part. If your cat's nails are dark and you can't see the quick, cut the nail just beyond the point where it starts to curve downward. Be quick and matter-of-fact about it. You may find that it's easier to just cut one paw, then return for another paw later in the day.

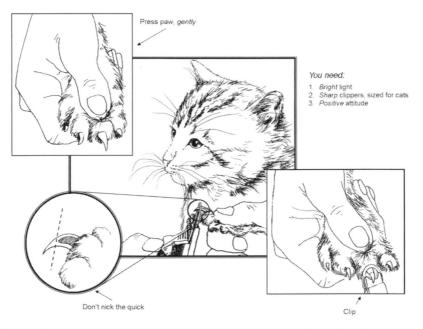

Press paw, *gently*

You need:
1. *Bright* light
2. *Sharp* clippers, sized for cats
3. *Positive* attitude

Don't nick the quick

Clip

Clipping the cat's nails. Squeeze the toe between your thumb and forefinger to extend the nail. Clip the clear part of the nail beyond the quick, just in front of the point where it curves downward.

If you accidentally cut into the quick, the cat will feel some pain and the nail will begin to bleed. Hold pressure over it with a cotton ball. The blood will clot in a few minutes. If it persists, styptic powder or cornstarch can be used to stop the bleeding.

Declawing is discussed on page 351.

Bathing

It is difficult to lay down specific guidelines on bathing, since this depends on the coat type and the lifestyle and fastidiousness of the individual cat. Some cats, particularly indoor cats, will never need a bath. Overbathing can remove natural oils essential to the coat. Regular brushing will keep the coat sleek and glowing and help eliminate the need for bathing.

However, while most cats keep themselves relatively clean, there are times when any cat might get very dirty or get something on her coat that is not safe for her to groom on her own. When the coat is badly stained, has a strong odor, or appears oily despite a thorough brushing, the only solution is a complete bath. Cats with skin conditions or parasite infestations may need to be bathed with medicated shampoos. And show cats are bathed periodically in preparation for cat shows. If you plan to show your kitten, kittens can be safely bathed after they are 3 months old.

How to Give Your Cat a Bath

This can be quite a challenge—particularly if your cat was not bathed as a kitten. Most cats dislike water, so expect to meet some resistance. If possible, have someone hold and soothe the cat while you give the bath. You can also take the cat to a professional groomer.

Begin by combing the coat to remove all knots and mats. Matted hair tends to "set" when wet and is more difficult to brush. Plug the cat's ears with cotton balls to keep out water. Use artificial tears ointment in the eyes to prevent soap burn (see *How to Apply Eye Medicines*, page 173).

The next question is what shampoo to use. Commercial pet shampoos now indicate on the label whether they are for dogs or cats. Always use a shampoo that is made for cats. Many dog shampoos contain ingredients that may be toxic to cats.

Place a bath mat on the bottom of the sink so the cat can have a nonslippery surface to grip. (You can also use a bathtub, but then you must bend over or get on your knees.) Fill the sink with warm water to a depth of 4 inches (10 cm). Holding the cat gently but firmly by the back of the neck, lower her into the sink with her back toward you (so you won't get clawed). Gently scoop some warm water over the cat's back using a plastic cup, then lather the coat with shampoo, keeping it out of the cat's eyes and ears. Rinse well with warm tap water or a spray; never spray water in the cat's face. Be sure to remove all traces of shampoo, because any soap left behind dulls the coat and irritates the skin. If the coat is especially dirty, you may need to give the cat a second sudsing.

Another method works well if you have a double sink. Fill both sinks to about 4 inches (10 cm) with warm water. Use the first sink for the soaping part of the bath, then transfer the cat to the second sink for rinsing.

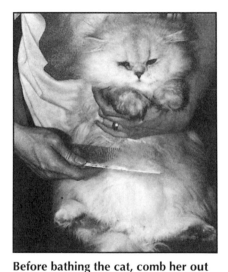

Before bathing the cat, comb her out thoroughly.

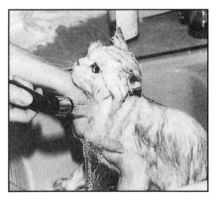

Plug her ears with cotton to keep out water.

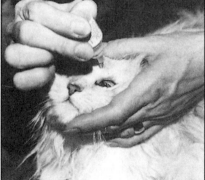

Instill a drop of mineral oil or artificial tears into the eyes to prevent soap burn.

Be sure to keep the spray out of the cat's face.

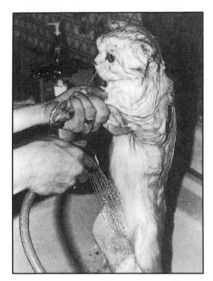

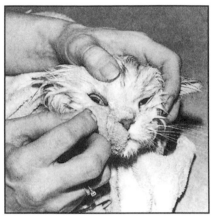

Wrap the cat in a towel and pat her dry. While she's wrapped, wash her face with a damp cloth.

Rinse the cat well to remove all lather.

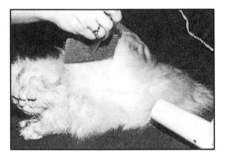

If your cat does not object to it, use a hair dryer on the cool air or fan setting (not hot!). Air drying may be easier; keep her in a warm room until she's dry.

Finally, fluff out the coat with a brush. For a show cat, you may want to add the air from a hair dryer to make the coat extra fluffy.

Special rinses are sometimes recommended to bring out qualities of the coat for show purposes. If you plan to use one, use it now—then rinse it out completely. *Do not use vinegar, lemon juice, or bleach rinses.* They are either too acidic or too basic and will damage the cat's coat and skin. Do not use any hair colorings or dyes, as these can damage the hair.

Now dry the coat gently with towels. Do not rub a longhaired cat, as that will mat the hair. Simply wrapping the cat in a towel and holding her for a few minutes will dry the coat quite a bit. The coat will take an hour or two to dry, and the cat should be kept indoors in a warm room until she is completely dry to avoid chilling. If your cat does not object to it, you can use an air comb. Do not use a hair dryer made for humans unless it has a cool air or fan function (the warm or hot air settings will damage your cat's coat). Even then, many cats will object to the noise.

Cats with an oily coat are especially prone to collecting dirt. In such cases, you can try "dry cleaning" the coat between baths. A number of products have been used successfully as dry shampoos. Make sure these are labeled as "cat safe." Calcium carbonate, talcum or baby powder, fuller's earth, and cornstarch are all effective. They can be used frequently without the danger of removing essential oils or damaging the coat or skin. Work the powder into the coat and leave it for 20 minutes to absorb oils. Then carefully brush or blow the powder out. Do not let your cat groom it off. If you show your cat, all traces of powder must be removed before you enter the judging ring.

SPECIAL BATH PROBLEMS
De-Skunking

The old remedy for removing skunk oil involved soaking the affected parts in tomato juice and then giving the cat a bath. What you usually ended up with was a pink cat who stilled smelled faintly of skunk. A new recipe appeared in *Chemical & Engineering* magazine and has been widely quoted on the Internet. It is far more effective and does not require repeated use. It can be used on dogs as well as cats. The recipe is as follows:

> 1 quart (1 l) 3 percent hydrogen peroxide (from the drugstore)
>
> ¼ cup (55 g) baking soda (sodium bicarbonate)
>
> 1 teaspoon (5 ml) liquid dish soap

Bathe the pet and work the solution into the coat. Follow with a tap water rinse. In longhaired cats, most of the challenge is getting the solution down to the skin.

Discard any unused formula because the release of oxygen caused by the chemical reaction could make the container explode.

Tar and Paint

When feasible, trim away any hair that contains tar, oil, or paint. To remove residual substances, saturate the effected parts with vegetable oil. Leave for 24 hours, then wash the coat with soap and water or give the cat a complete bath. If the substance is on the feet, apply nail polish remover and follow with a good rinsing. You must keep the cat from attempting to groom off the tar—and the oil. An Elizabethan or BiteNot collar may be needed.

Do not use petroleum solvents such as gasoline, kerosene, or turpentine to remove any substance from a cat's coat. These products are extremely harmful to the skin and are highly toxic if absorbed.

Gum

For sticky substances such as gum, put ice on the area and then try sliding the substance off. Otherwise, you may need to clip the hair.

Hairballs

Hairballs, also called trichobezoars, are the bane of many cat owners' existence. Because cats groom themselves so thoroughly, they ingest a fair amount of hair—along with anything that has settled on the surface of their coat. Most of the time, the cat will either pass the hair in the stool or vomit the hair back up. But hair can build up in the stomach or the intestines and, in rare instances, can even cause a blockage.

A cat preparing to expel a hairball will make an extensive coughing, gagging noise, similar to a cough. If your cat does this frequently and no hairball appears, the cough may have a more serious medical cause.

Treatment: The easiest way to control hairballs is to regularly groom your cat so she does not have to swallow so much hair. Dietary supplements have also been used to control hairballs. They generally fall into two categories: lubricants that help slide the hair along the digestive tract and fiber that helps push the hair along.

Petroleum-based laxatives lubricate the hair and move it along through the intestinal tract. These are often flavored and may be put on the cat's paws to encourage the cat to lick it off. If the taste is appealing enough, the cat may lick it off your fingers. Otherwise, some can be squeezed into the cat's mouth. Care must be taken, since petroleum-based laxatives interfere with the absorption of the fat-soluble vitamins, A, D, E, and K. Some commercial preparations for cats, such as Laxatone, include extra vitamins for this reason. It's also a good idea not to give your cat these kinds of products an hour before or after a meal.

High-fiber bulk additives can also be used to help move the hair through. Tablets, treats, powders such as Lax-eze, and special hairball control diets such as Science Diet Hairball Control Diet and Purina Pro Plan Hairball Management Formula work on this principle.

Prevention: The best way to prevent hairballs is to brush the cat more often, especially at shedding time (which, for indoor cats, may be year-round). Administer a commercial hairball preventive (such as described above), available at pet supply stores. A safe and effective home remedy for hairballs is white petroleum jelly. Use about half a teaspoon. The jelly melts in the stomach and lubricates the hairball for easier passage. Use once or twice a week.

Mineral oil is also effective. Add it to the cat's food once or twice a week at a dose of 1 teaspoon (5 ml) per 5 pounds (2.3 kg) body weight. Do not give by mouth because of the potential for inhalation. Keep in mind that mineral oil and petroleum jelly may decrease the absorption of fat-soluble vitamins, if given in large doses or for a prolonged period. There are also diets that help in hairball control, such as Science Diet Hairball Control and Purina ONE Advanced Nutrition Hairball Formula.

Sorting Out Skin Diseases

Skin disease is a common problem in cats. If you suspect your cat is suffering from a skin ailment, start by thoroughly examining the skin and coat. On shorthaired cats, run a fine-toothed comb against the lay of the hair to expose the skin. On longhaired cats, use a bristle brush. Check the appearance of the skin and examine the scrapings found on the comb and brush. The tables on pages 130 to 132 serve as an introduction to skin diseases and suggest where to look to find the cause of a problem.

Itchy skin disorders are characterized by constant scratching, licking, biting, and rubbing against objects. Allergies are a common cause of itching.

The itchy skin diseases in the first table are characterized by constant scratching, licking, and biting at the skin, and rubbing up against objects to relieve the itch. There will be crusty areas produced by scratching.

The second table lists a group of skin conditions that affect the appearance of the coat and hair. These diseases do not cause your cat much discomfort—at least not at first. Hair loss is the main sign. It may appear as impaired growth of new hair, or you may notice a patchy loss of hair from specific areas of the body. At times, the coat does not look or feel right and may be greasy or coarse and brittle. Many of these conditions are related to hormone production.

The third table lists diseases in which the predominant sign is skin infection or *pyoderma* on or beneath the skin. Pyoderma is characterized by *pus*, infected sores, scabs, *ulcers* of the skin, *papules*, *pustules*, *furuncles*, *boils*, and skin *abscesses*. Some cases are caused by self-mutilation and are late consequences of scratching and biting. Other pyodermas are specific skin diseases that occur by themselves.

During the course of grooming, playing with or handling your cat, you may discover a lump or bump on or beneath the skin. To learn what it may be, see the last table on lumps or bumps on or beneath the skin. Chapter 19, Tumors and Cancers, contains more information.

Itchy Skin Diseases

Allergic contact dermatitis: Similar to contact dermatitis, but rash may spread beyond the area of contact. Requires repeated or continuous exposure to allergen.

Chiggers: Itching and severe skin irritation between the toes and around the ears and mouth. Look for barely visible red, yellow, or orange chiggers (the larvae).

Contact dermatitis: Red, itchy bumps and inflamed skin at the site of contact with a chemical, detergent, paint, or other irritant. Can also be caused by rubber or plastic food dishes. There may be scales and hair loss.

Ear mites (ododectes): Head tilting and shaking, and scratching at the ears. Excessive brown, waxy, or purulent material in the ear canals.

Feline miliary dermatitis: Small bumps and crusts around the head, neck, and back felt beneath the haircoat. May be associated with fleas. May be complicated by pyoderma.

Flea allergy dermatitis: Red, itchy pimplelike bumps over the base of the tail, back of rear legs, and inner thighs. Scratching continues after fleas have been killed.

Fleas: Itching and scratching along the back, and around the tail and hindquarters. Look for fleas, or black and white gritty specks in hair (flea feces and eggs).

Food allergy dermatitis: Severe itching over the head, neck, and back. Swelling of eyelids. May only show as reddened ears. Often complicated by hair loss and oozing sores from constant scratching and biting.

Inhalant allergy (atopic dermatitis): Appearance is similar to feline miliary dermatitis. May have symmetrical hair loss over body.

Lice: Two-millimeter-long insects, or white grains of sandy material (nits) attached to the hair. Found beneath matted coats in poorly kept cats. May have bare spots where hair has been rubbed off.

Maggots (myiasis): Soft-bodied, legless fly larvae found in damp matted fur or open wounds. May be complicated by pyoderma.

Scabies (sarcoptic mange): Intense itching around the head, face, neck, and edges of the ears. Hair is rubbed off. Typical thick gray to yellow crusts. May be complicated by pyoderma.

Ticks: Large or very small insects attached to the skin, or possibly walking slowly through the hair. May swell up to the size of a pea. Often found around the ears, along the back, and between the toes.

Walking dandruff (cheyletiella mange): Large amounts of dry, scaly, flaky skin over the neck, back, and sides. Itching may be mild.

Diseases with Hair Loss

Congenital hypotrichosis: A genetic condition where kittens lose any hair they are born with by about 4 months of age.

Cortisone excess: Symmetrical hair loss over trunk and body, with darkening of the underlying skin. Seen with Cushing's disease. May also indicate a thyroid problem. Thinning of the skin is also seen with this condition.

Demodectic mange: Thinning and loss of hair around the eyes and eyelids, giving the cat a moth-eaten appearance. Not common in cats.

Eosinophilic granuloma: Raised, red circular plaque on the abdomen or insides of the thighs (eosinophilic plaque); or linear plaques on the backs of the hind legs.

Feline endocrine alopecia: Thinning or balding of the coat on insides of the back legs, lower abdomen, and genital area. Distribution is symmetrical. Occurs most often in neutered males and spayed females.

Hyperthyroidism (excess thyroid hormone): About one-third of cats with this endocrine problem will have hair that pulls out easily and hair loss.

Hypothyroidism (deficient thyroid hormone): Dry skin and thinning of the hair-coat. Hair becomes dull and brittle. Rare in cats.

Indolent (rodent) ulcer: Red shiny patches of hairless skin. Usually involves the middle of the upper lip and occasionally the lower lip. Not painful.

Psychogenic alopecia: Thinning of hair in a stripe down the back or on the abdomen. Caused by compulsive self-grooming.

Ringworm: A fungal infection. Scaly, crusty, or red circular patches ½ to 2 inches (12 to 50 mm) across. Patches show central hair loss with a red ring at the periphery. Sometimes just broken hairs around the face and ears. May become infected. Highly contagious, including to humans.

Stud tail: Greasy, rancid-smelling waxy-brown material at the top of the tail near the base. The site of the glands is usually devoid of hair.

Skin Diseases with Pus Drainage

Candidiasis (thrush): Moist white plaques that bleed easily when rubbed. Most common on mucous membranes.

Cellulitis or abscess: Painful, hot, inflamed skin or pockets of pus beneath the skin. Often caused by self-mutilation. Look for an underlying cause, such as an itchy skin disorder, foreign body, or bite or puncture wound.

Feline acne: Pimplelike bumps on the underside of the chin and edges of the lips. May be associated with plastic or rubber food and water dishes.

Impetigo: Pustules on the abdomen and hairless skin of young kittens.

Mosquito bite hypersensitivity: Crusty sores with erosions and scabs over the bridge of the nose and tips of the ears.

Lumps or Bumps on or Beneath the Skin

Abscess: A painful collection of pus at the site of a bite or puncture wound. Frequently found after cat fights. Forms a firm swelling that becomes soft with time. Purulent discharge.

Cancer: A lump that indicates cancer is characterized by rapid enlargement; appears hard or fixed to surrounding tissue; any lump growing from bone; a lump that starts to bleed; a mole that begins to spread or ulcerate; an unexplained open sore that does not heal, especially on the feet or legs. The only way to tell for sure is to remove and study the lump under a microscope. Better to check out a benign lump than to miss a malignant one.

Epidermal inclusion cyst: A firm, smooth lump beneath the skin. May grow slowly. May discharge cheesy material and become infected. Otherwise, not painful.

Grubs/Cuterebra: Inch-long fly larvae that form cystlike lumps beneath the skin with a hole in the center for the insect to breathe. Often found beneath the chin, on the neck, or along the abdomen.

Hematoma: A collection of clotted blood beneath the skin; often involves the ears. Caused by trauma. May be painful.

Mycetoma: Mass or nodule beneath the skin with an open tract to the surface draining a granular material. Caused by a fungus.

Skin papilloma: These grow out from the skin and may look like a wart or a piece of chewing gum stuck to the skin. Not painful or dangerous.

Sporotrichosis: Skin nodule with overlying hair loss and wet surface of pus at the site of a puncture wound or break in the skin. Caused by a fungus.

Fleas

The ordinary cat flea (*Ctenocephalides felis*) is the most common parasite on the cat's skin. All cats can be affected except for those living at higher elevations, because fleas do not live above 5,000 feet. Cats living indoors can have fleas year-round.

Fleas survive by jumping onto a host animal, cutting open their skin, and feeding on the blood. In most cases, they cause only a mild itch; but a heavy infestation, especially of kittens or older, ill cats, might cause severe anemia or even the death of the cat. Fleas also are an intermediate host of tapeworm. Some cats experience hypersensitivity to flea saliva. This produces intense itching and a localized or generalized skin reaction. Such cats require special attention (as described in *Feline Miliary Dermatitis*, page 153).

Flea infestation can be diagnosed by finding fleas on the cat or by seeing black and white, salt-and-pepper-like grains in the coat. These particles are flea feces (the "pepper") and flea eggs (the "salt"). Fecal material is made up of digested blood. When brushed onto a wet paper, it turns a reddish brown.

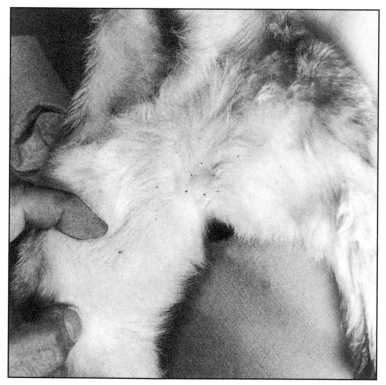

Fleas, seen here as black specks, are easier to see in the groin area, where there is less hair.

The adult flea is a small dark brown insect about 2.5 millimeters in size and can be seen with the naked eye. Although fleas have no wings and cannot fly, they do have powerful back legs and can jump great distances. Fleas move through the hair rapidly and are difficult to catch.

Look for fleas on your cat's back and around the tail and hindquarters by running a fine-toothed comb through her fur. Fleas are sometimes seen in the groin area, where it is warm and there is less hair. Itching is most pronounced in these areas.

THE FLEA LIFE CYCLE

An effective flea control strategy requires an understanding of the flea life cycle. Fleas need a warm, humid environment to flourish and reproduce. The higher the temperature and humidity, the more efficient their reproduction. The adult flea can live up to 115 days on a cat, but only one or two days off her.

After taking a blood meal, fleas mate on the skin of the cat. The female lays eggs within 24 to 48 hours, and may produce up to 2,000 eggs in a four-month life span. The eggs fall off and incubate in your home beneath furniture and in carpets, cracks, and bedding. Deep pile and shag carpets make an ideal environment for egg development.

In 10 days, the eggs hatch into larvae that feed on local debris. Larvae spin a cocoon and go into a pupal stage that lasts for days or months. Under ideal temperature and humidity conditions(65° to 80°F, 70 percent humidity, the presence of vibrations, and exhaled carbon dioxide), fleas can emerge rapidly. After hatching, immature adult fleas search for a host. If one is not found right away, they can live for one to two weeks without feeding.

A flea's life expectancy is affected by the cat's grooming. A cat who chews and licks at her skin because of the itch may destroy a large number of fleas and therefore have fewer than expected. Similarly, a cat who is not as sensitive to fleas may harbor a large number and show few signs of infestation.

At any given time, about 1 percent of the flea population is composed of adult fleas, while 99 percent remain in the invisible egg, larval, and pupal stages. An effective flea control program must eliminate this large reservoir. In other words, to control fleas on your cat, it is most important that you destroy a large number of fleas on the premises. Unless the yard and house are treated at the same time as you treat the cat, they will be a continuous source of reinfestation that no amount of insecticide on the cat can control. You must also treat all pets in the home, even if you only see fleas on one.

NEW METHODS OF FLEA CONTROL

New products such as Program, Advantage, and Frontline have practically replaced the use of dips, powders, sprays, and shampoos to treat and prevent fleas. The new products are more effective and safer than the traditional insecticides. They are also easier to administer. However, permethrins are toxic and any preparation that combines a chemical with permethrin is *not* safe for cats. If you have both dogs and cats, do not use permethrin products on your dog at all. Cats have developed toxicity just from sleeping with a dog treated with permethrins. The cat will show severe tremors or seizures, and diazepam is often not enough to control the symptoms. Methocarbamol may be needed and fluid therapy is also recommended.

Program (the brand name for lufenuron) was the first and remains one of the most popular agents for controlling fleas on cats. Program is a tablet or liquid given once a month with a meal. There is also an injectable form that is given every six months.

The active ingredient accumulates in the cat's subcutaneous tissue and the flea must bite the cat for Program to work. Program works by inhibiting flea eggs from growing and hatching. This leads to a steady drop in the number of new fleas in the environment. Its effect is limited to the hard outer shell of the flea, making it completely harmless to mammals. However, because mature fleas are not affected, it can take 30 to 60 days or longer for the adult fleas on the cat to die of old age before you notice a reduction in itching and scratching. All pets in the household must be on Program for it to be effective.

For more immediate results, and especially if the cat is suffering from flea allergy dermatitis, Program should be combined with a flea shampoo or some other topical insecticide treatment. Advantage or Frontline can be added to Program to kill adult fleas within one to two days. It may be necessary to eliminate fleas on the premises using insecticides, as well (see *Eliminating Fleas on the Premises*, page 139).

Advantage (imidacloprid) is a once-a-month topical liquid that kills fleas by direct contact. Fleas don't have to bite the cat for the preparation to work. Advantage comes in a tube and is applied to the cat's skin between the shoulder blades (you must carefully part the hair to make sure you get the liquid on the skin). One application protects the cat for up to 30 days. It is released through body oils and hair follicles. This is bitter tasting and cats who lick treated areas will drool, so try to place the topical where a cat can't reach it with her tongue.

Advantage kills fleas on direct contact and may reduce hatching eggs and larvae. Following application, 98 to 100 percent of adult fleas are killed within 12 hours. Thus, any new fleas that infest the cat should be killed before they have a chance to lay eggs. This breaks the flea life cycle and eventually eliminates fleas in the environment. Advantage is not absorbed into the cat's system, and therefore is nontoxic. Humans do not absorb the chemical after petting a treated cat. Advantage can be used on kittens 8 weeks and up.

Advantage Multi is a newer topical product that combines Advantage with moxidectin. Moxidectin prevents heartworms and kills ear mites, and both larval and adult stages of some intestinal parasites.

Frontline and **Frontline Spray** contain the active ingredient fipronil, which kills fleas on contact within 24 to 48 hours. The fleas do not need to bite the cat to be killed. Frontline is a topical liquid that comes in tubes and is applied as described for Advantage. The effectiveness of Frontline is not diminished if the cat's coat becomes wet. The product has a residual effect that lasts up to 90 days in some cats. Like Advantage, Frontline is not absorbed and thus appears to be nontoxic. One additional benefit is that it also kills ticks for up to 30 days. It can control chewing lice and aids in treating sarcoptic mange. Frontline should not be used on kittens under 8 weeks of age. This is released through body oils and hair follicles. Some cats may show sensitivity at the application site.

Frontline Plus has S-methoprene, which is labeled to kill adult fleas, flea eggs, and larvae. It also treats chewing lice and is used as part of a program to control sarcoptic mange. Frontline Plus is labeled for kittens 8 weeks of age and up. It is also labeled for use on breeding, pregnant, and lactating queens.

Revolution (selamectin), a heartworm preventive, is a once-a-month topical liquid that is applied to the skin of the cat's neck between the shoulder blades, as described for Advantage. It also controls adult fleas and prevents flea eggs from hatching. Selamectin can also be used to control ear mites, roundworms, and hookworms, as well as some ticks. It seems to be safe for pregnant and nursing cats.

Capstar with nitenpyram is a systemic product that kills adult fleas. It is given orally and has no residual activity, so it can be given frequently. It is rapidly eliminated in the urine. Kittens should be at least 4 weeks of age and weigh 2 or more pounds (.9 kg). This product is used by many shelters when cats or kittens are admitted with fleas.

Biospot Mist or **Topical** with pyriproxyfen or nylar have insect growth regulators. The topical form can be used on kittens 3 months of age and up and is applied every three months. The mist should only be used on cats 7 months of age or older and put on the cat every three months. It can also be used to spray the premises. This chemical is often combined with other chemicals that are not safe for use on cats, so always read ingredient lists carefully!

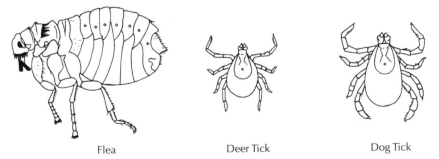

Flea   Deer Tick   Dog Tick

These pests are not drawn to scale, but the ticks are in relative proportion to one another.

TOPICAL INSECTICIDES FOR FLEA CONTROL

A variety of insecticide products are available to control fleas, but there are differences in safety and effectiveness. Be sure to read the label to make sure the product is specifically intended to control fleas on cats. Better yet, consult your veterinarian and use the products he or she recommends. *Do not* use flea products made for dogs on cats or rabbits! Also, many flea preparations should not be used on kittens and pregnant queens.

Permethrins are toxic to cats, as are many organophosphates. Amitraz is another chemical that is quite toxic to cats, but sometimes shows up in some flea-killing agents.

Flea shampoos kill only when they are on the cat. Once rinsed off, they have no residual effect. They are best used for mild to moderate flea infestation after treating the environment thoroughly. A variety of insecticide products are available as flea shampoos. Pyrethrin shampoos are generally safest to use on kittens. New cats coming into your home or into a shelter will benefit from a flea shampoo before entering. This will help prevent adding fleas to the environment.

Powders and dusts have more residual killing activity, but they must be worked thoroughly through the haircoat down to the skin. They tend to leave the coat dry and gritty. Dusting must be repeated two to three times a week, or as directed. Powders are best used along with shampoos, sprays, or dips. Always be sure these products say on the label that they are approved for use on cats; otherwise a cat may groom the product off and become ill or even die.

Sprays and foams are most effective when used between shampoos to kill late-hatching fleas that have eluded treatment of the living quarters. Most sprays have a residual killing action up to 14 days and use the same insecticides as described for shampoos. Water-based sprays are preferable to alcohol-based sprays, which are flammable and irritate the skin. Sprays and foams should not be used on kittens under 2 months of age.

When using a spray, begin near the cat's head and work toward the tail. This prevents fleas on the body from escaping the treatment by moving up onto the face. Gently massage the product into the coat—wearing gloves if recommended by the manufacturer.

Insecticide dips applied to the cat's coat and allowed to dry are extremely effective in ridding your cat of fleas. Dips penetrate the haircoat and have the most immediate killing action and longest residual activity. Organic dips containing d-limonene are among the safest for cats. However, even this ingredient has been associated with toxic reactions in cats. Before using a dip, read the instructions carefully. Use according to the manufacturer's recommendations. If your cat shows signs of toxicity, bathe or rinse her right away. Excess drooling, weakness, or instability in walking are all signs of mild toxicity. Most dips must be repeated every 7 to 10 days, but the product label must be consulted for recommended frequency. Dips should not be used on kittens under 4 months of age and must be properly diluted.

Flea collars are not generally considered to be as effective as other methods of flea control but may work in some situations. To avoid choking the cat, you should be able to get two fingers underneath the collar when it is on the cat. Extra portions of the collar should be trimmed off. Care must be taken that the cat cannot get caught or trapped by the collar. Collars with amitraz, permethrin, or organophosphates should *not* be used on cats.

A SUGGESTED FLEA-CONTROL PROGRAM

Start your cat on a monthly flea-prevention protocol (if possible, before the fleas attack), using a product such as Program, Advantage, or Frontline Plus. Prevention is the key to success.

If fleas have already become established, it is essential to kill them on the cat and prevent them from coming back. One way to do this is to shampoo or dip the cat to immediately eliminate the fleas. Thoroughly vacuum the environment and wash all cat bedding. Seal the vacuum cleaner bag and throw it away. Twenty-four to 48 hours later, apply Frontline or Advantage to kill new fleas hatching from eggs on the premises. Some veterinarians combine Frontline or Advantage with Program for more rapid results, and to minimize development of resistance. Because all of these products prevent fleas from reproducing, they eventually rid the environment of fleas.

For this approach to be successful, *it is essential to treat all the dogs and cats in the family, as well as any ferrets or house rabbits. Note that many products that are safe for dogs are not safe for cats or other pets.*

The following protocol for eliminating fleas can be used *only if your cat is not on a monthly flea-control program.*

- All dogs, cats, ferrets, and rabbits must be treated.
- Dip or shampoo all pets every other week using a solution containing pyrethrin. It is important to be sure the product is labeled as safe for cats. (If you are unable to treat every animal in the home, substitute sprays and foams at the maximum frequency allowed by the manufacturer.)
- Alternatively, use sprays or foams containing pyrethrins every other week. Apply to the cat's skin surface, not just the hair.
- For unaffected cats, a dip or a spray application (not both) twice a month is sufficient.
- Physically removing fleas using a flea comb (32 teeth per inch or per 2.5 cm) is effective on many cats with a mild infestation. The cat must be combed at least every other day. Comb the face as well as the body. Kill fleas on the comb by immersing it in alcohol or liquid detergent.
- Flea collars should not be used as the sole source of flea control.

A flea comb mechanically removes fleas. Use it on the face as well as the body.

ELIMINATING FLEAS ON THE PREMISES

If you are using a monthly flea control product such as Program, Advantage, or Frontline, the fleas in the environment should eventually be eliminated as they fail to reproduce. For this to be effective, all pets must be treated with the flea control product.

To immediately reduce fleas in the house or for severe infestations, thoroughly clean the entire house and then apply insecticides in the form of carpet shampoos and house sprays. On carpeted floors, electrostatically charged sodium polyborate powder (Rx for Fleas is the brand name) is most effective and lasts up to a year.

In households with cats and/or young children, the safest insecticides are the pyrethrins and the insect growth regulators methoprene and fenoxycarb. Insect growth regulators prevent eggs and larvae from developing into adult fleas. Methoprene must come into contact with the flea egg within 12 hours after it is laid to be completely effective, while fenoxycarb can contact the egg any time during its development to be effective.

Insecticides must be applied monthly to all floor surfaces. If pyrethrins are used alone, weekly spraying for the first three weeks is necessary.

Foggers generally contain permethrin or synergized natural pyrethrins (pyrethroids). Many of these are toxic to cats! Some contain insect growth regulators. One disadvantage of foggers is that the mist settles on top of carpets and may not settle into the cracks in upholstery and beneath furniture. Flea larvae and pupae, however, burrow deep into the nap and also seek out cracks and crevices. To offset this disadvantage, shampoo carpets and spray beneath furniture before activating the fogger.

Do not use foggers in rooms where toddlers and young children live or play. Although labels on these products say that rooms should be vacated for one to three hours, studies show that high residue levels can remain for a week or longer. Especially dangerous are exposed plastic toys and stuffed animals, which seem to attract the pesticide.

With a heavy flea infestation, mechanical cleaning and insecticide applications must be repeated at three-week intervals. It may take nine weeks to eliminate all visible fleas. With a heavy infestation, it may be advisable to enlist the services of a professional exterminator.

Outdoor control begins with the removal of all decaying vegetation before spraying or dusting. Mow, rake, and discard the debris. When applying sprays, give special attention to favorite resting places or flea "hot spots" (such as beneath the porch and in the garage). Insecticides effective in outdoor control contain chlorpyrifos or other organophosphate insecticides. Remember that these are toxic to cats! Fenvalerate, with or without an insect growth regulator, is a safer product for both your cat and the environment. Be sure the ground is dry before allowing pets outside.

Repeat the application every two to three weeks. Observe the manufacturer's precautions and follow directions about mixing, preparation, and application of the product. Try to prevent runoff into local water supplies, lakes, or rivers. Rodent control will help to decrease flea numbers outdoors.

Other Insect Parasites

Insect parasites are responsible for many of the skin ailments in cats and also figure prominently as transmitters of viral, protozoan, bacterial, and parasitical diseases of cats. Many of these parasites will be totally avoided if your cat remains indoors. If you groom your cat regularly, you can prevent many disorders caused by insects. If, despite adequate care, your cat still acquires fleas, mites, or some other external parasite, you are in a better position to seek consultation or start treatment before the problem becomes advanced.

Bees, wasps, and other insects that sting or bite are discussed in *Insect Stings, Spiders, and Scorpions*, page 43.

MITES

Mites are microscopic spiderlike creatures that live on the cat's skin or in the ear canals. Mites cause many skin conditions, from simple dandruff to irregular, moth-eaten patches of hair loss complicated by draining sores. Collectively, they are called mange. Mange can be classified according to the type of mite that causes it.

Ear mites (*Ododectes cynotis*) are a separate species and should not be confused with the mites that cause mange. Ear mites are one of the most common problems owners of cats who go outdoors are likely to encounter. These mites live in the ear canals and feed on skin and debris. They are discussed on page 212.

Feline Scabies (Head Mange)

Feline scabies is an uncommon skin ailment caused by the head mite *Notoedres cati.* The first sign is intense itching about the head and neck, along with hair loss and the appearance of bald spots. Due to the incessant scratching, the skin becomes red, raw, and excoriated. Typically, you will see thick gray to yellow crusts around the face, neck, and edge of the ears. The condition also may involve the skin of the paws and genitalia.

In severe or untreated cases the skin forms scabs, crusts, and thickened wrinkled skin on the head that gives the cat an aged look. With intense scratching, the wounds become infected.

Severe itching is caused by female mites tunneling a few millimeters under the skin to lay their eggs. Mite eggs hatch in 5 to 10 days. The immature mites develop into adults and begin to lay eggs of their own. The whole cycle takes three to four weeks. The diagnosis is confirmed by skin scrapings, or, in difficult cases, by skin *biopsy.*

Head mange is highly contagious. It is transmitted primarily by direct animal-to-animal contact. Dogs and even people can be infested, but only for short periods. Infestation in people produces an itchy skin condition that resolves spontaneously in two to six weeks, if all mites have been eliminated from the cat.

The *Notoedres* mite will reproduce only on cats. It is highly susceptible to drying and cannot live more than a few days off the host.

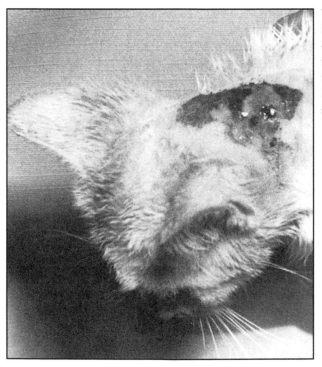

This wet, inflamed, infected skin was caused by self-mutilation. Head mange was the cause of the intense itching and scratching.

Treatment: Clip scabies-affected areas on longhaired cats and bathe the entire animal in warm water and soap to loosen crusts. Kittens may be dipped or shampooed but must be dried quickly to prevent chilling. Kill the head mites by dipping the cat in a 2.5 percent lime sulfur dip weekly. Continue for two weeks beyond apparent cure. Lime sulfur dips are safe for use on pregnant queens and kittens over 6 weeks of age. Other cats on the premises should be dipped once a week for three to four weeks, since they may harbor the mite and act as a reservoir for reinfestation.

An alternative to dips is selamectin (Revolution), with doses given a month apart. Ivermectin is also used by some veterinarians.

Mild shampoos can be used between insecticide dips to loosen scales. A cortisone product, such as 1 percent Cortaid, neomycin with cortisone, or Dermagard hydrocortisone spray, helps to relieve severe itching. Sores that look infected from self-mutilation should be treated by a soothing topical ointment.

Cheyletiella Mange (Walking Dandruff)

This type of mange is caused by a large reddish mite that lives on the skin and causes mild itching with a tremendous amount of dry, scaly material that looks like dandruff. The dandruff is heaviest over the back, neck, and sides. These mites often come in on contaminated bedding such as straw or old newspapers that have been stored in outdoor sheds. This type of mange is not common in cats.

The life cycle of the *Cheyletiella* mite is similar to that of the head mange mite. The entire life cycle takes four to five weeks. The diagnosis is confirmed by finding the mite in skin scrapings collected on paper and examined under a magnifying glass.

Walking dandruff is highly contagious. Humans can easily become infested. The signs are itching and the appearance of red, raised bumps on the skin. They look much like insect bites, which, in fact, they are. The *Cheyletiella* mite cannot live off the cat for more than two weeks. The owner's rash should improve as the cat is treated.

Treatment: All cats and dogs on the premises should be treated with a lime sulfur insecticide dip or a shampoo containing a pyrethrin insecticide. Continue to treat for two weeks beyond apparent cure. Treat the premises as described for *Eliminating Fleas on the Premises* (page 139). An alternative treatment is ivermectin.

Chiggers (Trombiculid Mites)

Chiggers, also called harvest mites or red bugs, live as adults in decaying vegetation. Only their larval forms are parasitic. Cats acquire the infestation while prowling in forest grasslands and fields where chiggers reproduce. Reproduction occurs in late summer or fall.

Larval mites appear as red, yellow, or orange specks barely visible to the naked eye but easily seen with a magnifying glass. They tend to clump in areas where the skin is thin, such as the webbed spaces between the toes or around the ears and mouth, but they can occur elsewhere on the body. The larvae feed by sucking on the skin. The result is severe irritation and the formation of red draining sores with overlying scabs. Patches of raw skin may appear.

The larvae can be either seen with the naked eye or identified by skin scrapings.

Treatment: Chiggers in the ear canals are eliminated by treating as you would for ear mites (see page 212). Those elsewhere on the body respond to a single application of a lime sulfur dip or pyrethrin shampoo. Fipronil is another effective treatment. Localized areas of chiggers can be treated with topical Tresaderm. Corticosteroids or antihistamines may be required to control intense itching. When feasible, prevent reinfestation by keeping your cat confined during the chigger season.

Demodectic Mange

This noncontagious form of mange is common in dogs, but fortunately, it is rare in cats. The demodex mite is a normal resident of the cat's skin and seldom causes more than mild, localized infection. The exception is in immune-suppressed cats suffering from FeLV, diabetes mellitus, chronic respiratory infection, cancer, or the immune-depressant effects of chemotherapy or excessive hydrocortisone.

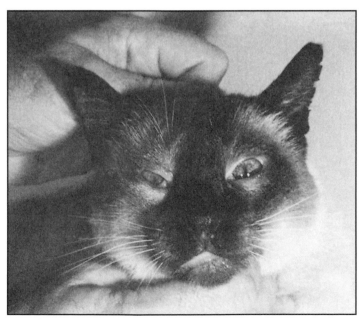

The moth-eaten look of hair loss around the eyes is characteristic of localized demodectic mange.

Cats have two versions of this mite: *Demodex cati* and *Demodex gatoi*. *D. cati* lives in hair follicles and *D. gatoi* lives on the skin surface. The diagnosis is confirmed by taking skin scrapings and identifying the characteristic mite under a microscope.

The localized form of demodectic mange, most often seen in young cats, produces one or more areas of hair loss around the head, neck, and ears, progressing to scaly, crusty sores that itch and become infected. After one or two months the hair begins to grow back. In three months, most cases are healed.

The generalized form is similar, but the condition extends widely over the body. The cat may be suffering from some other disease that also requires treatment.

Treatment: For localized demodectic mange, apply a topical keratolytic and antibacterial agent such as Pyoben or OxyDex shampoo. Follow with a lime sulfur dip or a local application of Rotenone. Ivermectin may also be used. Note that many of these treatments are not approved for use in cats or for this purpose, and should only be used under veterinary guidance.

Cats with generalized demodectic mange present a difficult problem. Shampoos are available that remove dead skin, kill mites, and treat secondary bacterial skin infection. Treatment is prolonged and repeated applications are necessary. Spontaneous remissions after several months have occurred in some cats.

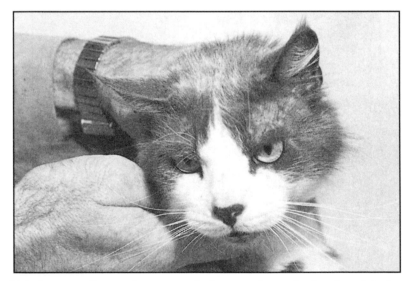

Hair loss over the eyes is common in free-roaming males in whom injuries from cat fights produce a buildup of scar tissue. It can resemble localized demodectic mange.

Deer tick

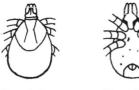

Dog Tick

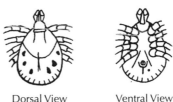

Dorsal view	Ventral view		Dorsal View	Ventral View

The abdomen edges are smooth on the dorsal view of the deer tick. On the ventral view, the anal opening is near the edge of the tick and is surrounded by a ridge of tissue.

Note that there are no ridges around the abdomen on the dorsal view of the dog tick. On the ventral view, you can see the anal opening near the middle of the tick.

Sarcoptic Mange

These mites occur frequently in dogs and produce a disease called sarcoptic mange. Fortunately, they are rarely seen in cats. Their effect and treatment is similar to that of head mange (see page 141). Skin scrapings are used to make the diagnosis. If no mites are found on multiple skin scrapes but other diagnoses have been eliminated, your veterinarian may recommend treatment anyway.

Treatment: Fipronil and milbemycin oxime have been used off label successfully.

TICKS

Ticks have a complicated life cycle. It involves three hosts, including wild and domestic animals and humans. Ticks begin as eggs that hatch into six-legged larvae. The larvae live and feed on animals for about a week before detaching and then molting. After the molt, the larvae become eight-legged nymphs. Nymphs feed on animals, engorge for 3 to 11 days, detach, and molt again into adult ticks.

Ticks do not run and jump as fleas do, but scuttle around slowly. They climb up grass and plants and hold their legs up to sense passing hosts. When a warm-blooded animal walks by, the adult tick crawls onto them and begins feeding.

Ticks can fasten to any part of the cat's skin, but they are commonly found around the ears, between the toes, and sometimes in the armpits. A severely infested cat may have hundreds of ticks all over her body, although cats often pull most ticks off themselves as they groom. The ticks insert their mouths, attach to their prey, and engorge themselves with a blood meal. During feeding, tick saliva can get into the host's body and bloodstream; this is how diseases are transmitted.

Males and female ticks mate on the skin of the cat, after which the female takes a blood meal and then drops off to lay her eggs. This usually occurs 5 to 20 hours after the cat acquires the ticks. Thus, prompt removal of ticks is an effective method of preventing tick-borne diseases.

Ticks may drop off a cat and transfer to people, although this is not common. Once a tick starts feeding on a cat, it will feed until it is engorged and will not seek a second host.

The male tick is a small, flat insect about the size of a match head. A blood tick is a pea-size female tick feeding on the host. Deer ticks are much smaller—the size of a pinhead.

Ticks can spread diseases to cats, including babesioisis, cytauxzoonosis, ehrlichiosis, haemobartonellosis, and tularemia.

Treatment: Since cats rarely have more than a few ticks, simply remove them individually. Keep in mind that the blood of ticks can be dangerous to people. Therefore, do not crush or squeeze a tick with your bare fingers. Before removing the tick, put on disposable rubber or plastic gloves.

Ticks that are not attached to the skin are easily removed with a pair of tweezers. There are also special tick-removing devices that are widely available, including Ticked Off, Protick Remedy, and Tick Nipper. Once removed, the tick can be killed by putting it in rubbing alcohol.

You must be careful if you find a tick with its head buried in the skin, because the head may detach and remain behind. Grasp the tick firmly with tweezers or a tick removal device, as close to the cat's body as possible without pinching her skin, and lift it off.

A drop of alcohol or nail polish applied to the tick may cause it to release its hold. If possible, remove the whole head and mouth parts. If left in the cat, these may cause a local infection.

Use the tweezers to place the tick in a jar or plastic dish with a little alcohol. Seal it well and dispose of the container in an outdoor garbage can. Don't flush it down the toilet, because the tick may survive the trip and infect another animal. Wash the tweezers thoroughly with hot water and alcohol.

Before you dispose of the tick, it can be a good idea to ask your veterinarian if they think it is important to bring the tick in for identification and to see if it is carrying any disease.

If the head or mouth parts remain embedded in the skin, redness and swelling is likely to occur at the site of the bite. In most cases, this reaction clears up in two to three days. A dab of antibiotic ointment will help prevent most skin infections. However, if it does not—or if the redness seems to be getting worse—consult your veterinarian.

Prevention: For outdoor control of ticks, cut tall grass, weeds, and brush. Treat the premises with an insecticide preparation as described for *Eliminating Fleas on the Premises* (see page 139). The use of topical flea control products that include with fipronil, selamectin, or pyrethrin will help in tick control.

LICE (PEDICULOSIS)

Lice are not common in cats. They occur primarily in malnourished, rundown cats who have lost the initiative to keep themselves groomed. Lice are usually found beneath matted hair around the ears, head, neck, shoulders, and perineal area. Because of the itching and constant irritation they cause, bare spots may be seen where the hair has been rubbed off. Lice are an intermediate host for the common cat tapeworm.

Cats may be infested only with biting lice (*Trichodectes felis* or *Felicola subrostratus*) that feed on skin scales. Adults are wingless, slow moving, pale insects about 2 to 3 millimeters long. They lay eggs called nits that look like white grains of sand and are found attached to hairs. They are difficult to brush off. Nits may look something like dandruff, but cats with ordinary dandruff do not itch as they do with lice. Inspection with a magnifying glass makes the distinction easy, because nits are well-formed, rounded eggs attached to hair shafts.

Lice are species-specific. Therefore, head lice that infest humans cannot come from the family cat.

Treatment: Lice show little resistance to insecticides and do not live long when off the cat. They can be killed by giving the cat a thorough bath, followed by an insecticide dip that is effective against fleas (see page 150). Three to four dips must be given at 10-day intervals. An alternative to a dip can be fipronil, selamectin, or imidacloprid topical preparations.

Heavily infested, severely malnourished cats might not be able to withstand the treatment and could go into shock. Consult your veterinarian before using an insecticide dip or a topical medication on such an individual. Infected bedding should be destroyed and the cat's sleeping quarters disinfected (see *Eliminating Fleas on the Premises*, page 139).

FLIES

Adult flies do not afflict the cat, but they may deposit their eggs on raw or infected wounds or in soil where larvae can penetrate the cat's skin.

Myiasis (Maggots)

This is a seasonal disease that occurs in warm weather. It is most often caused by the bluebottle or blow fly, which may lay eggs in open wounds or badly soiled, damp, matted fur. The eggs hatch in 8 to 72 hours. In 2 to 19 days, the larvae grow into large maggots that produce an enzyme in their saliva that digests the skin, causing "punched-out" areas. The maggots then penetrate the skin and enlarge the opening, thereby setting the stage for a bacterial skin infection.

With a severe infestation, the cat may go into shock. The shock is caused by enzymes and toxins secreted by the maggots.

Treatment: Clip the affected areas to remove soiled and matted hair. Remove all maggots with blunt-nosed tweezers. Wash infected areas with Betadine solution and dry the cat thoroughly. Use a nonalcohol spray or shampoo that contains a pyrethrin insecticide. Repeat the application as described for *A Suggested Flea-Control Program* (page 138) and check closely for remaining maggots. Be careful with the spray, as the pyrethrin can be absorbed through open wounds.

Virtually all cats with maggots have other health problems that left them open to these invaders. They should be seen immediately by a veterinarian. Cats with infected wounds should be treated with an oral antibiotic. The cat's health and nutrition must be stable to bring about a cure.

Grubs (Cuterebriasis)

The most frequent cause of grub infestation is the large botfly, which has a wide seasonal distribution in the United States. This fly lays eggs near the burrows of rodents and rabbits. The cat acquires the disease by direct contact with infested soil.

Newly hatched larvae penetrate the skin, forming cystlike lumps that have a small opening to the outside to allow the grubs to breathe. From time to time, inch-long grubs protrude from the skin through the breathing holes. In about a month, they emerge and drop to the ground. More than one grub may be found in the same area (usually along the jawbone, around the face, under the belly, or along the sides). In such cases they form large nodular masses.

Treatment: This should be handled by your veterinarian, who will clip away hair to expose breathing holes. He or she will then grasp each grub with a fine-tipped forceps and gently draw it out. The larva should not be crushed or ruptured during extraction, as this can produce anaphylactic shock. If necessary, a small incision should be made while the cat is under anesthesia to remove the parasite. Grub wounds are slow to heal and often become infected. Antibiotics may be required.

Using Insecticides

Dealing effectively with fleas, lice, mites, ticks, and other external parasites often involves using insecticides on your pets, your home, and your yard. Insecticides are incorporated into powders, sprays, dusts, and dips. They are also used to disinfect bedding, houses, catteries, runs, gardens, garages, and other spots where a cat might come into contact with the adult or intermediate insect forms.

Insecticides are poisons! If you decide to use an insecticide preparation, be sure to follow the precautions and directions on the label. Otherwise, you or your pets may be poisoned from improper exposure.

An overdose of an insecticide can cause your cat to twitch at the mouth, foam, collapse, convulse, or fall into a coma. Other signs of insecticide toxicity include diarrhea, asthmatic breathing, a staggering gait, and muscular twitching and jerking. These signs may be delayed by several days, depending on the dose of insecticide and the exact type of chemicals involved.

If you suspect that your cat might be suffering from an insecticide reaction, give her a bath in warm soapy water to remove any residual compound from the coat and keep her quiet. *Contact your veterinarian immediately.*

Lysol and other household disinfectants are not suitable for washing your cat and should not be used. Like insecticides, they are absorbed through the skin and can cause illness or death.

Insecticides should never be combined without consulting your veterinarian! There are five classes of insecticides in current use:

1. Pyrethrins (natural and synthetic)
2. Carbamates
3. Organophosphates
4. Natural insecticides, such as d-limonene
5. New topical products

In addition, there are insect growth regulators (IGRs) that, although they are not insecticides, do prevent insect reproduction.

Pyrethrin is a natural extract of the African chrysanthemum flower. It kills fleas quickly but has little residual activity because it is rapidly degraded in the environment by ultraviolet light. Pyrethrin has low potential for toxicity and is approved for use on both dogs and cats. It is found in many shampoos, sprays, dusts, dips, foggers, and premise sprays. Pyrethroids are synthetic compounds that resemble pyrethrin in structure but are more stable to sunlight and therefore have longer residual activity. Permethrin is the most commonly used synthetic pyrethrin, but there are others. Although pyrethrins tend to be quite safe, *virtually all permethrins and synthetic pyrethroids are toxic for cats!*

Carbamates include carbaryl (Sevin), an insecticide found in flea and tick powders and shampoos, and bendiocarb, commonly used by professional exterminators for premise control of fleas. Due to toxicity concerns, carbamates are rarely used for insecticide control any more.

Organophosphate insecticides are unstable and do not persist in the environment. They are among the most toxic to mammals and are particularly toxic to cats. Organophosphates should *not* be used on cats and should only be used in the environment under carefully regulated situations.

Natural insecticides are botanical compounds derived from roots and natural extracts of citrus fruit. Rotenone and d-limonene are moderately effective against fleas, ticks, and some species of lice and mites. D-limonene is effective against fleas in all stages, including the eggs; however, residual activity is less than for synergized pyrethrins. It is used in shampoos, dips, and sprays approved for both dogs and cats. D-limonene has recently been implicated in toxicity cases in cats, so it should only be used as a last resort and under veterinary guidance.

Insect growth regulators include methoprene (PreCor) and fenoxycarb, two hormonelike compounds that prevent flea larvae from developing into adults. They do not affect the cocoon or adult stages. Both are degraded by sunlight and therefore used mainly for indoor treatment. PreCor is used in foggers and premise sprays alone or in combination with pyrethrins to provide a spectrum of both egg and adult stage insecticides.

Among the **new topical products**, selamectin (Revolution) is a semisynthetic avermectin that acts by paralyzing the parasites. Imidacloprid (Advantage) is a synthetic nitroguanidine that acts on nerve receptors to cause central nervous system impairment and death. Certain insect species are more sensitive to these agents than are mammals. Fipronil (Frontline) is a phenylpyrazole antiparasitic agent that disrupts central nervous system activity in invertebrates.

With the development of pyrethrin compounds, natural insecticides, and IGRs, the more toxic insecticides are used less often for cats. Environmental concerns also favor use of the natural compounds. Because cats are especially sensitive to insecticide toxicity, it is important to use the least toxic product whenever possible.

INSECTICIDE DIPS

Dips are insecticide solutions that are sponged onto the body and dry on the hair and skin without rinsing. Choose a dip recommended by your veterinarian, or, if you decide to wash your cat with a commercial preparation, check the label to be sure it is effective against the insect in question and is *safe for cats*. Dips need to drip dry on the cat, so you must keep the cat from grooming and licking off the dip, as many can be toxic if taken internally. For this and other reasons, dips have been largely replaced by topical treatments.

Some worm medications contain chemicals similar to insecticide dips. If the cat has just been wormed, there could be a sudden accumulation of chemicals in the cat's system from powdering, shampooing, dipping, or spraying with an insecticide. Avoid using an insecticide dip within a week of worming the cat.

If your cat's hair is matted, dirty, or greasy, first wash with a gentle commercial cat shampoo. Then, while the coat is still wet, rinse thoroughly with an insecticide dip made according to the directions on the package. Apply ointment or mineral oil in the eyes, and plug the ears with cotton so you can treat head and ears with the dip. Immediately after dipping, while the cat is still wet, use a flea comb (32 teeth per inch [28 cm]) to mechanically remove insects.

Most dips must be repeated one or more times at intervals of 7 to 10 days to rid the dog of the parasite in question. Consult the label for recommended frequency. *Do not* exceed this frequency. Dips should not be used on kittens under 4 months of age.

DISINFECTING THE PREMISES

The goal here is to prevent reinfestation by ridding the environment of insects, eggs, larvae, and other intermediate stages of the parasite. This is accomplished by physically cleaning and then applying insecticides.

To eliminate all sources of reinfestation, it is essential to treat all animals in the household. All blankets, bedding, and rugs where the cat sleeps should be washed weekly at the hottest setting, or destroyed. Thoroughly clean the house, including vacuuming all carpets and rugs, spraying all furniture, and applying insecticide to corners and cracks, to help eliminate the insects, eggs, and larvae. This usually must be done two or three times. Floors should be mopped, giving special attention to cracks and crevices where organic debris and eggs accumulate.

With a severe infestation, steam cleaning carpets is highly effective in killing eggs and larvae. Insecticides can be used in the water of the steam cleaner. Specific products are now available where you rent the cleaner. You must check to be sure the products are safe to use around cats. Vacuum bags should be discarded immediately after use, because they provide an ideal environment for flea development. With heavy infestation, it is sometimes better to enlist the services of a professional exterminator.

After a thorough mechanical cleaning, the house and yard should be treated with insecticide applications as described in *A Suggested Flea-Control Program* (page 138). At least three applications, at two- to three-week intervals, are required to eliminate fleas. Afterward, the house should be treated periodically as needed. In warm, humid states, it may be necessary to re-treat every six to eight weeks.

The residual activity of outdoor insecticides depends on weather conditions. In dry weather, residual activity may persist for a month; in wet weather, one to two weeks. Re-treat accordingly. Some insecticide dips can be used as sprays on gardens, lawns, and other outdoor areas. Use according to the instructions on the label.

Diatomaceous earth, including the product Fleas Away, can be spread in areas of the yard where your cat likes to stay. You can also explore the use of beneficial nematodes that feast on flea larvae to help to keep your yard flea-free.

Discourage rodents such as squirrels, chipmunks, and mice that may be reinfesting your yard with fleas. You may need to trap them, or at a minimum, remove any bird feeders in the hopes the rodents will move elsewhere. Don't leave pet food outdoors because it attracts strays and wildlife. And be sure to securely cover all garbage cans.

Allergies

An allergy is an unpleasant physical reaction caused by the cat's immune system overreacting to a food, something inhaled, or something in the cat's environment. Without an immune system, any animal would not be able to build up resistance to viruses, bacteria, foreign proteins, and other irritating substances that get into the system. Sometimes, however, the immune system reacts to things that aren't really a danger. Certain foods or substances such as pollens, powders, feathers, wool, house dust, and insect bites trigger a reaction typified by itching and sometimes sneezing, coughing, swelling of the eyelids, tearing, or vomiting and diarrhea. This reaction occurs in cats as well as in humans. In rare instances, the immune system reacts against the cells of the cat's own body—these are *autoimmune* problems.

For a cat to be allergic to something, exposure must occur at least twice. What the cat is allergic to is called the *allergen*. The way the body responds to that allergen is called a hypersensitivity reaction or an allergic reaction.

There are two kinds of hypersensitivity reactions. The immediate type occurs shortly after exposure and produces hives and itching. Hives in the cat are characterized by sudden swelling on the head, usually around the eyes and mouth, and occasionally the appearance of welts elsewhere on the body. The delayed reaction produces itching that occurs hours or days afterward. Flea bite dermatitis is an example of both types. This explains why a cat may continue to itch even after fleas have been removed from the cat and the environment.

Allergens enter the body through the lungs (pollens, house dust, for example); the digestive tract (eating certain foods); by injection (insect bites and vaccinations); or by direct absorption through the skin. Although the target area for a reaction in people usually is the air passages and the lungs (producing hay fever and asthma), in the cat it is the skin or the gastrointestinal tract. The main sign of skin involvement is severe itching.

FOOD ALLERGY

Cats may become allergic to certain foods or substances in foods. The most common food allergens are chicken, fish, corn, wheat, and soy; cats may also develop a food allergy to beef, pork, dairy products, or eggs. An intensely itchy rash often develops on the head, neck, and back, and may be accompanied by swollen eyelids. You may see hair loss and oozing sores from constant scratching. Sometimes, only the ears will be involved. In those cases, the ears will be very red and inflamed and may have a moist discharge. Less frequently, food allergy produces diarrhea or vomiting (see *Inflammatory Bowel Disease*, page 270).

Treatment: Diagnosis is made by feeding the cat a diet without the suspected food for at least four to six weeks. The next step is exposing the cat to a suspected allergen and then watching to see if a reaction follows. There are numerous hypoallergenic diets available. Treatment is discussed at greater length in *Treating Diarrhea* (page 281) and *Food Intolerance* (page 265).

FELINE MILIARY DERMATITIS

This skin disease is caused by an allergic skin reaction to a number of possible allergens, including the bites of fleas, mosquitoes, mites, and lice. Bacterial and fungal skin infections, nutritional disturbances, hormonal imbalances, autoimmune diseases, and drug reactions can also produce miliary dermatitis. The affected cat breaks out along her back and around the head and neck with small bumps and crusts about the size of millet seeds beneath the hair-coat. There may or may not be itching.

Flea bite allergy is the most common cause of miliary dermatitis in cats. Other skin parasites, allergies, and infections should be considered for cats who have miliary dermatitis without fleas.

Flea-Bite Dermatitis

The skin is severely itchy and may break down, producing raw patches that become infected from intense scratching. Localized or generalized *eosinophilic plaques* may develop as a consequence (see *Eosinophilic Granuloma Complex*, page 166). A few cats are especially resistant to flea bites and can harbor many fleas without symptoms, but in the allergic reactor a single bite once or twice a week is sufficient to produce the response. Symptoms are most

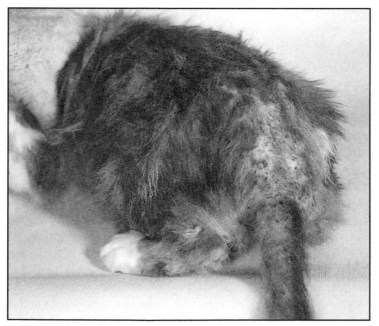

The typical appearance of a cat with flea-bite dermatitis: small crusts, bumps, and raw patches of skin, and hair loss due to licking and scratching.

prevalent in the middle of summer (peak flea season). However, once the cat is exposed, if fleas live in the house, itching may persist year-round.

The diagnosis is suspected by seeing the characteristic skin rash and by finding fleas on the cat. You can check for fleas by standing your cat over a sheet of white paper and brushing her coat. White and black grains of sandy material that drop on the paper are flea eggs and feces. The diagnosis is confirmed by an intradermal skin test. This is a hypersensitivity reaction of both immediate and delayed type; itching tends to persist long after fleas have been destroyed.

Treatment: When fleas are present, treat the infestation as described in *A Suggested Flea-Control Program* (page 138). In the absence of fleas, an effort must be made to determine the cause of the miliary dermatitis and to treat accordingly.

While treating for the fleas, cortisone tablets, such as prednisone, or injections that block the allergic reaction and relieve the itching are sometimes needed to make the cat comfortable. Steroids should only be given under veterinary guidance. Antihistamines and omega-3 fatty acids may also help to reduce the inflammation. Treat sores with a topical antibiotic/steroid ointment. Aloe ointments or an aloe plant's juice are also soothing and safe. If the cause of the allergy can be determined and eliminated from the cat's environment, such as removing all feather pillows, that would be ideal. However, this is not always possible. Hyposensitization (using injections of flea allergens of increasing strength to desensitize a cat's immune system) can make cats much more comfortable but requires multiple, long-term therapy.

IRRITANT CONTACT AND ALLERGIC CONTACT DERMATITIS

Irritant contact dermatitis and allergic contact dermatitis are two different conditions discussed together because they produce similar reactions. Both are caused by contact with a chemical. In contact dermatitis, the skin reaction is caused by a direct irritating effect of the chemical. In allergic contact dermatitis, repeated contact produces skin sensitization that results in an allergic response from subsequent exposure. Both types of dermatitis are rare in cats because their haircoat and their grooming habits protect the skin from sustained contact with chemicals. This is especially true for allergic contact dermatitis.

Both irritant and allergic contact dermatitis affect parts of the body where hair is thin or absent—the feet, chin, nose, abdomen, and groin. These areas are also the most likely to come in contact with chemicals. Liquid irritants may affect any part of the body.

Contact dermatitis of either type produces red, itchy bumps along with inflammation of the skin. Scaliness follows, and the hair falls out. Excessive scratching causes skin injury and, secondarily, infected sores. The rash from allergic contact dermatitis may spread beyond the contact area.

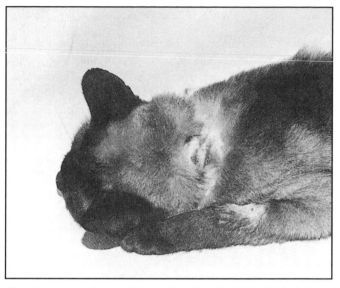

Allergic contact dermatitis produced by the insecticide in a flea collar.

Chemicals that can cause irritant dermatitis include acids and alkalis, detergents, solvents, soaps, and petroleum by-products. Substances that can cause an allergic reaction include flea powders, shampoos (particularly those containing iodine), poison ivy, poison oak and other plants, fibers (including wool and synthetics), leather, plastic and rubber food and water dishes, and dyes in carpets. Neomycin, found in many topical medications, can produce an allergic reaction, as can other drugs and medications.

Flea collar dermatitis is a reaction to the insecticide in the collar. It affects the skin around the neck, producing local itching and redness, followed by hair loss and crust formation. This condition may spread to other areas. In addition to causing local hypersensitivity, flea collars may cause toxicity from the absorption of chemicals, especially if there is contact between the collar and broken skin or open sores. Litter box dermatitis, in which the cat is allergic to the litter being used or an additive in the litter, affects the feet, the skin around the tail, and the anus.

Treatment: Consider the area of exposure and try to identify the skin allergen or chemical causing the problem. Prevent exposure. Treat infected skin as described in *Cellulitis and Abscesses* (page 164). Topical or oral corticosteroids or antihistamines, prescribed by your veterinarian, can help to reduce itching and inflammation. They do not cure the problem. Allergy shots and immune therapy may control the symptoms but do not cure the problem.

If an irritant substance gets on your cat, bathing immediately may minimize or even eliminate any symptoms.

ATOPIC DERMATITIS (INHALANT ALLERGY)

This is an allergic skin reaction caused by breathing pollens, house dust, molds, and other allergens indoors or outdoors. It may or may not occur seasonally. Signs and symptoms vary. They include itching on the head and neck, a rash along the neck and back similar to that described for feline miliary dermatitis (page 153), skin eruptions similar to those described in eosinophilic granuloma complex (page 166), and symmetrical hair loss over the body caused by excessive licking and grooming.

Atopic dermatitis is difficult to distinguish from other allergic skin disorders, such as those caused by insect bites, food hypersensitivity, and chemical contact. Diagnosis is best made by intradermal skin testing.

Treatment: Best results are obtained when the allergen can be identified and eliminated from the cat's environment. However, that is often not possible. Pollens, molds, and dusts can blow in through open windows and affect even indoor cats. Antihistamines or corticosteroids are beneficial in relieving symptoms but do not cure the problem. Allergy shots to hyposensitize the cat have been effective in some cases. Omega-3 fatty acids may also contribute to the cat's comfort and relieve some symptoms.

SEBORRHEA

Seborrhea can be a primary condition, in which case it is inherited, or it can occur secondary to almost any skin condition. Two versions are seen: a dry, scaly form that looks like dandruff, and an oily, scaly form that has an unpleasant odor as well as a greasy feeling. Some cats are itchy but others simply look poorly.

Treatment: Diagnosis usually depends on ruling out other primary skin conditions. If another condition is identified, treating that problem may clear up the seborrhea. Otherwise, the cat will benefit from seborrhea shampoos and fatty acid supplements.

IMMUNE-RELATED SKIN PROBLEMS

The pemphigus complex represents the most common *autoimmune* skin conditions in cats. This is a group of skin diseases involving inappropriate immunological attack against one of the normal layers of the skin. Different types of pemphigus involve different areas of the skin.

Pemphigus foliaceus is the most common form seen in cats. The feet and the head are affected first, with the appearance of *pustules* that progress to crusts. The nose often loses its pigment. The cat may itch and, if the feet are involved, she may be lame. Cats with a severe case may have a fever, lethargy, and loss of appetite. A *biopsy* is the ideal way to make a diagnosis. Treatment involves the use of corticosteroids, immunosuppressive drugs, and, in some cases, gold injections.

Pemphigus erythematosus is a milder form and may be related to sun exposure. Signs are usually limited to the face and ears. Topical steroids may control this condition.

Pemphigus vulgaris is the least common form of this problem. The cat will have large, ulcerated sores that crust over, especially on the head and even in the mouth. This is difficult to control, even with immunosuppressive doses of prednisolone and other drugs.

Lupus erythematosus is another autoimmune disease that can affect many body systems, including the kidneys and muscles, as well as the skin. Foot pads are often ulcerated and painful. Secondary bacterial infections are common. A blood test can be done, but biopsies are desirable for diagnosis. Prednisone and immunosuppressive drugs may be helpful in controlling the disease.

Fungal Infections
RINGWORM

Ringworm is not a worm. It is a plantlike growth that invades the hair and hair follicles. Most cases are caused by the fungus *Microsporum canis*. A few are caused by other species of fungus.

Ringworm gets its name from its appearance—a spreading circle with hair loss and scaly skin at the center and an advancing red ring at the margin. However, the typical form is not always seen, especially in cats. Occasionally, you will see only scaly patches, irregular hair loss, or just a few broken hairs around the face and ears. (Ringworm of the ear flap is discussed on page 215.) Ringworm may invade the claws; when the nails grow out, they are usually deformed. A few cats may show no symptoms at all but be carriers of the fungus.

Although simple ringworm is not usually an itchy condition, scabs and crusts can form, leading to draining sores that provoke licking and scratching. There can be extensive skin involvement. This problem usually occurs in young cats, poorly nourished cats, and cats whose immune system is depressed by disease.

The disease is transmitted by contact with spores in the soil and by contact with the infective hair of dogs and cats, which is typically found on carpets, brushes, combs, toys, and furniture. Cats can carry the fungus without showing any apparent infection and may represent a source of infection for other pets in the home. Humans can pick up ringworm from cats and can also transmit the disease to them. Children, who are especially likely to catch the disease, should avoid handling any animal with ringworm. Adults, except for the elderly and immunocompromised, seem relatively resistant.

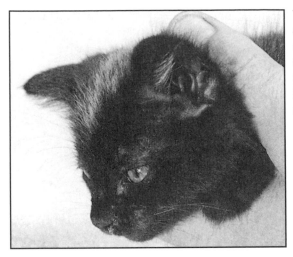

The typical ring form is not always seen, especially in cats. Occasionally, you will see only scaly patches, irregular hair loss, or just a few broken hairs around the face and ears.

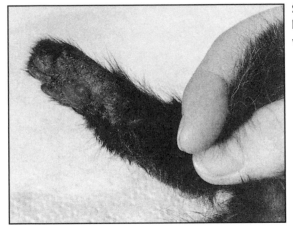

Scaly patches and irregular hair loss on the foot of a cat with ringworm.

Mild cases of ringworm, with just hair loss and local scaliness, often resemble demodectic mange. A diagnosis of ringworm can sometimes be made if the skin glows under ultraviolet light. This test is not positive in all cases. Microscopic examination of skin scrapings or fungal cultures are more certain methods of diagnosis. To grow a fungal culture, your veterinarian will remove some hairs from the affected areas and put them on a special culture medium. The medium will be checked daily for two to three weeks to see if anything grows. With growth, the media will change color and spores can also be examined to determine the exact species of fungus involved.

Treatment: Mild cases often regress spontaneously. Recurrence is uncommon in cats with normal immunity.

For localized infection, clip away the infected hair at the margins of the ringworm patches and cleanse the skin with Betadine solution. Apply an antifungal cream, ointment, or solution containing miconazole, chlorhexidine,

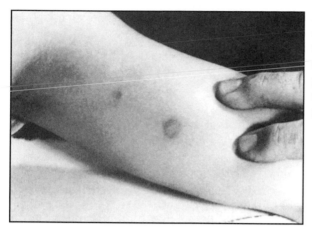

Ringworm is a highly contagious skin infection. On humans, the typical appearance is a round patch with scales at the center and an advancing red ring at the margin.

clotrimazole, or thiabendazole (such as Conofite, Nolvasan, Lotrimin, or Tresaderm) to the affected areas and surrounding skin and hair once a day. Treat infected sores with a topical antibiotic, such as triple antibiotic ointment. It is usually necessary to continue treatment for four to six weeks.

Generalized ringworm requires an extensive clip of all infected hair and a dip twice a week with an antifungal solution such as LymDyp (lime sulfur) or Nolvasan (chlorhexidine). Dips should be continued for two weeks beyond apparent cure. For information on dips, see page 137.

Oral antifungal drugs are often prescribed for generalized ringworm, especially in catteries, shelters, and multicat households. All cats should be treated, as some may be asymptomatic carriers. Griseofulvin (Fulvicin) is rarely used. Ketoconazole has been used, but itraconazole is now recommended because it has fewer side effects. Griseofulvin and ketoconazole should not be given to pregnant queens, as these drugs may cause birth defects. Antifungal drugs require close veterinary supervision and may need to be given for a month or more. Negative fungal cultures should be used to confirm a cure.

There is a vaccine for ringworm available for cats that may improve the clinical signs but does not appear to hasten a cure. It may reduce the severity of infection. This vaccine is not routinely recommended, but it may be useful in some cattery or shelter situations (see page 112).

Prevention: Spores, which can survive for up to one year, should be eliminated from the premises to prevent reinfection. The cat's bedding should be discarded. Grooming equipment should be sterilized in a 1:10 solution of bleach and water. The house should be thoroughly cleaned and carpets vacuumed weekly to remove infected hair. Mop and wash hard surfaces (floors, countertops, cattery runs) using diluted bleach. Technical Captan can be used as a spray in 1:200 dilution (in water) to spray a cattery or shelter, but not on cats themselves.

Strict hygienic precautions are necessary to prevent human infection. Rubber gloves should be worn while handling and treating infected cats. Boil contaminated clothing and fabrics or wash in bleach to kill spores.

MALASSEZIA

Malassezia pachydermatitis is a yeast that is commonly found on a cat's skin. Although normally it does not cause any problems, if there is overgrowth the cat will show clinical signs. Problems generally arise secondary to immune deficiencies, bacterial infections, or seborrhea. Hair loss is common and redness, including a moist redness, may be present in affected areas. Diagnosis is made by identifying the organism from skin scrapes or by dabbing the suspicious sites with a piece of tape or a glass slide and then examining the specimen under a microscope.

Treatment: Treatment generally consists of cleaning the areas with a benzoyl peroxide or chlorhexidine shampoo and then applying miconazole ointment. More generalized areas are treated with oral itraconazole or ketoconazole.

MYCETOMA

Mycetomas are tumorlike masses caused by several species of fungi that enter the body through wounds. The typical appearance is a lump beneath the skin with an open tract to the surface that drains a granular material. The color of the granules is white, yellow, or black, depending on the type of fungus involved. The condition may resemble a chronic abscess that does not heal, despite the administration of antibiotics. Some species of mycetoma can cause a fatal infection. This is a rare condition.

Treatment: Antifungal drugs are seldom effective. Complete surgical removal is the treatment of choice. Also see *Sporotrichosis* (page 99).

Hormonal Skin Diseases

Hormonal skin diseases are not common. Characteristically, they produce a symmetrical hair loss equally distributed along both sides of the body—one side being the mirror image of the other. They do not cause itching. The rare exception is the cat whose hormone disorder is complicated by a skin infection.

ALOPECIA

Alopecia is balding or hair loss. Feline endocrine alopecia is a type of balding seen most often in neutered males and spayed middle-age females. A hormone

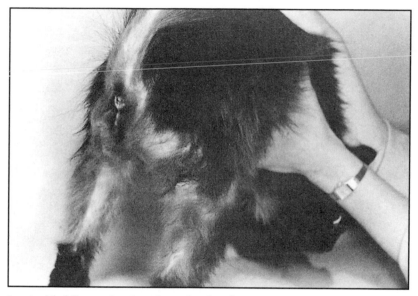

A cat with feline endocrine alopecia, showing symmetrical hair loss with normal skin.

deficiency has long been suspected as the cause of the problem, but hormone assays usually are normal. Psychogenic alopecia occurs in the same age range. It is possible that many cases attributed to hormone deficiency actually are cases of compulsive self-grooming.

Loss of hair occurs in a symmetrical pattern on the lower part of the abdomen, perineum, and genital areas and on the insides of the back legs. Only in severe cases is the remainder of the coat affected. Some cats grow back the hair, only to lose it again later. Itching is not a problem.

Grooming is often a response to stress by a cat. This might include a move, adding a new pet, even changing rugs or furniture. Siamese, Abyssinians, Burmese, and Himalayans are apparently predisposed to psychogenic alopecia. About one-third of all cats with hyperthyroidism will show areas of alopecia. The hair pulls out easily. See *Hyperthyroidism* (page 529).

Treatment: This is mainly a cosmetic condition. Treatment with sex hormones is not recommended because of serious side effects, which include liver and bone marrow toxicity.

In cases of psychogenic alopecia, behavior modification and possibly behavior modifying medications, such as amitriptyline, may be helpful.

HYPOTHYROIDISM

Hypothyroidism is rare in cats and most commonly follows surgery on the thyroid gland. A deficiency of thyroid hormone impairs new hair growth and prolongs the resting phase of hair shafts. Thus, there is a gradual thinning of the coat, which may appear dull and lifeless. Other signs of hypothyroidism include lethargy, constipation, weight gain, and mental dullness. In a congenital form of hypothyroidism, kittens show a disproportionate type of dwarfism characterized by an enlarged, broad head with a short neck and limbs. Diagnosis requires a thyroid blood test.

Treatment: Hypothyroidism is usually permanent and requires lifetime treatment with daily hormone replacement therapy.

CORTISONE EXCESS

This condition is due to the overproduction of cortisone by the adrenal glands. An adrenal gland tumor—or a tumor of the pituitary gland, which acts on the adrenal gland—can cause this problem. Both are extremely rare in cats. Administering cortisone by mouth or injection can, in time, lead to the same effect as if the adrenals were making too much cortisone. This happens infrequently in cats because they have a high degree of resistance to the side effects of cortisone.

The effect of excess cortisone is to produce loss of hair in a symmetrical pattern over the trunk, with darkening of the underlying skin. There is a pot-bellied look. Such cats gain weight, retain fluid, and may have associated disorders of the liver, pancreas, or urinary system.

Treatment: If your cat is taking cortisone by tablet or injection, your veterinarian may be able to gradually reduce the dosage or stop the medication altogether. This should not be done abruptly or the cat could become ill from too little cortisone (see *Hypoadrenocorticism*, page 391). Cortisone excess caused by a tumor of the pituitary or adrenal gland is treated by removing both adrenal glands and providing daily cortisone replacement tablets (see *Hyperadrenocorticism*, page 391).

SOLAR DERMATOSIS

Exposure to sunlight may lead to sunburn and a recurrent skin disease in cats. This is most often seen in white cats or cats with white noses and white ears. The recurrent inflammation may eventually predispose the cat to squamous cell carcinoma in those areas.

Treatment: Tattooing the white areas or applying sunscreen may help, but it is best to keep affected cats out of the sunlight, especially from 10 a.m. to 2 p.m.

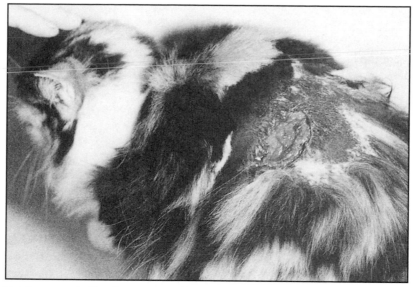

Pyoderma and skin abscess cause by a wound inflicted during a cat fight.

Pyoderma

Pyoderma is a bacterial infection of the skin. Ninety percent of cases are caused by the *Staphylococcus* bacteria. Pyoderma is classified according to the depth of skin involvement.

IMPETIGO

This is an infection of the dermis of the skin that occurs in newborn kittens. It is discussed in *Skin Infections of the Newborn* (page 473).

FOLLICULITIS

This is a localized infection of hair follicles. Scaling is often the most common sign, and this may occur concurrently with military dermatitis. It is often associated with more extensive skin involvement but may occur by itself. Deeper involvement of hair follicles is called *furunculosis*. When numerous hair follicles are affected, a carbuncle may form. (A carbuncle is a skin infection that often involves a group of hair follicles. The infected material forms a lump deep in the skin.)

Treatment: Cleaning the skin with medicated shampoos and, in severe cases, the use of antibiotics will often clear this problem.

FELINE ACNE

Feline acne develops in the sebaceous glands on the underside of the chin and edges of the lips. Blockage of skin pores by excess sebum or keratin is a predisposing cause. It is more common in cats with oily skin. It is not analogous to acne in people.

Feline acne is identified by finding blackheads or pimplelike bumps that come to a head and drain pus. Swelling of the entire chin and lower lips may be seen in severe cases.

A similar condition can be caused by an allergic reaction to rubber or plastic food and water bowls. In those cases, simply changing to stainless steel or ceramic dishes will clear up the condition.

Treatment: The infection usually responds to cleansing of the skin twice a day with an ointment or gel containing 2.5 to 5 percent benzoyl peroxide (OxyDex), chlorhexidine (Nolvasan) or povidone-iodine (Betadine). When excess sebum is a factor, the skin should be cleansed with a medicated shampoo for cats. An extensive or deep infection may require antibiotics. Because the underlying problem remains the same, acne often recurs when treatment is stopped. Some cats do better if switched from a wet to a dry food, or if the owner cleans their chin after every meal.

STUD TAIL

This condition is similar to acne because it is caused by oversecretion of the sebaceous glands. As you part the hair on top of the tail near its base, you may see an accumulation of waxy brown material. In severe cases, the hair follicles become infected. The hair becomes matted and greasy, develops a rancid odor, and may fall out. The condition is most common in unneutered males, but it may occur in females and neutered males.

Treatment: Wash the tail twice a day with a medicated shampoo for cats and sprinkle cornstarch or baby powder on the base. If the skin is infected, treat as you would for *Cellulitis and Abscesses* (page 164). Neutering may relieve the condition in males. This is a chronic condition and will require daily management. Oral retinoid may be used in severe cases, but it must be given under veterinary guidance.

CELLULITIS AND ABSCESSES

Cellulitis is an inflammation involving the deep layers of the skin. Most cases are caused by animal bites or scratches (such as wounds inflicted during cat fights). Puncture wounds allow bacteria to become established beneath the epidermis. Infection can be prevented in many fresh wounds if proper care is taken within the first few hours (see *Wounds*, page 47).

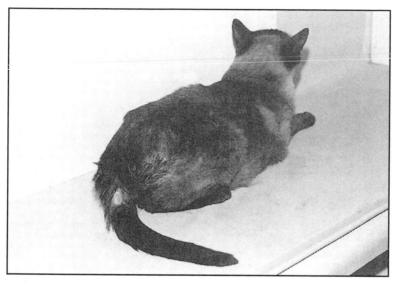

Stud tail is most common in unneutered males.

The signs of skin cellulitis include pain (tenderness to pressure), warmth (it feels hotter than normal), firmness (it's not as soft as it should be), and change in color (it appears redder than it should be). As the infection spreads from the wound into the lymphatic system, you may see red streaks in the skin and be able to feel enlarged lymph nodes in the groin, armpit, or neck.

Skin abscesses are localized pockets of *pus* beneath the surface of the skin. Pimples, *pustules, furuncles,* and *boils* are examples of small abscesses. The signs are the same as those for cellulitis, except that an abscess feels like fluid under pressure.

Treatment: Localize the infection by clipping away the hair and applying warm soaks three times a day for 15 minutes each. If hot packs are applied to an area of cellulitis, the heat and moisture assist the natural defenses of the body to surround the infection and make it come to a head. The skin over the top of an abscess thins out and ruptures, allowing the pus to be evacuated. Then the pocket heals from below. Ideally, an abscess should be kept open so that it heals from the inside out and does not close over prematurely, in which case a secondary abscess will form.

Pimples, pustules, furuncles, boils, and other small abscesses that do not drain spontaneously need to be lanced by your veterinarian. He or she will flush the cavity with a dilute antiseptic solution to keep it open and draining until it heals from below. Foreign bodies (such as splinters) beneath the skin must be removed with forceps because they are a continuous source of infection.

Antibiotics are used to treat wound infections, cellulitis, and abscesses. Most skin bacteria respond well to a variety of antibiotics, but cultures and antibiotic sensitivity tests may be needed to select the best drug.

Eosinophilic Granuloma Complex

Eosinophilic granulomas, formerly called lick granulomas, are a group of skin diseases producing ulceration and granulation of the skin. Some sores may be associated with an allergic skin disorder, such as feline miliary dermatitis, food hypersensitivity, or inhalant allergy. In others, the cat's immune system may be suppressed by a condition such as feline leukemia.

Indolent (rodent) ulcers are most often found on the middle of the upper lip, occasionally on the lower lip, or in the mouth behind the last upper molar. The ulcer is not itchy or painful. It has the potential to develop into cancer. (For more information, see *Eosinophilic Ulcers*, page 233.)

Eosinophilic plaque is an itchy skin condition that occurs in young to middle-age cats (the average age is 3 years). It is characterized by well-circumscribed, raised, red plaques with hair loss. These plaques are found on the abdomen and inner thighs. They are believed to be caused by an allergy, including flea allergies. The diagnosis is made by a *biopsy* of the plaque.

Linear granulomas, also called feline eosinophilic granulomas, occur in kittens and young cats (the average age is 1 year), more often in females than in males. They are circumscribed, raised, and red but present a linear rather than a circular appearance. They occur on the backs of the hind legs, in most cases on both sides, one side being the mirror image of the other. Linear granulomas also involve the foot pads and may occur in the mouth or on the chin. This condition is believed to be the result of an allergy. Cases just involving the foot pads may be a reaction to something in the litter. Diagnosis is like that for eosinophilic plaque.

Mosquito bite hypersensitivity affects the bridge of the nose and tips of the ears and produces itching of the pads of the feet. Characteristically, you will see crusty sores with erosions and scabs. When the condition is severe and generalized, it is accompanied by fever and swollen lymph nodes. It disappears in winter (when there are no mosquitoes). Cats with hypersensitivity to mosquito bites should be kept indoors.

Treatment: Identify the underlying cause of the problem, if possible, and treat it accordingly. Chlorpheniramine (Chlor-Trimeton) can help relieve the itching. Cortisone can be administered directly into the sore by injection. Oral cortisone preparations are required in most cases. Intramuscular injections of methylprednisolone acetate have also been used. Treatment should be vigorous, because eosinophilic granulomas are difficult to treat and tend to recur. Veterinary supervision is essential.

Lumps and Bumps on or Beneath the Skin

Any sort of lump, bump, or growth found on or beneath the skin is, by definition, a tumor, which literally means a swelling. Tumors are classified as benign when they are not cancer, and malignant when they are.

Classically, a benign growth is one that grows slowly, is surrounded by a capsule, is not invasive, and does not spread. However, there is no reliable way to tell if a tumor is benign or malignant without removing it and examining it with a microscope. If the tumor is benign, it won't come back if it is completely removed.

Cancers usually enlarge rapidly (a few weeks or months). They are not encapsulated. They appear to infiltrate into surrounding tissue and may ulcerate the skin and bleed. A hard mass that appears to be attached to bone or could be a growth of the bone itself is a cause for concern. The same is true for pigmented lumps or flat moles that start to enlarge, then spread out and begin to bleed (melanomas).

A hard gray or pink open sore that does not heal, especially on the feet and legs, should be regarded with suspicion. This could be a skin cancer.

Any unexplained nodules, bumps, or open sores on your cat should be checked by your veterinarian. Most cancers are not painful. Do not delay simply because your cat does not seem to be feeling uncomfortable.

To learn more about common growths on the skin, see chapter 19.

5

THE EYES

Cats' eyes have some special characteristics that set them apart from those of most other animals. Dogs use a combination of sight, hearing, and smell to orient themselves to their surroundings, but cats depend more on their sight, which is uniquely adapted to hunting and stalking. Cats will use their acute sense of hearing, with directional cues from their mobile ears, to tell them where a prey animal is moving. Then, their excellent vision guides them to the slightest movement.

The eyes of cats are unusually large. In fact, if humans had an eye of comparable size, it would measure almost 8 inches (20 cm) in diameter. The cornea, or outermost layer of the eye, is quite large, which allows more light in to the back of the eye. The eyeball is recessed in a fat cushion that protects the eyeball in a bony socket. Because it is deep-seated, eye movements are restricted. Especially adept at detecting movement out of the corner of the eye, a cat therefore turns his head rapidly to bring the object into focus. The cat is less skillful at identifying stationary objects and will watch them for long periods with an intense, steady, unblinking stare to detect the slightest movement. The fact that the eyes are located at the front of the head helps cats calculate the distance they need to leap to catch a prey animal—or a toy. Their field of vision is about 200 degrees (which means they have extraordinary peripheral vision), with an overlap, or binocular field, of about 140 degrees.

Cats do not see close objects in good focus and are considered to be farsighted—about a 20/100, compared to normal human vision of 20/20. This is because the muscles that change the shape of the lens are relatively weak, causing them to accommodate poorly (accommodation is the eye's ability to maintain focus as an object moves nearer). A cat's near vision is like that of a middle-aged person who is becoming farsighted and needs reading glasses. A cat's pupil is similar to that of a nocturnal reptile in that it is elliptical instead of round. This pupil shape allows the eye to open and close rapidly and to open more fully, allowing more light into the eye itself.

The cat's retina, a light-sensitive membrane at the back of the eye, contains two types of photoceptor nerve cells called rods and cones. Rods react to intensities of light. They enable cats to see black, white, and shades of gray. Cones provide color vision. Since the cat's retina has many rods and few cones, the cat is able to see well in dim light but has limited color vision. Cats are assumed to be similar in color vision to red-green colorblind people, although we don't really know this for sure.

The reason cats' eyes appear to glow in the dark is that they have a special layer of cells behind the retina called the tapetum lucidum. These cells act like a mirror, reflecting the light back onto the retina, doubly exposing the photoreceptors. It is this reflective process, plus the large number of rods in the retina, that is responsible for the cat's exceptional night vision, which is superior to that of most other animals. Although cats can't see in total darkness, they can see quite well in dim light or in fairly dark areas. Their minimal light threshold for vision is seven times less than that for most humans.

Like some other animals (including dogs), the cat has an extra eyelid, or nictitating membrane, normally not visible but resting on the eyeball at the inside corner. You can see this extra eyelid by recessing the eye. Press gently on the eyeball through the eyelid with your index finger. The third membrane will immediately slide out across the surface of the eye.

The third eyelid has an important cleansing and lubricating function and compensates for the fact that a cat seldom blinks. Like a windshield wiper, the third eyelid sweeps across the surface of the eye, dispersing tears and removing dust and foreign particles. It also helps protect the eye's surface from injury. By partially closing the upper and lower eyelids and protruding the nictitating membrane, a cat's eyes are protected while he is going through weeds and brush. This third eyelid will be visible in cats with certain eye problems or neurological problems, and in cats who are quite ill.

Structure of the Eye

The whole clear front part of the eye, which you can see when you look at your cat's face, is the cornea. The cornea is quite large relative to the size of the cat. It is covered by a layer of transparent cells and surrounded by a white rim called the *sclera*. In the cat, you can see very little of the sclera without drawing back the eyelids. The layer of tissue that covers the white of the eye is called the conjunctiva. It doubles back to cover the inner surface of the eyelids and both sides of the nictitating membrane but does not cover the cornea.

The cat's eyelids are tight folds of skin that support the front of the globe. They do not make direct contact with the surface of the eye because there is a thin layer of tears between them. The edges of the eyelids should meet when the eyes are closed. If this does not happen, the cornea dries out, causing eye irritation. Normally, cats do not have eyelashes, but when they are present and misdirected, they can irritate the surface of the eye.

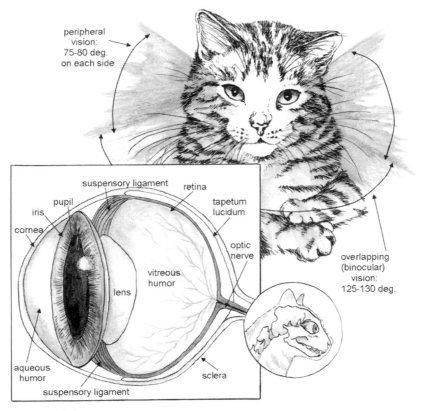

Anatomy of the eye.

The tears are secreted by glands found in the eyelids, nictitating membrane, and conjunctiva. Tears serve two functions: They cleanse, nourish, and lubricate the surface of the eye, and they contain chemicals that help with immunity to prevent bacteria from gaining a foothold and causing an eye infection.

A normal accumulation of tears is removed by evaporation. Excess tears are pooled near the eye's inner corner and carried via a drainage system to the nose. Excess tearing or watering of the eye indicates an eye ailment, a foreign substance in the eye that is an irritant, or a plugged tear drainage system.

The opening at the center of the eye is the pupil. It is surrounded by a circular or elliptical layer of pigmented muscle called the iris. The iris changes the size and shape of the pupil. As the iris expands, the pupil enlarges and becomes round, letting more light into the eye. As it contracts, the pupil narrows to a vertical slit, letting in less light.

Cats' eyes come in many colors. Eye color is the result of pigment in the iris and is genetically related to coat color. The most common iris colors are in the middle of the eye-color spectrum, from greenish-yellow to gold. Cats may also have blue, green, gold, or copper eyes. Occasionally, a cat is born with one blue iris and one green or gold iris, called odd-eyes. This may be associated with congenital deafness on the side with the blue iris. Congenital deafness can also occur in white-coated cats with blue irises. Not all cats with blue eyes are deaf, however—the defect is related to lack of pigment on internal ear structures.

The inner eye has two chambers. The anterior chamber is found between the cornea and the iris. The posterior chamber is a small area of fluid between the iris and the lens that has an opening into the anterior chamber, allowing two-way flow of the fluid and of cells. The vitreous chamber is the large chamber containing a clear jelly between the lens and the retina. Light enters the eye by passing first through the cornea and the anterior chamber and then through the pupil and the lens. The lens focuses the light, which then passes through the vitreous chamber and is received by the retina.

If Your Cat Has an Eye Problem

Your cat has an eye problem if there is matter in the eye; the eye waters; the cat blinks, squints, paws at the eye or gives evidence that the eye is painful; or the nictitating membrane is visible. The first thing to do is examine the eye and try to determine the cause. Eye problems can go from minor to serious very quickly. Be prepared to visit your veterinarian if you can't resolve the problem right away.

Signs of Eye Ailments

Eye problems are accompanied by a number of signs and symptoms. Pain is one of the most serious. *A cat with a painful eye needs prompt veterinary attention.*

- **Eye discharge:** The type of discharge helps define the cause. A clear discharge without redness and pain indicates a problem in the tear drainage system. A clear discharge with a reddened eye could be conjunctivitis, including from a viral infection. A thick, sticky, mucus or puslike discharge, along with a red (inflamed) eye suggests possible conjunctivitis as well, including from chlamydophila. Any discharge accompanied by a painful eye should alert you to the possibility of cornea or inner eye involvement.
- **Painful eye:** Signs of pain include excessive tearing, squinting (closing down the eye), tenderness to the touch, and avoidance of light. The cat may paw at the eye or try to rub it. The nictitating membrane often protrudes in response to pain. The usual causes of a painful eye are injuries to the cornea and diseases of the inner eye. These include serious vision-threatening problems, such as glaucoma and uveitis.

- **Film over the eye:** An opaque or whitish film that moves out over the surface of the eyeball from the inside corner of the eye is a protruded nictitating membrane. Causes are discussed in *The Nictitating Membrane* (page 183).

- **Cloudy eye:** There are certain diseases that change the clarity of the eye, turning it cloudy or making it seem as if the cat has a blind eye. This cloudiness can vary from a small, localized haziness to complete opacity of the eye. Loss of clarity or transparency of the eye indicates an inner eye disorder. Loss of clarity or transparency, accompanied by signs of pain, suggests keratitis, glaucoma, or uveitis. Corneal *edema*, the buildup of fluid in the normally clear cornea, will give the eye a uniform blue-gray appearance. This is usually associated with signs of pain. Cataracts are the most likely cause when the eye is not painful. When the eye is entirely opaque, you might think the cat is blind in that eye, but this is not necessarily true. A cloudy eye should receive immediate professional attention.

- **Hard or soft eye:** Changes in eye pressure are caused by disorders of the inner eye. The pupil may become fixed and unable to dilate or constrict. A hard eye with a dilated pupil indicates glaucoma. A soft eye with a small pupil indicates inflammation of the inner structures of the eye (uveitis).

- **Irritation of the lids:** Conditions that cause swelling, crusting, itching, or hair loss are discussed in *The Eyelids* (page 178).

- **Bulging or sunken eye:** A bulging eye occurs with glaucoma, tumors, and abscesses behind the globe, and with an eye out of its socket. A sunken eye occurs with dehydration, weight loss, eye pain, and tetanus. Some breeds, such as Persians and Himalayans, have eyes that normally bulge somewhat.

- **Abnormal eye movements:** Eyes that focus in different directions or jerk back and forth are discussed in *The Eyeball* (page 177).

- **Color change:** A change in the color of the eye may indicate the cancer known as melanoma. A yellowish tint to the sclera could be *jaundice*.

Do not neglect minor eye ailments. If there is any doubt about the diagnosis, and particularly if the eye has been treated at home but has not shown improvement in 24 hours, call your veterinarian. Eye problems can go from minor to serious in a very short time.

HOW TO EXAMINE THE EYES

The eye examination should be done in a dark room using a single light source, such as a flashlight, and a magnifying glass. With magnification, you can see fine details on the surface of the eyelids and the eyeball and may be able to inspect some of the inner-eye structures.

Many cats need to be restrained for an eye exam. Put the cat in a pillow-case and pin the case around the cat's neck, or hold the cat gently wrapped in a towel or on your lap if he is cooperative.

You can often get a clue to the cause of the problem by comparing one eye with the other. See if the eyes are of the same size, shape, and color. Do they bulge forward or are they recessed back in their sockets? Is there an eye discharge? Is the third eyelid visible over the inside corner of the eye? Does the eye look smoky, hazy, or cloudy?

To examine the outer surface of the eyeball, place one thumb just below the eye and the other over the bone just above the upper lid. Gently draw down on the lower lid and apply counter traction with the other thumb. The lower lid will sag out and you can look in and see the conjunctival sac and most of the cornea behind it. Reverse the procedure to examine the surface of the eye behind the upper lid.

Flash a light across the surface of the cornea to see if it is clear and transparent. A dull or dished-out (concave) spot is a sign of an injury. The pupils should be equal in size. They should narrow to vertical slits when light is flashed into the eye.

Push gently on the surface of the eyeball through the closed eyelid to see if one eye feels unusually hard or soft. If the eye is tender, the cat will give evidence of pain.

To test for vision, cover one of the cat's eyes and pretend you are about to touch the other eye with your finger. A cat who has vision will blink when your finger approaches. A cat will also blink if he feels even the slightest breeze from your hand movement, though, so this test is not always accurate.

HOW TO APPLY EYE MEDICINES

Other than artificial tears, no eye medications (ointments or drops) should be used without veterinary guidance. If the eye is painful, contact your veterinarian immediately.

To apply ointment, steady your cat's head with one hand and draw down on the lower eyelid to expose the inner surface. Rest the other hand containing the applicator against the cat's face, as shown in the photos on page 174. If the cat moves suddenly, your hand will also move, avoiding injury to the eye. Apply ointment to the inside of the lower lid; putting ointment directly on the eyeball is irritating and may cause the cat's head to jerk. Gently massage the eye with the lid closed to spread the medication evenly across the cornea.

Eyedrops are applied directly to the eyeball. Steady the hand holding the dropper against the side of the cat's head. Tilt the cat's nose upward, then drop

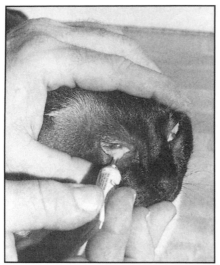

Apply ointment to the inside of the lower lid.

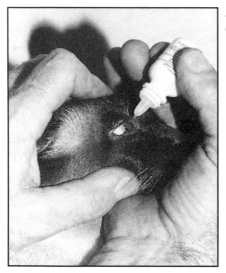

Apply drops to the inner corner of the eye.

the medication into the inner corner of the eye. Rub the eyelids gently to disperse the medicine. Eyedrops should be applied frequently, as directed by your veterinarian, since they tend to wash out with tears. Use only preparations that are specifically labeled for ophthalmic use. Check to be sure that the preparation is not out of date.

Your veterinarian may recommend that you clean the eye gently with artificial tears or saline solution before putting in medication. A warm compress may be needed to remove crusty buildup on the eyelids. Always follow directions carefully.

Prolonged administration of antibiotics in the eye can predispose the eyes to fungal infection or resistant bacterial infections.

If you need to give your cat atropine drops to help with dilating the eye and assisting in pain treatment, be aware that these drops taste quite bad. Cats may foam at the mouth for a minute or two if they get any atropine in their mouths. Cats with dilated eyes should be kept out of bright light.

The Eyeball
EYE OUT OF ITS SOCKET

This is an emergency. A hard blow to the head or a forceful strain can push the eyeball out of the socket. The lids may snap behind the eyeball, causing it to remain dislocated. This injury tends to occur in short-nosed breeds with large, prominent eyes, such as Persians. Shortly after the dislocation, swelling behind the eye makes it extremely difficult to manipulate the eye back to its normal position.

Treatment: Apply cold, damp compresses to prevent further swelling and bandage as described in *Eye Bandage* (page 54). Cover both eyes, as movement of the uninjured eye results in undesired movement of the dislocated eye. Seek immediate veterinary attention. The eyeball must be replaced as soon after the injury as possible. Try to keep the eyeball from drying out while transporting the cat to the veterinarian. Artificial tears, in the form of drops or ointment, can be used.

If you are in a place where it would be impossible to obtain veterinary services within one hour, attempt the following: First, restrain the cat (see *Handling and Restraint*, page 2). Then lubricate the eyeball with a few drops of artificial tears or mineral oil and gently draw the lids outward over the eyeball, allowing the eyeball to drop back into its socket. If you are unsuccessful, do not persist, as forceful manipulation and repeated attempts cause further swelling and lead to greater injury. It is also worth repeating that this is a last resort, *only* if veterinary care is unavailable.

There is a great risk that the cat will lose the vision in this eye. Even if you can replace the eyeball, you need to go to the veterinarian for follow-up care, which might include surgery to help keep the eyeball in its socket.

EXOPHTHALMOS (BULGING EYE)

In cats with this condition, swelling of tissue behind the eye pushes the eyeball forward. As seen from above, the affected eye appears to be more prominent. Major protrusion prevents the cat from closing his eyelids. If the nerves to the eye are stretched or damaged, the pupil dilates and does not constrict when a light is flashed in the eye.

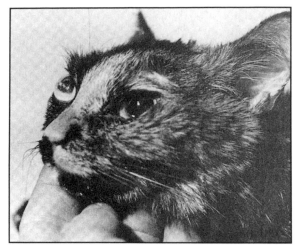

The bulging right eye is caused by a growth behind the eyeball.

This condition may be caused by an abscess. Exophthalmos may occur also after a blow that fractures the bones of the eye socket and causes a sudden buildup of blood or fluid behind the eye, called a *hematoma*. Infections that spread to the eyeball from the sinus also cause the eye to bulge. They are accompanied by extreme pain when the cat attempts to open his mouth and often a fever.

A growth behind the eyeball is another cause of eye protrusion. Most are malignant and respond poorly to treatment. You will notice a gradual bulging of the eye that gets worse over a matter of weeks. Finally, untreated chronic glaucoma can lead to increased size of the eye and protrusion (see *Glaucoma,* page 198).

Treatment: *All causes of exophthalmos require immediate veterinary attention.* They are extremely serious and may cause loss of vision. Drugs can be given to reduce the swelling produced by trauma. Antibiotics are required to treat infections behind the eye. Surgery may be indicated to drain blood or pus behind the eye or within an infected sinus, or to suture an eyelid over a bulging eyeball to protect that eyeball from injury and to keep it from drying out.

ENOPHTHALMOS (SUNKEN EYE)

Both eyeballs may recede when there is loss of substance in the fat pads behind the eye, as in dehydration or rapid weight loss. Many injuries or conditions may just affect one eye, however.

There is a retractor muscle that, when it goes into spasm, pulls the eye back into its socket. This can occur with a painful injury to the cornea. This is a temporary condition.

Tetanus produces retractor muscle spasms of both eyeballs, with the characteristic appearance of the third eyelids. Damage to a nerve trunk in the neck can result in a sunken eyeball and a small pupil (*Horner's Syndrome*, see page 184). This can occur as a consequence of a neck injury or a middle-ear infection. Finally, after a severe injury the eye may atrophy, becoming smaller and sinking into the socket.

As the eye begins to recess, the third eyelid or nictitating membrane becomes visible, and there is often an accumulation of mucus in the recessed space formed by the eye's sinking. This gives the eye a peculiar, rolled-back look. Because of the presence of a membrane across the eye, a sunken eye may be mistaken for a protrusion of the third eyelid.

Treatment: The treatment of enophthalmos is directed at the underlying cause of the problem.

STRABISMUS (CROSS-EYED GAZE)

Crossed eyes are quite common among Siamese cats—so much so that many owners accept them as normal. One eye looks ahead while the other eye turns in. This condition is inherited, and there is no way to correct it.

Other types of strabismus are caused by eye muscle paralysis. The eye cannot move in a certain direction. Brain tumors and injuries to the nerves and muscles of the eye are predisposing causes. This type of strabismus is rare.

NYSTAGMUS (JERKING EYE MOVEMENTS)

Involuntary movement of the eyes may be irregular side-to-side jerking of the eyeballs or rhythmic pendulumlike swings with a fast and slow phase. They

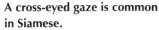

A cross-eyed gaze is common in Siamese.

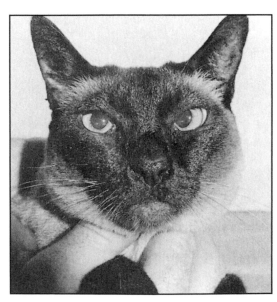

indicate a disorder of the vestibular system (see *Otitis Interna*, page 217). This movement may be called doll's eye, since the appearance is similar to that of a doll with movable eyes.

Treatment: The treatment is directed at the underlying cause of the problem.

The Eyelids

BLEPHAROSPASM (SEVERE SQUINTING)

Spasm of the muscles around the eye is induced by pain. This can have numerous causes, including irritation from a foreign body. The irritation causes tightening of the eyelid muscles, which partially closes the eye and rolls the eyelids inward against the cornea. Once rolled in, the rough margins of the lids rub against the eyeball, causing further pain and spasm.

Treatment: Anesthetic drops can be applied to the eyeball to relieve the pain and break the cycle. The relief is temporary if the underlying irritant is not found and removed.

BLEPHARITIS (IRRITATED EYELIDS)

Blepharitis, or inflammation of the eyelids, primarily occurs when the eyelids are injured during cat fights. Scratches and surface injuries can easily become

Severe squinting (blepharospasm) in this cat is associated with a painful eye condition.

infected. This leads to itching and scratching, crust formation, and the accumulation of pus and debris on the eyelids.

Blepharitis can also be caused by head mange mites (*Notoedres cati*), demodectic mange mites, or ringworm infection. Head mange causes intense itching. Because of persistent scratching, there is hair loss, redness, and scab formation. Ringworm affects the hair on the eyelid, causing it to become brittle and break off next to the skin. This is not an itchy condition. The skin may look scaly and crusted but is seldom red or irritated.

Treatment: Protect the eye by instilling mineral oil, and then loosen the scabs by soaking them with warm compresses. Keep the eye clean and *seek veterinary attention*. Antibiotics, topical or oral or both, may be required for infected eyelids. The cat may need to wear an Elizabethan or a BiteNot collar to prevent rubbing at the eyes. The treatment of ringworm and mange is discussed in chapter 4.

CHEMOSIS (SUDDEN SWELLING)

In cats with this condition, the conjunctiva and eyelids are fluid-filled, puffy, and soft. Water has passed out of the circulation into the tissues in response to the allergen.

Sudden swelling of the eyelids and conjunctiva is generally caused by an allergic reaction. Insect bites and allergens in foods and drugs are the most common causes. For more information, see *Allergies* (page 151).

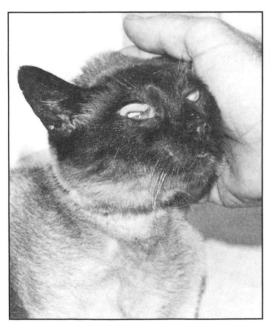

In this cat with chemosis, sudden swelling of the eyelids and conjunctiva was caused by an allergic reaction.

Chlamydophila and viral infections may also cause swelling, but it is primarily of just the conjunctiva.

Treatment: This is not a serious problem. It is of short duration and improves when the *allergen* is removed. Simple cases may be treated with drops or eye ointments prescribed by your veterinarian that contain a corticosteroid. Some cats may need systemic treatment for the allergic reaction, such as a corticosteroid or an antihistamine.

FOREIGN BODIES IN THE EYE

Foreign material such as dust, grass seed, dirt, or specks of vegetable matter can become trapped behind the eyelids and nictitating membranes. Although this is more common in cats who go outdoors, indoor cats may get hairs or dust in their eyes and on their corneas, as well. The first indication is tearing and watering, along with signs of irritation such as blinking and squinting. The third membrane may protrude to protect the irritated eye.

Treatment: First examine the eye as described in *How to Examine the Eyes* (page 172). You might be able to see a foreign body on the surface of the eye or behind the upper or lower eyelid. If not, the foreign body may be caught behind the third eyelid, and the cat will need a topical eye anesthetic before you can lift up the eyelid and remove the foreign matter. This is something your veterinarian should do, especially if your cat is not cooperative with being restrained.

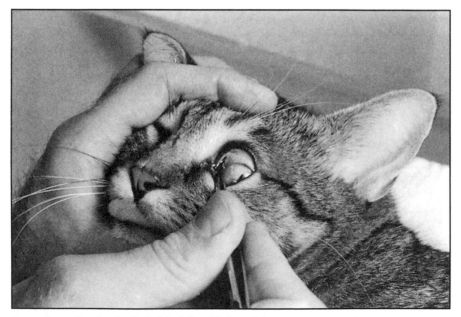

Removing a foreign body behind the third eyelid.

For dirt and loose debris in the eye, hold the eyelid open and flush the eye with artificial tears, a sterile saline eye solution, or cool water for 10 to 15 minutes. Soak a wad of cotton and squeeze it into the eye, or drop it into the eye from the bottle of solution. If a foreign body can be seen but cannot be removed by irrigation, you may be able to remove it by gently swabbing the eye with a moistened cotton-tipped applicator. The foreign body may adhere to it.

After you have removed a foreign object, apply to the eyeball a triple antibiotic or other ointment, as provided by your veterinarian.

Thorns that cling to the eyelid's surface can be removed with blunt-nosed tweezers, but unless they flush off with tears, you should contact your veterinarian. Foreign bodies that penetrate the surface of the eye should be removed by a veterinarian.

The cat may persist in rubbing the eye after treatment. Restrain the cat from doing this if possible. You may need to use an Elizabethan or a BiteNot collar. If the cat is rubbing at it, the foreign body may still be in the eye or there may be a corneal abrasion (see *The Cornea*, page 192). *Get help from your veterinarian.*

BURNS OF THE EYES

Chemical injuries to the conjunctiva and cornea can occur when acids, alkali, soaps, shampoos, or topical insecticides are splashed into the eyes. Toxic fumes can also irritate and injure the eyes. The signs are tearing, squinting, and pawing at the eye.

Treatment: Flush the eyes with cool water, artificial tears, or a sterile saline solution, as described in *Foreign Bodies in the Eyes* (page 180). This must be done immediately after exposure to prevent damage to the eye. Flush for a full 15 minutes. After you have completed the flushing, take your cat to the veterinarian for further evaluation and treatment.

Be sure to protect the eyes from shampoos and insecticides when bathing your cat.

TRICHIASIS

Normally cats do not have eyelashes, but there are exceptions. When present, they may grow in from the eyelid and rub against the cornea, producing eye irritation and injury.

Treatment: Eyelashes that are irritating the eyes should be removed by the roots by surgery or cryotherapy (freezing). Plucking them with blunt-nosed tweezers provides temporary relief but is not a permanent solution.

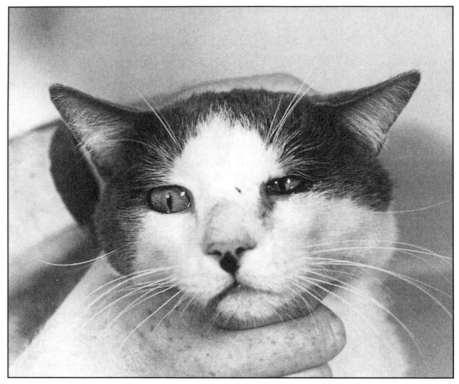

The severe squinting with eye discharge and loss of hair in one eye is indicative of chronic eye irritation, here due to entropion.

ENTROPION

This condition, in which the eyelid rolls in, occurs sporadically as a hereditary defect in Persians and related breeds, but it can occur in any cat because of scarring of the lower lid following a bout of purulent conjunctivitis or a lacerated eyelid. The rolled-in lid produces eye irritation with tearing and severe squinting.

Treatment: Entropion can be corrected surgically.

ECTROPION

In cats with this condition, the lower eyelid rolls out from the face, exposing the surface of the eye to irritants. It may be caused by a birth defect, but in most cases it is due to an improperly healed laceration of the lid. This condition is less common than entropion.

Treatment: Surgery may be necessary to tighten the lid and protect the eye.

TUMORS OF THE EYELIDS

In cats, growths on the eyelids tend to be cancers. Some are cauliflower-like growths, while others are *ulcerated*. Eyelid tumors usually occur in older cats. Malignant tumors grow rapidly and spread to the lymph nodes in the neck. Squamous cell cancer is the most common malignancy. White-coated cats are predisposed to squamous cell cancer of the eyelids, nose, and ears.

Treatment: All growths of the eyelids should be surgically removed and sent for tissue examination.

The Nictitating Membrane (Third Eyelid)

FILM OVER THE EYE

The third eyelid is not normally seen, but it may become opaque and/or visible in response to illness or injury. A few cats will have their third eyelid up when they are totally relaxed and resting, so it is important to know what is normal for your cat. In these cats, the membrane will retract quickly when they alert or startle, and then stay retracted for awhile. The length of time the membrane is exposed may vary, as though the cat is blinking, or it may remain visible. When the nictitating membrane is visible over the inside corner of the eye, it is protruding.

When associated with a bulging eye, causes of protrusion of the nictitating membrane include infection in the tissue behind the eyeball (*abscess*), bleeding behind the eye (*hematoma*), and tumor.

When associated with a retracted or sunken eye, causes of protrusion of the nictitating membrane include any painful eye illness resulting in spasm of the muscles around the eye; spasm of these muscles when caused by tetanus; and dehydration or chronic weight loss that reduces the size of the fat pad behind the eye. When only one eye is involved, suspect an illness related to that eye; when both eyes are involved, suspect a systemic illness such as feline viral respiratory infection.

Key-Gaskell Syndrome

This is a rare autonomic nervous system disorder of unknown cause, one sign of which is prolapse of the third eyelid. Other signs include dilated pupils, constipation, trouble eating, and a slow heart rate. Key-Gaskell syndrome is seen more often in Great Britain than elsewhere.

Treatment: Extensive nursing care for weeks to months is required. The prognosis is poor, with most cats ending up with aspiration pneumonia.

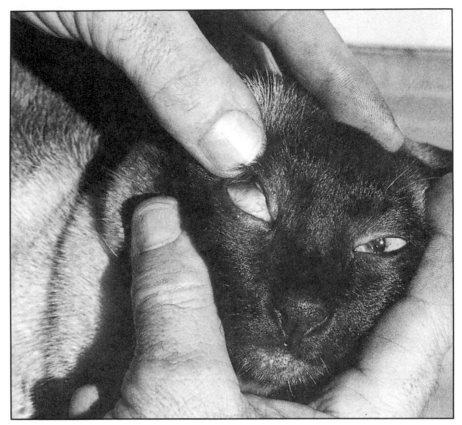

By recessing the eye, you can see a normal third eyelid.

Horner's Syndrome

Horner's syndrome can result in a sunken eye, prolapse of the third eyelid, and a small pupil. This can occur as a consequence of injury to (or cancerous involvement of) a nerve in the neck or a middle ear infection.

Treatment: There is no treatment, although the condition may resolve with time.

Haw Syndrome

This is a rather common but temporary protrusion of uncertain cause of the third eyelid. It affects otherwise healthy cats under age 2 and is frequently preceded by a gastrointestinal illness.

Treatment: The protrusion clears up within a few months without treatment. During this time, if the film interferes with your cat's vision, your veterinarian can prescribe an eyedrop solution containing 1 or 2 percent Pilocarpine, which reduces the size of the protrusion.

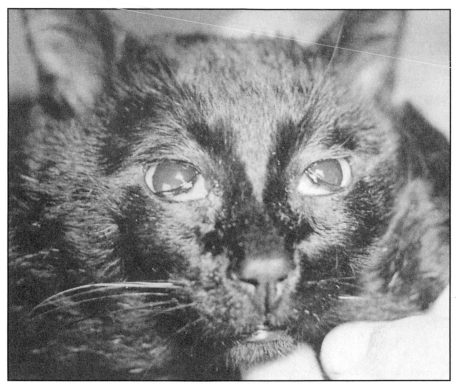

Protrusion of the nictitating membranes occurs with the haw syndrome.

CHERRY EYE

Eversion of the gland of the nictitans, known as cherry eye, occurs in cats, especially the Burmese breed. For unknown reasons, the cartilage of the third eyelid folds over, everting the gland. This condition is not only unsightly but can be uncomfortable and may cause corneal ulceration in the cat.

Treatment: At one time, eversions of the nictitans gland were treated by surgical removal, but that is not the ideal solution. Since part or all of the gland was usually removed at the same time, there was decreased tear production. This often led to secondary keratoconjunctivitis sicca. Now the gland is generally repositioned surgically.

The Tearing Mechanism
EPIPHORA (WATERY EYE)

There are a number of conditions that cause a watery or *mucus*-like discharge to overflow the eyelids and run down the sides of the face, staining the hair. Cats do not cry as people do, so this is not a factor to be considered as one of the causes. In all cats with a runny eye, the cause should be determined so that proper treatment can be given.

First, it is important to determine whether the eye is red or irritated. Irritating eye disorders are characterized by excessive tearing along with a red or painful eye. However, if the eye is *not* red, then a blockage in the tear drainage system is the problem.

Keep in mind that excessive tearing or a sticky, puslike discharge from the eyes or nose is frequently associated with feline viral respiratory infections (see page 79). This possibility should be investigated before the eye alone is treated.

Nasolacrimal Occlusion

In cats with this condition, the discharge is due to an overflow of tears caused by a blockage in the tear draining system. Inadequate tear drainage should be considered if the cat has a persistent eye discharge without redness.

A cat may be born with an inadequate tear drainage system. However, in most cases, nasolacrimal occlusion is the result of scarring from eyelid injuries acquired in cat fights. Other causes are chronic infection in the duct system and plugging of the ducts by thick secretions, dirt, or grass seeds.

To see if the drainage system is open, a veterinarian stains the pool of tears near the inner corner of the eye with fluorescein dye. If the dye does not appear at the nostril, the tear duct is blocked on that side. Nasolacrimal probes are inserted into the duct opening, and various flushing techniques are used to show the point of obstruction. The flushing often removes the blockage and opens the duct.

Treatment: Infection in the duct system is treated with antibiotics. In some cases, they are instilled into the duct or used to flush the system. The dosage, type, and route of administration should be determined by your veterinarian.

Occasionally, ducts are damaged beyond repair and you must simply deal with the mild chronic problem.

Tear Stains

An overflow of tears, accompanied by unsightly staining of the hair below the eyes, occurs in some cats with short noses, large, prominent eyes, and flat faces. The problem is seen most often in Persians and Himalayans, and other breeds with shortened muzzles. These breeds are subject to chronic eye irritations and infections that produce tearing. Their facial structure usually causes a narrowing of the nasolacrimal duct and a shallow tear lake at the inner corner of the eye. All these factors may contribute to the problem.

Treatment: If there is no correctable cause, symptoms can often be improved by administering a broad-spectrum antibiotic. If the cause is a chronic infection, the antibiotic will treat it. Tetracycline is the drug of choice. It is secreted in tears and also binds that part of the tears that stains the fur. If improvement is only due to the binding action of the drug, the face remains wet but not discolored. Tetracycline is given by mouth for three weeks. If the stain returns after treatment, then long-term administration might be considered. Some cat owners prefer to add low-dose tetracycline to the cat's food for long-term control. Tetracycline should not be given to growing kittens or pregnant queens, as it will cause problems with the development of teeth and bones.

When cosmetic considerations are important, you can improve your cat's appearance by clipping the hair close to his face.

KERATOCONJUNCTIVITIS SICCA (DRY EYE)

Keratoconjunctivitis sicca is a disorder of the tear glands that results in insufficient aqueous tear production and a correspondingly dry cornea. The tear film contains less of the aqueous layer and more of the mucus layer. In consequence, the classic sign of dry eye is a thick, stringy, *mucoid* to *mucopurulent* discharge. Since this type of discharge can also be seen in cats with conjunctivitis, cats with dry eye may be mistakenly treated for chronic conjunctivitis for long periods with little or no improvement.

Herpesvirus is considered to be a primary cause of dry eye in cats. Luckily, this disease syndrome is less common in cats than it is in dogs. A congenital form of this disease occurs in Burmese cats.

In a cat with dry eye, the bright, glistening sheen normally seen in the eye is replaced by a lackluster appearance in which the cornea is dry, dull, and opaque. Recurrent bouts of conjunctivitis are typical. Eventually, the cornea becomes *ulcerated* or develops *keratitis*. Blindness may ensue.

Dry eye can have several causes. Some specific conditions that predispose a cat to dry eye include the following:

- Injury to the nerves that innervate the lacrimal glands. A branch of the facial nerve that activates the tear glands passes through the middle ear. Infections in the middle ear can damage this branch, affecting the tear glands as well as the muscles on that side of the face. In this case, the opposite eye is not affected.

- Injury to the tear glands themselves. Partial or complete destruction of the tear glands can follow *systemic* diseases. For example, feline herpes may block the glands. Bacterial blepharitis or conjunctivitis can destroy the tear glands or block the small ducts that carry the tears into the eye. A number of sulfonamide drugs are toxic to tear glands. Tear gland injuries may be partially reversible if the underlying cause is eliminated.

The diagnosis of dry eye is made by measuring the volume of tears. The Schirmer tear test involves placing a commercial filter paper strip into the tear pool at the inner corner of the cat's eye and leaving it for one minute to see how much of the strip is wetted. Normally, the strip should be wet to a length of 12 to 22 mm.

Treatment: For many years, the frequent application of artificial tears was the only treatment available for dry eye. But use of ophthalmic cyclosporin has revolutionized treatment and greatly improved results. Cyclosporin reverses, or at least halts, the immune-mediated destruction of the lacrimal glands.

Cyclosporin ointment is applied to the surface of the affected eye. The frequency of application must be determined by your veterinarian. The result is not immediate. Artificial tears and topical antibiotics should be continued until the Schirmer tear test indicates that the volume of tears is adequate. Treatment is life-long.

When damage to the lacrimal glands leaves little or no functioning tissue, cyclosporin is not likely to be effective. This is also true if your cat's problem does not have an immune basis. Artificial tears (drops and ointments) prescribed by your veterinarian must then be instilled into the cat's eyes several times a day for life. Ointments are less expensive and do not need to be applied as frequently as drops. Saline drops should not be used because they aggravate the problem by washing away the lipid layer of the tear film.

Surgical treatment can be considered as a last resort, when medical management fails. The operation involves transplanting the duct of the parotid salivary gland up into the corner of the eye. The saliva takes the place of the tears. The operation has several significant disadvantages. One is that the volume of tears may be more than the drainage system can handle. This can result in a watery eye and the accumulation of mineral deposits on the cornea and face.

The Outer Eye
CONJUNCTIVITIS

Conjunctivitis is an inflammation of the membrane covering the back of the eyelids and surface of the eyeball up to the cornea. It is one of the most common eye problems in cats. Conjunctivitis in cats almost always has an underlying infectious cause. The most common cause is the herpesvirus (FHV-1), and the second most common is chlamydophila. Signs are a red eye, discharge, and pawing at the eye to relieve itching. The conjunctival tissues may be red and swollen. Untreated conjunctivitis may progress to vision-threatening problems.

Conjunctivitis is not painful—although it is itchy. If the eye is red, irritated, and painful to touch, consider the possibility of keratitis, uveitis, or glaucoma. Delay in treating these conditions could result in loss of vision.

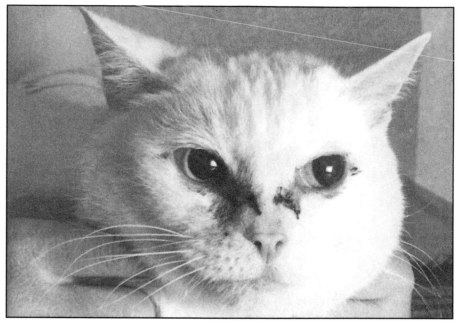

A clear watery discharge suggests serous conjunctivitis. The eye is not painful.

Serous Conjunctivitis

This is a mild condition in which the membrane looks pink and somewhat swollen. The discharge is clear and watery and is caused by physical irritants such as wind, cold weather, dust, or various allergens. This condition must be distinguished from a tearing problem.

Serous conjunctivitis may be the first sign of a feline viral respiratory disease or a chlamydophila infection. Eye worms (see page 192) are a rare cause of conjunctivitis.

Treatment: Mild, irritating forms of conjunctivitis can be treated at home. The eye should be cleansed with a dilute solution of boric acid for ophthalmic use, artificial tears, or a sterile ophthalmic irrigating solution that can be purchased over the counter and used as directed for people. You should see definite improvement within 24 hours. If not, bring your cat to the veterinarian.

Purulent Conjunctivitis

Purulent conjunctivitis begins as serous conjunctivitis that becomes *purulent*. Thick secretions crust the eyelids. The eye discharge contains *mucus* or *pus*. This suggests secondary bacterial infection.

When the discharge involves both eyes simultaneously, suspect a virus. This could be herpesvirus or calicivirus. When it involves one eye at first and progresses to the other eye several days later, suspect chlamydophila or mycoplasma. These microorganisms can be detected under a microscope by

This kitten has feline viral respiratory disease and purulent conjunctivitis.

your veterinarian, in scrapings taken from the conjunctival membrane. Ulcers on the cornea are diagnostic for herpesvirus conjunctivitis.

Conjunctivitis due to fungal infection is rare and requires special laboratory aid for diagnosis.

Treatment: Purulent conjunctivitis requires eye irrigations and sometimes warm soaks to loosen crusted eyelids. Antibiotics are applied to the eye surface several times a day. They should be continued for seven days beyond apparent cure. An ointment containing a combination of neomycin, bacitracin, and polymyxin (such as Neosporin ophthalmic ointment) often works well.

If the condition is caused by chlamydophila or mycoplasma, eyedrops containing tetracycline or chloramphenicol are the antibiotics of choice. Chlamydophila conjunctivitis can result from cats shedding organisms in their stool or urine after the infection appears to be cleared. This carrier state can be treated by your veterinarian with a three-week course of doxycycline or a week of azithromycin.

Deep-seated infections are difficult to clear up. In such cases, you should suspect involvement of the tear drainage system. Repeated cleansing of the eye, correction of any underlying problem, and specific topical and oral antibiotics tailored to cultures and sensitivities form the primary approach to this problem.

Antiviral eye medications are available for the treatment of viral conjunctivitis. They must be prescribed by a veterinarian. Cats with herpesvirus often have chronic recurrent conjunctivitis and may periodically be a source of infection for other cats. Research at Colorado State University is using a new antiviral drug, cidofovir, to treat cats with herpes conjunctivitis. This medication needs to be given twice a day and is not as irritating to the cat as other antiviral medications.

Follicular Conjunctivitis

This is a condition in which the small *mucous* glands (also called *follicles*) on the underside of the nictitating membrane form a rough, cobblestone surface that irritates the eye and produces a mucoid discharge. Various pollens, allergens, and infective agents are implicated as causes. After the initiating factor has been removed, these follicles may remain enlarged. The roughened surface of the conjunctiva then acts as a persistent irritant to the eye.

Chronic conjunctivitis with a thick mucus discharge from the eyes.

Treatment: A steroid-based eye ointment can be used to decrease the size of the follicles and smooth the surface. If steroids are not effective, your veterinarian can mechanically or chemically cauterize the follicles. Steroids should not be used unless an infectious cause has been ruled out.

Neonatal Conjunctivitis

This condition is due to a bacterial infection beneath the eyelids. Some cases are associated with the herpesvirus. It occurs in kittens before their eyes are open. For more information, see *Neonatal Conjunctivitis* (page 473).

EYE WORMS

Cats can have eye worms (*Thelazia sp.*) that are transmitted by flies feeding on eye secretions. The adult worms are about 1.5 inches (38 mm) long and appear in the conjunctival sac. If left unattended, they can damage the eye by abrading the cornea.

Treatment: Eye worms can be removed by your veterinarian with blunt-nosed tweezers under local anesthetic. Eye medications containing levamisole may be prescribed.

The Cornea

The cornea, or clear part of the eye, is covered by a protective layer of surface (*epithelial*) cells. Most destructive processes affecting the cornea begin with an injury to this layer. Any irritative process, such as a foreign body or cat scratch, can cause a surface injury. Cats with prominent eyes, such as Persians, are especially susceptible. Once the continuity of the epithelium has been destroyed, the injury either heals spontaneously or progresses to a more serious problem. The outcome depends on the magnitude of the injury, how quickly it is recognized, and whether the initiating factor has been identified and removed.

CORNEAL ABRASION

This is defined as an injury to the eye caused by a scratch. Corneal injuries are extremely painful. The cat squints, tears, and paws at the eye, and may be sensitive to light. Often, the third eyelid comes out to protect the injured eye. With an extensive injury, the surface of the cornea surrounding the injury becomes swollen due to edema giving it a cloudy, hazy, or opaque appearance.

The cause of the corneal abrasion can often be suspected from its location. Abrasions in the upper part of the cornea may be caused by misdirected eyelashes on the upper eyelid. Lower corneal abrasions suggest an imbedded foreign

The tearing, squinting, and protrusion of the third eyelid are caused by an extensive corneal abrasion.

body. Abrasions near the inner corner of the eye suggest a foreign body beneath the third eyelid. Even dust blowing onto the cornea may cause a mild abrasion.

Treatment: A cat with a suspected corneal abrasion should be seen by a veterinarian. This can rapidly progress to more serious eye injuries, including corneal ulcer or keratitis. Healing of a corneal abrasion usually takes place in 24 to 48 hours by a process in which the epithelium thins and slides over a small defect. Larger and deeper abrasions require more time. A corneal abrasion will not heal if a foreign body is imbedded in the cornea or beneath one of the eyelids. Accordingly, the cat should be examined for foreign bodies under the eyelids. Removal of foreign bodies is discussed in *Foreign Bodies in the Eye* (page 180).

CORNEAL ULCERS

Corneal ulcers are dangerous and must receive prompt medical attention. Most are caused by an injury to the cornea. Others are associated with an infection (virus, bacteria, fungus) or a nutritional deficiency. In some cases, the cause is unknown.

Large ulcers may be visible to the naked eye. They appear as dull spots or depressions on the eye surface. Smaller ones are best seen after the eye has been stained with fluorescein. Your veterinarian will gently put a drop of fluorescein liquid or put a tab of paper impregnated with fluorescein onto the eye. The eye is then examined with a blue light in a room with dim lighting. The corneal damage will glow brightly.

Treatment: Early treatment is vital to avoid serious complications or even loss of the eye. Treatment may include atropine drops for pain control (remember, these drops are quite bitter and cats will foam at the mouth if they get any atropine orally) and antibiotics to prevent secondary bacterial infections.

Cortisone, which is incorporated into many eye preparations used for conjunctivitis, *should not* be put into the eye if you suspect the cat has a corneal injury. This can lead to rupture of the cornea and blindness.

KERATITIS

Keratitis is an inflammation of the cornea, or clear window of the eye. This is a painful eye condition and should be distinguished from conjunctivitis. Signs of keratitis include squinting, discharge, rubbing the eye, and protrusion of the third eyelid. Conjunctivitis, on the other hand, is characterized by a chronic eye discharge with little, if any, pain.

There are different types of keratitis. All result in loss of transparency of the cornea, which may lead to partial or complete blindness in the affected eye. Keratitis must be managed by a veterinarian. Initially, topical drops or ointments may need to be given as frequently as hourly or every two hours.

Ulcerative Keratitis

An injury to the surface of the eye can result in the development of an abrasion or ulcer that does not heal and becomes secondarily infected. Trauma is the most common cause of ulcerative keratitis in cats.

An infectious form of ulcerative keratitis is caused by feline herpesvirus (see *Feline Viral Respiratory Disease Complex*, page 79). The signs of respiratory infection occur before or at the same time as eye involvement. One or both eyes may be affected.

Treatment: This involves antiviral eye medications, possibly including the new drug cidofovir. Vaccination for the herpesvirus will help but does not totally prevent this disease. Adding lysine to the diet may help, as this amino acid competes with the amino acid arginine, which is essential for herpesvirus replication.

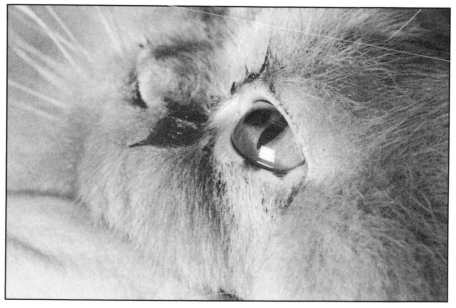

The round black spot on the clear window of the eye is a corneal sequestrum. This condition is unique to cats.

Chronic Degenerative Keratitis

This condition, unique to cats, occurs primarily in Persians and Himalayans, but has been seen in Siamese and domestic shorthairs, as well. Signs are similar to those of ulcerative keratitis, but in a cat with this condition, inflamed tissue forms a brown or black plaque on the corneal surface (the sequestrum). The exact cause is unknown, but it has been found in association with entropion, lack of normal tear production (keratoconjunctivitis sicca), and lagophthalmos, a condition in which the eyelids do not completely close.

Treatment: Treatment involves removing the sequestrum by stripping off the outer layer of the cornea. A conjunctival graft may be needed to cover a large defect. In this case, the eye may be closed temporarily to protect the cornea by suturing the third eyelid up to the top of the eye. Herpesvirus may be involved in these cases.

Eosinophilic Keratitis

In cats with this problem, many blood vessels grow across the cornea. A scrape of the outer layer of the cornea will show many *eosinophils* and mast cells—often associated with allergies and immune reactions. Herpesvirus may be involved, as well. You may notice a whitish plaque on the cornea and blood vessels growing onto the cornea.

Treatment: Anti-inflammatory agents, such as topical steroids or oral corticosteroids, may be effective, but the problem tends to recur. Due to concerns about reactivating a latent herpes infection, topical cyclosporine may be used instead; this is an immune-modulating medication. This problem is rarely cured, but it can be controlled in most cats.

The Inner Eye
BLINDNESS

Any condition that prevents light from getting into the eye will impair a cat's vision. Diseases of the cornea, such as keratitis, and of the lens, such as cataracts, fall into this category. Inflammations of the deep structures of the eye, including glaucoma and uveitis, also lead to blindness. A common cause of blindness in older cats is hypertension (high blood pressure). Finally, any disease that reduces the sensitivity of the retina to light impulses, such as retinal atrophy, or anything that affects the optic nerves or the sight center of the brain, including trauma, can produce various forms of visual disturbance, including blindness. Most cases of blindness are not evident on general observation of the eye itself. Ophthalmologic studies are required to make an exact diagnosis.

Shining a bright light into a cat's eyes to test for pupillary constriction is *not* an exact method of determining whether the cat sees. The pupil may become smaller simply because of reflex. This won't tell you if the cat's brain has the ability to form visual images. But there are other indications that might suggest your cat cannot see. For example, activities that require eye and body coordination, such as pouncing on a ball or jumping from a sofa to a chair, might be impaired. In a dimly lighted room, cats with little or no vision may bump into furniture or may hold their noses close to the ground and feel with their whiskers, which will be pointed forward.

Quite often, the eyesight of older cats begins to fail shortly after the onset of deafness. They then rely more and more on memory to find their way around the house. Many totally blind cats get along surprisingly well when kept in familiar surroundings. Do not rearrange the furniture, as the cat will have a mental map of where everything should be and can move about quite freely as long as things aren't moved. *One thing blind cats should never do is roam free.* They must be kept indoors or in enclosed areas, and taken outside only under supervision.

CATARACTS

A cataract is defined as any opacity on the lens that interferes with transmission of light to the retina. A spot on the lens that blocks out light, regardless of size, technically is a cataract.

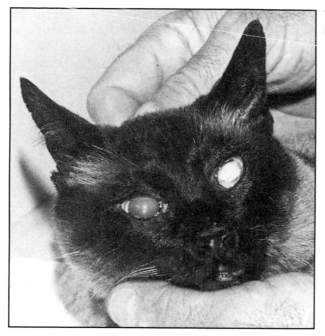

This cat has a cataract in the left eye.

Cataracts of all types are rare in cats. Most cataracts are caused by eye injuries and infections. Inherited cataracts can be accompanied by other eye birth defects, such as microphthalmia (an abnormally small eye) or persistent pupillary membrane (which is a tissue tag across the iris or from the iris to the cornea). Cataracts can develop in diabetic cats, but this is not common.

As a cat gets older, there is normal aging of the eye. New fibers, continually forming on the lens surface throughout the cat's life, push toward the center. The lens also loses water as it ages. These changes lead to the formation of a bluish haze seen on the lens behind the cornea in older cats. Usually this does not interfere with vision and does not need to be treated. This condition, called nuclear sclerosis, should be distinguished from a cataract.

Treatment: A cataract is significant only when it impairs vision. Blindness can be corrected by removing the lens (cataract extraction) and replacing it with an artificial one. There are three general techniques for cataract extraction: extracapsular lens extraction (ECLE), intracapsular lens extraction (ICLE), and phacofragmentation (also called phacoemulsification or "phaco" for short). ECLE is rarely done, and only if the lens is too hard for phacofragmentation. ICLE is mainly done for lenses that have slipped from their normal location. Phacofragmentation is the preferred technique of most veterinary ophthalmologists for cataract removal. This technique uses ultrasonic waves to liquefy the lens, to suck out lens fragments, and to irrigate the eye. An artificial lens can then be put in the eye to restore semi-normal vision. If the lens is not replaced, there is a loss of visual acuity because the lens is not present to focus light on the retina.

Cataract surgery tends to be reserved for cats with cataracts in both eyes who are having problems getting around. Before this surgery is done, the cat needs to have a thorough eye exam, including an electroretinogram (ERG) to verify that the retina and the rest of the eye are normal, so that removing the damaged lens will actually restore vision. If the retina is damaged, it makes no sense to put the cat through this surgery.

GLAUCOMA

Glaucoma is caused by an increase in fluid pressure within the eyeball. Normally, there is a continuous (although very slow) exchange of fluid between the eyeball and the venous circulation. Anything that upsets this delicate balance can cause a buildup of pressure and produce a hard, enlarging eye. When pressure within the eye becomes greater than the arterial blood pressure, arterial blood cannot enter the eye to nourish the retina.

Inflammations and infections within the eye are the most common causes of acquired or secondary glaucoma in cats (see *Uveitis*, page 199). Other causes are cataracts, eye injuries, and cancers within the eye. A lens that is out of alignment may block the outflow of aqueous fluid. Primary (congenital) glaucoma is rare but has been observed in Persians, Siamese, and domestic shorthairs.

A cat suffering from acute glaucoma exhibits mild to moderate tearing and squinting and there is a slight redness to the white of the eye. The affected pupil is slightly larger than the opposite pupil. The eye is painful when gently pressed and feels harder than the other eye. As fluid pressure increases to greater than 30 to 50 mmHg, the eye becomes noticeably larger and the surface begins to bulge. (Normal pressure is 10 to 20 mmHg.) In time, the retina is damaged. The lens may be completely or partially pushed out of alignment. This entire sequence can occur suddenly or over a matter of weeks.

To diagnose glaucoma, intraocular pressure is measured with a technique called tonometry, which uses an instrument placed on the surface of the eye. The interior of the eye must also be examined, and a procedure called gonioscopy checks the flow of fluid out of the eye. Ultrasound may also be used to evaluate the eye.

Every effort should be made to distinguish glaucoma from conjunctivitis and uveitis, both of which produce similar signs. It is critical to begin treatment of glaucoma before irreversible injury occurs to the retina. Some permanent vision may be lost before the disease is discovered.

Treatment: Acute glaucoma may require emergency hospitalization. Veterinarians use various topical and oral drugs to lower intraocular pressure. Mannitol may be used in the short term to lower pressure.

Maintenance drugs are used for chronic glaucoma. These might include carbonic anhydrase inhibitors topically or orally and, possibly, pilocarpine. Any underlying eye disorder should be treated. Treatment is for the life of the cat.

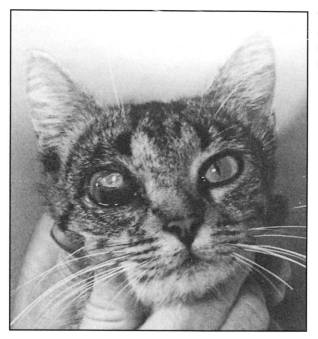

The bulging eye of chronic glaucoma, complicated by a corneal ulcer.

Failure to respond to medical management may suggest surgery is needed, if there is a potential to retain some vision. Surgery may try to decrease the fluid production or increase the rate of fluid escape from the eye, this reducing pressure within the eye. For an eye that is blind and painful, the best approach is to remove the entire eye. A prosthesis can be inserted for appearance.

It is felt that some glaucoma damage results from secondary nerve damage due to the cellular chemical glutamate. Glutamate is an amino acid and is extremely toxic to the retinal ganglion cells; basically, it overstimulates them. Drugs that block glutamate receptors, and calcium channel blockers—used to protect the retina and optic nerve—are being studied for possible therapy.

UVEITIS

Uveitis is an inflammation of the inner pigmented structures of the eye. It is one of the most common inner eye conditions of cats, in part because a number of feline infectious diseases can involve the eye. They include feline leukemia (FeLV), feline infectious peritonitis (FIP, especially the granulomatous form), feline immunodeficiency virus (FIV), toxoplasmosis, herpesvirus, bartonella, systemic fungal infections, and the larvae of roundworms and heartworms. Uveitis may also be caused by penetrating eye injuries, bloodborne bacterial infections, and eye tumors. Uveitis is a serious disorder that can lead to blindness.

Uveitis is painful. The cat squints, and the affected eye waters. Other distinguishing signs of uveitis are surface redness and a small pupil. When you push with your finger against the eyelid, the eye is tender and feels like a soft grape. Some cats will show a clouding or edema of the cornea and there may be new blood vessels growing across the cornea. Blood or *pus* may leak into the front area of the eye. The accumulation of inflammatory cells may cause the iris to stick to the lens and lead to secondary glaucoma as a result of scar-type damage.

Cats with acute uveitis will have low intraocular pressure. This can especially be seen when the pressures of both eyes are compared. *Serology tests* and *titers* may be done to look for the inciting cause.

Treatment: Any underlying infectious or systemic illness should be treated. Corticosteroids reduce intraocular inflammation, but they are used with caution to prevent exacerbating an underlying systemic illness. Eyedrops such as atropine may be used to dilate the pupil and relieve pain. Treatment must be administered under veterinary supervision. Antibiotics may be given as well to help battle infections. Clindamycin is often used, as well as azithromycin, to treat toxoplasmosis or bartonella.

Chronic uveitis that goes untreated may be associated with the development of intraocular cancer.

RETINAL DISEASES

The retina is a thin, delicate membrane that lines the back of the eye and is actually an extension of the optic nerve. In a healthy cat, the retina receives light, processes it, and passes it on to the brain. If the cells are damaged, it can't send anything on. In a cat with retinal disease, the retinal cells are damaged and the eye is no longer able to properly transmit information regarding the light it receives. The visual image may be blurred, and part or all of the visual field may be blacked out.

Retinal diseases usually begin with the loss of night vision. When this happens, the cat hesitates to go out at night or won't jump onto or off furniture in a darkened room.

Progressive Retinal Atrophy

Progressive retinal atrophy is the degeneration of the retinal cells over time. In cats, retinal diseases usually are not caused by genetic influences, although a hereditary form of progressive retinal atrophy occurs in Persians, Abyssinians, and possibly Siamese. The mode of inheritance appears to be autosomal recessive.

Treatment: Progressive retinal atrophy has no treatment and eventually leads to blindness. It is hoped that a genetic screening test will be available in the future so breeders can avoid this problem.

The dilated pupils of a blind cat with advanced retinal disease.

Retinitis

Retinitis is a disease in which inflammation of the retina leads to degeneration and destruction of the light receptors. It occurs in association with toxoplasmosis, feline infectious peritonitis, lymphoma, cryptococcosis, and systemic fungus infections. It may also occur as a consequence of hypertension, or eye injury, or for unknown reasons. In these cases, the retina may actually become detached from the back of the eye. High blood pressure or hypertension is one of the most common causes of this condition. The hypertension is usually associated with hyperthyroidism and/or renal failure. Immediate medical treatment may stop the progression of this detachment.

Treatment: The outlook for useful vision depends on the cause and extent of retinal damage at the time of diagnosis. Medical diseases, such as hypertension, are treatable. Control or cure can prevent further damage. If caught early, retinal detachments caused by trauma may sometimes be repaired—or at least, further damage can be prevented. This requires referral to a veterinary specialist.

Central Retinal Degeneration

A dietary deficiency of the essential amino acid taurine produces a type of retinal degeneration in cats that initially involves the central portion of the retina. Because this is the area where the cat sees best, he is unable to see stationary objects well. The cat retains some peripheral vision and thus is able to detect moving objects seen at the periphery. This dietary cause is rarely seen now, since cat food manufacturers have added supplemental taurine to most cat foods. (For more information on taurine deficiency see *Amino Acids*, page 495.)

The antibiotic enrofloxacin is also associated with a type of retinal degeneration. Some cases improve if the medication is stopped right away, but not all.

Treatment: Taurine deficiency is slowly progressive, but correcting the diet stops the process.

6

THE EARS

Hearing is one of a cat's keenest senses. Cats can hear sounds too faint for humans to detect. They can also hear noises pitched at a much higher frequency—even beyond the range of the dog. Cat hearing covers the range from 45 to 64,000 Hz. A cat's whole head turns toward the source of a sound. The ears move forward and backward or in a half circle to locate the angle of direction, and can move independently of one another. The eyes also focus in the direction of the sound. This combination of senses makes cats the excellent hunters they are, especially in dim light.

Cats also have a remarkable sense of equilibrium, due to a mechanism in the inner ear that enables the body to adjust with great speed and agility. When falling from a height in an upside-down position, cats can right themselves to land on their feet in less than two seconds. This is done by first rotating the forequarters to orient to the ground, and then rotating the hindquarters. With the aid of a strong tail, the body twists to bring all four feet down together for the landing. However, the fact that cats can land on all four feet does not mean they can fall from great heights without sustaining an injury. Veterinarians with urban practices report that falls from a height are a major cause of injury and death for cats. Be sure to keep screens on all your windows, because cats may jump with little or no regard for heights.

Along with hearing, cats' ears are also good indicators of mood. Ears turned sideways or back a little often indicate a cat who is getting agitated. A cat with ears flat back against the head is frightened, defensive, or aggressive. Ears forward and up mean the cat is relaxed. Ears swiveling show a cat is interested and listening.

Structure of the Ears

The ear is divided into three parts. The outer ear is composed of the ear flap (pinna) and ear canal (external auditory canal). The middle ear is made up of

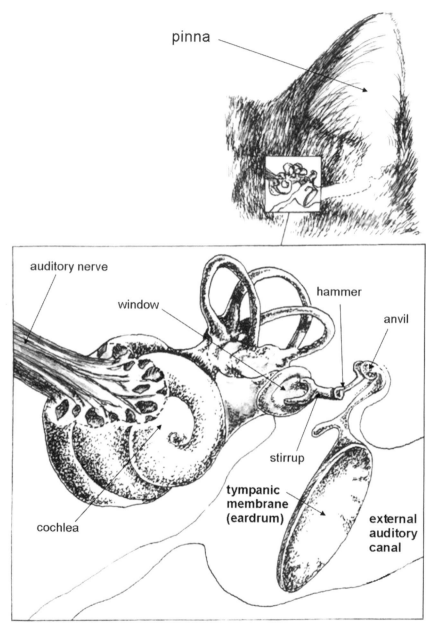

The anatomy of the ear.

the eardrum (tympanic membrane) and the auditory bones or ossicles. The inner ear contains the cochlea, bony labyrinth, and auditory nerves.

Sound, which is really vibrations of air, is collected by the pinna and directed down the ear canal to the eardrum. Movements of the eardrum are

The ear shape of the Scottish Fold is caused by a mutation of a single dominant gene that is linked to a skeletal abnormality. Breeding partners must be selected carefully.

transmitted by a chain of small bones, the ossicles, to the bony canals of the inner ear. The ossicles are the hammer, the stirrup, and the anvil.

The cochlea is a system of fluid-filled tubes in which waves are created by movements of the ossicles. Here, the waves are transformed into nerve impulses and carried via the auditory nerve to the brain.

Most cats' ears are carried erect—what's called a prick ear. The skin on the back of the pinna is covered by hair and, like the rest of the body, is susceptible to the same diseases. Skin on the inside is pale pink, occasionally with spots of pigment. A small amount of brown, waxy secretion in the ear canals is normal.

When a kitten is born, her ear canals are closed and it's likely that kittens are deaf (although we don't know for sure). They begin to open at 5 to 8 days. Kittens become oriented to sound at 13 to 16 days. They learn to recognize or distinguish between different sounds at 3 to 4 weeks. Knowing this sequence can help you to judge whether your kitten's hearing is developing normally.

In a few cat breeds, the ears are not erect. The American Curl is a breed with ears that curl back at the tips. The kittens are born prick eared, but by about 4 months of age you can tell if the ears will curl and just how much.

The ears of Scottish Folds fold down at about 3 to 4 weeks of age. In this breed, it is important never to breed cats with folded ears to other cats with folded ears. That's because the genetic mutation that caused folded ears is linked to gene that causes a skeletal abnormality. This is an incomplete dominant trait, and if you breed two carriers, at about 4 to 6 months of age a degenerative joint disease will become apparent in the offspring. The lower joints in the legs of these kittens will be fused and their tails will be shortened and stiff. If you breed a cat with prick ears to a cat with fold ears, you avoid this problem.

Your cat has an ear problem if you notice ear scratching, repeated head shaking, a bad odor emanating from the ear, or large amounts of waxy discharge or pus draining. In a younger cat, the most likely cause is ear mites, but other diseases of the ears (such as allergies) do occur. Diseases of the middle ear cause head tilt and the loss of hearing. Diseases of the inner ear affect the balance center. The cat wobbles, circles, falls and rolls over, and has trouble righting herself. The cat may show rapid jerking movements of the eyes (*nystagmus*).

Basic Ear Care

If you bathe your cat, prevent water from getting into her ears by inserting cotton balls at the opening of the ear canals. Wet ear canals can predispose a cat to ear infections. If your cat has been in a fight, check the ears for any cuts or bites that may need to be treated (see *The Pinna*, page 209).

Routine ear cleaning is not required. Some wax is necessary to maintain the health of the tissues. However, ears should be cleaned when there is an

To clean very dirty ears, instill an ear-cleaning solution and massage the base of the ear.

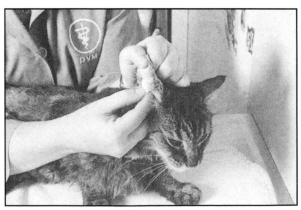

Gently wipe out the ear with a cotton ball.

excessive amount of wax, dirt, or debris. For small amounts of waxy debris, a damp cotton ball or a cotton-tipped swab works well. Many cats tolerate this well if you sit down and hold them in your lap, facing away.

Do not put any cleaning solution in the ear unless you are confident the eardrum is intact.

To clean a very dirty ear, apply a few drops of warm mineral oil, olive oil, a dilute vinegar solution (three drops white vinegar in 1 ounce [30 ml] of water), or a special ear-cleaning solution from your veterinarian (such as Oti-Clens, Epi Otic, Clear X Cleansing Solution, Virbac, Malacetic Otic, or Tris-EDTA products) to the *external* ear canal and massage the base of the ear to loosen dirt, excess wax, and debris. Then gently wipe out the ear with a cotton ball.

Ear folds and creases at the base of the ear are best cleaned with a cotton-tipped swab moistened with oil or a cleaning solution. *Do not* direct the applicator into the ear canal because this will push the debris deeper into the canal and pack it against the eardrum. *Do not* swab out or irrigate your cat's ears with ether, alcohol, or other irritating solvents, all of which cause pain and swelling of the tissues.

Many cats object to ear cleaning and should be gently restrained, as described in *Handling and Restraint* (page 2). Try to make this a positive experience by staying calm and quiet and giving your cat a treat or some play time right after the ear cleaning. Many cats hold their ears in strange positions right after a cleaning.

HOW TO APPLY EAR MEDICATIONS

Ear medications should be applied only to clean ear canals. Discuss with your veterinarian what cleaning solution will work best with the medications your cat needs.

Some ear medications come in tubes with long nozzles; others come with medicine droppers. Restrain your cat so the tip of the applicator does not accidentally lacerate the skin of the ear canal. Fold the ear flap back over the

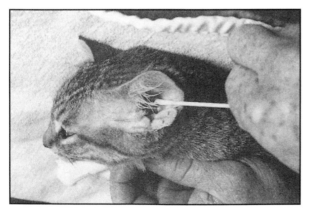

Clean folds and creases with a cotton-tipped swab. Do not insert the swab into the ear canal.

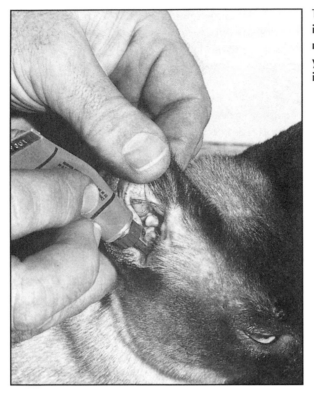

To apply medication, insert the tip of the nozzle only as far in as you can see and squeeze in a small amount.

top of the head. Insert the end of the nozzle or medicine dropper into the ear canal only as far as you can see. Unless directed otherwise by your veterinarian, squeeze in a small amount of ointment or instill three to four drops of liquid.

Because most infections involve the deep, horizontal part of the ear canal, it is important for the medicine to reach this area. Massage the cartilage at the base of the ear for 20 seconds to disperse the medicine. The massaging will produce a squishy sound. Use a cotton ball to wipe any excess medication off the inside of the ear flap.

Antibiotic Ear Medications

Antibiotic medications commonly used to treat external ear infections include Panolog, Tresaderm, Gentocin Otic, Otomax, Mometamax, Baytril, and others. Others are available that contain different antibiotics or combinations of medications. All ear preparations can damage the middle ear or inner ear if the eardrum has been ruptured. Medications should not be put into ears until a veterinarian has examined the cat and determined that the eardrums are intact. Sometimes the cat will need to be sedated by your veterinarian so that the ear canal can be thoroughly cleaned of wax and debris.

Problems associated with the prolonged use of antibiotic ear preparations include allergic skin reaction, the development of antibiotic resistant strains of bacteria, and overgrowth of yeast and fungi. Follow the directions of the manufacturer about frequency of application. Expect to see improvement in two to three days. If not, consult your veterinarian because further delay can be harmful.

The Pinna

The pinna is an erect flap of cartilage covered on both sides by a layer of skin. It is fragile and easily damaged. The signs of an outer or external ear problem are discharge, shaking the head, ear scratching, and tenderness about the ear. A cat with an itchy ear ailment may scratch so vigorously that the skin becomes severely abraded. The abraded skin may then become infected, leading to an abscess. Attempts to treat the traumatized pinna may not be successful until the initiating cause of the itching and scratching has been identified and treated.

BITES AND LACERATIONS

Cats give and receive painful bites and scratches that are prone to severe infection. The pinna is a frequent site for such injuries. Some occur during mating.

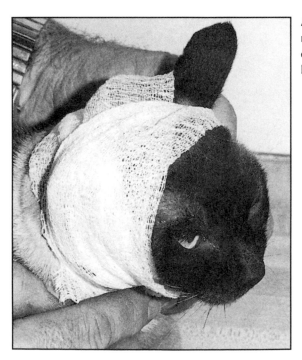

An ear bandage may be required to protect an ear injured by a bite or laceration.

Treatment: All cat bite wounds should be carefully cleaned and inspected. Trim the hair from the edges of the wound. Bathe the wound with a Betadine or a chlorhexidine wound cleansing solution to remove dried blood and foreign debris. Be careful to keep all solution out of your cat's eyes. Omit this step if there is fresh bleeding.

Then apply a topical antibiotic ointment, such as triple antibiotic ointment or Neosporin. Try to distract your cat for a minute or two after applying any ointment so that she does not immediately rub or lick it off.

Because claws and teeth produce deep wounds and punctures and almost always inject bacteria into the wound, injuries caused by cat fights are often complicated by abscesses. Some can be prevented by giving your cat a course of antibiotics (often a penicillin such as amoxicillin). Do not give any antibiotics without first consulting your veterinarian.

Large lacerations and those involving the margin of the ear or the cartilage should receive veterinary attention. Surgical repair is necessary to prevent scarring and deformity. With bite wounds from unknown animals, discuss rabies with your veterinarian.

SWOLLEN PINNA

Sudden swelling about the ear is due to an *abscess* or a *hematoma*. Abscesses are more common. They are caused by an infection of the skin of the ear and often occur after a fight. Severe scratching at the ear may produce skin infection and abscess. Abscesses are usually found below the ear. They are discussed on page 164.

A hematoma is a blood clot under the skin of the pinna. It, too, can be caused by trauma or by violent head shaking and scratching at the ear. Look for an itchy ear disorder, such as ear mites, or an infection involving the ear canal—which should be treated along with the hematoma.

Treatment: Blood should be expressed from a hematoma by a veterinarian, to prevent scarring and deformity of the ear when the clot retracts. Removing it with a needle and syringe usually is not effective, because serum accumulates in the pocket formerly occupied by the blood clot and the pocket fills again. Surgery, the treatment of choice, involves removing a window of skin to provide open and continuous drainage. A drain may be placed through the area. Sutures are then made through both sides of the ear to pull the skin down and eliminate the pocket. Expect your cat to need to wear a BiteNot collar or an Elizabethan collar to prevent her from pawing at the ear.

EAR ALLERGIES

Allergies are typified by itching and skin redness without drainage. Both food allergies and atopy (inhaled allergies) may first present as an otitis. They can

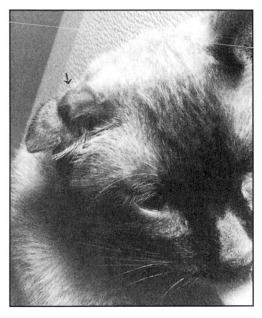

Hematoma of the pinna, caused by violent head shaking. Note the swelling and deformity.

affect the skin of the ear canals as well as the pinna. An allergic ear problem can closely resemble a yeast infection or may have a yeast infection secondary to an allergy, so check with your veterinarian before applying any medication at home. For more information, see *Allergies*, page 151.

Treatment: An allergic reaction is best treated with a 1 percent hydrocortisone cream, such as Cortaid. Because of the intense itching, the cat may traumatize her ears and set the stage for a secondary bacterial infection.

FROSTBITE

Frostbite affects the ears of outdoor cats in severe winter weather, particularly when there is high wind and humidity. The ears are especially susceptible because they are exposed and only lightly protected by fur, especially at the tips. After having been frozen, the ear tips of dark-coated or Siamese cats may become rounded and develop white hairs at their tips. Drooping of the pinna is another condition that follows prolonged exposure to wind and cold.

Treatment: Treatment of frostbite is discussed on page 21.

SUNBURN

Cats with white ears are particularly susceptible to sunburn. Hair is lost from the tips and edges of the ears. Then the underlying skin becomes reddened. Finally, because the cat will scratch at the ear, the skin breaks down and forms an open sore or ulcer. The condition grows worse with each passing summer.

In time, a squamous cell skin cancer is likely to develop in the ulcerated area. Other tumors also can grow on the skin of the ears. Most are malignant. Any growth on the ear is a cause for concern. Have it examined by your veterinarian.

Treatment: A cat with this condition should ideally be kept indoors. Keeping her inside only on sunny days does not address the entire problem, because the sun's ultraviolet rays, which are responsible for skin damage, can penetrate clouds. If a cat must be outdoors, she should only be let out at night. Sun block can also be applied to the ears. Try to distract the cat after applying it so she doesn't immediately groom it off. But be aware that she will eventually groom it off, so this is a less-than-ideal solution.

Surgery is indicated for a nonhealing sore. When the ear tips are ulcerated, they are rounded off surgically and removed. Small ulcers can be excised. Large ulcers, which are often malignant, may require removal of the entire pinna.

PARASITES

Head mange is caused by the head mite called *Notoedres cati*, which lives on the skin about the head and ears of cats. Itching is the predominant sign. Clean ear canals help distinguish this condition from an ear mite infection caused by *Otodectes cynotis*. Treatment is discussed on page 141.

Fleas frequently feed on the skin of the pinna. You may be able to see the actual fleas on the ears or elsewhere on the body, or you may see only black, crumbly crusts of dried blood. Treatment is discussed on page 138.

The Ear Canal

Signs of irritation or infection in the ear canals are discharge, shaking the head, and scratching and pawing at the ear. Common causes are listed here.

EAR MITES

Ear mite infection is one of the most common health problems seen in cats. Ear mites (*Otodectes cynotis*) are tiny insects that live in the ear canal and feed by piercing the skin. Mites are prolific. Kittens can be infected by their mothers while still in the nest. Suspect ear mites when *both* ears are affected.

The most frequent sign is intense itching, characterized by scratching and violent head shaking. This is worse if the cat suffers from an allergic reaction to the mites as well as simple irritation from them. You will see a dry, crumbly, dark brown, waxy discharge when you look into the ears. The discharge looks like coffee grounds and may be foul smelling. Constant scratching at the ears

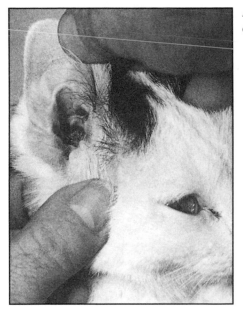

A dark brown, dry, waxy, crumbly discharge is typical of ear mites.

can cause raw areas, along with scabs and loss of hair around the ears. The initial problem may be complicated by a chronic bacterial infection.

Ear mites can be identified by your veterinarian by removing some earwax from a fold or crease with a cotton-tipped applicator and examining it under a magnifying glass, against a black background. Mites are white specks, about the size of the head of a pin, that move.

Demodex cati is another mite that can also affect the ears. Waxy debris is present; the mites can be found by examining a swab from the ears.

Ear mites can leave the ear canals and travel over the body. They are highly contagious among cats, house rabbits, ferrets, and dogs, but almost never humans. If mites are discovered on one pet, all pets in the household should be treated.

Treatment: Ear mites are a serious problem, and are deeply distressing and uncomfortable for your cat. They can crawl deep into the ear canals, where they may be difficult to treat. They can also lead to secondary infections of the ears. It is therefore very important to treat all cases of ear mites promptly and thoroughly.

Do not begin treatment until your veterinarian has positively identified ear mites as the cause of the symptoms. This is because other ear ailments can be complicated by using ear mite medications.

Clean the ears as described on page 206. This is *essential*. Dirty ear canals contain wax and cellular debris that shelters mites and makes it difficult for ear medications to destroy them.

Medicate the ears using a medication chosen by your veterinarian that is effective against mites. Some common ones are Nolvamite, Mitaclear, and

Tresaderm. Follow your veterinarian's instructions for dosage and frequency. It is very important to complete the recommended course of treatment, because a new crop of mites will reinfect your cat if the treatment is stopped too soon.

Ivermectin has been used successfully to treat ear mites. It is given as a single subcutaneous injection or with topical drops into the ear. Selamectin (Revolution) is also sometimes used for ear mites. *Demodex cati* mites are generally treated with ivermectin or lime-sulfur dips.

During treatment, mites can escape from the ear canals and temporarily take up residence elsewhere on the cat, causing itching and scratching. It is important to treat the *entire* cat with a topical insecticide preparation, as recommended by your veterinarian (see A *Suggested Flea-Control Program*, page 138). Since most cats sleep with their tail curled up next to their ears, be sure to treat the tail as well.

Clip the cat's nails to minimize injuries from scratching at the ear.

BACTERIAL OTITIS EXTERNA

Bacterial infections in the ear canal are frequently caused by scratches to the skin or cat bites. Some begin in an ear canal that contains excessive amounts of wax, cellular debris, or foreign material. Ear mite infections are often the cause of bacterial otitis.

Signs of an infected ear canal are shaking the head, scratching at the affected ear, and an unpleasant odor. The cat may tilt or carry her head down on the painful side and exhibit tenderness when the ear is touched. Examination reveals redness and swelling of the skin folds of the ear canal. There may be an excess amount of wax or a *purulent* discharge. There is often an unpleasant odor associated with the discharge.

An otoscope is needed to examine the deeper portions of the ear canal and look for a foreign body or other cause of chronic infection. This is best left to a qualified professional—your veterinarian or a veterinary technician.

Bacterial infections that progress over a long period produce thickening and reddening of the ear canal with considerable discomfort and pain. Treatment is prolonged. Inflammatory polyps and tumorlike masses may develop and block the ear passages. Surgery then becomes necessary to open the ear and promote drainage.

Treatment: The first step is to determine the cause. Mild cases—those without excessive discharge but perhaps associated with a dirty ear or the buildup of wax—may be treated at home after they have been diagnosed by a veterinarian.

Clean the ears as described on page 206. Remove crusts and serum with a cotton ball soaked in an ear-cleaning solution obtained from your veterinarian, being careful not to push the debris deeper into the canal. If there is a buildup of wax, instill a special wax-dissolving agent to soften the debris and make it easier to remove. Afterward, dry the ear canals with a cloth or cotton ball and apply an antibiotic ear medication, as described on page 207.

If the ear is extremely painful, you may need to leave your cat at the veterinary clinic for sedation and a thorough cleaning. A swab of the discharge may be examined under the microscope to look for the cause of the problem. Also, your veterinarian may take a sample for a culture and sensitivity test, especially if your cat has recurrent infections, to determine the best choice of antibiotic therapy. Some cats will need oral antibiotics as well as topical ones.

Clip the cat's nails to minimize injuries from scratching at the ear.

YEAST OR FUNGAL OTITIS EXTERNA

The prolonged use of topical antibiotics alters the natural bacterial flora in the ear canal, which improves conditions for the growth of yeast and fungi. A yeast otitis may therefore develop as a secondary problem in a cat with a long-standing bacterial or ear mite infection, or a food allergy. *Malassezia pachydermatis* is the most common culprit, including in cases of otitis related to food allergies and atopy.

Signs and symptoms of a yeast infection are not nearly as pronounced as the infection caused by bacteria. The ear is inflamed and painful, but less so. Sometimes the ear will simply be red and moist in appearance. The discharge is dark and waxy but not *purulent*. A rancid odor is characteristic.

Yeast and fungus infections tend to recur, and treatment is often prolonged.

Treatment: Your veterinarian may want to do a swab to look at cells from the ear to determine the exact cause of the problem and to determine whether the problem has cleared, because stopping treatment beforehand (not just at the remission of signs) frequently results in relapse. Topical medications may need to be supplemented with oral medications.

Treatment is similar to the treatment for bacterial otitis, except that an antifungal agent (such as nystatin or thiabendazole) is used. Panolog, which contains nystatin, is effective against the yeast *Candida albicans*. Tresaderm, which contains thiabendazole, is effective against *Candida* and most other common yeast invaders. Miconazole solutions are commonly prescribed as well.

FOREIGN BODIES OR TICKS IN THE EAR CANAL

Foreign bodies in the ear canal cause irritation and subsequent infection. Plant material (grass seeds or awns) is usually the problem; it first clings to hair surrounding the ear opening, and then drops down into the canal. Ticks can adhere to the skin of a cat's ear, or crawl into the ear canal.

Ears should be examined after a cat has been prowling in tall grass, weeds, and brush, especially if the cat is shaking her head and/or pawing at her ear.

Treatment: Foreign bodies in the ear canal should be removed by a veterinarian. When a foreign body is near the opening, it can be removed with blunt-nosed tweezers. Do not attempt this at home. Foreign bodies deep in the ear canal must be removed with special instruments. This is a sensitive area and requires anesthesia.

If a tick is easily accessible because it is on the pinna, it can be removed as described in *Ticks* (see page 145). Ticks in the ear canal should be removed by a veterinarian.

EAR POLYPS

Ear polyps are growths that are primarily seen in cats between 1 and 4 years of age, although cats of any age can develop them. They may be related to chronic inflammation or be the result of a developmental defect. Ear polyps often start in the middle ear and either grow out through the eardrum to the external ear canal or internally to the auditory canal. Any cat with recurrent ear infections should be carefully checked for an ear polyp.

Cats will shake their heads and sometimes have a discharge from the ear. The ear may be quite painful. A head tilt and a raised third eyelid are other possible signs. Some cats will have multiple polyps or another one in the nose or throat, and those cats may have breathing problems.

Treatment: Polyps are removed surgically, with care taken to remove the entire growth; otherwise, recurrence is common. Follow-up with corticosteroids may help reduce the chances of recurrence. Rarely, nerve damage will remain after removal. However, most cats have a complete recovery.

CERUMINOUS GLAND PROBLEMS

Benign ceruminous (wax) gland cysts are not uncommon in cats' ears. These cysts appear as dark lesions throughout the ear. They may cluster and look like a bunch of grapes. If these start to block the ear canal, they should be removed; otherwise they do not generally cause a problem.

Cats are also susceptible to ceruminous gland tumors in their ears, which are often malignant adenocarcinomas. These need to be distinguished from ear polyps.

Otitis Media

This condition, a middle ear infection, is not common in cats. Most cases result from an external ear infection that ruptures the eardrum. Tonsillitis and mouth and sinus infections can travel to the middle ear through the Eustachian tube, a passage that connects the middle ear to the back of the throat. Rarely, bacteria gain entrance through the bloodstream.

The first signs of otitis media are often masked by an ear canal infection that precedes it. However, as the middle ear becomes involved, the cat shows evidence of more severe pain, crouching low and tilting her head down on the affected side. The head is held as still as possible. The gait is often unsteady because balance is affected.

An otoscopic examination by a veterinarian may show perforation or loss of the eardrum. X-rays may show bone involvement. The face may droop on the affected side if the nerve that crosses the surface of the eardrum is involved. The third eyelid may be raised. Middle ear infections can extend to involve the inner ear.

Treatment: All infections of the middle ear should be treated by a veterinarian. Antibiotics, both oral and topical, may be required, but no cleaning or medicating should be done until the eardrum is examined.

Otitis Interna

Otitis interna is an inner ear infection—often one that started out as a middle ear infection. Suspect otitis interna if your cat vomits, staggers, or falls toward the affected side, circles toward that side, or shows rhythmic jerking movements of her eyeballs. These are signs of vestibular disease.

Most ear medications are capable of causing labyrinthitis and some permanent ear damage if they make direct contact with the sensitive structures of the inner ear. For this reason, the ears should not be flushed or medicated without first having your veterinarian examine the cat's ear canals to be sure the eardrums are not punctured or ruptured.

Other disorders that produce signs like those of an inner ear infection include brain tumor, drug intoxication, poisoning, and idiopathic vestibular syndrome (see *Vestibular Disorders*, page 342). The idiopathic syndrome is the more common. You should suspect one of these disorders when a cat shows signs of labyrinthitis without a prior ear infection.

Treatment: Infections of the inner ear should be treated by a veterinarian. Surgery may be required in cases of chronic and recurrent infections that don't respond to medical treatment. In rare cases, the ear canal itself may need to be removed.

Deafness

Some cats are born without the ability to hear because of developmental defects in the hearing apparatus. Cats may also be deaf in just one ear. Congenital deafness occurs most often in white cats with blue eyes, and is the result of an incomplete autosomal dominant gene. However, not all cats with blue eyes are deaf, and that includes not all white cats with blue eyes.

Longhaired cats with blue eyes have a higher risk of deafness than shorthaired cats with blue eyes. White cats with the Siamese dilution gene may have blue eyes with no hearing impairment. Still, white cats have a higher risk of deafness than other cats in general, and blue-eyed cats also have a higher risk of deafness—even if they have only one blue eye. *Congenitally deaf cats should not be bred.*

The table below lists the common cat breeds that have the white coat pigment gene and are therefore at higher risk for congenital deafness. This risk applies only to white cats of the breeds listed.

Common Breeds with the White Coat Pigment Gene	
American Shorthair	Manx
American Wirehair	Norwegian Forest Cat
British Shorthair	Oriental Shorthair
Cornish Rex	Persian
Devon Rex	Ragdoll
Exotic Shorthair	Scottish Fold
Maine Coon Cat	Turkish Angora

There have not been extensive studies on deafness in cats. If you suspect your cat is deaf, it would be beneficial to contact George Strain, PhD, at the veterinary school at Louisiana State University (strain@lsu.edu), who is a leading deafness expert.

Cats can be tested for deafness using the brainstem auditory evoked response (BAER) test. This test can be done at most veterinary colleges and some veterinary referral centers. Hearing is tested using an electroencephalogram (EEG) to record the brain waves produced in response to sounds of different frequencies. If the brain wave pattern remains unchanged, the sound was not heard. A BAER test can tell if a cat has normal hearing, is deaf in both ears, or is deaf in just one ear. Some cats can be tested while awake, but most will need sedation.

GRADUAL HEARING LOSS

Loss of hearing can be caused by old age, middle ear infections, head injury, blockage of the ear canal by wax and debris, and by certain drugs and poisons. In particular, the antibiotics streptomycin, gentamicin, neomycin, and kanamycin, if used for long periods, can damage the auditory nerves, leading to deafness and signs of labyrinthitis.

Gradual loss of hearing occurs in some older cats. Elderly deaf cats, however, often retain their ability to hear high-pitched sounds beyond the range of human hearing.

It is difficult to tell if a cat is going deaf. The ability to hear must be judged by observing the cat's actions and how she uses her ears. Cats who hear well cock their heads and look toward a sound. The ears swivel to pinpoint the source of the sound. Accordingly, lack of attentiveness is one of the first indications that a cat is not hearing well. One way to test this is to make a loud noise while the cat is asleep. If the cat does not startle and wake up, you can assume there is a significant loss of hearing. Suddenly touching a sleeping deaf cat without a warning could result in a scratch or a bite as the cat is startled when she wakes up. Stamping on the floor will attract a deaf cat's attention, because she can feel the vibrations.

Deaf cats get along quite well. They use their senses of sight and smell and the tactile sensations transmitted through their whiskers to compensate for the hearing loss. However, deaf cats should *not* be allowed outside.

7

THE NOSE

The tip of the cat's nose forms a triangle of skin, the color of which depends on genetics and the cat's basic coloring. Cats' noses can vary in color from light pink or salmon to slate blue, brown, black, or freckled. Pink-skinned cats are more susceptible to a squamous cancer of the nose and ears, especially when they are exposed to the sun over long periods of time. A cat with a pink nose may temporarily develop a white nose after being in cold weather or getting excited. A white nose—for no explainable reason—may indicate anemia.

The environment can greatly influence whether a cat's nose is warm and dry or moist and cool. A warm, dry nose is often the sign of a healthy cat, but it could also mean that a cat is dehydrated or has a fever. Occasionally, the reverse is true; a sick cat may have a cool, moist nose because of the evaporation of a runny discharge. A runny nose is never normal for a cat.

On either side of the nose, cats have sensitive whiskers on their cheeks (they also have whiskers on the chin, above the eyes, and at the backs of the legs). A cat's whiskers are sensitive tactile organs that transmit complex information about prey and surroundings to nerve bundles beneath the skin. Whiskers are extremely sensitive as they are closely connected to the nervous system. Any damage to his whiskers will cause your cat discomfort. Whiskers should *never* be clipped or trimmed.

The nasal cavity is divided by a midline partition into two passages, one for each nostril. These passages open into the throat. The cat has two large frontal sinuses that are connected to the nasal passages. Because of their small size, the nasal passages of cats must be examined under sedation or anesthesia. (See page 231 for the anatomy of the nasal cavity.)

The nasal cavity is lined by a mucous membrane (called the *mucociliary blanket*), which is rich with blood vessels and nerves. This blanket is lined with *cilia* and traps bacteria and foreign irritants, acting as the first line of defense against infection. Dehydration or prolonged exposure to cold stops the motion of the cilia and thickens the layer of mucus, reducing the effectiveness of the mucociliary blanket. *Brachycephalic* cats—those with shortened faces,

Brachycephalic cats, such as this Himalayan, are more prone to respiratory infections because of their flattened nasal cavity.

such as Persians and Himalayans—are prone to respiratory infections because they have less area for this protective mucociliary blanket.

The cat has an additional scent mechanism that people do not have. The vomeronasal organ (also called Jacobson's organ) is located in the roof of the mouth just behind the incisors, and consists of two fluid-filled sacs that connect to the nasal cavity via the nasopalatine ducts. Opening his mouth slightly enables the cat to open up these ducts so air containing scent molecules can pass into the vomeronasal organ. The appearance of the cat as he brings air into this organ has sometimes been likened to a smile or a grimace. This behavior, called flehman, can be seen in kittens as early as 2 months old.

We are not entirely sure what this type of scenting mechanism is used for, but it is thought to be associated with detecting pheromones (substances that possess a scent and are excreted outside the body). Pheremones help a cat find a mate and are excreted by cats as they rub the sides of their face against objects. They are very important in many cat behaviors and in behavioral therapies.

Cats have a sense of smell that is more than 14 times more sensitive than ours. This is partly why some cats reject scented litter and other cats refuse to use anything but a pristine litter box.

In the cat, the sense of smell is used primarily for self-orientation (which includes recognizing threatening odors). It is fair to say that cats know their world primarily through smell. Scent is also important for stimulating the appetite. Consequently, nasal obstruction is almost always accompanied by loss of appetite. Cats are very sensitive to spoiled food, and their sense of smell helps tell them if food is even the least bit tainted.

Cats also rely on their sense of smell to detect prey when hunting, and to identify one another and their people. Cats greet each other by first smelling each other's faces and then the anal areas.

Cats have personal scent glands on their faces, chins, heads, and tails with a scent that is unique to each cat. These glands can be used to mark territory by scratching (which leaves scent via glands on their paws) and by rubbing their heads, faces, and tails on objects—including humans! They can also mark using urine.

Certain odors are uniquely attractive to cats. Catnip, often put in toys, is a variety of mint that acts as a stimulant and seems to cast a spell over cats. They will approach catnip, sniff it, then usually lick or chew it. Afterward, the cat rolls on the floor or rubs against furniture. The effect lasts but a few minutes, and then the cat is typically quite relaxed. Catnip sensitivity is hereditary and is age-based. Young kittens and about one-quarter of all adults cats are unaffected. Interestingly, all members of the feline family, including lions and tigers, have the same attraction to catnip.

Cats are also attracted to the odors of garlic and onion. These flavorings used to be added to pet foods to enhance their appeal, but we now know these foods can be toxic to cats. The odor of citrus fruits, on the other hand, is repugnant. This fact can be used to keep cats away from certain spots in the house.

Signs of Nasal Irritation

RHINITIS (NASAL DISCHARGE)

A discharge from your cat's nose that persists for several hours indicates a problem. It is important to recognize early signs of illness, because professional attention may be required.

- A watery discharge with sneezing is caused by local irritation or allergic rhinitis. It can also appear early on in a cat with a viral infection.
- A *mucoid* discharge is characteristic of viral respiratory disease complex.
- A thick yellow, *purulent*, or puslike discharge suggests bacterial infection.

Very often a discharge will start out as fluid but will progress to *mucoid* and then *purulent*. This may be due to a progression of various infectious agents.

A discharge from both nostrils, often accompanied by fever, loss of appetite, eye discharge, drooling, coughing, or sores in the mouth suggests a feline viral respiratory disease. When both nostrils are blocked by swollen membranes, the cat sniffles, breathes noisily, and may breathe through his mouth. Because cats avoid mouth breathing whenever possible, you may see this sign only when the cat exercises. Any cat who is breathing through the mouth should be examined by a veterinarian.

Foreign bodies usually cause a discharge from just one nostril. This discharge can range from bloody to purulent. Allergic rhinitis usually affects both nostrils and the discharge is often *serous*.

Tumors, fungal infections, and chronic bacterial infections erode the nasal membranes producing a blood-tinged or bloody discharge. One or both nostrils may be involved. Cryptococcus is the most common fungal infection in the nose of cats (see page 98). When there is blood in the discharge, the cat needs to see a veterinarian.

SNEEZING

Sneezing is one of the chief signs of nasal irritation in cats. It is a reflex that results from stimulation of the lining of the nose. If the cat sneezes off and on for a few hours but shows no other signs of illness, it is most likely a minor nasal irritation or allergy. Irritants such as dust, cigarette smoke, and pollens could stimulate sneezing.

Sneezing that persists all day long could be the first sign of feline viral respiratory disease, especially herpesvirus (see page 78) or rhinotracheitis (see page 78). A sudden bout of violent sneezing, along with head shaking and pawing at the nose, suggests a foreign body in the nose (see page 224).

Bacterial infections also produce bouts of sneezing and sniffling. These tend to become chronic and quickly become associated with a mucoid to purulent discharge. Prolonged and severe sneezing can lead to a nosebleed.

Human cold viruses do not affect cats. However, cats are afflicted by a number of viruses that produce symptoms much like those of the human cold. Also, the same conditions that make us susceptible to viruses also make cats susceptible to viruses. These include crowding, poor ventilation, and stress. If your

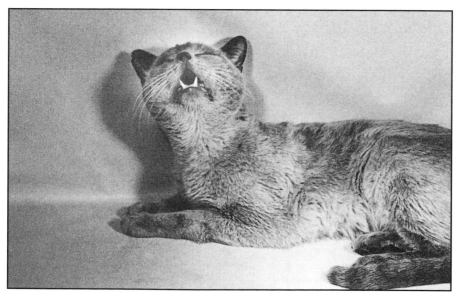

Sneezing is one of the leading signs of nasal irritation.

cat develops a runny nose along with a discharge from the eyes—and especially if the cat coughs, sneezes, and runs a slight fever—consult your veterinarian. (Also see chapter 10, *The Respiratory System*, and chapter 3, *Infectious Diseases*.)

LARYNGOSPASM (REVERSE SNEEZING)

Reverse sneezing is caused by a temporary spasm of the muscles of the larynx due to an accumulation of mucus at the back of the throat. This uncommon but harmless condition may be alarming because it sounds as if the cat has something caught in an air passage. During an attack, the cat violently pulls in air through his nose. This produces a loud snorting noise. The cat is perfectly normal before and after these attacks. Gently holding your hand over the cat's nose may help.

The Nasal Cavity

EPISTAXIS (NOSEBLEED)

Nosebleeds do not occur spontaneously in cats. However, the nasal cavity is extremely sensitive and bleeds easily when traumatized. Most nosebleeds are associated with a blow to the face that damages the nose. Others are due to an erosion of the nasal membrane caused by a foreign body, infection, tumor, or parasite. Rarely, a nosebleed may be a manifestation of a generalized clotting disorder such as that produced by a low platelet count, liver disease, or exposure to rodenticide anticoagulants.

When a cat's nose bleeds as a result of trauma, a midline fracture to the roof of the mouth may also have been incurred. Suspect this if the cat exhibits open-mouth breathing. This fracture can cause misalignment of the teeth, in which case the alignment must be adjusted and the teeth wired together to stabilize the upper jaw until it is healed. Any cat who has a nosebleed after trauma to the nose should be seen by a veterinarian.

Treatment: Nosebleeds may be accompanied by sneezing spasms that aggravate the bleeding. Keep the cat quiet and confined. Apply ice cubes or cold packs to the bridge of the nose to reduce blood flow and aid clotting. Slight bleeding usually subsides quickly, especially if the cat is kept quiet. Persistent bleeding is a cause for concern. Call your veterinarian.

FOREIGN BODY IN THE NOSE

Nasal foreign bodies are not common in cats because of the small size of their nasal passages. Nevertheless, pieces of straw, grass seeds and awns, fish bones, string, wood splinters, and, occasionally, insects can become wedged in the nose.

A noticeable sign is the sudden appearance of violent sneezing—at first continuous and later intermittent—along with pawing at the nose. The cat may tilt his head to the affected side, the eye on that side may squint, or the cat may drop his nose to the floor, extend his neck and try to breathe deeply. Repeated clearing of the throat suggests that the foreign object is trapped at the back of the nasal cavity. Some foreign bodies produce few signs and may go unnoticed.

Foreign objects that have been in the nose for a day or longer are associated with secondary bacterial infection and a *purulent* discharge (see *Nasal Infections*, page 226).

Cuterebra larvae can present as a purulent discharge from one nostril. These are fly larvae that are laid in the nasal passage, and the larvae then grow in that location. Anesthesia is often required to carefully remove the large larvae without damage to the cat's nose. You should not attempt this at home.

Treatment: If the foreign body is visible and close to the opening of the nostril, remove it with tweezers. Usually, however, it is lodged farther back. If you look down the throat, you may see a piece of string or grass bent over the soft palate projecting into the pharynx. Do not attempt to pull these out yourself. Go to your veterinarian.

If the foreign body is not visible and is not causing severe symptoms, the cat may yet expel it with time. If your cat is still uncomfortable after a couple of hours, though, you should contact your veterinarian. If the cat is unable to expel the foreign body, or if it is causing severe symptoms, the cat must be anesthetized by your veterinarian so they can locate and remove the object.

A cat with a foreign body that has been in the nose for a few days should be given prophylactic antibiotics to prevent secondary bacterial infection. Most foreign bodies do some tissue damage while in the nasal cavity, which opens the door for bacteria. The antibiotic should be continued for one to two weeks beyond the time when the foreign body was expelled or removed.

ALLERGIC RHINITIS (NASAL ALLERGIES)

Nasal allergies are characterized by periodic bouts of sneezing that last a short time and tend to recur day to day. Usually, there is a clear watery discharge from the nose. Most cases are caused by contact with environmental irritants and allergens (see *Allergies*, page 151). It makes sense to look for causes of this irritation. Cigarette smoke, dust, and pollen are common causes. A new carpet cleaner, deodorant powders or sprays, or even a new laundry soap could be the cause of nasal irritation. True nasal allergies are thought to be uncommon by most veterinary experts, and most cases that appear to be allergies are actually reactions to irritants.

Treatment: If possible, simply remove the source of the irritation. If that is not possible, this type of rhinitis responds well to medications that contain steroids and antihistamines. Never give your cat a medication containing a steroid without consulting your veterinarian. The antihistamines chlorpheniramine or cyproheptadine may be helpful, and your veterinarian may suggest anti-inflammatory eyedrops, which can be applied intranasally.

Chronic inflammation leads to lymphoplasmacytic rhinitis (an influx of *lymphocytes* into the nasal tissues), which is fairly common in cats. Systemic anti-inflammatory medications, such as meloxicam or corticosteroids, may be needed for control. These chronic inflammatory conditions may contribute to nasal lymphoma, which is the most common form of nasal cancer in cats.

NASAL INFECTIONS

Bacterial infections become established when the lining of the nose has been injured by a foreign body or nasal trauma or by a prior viral respiratory disease. Nasal infections can cause sneezing, nasal discharge, noisy breathing, and mouth breathing. When nasal congestion interferes with the ability to smell, the cat loses his appetite and stops eating.

On occasion, infection spreads to the nasal cavity from the frontal sinus (see *Sinusitis*, page 228). This is often associated with an infected tooth root. Nasal infections can also be secondary to tumors in the nasal cavity. The chief sign of bacterial involvement is a nasal discharge that is mucoid, creamy yellow, or puslike. A bloody discharge indicates deep involvement with ulceration of the nasal membrane. The cat may also have a fever and may not be eating well.

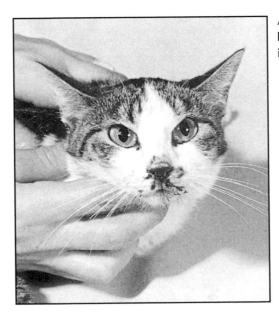

A thick, puslike discharge from both nostrils indicates nasal infection.

The feline viral respiratory disease complex (see page 78) is the most common cause of nasal infection. Eighty to 90 percent of cats who recover from an infection become carriers of herpesvirus or calicivirus. During periods of stress, immunity breaks down and the disease is reactivated. Calicivirus may be shed almost continuously, without clinical signs, which means the cat can infect other cats. In some cases, the nasal infection is mild; in others there is a chronic, *mucopurulent* discharge from the eyes and nose. (Also see chapter 3, *Infectious Diseases*.) Chlamydia (also called Chlamydophila) infections rank second to viruses for causing feline nasal infections.

Treatment: The objectives are to restore breathing, treat and prevent infection, and keep the cat as comfortable as possible. Isolate the ill cat if possible to prevent the spread of illness to other cats in the home. Gently wipe the nostrils with a moist cotton ball or soft, clean cloth to remove crusts and secretions. Unscented baby wipes also work well. Gently rub a drop of baby oil, aloe, or baby lotion on the nose to keep nostrils from cracking and drying. Vaporizers loosen secretions and help to restore the integrity of the mucociliary blanket. Even closing your cat in the bathroom while you shower can help loosen up nasal secretions.

Encourage the cat to eat by feeding his favorite aromatic foods. You can also add the juice from a can of tuna to your cat's regular food. Gently warming food to make the smell more pronounced can also encourage eating. Cyproheptadine is an antihistamine that has been used as an appetite stimulant; your veterinarian can prescribe it if necessary. Adding the amino acid lysine as a supplement may help decrease herpesvirus in the respiratory tract.

Shrink swollen nasal membranes by administering Afrin Children's Strength Nose Drops (.025 percent). Administer cautiously to prevent rebound congestion and excessive drying out of the mucous membranes, and use only under the guidance of your veterinarian. Administer one drop in one nostril the first day. The next day, administer one drop in the other nostril. Continue to alternate between nostrils because the medicine is absorbed and acts on both nostrils simultaneously. *Do not* use the decongestant for more than five days. Pediatric saline drops can provide some relief as well.

A *purulent* discharge signifies a bacterial infection and indicates the need for an antibiotic. When the discharge persists despite treatment, your veterinarian will need to do a culture and sensitivity test to select the most appropriate antibiotic.

In long-standing cases suspect a fungus. A fungus may be identified by examining a nasal swab under a microscope. Your veterinarian will do this for long-term or recurrent cases. Fungal infections require special long-term medications.

Some cats will need hospitalization for fluids and possibly feeding tubes to restore body condition. Kittens, in particular, can lose body condition and fluids quickly with an upper respiratory infection.

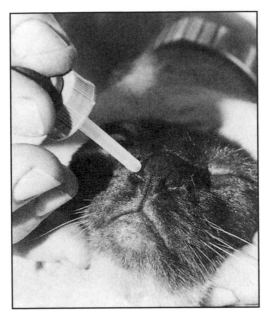

Nose drops help to shrink swollen membranes. This eases breathing and restores the cat's appetite.

Prevention: It is advisable to treat all nasal cavity injuries (such as those caused by a foreign body or a bite wound) with a prophylactic antibiotic to prevent bacterial infection.

SINUSITIS

The cat has two frontal and two sphenoid (wedge-shaped) sinuses. The small sphenoid sinuses don't often cause problems. But because respiratory infections are common in cats, secondary infections of the frontal sinuses occur with some frequency.

Signs of a chronic bacterial infection include a persistent, *purulent* nasal discharge, often just from one nostril, accompanied by frequent sneezing and sniffling. X-rays may show increased density of one sinus. The cat may appear to have a headache and sit with his eyes partially closed and his head hanging. Diminished appetite, another sign, can lead to rapid weight loss.

An abscessed tooth (usually the root of one of the top premolars) can lead to an abscessed frontal sinus. This produces a painful swelling below the eye. This problem is not common in cats.

Fungal infections (*cryptococcosis* and *aspergillosis*) are uncommon causes of sinus infection in the cat. These conditions are discussed in *Fungal Diseases* (page 98). With *cryptococcus* infection you may see facial deformities and skin ulcers on the nose. *Cryptococcus* is often associated with exposure to pigeons, even if it is simply the dust of pigeon excreta blowing in an open window.

Sinusitis can be suspected from the clinical signs and is usually confirmed by an X-ray.

Treatment: Treatment with an appropriate antibiotic, based on culture and sensitivity tests, is indicated. Sometimes this is not successful. A surgical procedure, which involves making an opening into the sinus through the skin to aid drainage, may be required. Flushing the sinus and leaving it open to heal is another treatment option.

NASAL TUMORS

Benign and malignant growths may arise in the nasal cavity and sinuses, usually on just one side. Early signs are sneezing and sniffling, eventually followed by obstructed breathing. Bleeding can occur through the affected nostril. Large tumors make one side of the face protrude more than the other. When tumors extend behind the eye, that eye will bulge. Such tumors are far advanced. Treatment generally is not possible.

Chronic rhinitis can predispose cats to nasal lymphoma.

Treatment: Radiation has been effective in treating many of these cancers in cats—often combined with surgery.

Nasopharyngeal Polyps

This is an uncommon upper respiratory condition that is unique to cats. Young cats are most often affected. These tumors block the eustachian tube at the back of the throat and produce middle ear infection (see *Otitis Media*, page 216).

Treatment: Treatment involves surgical removal.

THE MOUTH AND THROAT

The mouth is bounded on the front and sides by the lips and cheeks, above by the hard and soft palate, and below by the tongue and muscles of the floor of the mouth. Four pairs of salivary glands drain into the mouth.

The pharynx is a space formed by the nasal passages joining with the back of the mouth. Food is kept from going into the lungs by the epiglottis, a flap-like valve that closes off the larynx and the trachea when the cat swallows, sending food down the esophagus instead.

The average adult cat has 30 teeth. This is 2 fewer than humans and 12 fewer than dogs. Cats' teeth are designed for grasping, cutting, tearing, and shredding. The back teeth, like those in the front, are pointed and sharp. They are not designed to grind food. As a cat grasps a piece of meat with her front claws, she bites down on it with the four canine teeth (the fangs) in front, scissors the meat between her back teeth, and tears off a mouthful that is swallowed without chewing.

The surface of the cat's tongue has sharp hooks that are directed inward, toward the back of the throat. Hair clings to the rough tongue, making it an ideal comb for self-grooming.

The tongue will feel rough if your cat licks you. Unlike some animals, cats also are unlikely to lick their wounds extensively because the tongue's rough surface causes pain.

How to Examine the Mouth

Many mouth problems can be diagnosed by inspecting the lips, teeth, and oral cavity. However, a thorough examination of the mouth, especially if the cat is in pain, may require sedation—and so, of course, must be done by a veterinarian.

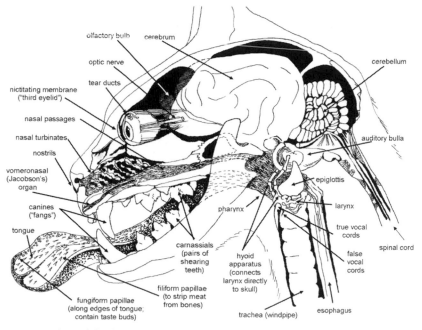

Cross-section of the head.

To examine the cat's bite, raise her upper lip while drawing down on the lower lip with your thumb. The bite is determined by seeing how the upper and lower incisor teeth meet (see *Malocclusion*, page 242). Raising the lips also exposes the mucous membranes of the gums. The appearance of the gums gives an indication of anemia and the state of circulation. This is easiest to evaluate in cats with pink gums (as opposed to pigmented gums).

To open the cat's mouth, place the thumb and forefinger of one hand against her upper cheeks and press in gently (see the photos on page 232). As the mouth begins to open wide, press down on the lower jaw with the index finger of your other hand. To see the tonsils and back of the throat, push down on the back of the tongue or tip the cat's head back. Many cats are reluctant to have their mouths examined and should be restrained to avoid a painful scratch or bite (see *Handling and Restraint*, page 2).

Signs of Mouth and Throat Disease

- **Failure to eat.** This is one of the first indications of mouth disease. In this case, not eating is caused by mouth pain rather than loss of appetite. The cat will often sit beside the food dish, giving every indication of wanting to eat, and may even begin eating, then drop the food quickly. If you attempt to examine the mouth, the cat draws back and struggles

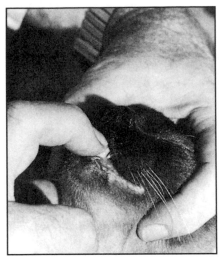 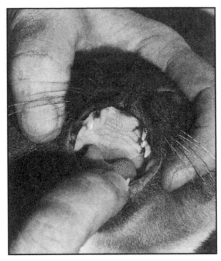

To open the cat's mouth, grasp the arch of the cat's face across the cheekbones and gently press in.

With the index finger of your other hand, press or pull down on the lower jaw.

to escape. Not eating is a serious problem in cats. Even going 24 hours without food can cause changes in liver function.

- **Unkempt appearance.** Because the mouth is used for grooming, another indication of a cat with a sore mouth is lack of grooming. When grooming is accompanied by drooling, the hair on the cat's chin and chest may be dirty and wet. A painful mouth is one of the main causes for drooling. The drool may be discolored—either brown or red from infection or bleeding.

- **Bad breath.** A persistent, disagreeable odor from the mouth is abnormal. The cause should be determined so proper treatment can be given. Some causes of bad breath are stomatitis and gingivitis. Excess tartar on the teeth is another cause of bad breath (see *Gingivitis*, page 236). A cat with bad breath who drools and resists having her mouth opened may be suffering from an infection or a cancer in the mouth. She should be seen by a veterinarian. Kidney disease can contribute to bad breath and/or cause oral ulcers.

- **Gagging, choking, drooling.** These all suggest a foreign object in the mouth, tongue, or throat. If an object is not immediately visible, or if you can see it but cannot remove it, the cat should be seen by a veterinarian. Rabies should be considered if the mouth sags open and the cat drools or foams at the mouth. This same picture can be seen in a cat with severe respiratory distress or a cancer in the mouth.

- **Difficulty opening the mouth or swallowing.** This commonly occurs with head and neck abscesses and injuries to the jaws.

The Lips

CHEILITIS

Cheilitis is an inflammation of the lips. It is recognized by serum crusts that form where the hair-covered areas meet the smooth areas of the lips. As the crusts peel off, the skin beneath looks raw and denuded and is sensitive to touch.

Inflamed lips are often caused by an infection inside the mouth that extends to the lips. Other causes are contact with weeds or brush that irritate the lips, giving them a chapped look. Electric shock, caused by grabbing or chewing on a live wire, can also cause cheilitis. Sometimes chronic moisture will cause a yeast (*Malassezia*) infection (see page 160).

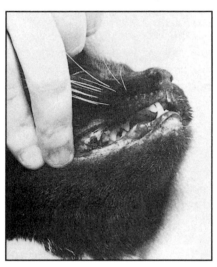

Inflammation of the lips (cheilitis) is often caused by a mouth infection.

Treatment: Clean the lips with warm water and a gentle shampoo. Warm compresses may be needed first to soften the crusts. Consult with your veterinarian about applying any ointment. Aloe ointments may be soothing. Even a chapped-lip lipstick made for humans (such as Chapstick) may offer some relief; designate an unflavored one just for your cat's use.

EOSINOPHILIC ULCERS (RODENT ULCERS, INDOLENT ULCERS)

A rodent ulcer begins as a yellow or pink shiny spot that deepens and becomes an open sore. Often, it begins on either side of center on the upper lip. Less commonly, it occurs on the lower lip or at the back of the jaw behind one of the last upper molars. Some cats will also develop an ulcer on the tongue. It is not itchy and seems to cause no pain. As the ulcer advances, the lip may be partly eroded by a large, ulcerated swelling that exposes teeth and gums.

This unsightly condition is unique to the cat. It may be found in cats of any age, and occurs three times more often in females than males. The exact cause of rodent ulcer is unknown, and there is actually no direct connection with rodents. The presence of *eosinophils* suggests an allergic reaction, parasite problem, or immune problem. It is thought to be part of the eosinophilic granuloma complex (see page 166). Hypersensitivity is strongly suggested, with causative agents including insects, environmental substances, and diet. Flea allergy should always be considered as a possible cause. Some cases are associated with dental infection. An underlying genetic predisposition is suspected.

Rodent ulcers have been found in cats who were exposed to the feline leukemia virus, further suggesting that impaired immunity may be a cause. However, not all cats with rodent ulcer test positive for the feline leukemia virus, nor does a rodent ulcer necessarily mean that a cat has feline leukemia. Note that a similar process involving ulceration and granulation occurs in other body parts (see *Eosinophilic Granuloma Complex*, page 166).

Diagnosis is suggested by the typical appearance and location of the ulcer. In questionable cases, a *biopsy* or needle aspirate *cytology* can be done to rule out malignant transformation. Cats with rodent ulcer should be tested for Feline Leukemia (see page 89).

Treatment: Veterinary care is required in all cases. Cortisone has proven to be the most effective treatment, but it should be given with an antibiotic, at least initially, to clear up any secondary bacterial infection. Cortisone is given either as pills (prednisone) or by injection (Depo-medrol). Depo-medrol is a long-lasting injection that is given at two-week intervals. Usually, three courses are necessary. Alternately, prednisone can be given daily until the ulcer disappears. If the ulcer recurs after either injectable or oral cortisone therapy, the cat is placed on prednisone maintenance—usually one pill every other day. Essential fatty acid supplements may also be beneficial.

In case this is the result of an allergen or irritant, do not use plastic or rubber food and water bowls. Stainless steel is a good alternative.

Cyclosporine, interferon, radiation therapy, and cryosurgery may all be effective. Gold salts, given as an injection, may also be used for treatment in cases that are difficult to treat.

Megestrol acetate (Megace) has been used in some cases of rodent ulcer. However, this progesterone drug is not approved for cats and has serious

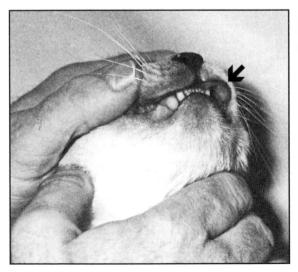

A rodent ulcer typically begins near the center of the upper lip.

undesirable side effects. It is best used as a last line of treatment under veterinary supervision. These ulcers are known to recur, so it is worthwhile to try to find and eliminate the underlying cause.

LACERATIONS OF THE LIPS, MOUTH, AND TONGUE

The soft tissues in the mouth are common sites for cuts. Most are caused by animal bites, including the bites of other cats. Some occur when a cat picks up or licks a sharp object, such as the rim of a food can. An unusual cause of tongue trauma is freezing to metal in extremely cold weather. When pulled free, the surface of the tongue is stripped off, leaving a raw, bleeding patch. Biting into an electric cord can leave wounds on the lips. These may appear as burns or ulcers.

Treatment: A cat with a painful mouth usually must be restrained (see *Handling and Restraint,* page 2). Bleeding can be controlled by applying pressure to the cut for five minutes. Use a clean gauze dressing or a piece of clean cotton cloth. Press the gauze directly against the wound. Bleeding from the tongue requires opening the mouth, as described on page 231. You may need to pull the tongue forward to see the bleeding site. Do not attempt to apply pressure to the tongue unless the cat is extremely agreeable to this.

Minor cuts that have stopped bleeding do not need to be sutured by your veterinarian. Stitching should be considered when the edges of the cut gape open, when lip lacerations involve the borders of the mouth, or when bleeding recurs after the pressure dressing is removed. It is essential that these be sutured as soon as possible; delaying treatment may make suturing impossible. All deep tongue wounds will need to be sutured. Puncture wounds are prone to infection. These are often not sutured or will be sutured but with a drain put in place. Proper early treatment of these wounds, as described in *Wounds* (page 47), is important.

As the wound is healing, cleanse the cat's mouth twice a day with 0.1 percent chlorhexidine antiseptic solution (such as Nolvadent or Peridex). Feed the cat an easily digestible diet with a strong scent to encourage eating, and avoid dry kibble, which requires chewing that may cause pain.

BURNS OF THE LIPS, MOUTH, AND TONGUE

Electrical burns of the mouth are caused by chewing on an electric cord. Although quite painful, most heal spontaneously. In some cases, a gray membrane appears on the surface of the burn and an ulcer develops. Surgical removal of the dead tissue back to healthy tissue will be necessary. Try to avoid this injury by taping cords down or running them through protective plastic coverings.

Chemical burns are caused by a variety of corrosives, including lye, phenol, phosphorus, household cleaners, alkalis, and others. Should the substance be swallowed, the throat may be burned as well, leading to a more serious problem (see *The Esophagus*, page 260). In addition, some products, such as phenols, may be toxic.

Treatment: *Immediately* flush the poison from the cat's mouth using large amounts of water while sponging and rinsing for several minutes. Aftercare for mouth burns is the same as for *Lacerations* above. Call your veterinarian immediately and *do not* induce vomiting.

The Gums

Healthy gums are firm and generally all pink, although some cats have spots of pigment on their gums. There is no room for food and debris to get down between the gums and the teeth, but pockets alongside the teeth are a source of gum infection and tooth decay.

Pale gums are a sign of anemia. Bluish gray gums indicate shock or lack of oxygen. Bright red gums may be an indication of carbon monoxide poisoning, heatstroke, or infection. Yellow tinged gums indicate jaundice.

You can check *capillary refill time*—a test of heart function and anemia—by gently pressing on the gum until it turns white and then observing how fast the color fills in. Normal capillary refill time is two seconds or less.

PERIODONTAL DISEASE

Periodontal disease is one of the most common problems seen in veterinary practice. It occurs in two forms: The first is gingivitis, a reversible inflammation of the gums. The second is periodontitis, an inflammation of the deeper structures supporting the teeth. Both begin when plaque and calculus are deposited on the teeth near the gum line. This occurs in about 85 percent of all cats over 2 years old, and it can be found in some cats even before they are 1 year old.

Gingivitis

The edges of healthy gums fit tightly around the teeth. In a cat with gingivitis, rough dental calculus builds up in an irregular fashion along the gum line, producing points at which the gum is forced away from the teeth. This creates small pockets that trap food and bacteria. In time, the gums become inflamed and then infected.

Plaque is a soft, colorless material that is not easily seen with the naked eye. It consists of food particles and other organic and inorganic material, plus millions of living and growing bacteria. It is yellow-brown and soft when first deposited.

The plaque quickly hardens into calculus (also called tartar), a mixture of calcium phosphate and carbonate with organic material. These calcium salts are soluble in acid but precipitate in the slightly alkaline saliva of the cat. Calculus is yellow or brown and produces the characteristic tartar stains. Calculus forms on irregular surfaces on the teeth, which creates an ideal environment for the formation of plaque. It begins to accumulate within one week of removal.

This buildup of calculus on the teeth is the primary cause of gingivitis. Gum infections may also occur with several diseases, including feline panleukopenia, feline viral respiratory disease complex, kidney and liver failure, nutritional disorders, and immune disorders.

The first sign is that the gums appear red, painful, and swollen, and may bleed when rubbed. Next, the edges of the gums recede from the sides of the teeth, allowing small pockets and crevices to develop. These pockets trap food and bacteria, which produces infection at the gum line and sets the stage for periodontitis and tooth decay. Other signs are loss of appetite, ungroomed appearance, drooling, and bad breath.

Treatment: Once signs of gingivitis are visible, a significant degree of dental tartar, calculus, and gum-pocket infection will be present. The teeth should be professionally cleaned by a veterinarian, after which the cat should be placed on a home dental care program (as described in *Taking Care of Your Cat's Teeth*, page 244). Brushing the teeth daily, or at least two or three times a week, will be required to prevent the recurrence of gingivitis. There are special diets formulated to reduce plaque and tarter and to prevent gingivitis (see *Taking Care of Your Cat's Teeth*, page 244).

Other diseases that may be contributing to the problem must be treated as a necessary part of restoring a healthy mouth.

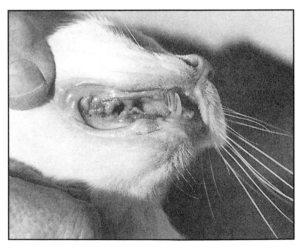

Gingivitis predisposes the cat to periodontal disease and tooth decay.

Periodontitis

Periodontitis is an infection of the teeth and gums with destruction or damage to the support structures of the tooth. It is the progression of untreated simple gingivitis. It is considered irreversible but, at least in some cases, treatable. Rarely, loose teeth will develop strong roots again with treatment. Periodontitis can lead to an abscess of the root of the tooth or teeth.

One of the first signs of periodontitis is an offensive mouth odor. It may have been present for some time—perhaps even accepted as normal. Another sign is a change in the cat's eating habits. Since it hurts to chew, the cat may sit by her food dish but decline to eat. Weight loss and an ungroomed appearance are common. Teeth may be loose or even have fallen out.

If you look closely at a cat with periodontitis, you will see tartar deposits on the premolars, molars, and canines. Pressure against the gums may cause pus to exude from pockets alongside the teeth. This can be very painful to the cat, so do not try it at home. It has been suggested that some cats are more susceptible to periodontitis than others. For example, periodontitis seems to be more common in the Siamese and Oriental Shorthair breeds. Increased susceptibility also seems to occur among cats who suffer from repeated viral respiratory infections,

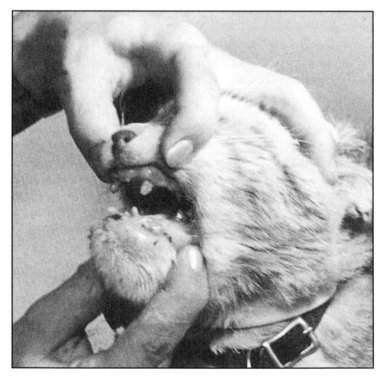

This cat has advanced periodontal disease and root abscesses. Note the swelling of the lower jaw because of bone infection.

especially calicivirus or bartonellosis, and among those who have had past exposure to the feline leukemia virus and feline immunodeficiency virus.

Normal chewing on hard, abrasive material cleans the teeth and reduces the formation of calculus. Special dental diets (see *Taking Care of Your Cat's Teeth*, page 244) help provide abrasive action. In the wild, cats would be chewing on small bones and the rough hair and feathers of prey animals, which help rub and clean the teeth.

Treatment: The mouth must be thoroughly cleaned and restored to a near normal condition. This involves removing dental tartar and calculus, draining pus pockets, extracting any damaged teeth, and polishing the teeth. This must be done by a veterinarian, because your cat will require general anesthesia for a thorough cleaning. While under anesthesia, the veterinarian will use a dental probe to see how deep the damage is to the gums. X-rays will reveal whether the teeth themselves are damaged. Antibiotic gels may be placed into deep pockets of infection.

Afterward, the cat should be placed on an antibiotic for at least 7 to 10 days. At this time, it is important to begin a good home dental program, as described in *Taking Care of Your Cat's Teeth* (page 244). Continuing regular home care is essential to treat periodontitis and to prevent further degeneration of the teeth.

LYMPHOCYTIC/PLASMACYTIC GINGIVITIS STOMATITIS

Cats can suffer from lymphocytic/plasmacytic gingivitis stomatitis (LPGS) or feline gingivitis stomatitis (FGS), a condition that is unique to their species. These terms refer to a severe inflammation that can affect the entire mouth as well as the gums. The gums will be very red and bleed easily if chafed. Some cats will have lesions that proliferate along the gums. Affected cats will have bad breath and may drool a great deal. These cats have extremely painful mouths and often will simply lick at their food, making no attempt to pick up pieces or chew.

Although most cats with this problem are middle-aged or older, there is a form that affects kittens just 3 to 5 months old. The kittens may outgrow the problem with extensive care, but most older cats do not. Abyssinians, Siamese, and Persians seem especially prone to the juvenile form of this problem.

The disease itself seems to be an immune reaction against dental plaque and/or the actual dentin of the teeth (the substance just under the enamel). The definitive cause is unknown. It appears to be an allergic or immune-based problem. About 15 percent of cats with LPGS will be positive for feline leukemia virus or feline immunodeficiency virus. An earlier exposure to calicivirus is considered to be a factor as well. The *Bartonella* species of bacteria are also implicated.

A *biopsy* may be needed to definitely diagnose this condition and rule out other similar problems that can result from renal failure, diabetes, or cancer. The fact that the lesions tend to be bilateral and symmetrical makes cancer less likely, but it should be considered and definitively ruled out. X-rays should be taken to check for tooth problems, including root resorptions (dissolving roots) and abscesses.

Treatment: Cats with LPGS will need to be treated for the inflammation with oral or injectable steroids. Antibiotics should be added, at least initially, to prevent bacterial overgrowth. Pain medications, such as a fentanyl patch, can be important to keep the cat comfortable. Laser surgery may be done to remove proliferative areas of inflamed tissue. Bovine lactoferrin (an iron-binding protein with immunomodulation capabilities) can be compounded for cats and used to flush the mouth. This product may act against calicivirus, as well, so it may be a double-edged weapon.

Cats with plaque and tartar buildup need to have that problem addressed. This may require cleanings under anesthesia as often as every four to six months. In addition, a diet for tartar control, such as Science Diet Oral Care, Purina D/H, Hill's Prescription Diet Feline t/d, or Royal Canin Feline Dental DD 27, may be helpful. CET Oral Hygiene freeze-dried meat chews for cats may also be useful.

Home care includes keeping the mouth and teeth as clean as possible with daily brushing and mouth washings. Switching from plastic or rubber to stainless-steel or ceramic food and water bowls may help some cats. Also, switching to a hypoallergenic, limited protein source diet, such as Royal Canin's Hypoallergenic HP 23, may be beneficial.

In many cats, LPGS will not clear up despite aggressive treatment and they will remain in discomfort until all of their teeth—or at least all of the teeth except the canines—are removed. Although this may seem a bit drastic, the cats do extremely well, regain lost weight, are clearly more comfortable and have no trouble eating—even dry kibble, in most cases.

Growths on the Gums

About 10 percent of all feline cancers occur in the mouth, and the majority of these are squamous cell carcinomas (the same cell type that occurs on white ear tips). This cancer tends to start at the base of the tongue—perhaps from cats licking off carcinogenic substances while grooming. This cancer is also associated with exposure to secondhand cigarette smoke.

Cats with oral cancers tend to drool, may sit with the mouth partly open, and often go to the food or water bowls but simply sit and do not try to eat or drink. There is often a bad odor associated with the mouth.

Eosinophilic ulcers (see page 233) can occur on the gums at the back of the jaw behind the last upper molars, although they are more likely to occur on the upper lip.

Treatment: Squamous cell carcinomas of the mouth respond reasonably well to surgery, followed by radiation if they are caught early. This is not a cure, but potentially provides some added quality time.

The Teeth

Dental problems in domestic cats are due, in part, to diet. Cats were designed to hunt and catch small prey, which they devoured more or less whole. The abrasive action of hair and feathers and bones from prey animals probably helped to keep their teeth clean. Current diets may predispose cats to tartar and plaque formation, as well as the development of feline oral resorptive lesions or cavities.

A cat's teeth should be inspected regularly. Many dental problems go undetected until they cause major symptoms. Cats resist examination, particularly when suffering from a painful mouth. A good program of home dental care will prevent many problems that would otherwise lead to a poor state of health and nutrition (see *Taking Care of Your Cat's Teeth*, page 244). There are also special diets that will also help prevent tartar buildup (see page 245).

DECIDUOUS AND PERMANENT TEETH

With rare exceptions, kittens are born without teeth. The incisors are the first deciduous (baby) teeth to appear, usually at 2 to 3 weeks of age. They are followed by the canine teeth at 3 to 4 weeks and the premolars at 3 to 6 weeks. The last premolar arrives at about 6 weeks of age. This sequence can be used to determine the approximate age of young kittens.

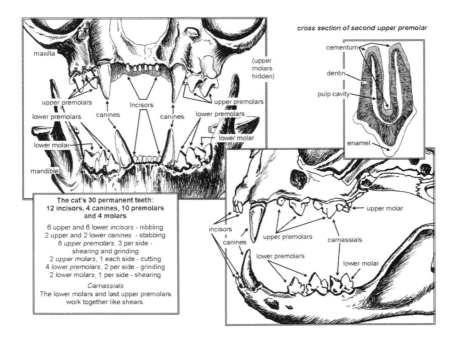

cross section of second upper premolar

cementum
dentin
pulp cavity
enamel

maxilla
(upper molars hidden)
upper premolars
lower premolars
canines
incisors
canines
upper premolars
lower premolars
lower molar
lower molar
mandible

The cat's 30 permanent teeth:
12 incisors, 4 canines, 10 premolars
and 4 molars

6 upper and 6 lower *incisors* - nibbling
2 upper and 2 lower *canines* - stabbing
6 *upper premolars*, 3 per side -
shearing and grinding
2 *upper molars*, 1 each side - cutting
4 *lower premolars*, 2 per side - grinding
2 *lower molars*, 1 per side - shearing

Carnassials
The lower molars and last upper premolars
work together like shears.

upper molar
incisors
canines
upper premolars
carnassials
lower premolars
lower molar

The average kitten has 26 deciduous teeth: On each side of the mouth, there are three upper and three lower incisors, one upper and one lower canine, and three upper and two lower premolars. Kittens do not have molars.

During teething, which lasts two to three months, a kitten may experience some soreness of the mouth. She may be off her food from time to time, but this should not affect growth and development. If a kitten is not growing, take her to a veterinarian right away.

Deciduous teeth are gradually replaced by the permanent (adult) teeth. At 3 to 4 months the incisors erupt, followed at 4 to 6 months by the canine teeth, premolars, and molars. By 7 months the cat's adult teeth are fully developed. Knowing this sequence can give you an idea of the approximate age of an older kitten.

The average adult cat has 30 permanent teeth: On each side of the mouth, there are three upper and three lower incisors, one upper and one lower canine, three upper and two lower premolars, and one upper and one lower molar.

Determining the age of an animal by checking the amount of wear on the cusps of the teeth is relatively reliable for horses and some other domestic animals, but less so for cats, whose teeth are not used for grinding. The general condition of the teeth and gums may allow a guess about the approximate age of the cat, but accurate determinations are possible only for very young cats. They are based on the time the deciduous (baby) and permanent (adult) teeth erupt, as just described.

Retained Baby Teeth

Normally, the roots of baby teeth are reabsorbed as adult teeth take their place. When this fails to happen, you will see what appears to be a double set of teeth. The permanent teeth are then pushed out of line, leading to malocclusion, or a bad bite (see below). Kittens at 2 to 3 months of age should be watched carefully to see that their adult teeth are coming in normally. Whenever a baby tooth stays in place while an adult tooth is coming in, the baby tooth should be pulled.

Abnormal Number of Teeth

It is not uncommon to see adult cats with fewer teeth than normal. Some cats are born with missing tooth buds. This has little or no effect on their health.

Rarely, you may find that your kitten has more than the usual number of teeth. This problem can cause the teeth to twist or overlap. One or more of the extra teeth will need to be extracted to make room for the rest.

MALOCCLUSION (INCORRECT BITE)

Most bite problems in young cats are hereditary, resulting from genetic factors controlling the growth of the upper and lower jaws. Some incorrect bites are caused by retention of baby teeth that push emerging adult teeth out of alignment. In older cats, an incorrect bite may be the result of trauma, infection, or cancer of the mouth.

A cat's bite is determined by how the upper and lower incisor teeth meet when the mouth is closed. In the even or level bite, the incisor teeth meet edge to edge. In the scissors bite, the upper incisors just overlap but still touch the lower incisors. An overshot bite is one in which the upper jaw is longer than the lower jaw, so the teeth overlap without touching. The undershot bite is the reverse, with the lower jaw projecting beyond the upper jaw. A wry mouth is the worst of the malocclusion problems. One side of the jaw grows faster than the other, twisting the mouth.

Incorrect bites interfere with the ability to grasp, hold, and chew food. Furthermore, teeth that do not align may injure the soft parts of the mouth.

Incorrect bites are much less common in cats than they are in dogs because cats' heads are quite similar in shape, despite differences in breeds. Short-nosed breeds, such as the Persian, are most susceptible to bite problems.

Treatment: The overshot bite may correct itself if the gap is no greater than the head of a match. Retained baby teeth displacing permanent adult teeth should be extracted by 4 to 5 months of age, at which time the jaw is still growing and there is opportunity for the bite to correct itself.

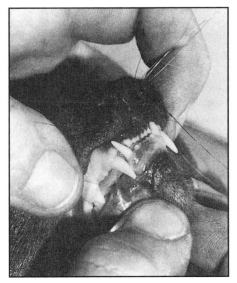

To examine the cat's bite, raise the upper lip while drawing down the lower lip. In this correct even or level bite, the incisors meet edge to edge.

FELINE ORAL RESORPTIVE LESIONS

Feline oral resorptive lesions (FORLs) can be found in anywhere from 28 to 67 percent of all adult cats. These are lesions on the teeth themselves, and range from barely penetrating the enamel at the neck of a tooth right above the gum line, to full-blown loss of the entire crown with gum tissues growing over the remaining root tip. The molars and premolars are most commonly affected, but these lesions can appear on any tooth and on any surface of a tooth.

Once the outer layer of enamel is gone, the teeth may become quite painful to the touch. The actual ringlike lesions can be seen, if you can examine the cat's mouth. Teeth may break off at the damaged sites, and cats sometimes show "jaw chattering" if the area is touched, due to pain. Many cats will not eat well because of the discomfort.

Many potential causes have been offered for this problem, ranging from existing periodontitis to viral exposures to renal or kidney problems. Any cat can suffer from this problem, although Siamese and Abyssinians seem predisposed. Shearing forces from eating dry cat food or highly acidic diets have also been suggested.

Your cat will need a full dental examination and treatment under general anesthesia. Oral X-rays will be taken to evaluate all the teeth.

Treatment: Some veterinarians have replaced the damaged enamel with glass ionomers, but this is not done routinely and is not usually successful. In most cases, it is best to simply remove the affected teeth. Pain medications and antibiotics may be needed as part of treatment.

CAVITIES

Cavities are not common in cats, primarily because a cat's diet is quite low in carbohydrates and sugars. The alkaline pH of cat saliva also helps to minimize the development of cavities. Cavities account for only a small percentage of lost teeth. When present, they develop along the gum line in association with periodontal disease and not on the crown of the tooth, as they do in humans.

True cavities are caused by bacteria. FORLs in cats (see page 243) are similar to what we call cavities in humans. Secondary bacterial infection can follow the initial inflammation.

Treatment: The affected tooth or teeth must be extracted.

BROKEN TEETH

Teeth can be chipped, broken, and lost—usually after a fight with another animal. FORLs can also lead to broken teeth due to the damage to the support structures. Broken teeth can lead to a tooth root abscess if the damage is deep enough. Teeth broken off above the dentin may do fine, but check them frequently for any signs of pain or infection.

Treatment: Extraction is the usual treatment.

TAKING CARE OF YOUR CAT'S TEETH

Many cats need preventive dental care by age 2 or 3. How often a dental examination, scaling, and polishing is needed will depend on the rate at which calculus forms on the cat's teeth. A program of dental hygiene will limit the rate at which this happens and help prolong the health and life of your pet. This includes the following:

- Feed your cat at least some dry kibble as part of her diet—preferably one of the dental diets listed here. (It's possible that the shearing forces generated when breaking nondental kibble predisposes cats to FORLs.) Dry foods are abrasive and help keep the teeth clean and sharp. Many cats do best with a diet primarily of canned food, so you may need to discuss this with your veterinarian and balance the food type according to your individual cat. Specific diets for cats to prevent dental disease include Hill's Prescription Feline t/d, Hill's Science Diet Oral Care, Friskies Dental Diet, Royal Canin Dental DD 27, and Purina Veterinary Diet DH (for Dental Health) Feline. However, if your cat suffers from other health problems, you may need to feed her a specific diet in which dental health is not the primary consideration.

- Start regular brushing once your kitten has her adult teeth, while gums are still healthy. Less effort is required to prevent gum disease than to treat it. You can maintain disease-free gums by brushing your cat's teeth two or three times a week. However, once the cat develops periodontal disease, *daily* brushing is necessary to keep the condition in check. (For advice on brushing your cat's teeth, see page 244.)

- Do not give your cat objects to chew that are harder than her teeth. CET has Oral Hygiene Chews that are safe for cats. There are special catnip chews and feline Greenies (dental treats) that may help your cat keep those teeth clean. Breath and Dental Care Treats, Feline, may also help with dental hygiene.

- There are currently at least two products you can add to your cat's drinking water that may help reduce tartar and plaque accumulation. These are Dental Fresh, and Pet Kiss Plaque and Tartar Control Liquid. If you add a supplement to your cat's water, *be sure she is willing to drink it.* It is better for her to go without the supplement than to forgo drinking. You could leave two bowls of water out—one plain and one with the supplement.

Brushing Your Cat's Teeth

Although it is only necessary to brush the cat's permanent teeth, it may be worthwhile to start a regimen of toothbrushing while your cat is still a kitten, just to get her used to the procedure.

Toothpastes and other dental products designed for people are *not* appropriate or healthy for cats. However, pastes, gels, sprays, and solutions are now available specifically for pets. There are cat toothpastes available that use

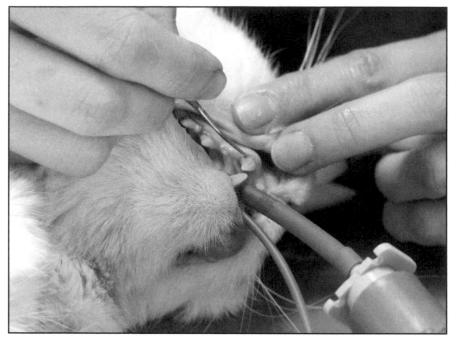

Good oral hygiene will make the need for professional dental cleaning less frequent.

baking soda as the base. Others use oxygenating substances to limit the growth of anaerobic bacteria. Virbac, Petrodex, Drs. Foster & Smith, and CET have lines of pet toothpastes. Many of these products now come in flavors that are attractive to cats, such as tuna and poultry. Nolvadent and Peridex oral washes contain 0.1 percent chlorhexidine, which is both antibacterial and antiviral. Maxi/Guard contains zinc ascorbate, which promotes the healing of diseased gums. Fluoride gels can be useful as well. Your veterinarian may suggest one of these products, especially if your cat has gum disease.

Cats may resist having their teeth brushed. However, a step-by-step approach often will lead to acceptance. Begin by rubbing the cat's muzzle over the teeth. This is easily accepted, as it mimics a natural behavior of face rubbing. Then raise the lip and massage the gums with your finger. When this becomes routine, wrap a piece of cloth or gauze around your finger and gently rub the cat's teeth and gums.

The next step is to introduce a toothbrush. Begin with a soft, small toothbrush (made for a young child). You can also purchase special fingertip brushes that fit on over a finger and give some added abrasive action. You can get small toothbrushes just for cats, too, but if you have trouble using one with your cat, try wrapping a gauze pad around your finger and putting some toothpaste on that.

Introduce the idea of toothpaste by first using the water from a can of tuna. Before using the actual toothpaste, introduce it to the cat by offering it on the tip of your finger.

Gently rubbing along the teeth inside the lip will work quite well. The most important part of the gum area to brush is the gingival sulcus, where the gum attaches to the teeth. Move the brush forward and back, parallel to the gum line, with the bristles in the gingival sulcus. It is not necessary to brush the tongue side. The cat's rough tongue will help distribute the dentifrice on the inside of the teeth.

Start when the cat is young and introduce toothbrushing gradually, and your cat will accept it as a routine procedure.

The Tongue
GLOSSITIS

Inflammation and infection of the tongue is called glossitis. It often accompanies immunodeficiency diseases such as feline leukemia, feline immunodeficiency virus syndrome, feline viral respiratory disease complex, and renal diseases. Cats can also irritate their tongues while removing burrs or other abrasive substances from their coats. Tongue burns can be caused by licking caustic materials off the body or by licking a metal surface in freezing weather. Cats may also injure their tongues by biting into electrical cords. Burns, scratches, and cuts on the tongue can become infected.

A cat with a sore tongue looks ungroomed. The fur on her neck may be dirty and wet from drooling. As the inflamed surface of the

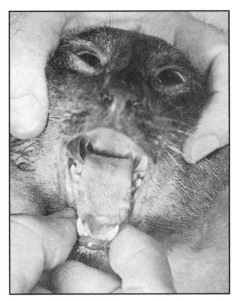

In this cat with glossitis, the tip of the tongue appears smooth and shiny. This condition is often associated with feline upper respiratory infections.

tongue is shed, the rough spikes are lost, causing the tongue to appear red and shiny. You may see ulcers and open sores on the tongue.

Treatment: Flush out the cat's mouth twice a day with 0.1 percent chlorhexidine solution. Ulcers must be assessed by your veterinarian, who may need to cauterize them. An antibiotic may be prescribed.

A cat with a painful tongue may have difficulty eating or drinking. Feed soft, canned food diluted with water or plain broth to a liquid consistency. Offer food and water at room temperature.

FOREIGN BODIES IN THE TONGUE

Small plant awns, burrs, splinters, and needles can become imbedded on the surface of the tongue. Signs are similar to those of *Foreign Bodies in the Mouth* (see page 251). A common place for a foreign body is the underside of the tongue. On lifting the tongue, you may see a grapelike swelling or a draining tract, which means the foreign body has been present for some time.

Treatment: In most cases, you will need to consult your veterinarian. Removing a foreign body can be tricky and difficult, especially if the cat is uncooperative. If a foreign body is visible and easily accessible, it can be removed with tweezers. A thread attached to a needle should not be pulled out, because the thread can be used to locate the needle.

Foreign bodies that have been present for some time are difficult to remove and require anesthesia. Afterward, your veterinarian will probably prescribe a prophylactic antibiotic for one week.

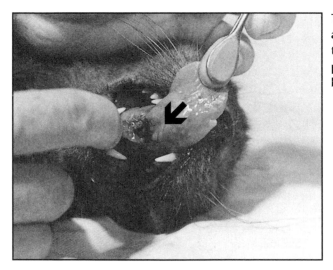

This cat has an ulcerating sore beneath the tongue, produced by a penetrating foreign body.

STRING AROUND THE TONGUE

Cats are attracted to all kinds of string, yarn, thread, and ribbon—to chew on or to play with. Often, this can lead to problems. Sometimes, as the cat swallows one end of a piece of string, the other end loops around the tongue. The more the cat swallows, the harder the string cuts into the base of the tongue. Eventually, the string may cut off the blood supply and cause strangulation of the tongue.

It may be difficult to locate the cause of this problem. The cat will be difficult to examine and the string could be as small as a thread. Close inspection is necessary to find and remove the cause of the constriction. Some cats will arrive at the clinic with a history of vomiting.

Treatment: This must be treated at the veterinarian's office, because most cats will require sedation or anesthesia. If the string is very long, one end could be under the tongue and the other end in the intestines. In these cases, abdominal surgery may be required to completely remove the string.

Carefully putting all toys with string, ribbons, and needlework away, safe from the cat, is the ideal prevention.

The Mouth

Any solid tumor growing in the mouth is a cause for concern. The majority are cancers. They require immediate professional attention.

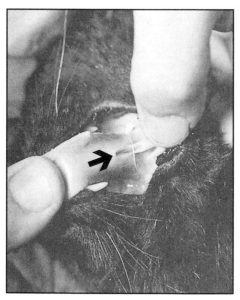

The arrow shows a string around the cat's tongue, which is cutting into the base.

STOMATITIS

Stomatitis is an inflamed, sore mouth, and should be suspected when you see drooling, refusal to eat, difficulty chewing, head shaking, pawing at the face, and reluctance to allow a mouth examination. The inside of the mouth looks reddened, inflamed, swollen, and tender. The gums may bleed when rubbed. Bad breath is present. Lack of self-grooming is evident. Cats may show pain when yawning or opening their mouths to eat.

Cats with any form of stomatitis must be examined by a veterinarian. In some cases, stomatitis is directly attributable to periodontal disease or a foreign object caught between the teeth or imbedded in the tongue. Other cases are associated with an immune deficiency disease such as feline immunodeficiency virus, feline leukemia, feline viral respiratory disease complex, or kidney failure. (Also see *Lymphocytic/Plasmacytic Gingivitis Stomatitis*, page 239.) Cases caused by a specific infection include the following.

Necrotizing Ulcerative Stomatitis (Trench Mouth)

This is an extremely painful stomatitis caused by a bacteria-like pathogen, a spirochete. There is a characteristic offensive mouth odor, usually accompanied by a brown, *purulent*, slimy saliva that stains the front of the legs. The gums are beefy red and bleed easily. Trench mouth occurs in cats with severe periodontal disease and in those who are run-down because of chronic illness or dietary deficiency. Frontal sinus infection can occur as a complication of trench mouth (see *Sinusitis*, page 228). Cats with diabetes, feline leukemia virus infection, or FIV may be predisposed to this disease.

Treatment: Your veterinarian may decide to thoroughly clean the cat's mouth under anesthesia. This provides the opportunity to treat any decayed roots, loose teeth, and dental calculus. Ulcers may be cauterized with silver nitrate. Infection is treated with an antibiotic. Afterward, the cat is placed on soft, canned food

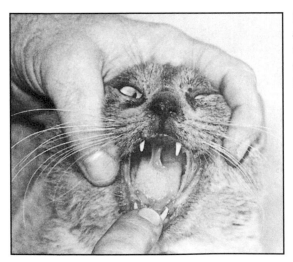

Note the shiny ulcerative appearance of the top of the tongue and the thick, slimy saliva in this cat with ulcerative stomatitis.

diluted with water or plain broth to a liquid consistency. Aftercare involves daily mouthwashes using 0.1 percent chlorhexidine solution, accompanied by a home program of good oral hygiene (see *Taking Care of Your Cat's Teeth*, page 244).

Ulcerative (Viral) Stomatitis

This is an extremely painful stomatitis in which ulcers form on the tip of the tongue and hard palate. The saliva is clear at first, then becomes blood-tinged and foul smelling. A yellow puslike *exudate* forms on the surface of the ulcers. Ulcerative stomatitis is seen most often in association with the feline respiratory disease complex, especially calicivirus.

Treatment: It is the same as for *Necrotizing Ulcerative Stomatitis* (page 250), except that antibiotics are not recommended unless the problem is complicated by a secondary bacterial infection.

Yeast Stomatitis (Thrush)

This is an uncommon form of stomatitis seen chiefly when a cat has been on a prolonged course of broad-spectrum antibiotics that alters the normal flora of the mouth and allows the overgrowth of yeast. It also occurs in immunodeficiency states associated with chronic illness. The mucous membranes of the gums and tongue are covered with soft white patches that coalesce to form a whitish film. Painful ulcers appear as the disease progresses.

Treatment: Nystatin and clotrimazole are the drugs of choice. Large doses of B-complex vitamins are also recommended. Ketoconazole may also be used for *Candida* infections. Correction of all predisposing causes is essential.

FOREIGN BODIES IN THE MOUTH

Foreign bodies that can lodge in the mouth include bone or wood splinters, gristle, slivers of wood, sewing needles, pins, porcupine quills, fishhooks, and

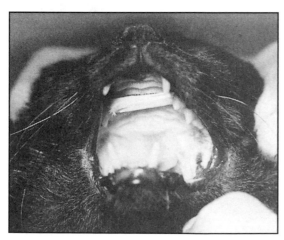

A foreign body is wedged across the roof of this cat's mouth.

plant awns. Some penetrate the lips, gums, and palate; others become caught between the teeth or wedged across the roof of the mouth. Pieces of string can become wrapped around the teeth and the tongue (see page 249).

Suspect a foreign body when your cat paws at her mouth, rubs her mouth along the floor, drools, gags, licks her lips, or holds her mouth open. Occasionally, the only signs are loss of pep, bad breath, refusal to eat, and an ungroomed appearance.

Treatment: Sit under a good light source and gently open your cat's mouth, as described on page 231. A good look may reveal the cause of the problem. It is possible to remove some foreign bodies using tweezers. Others will require the cat to be under general anesthesia—which requires a trip to the veterinarian.

To remove a fishhook when the barb is free, cut the shank next to the barb with wire cutters and remove the fishhook in two pieces. If the barb is embedded in the tissue, try to push the hook through until the barb is free. *Do not pull the hook back through the tissue.* Sometimes the hook can be removed with a good helper and firm control of the cat. In most cases, though, removing a fishhooks will require sedation at the veterinary clinic, unless the cat is very cooperative.

Foreign bodies left in place for a day or longer may cause infection. A broad-spectrum antibiotic is recommended for one week.

Porcupine Quills

Porcupine quills can penetrate the face, nose, lips, oral cavity, feet, and skin of the cat. If you decide to remove quills at home, restrain the cat completely, perhaps in a cat bag or wrapped in a large towel or blanket. Using a surgical hemostat or needle-nosed pliers, grasp each quill near the skin and draw it straight out on the long axis of the quill. If the quill breaks off, a fragment will be left behind to work in further, causing a deep-seated infection. If the cat is

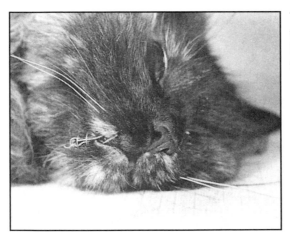

To remove a fishhook, push the barbed end through the lip. Cut the shank and remove the hook in two pieces.

becoming highly agitated or stressed, it is best to go to your veterinarian, where the cat can be sedated. This is less painful for the cat, as well.

Quills inside the mouth are difficult to remove and require general anesthesia.

The Throat
PHARYNGITIS (SORE THROAT)

Sore throats, by themselves, are not common in cats. Most are associated with a viral illness or mouth infection. The signs of sore throat are fever, coughing, gagging, vomiting, pain in the throat when attempting to swallow, and loss of appetite.

Foreign bodies in the throat cause symptoms much like those of sore throat and tonsillitis. This possibility should be considered.

Treatment: Veterinary examination and treatment of the basic disease process is required. Cats with a sore throat should be placed on soft, canned foods diluted with water or plain broth to a liquid consistency. Administer an antibiotic for one week. Pain medications may be needed.

TONSILLITIS

This also is rare in cats. The tonsils are aggregates of tissue, much like those of lymph nodes, and are located at the back of the throat, as they are in people. Usually, they are not visible unless they are inflamed. Infected tonsils cause symptoms much like those of a sore throat, except that fever is more pronounced (over 103°F [39.4°C]) and the cat appears more ill. Most cases are caused by a bacterial infection.

Tonsils can also be enlarged in certain cancers. If you suspect tonsillitis, your cat should be seen by a veterinarian.

Treatment: The treatment is the same as for *Pharyngitis* (above). Removal of chronically inflamed tonsils is seldom necessary.

FOREIGN BODIES IN THE THROAT (CHOKING AND GAGGING)

Some cats, especially kittens, may try to eat or swallow string, tinsel, cloth, fishhooks, and other small objects or toys. Depending on how far down the throat an object is lodged, the cat will exhibit gagging, neck extension on swallowing, and choking on swallowing.

If the signs are forceful coughing and the cat is having difficulty taking in air, the foreign body has passed into the larynx (see *Foreign Body in the Larynx*, page 302).

Treatment: Cats are extremely difficult to restrain when they are panicked. Struggling with them may cause a foreign body to work deeper into the throat. Do not try to open the cat's mouth. You may attempt a mini Heimlich maneuver (see page 303), but if this does not work immediately, do not delay. Calm the cat as best you can and proceed directly to the nearest veterinary hospital.

However, if the cat has fainted, the foreign body will have to be removed at once to reestablish the airway. Open the cat's mouth. This is now easily accomplished because the cat is unconscious. Take hold of the neck behind the object and apply enough pressure to keep the object from passing down while you hook it with your fingers. Work it loose as quickly as possible. Then administer *artificial respiration,* if needed (see page 11).

Prevention: Watch your cat carefully and do not let her play with small, easily torn toys. Do not feed a cat chicken bones or long bones that can splinter.

The Salivary Glands

There are four main salivary glands that drain into the cat's mouth. Only the parotid gland, located below the cat's ear at the back of the cheek, may be felt from the outside. The salivary glands secrete an alkaline fluid that lubricates the food and aids in digestion.

HYPERSALIVATION (DROOLING)

Healthy cats do not drool. However, it is common for cats to drool when they know they are going to be given an unpleasant-tasting medicine or receive an injection. This is psychological. A few cats will also drool when they are purring and very relaxed. It is important to know what is normal for your individual cat.

Keep in mind that an animal who drools excessively and acts irrationally could have rabies. Exercise great caution in handling such an animal.

Drooling accompanied by signs of ill health, such as watering of the eyes, is quite likely due to a feline viral respiratory infection. Young cats with liver shunts will drool excessively. Mouth infections and foreign bodies in the mouth are accompanied by drooling. Heat stroke can cause excess salivation, as can certain poisons (such as insecticides and arsenic).

Treatment: This is contingent on identifying the cause of the drooling.

SALIVARY GLAND TUMORS AND CYSTS

The salivary glands can be injured as a result of a fight or some other trauma to the head or neck area. The damaged gland may leak salivary fluid into the

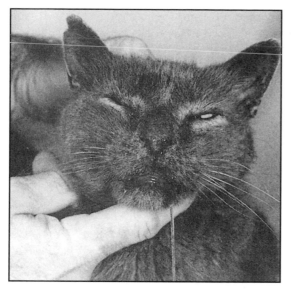

Excessive drooling caused by a severe mouth infection.

surrounding tissue, producing a cyst called a mucocele. When this occurs in the floor of the mouth on one side of the tongue, it is called a ranula. Mucoceles can enlarge and interfere with eating or swallowing.

Growths of the salivary gland are rare and occur in old cats. Most are cancers. They present as a slowly enlarging firm swelling or lump in the neck or on the side of the face.

Treatment: For mucoceles, treatment involves draining the cyst into the mouth or, for a more certain cure, surgical removal of the entire salivary gland. For growths, surgical cure is possible if it is done before the tumor has spread to other body parts.

Swollen Head
ALLERGIC REACTION

Sudden swelling of the face, lips, ears, and eyelids can be caused by a hivelike allergic reaction called urticaria. The cat's head may appear strangely out of proportion to her body, and the eyes may be swollen shut. Common causes are food allergy, contact and inhalation allergy, and the bites and stings of insects. Swelling may appear as much as 20 minutes after exposure to the allergen.

Treatment: Most reactions subside in three to four hours. Cool compresses may relieve some discomfort. Your veterinarian may choose to administer adrenaline or an antihistamine. You should try to find out what caused the allergic reaction so you can prevent your cat from coming into contact with that allergen again.

The addition of wheezing, respiratory distress, vomiting, or diarrhea indicates a potentially serious allergic reaction (see *Anaphylactic Shock*, page 15). Snakebite is another possibility. Seek immediate veterinary attention.

Head and Neck Abscesses

Head and neck abscesses appear suddenly and are accompanied by fever. They are extremely tender and may give a lopsided look to the head, face, or neck. Opening the mouth causes extreme pain in some cases. These cats refuse to eat or drink. Many have a high fever.

Most head and neck abscesses are caused by infected animal bites, mouth infections that spread to the frontal sinuses or the space behind the tonsils, or sharp foreign bodies such as wood splinters and quills that have worked back into the soft tissues.

Retrobulbar abscesses behind the eye cause tearing and protrusion of the eye. Submandibular abscesses cause swelling beneath the chin. An abscess in the frontal sinus causes swelling beneath the eye. Ear flap abscesses are discussed on in *Swollen Pina* (page 210).

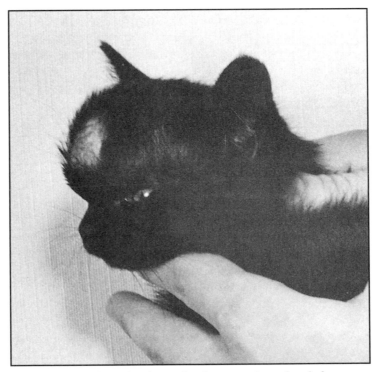

The swelling can be quite dramatic when a cat has a head abscess.

Treatment: In nearly all cases, incision and drainage by a veterinarian will be necessary when the abscess becomes soft. Your veterinarian may suggest applying warm saline packs for 15 minutes, four times a day to localize the infection before draining. Antibiotics are required. After incision and drainage, a wick of gauze may be used to keep the edges apart so that the wound can heal from the inside out. You may be required to change and dress the wound at home. If your cat paws at the site or licks at it, you may need to use an Elizabethan collar or a BiteNot collar.

9

The Digestive System

The digestive tract begins at the mouth and ends at the anus. The lips, teeth, tongue, salivary glands, mouth, and pharynx are discussed in other chapters of this book. The remaining digestive tract organs are the esophagus, stomach, *duodenum* (the first part of the small intestine), jejunum and ileum (also parts of the small intestine), colon, rectum, and anus. The organs that aid in digesting and absorbing foodstuffs are the pancreas, gallbladder, and liver. The pancreas is located next to the duodenum. The pancreatic enzymes drain into the pancreatic duct, which joins the bile duct from the liver; both ducts empty into the duodenum.

The esophagus is a muscular tube that carries food down to the stomach through a series of rhythmic contractions. The esophagus runs along the neck and into and through the chest cavity, on its way to the stomach. The lower esophagus enters the stomach at a sharp angle, which prevents food and liquids from refluxing back up into the esophagus. There is also a sphincter muscle that keeps the opening between the esophagus and the stomach closed, except when food is passed during swallowing.

The stomach grinds food into particles small enough to pass through a muscular sphincter called the *pylorus*. Food can remain in the stomach for three to six hours before passing through the pylorus into the duodenum and rest of the small intestine. Digestive juices from the pancreas and small intestine break the food down into amino acids, fatty acids, and carbohydrates. The products of digestion then pass through the wall of the bowel and into the bloodstream. Blood from the intestines flows to the liver. The liver has numerous functions connected with metabolism. Here the cat's meal is converted into stored energy and nutrients. Waste products are separated out.

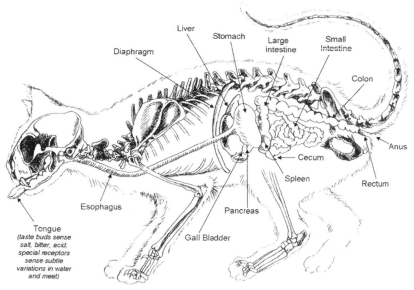

The gastrointestinal system.

Fiber and undigested food continue on through the small intestine into the colon. The function of the colon is to remove water and store waste material as feces.

Because of the cat's relatively relaxed abdominal wall, it is possible to feel many of the organs within the abdomen. Your veterinarian usually can tell whether the liver and spleen are enlarged and may be able to feel other swellings that could indicate a problem in the gastrointestinal or genitourinary systems.

The typical feline diet, based almost entirely on meat, is easy to digest, compared to the plant diet of an herbivore or even the mixed diet of an omnivore.

Endoscopy

An endoscope is an instrument used for viewing the interior of a body canal or a hollow organ such as the stomach or colon. Its use as a diagnostic tool is invaluable for digestive tract disorders, and more veterinary hospitals and clinics have acquired endoscopes.

While the cat is under general anesthesia, the flexible endoscope is inserted into the mouth or anus and fed through the gastrointestinal tract. A powerful light and a fiber optic cable are used to view the interior of the bowel. Tiny instruments passed through the scope are used to take biopsies and perform other procedures.

GASTROSCOPY

Gastroscopy, also called esophagogastroduodenoscopy (*EGD*), is the endoscopic procedure for exploring and biopsying the upper gastrointestinal (GI) tract. It is the best way to diagnose gastritis, stomach and duodenal ulcers, tumors, and foreign bodies. The endoscope is inserted into the mouth and passed through the esophagus into the stomach and duodenum. Foreign bodies, if encountered during the examination, can sometimes be removed from the esophagus and stomach using specially made instruments. Large objects may require open surgery.

COLONOSCOPY

Colonoscopy is a procedure in which the endoscope is passed through the anus into the rectum and colon. The ability to visualize the interior of the lower GI tract and biopsy the intestine has greatly simplified the diagnosis of colitis and other colon diseases.

The Esophagus

The esophagus is a muscular tube that propels food and water into the stomach. This is accomplished by a series of rhythmic contractions called peristaltic waves, which are coordinated with the act of swallowing.

Signs of esophageal disease include regurgitation, dysphagia (painful swallowing), drooling, and weight loss.

REGURGITATION

Regurgitation is the relatively effortless expulsion of undigested food, without retching. It occurs because the esophagus is physically blocked or there is a breakdown in the swallowing mechanism (peristalsis). In either case, the food accumulates until the esophagus is overloaded, after which the food is passively expelled.

Regurgitation should not be confused with vomiting. Vomiting is the forceful expulsion of stomach contents, preceded by retching. Vomited food is sour smelling, appears digested, or at least partly digested, and is often mixed with yellow bile.

Chronic regurgitation (the kind that comes and goes but seems to be getting worse) suggests a partial obstruction caused by megaesophagus, stricture, or tumor.

A serious complication of regurgitation is aspiration pneumonia, in which the lungs become infected as a result of food being aspirated (inhaled) into them. When regurgitated food ends up in the lungs, aspiration pneumonia is the result. Another potentially serious complication is nasal cavity infection. This occurs when food is regurgitated into the nose.

Bouts of severe coughing and gagging can be mistaken for either regurgitation or vomiting. It is important to distinguish between all three conditions, because each denotes a disease in a different system.

DYSPHAGIA (DIFFICULT, PAINFUL SWALLOWING)

If there is a partial blockage, swallowing can be difficult and painful, but the cat does not necessarily regurgitate. A cat with a painful esophagus makes repeated attempts to swallow the same mouthful and eats slowly. There may be noticeable weight loss, and as the condition becomes more painful, the cat may stop eating altogether.

Painful swallowing can be associated with mouth infections, dental infections, sore throat, or tonsillitis. Cats with these conditions also often have drooling and halitosis. Sometimes, the cat can eat softened or liquid foods but not hard or dry foods. Some cats will lick the "gravy" off canned foods but not eat the chunks.

MEGAESOPHAGUS (DILATED ESOPHAGUS)

Megaesophagus means "enlarged esophagus." When food is retained in the esophagus for an extended period, the esophagus becomes a storage organ and enlarges like a balloon. This process, called megaesophagus, is accompanied by regurgitation, loss of weight, and recurrent episodes of aspiration pneumonia caused by the reflux of food into the trachea.

There are two causes of megaesophagus. The first is a failure of the esophagus to contract and propel food into the stomach. This impaired motility occurs as a hereditary disorder in kittens and as an acquired disease in adults. The second cause of megaesophagus is a physical blockage, such as a foreign body, or a developmental problem with abnormal blood vessels that encircle the esophagus.

Congenital megaesophagus is a hereditary form of the disease that occurs in Siamese and other kittens. As the kitten swallows, the esophagus does not contract and does not propel food into the stomach. This is due to a developmental defect in the nerve plexus in the lower esophagus. Peristaltic activity stops at the level where the esophagus is paralyzed, and food can go no farther. In time, the esophagus above the inert segment enlarges and balloons out. This can be demonstrated by lifting up the kitten's back legs and looking for a bulging out of the esophagus at the side of the neck.

Kittens with congenital megaesophagus show signs at weaning, when they begin to eat solid foods. Characteristically, they approach the food dish with enthusiasm but back away after a few bites. They often regurgitate small amounts of food, which they eat again. After repeatedly eating the food, it becomes quite liquid and passes into the stomach. Repeated inhalation of food causes bouts of aspiration pneumonia.

This is a permanent condition and requires extensive care, such as feeding the cat in an upright position and maintaining that position after eating so that gravity can aid the movement of the food.

Another type of congenital megaesophagus is caused by retained fetal arteries in the chest (*aortic arch anomalies*). These arteries constrict the esophagus and prevent swallowing. Regurgitation and difficult swallowing appear as kittens are weaned from liquid to solid food. These kittens become malnourished and exhibit stunted growth. Surgery can correct some of these obstructions.

Adult-onset megaesophagus is an acquired condition seen in older cats. It can be a late manifestation of congenital megaesophagus, but it also can be caused by esophageal foreign bodies, tumors, strictures, nervous system diseases, autoimmune diseases, and heavy metal poisoning. In many cases, the cause is unknown.

A chest X-ray may show an enlarged esophagus, opaque material in the esophagus, or aspiration pneumonia. The diagnosis can be confirmed by administering a barium meal and then taking an X-ray of the chest.

Treatment: The primary goals are maintaining nutrition and preventing complications. Food and water should be given from a raised bowl to maximize the effect of gravity. A semiliquid or gruel mixture is easier for some cats to swallow; others do better with solids. Determine this by trial and error. After eating, the cat should be kept in an upright position so that gravity will help move food on into the stomach.

Even with dedicated care, many cats with megaesophagus will remain somewhat stunted and have bouts of aspiration pneumonia. Episodes of aspiration pneumonia require antibiotics, selected after culture and sensitivity tests. Signs of pneumonia are coughing, fever, and rapid, labored breathing (see *Pneumonia*, page 306).

Kittens rarely outgrow this condition. Older cats with acquired megaesophagus may respond to treatment of the stricture, tumor, or medical condition responsible for the symptoms.

FOREIGN BODY IN THE ESOPHAGUS

If a cat becomes suddenly distressed, drools, swallows painfully, or regurgitates food, suspect a foreign body, such as a small household object or a bone splinter, caught in the esophagus. A history of regurgitation and difficulty swallowing for several days or longer does not rule out a foreign body.

Sharp foreign bodies are particularly dangerous, because they can perforate the esophagus. Early diagnosis is important. A cat with a perforated esophagus exhibits fever, cough, rapid breathing, difficulty swallowing, and a rigid stance.

The diagnosis can usually be made by taking X-rays of the neck and chest. Ingesting a contrast material such as Gastrografin, followed by an X-ray of the esophagus, may be required.

Treatment: An esophageal foreign body is an emergency. Take your cat to a veterinarian at once. If you see a needle or thread, do not try to pull on it. It may be attached farther down the tract. Contact your veterinarian.

Many foreign bodies can be removed by gastroscopy. The cat is given a general anesthetic, after which an endoscope is passed through the mouth and into the esophagus. The object is located visually and removed with a grasping instrument. If the object cannot be withdrawn, it can often be pushed down into the stomach and removed surgically from the abdomen. Foreign bodies that cannot be dislodged using the endoscope require open esophageal surgery. The same is true for esophageal perforations.

ESOPHAGEAL STRICTURE

A stricture is a circular scar that develops after an injury to the esophagus. Injuries may be caused by esophageal foreign bodies, swallowed caustic liquids, or gastroesophageal reflux. The most common cause of stricture is esophageal injury caused by the reflux of stomach acid into the lower esophagus when a cat is under anesthesia. Strictures can also be caused by capsules or tablets that do not pass down the esophagus but sit along it and dissolve. Always encourage your cat to swallow after giving medications by immediately giving him a syringe full of plain water.

The principal sign of esophageal stricture is regurgitation. The diagnosis can be made by X-ray after the cat has been given a barium solution, or by an esophageal *endoscopy*. The stricture appears as a fibrous ring that narrows the esophagus.

Treatment: Most early strictures can be treated by stretching the wall of the esophagus with endoscopic dilators. Following dilatation, some cats swallow normally. Those that do not because megaesophagus (see page 261) has developed may require surgical removal of the stricture. Surgery in this area is often associated with complications. The cat may need a feeding tube sewn in to bypass the esophagus, and an extended hospital stay for healing.

In a cat with a stricture, overloading the esophagus with large meals aggravates the problem. Feed several small, semisolid meals a day from a raised food dish.

GROWTHS

Primary tumors of the esophagus are rare and most are malignant and occur in older cats. When a cancer (usually lymphosarcoma) involves the lymph nodes around the esophagus, these enlarged nodes can press on the esophagus, creating a physical blockage.

Treatment: Surgical removal of benign tumors (and malignant tumors that have not spread) offers the best chance for cure.

The Stomach

Stomach problems are often associated with vomiting. Since vomiting is so common in cats, it will be discussed in a separate section (see page 267).

ACUTE GASTRITIS

Gastritis is an irritation of the lining of the stomach that comes on suddenly. The principal sign is severe and continuous vomiting. Acute gastritis is severe and continuous vomiting that comes on suddenly. It is most likely caused by swallowing an irritant or a poison. Common stomach irritants include grass and other plants, hair, bones, spoiled food, and garbage. Certain drugs, notably aspirin, but also cortisone, butazolidin, and some antibiotics, produce gastric irritation. Common poisons include antifreeze, fertilizers, plant toxins, crabgrass killers, and rat poisons. If any of these is suspected, notify your veterinarian.

A cat with an acute gastritis vomits shortly after eating and later stops eating altogether and appears lethargic, sitting with his head hanging over the water bowl. His temperature remains normal unless the cat has an acute enteritis, a disease that also causes diarrhea.

Keep in mind that persistent vomiting is also associated with life-threatening diseases such as intestinal obstruction and peritonitis. Seek professional consultation in all cases where the cause of persistent vomiting is not known.

Treatment: Acute nonspecific gastritis is self-limiting and usually resolves in 24 to 48 hours if the stomach is rested and protected from excess acid. Follow the instructions in *Home Treatment of Vomiting* (page 269).

CHRONIC GASTRITIS

Cats with chronic gastritis vomit from time to time over a period of days or weeks, not always after meals. These cats appear lethargic, have a dull haircoat, and lose weight. The vomitus sometimes contains foreign material and food eaten the day before.

A common cause of chronic gastritis is swallowed hair that forms a hairball or *bezoar* in the stomach. Prevention is discussed in *Hairballs* (page 128). Other causes of chronic gastritis include persistent eating of plant matter, such as grass, or ingesting cellulose, plastic, paper, rubber, or other irritating products, and a diet of poor-quality or spoiled food.

Aspirin, when given to cats regularly, may cause thickening and peptic stomach ulceration, a condition that may be complicated by gastrointestinal bleeding. Aspirin and other nonsteroidal anti-inflammatory drugs should be given only under veterinary supervision.

Finally, if there is no apparent explanation for the sporadic vomiting, the cat may be suffering from an internal disorder such as liver disease, kidney failure, diabetes, tonsillitis, infected uterus, pancreatitis, hyperthyroidism, irritable bowel disease, or heartworm disease. The bacteria *Helicobacter pyloris* (see page 74) is a possible cause of chronic gastritis.

Treatment: This depends on finding and correcting the underlying cause. A cat with chronic vomiting should be examined by a veterinarian. Special diagnostic studies may be required. These may include a *biopsy* of the stomach or intestine by *endoscopy*, special dye studies with X-rays, or *ultrasound* examinations. Blood work is usually needed to rule out certain diseases. Cats with chronic vomiting often require a special, customized diet to fit the particular disease causing the vomiting. Famotidine (Pepcid) may be helpful.

FOOD INTOLERANCE

Some cats are unable to tolerate certain foods or specific brands of commercial cat food. This is determined by trial and error. Food hypersensitivity or intolerance could be the problem if your cat vomits about two hours after eating. Grains, especially wheat and corn, are common culprits. Cats may also develop an intolerance to a specific protein source, such as chicken or fish. This is usually accompanied by watery, mucuslike, or even bloody diarrhea (see *Diarrhea*, page 278).

Treatment: Commercial diets made without grain are now available. Special diets with limited protein sources or treated proteins can be prescribed by your veterinarian. Prescription diets for this problem include Eukanuba Response LB Feline, Royal Canin Hypoallergenic HP Feline, Royal Canin Neutral Formula Feline, Royal Canin's Limited Ingredients with duck, lamb, rabbit, or venison as the meat protein, Science Diet Feline d/d with duck, rabbit, or venison as the meat protein, and Science Diet z/d ULTRA Allergen Free Feline. Also see *Treating Diarrhea*, page 282.

MOTION SICKNESS

Many young cats suffer from motion sickness when traveling by car, boat, or air. The signs are restlessness followed by salivation, yawning, nausea, and then vomiting. Motion sickness is caused by overstimulation of the labyrinth system in the inner ear.

Treatment: If your cat is susceptible to motion sickness and you suspect your cat is going to be sick, your veterinarian may prescribe a drug such as dimenhydrinate (brand names Dramamine and Gravol, see *Over-the-Counter Drugs for Home Veterinary Use*, page 561). Follow your veterinarian's instructions for dosing. Unfortunately, the histamine receptors that cause motion sickness in dogs and people are not that important in cats, so drugs like dimenhydrinate or meclizine (Bonine) may not be helpful. Acepromazine may be prescribed for long trips.

Ginger is helpful for cats with motion sickness. Aromatherapy, particularly the use of lavender scents, may be helpful as well.

Cats travel best on an empty stomach, so it is best to withhold food before taking a trip. Try to keep the car cool, choose travel routes on smooth roads, and minimize stops and turns. Most cats with motion sickness become accustomed to riding in the car and eventually outgrow the problem.

ABDOMINAL DISTENSION

Several disorders may cause the abdomen to appear bloated or swollen. Overeating, eating fermented foods, and constipation can give a cat a somewhat bloated or pot-bellied look. Worm infestation can do this in kittens. Cushing's disease, heart failure, and feline infectious peritonitis often give cats a pot-bellied appearance.

Sudden swelling, accompanied by pain and signs of distress in the abdomen, indicate an urgent condition such as a bowel obstruction, bladder outlet obstruction, abscessed uterus, or peritonitis (see *Painful Abdomen,* page 15, and *Intestinal Obstruction,* page 274).

Acute gastric dilatation (bloat) or volvulus, which occurs in dogs, is extremely rare in cats but is an emergency when it occurs. In cats with gastric dilatation, the stomach distends with gas and fluid. With volvulus, the distended stomach rotates on its long axis. The spleen is attached to the wall of the stomach, and therefore rotates with the stomach. The signs are sudden abdominal swelling, a shocklike state, and peritonitis. *Rush your cat to the veterinary hospital.*

An abdominal swelling that comes on gradually over several days or weeks is most likely due to *ascites,* a condition in which fluid accumulates in the abdomen. Feline infectious peritonitis should be suspected. Other causes are right-sided heart failure and liver disease. Keep in mind that pregnancy and false pregnancy are common causes of abdominal enlargement in queens.

Treatment: Treatment depends on determining the exact cause. A veterinary examination is required.

STOMACH ULCER

Stomach ulcers are not common in cats. They are usually caused by drugs and medications—especially aspirin and other *NSAIDs* such as ibuprofen, naproxen, and butazolidin, and steroids. Vomiting is the most frequent sign. The vomitus contains old blood (which looks like coffee grounds) and occasionally fresh blood. Weight loss and anemia are accompanying features. Diagnosis is made by upper gastrointestinal X-rays or by *endoscopy*.

Treatment: Treatment involves discontinuing all ulcer-producing medications. Drugs are available to treat ulcers in cats. These include ranitidine, famotidine, cimetidine, omeprazole, and sucralfate.

Vomiting

A number of diseases and upsets in the cat are associated with vomiting. It is one of the most common nonspecific symptoms you are likely to encounter.

Cats vomit more easily than most other animals. Some cats seem to do so almost at will, at times for no apparent reason. A cat may vomit undigested food immediately after eating, then eat it again. A mother vomits food so her kittens will have a predigested meal.

All vomiting is the result of stimulation of the vomiting center in the brain by numerous receptors located in the digestive tract and elsewhere. As the need to vomit is perceived, the cat appears anxious and may seek attention and reassurance. You will also see the cat begin to salivate and make repeated efforts to swallow.

As vomiting starts, a simultaneous contraction of the muscles of the stomach and abdominal wall occurs. This leads to an abrupt buildup in intra-abdominal pressure. At the same time, the lower esophageal sphincter relaxes. The stomach contents travel up the esophagus and out the mouth. As the cat vomits, it extends its neck and makes a harsh gagging sound. This sequence should be distinguished from the passive act of *regurgitation* described earlier.

CAUSES OF VOMITING

The most common cause of vomiting is swallowing hair or some other indigestible foreign material, such as grass, that is irritating to the stomach. Most cats experience this at one time or another. Intestinal parasites may also cause stomach irritation. Other common causes are overeating or eating too fast. When kittens gobble their food and exercise immediately thereafter, they are likely to vomit. This kind of vomiting is not serious. It may be the result of feeding several kittens from a single pan, which encourages rapid eating. Separating kittens or feeding smaller meals often eliminates this problem. (For more on vomiting in kittens, see chapter 17.)

If the cat vomits once or twice but appears perfectly normal before and after, the problem is not serious and can be treated at home (see *Home Treatment of Vomiting*, page 269). Vomiting unrelated to eating is frequently a sign of an infectious disease, kidney or liver disease, or a central nervous system disorder. Diseases frequently associated with vomiting include feline panleukopenia, tonsillitis, sore throat, inflammatory bowel disease, and infected uterus (acute metritis). Other signs of illness will be present. In young cats, sudden vomiting with fever is suspicious of panleukopenia.

Another serious cause of vomiting is ingesting poison or a drug. Poisons are discussed on page 26. A most serious cause of vomiting is associated with peritonitis. *This is an emergency.* Causes are discussed in *Painful Abdomen* (page 15).

It is often possible to understand your cat's problem by noticing *how* and *when* he vomits. Note whether it is repeated, and if so, whether it is sporadic or persistent. How soon after eating does it occur? Is it projectile? Inspect the vomitus for blood, fecal material, and foreign objects.

Persistent Vomiting

The cat vomits, then continues to retch, bringing up a frothy, clear fluid. This suggests spoiled food, grass, hairballs, other indigestibles, and certain diseases such as *infectious enteritis,* which irritate the stomach lining. If the vomiting is accompanied by diarrhea, consult *Diarrhea,* page 278.

Sporadic Vomiting

Sometimes a cat vomits off and on over a period of days or weeks. There is no relationship to meals. The appetite is poor. The cat has a haggard look and appears listless. Suspect liver or kidney disease, or an illness such as chronic gastritis, irritable bowel disease, hairballs, a heavy worm infestation, or diabetes mellitus.

A foreign body in the stomach is another possibility. In an older cat, suspect a gastric or intestinal tumor. A veterinary checkup is in order.

Vomiting Blood

Red blood in the vomitus indicates active bleeding somewhere between the mouth and the upper small bowel. This is most commonly caused by a foreign body. Material that looks like coffee grounds is old, partially digested blood. This also indicates a bleeding point between the mouth and upper small bowel.

Any cat who vomits blood has a serious condition and must be seen right away by a veterinarian.

Vomiting Feces

A cat who vomits foul material that looks and smells like feces is most likely suffering from intestinal obstruction or peritonitis. Blunt or penetrating abdominal trauma is another cause of fecal vomiting. Seek immediate professional treatment.

Projectile Vomiting

Projectile vomiting is forceful vomiting in which the stomach contents are ejected suddenly, often a considerable distance. It indicates a complete blockage in the upper gastrointestinal tract. Foreign bodies, hairballs, tumors, and strictures are possible causes. Brain diseases that cause increased intracranial pressure also produce projectile vomiting. They include brain tumor, encephalitis, and blood clots.

Vomiting Foreign Objects

Hairballs may form wads too large to pass out of the stomach. Other foreign objects cats may vomit include pieces of cloth, bone splinters, sticks, stones, and small household objects. For more information, see *Gastrointestinal Foreign Bodies* (page 273). Kittens with a heavy roundworm infestation may vomit adult worms. These kittens should be treated as described in *Ascarids*, page 60.

HOME TREATMENT OF VOMITING

If there is any question about the cause or seriousness of the vomiting, seek veterinary help. Vomiting cats can rapidly become dehydrated as they lose body fluids and electrolytes. If vomiting is combined with diarrhea, the likelihood of dehydration increases dramatically. *Consult your veterinarian if vomiting persists for more than 24 hours*, if the cat becomes dehydrated, or if vomiting recurs.

Home treatment is appropriate only for normal, healthy adult cats who show no signs other than vomiting. Kittens, cats with preexisting health conditions, and older cats are less able to tolerate dehydration and should be treated by a veterinarian.

When the stomach responds promptly, the foreign material is expelled. Afterward, an important initial step is to rest the stomach by withholding food and water for a minimum of 12 hours. If your cat appears thirsty, allow him to lick ice cubes.

After 12 hours, if the vomiting stops, offer sips of water. A pediatric electrolyte solution (see *Home Treatment of Diarrhea*, page 281) can be given in small amounts, in addition to the water.

If the water is well tolerated, advance to a strained meat baby food (low in fat and with no onion powder). Offer four to six small meals a day for the next two days. Then return to a regular diet.

Stop all food and water and obtain immediate veterinary assistance when

- Vomiting persists even though the cat has received no food or water for several hours.
- Vomiting recurs during attempts to re-introduce food and water.

- Vomiting is accompanied by diarrhea.
- The cat vomits fresh blood or material that looks like coffee grounds (partially digested blood).
- The cat becomes weak and lethargic or shows other signs of systemic illness.

Small and Large Bowels

Cats have relatively short intestines; most of their nutrition comes from meat, which requires less surface area for digestion. Problems in the small and large bowel are associated with three common symptoms: diarrhea, constipation, and passing blood. Diarrhea is by far the most common and will be discussed in a separate section (see page 278).

INFLAMMATORY BOWEL DISEASE

There are three bowel problems in cats characterized by chronic and protracted diarrhea, sporadic vomiting, malabsorption and, in long-standing cases, weight loss, anemia, and malnutrition. Together, these are classified as inflammatory bowel disease (IBD). Some affected cats show clinical signs in a cyclical pattern, while others are constantly in discomfort.

All of these diseases are *immune-mediated* reactions of the gastrointestinal system to food, bacteria, or parasite *antigens*. These reactions get out of control, with large numbers of inflammatory cells collecting along the gastrointestinal tract and interfering with digestion and absorption. These syndromes can be managed but are seldom cured, and over the long term may lead to ulcers or cancer, such as lymphosarcoma.

Other health problems, such as parasites, hyperthyroidism, and kidney disease, must be ruled out first. Blood work and *ultrasound* or X-ray studies of the gastrointestinal tract may be needed.

The role of bacteria in these syndromes has not been clearly established in cats but has been suggested, since cats tend to have higher concentrations of bacteria in their small intestines than many other mammals. This may be related to their being obligate carnivores and having a relatively short intestinal tract. Some scientists believe that cats fed a high-protein, low-carbohydrate diet that is more like a wild cat's natural diet are less likely to develop these problems.

In each disease in the IBD complex, a different type of inflammatory cell (plasma cell, eosinophil, lymphocyte, macrophage) accumulates in the mucous lining of the small or large intestines. Pancreatitis and intestinal cancer may cause similar signs. A definitive diagnosis is made by *endoscopy* or exploratory surgery, during which biopsies are taken of the intestinal wall.

Treatment: This is an illness for which the realistic goal is control, not cure. Treatment tends to be lifelong for most cats. Although the exact medications may vary for the three versions of IBD, all three types often respond, at least partially, to dietary changes as described for lymphocytic-plasmacytic enterocolitis. Along with immunosuppressive drugs such as prednisolone and azathioprine, omega-3 fatty acids, antioxidants, and probiotics such as acidophilus may be helpful. Metronidazole, which is used to lower bacterial counts, can reduce symptoms. Budesonide is a new drug being looked at for treating IBD. This is a version of a corticosteroid, but it may have milder side effects. More research must be done before this drug can be recommended.

Lymphocytic-Plasmacytic Enterocolitis

This is the most common inflammatory bowel disease in cats. Lymphocytes and plasma cells are the predominant inflammatory cells seen on biopsy of the small and large intestines. The disease has been associated with giardiasis, food allergy or intolerance, and an overgrowth of intestinal bacteria. Vomiting is a common sign but is not present in all cases.

Treatment: An antibiotic (metronidazole) is given to treat bacterial overgrowth and giardiasis. Immunosuppressant drugs such as azathioprine (Imuran) and/or prednisone are used if other treatments are not successful. As a general measure, the cat should be placed on a hypoallergenic diet, either homemade (baby foods or boiled chicken) or commercially obtained from your veterinarian. The diet should be highly digestible and low in fat. If colitis is present, fiber may need to be added. A homemade diet may be developed by consulting a veterinary nutritionist. Raw diets are not recommended because the cat already has a stressed immune system.

Eosinophilic Enterocolitis

On biopsy, *eosinophils* may be found in the stomach, small intestine, or colon, and the eosinophil count in the blood may be elevated. Some cases are thought to be associated with food allergy or the tissue migration of roundworms and hookworms.

Treatment: Treatment involves the use of high-dose corticosteroids, such as prednisolone, that are tapered as symptoms are controlled. The cat should be tested for food allergies and intestinal parasites and treated accordingly. Dietary changes, as described for lymphocytic-plasmacytic enterocolitis, may be beneficial. This form of IBD is the most difficult to treat successfully and has the poorest outlook.

Granulomatous (Regional) Enteritis

This is a rare disease, similar to Crohn's disease in humans. There is thickening and narrowing of the terminal small bowel due to inflammation of surrounding fat and lymph nodes. Macrophages, which are cells, found in tissues, that fight infections, are found when the colon is biopsied. The diarrhea contains mucus and blood. Biopsies are processed with special stains to exclude histoplasmosis and intestinal tuberculosis.

Treatment: Corticosteroids and immunosuppressive drugs are used to reduce inflammation and scarring. A course of metronidazole may be of benefit. Surgery may be required for a strictured bowel.

ACUTE INFECTIOUS ENTERITIS

Enteritis is an infection of the gastrointestinal tract characterized by the sudden onset of vomiting and diarrhea, rapid pulse, fever, apathy, and depression. The vomitus and diarrhea may contain blood. Dehydration occurs rapidly. Cats under 1 year of age and those over 10 are particularly susceptible to the effects of dehydration and shock.

The parvovirus that produces feline panleukopenia is a common cause of infectious enteritis in cats. Less commonly, it is caused by bacteria (*Salmonella*, *E. coli*, *Campylobacter*), protozoa (coccidia, giardia, toxoplasma), or intestinal parasites (roundworms, tapeworms, hookworms). These diseases are discussed in chapter 3.

Treatment: This is directed toward prompt replacement of fluids and electrolytes. Intravenous fluids may be necessary. Antibiotics that are effective against the causative bacteria may be administered. Medications to control vomiting and/or diarrhea may also be needed.

COLITIS

This is an inflammatory disease of the large bowel or colon, usually occurring as a manifestation of inflammatory bowel disease, occasionally as a manifestation of acute infectious enteritis or a parasitic infestation.

Signs of colitis include urgent straining, painful defecation, prolonged squatting, flatulence, and passing many small stools mixed with blood and mucus. These signs should be distinguished from constipation (see page 276). In a cat with colitis, the stools are generally soft or watery. In a cat with constipation, the stools tend to be hard and dry, although a cat with colonic impaction (constipation) may pass only fluid, mimicking diarrhea.

Antibiotics can upset the normal flora of the colon and result in an overgrowth of virulent bacteria that then produce an acute pseudo-membranous colitis. This is common in people but uncommon in cats.

Treatment: Colitis is complicated and requires veterinary diagnosis and management. High-fiber diets, as described for the treatment of chronic constipation (see page 276), may be beneficial. These diets include Science Diet w/d, Eukanuba Low Residue, and Royal Canin HiFactor Formula.

MALABSORPTION SYNDROME

Malabsorption is not a specific disease but occurs as a consequence of some underlying disorder of the small bowel, the liver, or the pancreas. In malabsorption syndrome, the cat either does not digest food or does not absorb the products of digestion from the small intestine. The absorption of nutrients requires both the presence of digestive enzymes and a healthy bowel lining. Failure to digest or absorb food leads to loose, unformed stools containing large amounts of fat.

This syndrome can have a variety of causes. Liver and pancreatic disease can be associated with failure to produce or secrete digestive enzymes, while inflammatory disease of the small intestine may permanently damage the intestinal lining. The crowding out of normal cells in the bowel wall by malignant cells, which occurs with intestinal lymphosarcoma, is another consideration.

Cats with malabsorption syndrome are thin and malnourished, despite a large appetite. The stool contains large amounts of undigested fat, giving it a rancid odor. The hair around the anus is oily or greasy. The exact cause of malabsorption can usually be determined by specific tests or intestinal *biopsy*.

Treatment: This is directed at the underlying disease. When pancreatic disease is the problem, the cat can be given the missing pancreatic enzymes orally with his meals (see *Pancreatitis,* page 295).

Cats with malabsorption syndrome should be placed on a low-fat diet. Suitable homemade diets include boiled chicken or lamb, with supplements, as directed by a veterinary nutritionist. Prescription diets are available through your veterinarian and include Science Diet i/d, Eukanuba Low Residue, Purina EN Feline, Royal Canin Neutral Formula, and Royal Canin HiFactor Formula. Supplemental B-complex and fat-soluble vitamins should be given.

GASTROINTESTINAL FOREIGN BODIES

Hairballs rank as the number one cause of foreign material in the gastrointestinal tract. As cats groom their coat, they pick up and swallow hair. The hair forms tubular wads. Other material, such as wool, may be incorporated into the wad of hair, resulting in the formation of a *bezoar*. Eventually, the bezoar becomes too large to pass out of the stomach and produces bouts of vomiting and symptoms like those of chronic gastritis. Hair that passes into the colon contributes to constipation. If you find that your cat vomits wads of hair or if his stool has quite a bit of hair in it, anticipate a problem and take the preventive measures described in *Hairballs* (page 128).

Objects sometimes swallowed by cats include pins and needles, wood splinters, nylon stockings, rubber bands, feathers, cloth, tinsel, plastic, and string. Most pass through the intestinal tract without causing problems, although sharp objects have the potential to perforate the bowel. Fortunately, this is

Do not allow your cat to play unsupervised with string or other objects he could swallow. Pick up all such items when you are not present and supervising.

not common, even when a pin is swallowed. Should perforation occur, it leads to signs of painful abdomen. Seek immediate professional attention.

Treatment: If your cat swallows a sharp object or any object that you suspect may be too large to pass through his intestinal tract, *do not induce vomiting.* Consult your veterinarian. *Do not* attempt to pull a string out from your cat's mouth or from under or around the tongue. Pulling may lacerate his intestines. One end of the string often knots while the other gets caught in food that has already been eaten. Tension on the string can cause it to cut through the wall of the bowel. Your cat will need anesthesia and most likely surgery.

Prevention: Do not allow your cat to play with string, cloth, or plastic toys he could tear and swallow. If you use items such as fishing pole toys for interactive play, put them away when the play session is over.

Be careful not to leave ribbon, small craft objects, tinsel, and other easily swallowed items where your cat can get them. Examine his toys frequently for any small parts that may be coming loose.

INTESTINAL OBSTRUCTION

Any problem that interferes with the passage of intestinal contents through the GI tract results in a blocked bowel. The most common cause is a gastrointestinal foreign body. Other causes are tumors and strictures of the small and large intestines, adhesions following abdominal surgery, navel and groin hernias, and intussusception—a condition in which the bowel telescopes in upon itself, much like a sock pulled inside out. On occasion, obstruction of the colon may be caused by a fecal impaction or tumor. An intestinal blockage can be partial or complete.

Partial or intermittent obstruction, such as that caused by a tumor or stricture, may cause signs that come and go. These include weight loss and intermittent vomiting or diarrhea. Tumors tend to occur in older cats, and most of them are malignant. They often become large before being discovered, usually by feeling a mass in the abdomen.

Signs of complete blockage include sudden pain, vomiting without relief, dehydration, and swelling of the abdomen. When the blockage is in the upper small bowel, the vomiting may be projectile. Blockages in the lower GI tract cause abdominal distension and the vomiting of brown, fecal-smelling material. Cats with complete obstruction pass no stool or gas through the rectum. In general, cats with lower bowel obstruction are less sick than those with upper intestinal obstruction.

Treatment: Intestinal obstruction leads to death unless treatment is instituted immediately. The cat's condition is most urgent when there are signs of strangulation or interference with the blood supply to the bowel. This is characterized by sudden distress, an extremely tender, boardlike abdomen, shock, and prostration. Surgical exploration and relief of the blockage is necessary. Strangulation requires immediate surgery. A dead segment of bowel must be removed and the bowel restored by an end-to-end hookup. There are often complications associated with these surgeries.

FLATULENCE (PASSING GAS)

Cats who frequently pass gas can embarrass or distress their owners. Flatulence is caused by eating highly fermentable foods, such as beans, cauliflower, cabbage, and soybeans; drinking large quantities of milk; and swallowing large amounts of air during meals. Diets high in carbohydrates and fiber contribute to it. Flatulence also occurs with malabsorption. This is related to incomplete digestion of carbohydrates. If your cat has a robust appetite and passes a large amount of soft stool, see *Malabsorption Syndrome*, page 273.

Treatment: It's important to first rule out any malabsorption syndrome. Change the cat's food to a highly digestible, low-fiber diet, and avoid giving table scraps. If dietary manipulation fails to control the problem, switch from commercial food to a highly digestible prescription diet, such as Science Diet i/d or one of the diets for food allergy or intolerance. Low-carbohydrate diets are often helpful. Free feed to prevent greedy eating and gulping air, unless your cat is overweight. A medication combining simethicone and activated charcoal (Flatulex) is available for people and can be used in cats. See *Over-the-Counter Drugs for Home Veterinary Use* (page 561) for dosage. This medication should not be given to cats with liver or kidney problems.

Overweight cats are more likely to suffer from flatulence, so work on weight control and provide plenty of exercise.

Constipation

Most cats have one or two stools a day. However, some cats have a bowel movement every two or three days. These cats are quite likely to be constipated. Constipation is the infrequent passage of small, hard, dry stools. When feces are retained in the colon for two to three days, they become dry and hard. This results in straining and pain during defecation.

Straining also occurs with colitis and feline lower urinary tract disease (FLUTD, page 380). Be sure the cat is not suffering from one of these conditions before treating for constipation. An overlooked urethral obstruction is especially serious, since it can cause damage to the kidneys and death.

Chronic Constipation

Dehydration, such as occurs in a cat with renal disease, is a common cause of constipation. The problem is intensified if the cat does not drink enough water. In fact, because they are descended from wild cats who inhabited an arid climate, cats tend to drink less water than most other animals.

Hairballs are a common cause of hard stools, particularly in longhaired cats. Suspect this if your cat vomits hair or if you see hair in his stool. Preventing hairballs is discussed in *Hairballs*, page 128. Other indigestible substances, such as grass, cellulose, paper, and cloth can lead to constipation or fecal impaction.

The urge to defecate can be overridden voluntarily. Many cats will not defecate when in unfamiliar surroundings; others may refuse to use a dirty litter box. Older, less active cats experience reduced bowel activity and the muscles of the abdominal wall may weaken. Either can lead to prolonged retention and increased hardness of stools. Obese cats are also more likely to suffer from constipation.

Occasionally, chronic constipation is due to or results in an enlarged, sluggish, poorly contracting colon, a condition called megacolon (see page 278). Cats with this condition require lifelong treatment with stool softeners and special diets. Veterinary supervision is necessary.

A chronically constipated cat may have a bloated look, seem lethargic, and pick at his food.

Constipation and fecal incontinence can occur in tailless cats, such as the Manx, who have developmental deformities of the spine and incomplete enervation of the colon. Also, cats who have suffered from a broken pelvis may have nerve damage to the colon or a mechanical narrowing of the pelvic canal, causing a partial obstruction.

Treatment: Cats with chronic or recurrent episodes of constipation may benefit from a high-fiber diet. Some commercial weight-loss cat foods and some hairball prevention formulas are high in fiber. There are also prescription high-fiber diets, such as Science Diet w/d, Royal Canin HiFactor Formula, and Purina OM Feline Formula. However, some veterinarians believe that a low-carbohydrate (and, therefore, low-fiber) diet may be better for constipated cats. They suggest feeding the cat only canned foods for the increased water and lower carbohydrate content, adding 1 teaspoon (1.2 g) of rice bran or powdered psyllium, if needed. For mild constipation, adding bulk-forming laxatives is beneficial. These laxatives absorb water in the colon, soften feces, and promote more frequent defecation. Wheat bran (1 tablespoon, 3.6 g, per day), canned plain pumpkin (1 teaspoon, 5 g, twice a day) or Metamucil (1 teaspoon, 5 g, per day mixed into wet food) is recommended. Lactulose, a synthetic sugar that draws water into the bowel, is often helpful and can be powdered and put in capsules if your cat won't eat it in with his food. Bulk laxatives can be used indefinitely without causing a problem.

Pediatric glycerin suppositories are sometimes useful for periodic treatment.

Stimulant laxatives are effective for simple constipation but repeated use may interfere with colon function. Several products are available that are made for cats, including Kat-a-lax and Laxatone. The latter is especially effective for cats with hairballs. These products should never be used if there is any possibility of an obstruction. Always consult with your veterinarian before giving your cat any laxative product.

Kitty litter should be scooped at least once a day and changed frequently, so that the box is always clean and fresh. Daily exercise is beneficial.

FECAL IMPACTION

A fecal impaction is a large mass of dry, hard stool that can develop in the rectum due to chronic constipation. This mass may be so hard that it cannot come out of the body. Watery stool from higher in the bowel may move around the mass and leak out, causing soiling. Affected cats often pass blood-tinged or watery, brown stool. This may be mistaken for diarrhea. Fecal impaction is confirmed by digital examination by your veterinarian using a well-lubricated glove.

Treatment: The removal of impacted feces requires both a laxative and an enema. As you may imagine, giving a cat an enema is no easy task, so it is best left to a veterinarian or a veterinary technician. For a severe impaction accompanied by dehydration, fluid replacement is necessary before attempting to remove the impaction.

Enemas may be repeated as necessary to evacuate all fecal material. Soap suds enemas and Fleet enemas should not be used because of potential toxicity in cats.

If a fecal impaction is too large or hard to evacuate with enemas, manual extraction by your veterinarian with forceps will be required; the cat must be anesthetized.

MEGACOLON

Megacolon is a stretching of the wall of the large intestine or colon caused by large amounts of fecal material building up inside. The motility of the intestine is also affected. This appears to be a muscular problem as opposed to a purely neurological one. About 62 percent of cases have no known cause.

Shorthaired, middle-aged male cats are most commonly affected, but about 12 percent of the cases are Siamese cats. Manx cats with pelvic problems may also develop a secondary megacolon. Obesity may be a predisposing factor.

Cats with megacolon may be depressed and not groom well. They will not be passing feces and a large mass can be felt in the abdomen or rectally.

Treatment: Veterinary treatment is required. Removing the feces often requires anesthesia and repeated enemas, as well as manual extraction of the hard, dried mass of fecal material. Many of these cats are dehydrated and need fluid therapy.

Long-term dietary changes, such as adding fiber (either canned pumpkin at 1 to 3 teaspoons, 5 to 15 g, per meal; or wheat bran at 1 to 3 teaspoons, 1.2 to 3.6 g, per meal), may help. Other cats benefit from a highly digestible diet such as Iams Low Residue. Occasional laxative use may also help. You may have to customize treatment to the individual cat. Cisapride is a motility drug that benefits some cats.

In severe and recurrent cases, surgery to remove the affected areas of large intestine may be needed.

FECAL INCONTINENCE

Loss of bowel control may follow a spinal cord injury, especially one in which the cat's tail is run over by a car. The bladder may also be paralyzed. The sacral or coccygeal vertebrae are pulled apart, damaging the nerves to the rectum, bladder, and tail. An injured cat with a limp tail should be X-rayed to see if he has a spine injury.

Loss of function may be temporary or permanent, depending on the severity of the nerve injury (see *Spinal Cord Injuries*, page 343). Loss of the ability to urinate or defecate is particularly serious. If untreated, it leads to kidney failure and death.

Treatment: Some cats will regain neurological function. Nursing care in the meantime may include expressing the bladder and administering enemas. Your veterinarian can guide you on supportive care.

Diarrhea

Diarrhea is the passage of loose, unformed stool. In most cases, there is a large volume of stool and an increased number of bowel movements. Diarrhea is a symptom—not a disease. A common cause of diarrhea is overfeeding. Dietary overload presents the colon with more volume than it can handle easily.

Food in the small intestine takes about eight hours to get to the colon. During this time, the bulk of it is absorbed. Eighty percent of water is absorbed in the small bowel. The colon concentrates and stores the waste. At the end, a well-formed stool is evacuated. A normal stool contains no mucus, blood, or undigested food. But when food passes rapidly through the small intestine, it is incompletely digested and arrives at the rectum in a liquid state. This results in a loose unformed bowel movement. Transit time in the intestinal tract can be speeded up by a variety of irritating substances, including

- Dead animals, including rodents, and birds
- Garbage and decayed food
- Rich foods, gravies, salts, spices, and fats
- Indigestible items, such as sticks, cloth, grass, paper, and plastic
- Intestinal parasites

Diarrhea from eating toxic substances is not common in cats, because they are quite careful of what they eat and tend to eat slowly. However, toxic substances can be ingested when cats clean their feet or groom their coat. Many of these substances are also toxic to the stomach and cause vomiting. Some toxic substances that can cause diarrhea include

- Gasoline, kerosene, oil, and coal tar derivatives
- Cleaning fluid and refrigerants
- Insecticides, bleaches, toilet bowl cleaner inserts
- Wild and ornamental plants, mushrooms
- Building materials (cement, lime, paints, caulks)

Some adult cats (and occasionally kittens) are unable to digest milk and some milk byproducts. This is because they lack adequate amounts of the enzyme lactase, which aids in the digestion of milk sugars—present in all dairy products. The unabsorbed sugar, called lactose, holds water in the small intestine, producing increased motility and a large volume of stool. Other foods that some cats may be unable to tolerate include beef, pork, chicken, horse meat, fish, eggs, spices, corn, wheat, and soy—either in people foods or commercial cat foods. At times, even a simple change in diet may cause diarrhea. Diarrhea in kittens is discussed in chapter 17.

Cats can experience emotional diarrhea when they are excited or stressed.

To narrow the search for the cause of the diarrhea, begin by examining the color, consistency, odor, and frequency of stools. The table on page 280 details what to look for.

Characteristics of Diarrhea

	Likely Cause	Likely Location
Color		
Yellow or greenish	Rapid transit	Small bowel
Black, tarry	Upper GI bleeding	Stomach or small bowel
Red blood or clots	Lower GI bleeding	Colon
Pasty, light	Lack of bile	Liver
Large, gray, rancid	Inadequate digestion or absorption	Small bowel or pancreas
Consistency		
Watery	Rapid transit	Small bowel
Foamy	Bacterial infection	Small bowel
Greasy, often with oily hair around the anus	Malabsorption	Small bowel, pancreas
Soft, bulky	Overfeeding, or poor-quality diet high in fiber	Small bowel (rapid transit)
Glistening or jellylike	Contains mucus	Colon
Odor		
Foodlike, or smelling like sour milk	Rapid transit, inadequate digestion or absorption (suggests overfeeding, especially in kittens)	Small bowel
Rancid or foul	Inadequate digestion with fermentation	Small bowel, pancreas
Putrid	Intestinal infection, bleeding	Small bowel
Frequency		
Several small stools in an hour, with straining	Colitis	Colon
Three or four large stools a day	Malabsorption, inflammatory bowel disease	Small bowel, pancreas
A week or longer	A chronic ailment such as colitis, inflammatory bowel disease, parasite infestation, or malabsorption syndrome	Throughout the intestinal tract
Condition of the cat		
Weight loss	Inadequate digestion or absorption	Small bowel, pancreas
No weight loss, normal appetite	Large bowel disorder	Colon
Vomiting	Enteritis	Small bowel, rarely colon

TREATING DIARRHEA

The first step is to identify and remove the underlying cause. For example, if a cat has a lactase enzyme deficiency (lactose intolerance), dairy products can be removed from the diet without causing a nutrient deficiency because they are not a necessary part of an adult cat's diet. Diarrhea caused by overeating (characterized by several large, bulky, unformed stools) is controlled by cutting back the overall food intake and feeding the cat three small meals instead of one large meal a day. Unfamiliar water can cause diarrhea. Give the cat water brought from home or bottled water when you are traveling. When irritating or toxic substances have been ingested, identify the agent because specific antidotes may be required (see *Poisoning*, page 22).

Diarrhea caused by food allergy or intolerance is treated by placing the cat on a homemade or commercial hypoallergenic diet prescribed by your veterinarian for about eight weeks. If the diarrhea disappears, the cat can remain on this diet, or various foods can be added one by one until the offending food allergen is detected by a return of symptoms. This food substance is then eliminated from the diet.

Food intolerance is a non-immune-mediated cause of diarrhea and vomiting. This could be a response to a dietary protein, a preservative, a flavoring, or anything else in the cat's diet. Again, removing the offending substance will stop the problem. Prescription diets for this problem include Eukanuba Response LB Feline, Royal Canin Hypoallergenic HP Feline, Royal Canin Neutral Formula Feline, Royal Canin's Limited Ingredients with duck, lamb, rabbit, or venison as the meat protein, Science Diet Feline d/d with duck, rabbit, or venison as the meat protein, and Science Diet z/d ULTRA Allergen Free Feline.

Diarrhea that persists for more than 24 hours is potentially serious. *Consult your veterinarian without delay.* Always remember to bring a sample of the diarrhea so that it can be examined for parasites and bacteria. A cat dehydrates quickly when fluid losses go unchecked, and this can lead to shock and collapse. Other indications to consult your veterinarian include bloody diarrhea and diarrhea accompanied by vomiting, fever, and signs of toxicity. The cause of chronic diarrhea is difficult to diagnose and requires laboratory analysis and close professional monitoring.

Diarrhea of short duration without excessive fluid loss can be treated at home. Withhold all food for 24 hours. Periodically give him very small amounts of water or ice cubes to lick. As the cat begins to recover, introduce food gradually, feeding three to four small meals a day. Begin with a diet high in meat protein. Strained meat baby food, the diets recommended earlier for food allergy and intolerance, and Hill's Prescription Diet Feline i/d are good examples. Avoid high-carbohydrate foods and dry cat foods. Cats have a low tolerance for carbohydrates and high-carb diets are likely to prolong the diarrhea. Gradually return to the usual food when the cat has fully recovered.

Loperamide (Imodium) may be used upon the advice of your veterinarian. However, if an infectious cause is suspected, loperamide might be contraindicated

Cats with severe diarrhea dehydrate quickly and should be given intravenous fluids to prevent shock and collapse.

because it will keep the infectious organism in the bowel longer by slowing the body's efforts to expel it. Loperamide is also somewhat controversial, as it may cause excitement in some cats. Avoid any diarrhea medicines that contain salicylates. (See *Over-the-Counter Medications for Home Use*, page 561.)

The Anus and Rectum

Signs of anal and rectal disease are pain when defecating, severe straining, scooting, passing bright red blood, and licking repeatedly at the rear. Cats with anal and rectal pain often try to defecate while standing upright, rather than squatting.

Bleeding from the anus or rectum is recognized by finding blood on the outside of the stool rather than mixed in with it.

Scooting along the ground is a sign of anal itching. It can be caused by flea bites, inflammation of the anus, anal sac disease, roundworms, or tapeworms.

PROCTITIS (INFLAMED ANUS AND RECTUM)

Inflammation of the skin around the anus is often caused by feces adhering to the hair around the anus. Irritation of the anal canal itself can occur when the cat passes hard or sharp objects and hard, dry stools. Repeated bouts of diarrhea, especially in kittens, cause an inflamed anus and rectum. Other causes are insect bites and internal parasites.

Straining is the most common sign of proctitis. Other signs are scooting, biting, and licking at the rear. The rough surface of the cat's tongue may aggravate the problem, causing further ulceration and extreme discomfort.

Treatment: Clip away any matted hair and stool, if present, to let air get to the skin. An irritated anus can be soothed by applying ointment such as triple-antibiotic ointment, aloe, or a hydrocortisone cream. See *Constipation* (page 276) if the cat has hard dry stools. See *Diarrhea* (page 278) if this is a contributing factor. Put your cat on an appropriate diet. Feed smaller amounts of food more often until the condition is healed.

Cats may be kept from licking their rear by applying bad-tasting repellent medication obtained from a veterinarian.

ANAL AND RECTAL PROLAPSE

With forceful and prolonged straining, a cat can force the lining of the anal canal to protrude. A partial prolapse is confined to the mucous membrane. In a cat with a complete prolapse, a segment of intestine two to three inches long may protrude. This difference is quite evident. Protrusion of anal tissue could be mistaken for hemorrhoids, but cats do not get hemorrhoids.

Conditions that produce forceful straining and predispose a cat to prolapse include infectious enteritis, fecal impaction, prolonged labor, colitis, and FLUTD. Kittens younger than 4 months have the highest incidence of prolapse, which may be related to parasite infestations. Manx cats also have a higher incidence.

Treatment: The underlying cause of straining must be identified and treated. A partial prolapse is treated in the same manner as described for *Proctitis* (page 282).

A complete rectal prolapse should be replaced manually by your veterinarian. Until you can reach your veterinarian, it is important to keep the prolapsed tissue healthy. Clean the tissue using a wet cloth and lubricate it with petroleum jelly. Then try to gently push it back through the anus. Even if it goes in, get your cat to the veterinarian.

To prevent recurrence, your veterinarian may suggest taking a temporary purse-string suture around the anus to hold everything in place until healed. The cat should be placed on a stool softener such as Colace liquid, 1 percent, as prescribed by your veterinarian. Feed a highly digestible diet—preferably a canned one.

IMPACTED ANAL SACS

The cat has two anal glands, or sacs, located at about four o'clock and eight o'clock in reference to the circumference of the anus. A cat's anal glands are

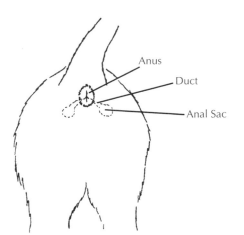

Position of the anal sacs.

Anus

Duct

Anal Sac

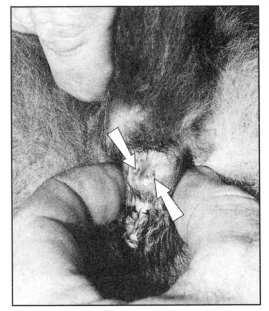

The arrows indicate the anal sac openings.

about the size of peas. The openings of the anal sacs are found by lifting up the cat's tail, drawing down on the skin of the lower part of the anus, and looking for the openings in those locations.

These sacs are sometimes referred to as scent glands. In the cat they mark the stool with an odor that identifies that particular individual—which helps the cat establish his territory.

Normally, the anal sacs are emptied naturally by rectal pressure when the cat defecates. The secretions are liquid, malodorous, and light gray to brown. At times they may be thick, creamy, or yellowish. It is not necessary to express the cat's anal glands manually unless there is some medical reason to do so. However, when frequent odor poses a problem (for example, in a cat with overactive anal sacs), you can control it by expressing the sacs yourself.

Impaction (the sacs become filled and cannot empty) is uncommon and occurs when the sacs fail to empty normally. This may happen if the small ducts are plugged by their pasty secretions. Often, it is not recognized until infection is present. Some complications that may occur from anal gland impaction include infection and abscess.

Uncomplicated anal sac impaction is treated by manual emptying (see below). If no discharge is noted, you may need to put a warm compress on the area for five to ten minutes twice a day to loosen up the secretions. Try emptying the anal sacs *after* the compress treatments.

How to Empty the Anal Sacs

Raise the cat's tail and locate the openings as shown in the illustration on 284. You can feel the sacs as small pea-size lumps in the perianal areas at the four o'clock and eight o'clock positions. Grasp the skin surrounding the sacs with your thumb and forefinger and squeeze together. As the sacs empty, you will note a pungent odor. Wipe the secretions away with a damp cloth. If the discharge is bloody or purulent, the anal sacs are infected and you should contact your veterinarian.

ANAL SACCULITIS (ANAL SAC INFECTION)

This condition complicates impaction. Signs of infection include the presence of blood or pus in the anal sac secretions, swelling on one or both sides of the anus, and the presence of anal pain and scooting. You may notice the cat licking the area more than usual. These signs also occur with anal sac abscess.

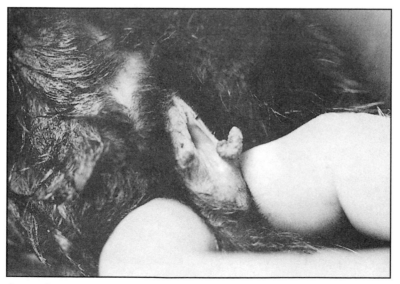

The anal sacs are emptied by pinching the anal skin between the fingers.

Treatment: The anal sacs should be expressed and emptied daily, after which an antibiotic may be put into the sac through the opening. This procedure is difficult and should only be done by a veterinarian. Your veterinarian may show you how to do some of the care.

You can help to resolve infection by applying warm wet packs to the anal area for 15 minutes three times a day for seven to ten days. A systemic antibiotic may be prescribed by your veterinarian, in addition to the topical antibiotic.

Anal gland infections seem to be more common in overweight, inactive cats. Weight loss and increased exercise may help prevent recurrence. Some cats do well with a change in diet, as well. Cats with recurrent anal sac infections may benefit from a dental diet such as Hill's Prescription Diet t/d. Cats with recurrent anal gland infections may need to have the glands removed.

ANAL SAC ABSCESS

An abscess is recognized by the signs of infection and swelling at the site of the gland. The swelling is red at first, then turns a deep purple. The cat may have a fever until the abscess is opened and drained. You may notice the cat licking at the area more than normal.

Treatment: An abscess is ready to drain when it becomes soft and fluidlike. At this point, it should be lanced by your veterinarian so that pus and blood will drain out. The abscess cavity must heal from the inside out. Keep the edges apart by flushing the cavity twice a day with a topical antiseptic such as

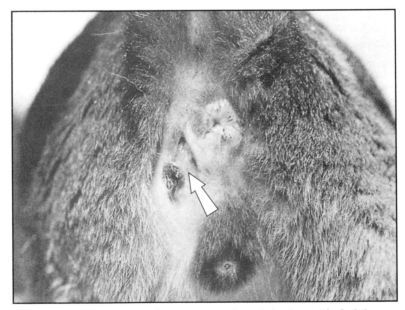

The arrow shows the site of recurrent anal sac infection with draining abscess and skin tracts.

dilute (tea-colored) Betadine solution for 10 to 14 days, and applying warm wet packs to the anal area for 15 minutes three times a day for 7 to 10 days. An oral antibiotic is normally administered. Culture and antibiotic sensitivity tests may be warranted. Some abscesses leave scarring so that the anal gland is no longer functional. This is not a problem for most cats.

POLYPS AND CANCER

Polyps are grapelike growths that occur in the rectum and protrude from the anus. They are not common and should be removed.

Cancer of the anal canal is not common. It appears as a fleshy growth that ulcerates and bleeds. Signs are similar to those of prolonged proctitis—straining being one of the most common. The diagnosis is made by obtaining a fragment of tissue for microscopic examination. Anal glands can sometimes develop cancers, but that is much more common in dogs than in cats.

The Liver

The liver has many vital metabolic functions, including synthesizing proteins and sugars, removing wastes from the bloodstream, manufacturing blood-clotting factors, and detoxifying many drugs and poisons.

A common sign of liver disease is *jaundice*, in which bile accumulates in the tissues, turning the skin and whites of the eyes yellow and the urine tea-colored. Jaundice may also be caused by *immune-mediated* destruction of red blood cells. Sometimes this color change is first noted on the inside of the ears.

Ascites is the accumulation of fluid in the abdomen. It can be caused by increased pressure in the veins of the abdomen. It can also be the result of decreased protein synthesis by the liver, so that fluids leak out of the blood vessels. A cat with ascites has a swollen or bloated look to the abdomen. Feline infectious peritonitis is the most common cause of ascites.

Spontaneous bleeding is a sign of advanced liver disease. Common sites of bleeding are the stomach, intestines, and urinary tract. Pinhead-size areas of hemorrhage occur in the mouth (especially on the gums) or may be noted on the skin, especially in the groin area.

Cats with impaired liver function appear weak and lethargic, lose their appetite and lose weight. They may also vomit and have diarrhea, drink excessively, and have pain in the abdomen. Signs of central nervous system involvement—head pressing (the cat has a bad "headache" and actually puts his forehead against a wall), intermittent apparent blindness, stupor, seizure, and coma—indicate advanced liver failure. These signs may be designated as hepatic encephalopathy.

Causes of Liver Failure

The most common cause of liver failure in cats is idiopathic hepatic lipidosis (discussed below). The next most common cause is cholangiohepatitis (see page 289). Infectious diseases that involve the liver include feline infectious peritonitis and toxoplasmosis. Feline leukemia and cancers that begin in the liver or spread there from other locations are other causes of liver insufficiency.

A blockage of the bile ducts by gallstones or parasites (liver flukes) is not common but should be considered when a cat has unexplained jaundice.

Chemicals known to cause liver toxicity are carbon tetrachloride, insecticides (such as the chlorinated hydrocarbons chlordane and dieldrin) and toxic amounts of copper, lead, phosphorus, selenium, and iron.

Drugs that adversely affect the liver include acetaminophen (Tylenol), some inhaled anesthetic gases, some antibiotics, diuretics, sulfa preparations, anticonvulsants, arsenicals, diazepam (Valium), and some steroids. Most drugs cause problems only when recommended doses are exceeded or when administered for long periods.

Treating liver failure depends on making the diagnosis. Special laboratory studies (blood work for bile acid assays, ultrasound, CT scan, liver biopsy) may be needed to determine the exact cause. The prognosis for recovery is related to the duration and extent of the damage and to whether the cause can be corrected. Luckily, the liver is noted for its regenerative powers, and for many diseases, if the cat can be given prompt supportive care, the liver will gradually heal.

Hepatic Lipidosis

This disease, unique to cats, is the most common metabolic cause of liver failure. Although the precise cause(s) may be unknown, this syndrome appears to be a type of anorexia that occurs when a cat has a sustained loss of appetite and stops eating. The liver plays a major role in fat (lipid) metabolism. With starvation, fat accumulates in liver cells. Lipid mobilization (lipid molecules are moved out of storage in the tissues) throughout the body, along with related secondary nutritional deficiencies, seems to be the critical path to disease.

The liver becomes yellow, greasy, and enlarged. Signs of liver failure (especially jaundice) appear as liver function deteriorates. Drooling is common, and the cat may have an enlarged liver on palpation, X-rays, or ultrasound examination. Usually, the loss of appetite has been going on for two to three weeks, but cases do occur in which anorexia is present for just a few days.

Often, hepatic lipidosis is secondary to a systemic problem, such as hyperthyroidism, diabetes mellitus, urinary tract conditions, or upper respiratory infections. Illnesses in which the cat cannot keep down food may also cause the disease. However, anywhere from 15 to 50 percent of cases have no obvious primary cause.

Hepatic lipidosis occurs in cats of both sexes and all ages. Being overweight is a predisposing cause. Often, stress is the initiating factor, but frequently the cause of the anorexia is unknown (idiopathic hepatic lipidosis). Diagnosis is confirmed by liver *biopsy* and blood work. Cats who are severely ill are at high risk for complications during anesthesia for biopsy, so it may be best to wait on the biopsy and start treatment. A *needle aspirate* under ultrasound guidance may be adequate, and even that should only be done after a clotting profile.

Treatment: Early intensive fluid replacement and forced feeding offer the best chance for reversing the process. Cats who receive early and aggressive nutritional support, such as the placement of feeding tubes, have a 90 percent chance of survival. If the cat does not get this quick, aggressive treatment, the survival rate goes down to 10 to 15 percent.

Appetite stimulants may be prescribed by your veterinarian, but they are only effective if the cat is still eating at least a little on his own. In most cases, nutritional support involves special diets and formulas administered by your veterinarian by stomach tube or gastrostomy, an operation in which a feeding tube is placed into the stomach through a small incision in the abdominal wall. Nutritional support is continued until the cat recovers and begins to eat on his own. Any nutritional supplements given through a feeding tube should be warmed to room temperature.

Fluids should be free of carbohydrates. Cats with this problem need high-quality protein and extra vitamins and nutrients, including the amino acids carnitine, taurine, and arginine. If the cat is showing extensive neurological signs, the amount of protein may need to be reduced to minimize ammonia production. Small, frequent feedings are best at first. Phosphorus and potassium levels need to be monitored. Cimetidine and ranitidine (acid blockers) are important if the cat shows any signs of ulcers in the gastrointestinal tract. Neomycin and metronidazole (antibiotics) may be helpful if the cat has neurological signs. SAMe is an antioxidant that is important in fighting liver disease, as is the herb milk thistle. N-acetylcysteine, another antioxidant, may be beneficial for many cats.

Recovery may take two to three months and requires home nursing care and complete dedication by the owner. Survival of the first four days of intensive treatment is a very good sign, with 85 percent of those cats going on to recovery. If pancreatitis is also present, the prognosis is poor.

When cats stop eating for even a day or two, they are prone to liver disease. Seek veterinary attention whenever your cat refuses to eat for more than two days.

CHOLANGIOHEPATITIS

Cholangiohepatitis is the second most common liver disease of cats. This disease involves inflammation of the liver and the bile ducts. Bile is the product of the gallbladder and is important in managing fats and collecting toxins to be removed from the blood. When bacteria from the duodenum (small intestine) come up the bile duct (instead of bile going down), they can gain access to the gallbladder and the liver. This liver infection is often associated with inflammatory bowel disease and/or pancreatitis.

There are believed to be three forms of cholangiohepatitis, with the distinctions based on the cause and the reactive type cells seen in the tissues. Neutrophilic is generally associated with bacterial infection. Lymphocytic tends to be *immune-mediated,* with 80 percent of affected cats having associated inflammatory bowel disease and 50 percent having associated pancreatitis. Chronic cholangitis is the third form, and tends to be associated with liver fluke infestations.

Some cats will become acutely ill, but many simply show anorexia and possibly jaundice and an enlarged liver. Some cats will have vomiting, diarrhea, depression, and weight loss.

Diagnosis is done with blood work and possibly a liver *needle aspirate* or a *biopsy.* An aspirate of bile for culture can be helpful as well, as can ultrasound. Cats should also be screened for hyperthyroidism.

Treatment: Treatment requires supportive care, including fluids and nutritional support—maybe even a feeding tube placed by your veterinarian. Antibiotics are important, as this is a bacterial infection. Antibiotics may be needed for three to six months. SAMe and vitamin E are useful antioxidants that can help the liver heal, and milk thistle is an herb with liver-protectant qualities. If inflammatory bowel disease is also involved, the cat may need immunosuppressive drugs such as prednisone.

Ursodeoxycholic acid (Actigall) is a human medication that has been used *off-label* in cats with cholangiohepatitis, and is important as an anti-inflammatory as well as for improving bile flow.

Survival rate is about 50 percent—higher if the cat is diagnosed and treated aggressively early in the course of the disease. This often includes supplemental feeding through a tube.

PORTOSYSTEMIC SHUNT

A portosystemic shunt is an inherited anatomical defect that is present at birth. In a normal kitten or cat, food is eaten and digested, then absorbed through the intestines into a large vein called the portal vein. This vein carries digestive products to the liver, where nutrients are metabolized, detoxified, and used to create new substances. In cats with portosystemic shunt, an abnormal portal vein bypasses the liver and takes blood directly to the heart. This means the nutrients and waste products are not processed by the liver. Ammonia products build up in the cat's system and many behavioral abnormalities may be seen such as circling, head pressing, or seizures (see *Hepatic Lipidosis,* page 288). Weight loss, excessive drooling, vomiting, and diarrhea may be seen.

Diagnosis is done via blood work and looking at special X-ray studies and ultrasound evaluations.

Treatment: Medical management is usually a temporary step. Protein that has not been properly metabolized is the biggest offender, so the cat needs to go on a low-protein diet. Many cats will also have stomach ulcers that must be managed with diet and medication.

Most cats end up going for surgery. The goal is to change the blood flow so most of the blood from the intestines goes to the liver. This is accomplished by reducing the blood flow through the abnormal vessel and encouraging other blood vessels that do go to the liver to take up the extra flow. Ideally, the surgeon can tie off the abnormal vessel, but if the pressure rises too high in the other blood vessels, only a partial occlusion is possible.

This intricate surgery is normally only done at veterinary referral centers. A new device, called an ameroid constrictor, is helping surgeons. This is a metal band lined with dehydrated protein. As the band is placed around the offending vessel, the dehydrated protein will gradually expand inward, slowly closing off the blood flow through that vessel. So far, the use of this device in cats is experimental.

Cats who come through surgery successfully often go on to live normal lives.

The Pancreas

The pancreas has two main functions: to provide digestive enzymes, the insufficiency of which causes malabsorption syndrome; and to make insulin for sugar metabolism.

DIABETES MELLITUS (SUGAR DIABETES)

Diabetes mellitus, or sugar diabetes, is a commonly diagnosed disease in cats and ultimately affects all the organs. It develops in about 1 in 400 cats. It is due to inadequate production of insulin by the beta cells in the pancreas or inadequate response of the cells to insulin. Insulin is secreted directly into the circulation. It acts upon cell membranes, enabling glucose to enter the cells, where it is metabolized for energy. Without insulin, the body can't utilize glucose. This results in elevated blood sugar levels (*hyperglycemia*). In diabetic cats, excess glucose is eliminated by the kidneys, producing frequent urination. There is a need to compensate for the increased urination by drinking unusual amounts of water.

Pancreatitis, hyperthyroidism, medications such as megestrol acetate (Megace), and some corticosteroids, all have the potential to cause or mimic diabetes in a cat. Obesity is a predisposing factor for all cats, and Burmese cats may have a genetic predisposition. Male cats have twice the risk of females. At greatest risk are neutered male cats over 10 years of age and over 15 pounds in weight.

Glycosuria is sugar in the urine. When a urine glucose test is positive, suspect diabetes. Some cats will show high glucose levels in urine and blood due to stress, however, so a repeat test may be needed to verify the results. Defects in the kidney tubule function, such as with antifreeze poisoning, may also cause high glucose levels in the blood and urine.

Ketones (the end-product of rapid or excessive fatty-acid breakdown) are formed in the blood of diabetics because of the inability to metabolize glucose. High levels lead to a condition called ketoacidosis. It is characterized by acetone on the breath (a sweet odor like nail polish remover); rapid, labored breathing; and, eventually, diabetic coma.

In the early stages of diabetes, a cat will try to compensate for the inability to metabolize blood glucose by eating more food. Later, with the effects of malnourishment, there is a drop in appetite. Accordingly, the signs of early diabetes are frequent urination, drinking lots of water, a large appetite, and unexplained weight loss. The laboratory findings are glucose and possibly ketones in the urine and a high blood glucose level.

In more advanced cases, there is loss of appetite, vomiting, weakness, acetone breath, dehydration, labored breathing, lethargy, and, finally, coma. Unlike dogs, diabetic cats rarely develop cataracts. A muscle weakness, usually shown by an unusual stance in the rear with the cat walking down on her hocks instead of up on her toes, is often seen if glucose regulation is poor.

Three types of diabetes are seen in cats. Type I diabetic cats are insulin dependent and need to receive daily insulin injections because the beta cells of their pancreases are not making enough insulin. In cats with type II diabetes, the cat's pancreas may make enough insulin but the cat's body does not use it properly. This is the most common type of feline diabetes. Some of these cats will require insulin as well, but others may get by on oral drugs to control blood glucose and dietary changes. About 70 percent of all diabetic cats will require at least some insulin.

The third type is known as transient diabetes. These are type II cats who present as diabetics and require insulin initially, but over time, their system re-regulates so they can go off insulin—especially with a change to a high-protein, low-carbohydrate diet.

Treatment: Dietary management (see page 294) and daily injections of insulin can regulate most diabetic cats, enabling them to lead normal lives. The amount of insulin needed cannot be predicted based on the cat's weight, and must be established for each individual. It is important for the success of initial therapy that the cat be hospitalized to determine his daily insulin requirement. While in the hospital, a glucose curve will be traced, using periodic blood samples to track how your cat responds to insulin and how much insulin will be needed. Most cats need one or two injections a day, and your veterinarian will show you how to give them. Luckily, the amounts are very small, the needles are tiny and very sharp, and most cats tolerate the subcutaneous injections with no problem.

Fructosamine (a test that gives an "average" glucose reading over the previous two weeks, rather than at a single point in time) or periodic blood glucose tests are done at the veterinary clinic to check the correct insulin dose for your cat. At home, you may use special strips to check his urine glucose, or even a special kitty litter additive such as Purina Glucotest Feline Urinary Glucose Detection System, which changes color if there is glucose in the urine. Many owners of diabetic cats do home glucose monitoring using ear pricks and home glucose monitors made for humans.

Cats who are on oral medications may eventually need insulin injections. Oral drugs include glypzide, which enhances insulin production but may be falling out of favor due to side effects, such as vomiting; acarbose, which blocks glucose absorption from the intestines and shows promise; and troglitazone, vanadium, and chromium, which make the cat's body more sensitive to his own insulin.

Because insulin requirements vary with the diet, it is important to keep the cat's caloric intake constant from day to day (see *Dietary Management*, page 294). It is equally important to maintain a strict schedule for insulin injections and exercise. Cats require small amounts of insulin, so it is necessary to dilute the insulin for accurate dosing. How to prepare and inject the insulin will be explained to you by your veterinarian.

Many cats go through periods when the diabetes seems to correct itself, and they do not require insulin. They may remain in this state of spontaneous remission for varying periods before again needing insulin to control their diabetes.

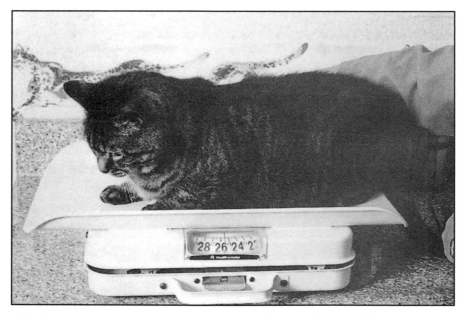

Obesity greatly reduces a cat's response to insulin. Sometimes, weight loss alone may be enough to reduce or even eliminate a cat's need for insulin.

It is important to regularly check the cat's urine for glucose to assist in the early detection of this transient nondiabetic state to avoid insulin overdose.

Dietary management: In the past, diabetic cats were placed on a high-fiber diet that was thought to slow the absorption of nutrients, with the goal of stabilizing blood glucose levels. However, recent research has shown that this is not the ideal diet for diabetic cats. Because cats primarily metabolize protein, not carbohydrates, for glucose, high-protein, low-carbohydrate diets have proven to be more efficiently metabolized and of great help in controlling diabetes. Prescription diets for diabetic cats that fit this profile include Purina DM Feline, Royal Canin Diabetic DS 44, and Science Diet m/d Feline. Some veterinarians also advise their clients to add meat to the cat's diet, and some prefer to avoid dry foods because a carbohydrate source must be added to make the kibble. Consult with your veterinarian for specific guidelines for your cat. Occasionally, an obese diabetic cat responds to dietary management alone and does not require insulin to keep his blood glucose well controlled.

Obesity greatly reduces tissue responsiveness to insulin and makes diabetes difficult to control. Accordingly, overweight cats should be put on a diet until they reach their ideal body weight. Prescription diets are available for weight reduction. These diets may or may not be suitable for diabetic cats. Consult with your veterinarian.

Daily caloric requirements are determined by the weight and activity of the individual cat. Once this is established, the quantity of food offered each day can be determined by dividing the daily caloric requirements by the amount of calories per cup or can of food. To prevent high levels of blood glucose after eating, avoid feeding the whole day's calories at one meal. Divide the daily ration into a number of smaller meals. For cats on once-daily insulin, feed half the food at the time of injection and the rest at peak insulin activity—8 to 12 hours later, as indicated by your cat's glucose curve. With two injections daily, the ration can simply be split in half and fed at the time of the injections. Cats on oral medications should be given small meals throughout the day.

HYPOGLYCEMIA (INSULIN OVERDOSE)

An overdose of insulin drops the blood sugar well below normal. This condition is called hypoglycemia. Suspect this condition if your cat appears confused, disoriented, or drowsy, or if he shivers, staggers about, collapses, falls into a coma, or has seizures.

Treatment: If the cat remains conscious and is able to swallow, give a sugar solution (corn syrup, glucose paste, honey). If the cat is not able to swallow, rub the solution into the mucous membranes of the cat's cheeks. Recovery occurs within minutes. Then *immediately take your cat to a veterinarian.*

PANCREATITIS

Pancreatitis is an inflammation of the pancreas, which often primarily affects the exocrine or digestive enzymes. It can be acute or chronic, with the chronic form being more common in cats.

Pancreatitis can have many causes, including trauma, parasites, infection, and drug reactions. However, more than 90 percent of all pancreatitis cases in the cat have no identifiable cause. Siamese cats may have a genetic predisposition.

Unlike dogs, cats with pancreatitis do not usually show vomiting or abdominal pain as their initial sign. In more than 50 percent of affected cats, lethargy, poor appetite or not eating, dehydration, increased respiratory rate, and a lower-than-normal body temperature are the initial signs. Many cats may have concurrent hepatic lipidosis, cholangiohepatitis, or inflammatory bowel disease. Only about 35 percent of the cats with pancreatitis will vomit.

Diagnosing pancreatitis can be problematic. Ultrasound is one of the best methods, in the hands of an experienced examiner. New blood tests for feline trypsinlike immunoreactivity and pancreatic lipase immunoreactivity both show promise. If the cat is not in severe, acute distress, a pancreatic *biopsy* is diagnostic, but severely ill cats are anesthetic risks. Anemia may be present. Hypoalbuminemia may lead to fluid accumulation in the abdomen.

Treatment: Treatment is complicated. All cats with pancreatitis will need extensive fluid therapy and careful monitoring of their electrolytes. If the cat is vomiting, food may need to be withheld, but ideally not for more than 48 hours or hepatic lipidosis (see page 288) can occur. A feeding tube inserted by your veterinarian into the small intestine, or special liquid nutrition given via an intravenous line, may be needed for as long as seven to ten days. Pain control is essential.

Dopamine to stimulate blood flow can be beneficial. Medications to control vomiting and gastric acid may be needed. Antibiotics are rarely indicated. Corticosteroids and metronidazole may be important for chronic cases.

Severe acute pancreatitis can lead to rapid kidney failure, respiratory failure from pulmonary edema, disseminated intravascular coagulation, and death. Plasma administration may be very important for these cases. Peritoneal dialysis, which is only available in certain veterinary referral centers, may be valuable with acute cases.

PANCREATIC ISLET CELL TUMORS

Insulinomas, or pancreatic tumors of the cells that produce insulin, are quite rare in cats. They occur most commonly in older, neutered male Siamese. These cats show low blood glucose, weakness, and possibly seizures.

Treatment: Treatment ideally is surgical removal of the cancer, but most of these are malignant and have already spread by the time of diagnosis.

10

THE RESPIRATORY SYSTEM

The cat's respiratory system is composed of the nasal passages, throat, larynx (voice box), trachea (windpipe), and lungs. Lungs are composed of bronchial tubes (branching airways), alveoli (air sacs), and capillaries. Air is breathed in primarily through the nose. It travels down through the trachea and then through the bronchial tubes in the lungs. At the ends of the smallest bronchial tubes are groups of alveoli, which have very thin walls that are laced with capillaries. Oxygen passes from the alveoli into the blood that is in the capillaries. At the same time, carbon dioxide passes from the blood into the alveoli and is eventually exhaled. This process is called gas exchange.

The lungs function using a vacuum action. The ribs and muscles of the chest, along with the diaphragm, act as a bellows, moving air into and out of the lungs.

A cat at rest takes about 25 to 30 breaths per minute—about twice as many as a human. It takes a cat about twice as long to exhale as it does to inhale.

Purring

A cat's purr is unique, and we are still not exactly sure how it works. It is believed that breathing in and out alternately tenses and relaxes the muscles of the larynx and diaphragm, creating pressure changes that result in turbulent airflow through the trachea. These cyclic and rapid pressure changes are superimposed on normal breathing and create the characteristic vibrations of purring. Other theories suggest that purring is a rapid contraction of muscles in the larynx and diaphragm in a constant rhythm.

Purring is instinctive. Kittens purr as early as 2 days of age. Large cats such as lions do not purr well, but cheetahs can purr.

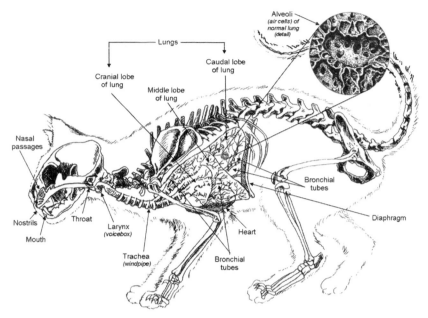

Alveoli
*(air cells) of
normal lung
(detail)*

Lungs

Caudal lobe
of lung

Cranial lobe
of lung

Middle lobe
of lung

Nasal
passages

Bronchial
tubes

Diaphragm

Nostrils   Throat

Larynx
(voicebox)

Heart

Mouth

Trachea
(windpipe)

Bronchial
tubes

The respiratory system.

A common misconception about purring is that it always indicates a state of pleasure. Sometimes it does, but cats also purr when they are hungry, stressed, or in pain. Cats have been known to purr just before dying. Some behaviorists believe purring is a signal to other cats and animals that they are not a threat.

Cat purrs are in the frequency range of 25 to 150 Hz. This frequency range is also considered to be beneficial to healing. So, perhaps cats are attempting to heal themselves at the cellular level.

Signs of Abnormal Breathing

A cat's respiratory motion should be smooth, even, and unrestrained. Rapid breathing at rest, coarse breathing, wheezing, rasping, coughing, and bubbling in the chest are all abnormal. (However, when a cat is intently sniffing an object, the respirations may appear abnormal for a brief time.) Possible causes of abnormal breathing are discussed in this section, along with their signs. Many feline respiratory problems have infectious causes (see chapter 3, *Infectious Diseases*).

- **Rapid breathing.** This can be caused by pain, stress, fever, or overheating. Other conditions to consider are shock, dehydration, anemia, lung disease, heart disease, and a buildup of acid or toxic substances in the blood (diabetes, kidney failure, or poisoning). An increased rate of breathing at rest means a veterinary examination is necessary. X-rays and other tests may be needed to help identify the exact cause.

- **Slow breathing.** A very slow rate of breathing is found in cats with narcotic poisoning, encephalitis, or a blood clot pressing on the brain. In late stages of shock or collapse, it usually signifies a terminal condition.

- **Panting.** Panting is a normal process after exercise. It is one of the chief ways in which a cat lowers her body temperature, as water evaporates from the mouth, tongue, and lungs and warm air is exchanged for cool. Cats also cool themselves by licking their fur and by perspiring through the pads of their feet. When panting is rapid, labored, and accompanied by anxiety, heat stroke should be considered. Some cats will pant and breathe with an open mouth when they are frightened.

- **Shallow breathing.** Shallow breathing is seen in cats with conditions that restrict the motion of the rib cage. To avoid the pain of a deep breath, a cat breathes rapidly but less deeply. The pain of pleurisy or rib fractures can cause shallow breathing. Blood, pus, or serum in the chest produces restricted breathing, but normally without pain. This condition, called *pleural effusion*, is the most common cause of respiratory distress in cats.

- **Noisy breathing.** Noisy breathing indicates obstructed airways and is a cardinal sign of upper respiratory disease. Cats with shortened muzzles, such as Persians, may always make some noise when they breathe.

- **Croupy breathing.** This refers to the high, harsh sound caused by air passing through a narrowed larynx. When the onset is sudden, the most likely diagnosis is a foreign body in the larynx or a swelling in the throat.

- **Wheezing.** A wheeze is a whistling sound that occurs when a cat breathes forcefully in or out. It indicates narrowing or spasm in the bronchial tubes. Tight, deep-seated wheezes are best heard with a stethoscope. Causes of wheezing include feline asthma, lungworms, heartworms, and tumors or growths in the bronchial tubes.

- **Meowing (crying).** A cat who meows continuously is most likely in pain or some sort of discomfort or distress. You should determine the cause of this anxiety and seek veterinary attention. Excessive meowing can lead to laryngitis.

Coughing

Coughing is a reflex initiated by an irritant in the bronchial tubes. It can be caused by a respiratory infection; inhaled irritants such as smoke and chemicals; foreign objects such as grass seeds, dust and food particles; pressure from a tight collar; or growths arising in the bronchial tubes. Some coughs are triggered by an allergic reaction. The type of cough often suggests the location and probable cause:

- A cough accompanied by sneezing and watery red eyes suggests feline viral respiratory disease complex.
- A deep, paroxysmal cough with the cat's neck extended and the production of phlegm suggests chronic bronchitis.
- A sudden coughing attack accompanied by wheezing and difficulty breathing suggests feline asthma.
- Sporadic coughing with weight loss, listlessness, and depressed appetite is seen in cats with heartworms, lungworms, and fungal diseases.
- Spasms of coughing that occur after exercise suggest acute bronchitis.
- Some cardiac problems, including cardiomyopathy, will cause a cat to cough.

Coughs are self-perpetuating. Coughing irritates the bronchial tubes, dries out the mucous lining, and lowers resistance to infection—leading to further coughing.

The diagnostic workup of a cat with a chronic cough includes a chest X-ray and *transtracheal washings*. These washings are obtained by placing a sterile tube into the trachea with the cat under light anesthesia. Microscopic examination of recovered cells leads to a specific diagnosis.

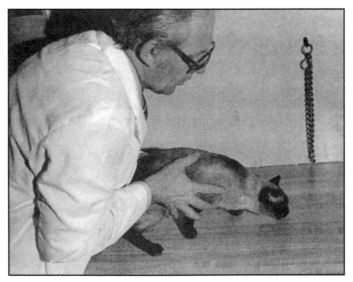

This cat's cough is due to bronchitis. Note the typical posture, with hunched-up shoulders, lowered head, and stretched neck.

Bronchoscopy is an excellent method of evaluating bronchial tube disease. A fiber-optic instrument is passed into the trachea, again with the cat under anesthesia. The bronchial tubes can be viewed directly, biopsies taken, and phlegm removed via bronchial *lavage* for microscopic exam and culture and sensitivity testing.

Treatment: Coughs accompanied by fever, difficulty breathing, discharge from the eyes and nose, or other signs of a serious illness should be treated by a veterinarian. Also, if your cat's appetite is off and she is coughing, she should be taken in for a veterinary exam.

It is important to identify and correct contributing problems. Air pollutants such as cigarette smoke, aerosol insecticides, house dust, and perfumes should be eliminated from the atmosphere. HEPA filters can assist in this effort. Any nose, throat, lung, or heart disorders should be treated.

Only minor coughs of brief duration should be treated at home. A variety of cough suppressants used for children are available at drugstores to treat mild coughs. However, *medications containing acetaminophen (Tylenol), codeine, and other narcotics are toxic to cats and must never be used.* Plain Robitussin is an example of a safe and effective cough preparation for cats. It contains an expectorant called guaifenesen that does not suppress the cough reflex but liquefies mucus secretions so they can be coughed free. Robitussin-DM contains the cough suppressant dextromethorphan—the only cough suppressant that is safe for cats. (The correct dosage for these cough preparations is given in the table *Over-the-Counter Drugs for Home Veterinary Use* on page 561.) These medications are not approved for use in cats and should not be used without consulting your veterinarian. In fact, *no medication*, even an over-the-counter one for children, should be given to your cat without first consulting your veterinarian.

Although cough suppressants decrease the frequency and severity of the cough, they do not treat the disease or condition causing it. Their overuse may delay a proper diagnosis and treatment. Cough suppressants (but not expectorants) should be avoided when phlegm is being brought up or swallowed. These coughs are clearing unwanted material from the airway.

The Larynx

The larynx is a short, oblong box located in the throat above the trachea. It is composed of cartilage and contains the vocal cords. In the domestic cat, the larynx is connected directly to the base of the skull by the hyoid bone. In lions, tigers, leopards, and other members of the large cat family, the hyoid bone is partly replaced by cartilage. As a result, the vocal apparatus of large cats is able to move freely and produce the characteristic full-throated roar. In contrast, small cats can make only a small roar.

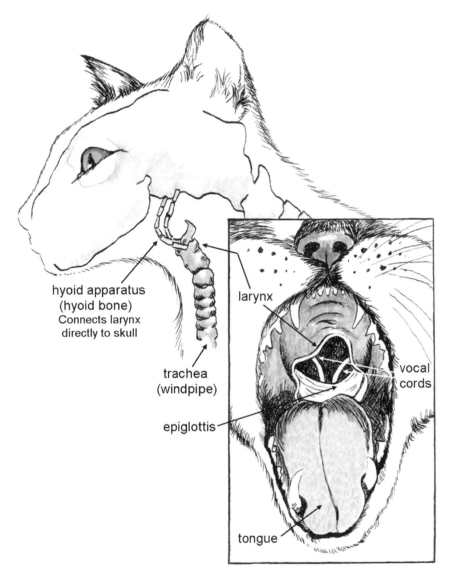

The larynx.

At the top of the larynx is the epiglottis, a leaflike flap that closes during swallowing, keeping food from going down the trachea. Disorders of the larynx give rise to coughing, croupy breathing, and loss of voice. The larynx is the most sensitive cough area in the body.

The larynx may also be affected by benign polyps (see *Nasal Tumors*, page 229, and *Ear Polyps*, page 216).

LARYNGITIS

Laryngitis is an inflammation of the mucous membranes of the larynx. Signs of laryngitis include hoarseness and loss of voice. The most common causes are excessive meowing and a chronic cough. Both cause vocal cord strain.

Laryngitis can be associated with tonsillitis, throat infections, tracheobronchitis, pneumonia, inhalant allergies, and (rarely) tumors in the throat. The lining of the larynx is not coated with cilia. Therefore, mucus frequently accumulates in the larynx. Exaggerated throat clearing is needed to dislodge it. This further irritates the larynx and lowers resistance to infection.

Treatment: Laryngitis due to excessive meowing usually responds to removing the cause of the cat's anxiety or distress. If the problem is due to prolonged coughing, seek veterinary attention to investigate and eliminate the cause of the chronic cough.

FOREIGN BODY IN THE LARYNX

The sudden onset of forceful coughing, pawing at the mouth, and respiratory distress in a healthy cat suggests a foreign object caught in the larynx. Foreign bodies caught in the larynx are not common. Most food particles are of little consequence because the resulting cough expels them.

If your cat is *choking* with gagging, retching, and respiratory distress, assume there is a foreign body caught in the cat's throat and seek emergency treatment (see *Foreign Bodies in the Throat*, page 253).

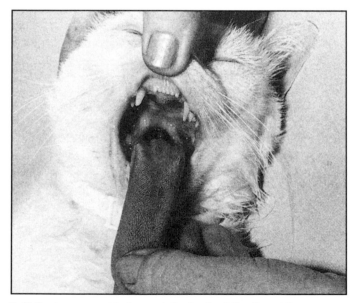

Pull the tongue out to inspect the back of the throat for an obstructing foreign body.

Treatment: This is an emergency. If the cat is conscious and able to breathe, go at once to the nearest veterinary clinic.

If the cat collapses and is unable to breathe, lay the cat on her side with her head lower than her body. Open her mouth, pull out her tongue, and look for the foreign body. When you see it, take hold of the cat's neck behind the lodged object and apply enough compression to keep the object from passing down. With your fingers in the cat's mouth, work the object loose as quickly as possible. If unsuccessful, proceed to the Heimlich maneuver.

The Heimlich Maneuver

- Place one hand along the cat's back and the other just below the sternum or rib cage.
- With both hands in position, give four forceful thrusts by pressing in and up.
- Next, check the mouth for the foreign body with a finger sweep.
- Then give two breaths, mouth to nose, as described in *Artificial Respiration* (page 11).
- Repeat cycles of compression and artificial respiration until the object is dislodged.

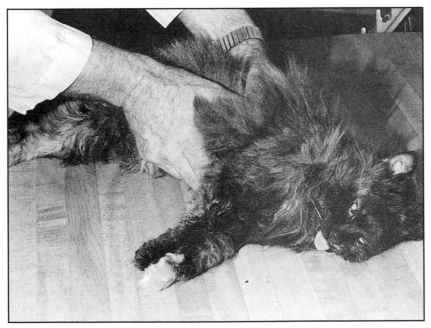

The Heimlich maneuver. Place your hands as shown and give four quick thrusts, pressing up and in.

Trachea and Bronchi
FOREIGN OBJECT IN THE TRACHEA

Grass seeds and food particles are the most common foreign material of sufficient size to lodge in the trachea or bronchial tubes. Most of these are quickly coughed up. If the object becomes fixed in a bronchial tube, it causes intense irritation and swelling.

Sudden attacks of coughing after a cat has been prowling in weeds or long grass, or immediately after vomiting, suggest aspiration of a foreign body.

Treatment: *Have the cat examined by your veterinarian.* Do not give her cough medicine, since it serves no purpose and only delays treatment. Foreign objects can sometimes be located by chest X-ray or located and removed by *bronchoscopy*.

BRONCHITIS

Inflammation of the smaller bronchi is called bronchitis. It is characterized by repeated coughing, which further irritates the lining of the tubes and spreads infection to the trachea. The trachea and the bronchi have a protective layer of mucus that traps foreign materials and infectious agents. Along with hairlike cilia that move foreign material toward the mouth, this mucus layer serves as a major defense system against infection. Conditions that interfere with the function of the mucociliary blanket—such as chilling; breathing cold, dry air; and dehydration—predispose a cat to bronchial infection.

Acute bronchitis is most commonly caused by an upper respiratory infection (see *Feline Viral Respiratory Disease Complex*, page 79). Secondary bacterial infections are common and frequently lead to persistent cough and chronic bronchitis. The cough of acute bronchitis is harsh, dry, and hacking, and it is aggravated by exertion and cold, dry air. Therefore, warm, humid air and restricted exercise are of great therapeutic value.

Chronic bronchitis refers to bronchitis that persists for several weeks. Many cases begin as acute bronchitis; others occur as a sequel to feline asthma. After a period of chronic coughing, a secondary bacterial infection becomes established. The cough of chronic bronchitis is moist or bubbling and often ends with retching and the expectoration of foamy saliva. This may need to be distinguished from hairballs.

Chronic bronchitis can severely damage the bronchial tubes, and infected mucus and pus can accumulate in partially destroyed bronchi. This condition is called bronchiectasis. Chronic coughing can also lead to a breakdown and enlargement of the alveoli, a condition called emphysema. These conditions are not reversible but can be managed medically in most cases. For these reasons, chronic coughs require veterinary examination and professional management. The diagnostic workup is similar to that described in *Coughing* (page 298).

Treatment: Rest and humidification of the atmosphere are important. Confine your cat in a warm room and use a home vaporizer. Cough suppressants interfere with host defenses and prevent the elimination of *purulent* secretions, and they should not be given to cats with chronic bronchitis. Expectorants may help. Bronchodilators (such as Theophylline) relax the breathing passages and reduce respiratory fatigue. Phlegm should be cultured and specific antibiotics selected by your veterinarian.

Cortisone preparations reduce the inflammatory response caused by coughing. However, cortisone is contraindicated in the presence of bacterial infection and should be used only with caution under professional supervision.

FELINE ASTHMA (FELINE ALLERGIC BRONCHITIS)

Asthma is a hypersensitivity to environmental allergens. This acute respiratory disease in cats resembles bronchial asthma in humans. Feline asthma affects approximately 1 percent of all cats. Siamese may have a slightly increased risk. Some of these cats present as an acute emergency with severe respiratory distress; others have a chronic history of coughing and wheezing. Cats with a chronic cough may need to be distinguished from cats with a hairball problem. In some cats, there will be seasonal triggers, and the asthma will be acutely exacerbated at those times.

In some cases, asthmatic attacks may be triggered by exposure to inhaled allergens, such as tobacco smoke, kitty litter dust, various sprays, and carpet deodorizers. Heartworm may well be a leading cause of asthma. In many cases, the initiating cause is unknown.

An acute attack begins with the sudden onset of difficulty breathing, accompanied by wheezing and coughing. This is associated with a sudden contraction of the smooth muscles surrounding the bronchi. The bronchial tubes are then dramatically narrowed. The wheezing is heard as the cat exhales, and usually it is loud enough to be heard with the naked ear.

During a severe attack, the cat may sit with her shoulders hunched or lie chest down with her mouth open, straining to breathe. The mucous membranes are a bluish color due to the lack of oxygen (*cyanosis*). Only two other conditions produce similar signs and symptoms: They are *pleural effusion* and *pulmonary edema* (see *Heart Failure*, page 315).

Treatment: Immediate veterinary attention is needed to relieve bronchial spasm and ease respiratory distress. Epinephrine may be needed as an emergency treatment. Bronchodilators, such as terbutaline, and cortisone are effective during the acute attack. Antihistamines and cough suppressants should not be used because they interfere with the cat's ability to clear her own secretions. Asthmatic cats may have to be hospitalized for sedation and to remove them from an allergenic environment. Supplemental oxygen, such as an oxygen cage, may be needed for acute cases.

Feline asthma is a chronic condition with recurring attacks. These attacks are often controlled with maintenance doses of an oral corticosteroid. To avoid dependency, the medication is usually given every other day. Some cats may respond favorably to tapering the drug, whereas others experience an immediate relapse and require lifelong medication. If the trigger for the attacks is a seasonal one, such as certain pollens, the cat may only need medication at those times of year.

Many asthmatic cats are now treated with specially designed inhalers, such as Aerokat. Medications prescribed by your veterinarian are administered by having the cat breathe through the inhaler mask. Albuterol (a bronchodilator) and steroids, such as fluticasone, are the most commonly used inhalant drugs. This method minimizes side effects from steroids and provides rapid relief.

Antibiotics are rarely needed, unless the cat has a concurrent *Mycoplasma* infection.

Try to minimize exposure to the inciting allergens. A HEPA air filter in the house may be useful.

The Lungs
PNEUMONIA

Pneumonia is an infection of the lungs and is classified according to cause: viral, bacterial, fungal, parasitic, or inhalation.

Pneumonia can follow one of the feline viral respiratory illnesses, when the cat's natural defenses are weakened by the primary infection. This allows secondary bacterial invaders to gain a foothold. Individuals most likely to develop pneumonia are kittens, old cats, cats who are malnourished or immunosuppressed, and cats with long-standing respiratory diseases such as *chronic bronchitis*.

Aspiration of foreign material during vomiting (perhaps while the cat is under anesthesia) and the unskilled administration of medications or supplemental feedings account for occasional cases. Tuberculosis and systemic fungus infections are infrequent causes of pneumonia. These illnesses are discussed in chapter 3, *Infectious Diseases*.

The general symptoms of pneumonia include high fever, rapid breathing, splinting, cough, fast pulse, and rattling and bubbling in the chest. When the disease is severe enough to cause an oxygen deficiency, you will notice a blue cast to the mucous membranes of the mouth. The diagnosis is confirmed by laboratory tests and a chest X-ray.

Treatment: *Pneumonia is a serious illness requiring urgent veterinary attention.* Until veterinary help is available, move your cat to warm, dry quarters and humidify the air. Give her plenty of water. *Do not use cough medications*, because coughing in a cat with pneumonia helps to clear the airways.

Pneumonia usually responds to an antibiotic selected specifically for the causative agent. Your veterinarian can select the proper antibiotic. A nebulizer may be used as the best method of getting antibiotics into the cat's lungs. Your cat may need to be hospitalized for fluids and oxygen therapy.

Cats with severe respiratory infections may not want to eat because they can't smell the food. Strong-smelling food, such as canned tuna, may help to stimulate appetite. Gently warming the food will also make it more aromatic.

ALLERGIC PNEUMONITIS

Allergic pneumonitis is a hypersensitivity reaction that affects the lungs. Possible causes include migrating parasites, such as heartworms or lungworms. The degree of illness will vary greatly, with some cats showing a chronic cough but no fever. The condition is typically diagnosed with X-rays and a *bronchial lavage*. Many *eosinophils*, cells associated with allergic reactions, will be found in the tissues and in lavage samples.

Treatment: Steroids are normally used to reduce the inflammation. Treatment of the underlying cause is also important.

PLEURAL EFFUSION

The most common cause of difficult breathing in cats is *pleural effusion*—fluid accumulation in the pleural space surrounding the lungs. The fluid compresses the lungs and keeps them from filling with air. This condition is much more common in cats than it is in other animals. The reason is that cats suffer from two diseases that produce pleural effusion: feline infectious peritonitis and feline leukemia. Other causes of pleural effusion include cancers, congestive heart failure, and liver disease.

Infections in the pleural space follow puncture wounds of the chest, often acquired in fights with other animals, including other cats. The infection leads to pus formation in the lungs, a condition called empyema or pyothorax.

Bleeding into the chest cavity and lungs often follows chest trauma. A severe blow to the abdomen can rupture a cat's diaphragm, allowing the abdominal organs to enter the chest cavity and compress the lungs. This is a diaphragmatic hernia. These cats can show evidence of shock (see page 13).

Depending on the cause, cats can show acute distress or more gradual, chronic signs of pleural effusion. However, in all cases, the cat will have difficulty breathing. Cats often sit or stand with elbows out, chest fully expanded, and head and neck extended to draw in more air. The animal may be unable to lie down. The least effort produces sudden distress or collapse. Breathing is open-mouthed, and the lips, gums, and tongue may look pale or appear blue or gray. The blue-gray color, called *cyanosis*, is due to insufficient oxygen in the blood. Depending on the cause of the fluid accumulation, other signs of illness may include weight loss, fever, anemia, and signs of heart or liver disease.

Treatment: When fluid builds rapidly in the chest, *urgent veterinary attention is required to prevent respiratory failure and sudden death*. The fluid will need to be drained. The cat should be hospitalized for care and further diagnosis. A chest drain may need to be placed, antibiotics and pain medications are usually required, and surgery may be necessary. An oxygen cage may be required until the cat is stabilized.

PNEUMOTHORAX

Pneumothorax is a life-threatening condition caused by free air (air that is not within the lungs) present in the chest. The presence of free air destroys the vacuum that helps the lungs expand and contract. Trauma is the most common cause of pneumothorax.

The cat will obviously have a problem on inhalation and may quickly become blue. Cats with a pneumothorax will try to stay in sternal recumbency—lying on their chest with their head up.

Treatment: This is an emergency situation and you should head to the veterinarian as quickly as possible. If there is an obvious wound opening on the chest, apply a pressure bandage. The cat may need surgery, and often a special one-way drain will be placed in the chest to prevent air buildup as the wounds heal.

TUMORS

Most lung cancers in cats are metastatic cancers from other primary locations in the body. Primary cancers of the lungs are not common in cats. There does seem to be a predisposition, however, in cats who are routinely exposed to cigarette smoke. Primary carcinomas may metastasize to the digits and the tail.

Lung cancers of any type are often accompanied by pleural effusion (see page 307). Many cats will not have direct respiratory signs, such as a cough or wheeze, but instead will show lethargy, weight loss, and depression.

Diagnosis is generally done by X-ray, with three views recommended. A *bronchial lavage* may yield cancer cells.

Treatment: Depending on the type of cancer, surgery, radiation, or chemotherapy may be recommended. The prognosis is not good.

PARASITES IN THE LUNGS

In addition to the parasites in this section, heartworms can also be a major cause of pulmonary disease. For more information, see page 326.

Lungworms

Lungworms are slender, hairlike parasites about 1 centimeter in length. There are several species, but only two commonly affect cats. *Aeleurostrongylus abstrussus*, which is the most common of the two, has a complicated life cycle. Larvae are passed in the feces. They are taken up by snails and slugs that in turn are eaten by birds, rodents, and frogs. When these transport hosts are eaten by the cat, lungworm eggs hatch in the intestines. Adult worms migrate to the lungs and lay eggs. Larvae migrate up the trachea, are coughed up, swallowed, and passed in the feces.

The second common lungworm, *Capillaria aerophila*, is acquired by the direct ingestion of infective eggs or a transport host.

Most cats do not show signs of clinical infection. Others may have a persistent dry cough that is caused by a secondary bacterial infection. Occasionally, a cat will experience fever, weight loss, wheezing, and nasal discharge. These symptoms might suggest other respiratory illnesses as well. A chest X-ray is often normal.

Microscopic diagnosis is made by finding coiled or comma-shaped larvae in feces or sputum (in the case of *A. abstrussus*). The ova of *C. aerophila* are easily confused with the eggs of whipworms. Many cases that are thought to be whipworm infestations are probably due to lungworms.

Treatment: Lungworms are difficult to eliminate. Ivermectin and fenbendazole are effective in some cases. Secondary bacterial bronchitis or pneumonia is treated with antibiotics. Veterinary management is required. Preventing a cat from going outside and hunting should minimize the chances of the cat acquiring lungworms.

Lung Flukes

The lung fluke *Paragonimus kellicotti* is sometimes found in cats. Cats will cough and show a loss of condition. Cats cough up the eggs, which are then swallowed and eventually passed in the feces. Eggs from the flukes may be detected in the feces. Cats acquire lung flukes by eating raw crabs or raw crayfish.

Treatment: Lung flukes may be treated with fenbendazole or praziquantal.

11

THE CIRCULATORY SYSTEM

The circulatory system is made up of the heart, the blood vessels, and the blood. There are about 8 ounces (240 ml) of blood in the circulatory system of a 7-pound (3-kg) cat. Roughly 5 percent of the cat's body weight is blood. Feline blood donors typically donate only 60 ml of blood at a time, and they need fluid replacement to compensate for the volume loss.

The Heart

The heart is a pump made of four chambers: the right atrium and right ventricle, and the left atrium and left ventricle. The two sides are separated by a muscular septum. In a normal heart, blood cannot pass from one side to the other without first going through either the general, *systemic*, or the pulmonary circulation. Four valves keep the blood flowing in one direction. When the valves are diseased, blood leaks backward, causing the heart to pump less effectively. If there is a hole in the septum, blood can also leak backward.

Blood enters the heart through two large veins, the inferior and superior vena cava, emptying oxygen-poor blood from the body into the right atrium. It then flows through the open tricuspid valve into the right ventricle. When the right ventricle is full, the tricuspid valve shuts, preventing blood from flowing backward into the atrium while the right ventricle contracts.

Blood leaves the right ventricle through the pulmonic valve and flows into the pulmonary artery. The pulmonary artery branches into smaller vessels and finally into capillaries around the air sacs. Oxygen passes through the walls of the capillaries and into the blood. At the same time, carbon dioxide, a waste

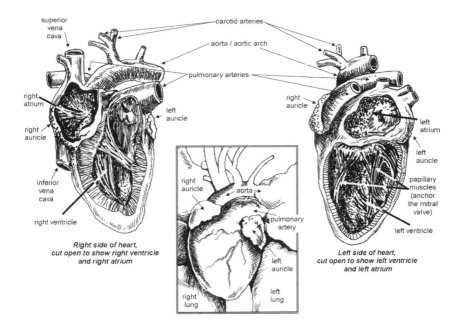

Right side of heart,
cut open to show right ventricle
and right atrium

Left side of heart,
cut open to show left ventricle
and left atrium

product of metabolism, passes from the blood into the air sacs of the lungs, and leaves the body when the cat exhales.

The oxygenated blood flows through the pulmonary veins to the left atrium. It then flows through the open mitral valve into the left ventricle. When the left ventricle is full, the mitral valve shuts, preventing blood from flowing backward into the atrium while the left ventricle contracts.

Blood then leaves the heart through the aortic valve, flowing into the aorta. It passes through progressively smaller arteries until it reaches the capillary beds of the skin, muscle, brain, and internal organs. At these end locations, oxygen is released and carbon dioxide is collected. Blood is carried back to the heart through progressively larger veins, thus completing the cycle.

The arteries and veins are under the control of the nervous system and of the hormones. They can expand or contract to maintain a correct blood pressure.

The heartbeat is controlled by an internal nerve system that releases electrical impulses. This system is responsive to outside influences, so the heart speeds up when the cat exercises, becomes frightened, overheats, goes into shock, or requires greater blood flow to tissues. Heart rhythms follow a fixed pattern that can be seen on an electrocardiogram (EKG or ECG). Whether the beat is fast or slow, the sequence in which the various muscle fibers contract remains the same. This sequence causes a synchronized beat, allowing both ventricles to empty at the same time.

If the heart rate is very slow, this is called bradycardia. If the heart rate is too fast, this is called tachycardia. When the rate is so fast that the normal sequence of contraction is disturbed, the condition is called fibrillation.

Arrhythmia, an absence of a regular rhythm, upsets the normal pattern of the heart muscle contraction, causing inefficient pump action. Pacemakers have been used in cats with arrhythmias, but not very successfully. This may be due, in part, to the small size of cats. Some cats with arrhythmias develop secondary chlothorax (accumulation of lymph fluid in the chest).

Evaluating the Circulation

There are physical signs that can help determine whether a cat's heart and circulation are working properly. Familiarize yourself with what is normal for your cat, so that you can recognize abnormal signs if they appear.

PULSE

The pulse is easily detected by feeling the femoral artery in the groin. With your cat standing or lying belly up, feel along the inside of the thigh where the leg and body join. Press lightly with your fingers until you locate the pulse. Alternately, take the pulse by pressing against the cat's rib cage over the heart. With the cat standing, feel the pulse or direct heartbeat just behind the elbow.

The pulse rate can be determined by counting the number of beats per minute. Adult cats have a normal pulse rate of 140 to 240 beats per minute. The pulse should be strong, steady, and regular. A fast pulse indicates excitation, fever, anemia, blood loss, dehydration, shock, infection, heat stroke, or heart (and lung) disease. A slow pulse indicates heart disease, pressure on the brain, hypothermia, or an advanced morbid condition that is causing collapse of the circulation. An erratic, irregular pulse indicates an *arrhythmia*. Various drugs can affect the rate and rhythm of the heart.

HEART SOUNDS

Veterinarians use a stethoscope to listen to the heart. You can also listen to the heart by placing your ear against the cat's chest. The normal heartbeat is divided into two separate sounds. The first is a LUB, followed by a slight pause, and then a DUB. Together, the sound is LUB-DUB, evenly spaced and steady. When the heart sounds can be heard all over the chest, the heart is enlarged. This can also occur with a very thin cat.

Murmurs

Murmurs are caused by turbulence in the blood flow through the heart. Serious ones are due to feline cardiomyopathy and anatomical birth defects. Hyperthyroidism can cause heart murmurs. Systemic hypertension (high blood pressure), as well as anemias, can also have associated murmurs.

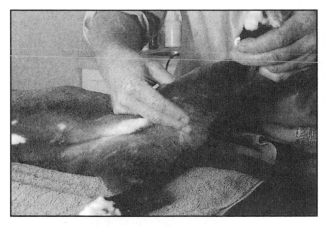

Taking the femoral pulse. Feel along the inside of the cat's thigh. Press with your fingers to locate the pulsation.

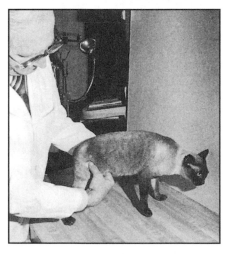

Taking the pulse with the cat standing.

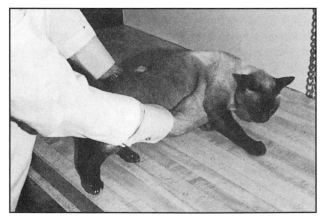

Another way to take the pulse is to feel for the heartbeat behind the elbows.

Not all murmurs are serious. Some are functional or physiological—that is, there is no disease, just a normal degree of turbulence. A murmur will be graded by your veterinarian from 1 to 6, with grade 6 being the most serious. Many cats with low-grade murmurs lead basically normal lives. An echocardiogram (ultrasound of the heart), combined with lab work and possibly X-rays, are needed to determine the cause of most murmurs.

Thrills

A thrill is caused by turbulence of such a degree that you can feel a buzzing or vibration over the heart. It suggests an obstruction to the blood flow—for example, a narrowed valve or a hole in the muscle wall between two chambers of the heart. If the heart is enlarged or diseased, you may also be able to detect a buzzing or vibration over the chest wall. A thrill indicates a serious heart condition.

CIRCULATION

By examining the cat's gums and tongue, you can determine both the adequacy of a cat's circulation and whether he is anemic. Deep pink is a sign of normal red blood cell volume. A gray or bluish color is a sign of inadequate oxygen in the blood (*cyanosis*). Cyanosis can be seen in a cat with heart and lung failure. Pale pink or whitish gums suggest anemia. Bright red can mean cyanide or carbon monoxide poisoning.

The adequacy of the circulation can be tested by noting the time it takes for the tissues to pink up (or refill) after the gums have been pressed firmly with a finger. This is called *capillary refill time* (CRT). With normal circulation, the response is immediate (one second or less). More than two seconds suggests poor circulation. When the finger impression remains pale for three seconds or longer, the cat is in shock.

Blood Types

Cats have three different blood types: A, B, and AB. Type A is the most common; about 95 percent of all cats are type A. Siamese and Oriental breeds are virtually all type A. Type AB is quite rare and has been noted in certain families of Birmans, British Shorthairs, Scottish Folds, Somalis, and Sphynxes. Type B is seen in some geographic areas and in certain breeds. The northwestern region of North America, for example, has about 6 percent type B cats. In the Devon Rex breed, about 41 percent of the cats have type B blood; and in the British Shorthair breed, about 36 percent are type B.

Percentages of Blood Types in Selected Breeds	
Type A only	Siamese, Burmese, Tonkinese, American Shorthair, Oriental Shorthair
1% to 10% type B	Maine Coon Cat, Norwegian Forest Cat
10% to 25% type B	Abyssinian, Birman, Himalayan, Japanese Bobtail, Persian, Scottish Fold, Somali, Sphynx
25% and higher type B	British Shorthair, Devon Rex, Cornish Rex

Source: www.pandecats.com/x/blood_type_incompatibility.htm (Reviewed by Urs Giger, PhD, Dr.Med.Vet., MS, FVH, Chief of Section of Medical Genetics, University of Pennsylvania).

Reprinted with permission from Vella & McGonagle, *Breeding Pedigreed Cats*, 2nd ed., 2006.

As with humans, blood must be typed before a cat gets a transfusion. If a cat is given blood that is not his blood type, a life-threatening reaction can result. This can happen the very first time an adult cat gets a transfusion of the wrong type blood. Therefore, all blood donor cats should be typed.

Blood type is also a factor if you are breeding cats. Even if they have never been exposed to type A blood, all type B cats will have antibodies against type A blood by about 3 months of age. This means that if a female cat with type B blood is bred to a type A male, the kittens born with type A blood may be affected by neonatal isoerythrolysis (see page 469) as a result of nursing, which exposes them to the type A antibodies in their mother's milk. By the time you notice signs of neonatal isoerythrolysis, it may be too late to save the kittens.

Adults cats to be used for breeding should be blood typed (both the tom and the queen). Typing can be done at the University of Pennsylvania using blood samples and by the Veterinary Genetics Laboratory at the University of California using a genetic test. Kittens born to queens of a different blood type should not be allowed to nurse. If you are breeding a type B queen to a type A tom, assume all the kittens are type A and do not allow them to nurse at all. Caring for the kittens will therefore require advance preparation and a serious commitment.

Heart Failure

Heart failure is the inability of the heart to pump enough blood to provide adequate circulation and meet the body's needs. It is the result of a weakened or damaged heart muscle. The liver, kidneys, lungs, and other organs eventually become affected due to a lack of oxygen, causing a multiple organ system problem. When a diseased heart begins to weaken, the resulting signs will suggest whether the failure is on the right side or the left side of the heart.

Any cat with signs of heart failure should avoid stress as much as possible. Medically speaking, these are fragile cats. Cats are extremely good at hiding signs of illness, especially heart problems. They will lie quietly, conserving energy and not stressing their heart. Often, by the time signs are apparent, they are extremely ill.

LEFT-SIDED HEART FAILURE

As the left ventricle begins to fail, pressure backs up in the pulmonary circulation. This results in lung congestion and the accumulation of fluid in the air sacs (*pulmonary edema*). In the late stages of pulmonary edema, the cat is extremely short of breath, coughs up bubbles of red fluid, and can't get enough oxygen. Pulmonary edema is likely to be brought on by exercise, excitement, or any stress that causes the heart to accelerate. Fluid may accumulate around the lungs in the chest space, pressing on the lungs and causing further breathing difficulties. This is called *pleural effusion*, a common cause of respiratory distress in cats (see page 307).

The two early signs of left-sided heart failure are fatigue and rapid breathing after exercise. They are less apparent in sedentary cats. In advanced cases, breathing is labored and the cat assumes a characteristic sitting position with elbows apart and head extended to take in more air. The pulse is rapid, weak, and irregular. Murmurs or thrills may be detected over the chest. Arrhythmia can cause fainting, which may be mistaken for a seizure.

RIGHT-SIDED HEART FAILURE

Right-sided heart failure is less common than left-sided failure. When the right ventricle starts to fail, pressure backs up in the veins of the general circulation, causing heart failure due to fluid backup in the circulation. You will see fluid beneath the skin of the abdomen and swelling or edema of the limbs.

Fluid may also build up in the abdominal cavity, giving the cat a pot-bellied look. This is called *ascites*. It may suggest lymphosarcoma or the wet form of feline infectious peritonitis. Fluid retention is made worse by the kidneys, which respond to the sluggish blood flow by retaining salt and water.

Cardiovascular Disease

Congenital heart defects, those that are present at birth, account for about 15 percent of all cases of cardiovascular disease. Valvular heart disease and heartworms account for a few cases. Congenital heart defects usually produce heart failure by 10 months of age.

Cardiomyopathy is the major cause of heart disease in cats. It affects young to middle-aged cats. Occasionally, symptoms will not become apparent until a cat is older.

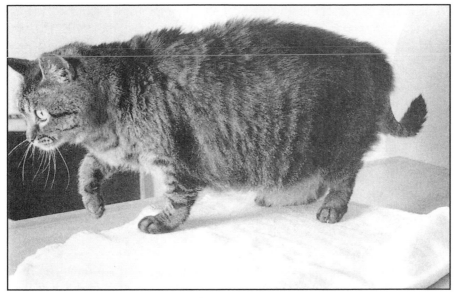

The swollen, pot-bellied abdomen of a cat with ascites.

Coronary artery disease of the type humans get from, for example, high blood cholesterol, almost never occurs in cats.

CONGENITAL HEART DEFECTS

Congenital heart defects are not common in cats, affecting from .2 to 1 percent of all cats. The most common congenital defects involve the heart valves or the septum that separates the two sides of the heart.

Septal defects are windows that allow blood to go from one side of the heart to the other without passing through the circulation, thus mingling unoxygenated blood with oxygenated blood. The most common heart defects in cats are ventricular septal defects and tetralogy of Fallot. In tetralogy of Fallot, the cat has an opening between the ventricles of the heart and also a narrowing of the pulmonary artery. Siamese, Burmese, and domestic short-haired cats are affected most often. A ventricular septal defect is a hole between the heart's two lower chambers (the ventricles).

Cats with congenital cardiac defects may turn blue easily, have limited ability to exercise, and many go on to full heart failure. The extent and severity of the symptoms depend on the type and location of the defect. More than one defect may exist at the same time. Examination of an asymptomatic kitten may disclose a murmur. However, the first indication usually is the appearance of heart failure.

Cardiac defects are diagnosed through physical examination, an EKG, X-rays of the chest, and echocardiograms (cardiac ultrasound), especially with Doppler technology to follow the flow of the blood.

Treatment: Most kittens with congenital heart defects die within the first year. Early detection in some cases may allow for surgical repair. Kittens with mild conditions may be managed medically through a low-salt diet, diuretics, and drugs to manage heart functions.

CARDIOMYOPATHY

Cardiomyopathy is a disease of the heart muscle. There is more than one form. Thus, cardiomyopathy is not a specific disease but is the result of some disturbance affecting the muscle of the heart. The difference among the forms is in how the disease process affects the heart walls. Either they thicken (as in hypertrophic and restrictive cardiomyopathy) or they stretch (as in dilated cardiomyopathy). In all forms, the heart's function is significantly compromised. An accurate diagnosis is necessary to establish which form of cardiomyopathy the cat has and to provide the proper treatment.

Hypertrophic Cardiomyopathy

This is the most common cause of heart disease in cats and the most frequent cause of spontaneous death in indoor adult cats. In cats with this condition, the walls of the ventricles become thick. However, because the muscle fibers are replaced by fibrous connective tissue (scar tissue), the thicker heart walls do not translate into increased pumping power. In fact, the heart is actually weakened as the affected wall of the heart becomes less elastic and the heart chambers get smaller.

Early signs of hypertrophic cardiomyopathy are vague and indefinite. Increased heart rate and a murmur are common signs. Decreased appetite, weight loss, and an increase in respiratory rate may all be noted. Loss of pep

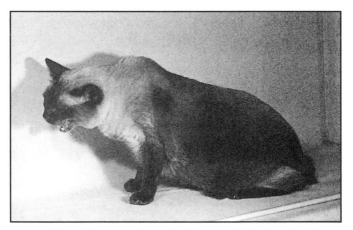

A cat with cardiomyopathy typically extends the head and neck, straining to breathe.

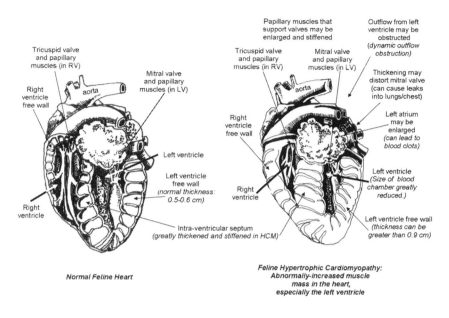

Papillary muscles that support valves may be enlarged and stiffened

Outflow from left ventricle may be obstructed (dynamic outflow obstruction)

Tricuspid valve and papillary muscles (in RV)

Mitral valve and papillary muscles (in LV)

Right ventricle free wall

aorta

Left ventricle

Right ventricle free wall

Left ventricle free wall (normal thickness: 0.5-0.6 cm)

Right ventricle

Intra-ventricular septum (greatly thickened and stiffened in HCM)

Tricuspid valve and papillary muscles (in RV)

Mitral valve and papillary muscles (in LV)

aorta

Thickening may distort mitral valve (can cause leaks into lungs/chest)

Left atrium may be enlarged (can lead to blood clots)

Left ventricle (Size of blood chamber greatly reduced.)

Right ventricle

Left ventricle free wall (thickness can be greater than 0.9 cm)

Normal Feline Heart

Feline Hypertrophic Cardiomyopathy:
Abnormally-increased muscle mass in the heart, especially the left ventricle

and appetite and reduced exercise tolerance may go unnoticed, because cats are able to recognize their own physical limitations and restrict their activities accordingly. Other than possibly hearing a heart murmur, it is unusual to detect heart disease before signs of congestive heart failure. The first and only sign may be sudden death.

Coughing is rarely a sign of cardiovascular disease in cats. A chronic cough is more likely to indicate bronchitis or feline asthma. As the left ventricle loses its function, cats may show signs of pulmonary edema and pleural effusion, though, and these cats may cough.

The appearance of a blood clot in an artery, as described in *Feline Aortic Thromboembolism* (see page 322), may be the first indication of cardiomyopathy of any type.

Diagnosis is by chest X-ray, electrocardiogram, ultrasound of the heart, and thyroid function tests. Echocardiograms, especially with Doppler technology, are excellent diagnostic tools.

Hypertrophic cardiomyopathy tends to affect cats 1 to 5 years of age. It has been detected in kittens as young as 3 months, however, and in cats as old as 10 years. Maine Coon Cats, Ragdolls, British Shorthairs, American Shorthairs, and Devon Rexes show a familial inheritance. In Maine Coon Cats, signs of hypertrophic cardiomyopathy usually show up in affected males by 2 years of age and affected females by 3 years of age. Ragdolls usually show signs by 1 year of age.

In the Maine Coon Cat and the Ragdoll, genetic mutations have been identified that are associated with the development of hypertrophic cardiomyopathy. These genetic defects both involve the myosin Binding Protein C in the heart muscle, but the specific defects are different for the two breeds.

It is estimated that 25 to 33 percent of all Maine Coon Cats carry a copy of the defective gene, which is an autosomal dominant. It affects both males and females, and even one copy of the gene may lead to disease. Through the Veterinary Cardiac Genetics Laboratory at the Washington State University College of Veterinary Medicine, cats can be tested for this defect using a cheek swab or a blood test. So far, about 4 to 5 percent of the Maine Coon Cats tested are homozygous for this trait, with two copies of the defective gene. The same lab developed the test for Ragdolls, but the test is still quite new at this writing and statistics are not available.

These tests are excellent tools for Maine Coon Cat and Ragdoll breeders who are trying to remove this trait from their breeds. It is not a foolproof test for this health problem, however, because other genes also seem to be involved in the development of the disease. It is recommended that breeding cats be tested for this problem but also continue to have an echocardiogram yearly to catch the disease early on.

Treatment: Cats with hypertrophic cardiomyopathy require drugs that relax the heart and increase its efficiency. Most of the drugs used to treat heart disease in people are used for similar purposes in small animals. The specific drug chosen depends on the stage of illness and presence or absence of complicating factors, such as arrhythmia. Drug choices include diuretics, calcium channel blockers, beta blockers, and ACE inhibitors. Most of these medications are not approved for cats and should only be used directly under your veterinarian's guidance. Do not give your heart medications to your cat!

Aspirin may be used to try to prevent clot formation, and low-salt diets such as Hill's Prescription Diet Feline h/d or Purina's CV Cardiovascular for cats, are recommended. Cats metabolize aspirin very slowly and the dose and frequency must be prescribed by your veterinarian.

Restricting the cat's activity reduces the strain on the heart. Your veterinarian may prescribe a period of cage rest. These measures often yield substantial results in a longer, more comfortable, and active life for your cat.

Dilated Cardiomyopathy

Dilated cardiomyopathy occurs when the heart muscle loses its tone and becomes flaccid. The heart chambers overfill, the walls of the ventricles become thinner, and the chambers enlarge. One cause of dilated cardiomyopathy is taurine deficiency. Taurine is an essential amino acid present in high concentrations in animal tissue. Feeding dog food or a grain-based cat food could lead to taurine deficiency. Most commercial cat foods are currently supplemented with taurine. Dog foods are not, so a cat eating dog food has a high risk of developing dilated cardiomyopathy.

Another cause of dilated cardiomyopathy is myocarditis, which is inflammation of the heart muscle. Viruses and autoimmune diseases have been implicated as the cause of myocarditis in humans, although its cause is unknown in cats.

Dilated cardiomyopathy is often a rapid-onset disease that progresses over two or three days as the heart begins to fail. The most frequent sign is labored breathing at rest. The cat often sits with his head and neck extended and elbows out, straining to take in air. Cool feet and ears and a body temperature below normal are signs of poor circulation. Heart murmurs are common. The pulse is often rapid and thready and may be irregular or even slow. Loss of appetite, rapid weight loss, weakness, fainting attacks, and crying out spells often accompany the signs. A clot blocking the vascular pathway to the rear legs may be the first sign (see *Feline Aortic Thromboembolism*, page 322). Echocardiography is the best method for diagnosing dilated cardiomyopathy.

Treatment: Treatment of dilated cardiomyopathy is directed at correcting any taurine deficiency and controlling fluid retention. Fluid retention is best managed using diuretics such as furosemide (Lasix). Cats with taurine deficiency cardiomyopathy who survive the first week of supplementation have an increased chance for survival, but it can take four to six months for the heart muscle to heal.

Aspirin may be administered in an attempt to reduce the risk of blood clots forming. Calcium channel blockers, such as diltiazem, or beta blockers, such as propranolol, may be prescribed by your veterinarian. These drugs are not approved for use in cats, however. An ACE inhibitor such as enalapril may also be part of the therapeutic plan.

A restricted mineral and sodium diet, such as Hill's Prescription Diet Feline h/d or Purina's CV Cardiovascular for cats, is recommended. Antithyroid drugs are used to treat hyperthyroidism, when present.

Sudden death is always a possibility.

Restrictive Cardiomyopathy

Restrictive cardiomyopathy occurs when the heart becomes constricted in its ability to pump blood due to a loss of elasticity throughout the heart muscle, although the heart wall is not thickened. Scar tissue, or in other cases inflammation of the muscles, may be responsible for these changes. Rhythm disturbances and murmurs may be heard. Cats with this condition tend to have a very distended left atrium and are at a high risk of developing blood clots and congestive heart failure. The causes of both this form and unclassified cardiomyopathy are unknown.

Treatment: Treatment is similar to that for hypertrophic cardiomyopathy (see page 318) and the outcome is generally poor.

Arrhythmogenic Right Ventricular Cardiomyopathy

This is a newly recognized type of cardiomyopathy, and the cause is not yet known. This disorder is characterized by progressive atrophy of the right ventricle, the infiltration of fat into the heart walls, and ventricular tachycardia—a rapid heart rate.

Treatment: Affected cats may benefit from anti-arrhythmic medications as well as the standard drugs used to treat heart failure.

Unclassified Cardiomyopathy

Some heart muscle diseases have features that do not fit into any of the other categories, or display characteristics of more than one type of cardiomyopathy. They are termed unclassified cardiomyopathy.

Treatment: Treatment is similar to that for hypertrophic cardiomyopathy (see page 318).

FELINE AORTIC THROMBOEMBOLISM

This is characterized by the passing of a blood clot (*embolus*) from the left side of the heart into the general circulation, where it becomes lodged in an artery. The resulting obstruction to the flow of blood leads to clotting of the artery (thrombosis).

The most common site for blockage is the point at which the abdominal aorta branches into the main arteries that supply the rear legs. Arteries elsewhere in the body can be affected, particularly in the kidneys. Diagnosis of the rear limb problem can be based on signs such as rear limb paralysis, swollen muscles, the absence of a pulse in the groin, and blue nails due to *cyanosis*. If the renal arteries are blocked, acute kidney failure may result. If a cerebral artery is blocked, seizures may occur. Cats with thrombi can be in quite serious pain.

Formation of a blood clot in the heart and subsequent arterial *thromboembolism* occurs in about half of all cats suffering from cardiomyopathy. It may be the first indication of heart disease. Suspect this possibility if your cat

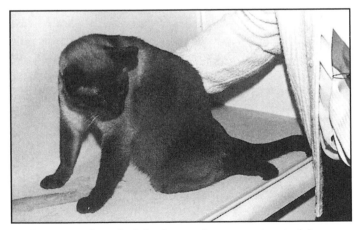

Sudden onset of paralysis in the rear legs suggests arterial thromboembolism or ruptured disc.

experiences the sudden onset of weakness in the rear legs. Look for cold legs, bluish skin, and faint or absent pulses in the groin. One leg may be more severely blocked than the other. The colder leg with the weaker pulse is the more severely affected. Ultrasound can be very useful in localizing all potential areas of thrombosis.

Treatment: This depends on the severity of the blockage. Your veterinarian can prescribe medications to try to dissolve the clot. Heparin seems to be the most useful drug for this condition. Aspirin may also be used, and a new product called Fragmin, which is a molecular weight heparin (a version of heparin that is smaller in size—molecular weight—than standard heparin), may also be useful, but it is very expensive and is not approved for use in cats at this time. Clopidogrel is currently being tested at Purdue University to see if it will reduce the recurrence rate of thromboembolism. Surgery has not been found to have a high success rate.

Since these cats are almost always also suffering from severe heart disease, management can be difficult. Potassium levels must be monitored carefully, as the damaged muscles release potassium into the circulation. Kidney function must also be monitored in case a clot lodges in the renal artery and causes acute kidney failure.

Cats who do recover from an initial thrombus are at risk for repeated injuries. Physical therapy may be necessary as healing progresses to restore muscle and joint function. Some cats will develop collateral circulation, where blood vessels grow around the clotted thrombus to provide nutrients and remove toxins in that area, but they are in the minority.

ACQUIRED VALVULAR DISEASE

Acquired valvular heart disease is rare in cats. It is caused by a blood-borne infection. Bacteria lodge on the heart valves, forming clumps of infective material containing fibrin (a protein involved in blood clotting) and debris that damages the valves. Heart failure develops as a consequence of impaired valve function.

The disease can be prevented by effectively treating skin abscesses, oral infections, and other infections that are likely to invade the bloodstream.

Treatment: The heart failure must be treated as described for *Feline Aortic Thromboembolism* (page 322). Surgery to correct the condition is rarely done.

Anemia

Anemia is a deficiency of red blood cells in the circulation. Red blood cells carry oxygen to the tissues; therefore, the symptoms of anemia are due to insufficient oxygen in the blood and tissues. In adults, anemia exists when there are fewer than five million red cells in 1 milliliter of blood or when the percentage of red cells in whole blood is less than 25 percent by volume. Normal values are somewhat lower in young kittens. Once anemia is identified, its cause can be determined by other tests.

CAUSES OF ANEMIA

Anemia can be caused by blood loss or inadequate red blood cell production. In some cases, the body produces red cells rapidly, but not fast enough to keep up with the losses. It may take three to five days for the bone marrow to respond to a blood loss by producing new red blood cells.

Blood Loss

Rapid blood loss is caused by trauma and major hemorrhage. Shock will ensue. (Shock is discussed on page 13.) Treatment of shock using intravenous electrolyte solutions and blood transfusions is directed at controlling the bleeding and restoring fluid volume and red blood cells.

A less obvious blood loss takes place through the gastrointestinal tract as a result of hookworm or coccidia infestation, tumors, or ulceration. External parasites such as fleas and lice can cause a cat to lose surprising amounts of blood.

The average life span of red cells in the cat is 66 to 78 days. A shortened life span occurs when red cells are prematurely destroyed within the circulation. This condition, called hemolysis, can occur with autoimmune hemolytic anemias, toxic drugs, and infectious microorganisms. One cause of hemolysis is a blood transfusion with an incompatible blood type.

Inadequate Blood Production

Eighty percent of feline anemias are due to inadequate red blood cell production. Iron, trace minerals, vitamins, and essential fatty acids are incorporated into red blood cells, so a deficiency in building materials will result in a failure to manufacture the final product.

Iron deficiency is a cause of anemia. Some cases are caused by diets low in iron and other essential nutrients. However, most cases are caused by chronic blood loss. Each milliliter of blood lost contains 0.5 mg of iron.

A number of diseases and toxic agents interfere with the production of red blood cells in the bone marrow. They include feline leukemia and feline infectious peritonitis, some cancers, drugs such as chloramphenicol, kidney failure with uremia, and various chemicals and poisons. Kidney failure leads to a deficiency of erythropoietin, a hormone that stimulates red blood cell production in the bone marrow. In fact, any chronic illness can depress the bone marrow and lead to anemia.

Pyruvate kinase deficiency is a genetic enzyme deficiency that leads to anemia. It is seen in Abyssinians and Somalis. This defect can be detected through blood tests, but there is not yet a genetic test for carriers. Treatment may consist of the use of steroids and, sometimes, removal of the spleen.

Infectious Anemias

There are two known infectious agents that can cause anemia in cats. *Cytauxzoon felis* is not very common and is passed to cats by ticks. Bobcats and the Florida panther may be reservoirs of infection. Most cases occur in cats living in rural, wooded areas of the Southeast. Depression, not eating, and a fever may be noted in cats with this type of infection. Some will develop jaundice. Cytauxzoonosis is usually fatal to domestic cats, and death occurs rapidly. There is no standard treatment, but imidocarb dipropionate and diminazene aceturate have been suggested as possible treatments if cases are detected early on.

More common is infection with *Mycoplasma haemophilus* (formerly called *Hemobartonella felis*). A variant is *Mycoplasma haemominutum*. This blood parasite is primarily passed to cats through tick and flea bites, but it can also be spread by cat bites and *in utero* or from infected queens to nursing kittens. Red blood cells are destroyed by the cat's own immune reactions to the parasites. *Mycoplasma haemophilus* may also work in concert with feline leukemia virus to stimulate bone marrow cancers.

Cats with this type of infectious anemia are often weak and may have fevers. Some cats eat dirt or their litter in an attempt to add minerals to their diet. If left untreated, up to 30 percent of affected cats may die.

Some cats will remain carriers even after treatment, which consists of antibiotics.

SIGNS OF ANEMIA

Signs may be overshadowed by a chronic illness. In general, anemic cats lack appetite, lose weight, sleep a great deal, and show generalized weakness. The mucous membranes of the gums and tongue are pale. In cats with severe anemia, the pulse and breathing rate are rapid. These signs also occur with heart disease, and these two conditions can be confused.

Anemia is usually diagnosed by blood tests that look for the red blood cell count and also for the numbers and types of red blood cells present on a smear. Blood parasites are often detected on a smear, but special polymerase chain reaction (PCR) tests may be needed in some cases. A bone marrow sample may also be useful in determining the cause of the anemia.

Treatment: Uncomplicated nutritional anemia responds well to replacement of the missing nutrients and restoring the cat to a nutritionally complete diet.

Iron deficiency anemia should alert you to the possibility of chronic blood loss. A stool check will show whether there are ova and parasites or traces of blood in the feces. Work with your veterinarian to treat any external parasites (see chapter 3).

Infectious anemias respond to antibiotics such as doxycycline and enrofloxacin. Prednisolone may be needed as well to stem the destruction of the red blood cells.

Blood transfusions may be needed for cats with severe anemias.

Heartworms

Heartworm disease, so named because the adult worms live in the right side of the heart, is common in dogs, less so in cats. In fact, cats may be accidental hosts only, and certainly they are less perfect hosts for this parasite than dogs are.

HEARTWORM LIFE CYCLE

A knowledge of the life cycle of this parasite (*Dirofilaria immitis*) is needed to understand how to prevent and treat it. Infection begins when L_3 infective larvae in the mouthparts of a mosquito enter the cat's skin at the site of a bite. The larvae burrow beneath the skin and undergo two molts that eventually lead to the development of small, immature worms. The first molt (L_3 to L_4) occurs 1 to 12 days after the cat is bitten by the mosquito. The larvae remain in the L_4 stage for 50 to 68 days, and then molt into the L_5 stage (immature worms).

Immature worms make their way into a peripheral vein and are carried to the right ventricle and the pulmonary arteries. In cats, the larvae may become disoriented and migrate into body cavities and the central nervous system. Approximately six months after entering the cat's body, they mature into adults. Adults can grow from 4 to 12 inches (10 to 30 cm) long and live up to two to three years.

In dogs, mature heartworms produce larvae, called microfilaria, that circulate in the bloodstream. This is much less common in cats, possibly because the cat's immune system removes the microfilaria or because low numbers of adult worms or same-sex worms actually prevent the production of microfilaria to begin with.

HEARTWORM DISEASE

Because of the small size of the cat's heart, one or two worms may be enough to cause serious heart trouble or even sudden death. Signs of heartworm infestation include a cough made worse by exercise, lethargy, loss of weight and

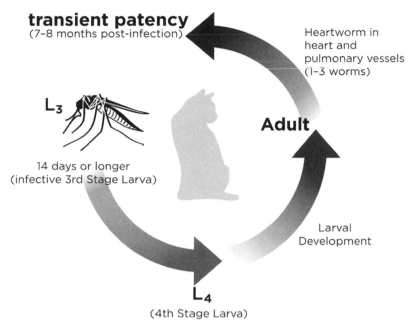

transient patency
(7–8 months post-infection)

Heartworm in
heart and
pulmonary vessels
(1–3 worms)

L₃

14 days or longer
(infective 3rd Stage Larva)

Adult

Larval
Development

L₄
(4th Stage Larva)

Life cycle of the heartworm.

coat condition, and bloody sputum. At this point, it may appear that the cat has asthma or allergic bronchitis. The cat's pulmonary artery response to heartworms is much more severe than is the dog's.

Cats who pass through this phase of infection may be relatively fine until the adult heartworms start to die in two to three years. Labored breathing and mild, low-grade, chronic respiratory signs may go on for a while. Congestive heart failure, along with heart murmurs, loss of condition and appetite, and intermittent vomiting may all appear late in the disease. Worms may be discovered at autopsy following sudden, unexplained death.

Diagnosis is generally done by blood tests looking for the heartworm antigens or antibodies produced to fight them. Both types of tests are valuable before starting treatment for a suspected infection. X-rays of the chest and the use of echocardiography can be especially helpful in diagnosing heartworms in cats.

Treatment: Treatment is complex and potentially dangerous. If the cat seems reasonably healthy, monitoring his condition and following the lifespan of the heartworms may be the best option. Medical support may be needed for any respiratory or cardiac signs. Corticosteroids may be useful in reducing reactions to the worms. Ivermectin has been used to treat heartworm infections in cats, but the drug is still considered experimental as a treatment. Surgery can also be done to physically remove any heartworms, but it is not common.

Prevention: Heartworms are spread by mosquitoes, and areas along coastal regions with swamps or other brackish water provide ideal conditions for mosquitoes to breed. Areas with warm temperatures most of the year have a longer mosquito season, and any nearby areas of standing water can provide a mosquito habitat. In theory, the best way to prevent heartworms is to keep your cat from being bitten by a mosquito. Since mosquitoes have a flight range of one-quarter mile (402 m), in many cases spraying around catteries can be partially effective. Cats can get some protection by being kept indoors in the late afternoon and evening, when mosquitoes are feeding.

Even indoor-only cats can become infected, however, because mosquitoes often get through screens or open doors and windows, or come in on other pets. Preventive drugs for cats include ivermectin, selamectin, and milbemycin oxime, all of which guard against some internal parasites as well. A heartworm test (preferably both antigen and antibody) is recommended but is not absolutely necessary before starting your cat on a preventive regimen. Many practitioners now advocate year-round prevention, although theoretically cats need not be protected in the winter months in cold areas, because there are no mosquitoes alive outside.

12

THE NERVOUS SYSTEM

The cat's central nervous system is composed of the cerebrum, cerebellum, midbrain (which includes the brain stem), and spinal cord.

The cerebrum has two hemispheres and is the largest part of the brain. It controls learning, memory, reasoning, and judgment. A cat's voluntary actions are initiated here. Diseases affecting the cerebrum are characterized by changes in personality and learned behavior. A well-behaved cat may begin to eliminate outside the litter box, grow irritable or become aggressive, or exhibit compulsive pacing, circling, or apparent blindness. Seizures are frequently associated with cerebral disease.

The cerebellum is large and well-developed in the cat. It also has two lobes. Its main function is integrating the motor pathways of the brain to maintain the cat's coordination and balance. Injuries or diseases of the cerebellum result in uncoordinated body movements such as jerking, stumbling, falling, and overreaching with the paws.

In the midbrain and brain stem are the centers that control the respiration, heartbeat, blood pressure, and other activities essential to life. At the base of the brain are centers for responses such as hunger, rage, thirst, hormonal activity, and temperature control. Closely connected to the midbrain and brain stem are the hypothalamus and the pituitary gland.

A set of 12 nerve pairs called the cranial nerves pass directly out from the midbrain into the head and neck through special holes in the skull. Especially important among these cranial nerve pairs are the optic nerves to the eyes, auditory nerves to the ears, and olfactory nerves to the scent organs.

The spinal cord passes down a bony canal formed by the arches of the vertebrae. The cord sends out nerve roots that combine with one another to form the peripheral nerves, which carry motor impulses to the muscles and receive sensory input from the skin and deeper structures.

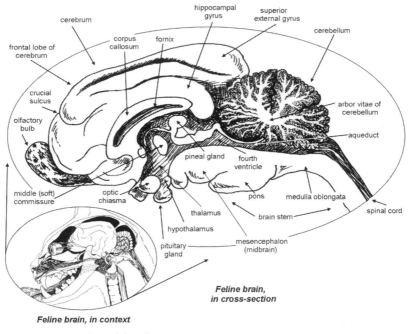

Feline brain, in context

Feline brain, in cross-section

Cross-section of the feline brain.

In assessing brain and nerve diseases, the cat's history is very important. Your veterinarian will ask if your cat has been in an accident or has received a blow to the head. Was she recently poisoned? Is the cat taking any drugs? Has she been exposed to other cats who are ill? When did you first notice the symptoms? Have the symptoms progressed? If so, has the progression been rapid or gradual? These are all important points to consider.

To further evaluate a neurological disorder, special tests may be needed. A neurological physical exam may be done, in which the cat is manipulated to determine which nerves are involved in the problem. X-rays, electroencephalography (*EEG*), CT scan, MRI, and spinal tap (a procedure in which fluid is removed from the spinal canal and submitted for laboratory analysis) may also be necessary. Blood work, including a blood chemistry panel, may be needed to search for metabolic problems. In a few cases, DNA testing, such as for metabolic disease, may shed light on the cause of neurological problems.

Head Injuries

Forty percent of cats who are hit by a car suffer a head injury. This can range from a broken jaw to severe damage to the skull. Other causes of head injury are falls and blows to the skull.

SKULL FRACTURES

Since the brain is not only encased in bone but also surrounded by a layer of fluid and suspended in the skull by a system of tough ligaments, it takes a major blow to fracture the skull and injure the brain. Injuries of sufficient magnitude to fracture the skull are often accompanied by bleeding into the brain from ruptured blood vessels.

Skull fractures can be linear, star shaped, depressed, compound (open to the outside of the body), or closed (under the skin). Fractures at the base of the skull often extend into the ear, orbit (the bones around the eye), nasal cavity, or sinuses, creating openings for brain infection.

BRAIN INJURIES

In general, the magnitude of the skull fracture is an indication of the severity of brain injury. Nevertheless, even head injuries without skull fracture can cause severe brain damage. Brain injuries are classified according to the severity of the damage to the brain.

- **Bruising (contusion).** This is the mildest injury; there is no loss of consciousness. After a blow to the head the cat remains dazed, wobbly, or disoriented. This condition then gradually clears.
- **Concussion.** A concussion means the cat was knocked out or experienced a brief loss of consciousness. Upon returning to consciousness, the cat exhibits the same signs as those of a contusion.
- **Cerebral edema.** Following severe head injury, there may be swelling of the brain or the formation of a blood clot from ruptured vessels. Both produce increased intracranial pressure. Cerebral edema, swelling of the brain, is always accompanied by a depressed level of consciousness and often coma. Since the brain is encased in a bony skull, brain swelling leads to pressure on the brain stem. As the cerebellum is forced down through the spinal cord opening at the base of the skull, the vital centers in the midbrain become squeezed and compressed. When this happens suddenly, it quickly leads to death.
- **Blood clot.** A blood clot on the brain produces localized pressure symptoms that do not, at least initially, compress the vital centers. There is a depressed level of consciousness. Often one pupil is dilated and will not constrict down when a light is flashed in the eye. A paralysis or weakness may be present on one side of the body. This is similar to a stroke in a person.

Death and damage to certain areas of the brain also occur when the brain is deprived of oxygen. Complete interruption of the oxygen circulation for only five minutes produces irreversible damage to the cells of the cerebral cortex—the part of the brain that controls many conscious actions. This could happen with suffocation, drowning, or cardiac arrest.

Signs of Increased Intracranial Pressure

Following a blow to the cat's head, you should watch for signs of brain swelling or the development of a blood clot. These signs can appear any time during the first 24 hours after the injury.

The most important thing to observe is the level of your cat's consciousness. An alert cat is in no immediate danger. A stuporous cat is sleepy but will still respond to you. A semicomatose cat is sleepy but can still be aroused with effort. A comatose cat cannot be aroused.

After physical or emotional stress, cats tend to sleep as the excitement wears off. Awaken your cat every two hours for the first 24 hours to check her level of consciousness. Also look for these other signs:

- **Slight pressure on the brain.** The cat is stuporous and may stumble or stagger. Breathing is normal. The pupils remain small and constrict when a light is flashed in the cat's eyes.

- **Moderate pressure on the brain.** The cat is reclining and is difficult to arouse. Breathing is rapid and shallow. The cat is generally weak. Eye movements and pupils are normal.

- **Severe pressure on the brain.** The cat is in a coma. All four legs are rigid, then become flaccid. Breathing is gasping or irregular. Pupils are dilated and do not react to light. The heart rate is slowed. Eye movements are slight or absent.

Close and frequent observations are important, particularly if the signs change and indicate an increase in intracranial pressure. *Notify your veterinarian without delay.* Early treatment, preferably within the first hour, greatly enhances the prognosis for successful recovery. When treatment is delayed for just a few hours, the opportunity to prevent irreversible brain damage is lost.

Most cats with head injuries should be hospitalized at least for 24 hours in an emergency facility with 24-hour coverage. That way, treatment can be instituted immediately if the cat shows a change in condition.

TREATING HEAD INJURIES

Treating shock takes precedence over management of the head injury (see page 13). If the cat is unconscious, establish an open airway by extending her head until her neck is straight and pulling her tongue forward.

With a severe brain injury, the cat may exhibit few, if any, signs of life. Signs of death are no pulse, no effort to breathe, dilated pupils, and a soft eye (an eye with abnormal pressure due to the trauma). Whether sudden death is

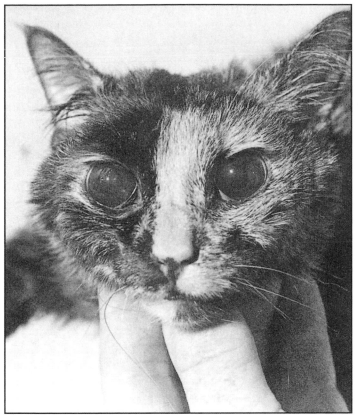

The dilated pupils indicate severe pressure on the brain. This cat had a terminal brain injury.

caused by a head injury or a state of shock from internal bleeding is usually impossible to know. It is wise to administer cardiopulmonary resuscitation immediately if there is no pulse (see *CPR*, page 13).

At the scene of an accident, follow these instructions for transporting the cat to the nearest veterinary hospital:

1. Control bleeding as described in *Wounds* (page 47).
2. Place the cat on a flat stretcher, as described in *Spinal Cord Injuries* (page 343).
3. Stabilize all fractures, if possible (see *Broken Bones*, page 16); cover the cat with a warm blanket.
4. Record a baseline neurological exam (level of consciousness, limb movement, and pupil size).
5. Transport the cat to an emergency veterinary hospital with her head higher than her rear; this helps lower intracranial pressure.

Cerebral edema is treated with steroids, oxygen, and diuretics (Mannitol) to reduce brain swelling. Severely depressed and open skull fractures require surgical cleansing and removal of devitalized bone, or elevation plus replacement of a depressed fragment to relieve pressure on the brain. Antibiotics are sometimes needed to prevent infection. Uncomplicated skull fractures can be simply observed.

The outlook following head trauma depends on the severity of the injury and whether immediate treatment is successful. When both pupils are fixed and dilated, the injury is usually irreversible. When a coma persists for more than 24 hours, the outlook is poor. However, if the cat shows steady improvement throughout the first week, the outlook is good.

Cats who recover from a brain injury may have permanent behavior changes, head tilt, blindness, partial paralysis, lack of coordination, or seizures. Some of these changes can be improved through physical therapy.

The Central Nervous System

Central nervous system disorders affect less than 1 percent of cats. The most frequent is head trauma. Next in frequency are drug intoxication, poisoning, cerebrovascular disease, and *encephalitis*. Other conditions seen less frequently are tumors, vitamin deficiencies, and congenital abnormalities.

ENCEPHALITIS

Encephalitis is inflammation of the brain caused by an infection. Symptoms are caused by the destructive effect of the infectious agent and by secondary *cerebral edema*. They include fever, behavioral and personality changes (especially aggression), loss of coordination, unstable gait, stupor, seizures, and coma.

Viruses that cause encephalitis include feline infectious peritonitis, panleukopenia, feline leukemia, rabies, and pseudorabies. These are discussed in chapter 3.

Panleukopenia is a problem in the newborn kitten when it produces cerebellar hypoplasia (lack of development of the cerebellum, the coordination center of the brain). These kittens are infected *in utero* or shortly after birth. They show a lack of coordination and may have tremors. Luckily, these conditions are not progressive and at least some of these kittens can still be acceptable pets.

Bacteria also can cause encephalitis. Most bacteria gain entrance to the brain via the bloodstream or by direct extension from an infected sinus, nasal passage, or eye, or from head and neck abscess. Fungal brain infection (*Cryptococcus*) is a rare cause of encephalitis, as is the protozoan Toxoplasmosis (see page 67).

Granulomatous meningoencephalitis (GME) is an inflammatory disease of unknown cause at this time. It is rare in cats. Cells associated with inflammation build up in the central nervous system (brain and spinal cord) and interfere with normal nerve cell functions. The focal form attacks one or two sites in the brain. The disseminated form spreads throughout the central nervous system. The ocular form primarily affects the nerve cells of the eye. Signs vary, depending on the location of the inflammation; affected cats may show neck pain, a rigid stance, and fever. *Paresis* and paralysis slowly progress over one to two months.

Treatment: This is directed at the primary cause. Steroids are used to reduce brain swelling. Radiation therapy may be added to the treatment regimen to provide short-term relief for cats with GME. Antibiotics are needed for bacterial infections. Most cats with encephalitis will need to be hospitalized, at least initially.

CEREBRAL HEMORRHAGE (STROKE)

Strokes in cats are caused by ruptured blood vessels bleeding into the brain. True strokes are not common in cats, but hypertension (high blood pressure, see page 380) can lead to strokes and similar damage to the brain. In most cases, the initiating cause of cerebral hemorrhage is unknown. However, preceding the stroke, there may have been a recent upper respiratory infection or an illness that produced a fever.

Signs that often come on suddenly include spasms of the face and limb muscles, paralysis, loss of coordination, and blindness. Increased vocalizations may also be a sign. Usually, only one side is affected. Residual signs include behavior changes, pacing and circling, and seizures. Diagnosis of a stroke can be made from the history and physical findings. However, it can be confirmed only by special studies that are not generally available to most practitioners.

Treatment: The only treatment is supportive care until the cat has adapted to her dysfunction.

BRAIN TUMORS

Brain tumors are rare in cats. Lymphosarcoma is the most common tumor seen in the central nervous system, and has often *metastasized* there from a primary tumor elsewhere in the body. It affects the spaces around the brain and the spinal cord. Signs of brain tumor are like those of a stroke (discussed above), except they tend to come on gradually as the tumor grows.

Meningiomas (tumors growing from the covering of the brain) are the most common true brain cancer in cats. This type of cancer is seen in older cats, with males having a slightly higher risk. Signs can include behavior changes, changes in vocalization, vision deficits, circling, and, eventually, *paresis*. Diagnosing this cancer almost always requires an MRI or CT scan.

One dilated pupil may suggest a brain tumor or a blood clot on the brain.

Treatment: Surgery is the ideal treatment and should be done by an experienced surgeon. Postoperative hemorrhage is a risk, but cats who avoid that risk often do quite well.

NUTRITIONAL DISORDERS

Nutritional disorders can sometimes affect the central nervous system.

Hypoglycemia, or low blood sugar, can produce seizures, a depressed level of consciousness, and coma. It is sometimes associated with prolonged chilling. Insulin overdose in a diabetic cat is a common cause. See *Diabetes Mellitus,* page 291, for more information on this disease.

Hypocalcemia, or low blood calcium, causes signs and symptoms much like those of hypoglycemia. It is discussed in *Eclampsia* (page 448).

Thiamin deficiency occurs when a cat fails to eat regularly or is fed an unbalanced diet containing large amounts of raw fish. Raw fish has an enzyme that destroys vitamin B1. Signs of brain involvement are similar to those described for *Vestibular Disorders* (page 342), and are frequently accompanied by seizures. When lifted up, cats often flex their necks, dropping chin to chest.

Injections of thiamin and switching to a balanced diet lead to recovery—but only when the deficiency is discovered and treated before the cat becomes comatose.

INHERITED METABOLIC DISEASES

These are a group of genetically determined disorders that produce degenerative changes in the central nervous system. In each case, a specific enzyme required for nerve cell metabolism is missing. Although these diseases are

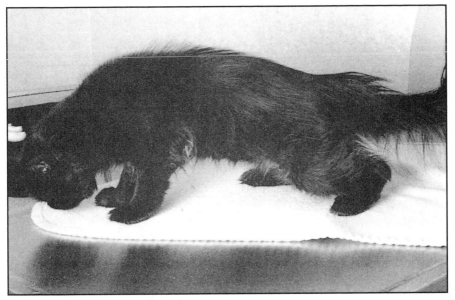

The wide-based stance and wobbly gait of a kitten with metabolic nervous system disease.

The kitten uses her head to keep her balance.

quite rare, cat breeders should recognize them and work to eliminate carriers from their breeding program.

Metabolic nervous system diseases are generally inherited as autosomal recessive traits. Siamese and various domestic shorthair cats are most often affected. Both parents must carry the gene and each must pass it on to an affected kitten. Littermates who do not show signs of the disease may carry the trait. Accordingly, when one of these diseases is discovered in a family or bloodline, carriers should be identified by special enzyme or DNA tests, so that steps can be taken to eliminate the trait from the bloodline.

Signs first appear at weaning or shortly thereafter. They include muscle tremors and loss of coordination. The kitten's gait may be wobbly and unstable. As the disease progresses, the kitten develops late signs that include weakness, paralysis of the back limbs, blindness, and seizures.

Many of the problems noted here involve enzyme deficiencies or defects in metabolism, leading to the buildup and storage of metabolic waste products. These conditions can be identified by specialized blood work and, in a few cases, by DNA testing. There is no treatment for most of these conditions. Therefore, the best option is to eliminate carriers from a breeding program.

- **GM1 (gangliosidosis).** Seen in Oriental breed cats. Signs include corneal clouding and cerebellar signs such as *ataxia*.

- **GM2 (familial amaurotic idiocy).** Seen in domestic shorthair and Korat cats. Signs include behavioral and visual deficits, along with progressive ataxia and head tremors.

- **Niemann-Pick (sphingomyelinosis).** Autosomal recessive inheritance in Siamese cats. There are cerebellar signs and an enlarged abdomen due to enlarged liver and spleen. Deficits vary according to the exact subtype of the disease.

- **Mannosidosis.** Seen in domestic shorthair, domestic longhair, and Persian kittens. There will be cerebellar and behavioral abnormalities, visual deficits, and bone abnormalities. A DNA test is available from PennGen at the University of Pennsylvania.

- **Glycogenolysis type IV.** Autosomal recessive inheritance in Norwegian Forest Cats. Signs include fever, abnormal gait, muscle atrophy, and seizures.

- **Mucopolysaccharidosis type 1.** Seen in domestic shorthairs. Signs include flattened face, lameness, corneal clouding, and bone dysplasias. Signs are not progressive after 9 months of age. A DNA test is available from PennGen at the University of Pennsylvania.

- **Mucopolysaccharidosis type VI.** Seen in Siamese. Signs include flattened face, abnormal bones, rear limb *paresis*, and, rarely, seizures. A DNA test is available from PennGen at the University of Pennsylvania.

- **Ceroid lipofuscinosis.** Seen in Siamese, possibly an autosomal recessive trait. Signs include visual deficit, ataxia, and seizures.

- **Hereditary hyperchylomicronemia (hyperlipidemia).** An autosomal recessive trait. Mild neurological signs such as ataxia start at about 8 months of age. A low-fat diet may be helpful.

- **Spongiform degeneration.** Seen in Egyptian Maus and Burmese. Signs include ataxia, hypermetria (exaggerated height to the steps), tremors, and behavior problems. Poor prognosis for survival.

Inherited metabolic diseases should be distinguished from cerebellar hypoplasia (see page *Neonatal Feline Panleukopenia*, page 472), which follows intrauterine exposure to the virus of feline panleukopenia. In addition, other congenital malformations do occur, although they are rare. Microencephaly is a problem noted in Korat cats. The small brain leads to seizures and behavior abnormalities. Hydrocephalus is an enlargement of the dome of the skull due to a blockage in the circulation of cerebral spinal fluid.

Seizures

A seizure is a sudden and uncontrolled burst of activity that may include one or more of the following signs: champing and chewing, foaming at the mouth, collapse, jerking of the legs, and loss of urine and stool. An altered level of consciousness is followed by a gradual return to normal.

Some seizures are atypical. Instead of the classic convulsion, the cat exhibits strange and inappropriate behavior, such as sudden rage or hysteria. Cats may lick and chew themselves, scratch or bite their owner or another cat. This is called a psychomotor seizure.

Most classic seizures in cats are caused by acute poisoning. Seizures after head injury may occur at the time of the accident, but in most cases appear several weeks later as a result of scar tissue on the brain. Stroke, metabolic disorders, and epilepsy are other causes of seizures.

Common poisonings that induce seizures include strychnine, antifreeze (ethylene glycol), lead, insecticides (chlorinated hydrocarbons, organophosphates), and rat poisons (see *Poisoning*, page 26). Organophosphates characteristically produce seizures that are preceded by drooling and muscle twitching. A history of exposure to an insecticide (spray, dip, or premise treatment) suggests this diagnosis (see *Insecticides*, page 36).

Kidney and liver failure, accompanied by the accumulation of toxins in the blood, can cause seizures and coma.

Epilepsy is a recurrent seizure disorder that originates in the brain. It can be caused by outside influences, such as trauma, which is acquired epilepsy, or from a defect in neurochemicals in the brain, which is idiopathic epilepsy. Idiopathic epilepsy always has symmetrical signs. It is far less common in cats than it is in dogs.

To establish a diagnosis of epilepsy, the attacks must be recurrent and similar. Toward this purpose your veterinarian will ask you to provide a complete description of your cat's behavior before, during, and after the seizures.

Narcolepsy-cataplexy is a rare condition in which the cat suddenly falls asleep and drops to the ground. The cat may have one or dozens of such attacks in a day, lasting a few seconds or up to 20 minutes. The attacks can be reversed by petting the cat or making a loud noise. The cat is completely normal when awake.

There are a number of conditions that, while not true seizures, can easily be mistaken for them. Bee stings, for example, can cause shock and collapse. Fainting spells associated with advanced heart or lung disease may look like seizures.

A cat who has suffered from a seizure should have a complete veterinary workup, including blood chemistries, a neurological exam, and, if available, an MRI or CT scan.

Treatment: If your cat is having a classic seizure, cover the cat with a blanket and stand aside until the animal quiets down. Do not put your fingers in the cat's mouth or try to wedge something between the teeth. Cats cannot swallow their tongues while having a seizure, and this will simply result in you being badly bitten. Then take your cat to the veterinarian so they can determine the cause of the seizure.

Seizures lasting over five minutes (continuous seizures or status epilepticus) are very dangerous. They must be stopped to prevent permanent brain damage. Valium is given by your veterinarian to stop a continuous seizure.

Recurrent seizure disorders can often be controlled with medications. Although there is no cure for idiopathic epilepsy, seizures can generally be controlled medically. For acquired epilepsy or seizures of other causes, the inciting cause must be treated.

The same drugs used in treating seizures in people and dogs, such as potassium bromide, phenobarbital, and diazepam (Valium) may be tried for treating a cat with seizures. However, in cats, all of these medications can be quite toxic and require close veterinary supervision. Potassium bromide has been connected to respiratory problems in about 35 percent of the cats who have taken it. Blood tests should be done periodically to guard against toxic effects. Families should keep track of any seizure activity on a calendar so they can look for any pattern to the seizures.

Coma

Coma is a depressed level of consciousness. It begins with confusion, progresses through stupor, and ends in complete loss of consciousness. Following a blow to the head, coma can occur without progressing through the earlier stages. No matter what the cause, coma is a potentially fatal condition.

Coma is associated with oxygen deprivation, brain swelling, brain tumor, encephalitis, poisoning, and death. Disorders that cause seizures can also cause coma, depending on whether the brain is made more excitable or less by the disorder.

Another cause of coma is prolonged chilling, or hypothermia. In this case, the cat's temperature is subnormal—well below the normal level on the thermometer. Treatment involves slow warming and intravenous glucose. Coma associated with insulin overdose is discussed in *Diabetes Mellitus* (see page 291).

With a comatose cat, the most important thing to observe is the level of consciousness. This cat cannot be aroused.

Coma may also be associated with brain trauma or the late stages of kidney and liver disease, and is a sign of very serious illness. Coma accompanied by high fever or heat stroke is also a grave sign. Vigorous efforts to bring down the fever are needed to prevent permanent brain damage (see *Heat Stroke*, page 24).

If you find your cat in a coma for which there is no apparent explanation, your cat may have been poisoned. Common poisons that cause coma are ethylene glycol, barbiturates, turpentine, kerosene, arsenic, cyanide, dinitrophenol, hexachlorophene, amphetamines and lead salts. A cat left too long in an airtight space may have smothered or developed carbon monoxide poisoning. All these conditions are discussed in chapter 1.

Treatment: First, determine whether the cat is alive and the level of consciousness (as described in *Signs of Increased Intracranial Pressure*, page 332). An unconscious cat can inhale her own secretions and strangle on her tongue. Pull the tongue forward and clear the airway with your fingers. Lift the cat by the rear legs and set the animal on a table with her head hanging over the side.

If the cat is alive, wrap her in a blanket and go at once to a veterinarian. If the cat shows no signs of life, begin CPR (see page 12). Cats are remarkable in their ability to survive serious conditions—hence, their reputation for having nine lives!—so do not give up your efforts until a veterinarian has pronounced the cat dead.

Vestibular Disorders

Vestibular disorders are common in cats. The vestibular apparatus (called the labyrinth) is a complex sense organ composed of three semicircular canals, plus the utricle and the saccule. The labyrinth is stimulated by gravity and rotational movements. It plays an important role in balance and orienting the body in space. Inflammation of the labyrinth is called labyrinthitis.

A cat with labyrinthitis has a problem with balance. The animal wobbles, circles, falls and rolls over, and has trouble righting herself. She may lean against the wall for support and crouch low to the floor when walking. The cat often shows rapid jerking eye movements (*nystagmus*), and her head will usually tilt down on one side. When picked up and turned in a circle, the cat will act even more dizzy. There may be vomiting and deafness.

A common cause of labyrinthitis is inner ear infection. Other causes include stroke, brain tumor, head trauma, brain infection, drug intoxication (especially by the aminoglycoside antibiotics), and thiamin deficiency.

A *congenital* vestibular defect is seen in Oriental breeds. Kittens show a head tilt, circling, and rolling behaviors. Siamese kittens with this condition may also be deaf. There is no cure.

Idiopathic vestibular syndrome is the most common cause of labyrinthitis in cats. The onset is sudden and the cause is unknown. The signs include a head tilt and nystagmus, and cats may have difficulty walking. There is an increase in these cases in July and August in the northeastern United States, suggesting an environmental cause.

Treatment: With cases of idiopathic vestibular syndrome, in two to three days, the cat begins to recover on her own. In most cases, the cat is well in three weeks, although some cats retain a permanent head tilt. During the recovery period, the cat will need supportive care.

The Spinal Cord

Injuries and diseases of the spinal cord produce a variety of neurological signs. Following injury, there may be neck or back pain; weakness or paralysis of one or more legs; a stumbling, uncoordinated gait; loss of pain perception in the limbs; and urinary or fecal incontinence.

Other conditions producing limb weakness or *paralysis* that may be mistaken for a spinal cord problem are arterial thromboembolism, nerve injury, and broken bones. Arterial thromboembolism can be distinguished by absent or reduced pulses in the groin.

A pelvic fracture is frequently mistaken for a broken back. In both cases, the cat is unable to use her back legs and will show pain when handled in the area of the injury. An X-ray may be needed to distinguish the two conditions. It is important to ascertain that the urinary bladder hasn't ruptured. It might

When both rear legs are paralyzed, consider spinal cord injury or arterial thromboembolism.

appear that the outlook is poor, even though cats with a broken pelvis usually recover completely.

Acute abdominal pain (caused by peritonitis, lower urinary tract disorder, or a kidney or liver infection) produces a peculiar hunched appearance that can be mistaken for a spinal cord problem. The acute abdomen will show signs of pain when pressure is applied to the abdominal wall (see *Painful Abdomen*, page 15).

SPINAL CORD INJURIES

Traumatic spinal cord injuries are usually caused by car accidents, falls, and abuse. A cat can get caught in the blades of an automobile fan when the car is started, because outdoor cats frequently will huddle up next to a warm car radiator in cold weather.

A common injury occurs when a car runs over a cat's tail, pulling apart the sacral-lumbar or coccygeal vertebrae and stretching the nerves that go to the bladder, rectum, and tail. The signs are paralysis of the tail (which hangs loosely like a rope) and urinary or fecal incontinence. The anal sphincter is completely relaxed. The bladder is paralyzed and greatly overdistended. If the condition is not recognized and treated shortly after the accident, bladder paralysis remains even though nerve function is restored. As a result, *any cat with a limp tail must be seen by a veterinarian and X-rayed for sacral injury.* Many

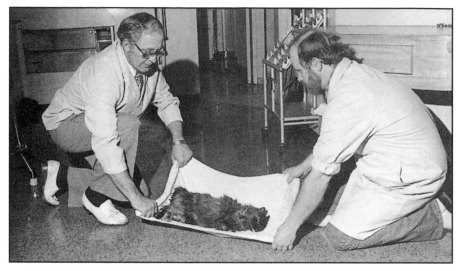

Protect the cat's spine. Use a blanket or towel to lift her onto a flat surface, such a board, before transporting.

of these cats will need to be hospitalized so the bladder can be manually emptied and treatment can be started to attempt to heal the nerves controlling urination and defecation.

Treatment: All spinal cord injuries require *immediate* veterinary attention. A cat with spinal cord trauma may also have other life-threatening injuries that take precedence. All cats who are unconscious or unable to stand should be considered to have spinal cord injury and must be handled with great care to protect the spine.

At the scene of the accident, move the cat as gently as possible onto a rigid, flat surface, such as a plywood board or a folded-down cardboard box, and transport to the nearest veterinary clinic. Sliding the cat onto a blanket or large towel and lifting the corners is a satisfactory way of transporting the cat if no board is available.

Spinal cord injuries are treated at the veterinary hospital with corticosteroids and diuretics to prevent the cord from further swelling. A cat with a mild contusion or bruising of the spinal cord will begin to recover in a few days. However, if the cord has been severed, it cannot regenerate and paralysis will be permanent.

PROTRUDING DISCS

Protruding discs are common in older cats but seldom produce weakness or paralysis as they do in dogs. They may cause pain. Most are the result of trauma. There is an increase in the incidence of disc damage with age, and ruptured discs are primarily seen in cats over 15 years of age.

Treatment: Treatment may include pain relief and/or surgery for severe cases.

SPONDYLITIS

Spinal arthritis, sometimes called spondylitis, is a condition in which spurs of calcium develop on the vertebrae. These spurs can exert pressure on the spinal cord or the roots of the spinal nerves, occasionally causing pain and, rarely, weakness of a limb. Although this change is commonly seen in older cats, it does not usually cause any clinical problems.

Treatment: Basic arthritis care can be helpful (see page 362), such as a shallow litter box to make it easier for the cat to get in and out. Pain relief medications may also be helpful.

SPINAL MUSCULAR ATROPHY IN MAINE COON CATS

This is a genetic defect that occurs in Maine Coon Cats. Spinal cord nerves that control the skeletal muscles of the body and legs die off. The disease is evident at about 3 to 4 months of age. Kittens move with a sway in the rear end, and by 5 or 6 months of age they can't jump up. Muscle mass is decreased. The cats do not appear to be in pain and may lead fairly normal lives as indoor pets. There is no treatment.

This is an autosomal recessive trait. A DNA test has been developed at the Laboratory of Comparative Medical Genetics at Michigan State University, so cats can be tested by sending in a cheek swab to see if they are carriers before being bred.

SPINAL CORD INFECTIONS

Spinal cord infections are not common. Most of them are due to a neighboring abscess, caused by a penetrating wound such as a bite or a laceration.

Meningitis is an infection of the lining of the spinal canal and the brain. On rare occasions, it may be caused by blood-borne bacteria. Diagnosis of a spinal cord infection may require a spinal tap—withdrawing cerebral spinal fluid from around the spinal cord to look for cells and bacteria. Most cats with meningitis will have a fever and changes in their blood work.

Treatment: The treatment depends on the cause and may require long-term antibiotics.

TUMORS OF THE SPINAL CORD

Lymphosarcoma is the most common tumor along and around the spinal cord in cats. Pressure from the growth will lead to damage to the nerves and result in clinical signs such as weakness or paralysis. Specialized X-rays, called myelograms, may be needed for a diagnosis. Dye is injected around the spinal cord, with the hope that it will outline any growths present. MRI and CT scans are also very useful.

Treatment: Chemotherapy may be helpful. Rarely, surgery can be done to remove a discrete mass.

SPINA BIFIDA

Spina bifida is a developmental defect in the closure of the bones in the lower back. With this problem, the spinal cord is not protected by the bony vertebral column and is easily damaged and prone to infections. It is common in the Manx breed and any cat born without a tail. Signs include a lack of bladder and bowel control. These cats can exhibit weakness of the hind legs and a peculiar gait that resembles a bunny hop.

Treatment: There is no treatment beyond supportive care.

Nerve Injuries and Diseases

An injury to one of the peripheral nerves results in loss of sensation and motor function in the area controlled by that nerve. Common injuries are stretches, tears, and lacerations. Tumors are rare, but include schwannomas and neurofibromas. Diabetic cats can develop nerve weakness related to their disease.

Brachial and radial nerve injuries involve one of the front legs. They are usually caused by an auto accident, during which the leg is jerked backward away from the trunk. The leg hangs limp. With partial paralysis, the cat can often stand but will stumble when taking a step. If the leg is paralyzed, amputation may be the best course of action.

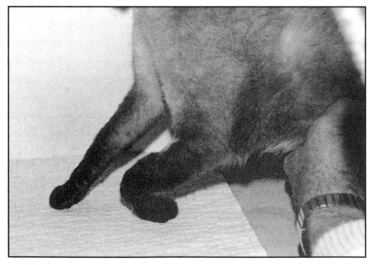

Paralysis of the front leg due to nerve injury.

Another cause of temporary nerve paralysis is the injection of an irritating medication into the tissue surrounding a nerve. This problem is infrequent but can be a source of concern. The correct procedure for giving injections is described on page 557.

PARALYSIS OF THE TAIL

Paralysis of the tail occurs when a car runs over the tail while the cat is trying to escape or the tail is caught in a door as the cat darts in or out of a room. This is a common injury, and is discussed on page 343. Amputation of the tail may be indicated if movement and sensation do not return after six weeks, because the paralyzed tail tends to remain soiled, gets caught in doors, and presents a significant handicap to the cat.

Treatment: Lacerated nerves must be repaired surgically, if there is any hope for restoration of function. Stretched nerves may (but often do not) return to normal. Those that do recover begin to improve in three weeks and may continue to improve for six months. If recovery does not occur, cats often benefit from amputation of the flail leg or "dead" tail.

HORNER'S SYNDROME

This is a neurological condition, usually caused by trauma or middle or inner ear infections. In this case, the cat will have a small pupil in one eye, along with protrusion of the third eyelid on the same side. The upper eyelid will droop and the eye will appear sunken.

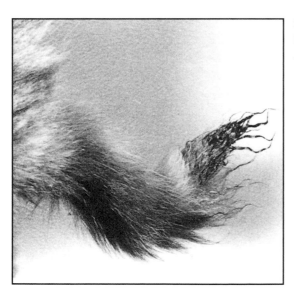

Self-mutilation of a paralyzed, desensitized tail. Amputation was curative.

Treatment: This condition may clear up with time and anti-inflammatory medications.

IDIOPATHIC FACIAL PARALYSIS

This disorder involves the cranial nerves of the facial region. Most often seen in domestic longhaired cats, this condition can be unilateral or bilateral. The cat can't blink, the ear and lip on that side droop, and drool will pool from the mouth.

Treatment: The symptoms are treated with artificial tears. Some cats will improve over time.

FELINE HYPERESTHESIA SYNDROME

This condition usually first appears in cats at about 1 to 4 years of age. Cats will have episodes when their skin twitches, their tail whips, and they don't want to be touched—almost as if their skin was supersensitive. Pupils are often dilated. It is not certain if this is truly a neurological problem or a behavioral one. It is more commonly seen in Siamese, Burmese, Himalayans, and Abyssinians.

Treatment: Treatment might include anti-seizure medications, steroids, or medications that modify behavior. With a behavioral cause, a program of behavior modification may also be helpful.

CHRONIC INFLAMMATORY DEMYELINATING POLYNEUROPATHY

This is an autoimmune problem seen in older cats—generally 6 years of age and older. The disease tends to start in the rear legs with weakness and an *ataxic* gait. This is a chronic condition with periodic relapses.

Treatment: Most cats respond very well to corticosteroid therapy. Immunosuppressive medications may work for cats who relapse and don't respond to the steroids.

THE MUSCULOSKELETAL SYSTEM

13

The cat's skeleton is made up of about 244 individual bones—approximately 40 more than humans have. Nearly half the difference is made up by the cat's tail, which contains 19 to 28 small vertebrae. The number of bones each cat has may vary, depending on the length of his tail. Japanese Bobtail and Manx breeds, and other cats with short, bobbed, or missing tails, have fewer vertebrae.

The outside of a bone is called the cortex. It gives the bone rigidity. Nutritional deficiencies can result in demineralization of the cortex, making fractures more likely. Inside is the marrow cavity, which is important in blood cell production.

Bones are held together by connective tissue called ligaments. The place where two bones meet is called a joint (also known as an articulation). In some joints, a cushioning pad of cartilage (called the *meniscus*) is interposed between the two bone surfaces. Although cartilage is tough and resilient, it still can be damaged by joint stress and trauma. Once damaged, it may deteriorate and become calcified, acting as a foreign body and irritating the joint surfaces.

Each joint is held in position by ligaments, tendons (which join muscle to bone), and a tough fibrous capsule around the joint. These combine to provide stability and tightness. Joint laxity, caused by loose ligaments or a stretched capsule, causes slippage of the articulating surfaces and leads to cartilage injury and, later, arthritis.

Cats owe much of their flexibility to their extremely mobile vertebrae. These bones are less tightly connected than in most other animals, and the

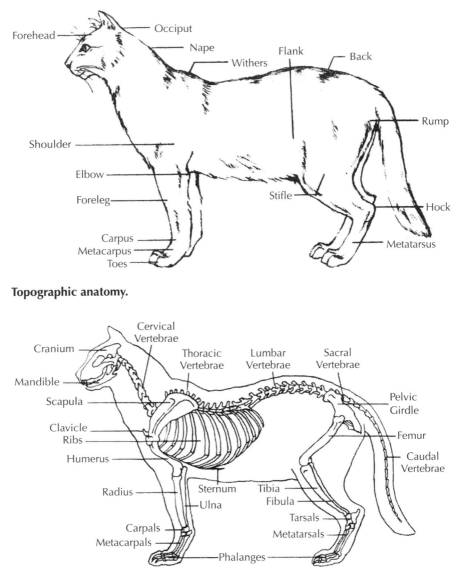

Topographic anatomy.

Skeletal anatomy.

discs that sit between and cushion each vertebra are exceptionally thick and spongy. Although the degree of movement between individual vertebrae is small, when taken together, the flexibility of the vertebral column is considerable. This means a cat can bend, twist, and rotate his front and back body parts independently. He can also compress or stretch out his spine, making himself smaller to curl up in tight spots or longer to leap across wide gaps.

The skeletal anatomies of humans and cats have much in common, including similar terminology, but there are significant differences in angles, lengths, and positions of bones. The cat's hock is our heel. So while we walk on the soles of our feet, cats walk on their toes. The collar bone (clavicle) is quite small in the cat and may even be absent in some cats. When it is present, it is not attached to the main body of the skeleton. This narrows the chest and enables cats to keep their legs and feet close together—thereby providing speed, flexibility, and the ability to squeeze through tight spaces. It also enables the front legs to more efficiently absorb the shock of landing.

Veterinarians, cat breeders, and judges use certain terms to describe a cat's overall composition and structure. *Conformation* is how the various angles, shapes, and parts of the cat's body agree or harmonize with one another, and conform to the breed standard. Standards for purebred cats describe the ideal conformation for each particular breed. At one end of the scale is the strong, sturdy, blocky structure typified by the American Shorthair, Persian, British Shorthair, and Maine Coon Cat. At the other end is the lithe, sleek, fine-boned silhouette, exemplified by Oriental breeds such as the Siamese. Other breeds, such as the Abyssinian, embody characteristics of both. Standards also describe head features, length of coat, color and markings, overall balance, and personality of the breed.

Another term, *soundness*, is used to assess the physical attributes of an animal. When applied to the musculoskeletal system, soundness means all the cat's bones and joints are in correct alignment and are functioning efficiently.

Declawing

All the members of the feline family except cheetahs have retractable claws. When a cat is walking around, the claws are retracted and don't catch on anything. This is also partly why cats can be so stealthy. The claws grow somewhat like human fingernails, but also will shed the outer sheath periodically, leaving a sharper claw beneath. To aid in removing the sheaths, cats scratch, often by stretching up and pulling downward. This action also helps to stretch out the spine and leaves a scent mark.

Scratching is a natural and necessary behavior for cats. You cannot teach them never to scratch. However, you can provide an adequate scratching surface and then teach them to scratch only on that surface. It is very important to provide appropriate scratching opportunities for cats right from kittenhood, so they learn where and where not to scratch.

Scratching posts must be tall enough and sturdy enough that the cat can stretch his full length and pull down. (This means many scratching posts on the market are not tall enough.) Posts can be made attractive by offering a variety of surfaces (carpeting is often the least attractive to cats, while wound sisal is the most attractive), providing horizontal and vertical areas, and rubbing catnip on the scratching surface.

Most scratching damage is caused by the front claws. Cats who claw and scratch indiscriminately may end up being put to death or abandoned due to this easily controlled behavior.

Trimming your cat's claws every week or so will greatly limit any unwanted scratching damage, and most cats tolerate this well. Start with your kitten and do just one foot or even one toe at a time to accustom the cat to the handling. Gradually work up to trimming a whole paw, then two, then four. End each trimming session with a treat and some happy playtime. There are also soft gel caps that can be applied over the claws to minimize scratching damage. These are temporary and need to be replaced periodically. Your veterinarian or a professional groomer can show you how to apply them.

Declawing surgery, despite its name, is not simply the removal of the cat's claws. It is the removal of the last bone in each toe of the foot. This is generally done just on the front feet. The removal of this joint is necessary to remove the entire claw and prevent any regrowth.

The surgery, done under general anesthesia, involves the removal of the claw to include the nail matrix and all of the last bone of the toe. It is akin to removing the last joint on each human finger. Laser surgery is sometimes used in place of a scalpel. In most cases, only the front claws are removed; the back claws are not used to scratch furniture, and they do help the cat run, leap, and balance.

A tendonectomy, severing the tendon that enables the cat to extend his claws, is not widespread. The problem is that the nails continue to grow and are not worn down, which means they can grow into the pads, causing pain and infection.

Pain medication is important postoperatively in all declaw procedures, and there may be complications. These range from slight bleeding, to bone chips left, or continued, ongoing pain.

The feet are firmly bandaged. Some veterinarians choose to suture the skin closed with absorbable suture material. Dressings are removed in a day or two and the cat can go home. The feet will be tender for several days, so filler in the litter box should be replaced with shredded paper to prevent litter from getting into the healing incision. Most cats heal reasonably well.

There is controversy about whether a cat should be declawed, and the practice is outlawed in some countries. Scientific studies have not shown that declawing leads to behavior problems, but anecdotally, many behaviorists believe this is the case. Behavior problems can include mouthy behavior, irritability, and defensive behaviors.

Cats who live outdoors or go outdoors should never be declawed. Their claws are vital for their ability to climb, defend themselves, and escape dangers. Even indoor cats use their claws for balance when they leap, and to grasp and manipulate objects.

Declawing may be recommended for families with immunocompromised members who could not tolerate even an accidental scratch, but there are no feline medical reasons for a cat to be declawed. The American Association of Feline Practitioners advises veterinarians to provide full education about scratching behavior and alternatives before discussing declawing and never to present declawing as a routine procedure.

If declawing is done at all, it is best done when a kitten is 3 months of age or older. Many veterinarians suggest that the operation be deferred until a kitten is 4 to 5 months old. Young cats learn to cope without claws more quickly than do adults. Overweight cats tend to have a very difficult time recovering from this surgery.

Ideally, cats should be trained to use a scratching post (see page 485), eliminating the need for this surgery.

Limping or Lameness

Limping indicates pain or weakness in the involved leg. It is not only the most common sign of bone or joint disease but also of muscle or nerve damage.

DETERMINING THE CAUSE

Consider the history and circumstances surrounding the appearance of lameness. Did the lameness appear spontaneously or was there an injury? Which leg is involved? A cat often holds up the paw or places less weight on a painful leg, especially one that has been recently injured. A cat usually takes shorter steps on a painful or weak leg. The cat's head bobs up on the painful side and down on the side with the sound leg. With chronic lameness, the cat may simply take very short strides with no obvious limp. This is also true if more than one leg is injured or hurts. Such a cat may also be reluctant to leap or jump.

Having identified which leg is involved, try to identify the specific site and possible cause. Be gentle and careful, because even the sweetest cat may scratch or bite when he's in pain. First, examine the foot and look between the toes. Many cases of lameness are due to foot injuries such as sprains, pad lacerations, broken nails, and penetrating puncture wounds. Carefully feel the leg from the toes up. Locate areas of tenderness by applying very gentle pressure. You may also feel areas of swelling.

Next, flex and extend all joints from the toes to the shoulder or hip looking for resistance (lack of easy movement). Resistance is a sign of joint pain, which will be evident when the cat attempts to pull the leg free. If you aren't sure if something you feel is normal, check the cat's other leg. You have one for a comparison for both front and rear leg problems.

Having located the site of pain, the next step is to try to determine the cause of the pain. Consider the following:

- **Infected areas** are red, warm, and tender, and are often associated with skin lacerations or bite wounds. There may be a discharge, initially bloody, and then *purulent* with time. The limp grows steadily worse. An abscess may be developing. The cat may have a fever. Cats often lick at abscessed or wounded areas. Infected cat fight wounds are the most common cause of lameness.

- **Sprains and strains** of joints, tendons, or muscles occur suddenly and are often accompanied by swelling and, sometimes, bruising. They gradually improve. The cat usually has partial use of the leg even when it is injured. Pain is mild. There is no fever. The lameness may persist for days or weeks.

- **Fractures and dislocations** cause severe pain and the cat is unable to bear weight on the leg. There is some degree of deformity. Moving the involved part produces a gritty sound. The tissues are swollen and discolored from bleeding.

- **Spinal cord injuries and peripheral nerve injuries** (discussed in chapter 12) produce weakness or paralysis in one or more limbs but do not produce pain, since the nerves that signal pain are also damaged in most cases.

- **Inherited orthopedic diseases** generally come on gradually. There may be few local findings to explain the lameness. Swelling, if present, is often slight. The lameness persists and grows worse with time.

- **Degenerative joint disease,** also called arthritis or osteoarthritis, is the most common cause of lameness in older cats. The lameness is worse when the cat wakes up and improves as he moves about.

- **Metabolic storage diseases** (see page 336) can also cause bone or muscle defects.

- **Bone tumors** are evidenced by a firm mass or swelling with or without signs of inflammation (see page 515). Pressure over a bone tumor causes varying degrees of pain. Consider this diagnosis in a mature cat with an unexplained limp.

DIAGNOSTIC TESTS

X-rays of the bones and joints are used to diagnose fractures and dislocations. They are also helpful in distinguishing bone growths from soft tissue swellings. Note that many cases of lameness occur without positive findings on conventional X-rays.

A bone scan (also called nuclear scintigraphy) is an imaging technique that uses radioactive isotopes injected into the body and X-ray equipment to form a picture of the bone and surrounding tissue. These scans are especially useful in diagnosing bone cancers and determining the extent of their spread. Because of the cost and the restrictions on using radioactive isotopes, bone scans are performed only at medical centers and schools of veterinary medicine.

A *CT scan* or *MRI* may be of benefit in special circumstances, particularly with tendon, ligament, and muscle damage, but their availability and the cost of these studies limit their usefulness.

Synovial fluid is a viscous joint lubricant that contains hyaluronic acid. The fluid can be removed using a sterile needle and syringe. Analyzing this fluid helps determine the cause of joint swelling. Normal synovial fluid is clear and pale yellow. Blood in the fluid indicates recent joint injury. Pus indicates joint infection (septic arthritis).

Muscle, Bone, and Joint Injuries

Emergency treatment for fractures is discussed in *Broken Bones* (page 16). A fracture (or even a suspected fracture) is always an emergency and requires immediate veterinary attention.

SPRAINS

A sprain is a joint injury caused by a sudden stretching or tearing of the ligaments. The signs are pain over the joint, swelling of the tissues, and temporary lameness. If the cat refuses to put weight on a leg, have him examined by a veterinarian to rule out a fracture or dislocation. The same is true for any injury that fails to improve in four days. X-rays should be taken.

Treatment: The primary treatment is to rest the injured body part. Ice packs help to reduce pain and swelling. Add crushed ice to a plastic bag. Place the bag over the injured joint and hold in place with an elastic bandage or your hand. New commercial cool packs work well, as do bags of frozen vegetables. Apply the cold pack for 15 minutes every hour for the first three hours. If it is left too long, it may cause tissue damage.

Consult your veterinarian for safe pain and anti-inflammatory medications. Never give a cat acetaminophen (Tylenol) or any other over-the-counter pain medication.

TENDON INJURIES

A tendon may be stretched, partly torn, or completely separated (ruptured). An irritated or inflamed tendon is tendonitis. Strained tendons follow sudden wrenching or twisting injuries. The tendons in the front and back paws are the ones most often strained. Signs of tendonitis include temporary lameness,

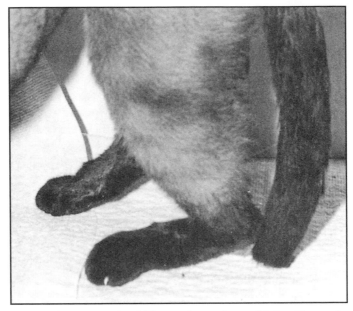

A cat with a ruptured Achilles tendon walks on his heel instead of the toes.

pain on bending and straightening the joint, and tenderness and swelling over the length of the tendon.

Rupture of the Achilles tendon that attaches to the hock joint is caused by sudden and extreme flexion. This tendon is most often injured in auto accidents and cat fights.

Treatment: Stretched tendons are treated in the same way as sprains (see page 355). A ruptured tendon is an emergency and requires immediate veterinary attention. Surgery will be performed and the cat may need a splint or cast, as well as pain medications and follow-up physical therapy.

MUSCLE STRAINS AND CONTUSIONS

A bruised or torn muscle can be caused by sudden stretching of the muscle fibers, overexertion from prolonged use, or a blow to the muscle. Signs are lameness, knotting of the muscle, tenderness over the injured part, and discoloration caused by bleeding. Muscle *atrophy*, the gradual decline in muscle mass due to a lack of use, starts as soon as 24 to 48 hours after a muscle is injured and not used.

Treatment: Rest and cold packs are recommended (see *Sprains*, page 355). Massage may be helpful, and physical therapy exercises may speed healing. Check with your veterinarian.

LUXATION (DISLOCATED JOINT)

Major force is necessary to rupture a joint and displace the bones. Such injuries usually are the result of falls, fights with other animals, or car accidents. The cat may also be in shock and have internal bleeding from injured organs. Signs of dislocation are sudden pain with the inability to bear weight on the limb. There is an observable shortening of the limb when compared with the opposite side.

The hip is the most commonly dislocated joint in the cat. It can be recognized by signs of pain on movement of the hip, a gritty sensation, and shortening of the leg by about 1 inch (25 mm). Other joints less frequently dislocated are the patella (kneecap), hock, and jaw. A dislocated kneecap occurs with some frequency in the Devon Rex; the breed has a hereditary predisposition. It is also seen in Maine Coon Cats.

Treatment: Veterinary examination is necessary to rule out an associated fracture and to replace the joint in its socket. Treating other injuries may take precedence, because a dislocated joint is not life threatening. Replacing a joint in its socket often requires sedation or anesthesia, and the cat may need to wear a splint or wrap to hold the joint in place for a short time while the damaged tissues heal. If a joint has been dislocated for a long time, surgery may be required to replace it or, in extreme cases, the involved joint may need to be removed; for example, in some hip dislocations the femoral head is removed.

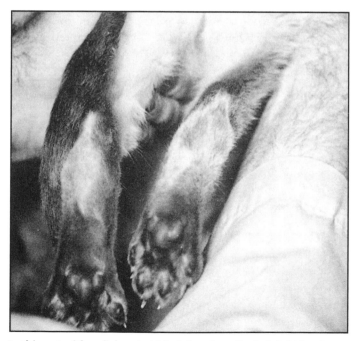

In this cat with a dislocated hip joint, the affected right leg is shorter than the left one.

RUPTURED CRUCIATE (TORN KNEE LIGAMENT)

The knee is stabilized by two internal cruciate ligaments that cross one another in the middle of the knee joint. A pad of cartilage (the *meniscus*) sits between the bones of the joint as padding. The knee ligaments may rupture and the meniscus can tear after a car accident or a fall from a height. Signs of injury include joint swelling, pain on flexing and extending the knee, and looseness of the joint. You may be able to detect a click in the joint, which is a sign of a torn meniscus.

Treatment: Immediate surgical repair of a badly damaged knee joint is the treatment of choice. A mild injury, perhaps limited to the meniscus, can be treated with cage confinement for three to five weeks to rest the joint and allow it to heal by itself. If lameness persists, surgery should be considered. TTouch (a trademarked form of physical therapy) techniques, massage, and physical therapy, even hydrotherapy, can help the healing process for a cat with a ruptured cruciate.

Degenerative arthritis follows trauma to the knee joint. Scar tissue develops in and around the joint, causing pain and stiffness. These arthritic problems are less likely to occur if the joint is repaired surgically. Chondroprotective supplements can greatly aid in delaying the onset of arthritis (see page 363).

OSTEOMYELITIS (BONE INFECTION)

Bone infection is more common in cats than in dogs because cat bites, being puncture wounds, are more likely to become infected and progress to involve the bone. Other causes of bone infection are open fractures and surgical procedures on bones.

The signs of osteomyelitis include lameness, fever, pain, swelling, and discharge through a sinus tract connecting the bone to the skin. The diagnosis is confirmed by X-ray and bone *biopsy*.

Treatment: Bone infection is difficult to eliminate. Bacterial cultures aid in selecting appropriate antibiotics. Some cases require surgical cleansing with removal of devitalized bone and overlying tissue, and wide-open drainage. Treatment is prolonged.

Inherited Orthopedic Diseases

Congenital bone defects occur with some frequency in cats but seldom produce a physical handicap. They include an absent or kinked tail, extra toes, and cleft foot. Breeding two Scottish Fold cats with folded ears leads to bony deformities (see *Structure of the Ears*, page 205; also see metabolic disorders of the central nervous system, page 336).

Polydactyly is the term used for cats with extra toes. Normally, cats have five toes on each front paw and four toes on each rear paw. Generally, any extra toes are on the front paws, but they can appear in both front and rear. This is a genetic trait. Extra toes can cause a problem because the claws on those toes often do not get any wear and might grow around into the pads. Regularly trimming the nails will prevent this problem.

Inherited bone and joint diseases have a genetic basis, despite the fact that only a certain number of offspring will be affected. If, after a careful veterinary examination, one of these conditions is diagnosed in your cat, do not breed the animal.

HIP DYSPLASIA

Hip dysplasia is a disorder caused by abnormal development of the hip joint. It is a polygenetic trait, which means more than one gene is involved in its development. A normal hip joint is a fairly tight ball-and-socket joint; the ball is the head of the femur and the socket is the acetabulum of the pelvis. In a dysplastic hip, the head of the femur fits loosely into a poorly developed, shallow acetabulum. Joint instability occurs as muscle development lags behind the rate of skeletal growth. As the stress of weight-bearing exceeds the strength limits of the supporting connective tissue and muscle, the joint becomes loose and unstable. This allows for free play of the femoral head in the acetabulum; degenerative changes develop on the bones and in the joint, potentially causing pain and abnormal movement.

Cats are fairly small, so many cats with dysplastic hips do not show pain or changes in their gait. Cats who are clinically affected may walk stiffly and often are hesitant to jump or to climb. The gait may also sometimes be described as rolling. Some of these cats will also have patella luxations (see page 360).

Diagnosis of hip dysplasia often starts with careful palpation by a veterinarian, but X-rays are necessary for a definitive diagnosis. Standard hip evaluation techniques developed by the Orthopedic Foundation for Animals (OFA) and the University of Pennsylvania Hip Improvement Program (PennHIP) for use in dogs can be adapted to cats. On the X-rays, veterinary specialists look for any arthritic changes, abnormal structure, and joint laxity. Through OFA, X-rays may be submitted and evaluated, and cats over 2 years of age can be certified as clear of hip dysplasia. PennHIP looks at laxity of the joint—greater laxity is associated with later arthritic changes. Cats receive a distraction index (DI) reading.

As with dogs, the cats most commonly affected with hip dysplasia tend to be males and of the larger, big-boned breeds such as Persians and Maine Coon Cats. Of all the X-rays submitted to OFA from Maine Coon Cat breeders, about 23 percent have dysplastic hips. Most of these cats are only mildly affected,

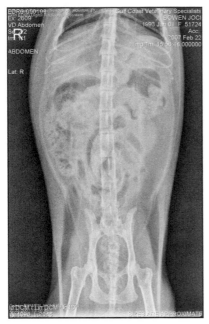

This is an X-ray of a cat with normal hips.

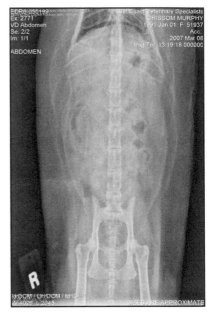

This cat has severe dysplasia without any subluxation. Note the very different position of the ball of the hip in the socket.

but they should not be bred. Any cat can suffer from hip dysplasia—mixed breeds and smaller cat breeds as well.

Treatment: Most dysplastic cats do quite well as long as they are kept at a correct weight and given moderate exercise to keep the muscles that support the hip joint strong. Chondroprotective supplements, such as Sea Flex, Cosequin, Glycoflex, and other glucosamine-chondroitin combinations are helpful (see *Chondroprotectants*, page 363). Make sure any joint supplement you buy is specifically formulated for cats.

Cats with actual lameness may benefit from pain medications and/or anti-inflammatories. *Always* check with your veterinarian before giving any supplements or medications to your cat.

Rarely, cats with severe hip dysplasia will have surgery to actually remove the head of the femur. Although this sounds drastic, the muscle and remaining bone form a false joint and the cat is usually pain-free and can return to normal activity.

PATELLA LUXATION (SLIPPING KNEECAP)

The patella, or kneecap, is a small bone that protects the front of the stifle joint on the rear leg. The patella is anchored in place by ligaments and slides in a groove in the femur called the trochlea. If the groove is too shallow, the patella will slip out when the knee bends. When the patella slips out to the inside of the knee joint, it's called medial luxation. When it slips out to the outside, it's called lateral luxation.

Medial luxation is far more common in cats. Cats with a loose or slipping patella will often skip in their gait. The degree of lameness will vary with the extent of the luxation.

Cats can be evaluated for patella problems by a careful physical examination. The diagnosis of luxation is made by attempting to push the patella out of the trochlear groove. This manipulation should only be done by a veterinarian experienced in this technique.

Patella luxation is usually an inherited developmental defect. Rarely, it is acquired through trauma. In one study done at the University of Pennsylvania, cats with patella luxation had a three times greater risk of also having hip dysplasia. These two defects may be associated. The OFA maintains a registry for cats certified free of patella luxation.

Treatment: A few cats with mild cases will do fine simply with weight control. A number of orthopedic surgeries can be done that tighten up the stifle joint and allow for normal movement. Over time, arthritis will develop in the stifle joint if the patella luxation is not treated.

Arthritis

Arthritis can affect one or more joints. Most cases occur in joints that have been severely stressed, dislocated, or fractured. It can also occur with repeated wear and tear on joints that aren't perfectly aligned to begin with. Months or years after the injury, bone spurs develop in and around the joint, causing pain and restriction. Inflammatory conditions can also contribute to arthritis by depositing debris in joint spaces. Some cases of arthritis are related to an immune-mediated joint disease or a joint infection. Calicivirus (see page 84) may also cause an inflammatory lameness. Most cats recover from this temporary lameness on their own. Some of them will also show respiratory signs.

OSTEOARTHRITIS (DEGENERATIVE JOINT DISEASE)

Osteoarthritis, also called degenerative arthritis or degenerative joint disease, is the most common form of arthritis in cats. Still, it is less common in cats than it is in dogs and produces milder symptoms. In a cat with degenerative joint disease, the cartilage covering the articulating surface of a joint wears out and the underlying bone develops a roughened surface that damages the joint. Osteoarthritis occurs in joints that have been severely stressed, dislocated, or fractured. Proper early care of joint injuries may reduce the severity of any subsequent lameness.

Although osteoarthritis may begin during the first half of life, symptoms generally do not appear until much later. The signs are mainly stiffness and lameness. Lameness is usually worse when the cat wakes up but gets better as the day wears on. Cats may show swelling around affected joints and muscle atrophy on legs with arthritic conditions. There may be a reluctance to jump and leap. They often exhibit irritability and behavioral changes associated with increasing disability. Cold and damp surroundings increase pain and stiffness.

The diagnosis of osteoarthritis is made by joint X-rays that show bone spurs at points where the ligaments and the joint capsule attach to the bone. There may be varying degrees of joint space narrowing and increased density of bone around the joint.

Treating Osteoarthritis

Osteoarthritis is incurable, but treatment can substantially improve the cat's life. Keeping cats at a trim weight will take stress off their joints. It also helps to provide warm places for cats to sleep and rest. An arthritic cat may need steps to get to favorite places, such as the bed, the couch, and the windowsill. Massage, TTouch, and physical therapy may be beneficial. Acupuncture can be helpful for many cats, and if the cat is willing to swim, hydrotherapy can be a great boon.

Many cats will benefit from chondroprotective supplements such as glucosamine-chondroitin products to repair joint cartilage and prevent further damage. In severe cases, analgesics and corticosteroids may be used to relieve pain and improve function.

Physical Therapy

Moderate exercise is beneficial because it maintains muscle mass and preserves joint flexibility. Excessive exercise, however, is counterproductive. Arthritic cats should never be encouraged to stand up on their back legs. There are veterinary physical therapists who can help design an exercise (and weight-loss) program.

Overweight cats should be encouraged to lose weight, as described in Obesity (page 510). Being overweight seriously complicates the treatment of osteoarthritis.

Medications

There are many new medications that can be used to treat pain and inflammation in cats. They should only be used under the guidance of your veterinarian. Unfortunately, many of the medications developed to treat arthritis in dogs are not safe for cats and can be toxic. The same is true of medicines developed for humans. Tylenol (acetaminophen), in particular, must *never* be used. Fortunately, pain or severe lameness in cats is infrequent and seldom produces significant disability.

Chondroprotectants

These compounds appear to modify the progression of osteoarthritis by preventing the further breakdown of cartilage. Breakdown of cartilage is the first step in the development of osteoarthritis. Chondroprotectants are most effective when used early in the course of the disease.

Chondroprotective agents are nutraceuticals—products that lie somewhere between a nutrient and a drug. Nutraceuticals are believed to have medical value based on subjective evidence of their effectiveness, although clinical evidence based on controlled studies is lacking for many of these. Unlike drugs, nutraceuticals do not undergo an approval process and are not regulated by a federal agency. Numerous controlled studies in humans, limited studies done on dogs and cats, and anecdotal reports suggest these substances do have medical value for arthritic cats. Many of the supplements mentioned in the chart below are used based on anecdotal information, not clinical studies. So far, however, these compounds appear to be both safe and effective.

Most nutraceuticals used to treat osteoarthritis contain glucosamine, polysulfated glycosaminoglycans, and chondroitin sulfates—compounds known to be involved in the synthesis and repair of joint cartilage. Examples include Cosequin, Glycoflex, and Sea Flex. These compounds are given orally, some as treats. Because cats are small animals, it is important to choose joint supplements that are formulated specifically for cats.

Chondroprotectants and Other Supplements

Supplement	Use	Side Effects
Perna cannaliculus, green-lipped mussel	Cartilage protection and repair	Minimal
Sea cucumber, sea jerky	Cartilage protection and repair	Minimal
Chondroitin sulfate	Cartilage production and repair, prevents damage, controls pain	Minimal
Glucosamine	Cartilage production and repair	Minimal
Methylsulfonylmethane, MSM	Sulfur supplement, controls pain	Minimal
Polysulfonated glycosamino glycan (must be given by injection)	Cartilage protection and repair	Minimal (Not approved for cats, but has been used safely)
Omega-3 fatty acids	Anti-inflammatory	Minimal
Vitamins C and E	Antioxidants	Minimal, but excessively high doses can result in toxicity
Boswellia	Anti-inflammatory herb	Minimal
Yucca	Anti-inflammatory herb containing steroidal saponins	Minimal

SPONDYLITIS

When the vertebral column is involved in the progression of arthritis, it is called spondylitis. In cats with this kind of spinal arthritis, developing bone spurs can create pressure points on the nerve roots.

Bacteria or fungus can get into the bony vertebrae, and possibly the discs between vertebrae. Cats who live in areas with small plant awns, such as fox-tails, and go outside seem to have this problem more often, because the awns can migrate through the skin. An unusual cause of spondylitis is a dietary intake of excessive amounts of vitamin A.

Affected cats may have a fever, back pain, and weight loss, and may be inactive. Many are reluctant to jump and run as they normally would. Diagnosis may involve X-rays, blood culture, and a spinal fluid tap.

Treatment: Medical therapy is often long term, with either antibiotics or antifungal medications.

FELINE PROGRESSIVE POLYARTHRITIS

Feline progressive polyarthritis (also sometimes called feline chronic progressive polyarthritis) is an inflammation involving a number of joints. This is an *immune-mediated* disease that may be associated with the feline leukemia virus and the feline syncytial virus. It affects male cats, both intact and neutered.

Signs generally begin at 1½ to 5 years of age. The joints most likely to be involved are the carpus (wrist) and the tarsus (hock), as well as bones in the feet. There are two forms. In the milder form, new bone is formed around the involved joints, which lessens joint motion and may cause pain. In the severe form, the cartilage may wear down to sensitive bone and cause a great deal of pain, along with fever and joint swelling. Initially, signs may move from one leg to another. Diagnosis is generally done by X-rays but may also involve checking joint (synovial) fluid.

Treatment: Corticosteroids such as prednisone may be used to reduce inflammation caused by the immune response, although the condition is progressive. Some cats may need strong immune modulators such as cyclophosphamide. Eventually, many cats end up being euthanized due to extreme pain.

SEPTIC ARTHRITIS

Septic arthritis is an arthritis related to an infection in the joint. It is more common in cats than in dogs, because cats are more likely to acquire deep bacterial infections from bite wounds that penetrate joints.

Treatment: Treatment of a septic joint is similar to that described for *Osteomyelitis* (page 358). Lavage (flushing the joint) may help to speed healing.

Long-term antibiotics may be necessary. Culturing joint fluid can aid in prescribing the most effective antibiotics.

Metabolic Bone Disorders
PARATHYROID DISORDERS

The parathyroids are four small glands in the neck located near the thyroid gland. The parathyroid glands secrete the hormone PTH, which is essential to bone metabolism and blood calcium regulation. As the blood calcium level falls, the parathyroid glands compensate by releasing more PTH, which raises the calcium level in the blood by drawing calcium out of the bones. High serum phosphorus levels will also stimulate the body to secrete PTH. Accordingly, either a low serum calcium or a high serum phosphorus will cause an excess of PTH in the blood. When this situation goes unchecked, the bones become demineralized, thin, and often look cystic (small holes in the bone) on X-ray. Minor stress can cause a fracture.

There are several conditions related to abnormal parathyroid gland metabolism.

Hypoparathyroidism

Low levels of parathyroid hormones are almost always associated with the inadvertent removal of the parathyroid glands during surgery for hyperthyroidism (see page 529). In this case, cats have a low level of blood calcium and may have muscle tremors.

Treatment: Treatment involves oral or even intravenous calcium supplementation. Many cats adapt to this problem with time and medication, but it can be serious immediately after the surgery.

Primary Hyperparathyroidism

This rare condition is due to a parathyroid gland tumor that produces excess hormone. These are usually benign adenomas and are seen in older cats.

Treatment: Surgical removal of the affected gland is the only possible treatment.

Renal Secondary Hyperparathyroidism

This condition is the result of long-standing kidney disease that causes the cat to retain phosphorus. The high serum phosphorus stimulates the parathyroid glands to produce excessive amounts of PTH. Effects on the bones are the same as those of nutritional secondary hyperparathyroidism (page 366). However, signs of kidney failure are usually the main symptoms.

Treatment: Treatment is directed toward correcting the kidney disease, as described in *Kidney Failure* (page 375).

Nutritional Secondary Hyperparathyroidism

The cause of this nutritional bone disease is a diet consisting primarily of organ meats, such as hearts, livers, and kidneys. Such a diet is too high in phosphorus and too low in calcium and vitamin D. (Vitamin D is necessary for calcium to be absorbed from the small intestine.)

Kittens are at particular risk because they require large amounts of calcium for growth and development. The daily calcium, phosphorus, and vitamin D requirements for young kittens and adult cats are found in the table on page 493. When a kitten's sole source of nourishment is meat, he's getting too much phosphorus and not enough calcium. This results in overactivity of the parathyroid glands.

Symptoms appear after the kitten has been on a high-meat diet for about four weeks. Affected kittens are reluctant to move, and they develop an uncoordinated gait and lameness in the back legs. The front legs are often bowed. Their thin bones are easily fractured. These fractures, often multiple, tend to heal rapidly and may even go unrecognized. Because the meat diet supplies adequate calories, kittens often appear well-nourished and have a healthy coat despite their metabolic bone disease.

Osteoporosis is the adult form of this disease. It occurs in older cats who receive large quantities of meat at the expense of other nutrients. Other feeding practices that can lead to osteoporosis include vegetarian diets, dog food diets, and diets that consist primarily of table scraps and leftovers.

Since adult calcium requirements are lower than those for kittens and adult cats have more calcium in their bones to draw out, bone demineralization takes longer (5 to 13 months). The first sign of demineralization is thinning of the jaw bones with exposure of the roots of the teeth. The loose teeth are then expelled.

Treatment: Dietary correction is required. Diets that meet all the nutritional requirements for growing kittens and adult cats are discussed in chapter 18. Calcium and vitamin D supplements should not be given to kittens unless prescribed by a veterinarian for a specific deficiency. Oversupplementation can be just as dangerous as deficiencies (see page 367).

Kittens with nutritional secondary hyperparathyroidism should be kept quiet and confined to prevent bone fractures while their diet is adjusted. Bone deformities tend to be permanent, so early recognition and treatment is important.

Older cats with advanced periodontal disease or fixed eating habits that do not include a balanced diet should be evaluated by a veterinarian and considered for nutritional supplements.

NUTRITIONAL DISORDERS
Osteomalacia (Rickets)

Rickets is caused by a deficiency of vitamin D. Since this vitamin is active in the absorption of calcium and phosphorus from the intestines, these minerals may also be deficient. This disease is rare in cats because only small amounts of vitamin D (50 to 100 I.U.) are required daily. Many cases classified as rickets are probably due to nutritional secondary hyperparathyroidism.

Signs include a characteristic enlargement of the joints where the ribs meet the cartilage of the sternum. Bowing of the legs and other growth deformities in kittens, along with fractures in adults, are common in severe cases.

Treatment: It is the same as for nutritional secondary hyperparathyroidism (see page 366).

Pansteatitis

This disease is caused by a deficiency of vitamin E. It is one of the most important vitamin deficiency diseases of cats. Young and overweight cats are most commonly affected. It occurs among cats who are fed excessive amounts of unsaturated fatty acids, found especially in dark meat tuna. Fatty acids oxidize and destroy vitamin E. In addition, unlike tuna-flavored cat foods, canned tuna for human consumption is not supplemented with this vitamin. Therefore, cats who eat tuna as a major part of their diet are at risk.

Some petroleum-based hairball remedies also inhibit the absorption of vitamin E in the intestines, which is why they should not be given an hour before or after meals. Many of these remedies are now supplemented with extra vitamins.

Vitamin E deficiency causes a yellow pigment to be deposited in fat. This pigment acts like a foreign body, producing inflammation. Affected cats run a fever, are reluctant to eat and move, and exhibit pain when handled or stroked. Digestive disturbances caused by inflammation and degeneration of fat in the abdomen may dominate the findings. The disease is difficult to diagnose but can be suspected by the feeding history. A fat biopsy confirms the diagnosis.

Treatment: The disease is reversed by giving the cat a daily dose of vitamin E. Corticosteroids can be administered to decrease the inflammatory reaction. Full recovery takes one to four weeks. Pansteatitis can be prevented by feeding a nutritionally complete cat food and by feeding fish products only as occasional treats.

Vitamin Overdose

Growing kittens do not need supplemental vitamins and minerals. Modern high-quality commercial kitten foods supply the needed vitamins and minerals to sustain normal growth, provided the kitten or young cat eats that food as his main or sole source of nutrition. Vitamins and minerals in excess of those needed for growth and development will not add more coat or substance to the growing animal.

When calcium, phosphorus, and vitamin D are given beyond the animal's capacity to use them normally, growth and development can be adversely affected. Overdosing with vitamin D causes the bones to calcify unevenly. Also, calcium may be deposited in the lungs, heart, and blood vessels, causing those tissues to lose their elasticity.

High levels of vitamin A can cause bone spurs to develop in and around the joints, particularly those of the neck and back. These spurs result in a loss of flexibility and produce pain on joint movement. Symptoms include joint swelling, lameness, pain in the neck and back, and hypersensitivity of the skin to touch. Diets containing high levels of vitamin A (liver and milk diets) have been found to cause this problem. Treatment involves dietary correction and the discontinuation of vitamin A supplements. However, once bone spurs have developed, symptoms will not disappear.

Vitamin and mineral supplements are most useful when given to queens in late pregnancy and during lactation, and are not always needed even then. They may also be of some benefit to elderly cats with poor eating habits, who may have developed a dietary deficiency. To avoid complications associated with vitamin overdosing, any supplementation should be determined by your veterinarian.

Muscle Disorders
MYOTONIA CONGENITA

This is a genetic defect that leads to continued muscle contractions, even after movement has stopped. Signs are first noticed when kittens start to move and will be worse after a period of rest. The gait is very stiff and startled kittens may actually fall over due to hyperextension of their legs. They will often snag their claws in carpets as they walk. The meow may be abnormal and eventually the kittens get muscle hypertrophy from all the activity.

Treatment: Drugs to stabilize muscle membranes may help, but they are still experimental.

HYPOKALEMIC MYOPATHY OF BURMESE CATS

This is an autosomal recessive genetic defect that is seen in young Burmese kittens. Signs are usually noticed at about 3 to 4 months of age. These kittens show episodes of paralysis or weakness and tend to keep their necks flexed downward.

Treatment: Supplementing the diet with potassium reverses the signs. This supplementation may be needed for variable amounts of time, until the kittens can regulate their own potassium metabolism.

DEVON REX HEREDITARY MYOPATHY

This is another autosomal recessive genetic defect—this time seen in Devon Rex kittens. At 4 to 7 weeks of age, the kittens have a low exercise threshold and keep the head and neck flexed downward even when walking or eliminating. *Megaesophagus*—an enlargement of the esophagus related to swallowing disturbances—is usually present.

A specific kind of hypokalemic myopathy affects Burmese cats.

Treatment: There is none. Most of these kittens do not do well and have short lives.

FELINE HYPOKALEMIC POLYMYOPATHY

This condition is a generalized muscle weakness due to low blood potassium. The cause could be too little potassium in the diet or high potassium losses via urination. Cats with low serum potassium are weak, hold the neck flexed downward, walk stiffly, and show muscle pain. Appetite is usually depressed.

Treatment: Treatment consists of dietary and/or IV potassium supplementation. Caught early on, most cats recover fully.

14

THE URINARY SYSTEM

The urinary system is composed of the kidneys and ureters, bladder, and urethra. In male cats, there is also a prostate gland. The kidneys are paired organs located on each side of the backbone just behind and below the last rib. Tucked in along with the kidneys are small organs called the adrenal glands. Each kidney has a renal pelvis, which acts as a funnel that siphons the urine into a ureter. The ureters pass down to the pelvic brim and empty into the bladder. The passageway that connects the neck of the bladder to the outside of the cat is the urethra. The opening of the urethra is found at the tip of the penis in the male and between the folds of the vulva in the female. In the male, the urethra also serves as a channel for semen. The urethra in the male is much narrower than it is in the female.

The chief functions of the kidneys are to regulate fluid, electrolyte, and acid-base balance, and to excrete the wastes of metabolism. This is accomplished by millions of *nephrons,* the basic working units of the kidneys. A nephron is composed of a globe of blood vessels (called the glomerulus) that filters waste from the blood plasma and passes it through a system of tubules that reabsorb water and electrolytes. This concentrates the liquid waste, which is now urine. Damage to nephrons or tubules leads to kidney failure.

Normal urine is yellow and clear. Its color can be altered by the concentration of waste products, the presence of cells such as red blood cells, the cat's overall state of hydration, and by various drugs, diets, and diseases.

The act of voiding is controlled by the central nervous system. A cat can decide when to void. This is the basis for successful litter box training. Once the decision to void is reached, the actual mechanism of emptying the bladder is carried out by a complicated spinal cord reflex and is not under conscious control.

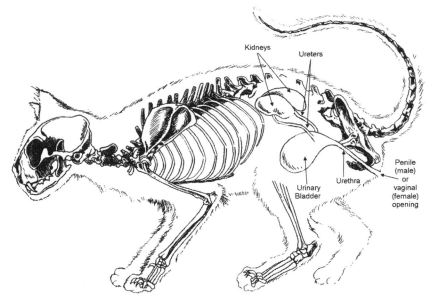

Kidneys

Ureters

Penile
(male)
or
vaginal
(female)
opening

Urethra

Urinary
Bladder

The urinary system.

Signs of Urinary Tract Disease

Most urinary tract diseases are associated with a disturbance in the normal pattern of voiding. That is why it is so important to get a veterinary checkup for any cat who has been using the litter box faithfully and suddenly stops doing so. Signs include the following:

- **Excessive urination (polyuria).** Frequent voiding of normal amounts of urine suggests kidney disease. A cat compensates for a high urine output by drinking large amounts of water (polydipsia). You may notice the increased drinking first. Diabetes mellitus and hyperthyroidism are among the other causes of excessive thirst and urination.

- **No urine (anuria).** This refers to a cat who is not producing any urine. If a cat cannot urinate, deadly toxins will build up in her system. This could be the result of a urinary blockage or severe kidney failure.

- **Painful urination (dysuria).** This is characterized by distress during urination with prolonged squatting and straining; failure to pass urine after many tries; and passage of mucus, blood clots, or bloody urine. The cat may spend an unusual amount of time licking at the urogenital area. Pain and swelling within the lower abdomen suggest an overdistended bladder. Cats will sometimes urinate in unusual locations, rejecting the litter box. Bathtubs and sinks are common alternative sites.

- **Blood in the urine (hematuria).** When accompanied by painful urination, blood in the first urine flow indicates a problem in the urethra or bladder. A uniformly bloody urine without pain suggests kidney disease.

- **Urinary incontinence.** This is characterized by the loss of voluntary control over voiding or by inappropriate urination—often the result of neurological disease. The cat may void frequently, and/or dribble and urinate in unusual places. Because of overlapping symptoms and the possibly of more than one problem at the same time, it is difficult to make an exact diagnosis based on the symptoms alone. Physical urinary incontinence needs to be distinguished from behavioral urination elimination problems. This can only be done by a veterinarian, possibly working with a behaviorist.

HOW TO COLLECT AND TEST URINE

In the diagnosis of urinary tract disease, laboratory analysis is of considerable help. Routine tests are urinalysis, blood chemistries, and a complete blood count (see appendix C). Your veterinarian may request a sample of your cat's urine. The procedure for collecting a urine sample at home is as follows:

- Thoroughly clean and dry the litter box, then replace the normal kitty litter with an inert substance, such as Styrofoam packing, aquarium gravel (which does not absorb urine and can be washed between samples), or a special litter called No-Sorb, available from your veterinarian.

- After the cat has voided, pour the urine from the litter box into a small, clean, sealable plastic or glass container. This container should be thoroughly cleaned and dried before the sample is poured into it.

- To store the sample, if necessary, place it in the refrigerator in the sealed container. The sample should be taken to the veterinarian within two hours. After this time, evaluation of the urine for crystals may be inaccurate.

If you have more than one cat, it will be necessary to isolate that cat with her own litter box.

You may be asked to test the urine pH with a laboratory strip provided by your veterinarian. Follow the instructions exactly.

There are also diagnostic litters that can be used to indicate various health conditions. Scientific Professional Cat Litter will change colors (becoming progressively pinker) with changes in urine pH. Purina Glucotest Feline Urinary Glucose Detection System uses a litter additive to indicate urinary glucose levels. Hemalert detects blood in the urine.

The samples you collect from your cat will not be sterile and are not ideal for culturing. A sterile urine sample can only be obtained by your veterinarian.

The veterinarian will either pass a sterile catheter into the cat's bladder to take a sample or draw a sample through the body wall with sterile equipment—this procedure is called cystocentesis.

Additional diagnostic studies are often needed. They include urine cultures, ultrasound examination, and X-ray examinations of the abdomen. The intravenous pyelogram is an X-ray examination in which a dye is injected into the circulation. It is excreted by the kidneys and outlines much of the urinary tract. A cystogram is an X-ray examination that involves injecting dye (positive contrast cystogram) or air (negative contrast cystogram) through a urethral catheter into the bladder. Other selective studies may be performed when needed. They include CT *scan*, surgical exploration, and *biopsy*.

The Kidneys

Although many signs of kidney disease are the same as those for any problem with the urinary tract, there may be some differences. Cats with kidney disease may show these symptoms:

- Increased drinking and urination (polydipsia and polyuria)
- Urination outside the litter box
- Decreased or even complete lack of urination
- Blood in the urine
- Vomiting
- Loss of appetite, probably due to nausea
- Weight loss
- Pain in the lower back area
- Sitting hunched or walking stiffly
- Poor haircoat, partly due to decreased grooming
- Ulcers in the mouth and/or drooling
- High blood pressure, possibly with associated retinal damage
- Anemia

PYELONEPHRITIS

Pyelonephritis is a bacterial infection of the kidney and renal pelvis (the urinary collection system). It usually ascends from an infection in the bladder. Occasionally, it is blood-borne.

Acute pyelonephritis begins with fever, vomiting, and pain in the kidney area (the lower back). A stiff-legged gait and a hunched posture are characteristic signs. The cat's urine is often bloody.

Chronic pyelonephritis is an insidious disease that may or may not be preceded by signs of acute infection. When the disease is of long duration, you will see weight loss and signs of kidney failure. If it is diagnosed before irreversible changes occur in the kidneys (that is, during a regular health checkup), treatment may prevent complications, or at least slow the progression of the disease.

Treatment: The cat's urine should be cultured. Antibiotics that concentrate in the urine will be selected by your veterinarian based on bacterial sensitivity testing. Chronic pyelonephritis should be treated for at least six weeks. Many cats will require dietary adjustments. Most cats will need added fluid therapy—this may be done in the veterinary hospital intravenously or at home with subcutaneous injections. Also see *Kidney Failure* (page 375).

NEPHRITIS AND NEPHROSIS

Nephritis and nephrosis are a group of diseases of the kidneys that produce scarring and kidney failure. Many cats with these conditions also have high blood pressure and a tendency to develop blood clots. Abdominal ultrasound and a kidney biopsy may be required to make an exact diagnosis.

Nephritis is an inflammation of the kidneys, regardless of cause. Chronic interstitial nephritis is perhaps the most common form, but even this may not be a single disease, but rather, the result of various toxins, drugs, poisons, or viruses. In cats with this condition, the kidneys become small and scarred due to repeated insults.

Glomerulonephritis is an inflammatory disease affecting the filtering mechanism of the kidneys. The disease appears to be related to the cat's immune system, and is found in association with feline leukemia, feline infectious peritonitis, feline progressive polyarthritis, some types of infections, and certain types of cancer. This tends to be a disease of cats in their prime, with the mean age about 4 years old.

Amyloidosis is a rare disorder in which a substance called amyloid (fibrous proteins) is deposited in the cat's kidneys and other organs. This may occur as part of a hereditary condition or with certain cancers and metabolic problems. Depending on the exact type of amyloidosis, there may be a great deal of protein in the urine or virtually no protein in the urine. Treatment is aimed at correcting general kidney failure and hypertension (high blood pressure), along with very low dose aspirin to try to avoid the formation of blood clots. Abyssinians may be predisposed to this problem.

Nephrosis refers to kidney diseases accompanied by destruction of the nephrons and loss of functioning kidney cells. In a cat with nephrotic syndrome, protein leaks through the kidney filtering system in large amounts and is lost in the urine. This results in abnormally low serum proteins. Protein in the serum maintains osmotic pressure that keeps fluid from passing out of the bloodstream into the cat's tissues. Because of the low serum protein, fluid accumulates beneath the skin of the legs (*edema*) and inside the abdomen (*ascites*). The signs are like those of right-sided heart failure (see page 316). Laboratory studies will distinguish between these conditions. Hydronephrosis is caused by an obstruction in the ureter (such as a urolith), which causes urine to back up into the kidney, destroying its architecture.

Treatment: Nephritis and nephrosis are not usually recognized until a cat develops signs of kidney failure. Steroids and special diets may be of temporary help (see treatment of *Kidney Failure*, page 376).

KIDNEY FAILURE (UREMIA)

Kidney failure is the inability of the kidneys to remove waste products from the blood. The buildup of toxic wastes produces the signs and symptoms of uremic poisoning. Kidney failure can come on acutely or occur gradually over weeks or months. Chronic renal failure is a leading cause of death in pet cats.

Causes of *acute* kidney failure include the following:

- A blockage in the lower urinary tract associated with feline lower urinary tract disease (FLUTD, see page 380) or a congenital bladder defect
- Trauma to the abdomen, especially when accompanied by pelvic fracture and rupture of the bladder or urethra
- Shock, when due to sudden blood loss or rapid dehydration
- Arterial thromboembolism (a blood clot blocking the artery), particularly when both renal arteries are obstructed
- Heart failure, when associated with a persistently low blood pressure and reduced blood flow to the kidneys
- Poisoning, especially from ingesting antifreeze or Easter lilies

Causes of *chronic* kidney failure include these:

- Nephritis and nephrosis, in which case the failure is usually of the renal tubules, not the glomeruli.
- Infectious diseases, especially feline infectious peritonitis and feline leukemia.
- The use of nonsteroidal anti-inflammatory drugs (NSAIDs), especially during periods of hypotension (low blood pressure such as occurs during anesthesia).
- Various toxins. Antibiotics that are poisonous to the kidneys when given for prolonged periods or in high doses include polymyxin B, gentamicin, amphotericin B, and kanamycin. The heavy metals mercury, lead, and thallium are also toxic to the kidneys.
- Most elderly cats, if they live long enough, will have some degree of kidney insufficiency.

- Chronic renal failure and hyperthyroidism seem to often go hand in hand, since they are both geriatric diseases. Treatment of hyperthyroidism may unmask underlying chronic renal failure.

Cats with kidney diseases do not begin to show signs of uremia until about 70 percent of their nephrons are destroyed. Thus, a considerable amount of damage occurs before any signs are noted. The degree of renal failure can be determined by looking at laboratory data and tracking the progression of certain parameters.

One of the first signs of kidney failure is an increase in the frequency of voiding. Because the cat is voiding frequently, it might be assumed that her kidneys are functioning properly. Actually, the kidneys are no longer able to conserve water efficiently. Cats will go to the litter box several times a day and may also begin to urinate outside the box, since the box is getting dirty faster. This large urine output must be compensated for by increased fluid intake, and the cat will drink a lot more than usual. Also, because the urine is dilute (not concentrated), bacterial infections of the bladder and kidneys are much more common.

As renal function continues to deteriorate, the cat begins to retain ammonia, nitrogen, acids, and other waste products in the bloodstream and tissues (uremic poisoning). Blood chemistries will determine the exact levels of these metabolic products. Cats in the later stages of kidney failure may produce less urine than normal and, eventually, no urine at all, which leads to rapid decline.

Signs of uremia include apathy and sluggishness, loss of appetite and weight, dry haircoat, a brownish discoloration to the surface of the tongue, and ulcers on the gums and tongue. The breath may have an ammonialike odor. Vomiting, diarrhea, anemia, and episodes of gastrointestinal bleeding can occur. Eventually, the cat falls into a coma and dies.

Diagnosing kidney failure may require a number of techniques. X-rays, with or without dye studies, along with ultrasound evaluations, can be important. Blood work, especially blood chemistry panels that look for toxic waste levels in the blood, should be done. Many cats will show increased levels of BUN (blood urea nitrogen), creatinine, and phosphorus. Anemia will show up in cats with chronic renal failure.

A urinalysis will show if the kidneys can still filter and concentrate the urine. Looking at urine sediment may suggest a cause for the kidney failure. ERD-HealthScreen is an early detection test that looks for the protein albumin in the urine (microalbuminuria). It is hoped that with early detection and treatment, the progression of kidney failure can be slowed. However, many inflammatory conditions, such as gingivitis, may also cause microalbuminuria.

Treatment: The outlook for a cat with kidney failure depends on a number of factors. Your veterinarian may want to make an exact diagnosis by ordering special tests to determine whether the disease is potentially reversible. A renal *biopsy* may be needed to determine the exact cause of the problem.

Acute kidney failure can be reversed if the underlying cause can be corrected before it permanently damages the nephrons. If the insult is severe,

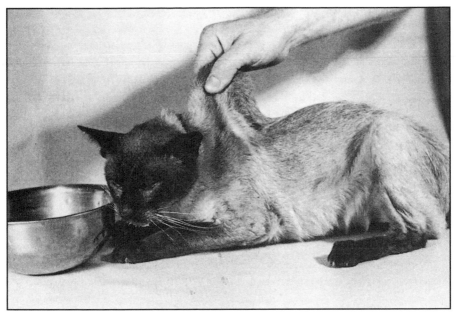

Severe dehydration, revealed by the loose skin that does not spring back into place, is characteristic of this cat in kidney failure.

hemodialysis (more commonly called dialysis) may be necessary to try to give the kidneys a chance to heal. Dialysis is most commonly used short term to treat acute renal failure or toxicities, or while a search is conducted for a transplant candidate (see page 378). Dialysis is extremely expensive, can only be done at a few veterinary referral centers, and still requires extensive medical management of the cat in addition to the dialysis sessions.

Most cases of chronic kidney failure occur in cats who have sustained irreversible damage to the kidneys. However, these cats may still have many happy months or years of life ahead, with proper treatment. It is extremely important to be sure these cats take in enough water to compensate for their large urine output. A supply of fresh, clean water should be available at all times. Many cats will need supplemental fluids, given either intravenously at the veterinary hospital or subcutaneously at home.

The diet of a uremic cat should include protein of high quality, but lower in total amount, to minimize the amount of phosphorus and nitrogen that must be excreted by the kidneys. Special diets are available through your veterinarian. Canned foods are better than dry foods, because the canned food adds fluid to the diet. Prescription diets that are used for cats with kidney failure include Eukanuba MultiStage Renal, Purina Veterinary NF, Hill's Science Diet k/d, Royal Canin Modified Formula, and Royal Canin Renal LP 21. Your veterinarian can also guide you to appropriate homemade diets.

Phosphorous restriction in the diet is important, although phosphate binders, such as aluminum hydroxide salt (Amphogel) can also be given. Vetoquinol has produced a veterinary product called Epakitin that is a palatable powder that also binds phosphates. However, this product also contains calcium, which may be contraindicated in the later stages of renal failure.

Large amounts of B vitamins are lost in the urine of uremic cats. These losses should be replaced by giving vitamin B supplements. Sodium bicarbonate tablets may be indicated to correct an acid-base imbalance. Potassium may also need to be supplemented. The kidneys are also important in the production of vitamin D. Cats in chronic renal failure may benefit from the addition of calcitriol to their therapeutic regimen. Your veterinarian may need to order special compounded versions of calcitriol to get the appropriate dosage for a cat.

Vomiting may need to be controlled with medications such as famotidine, ranitidine, omeprazole, or others, until the renal condition is stabilized.

Erythropoietin may be used to help counteract the anemia associated with long-term renal failure. Currently, human recombinant erythropoietin is used, which may lead to immune-based destruction of red blood cells and a renewal of the anemia over time. Research is continuing for a safe feline alternative.

Cats with hypertension will need therapy to lower their blood pressure (see page 380).

A uremic cat who becomes ill, dehydrated, or fails to drink enough water may suddenly decompensate; this is known as a uremic crisis. The cat should be hospitalized and rehydrated with appropriate intravenous fluids and balanced electrolyte solutions.

Some exercise is good for a uremic cat, but stressful activity should be avoided.

Kidney Transplant

Another option to consider for cats with terminal kidney failure is a kidney transplant. Kidney transplants are only done at a few veterinary referral centers but are becoming more common. As with human transplant patients, drugs must be given post-transplant to prevent rejection problems. These drugs are quite expensive and must be carefully calibrated to minimize side effects. Also, it was recently reported that cats are at a higher risk for developing diabetes due to the use of these drugs.

The current method for finding kidney donors is to test shelter cats for tissue compatibility. The shelter cat then donates one kidney—cats, like people, can do fine with just one healthy kidney. The shelter cat is then adopted by the family of the recipient cat, who must agree ahead of time to provide a home for the donor cat for the rest of her life.

TUMORS

Kidney tumors are rare in cats. Lymphosarcoma is the most common. About half of all cats with lymphosarcoma of the kidney are positive for feline leukemia virus. Therefore, when a growth or mass occurs in the kidney, the prime consideration is that feline leukemia as an underlying cause. About 45 percent of all cats with lymphoma in the abdomen will have kidney involvement—many of them bilateral (involving both kidneys).

Treatment: If the cat is positive for the feline leukemia virus, the prognosis is poor. Chemotherapy may be attempted in cats with renal lymphosarcoma, but if both kidneys are involved, the prognosis is poor.

CONGENITAL DEFECTS

Cats may be born with various malformations of the kidneys. These include cystic kidneys (see *Polycystic Kidney Disease*, below), malpositions, and incomplete development. Such defects are often accompanied by abnormalities in the reproductive tract. Severe defects cause neonatal death. Others do not cause symptoms until later in life, when kidney damage reaches the point of failure.

Congenital obstructions in the urinary tract can cause swollen or infected kidneys. It may be difficult to tell whether the condition is congenital or acquired without special examinations. This could make a difference in treatment. A complete veterinary workup is desirable.

Treatment: If the cat has one functioning kidney, the defective kidney may be removed surgically.

POLYCYSTIC KIDNEY DISEASE

Polycystic kidney disease (PKD) is an inherited condition seen in Persians and Persian-cross or Persian-related cats, such as Himalayans. It is estimated up to 37 percent of these cats may carry the gene for PKD. This is an autosomal dominant condition, meaning it will affect both male and female cats, and cats with just one copy of this gene will develop the disease. It can be difficult to predict exactly when a cat will show clinical signs of kidney failure.

A cat with PKD will develop multiple cysts that replace the kidney tissue and often enlarge the kidney size, but with useless tissue. The PKD progresses as the cat ages, and many cats do not actually show signs of kidney failure until they are about 7 years of age. Eventually, the enlarged kidneys can be detected by X-rays—although with ultrasound the diagnosis in 10-month-old kittens is about 98 percent accurate with an experienced evaluator. Sometimes cysts can be detected in kittens as early as 8 weeks of age.

A DNA test developed by VetGen (see appendix D) can be done on very young kittens—literally as soon as the cheek swab fits into their mouths. Genetic testing is recommended for all cats used in a breeding program, and affected animals should not be bred.

Treatment: Treatment is as described for *Kidney Failure* (page 375).

Hypertension (High Blood Pressure)

Hypertension in cats is usually a secondary problem. Chronic renal failure is generally regarded as the most common cause of hypertension, with studies reporting anywhere from 20 to 61 percent of all cats with renal failure also suffering from hypertension. The second most common cause is hyperthyroidism (see page 529). About 87 percent of all cats with hyperthyroidism also have hypertension.

The normal blood pressure for a cat is about 124 mm Hg. Older cats normally tend to run higher than this. Any cat with a reading over 150 should be checked carefully. (Since cats have such small arteries, most techniques simply involve taking a systolic reading. The 124 compares to the first number generally seen in blood pressure reports for humans.)

Cats with hypertension may have damage to the eyes, kidneys, heart, and nervous system because these organs are not receiving the appropriate blood flow. Some cats will initially be diagnosed after retinal damage is found on an exam or a cat suddenly goes blind. Enlargement of the heart, with corresponding murmurs, may be noted.

Kidney failure and hypertension aggravate one anther in a vicious cycle, leading to a faster progression of kidney failure. Neurological signs, such as *ataxia* or even seizures, may be secondary to hypertension.

Hypertension is diagnosed by using a small blood pressure cuff on either the forelimb or the base of the tail. An ultrasound probe may be used as an adjunct to detecting the pulse.

Treatment: Treatment involves the use of ACE inhibitors, such as enalapril and amlodipine, a calcium channel blocker—both medications are used in humans. Cats with acutely high blood pressure may need a single treatment with sodium nitroprusside, which rapidly lowers blood pressure. This must be closely monitored or the pressure can drop too low and leave the brain without adequate blood flow. Cats with hypertension should have regular rechecks to evaluate the success of their medications. Once hypertension is controlled, it is possible that some damage to the vision may correct itself.

Feline Lower Urinary Tract Disease (FLUTD)

Feline lower urinary tract disease, also called feline urologic syndrome (FUS), is the most common disorder affecting the lower urinary tract in cats. The lower urinary tract is the urinary bladder, bladder sphincters, and urethra. Therefore, conditions affecting any of these organs can cause FLUTD. Cystitis, meaning inflammation of the bladder, is another term commonly used, but should be specifically reserved for conditions affecting only the urinary bladder.

Lower urinary tract problems are by far the major health concern of cat owners—although they do not occur in most cats. One reason is that FLUTD has a 50 to 70 percent rate of recurrence. Although FLUTD can occur in cats of all ages, it is seen most commonly in those older than 1 year. It occurs in both sexes, but the anatomy of the male increases the likelihood of bladder obstruction. It is more common in obese cats, possibly due to mechanical interference with voiding or to infrequent voiding in a less active cat.

The signs of FLUTD include prolonged squatting and straining; entering and leaving the litter box often, sometimes without voiding; frequent urination; passing bloody urine; urinating in unusual locations (possibly because the litter box becomes associated with pain); licking the penis or the vulva excessively; and crying out during the act of voiding.

FLUTD accounts for the great majority of feline urinary tract symptoms (dysuria, hematuria, and anuria), and although the signs of FLUTD might suggest a bladder or urethra infection, studies have shown that in most cases a bacterial infection is not present—at least not initially. Therefore, veterinarians have had to revise their thinking about the association of bacterial infections with urinary tract symptoms in the cat. The following points should be considered in this regard:

- There is a normal bacterial flora in the terminal portion of the cat's urethra. Accordingly, cultures taken from voided urine specimens are contaminated and show growth of bacteria even though the bladder urine is sterile. Cultures taken by catheter or bladder aspiration, called cystocentesis, are more accurate.

- The lining of the normal cat's urethra and bladder contains antibodies and immune substances that destroy harmful bacteria. The process of emptying the bladder flushes out the lower system and keeps the channel clean.

- Valves at the junction of the ureters and the bladder prevent reflux of infected urine up into the kidney.

- The concentrated urine of cats contains acids, urea, and other substances that create an unfavorable living environment for most bacteria. Dilute urine is more likely to support bacterial growth. However, heavily concentrated urine that contains sediment is not desirable and may predispose the cat to FLUTD.

- FLUTD symptoms wax and wane—so although it may appear the symptoms are responding to antibiotic therapy, it's likely they would have diminished without antibiotic therapy.

Some breakdown in either local immunity or normal bladder function must occur for a cat to develop a bacterial urinary tract infection. This breakdown allows harmful invaders to gain a foothold. Some processes that lead to a breakdown are as follows:

- Repeated attacks of obstruction, which scar the urethra and further obstruct the bladder outlet.

- Repeated catheterization, which injures the lining of the urethra and enables bacteria to enter the bladder.

- Tumors or growths in the bladder and strictures of the urethra—which impair the flushing effect of urination and leave a residual pool of urine for bacterial growth.

- A prior urinary tract infection, which leads to tissue injury and reduced local resistance. Cats who have had one urinary tract infection are more likely to have others.

- Female cats, because of their short, wider urethra, are more prone than males to ascending urinary tract infections from vaginal or fecal contamination.

In summary, FLUTD in cats does not always mean infection. Infections are preceded by some process that damages the cat's normal defense mechanisms and sets the stage for bacterial invasion. Once established, recurrent infections are common. Some of these infections become resistant to commonly used antibiotics, so a urine culture and sensitivity test is essential. Failure to promptly correct the initial problem makes repeated infections almost a certainty.

CAUSES OF FLUTD

There are a number of important contributing factors that explain why some cats get FLUTD, but no one circumstance accounts for all cases. It is known that

- FLUTD can be caused by the urethra being plugged by a pastelike, gritty, or sandy material composed primarily of mucus and struvite (magnesium-ammonium-phosphate) crystals, which are about the size of grains of salt. Although struvite crystals constitute a major part of most plugs, other types of crystals may be found. Some plugs are composed primarily of mucus, blood, and white cells.

- FLUTD can also be related to uroliths—crystals or stones—found in the urinary tract (see page 388). The type of urolith will vary depending on the cat's diet and urine pH factors. The two most common types are struvite (magnesium phosphate) and calcium oxalate. Factors influencing urolith formation in cats include concurrent bacterial infections; infrequent urination caused by a dirty litter box; reduced physical activity; and reduced water intake due to poor quality or no water available, or feeding exclusively dry cat food.

- Cat urine is normally slightly acidic. Factors that favor an alkaline urine include the type of food eaten and the presence of bacterial urinary tract infection. Acid urine has antibacterial properties. Despite this observation, some cases of FLUTD occur in cats with acid urine. These cats may suffer from calcium oxalate uroliths. If the urolith occurs in the urethra, a life-threatening obstruction may occur.

- Bacterial cystitis (see page 386) and urethritis (inflammation of the urethra) have long been accepted as basic causes. Current research indicates that bacteria are not involved in most cases, at least not at first. However, bacterial cystitis may be a very important cause of recurrent attacks. Also, keep in mind that the potential for infection increases with obstruction. Again, recurrent infections may be the result of antibiotic resistance, so the urine should be cultured before beginning any treatment.

- Diet and water intake have been proposed as contributing factors. Cats who eat dry food take in less water with their meals and also lose more water in their stools. Presumably, dry cat food leads to a more concentrated urine and a greater amount of sediment. Cats who eat dry food exclusively do not urinate as frequently and therefore sediment and bacteria are not as effectively flushed from the urinary tract.

- Stress also may play a role in sterile (negative bacterial culture) outbreaks. Signs of dysuria often flare up associated with emotional or physical upheavals in the household.

In summary, no one theory accounts for all cases of FLUTD. It does seem likely that reduced water intake, diets that contain large amounts of such crystal precursors as magnesium and calcium, urinary pH, as well as other currently unknown factors all contribute. Bacterial infection, once established, is an important cause of recurrent attacks.

URETHRAL OBSTRUCTION

Major obstructions of the urethra can occur with the first episode of FLUTD or during subsequent attacks. With partial or complete obstruction of the urethra, the lower abdomen becomes distended and painful to touch. An obstructed cat spends a lot of time straining to urinate (many owners mistake this for constipation) without producing any urine.

Female cats do not obstruct as frequently as males, because their urethra is wider and crystals and plugs pass easier. However, females can become obstructed with urethral uroliths.

As pressure increases in the upper urinary tract, the kidneys fail and stop making urine. Wastes build in the blood, leading to uremia (a toxic buildup of urea). The cat loses her appetite, acts sluggish, and begins to vomit. If unrelieved, irreversible kidney damage occurs, leading to death. Thus, *it is of vital importance to relieve the obstruction as soon as possible.* Keep in mind that cats often seek seclusion when they are ill or in pain; therefore, a cat with symptomatic FLUTD should not be allowed outdoors.

Treatment: A cat with a plugged urethra needs immediate veterinary attention. This is an emergency with potentially life-threatening consequences. An obstructed male often protrudes his penis. You can massage the penis by rolling it between your thumb and index finger. This may crush the plug and allow the material to be expelled. Even if this is successful, veterinary attention and possible hospitalization are required.

Even if you can remove the plug so the cat can now urinate, you must take the cat to your veterinarian for follow-up veterinary care. Any plugs or crystals that are passed or collected should be analyzed so the correct treatment plan can be developed.

To relieve an obstruction, your veterinarian should first relieve the pressure in the bladder by emptying it via cystocentesis, a procedure in which a fine needle attached to a syringe is inserted into the bladder through the abdomen and urine is drawn into the syringe. This allows time for the kidneys to start functioning again and the cat to be stabilized with intravenous fluids prior to sedation. Relieving the obstruction must be done under sedation or anesthesia. Your veterinarian will insert a small, soft, rubber or flexible polyethylene catheter through the urethra into the bladder to relieve the obstruction. Intravenous fluids are continued to rehydrate the cat and increase the flow of urine. Antibiotics may be prescribed to prevent or treat an associated bladder infection. After obstruction, many cats need continued intravenous or subcutaneous fluids for several days, until kidney function returns to normal and the cat is voiding normally.

Following discharge from the veterinary hospital, the cat should be placed on a special diet; which diet depends on the type of crystals found in the urine. For cats with magnesium phosphate crystals, diets such as Hill's Prescription Diet Feline s/d, Eukanuba Low pH/S, Purina UR St/Ox, Royal Canin Control Formula, Royal Canin Dissolution Formula, and Royal Canin Urinary SO 30 help dissolve any residual struvite crystals or stones in the urinary bladder. These foods are low in magnesium and aid in maintaining a normal acid urine. In cats fed these special diets exclusively, signs associated with FLUTD will normally cease within the first five to seven days. To completely dissolve all residual struvite crystals or stones, the diet should be followed for one to two months. These diets, however, are high in salt and ordinarily are not used as a maintenance food (see *Preventing FLUTD*, page 387). It is important to feed only the prescribed diet. Do not feed fish, shellfish, cheese, vitamin-mineral supplements, or table scraps. These foods contain extra magnesium and also produce an alkaline urine.

During and immediately after the dissolution process, you may be asked to monitor your cat's urine pH at home or to bring in a urine specimen to be checked for struvite crystals under the microscope (see *How to Collect and Test Urine*, page 372).

For those plugs or stones that consist of nonstruvite compounds, such as calcium oxalate, there are also diets that will be of some assistance to prevent recurrence. These include Eukanuba Moderate pH O, Purina UR St/Ox, and Royal Canin SO 30.

No matter what type of urolith is present, surgery may be the best option for your cat, especially if the obstruction cannot be resolved. Your veterinarian will discuss the options with you. There is an operation for male cats in

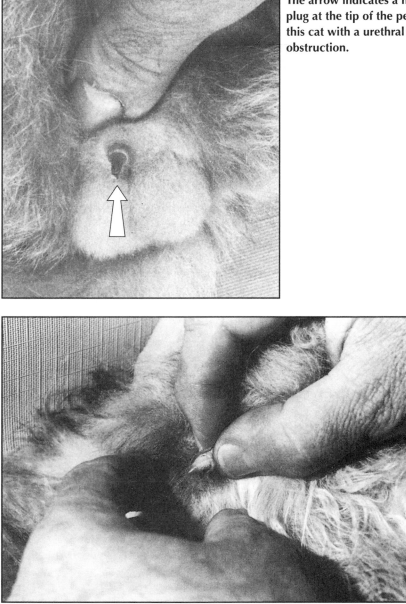

The arrow indicates a mucus plug at the tip of the penis in this cat with a urethral obstruction.

Rolling the penis between your finger and thumb may crush the plug and clear the passage. The cat still needs to see a veterinarian.

which part of the penis is removed to enlarge the opening of the urethra. The surgery is called a perineal urethrostomy. Upon recovery, cats are still able to control their urination and use a litter box, but tend to be more prone to bacterial infections of the bladder due to the now shorter, wider urethra.

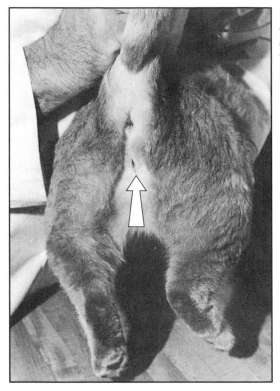

In a perineal urethrostomy, the entire penis is removed to enlarge the urethral opening. The cat now is able to control his urine.

However, this surgery allows small uroliths and urethral plugs to be passed in the urine without causing an obstruction.

CYSTITIS

Cystitis is an inflammation of the bladder and is part of the FLUTD complex. Inflammation may be caused by stones (uroliths), tumors, bacterial infections, or may be *idiopathic*. Affected cats show frequent urination and straining, similar to an obstructed cat except urine is being produced frequently in small amounts.

Idiopathic cystitis in cats may be similar to interstitial cystitis in people. Affected cats urinate frequently, almost always with blood visibly present in the urine. Bacteria and uroliths or crystals are rarely found. An accurate diagnosis may require cystoscopy (evaluating the bladder with an endoscope) or a bladder *biopsy*. Stress appears to be a major factor in this disease in cats—which is very similar to the interstitial cystitis condition in humans that is also exacerbated by stress.

Urine should be submitted for culture and sensitivity tests to rule out infection or, if an infection is present, to determine which antibiotic to use. Ultrasound examination and X-rays (with or without contrast materials) are needed to determine the possible cause. Idiopathic cystitis can only be diagnosed if other causes are ruled out.

Treatment: Unfortunately, some cats with cystitis will also retain urine and form uroliths or urethral plugs. These cats should be treated for uroliths (see page 388) or urethral obstruction (see page 383).

Most cases resolve without medical treatment, but reducing stress can hasten healing and decrease the likelihood of recurrence. It may be necessary to work with a feline behaviorist on the causes of your cat's stress. Feliway, an antianxiety pheromone, can also help calm the cat. Sometimes antianxiety drugs (such as amitriptyline) are prescribed for the cat.

There is some evidence that supplementation with glucosamine and chondroitin sulfate may be beneficial in preventing recurrence, as these substances are thought to protect the lining of the bladder. Feeding canned foods as opposed to dry foods seems to be helpful in preventing recurrences, as frequent voiding flushes bacteria and crystals out of the bladder. Diets such as Hill's c/d, which tend to provide near-neutral urine pH, seem to be best. Pain medications may keep the cat more comfortable.

PREVENTING FLUTD

Many cats experience a recurrence of FLUTD when they return to their former food. To prevent recurrence, your veterinarian may suggest feeding your cat a prescription diet, such as Hill's Feline c/d(s) for struvite uroliths or c/d(o) for calcium oxalate uroliths, for six to nine months. Switch to the prevention diet when your veterinarian has determined that your cat is free of symptoms and the urine is free of crystals. The procedure for introducing a new diet is to gradually mix it in with old food over the course of about ten days, adding more and more of the new food and less and less of the old until the switch is complete.

If the cat remains free of symptoms and urinary crystals for six to nine months, your veterinarian may suggest a moderately restricted magnesium diet, or some combination of prescription diets that produce an acidic or alkaline urine, depending on your cat's situation. High-acid diets are not recommended for elderly cats. Cranberry capsules may be a safe long-term additive to encourage bladder health.

The cat's urine should be checked every six months. If the cat develops new signs of illness while on a maintenance diet, your veterinarian may advise you to switch back to one of the prescription diets already mentioned.

There are also other steps you can take to reduce the likelihood of the cat developing excessive urinary sediment or infection.

- Keep the litter box clean. It should be scooped at least twice a day and the litter changed whenever it smells. Some cats refuse to use a dirty litter box. This can result in voluntary retention of urine.

- Encourage water consumption by keeping clean, fresh water available at all times. Feeding canned foods will also provide your cat with more liquid in her diet. Some cats can be induced to drink more by providing a small water fountain or leaving a faucet dripping.

- Prevent obesity. Maintain normal body weight by restricting food intake, as discussed in chapter 18. Encourage your cat to exercise by engaging in regular interactive play sessions.

- Minimize stress as much as possible.

- Glucosamine supplements may be beneficial in preventing a recurrence, as these substances are thought to protect the lining of the bladder.

- Occasionally, a cat will not consume a prescription diet. Your veterinarian should be able to recommend other diets, supplements, or recipes for home-cooked diets.

Cats with repeated attacks of FLUTD that don't respond to the preventive measures listed here should have complete veterinary evaluation, searching for uroliths and other abnormalities in the urinary tract

The question arises about whether all adult cats should be placed on a special diet as a prophylactic measure to prevent FLUTD. Considering that 99 percent of cats are not affected by FLUTD, regardless of diet, and that other factors besides diet are important in the etiology of this syndrome, feeding a severely restricted diet to all cats probably is not justified. However, feeding canned food is desirable for this and many other reasons.

Most cat food manufacturers have reduced the levels of magnesium in their products and added L-methionine, a urinary acidifier. This should provide some protection against FLUTD when it involves struvite crystals or uroliths. Remember that while most dietary information for cats with urinary problems relates to struvite uroliths, many cats suffer from calcium oxalate uroliths and need a different therapy plan.

Uroliths (Bladder Stones)

Most bladder stones in cats cause symptoms of FLUTD. The same process that causes small crystals or crystalline material to plug the urethra also causes stones to form in the bladder. Stones are more likely to form in a persistently infected bladder and in a bladder that is partially obstructed. Stones irritate the bladder wall, prolong infection, and produce symptoms of FLUTD. Cats with bladder stones may not have any crystals present in urine samples. Some affected cats show no clinical signs.

The two most common types of uroliths are struvite (magnesium phosphate) and calcium oxalate. There are also other types of uroliths. Two factors of primary importance in struvite stone formation are high concentrations of magnesium in the urine and a urine with an alkaline pH (over 6.8). Factors of primary importance in calcium oxalate urolith formation include urine with an acidic pH and lower levels of magnesium in the diet.

Female cats have a higher risk of developing struvite uroliths, especially female cats 1 to 2 years of age. However, struvite uroliths have been found in kittens as young as 1 month and cats as old as 20 years. Calcium oxalate uroliths tend to occur more often in male cats, particularly 10- to 15-year-old neutered males.

General Feline Urolith Facts

Struvite	Calcium Oxalate
Female cats	Neutered male cats
1 to 2 years of age	10 to 15 years of age
	Persians, Himalayans, Burmese predisposed
Alkaline urine is a risk	Acidic urine is a risk
About 50 percent of all uroliths	About 39 percent of all uroliths
More than 85 percent of all urethral plugs	Less than 15 percent of all urethral plugs

The Minnesota Urolith Center at the University of Minnesota College of Veterinary Medicine, established by Dr. Carl A. Osborne, is well known for its work on uroliths in cats. Among other things, the center analyzes uroliths removed from cats and sent in for study. From 1981 until about 2002, the percent of struvite uroliths dropped from close to 98 percent to just 33 percent. This is undoubtedly due to changes in feline diets that led to acidic urine.

Meanwhile, the percentage of calcium oxalate uroliths rose from 2 percent to 55 percent. For a few years since 2002, the two types of uroliths were about equal in number, as judged by samples sent to the lab. Struvite uroliths are now on the rise again.

In evaluating the content of urethral plugs submitted to the lab, struvite has continued to dominate—often 85 percent or higher. It is not known why there is the discrepancy between the composition of urethral plugs and that of uroliths.

Treatment: Struvite stones will usually dissolve in one to three months under the same treatment protocol described for FLUTD (see page 380). Abdominal X-rays are taken periodically to monitor the progress of dissolution. Any associated bacterial infection is treated as described for *Cystitis* (page 386).

Stones that do not dissolve must be removed surgically. Calcium oxalate stones almost always require surgical removal. Following treatment, a cat should be placed on the same protocol as described for *Preventing FLUTD* (page 387). The dietary regimen will vary with the type of urolith. Stones should be sent for analysis, to determine the proper course of treatment. The Minnesota Urolith Center is the recommended laboratory (see appendix D).

Urinary Incontinence

Incontinence is defined as abnormal voiding behavior showing a loss of voluntary control over the act of voiding with inappropriate urination. It should be distinguished from housetraining lapses and psychological causes, which are discussed in *Inappropriate Urination* (page 393).

One cause of incontinence may be an ectopic ureter—an abnormality in development in which instead of attaching to the bladder in the normal location, the ureters may attach very close to the neck of the bladder or even directly to the urethra, therefore bypassing the control sphincters. Since this is a congenital defect, signs are usually noted in cats under 1 year of age. Surgery may be attempted to move the ureter to a more normal location, or the kidney and ureter on that side may be removed. Cats do quite well with just one normal kidney.

When urinary incontinence is associated with FLUTD, the cat may at first experience sudden urges to void, urinate in locations other than the litter box, and void frequently in small amounts. These symptoms are caused by urgency and pain upon urination, but the cat retains some control over the act of voiding. However, if obstructions recur, the repeatedly overdistended bladder loses the ability to contract and empty. A more or less constant dribbling of urine occurs from the inert, overloaded bladder. Spinal cord injury, especially that associated with pulling apart the sacral-lumbar or coccygeal vertebrae when a car runs over a cat's tail, is a common cause of bladder paralysis, overdistension, and subsequent urinary incontinence. Spinal cord diseases and brain diseases can also lead to loss of bladder and bowel control. The spinal cord defect sometimes seen in Manx cats and associated with their tailless gene may also cause incontinence. Dysautonomia is an unusual neurological problem that often presents with incontinence as one of the signs. Incontinence related to these problems may improve if the primary condition responds to therapy.

Geriatric cats may lose some or all of their control over urination and leak, especially when sleeping. Cats suffering from feline leukemia sometimes show incontinence, as well.

Treatment: Treating incontinence is directed at finding the underlying cause and correcting it if possible. Drugs that act on the bladder muscle may be useful in selected cases.

The Adrenal Glands

The adrenal glands are small endocrine organs located right next to the kidneys. The adrenals produce substances that go into the bloodstream, such as hormones, and regulate various metabolic functions.

HYPERADRENOCORTICISM (CUSHING'S DISEASE)

This disease occurs when too much cortisol is produced by the adrenal glands, usually as the result of a cancer. About 80 percent of the time, this is cancer in the pituitary gland, which signals the adrenals to continue hormone production beyond what is needed. In the other 20 percent, it is from a cancer in part of the adrenal gland itself.

Middle-aged and older cats, particularly females, are seen with this problem. Normally, the first clinical signs are increased drinking and urination, with very dilute urine. About 75 percent of these cats will also have diabetes mellitus. The cat may appear potbellied and have a poor haircoat with easily damaged skin.

Diagnosis involves blood work, though ultrasound may show an adrenal tumor.

Treatment: Surgery can be used to treat tumors of both the adrenal and pituitary glands but should be done at a referral center by an experienced surgeon. If both adrenal glands are affected and are surgically removed, the cat will need to be on supplements for life to replace the adrenal secretions. These supplements include glucocorticoids and mineralocorticoids. Nonsurgical treatments with trilostane and mitotane have been used. These drugs affect the amount of cortisol produced by the adrenal glands.

HYPOADRENOCORTICISM (ADDISON'S DISEASE)

This disease occurs when not enough secretions are produced by the adrenal glands. It is quite unusual in cats. Cats with this problem are inactive, lose weight, and may suddenly collapse.

Blood work is the method of choice for diagnosis. Some affected cats will show an increase in potassium as well as poor concentration of urine, so renal failure may be suspected. Lab work can differentiate the two problems.

Treatment: Cats with hypoadrenocorticism will need supplementation for life with glucocorticoids and mineralocorticoids.

HYPERALDOSTERONISM

This syndrome is diagnosed with increasing frequency in cats. Most cases involve a unilateral cancer of one adrenal gland. In this case, the cancer is primarily of the cells that produce aldosterone, a hormone that regulates sodium and potassium balance in the cat's body. Too much aldosterone leads to low levels of potassium in the blood and associated weakness, flexion of the head and neck, and increased drinking and urinating. These cats may also have high blood pressure and associated vision problems due to retinal injury.

Treatment: Surgery is the treatment of choice at this time, especially with unilateral cancers. Some cats have done well with amlodipine, or amlodipine and potassium supplementation, or other medical management.

Pheochromocytomas

The adrenal gland also produces epinephrine, which can affect heart rate and blood pressure. Occasionally, the adrenal gland is affected by an epinephrine-producing tumor. These tumors are very aggressive and have a grave prognosis.

Treatment: The tumor should be removed, if possible, by an experienced surgeon. Medical control of the heart rate and blood pressure should be attempted.

Litter Box Issues
Litter Box Training

Contrary to popular belief, mother cats do not teach their kittens to use the litter box. Kittens begin to dig in and use dirt and dry, loose material at about 4 weeks old without ever having observed their mothers doing so. This natural instinct is used in training kittens to use the litter box. Begin as soon as the new kitten arrives in your home.

Buy the largest litter box you can find; your kitten will soon grow into a cat, and will appreciate having the room. Make sure at least one side is low enough that your kitten can easily climb in and out of the box. And make sure the box is in a spot that is easy to get to. (These are also important considerations for a geriatric cat, who may have limited mobility.) Place the box away from heavy traffic and loud distracting noises so the cat can have privacy. If it becomes necessary to move the box, make the change gradually, moving it step by step.

If the kitten was trained to use a litter box by her previous owner, use the same type of box and litter. A kitten who has been living outside may need dirt or sand in the litter box at first, as that is what she is accustomed to using. Gradually replace the dirt with more and more litter, until you have completely switched over. This method works for switching the litter for any cat.

Place the kitten in the litter box after a nap, a meal, a play session, and whenever your kitten appears inclined to urinate or defecate. Praise her when she goes. If mistakes occur, pick up the kitten and set her down in the box. Do not discipline *just before* placing the kitten in the box. The kitten will associate any reprimand with being placed in the litter box and will assume the litter box is the wrong place to go.

Never rub cat's nose in a mess or bring her over to it for a reprimand. She will have no idea why she is being reprimanded, but she may be inclined to eliminate in hidden spots (such as behind the sofa) to avoid another reprimand.

When your kitten is still learning to use the box, leave a tiny bit of urine or feces behind in the box, so the scent will remind her what the box is for. As soon as she is using the box reliably (and this could be as quickly as a day or two) remove all liquid and solid waste regularly. Scoop out solid material once or twice a day, and stir the litter to keep the surface dry. If you are using a clumping litter, scoop the liquid wastes at the same time. Change nonclumping litter every week—more often if necessary. Change clumping litter as soon as you notice that the box has even the slightest odor after you have scooped. Wash the box thoroughly and let it dry completely before adding fresh litter.

KITTY LITTER

The choice of litter is very important to your cat. The ideal litter is as dust-free as possible, unscented, absorbent, and easy to dispose of. Dust can be a serious problem for cats because they are digging in the litter and can inhale dust, leading to respiratory problems. This is especially problematic in enclosed litter boxes—which many cats don't like, either.

While scenting the litter makes the humans feel good, the smell may be overpowering to the cat, who will choose to retain urine or eliminate elsewhere. Applying feline pheromones, such a Feliway, near the litter box is an exception.

Clumping litter is often preferable because it is easier to remove all solid and liquid waste from the box daily. Discussions have been held about the dangers of cats licking granules of clumping litter off their feet, but no case of a cat being harmed as the result of ingesting clumping litter has ever been verified. (Dogs who like to raid the litter box and ingest fairly large amounts of litter may suffer from dehydration.)

Cats who are recovering from surgery and have sutures may benefit from a non-clay-type litter such as those made from corn, wheat, pine, and recycled newspaper pellets. Many of these are flushable as well, which makes them convenient for you.

There are also diagnostic litters. These include Scientific Professional Cat Litter, which changes color with changes in urine pH, and Purina Glucotest Urinary Detection System, which uses an additive to indicate urine glucose levels to help monitor diabetic cats. Hemalert, also made by Purina, detects blood in the urine—a possible sign of FLUTD.

It is important to place litter boxes in relatively quiet areas that are easily accessible to the cat. Litter should be scooped at least once every day and the boxes thoroughly cleaned weekly. Ideally, you should have one litter box per cat in the household, plus a spare. They should not all be in the same room.

INAPPROPRIATE URINATION

Inappropriate urination is the most common behavior problem reported by cat owners. Male and female cats share the problem equally. Many medical problems can cause inappropriate urination, so it is extremely important to rule out any medical cause before assuming it's a behavior problem.

Inappropriate urination can be regarded as two separate behaviors. One is urine marking (which includes spraying). The other is regularly urinating outside the litter box. Male and female cats both urinate in the squatting position. The urine is voided downward onto a flat surface.

Spraying occurs in the standing position. The tail is held straight up and typically quivers. Urine is sprayed horizontally onto walls and furniture. Both male and female cats spray, although males are more likely to do so than females. Females in estrus may urine-mark in the squatting position. A spraying cat continues to use the litter box for defecation and *most* or at least some urine elimination.

Urine Marking and Spraying

Urine marking may be used to establish territory. It is then often associated with rubbing pheromones from the chin and tail on prominent objects. A cat may also mark when she feels threatened or stressed. Marking can advertise that sex is available—this is far more common in unaltered cats. This kind of marking increases during the mating season and especially during courtship.

A number of situations may elicit urine marking or spraying. An indoor cat looking out a window may observe a neighborhood cat entering the backyard or coming near the house. The indoor cat initiates defensive activity that involves spraying and may include threat behavior such as running to the door, hissing or growling at the windows, and intensely watching the "intruder." The introduction of a new cat to the household may elicit spraying by either the resident cat or the newly arrived cat. Multicat households in which cats feel crowded may elicit spraying from one or more cats. And any disturbance in a cat's routine that arouses the cat or is perceived as a threat can elicit spraying.

Treatment: Intact cats should be spayed or neutered. This is effective in 80 to 90 percent of cases. Spaying or neutering a cat before spraying behavior begins (usually, before 6 months of age) will often head it off entirely—especially in males. Unneutered males *will* spray, and that behavior cannot be eliminated unless the cat is neutered.

Neutered cats who continue to spray or urine mark often respond to modification of the environment and behavior modification techniques. Environment modification techniques are effective if the situation that elicits urine marking and spraying can be identified and removed. For example, competition between an indoor and outdoor cat can be lessened by driving the outdoor cat away or by preventing the indoor cat from seeing the outdoor cat. Simply close the door to the viewing room. If that is not possible, you may need to block the view outside using blinds, curtains, or shades. A motion-activated water sprinkler may help keep roaming cats away from your home.

Treat conflict between indoor cats by reducing competition, separating the cats, or reducing the number of cats in the household. If having fewer cats is not possible, increase the available territory by adding several multi-tier cat trees.

If spraying occurs in one or two locations, it may be possible to create an aversion to these locations by spraying the area with a commercial cat repellent. Other substances that may repel the cat are mothballs in cloth bags, orange peels, and rubbing alcohol. Placing upside-down carpet runner (pointy side up) around a favorite spraying area may also work.

Feliway is a commercial brand synthetic pheromone that is similar to cat cheek gland scent markers. This can help to relieve stress and keep cats away from an area where they sprayed.

There are now a variety of behavior modification drugs that are used for cats, especially for house-soiling problems. See *Drug Treatment of Behavior Disorders*, page 551.

Urinating Outside the Litter Box

One or more of the following may explain why some cats fail to use the litter box:

- The cat may develop a dislike for the litter box, the litter, or the box's location.
- The cat may develop a surface or location preference.
- The cat may have a behavioral problem or excessive stress that is expressed as inappropriate urination.
- In a multicat household, one or more cats may be bullied or threatened while in or attempting to get to the litter box.
- The cat may have had a negative experience while in the litter box.
- The cat may be avoiding the litter box as a residual behavior from a medical problem.
- The cat may be physically unable to get into or out of the litter box or the area where the box is kept (especially a problem with kittens and older cats).
- The cat may have forgotten where the litter box is (especially a problem with kittens and older cats).

Cats who eliminate outside the box once tend to do so again. A common belief is that cats are attracted to the odors of urine and feces, and mainly because of that attraction, they return to the same spot to eliminate. This belief is at odds with the observation that cats avoid dirty litter boxes and do not like to eat or play in areas where they eliminate. Accordingly, there must be other explanations for the cat's consistent return to the same spot.

Cats who regularly use a litter box dig and paw in the litter and often bury the urine and feces—but not always. A cat may dig in the litter before eliminating and not afterward, or vice versa. The pawing and digging is not simply to cover the elimination. The movement of the paws through the litter and the feel of the litter as the paws are drawn through it seem to provide a tactile-kinesthetic sensation that gratifies the cat and eventually becomes associated with elimination. It follows, then, that cats prefer to dig in litter or on surfaces that give the best sensation of digging and are averse to digging in material that provides the least positive sensation. In fact, evidence from several studies suggest that coarse-grained litter, either sand or clay, is less satisfying to cats and that a fine-grained, clumping litter is much preferred.

It has also been observed that cats acquire a preference for eliminating on specific substrate. This can come from the earliest experiences with an elimination substrate. Outdoor cats use a variety of surfaces, such as loose dirt, leaves, or sand in which to dig and scratch, eliminate, and cover their excrement. Indoor cats have fewer options. An indoor cat can dig either in the litter provided, or dig on the carpet or the potted plants or the basket of dirty laundry. Cats who dig and scratch with their paws outside the litter box, either before or after eliminating, may also acquire a preference for the new surface and begin to eliminate on that surface. Adjustments such as covering the surface with plastic, moving the litter box, and cleaning the carpet with cleaners made specifically to remove animal waste odors can help.

A cat may begin to soil outside the box because the litter is dirty or a cover was placed on the box. A cover can make the litter box unattractive by preventing dissipation of disagreeable odors and interfering with the cat's normal posture or the ability to dig and paw in the litter. Because of an acquired preference for the carpet, the cat may continue to use the carpet even after the box is cleaned or the cover removed.

A cat who is frightened by a loud noise or chased or threatened by another cat while using a litter box may seek and find another location with more privacy. Scolding a cat for a lapse in training and immediately placing her in the box can lead to future avoidance.

A cat with a urinary tract problem such as FLUTD may experience pain upon urination and then associate the box with pain. Even after the condition has cleared up, the cat may avoid the box.

Cats with mild litter box aversion typically do not dig, cover, and bury their waste and may stand on the edges of the box to avoid physical contact with the litter, run quickly out of the box, and show other signs of distaste for the litter box or its substrate. They may still continue to use the box part-time. Cats with an intense aversion rarely, if ever, use the box.

Cats learn to associate specific activities with specific locations. They prefer certain spots for sleeping, sunning, eating, grooming, and eliminating. A cat may use a litter box consistently primarily because of that specific location. When the box is moved, the cat may eliminate on the floor where the box had been located.

Stress can also cause inappropriate urination. Cats do not eliminate outside the litter box out of spite or anger. These emotions are not in the feline repertoire. They do not urinate inappropriately to "get even" with you. Litter box accidents are often associated with changes in the household or the owners going away on vacation, but the cat's resulting reaction is due to stress, not a desire for revenge. Studies show that stress alone can alter the pH of a cat's urine, causing irritation that can lead to FLUTD. Cats may also derive comfort from urinating on their owner's clothing or bedding—thereby mixing their own scent with that of their owners.

Treatment: Determine why the cat is not using the box, keeping in mind that one reason may have initiated the problem and another is now maintaining it.

For a litter box aversion, clean the box more frequently, as described in *Litter Box Training* (page 392). Use an unscented litter without additives. Switch to a fine-grained, clumping litter. Do not cover the box. If the cat scatters the litter, try using a bigger box or one with higher sides. If you are dealing with a feral cat, you may need to use dirt in the litter box at first and gradually switch over to litter.

For a location aversion, increase the number of litter boxes, placing a new one where the cat is now soiling. Later, remove any unused litter boxes. Prevent sneak attacks by another cat while the first is using the box by placing boxes in locations that offer clear escape routes. Avoid stimuli that frighten the cat while she is using the litter. Often this means not putting the box in the laundry room, where the sudden start of the spin cycle can startle a cat.

For location and surface preferences, make sure the litter or litter box are not being rejected by looking for signs of litter aversion. If none are apparent, move the litter box to the site of soiling. If this is effective, the litter box should not immediately be moved back to its original location. Instead, the box should be moved several inches each day for the first several days, and then progressively greater distances until the box is in a more convenient site.

Other possible actions include removing a rug, adding a rug, or covering the area that is being soiled with a hard surface material—but only if it seems that this would not cause the problem to become generalized and involve other similar surfaces in the house. Create an aversion to the new location by feeding or playing with the cat at the site of soiling.

For stress-related problems, decrease the amount of time the cat is alone. Provide a cat sitter who will play with and pet the cat during your absence. Increase the time you spend playing with the cat every day. Consider a companion cat. Provide stimulation for the cat—perhaps a "cat video" or television left on to animal programs. Reading a book into a tape recorder and leaving that playing all day may soothe a stressed cat.

There are now a variety of behavior modification drugs that are used for cats, especially for house-soiling problems. See *Drug Treatment of Behavior Disorders*, page 551.

Consultation with a behaviorist may be very helpful in working through this situation.

15

SEX AND REPRODUCTION

The majority of cats living as household pets are not pedigreed. They are born of parents who are themselves unregistered and, in most cases, are of mixed ancestry. Such cats are called mixed breeds, domestic shorthairs, or domestic longhairs. Although these cats are delightful companions, there is no reason to breed them. The number of homeless cats far exceeds the number of loving homes available for them, and breeding more cats only contributes to this problem.

A female cat will cycle continuously throughout most of the year. During this time, she will howl, act erratically, and attract *intact* males who will spray very strong-smelling urine around your house and yard. So, along with adding to the unwanted pet population, you may find you are going crazy from these behaviors. Most families choose to *spay* their female cats and *neuter* their males. Breeding is not for the faint of heart.

Breeding pedigreed cats is a different matter. Pedigreed cat breeding has greatly enhanced our understanding of feline health and genetics. However, to have a breeding program with a high degree of excellence demands careful attention to detail and great patience.

The object of any breeding program is to preserve the essential qualities and distinct attributes of the breed, while also breeding cats of excellent health and temperament. Accordingly, a thorough understanding of the breed standard is a basic requirement. Pedigrees are also important, because they are the means to study bloodlines and understand the relationships between the two individuals in a proposed mating. They are of the greatest value when the individual cats are known or actually have been seen, because a pedigree only ensures that the animals are registered specimens of the breed. It does not testify to the quality of the cats in question.

Championships do indicate merit and give some indication of quality. However, they do not always give a complete picture, because some cats do a lot of winning because they get a lot of exposure, and others do not win many ribbons because of lack of exposure. In addition, the modern breeder has far more information on cat genetics than in the past and also has the product of many generations of selective breeding on which to base a successful program.

Since it is the genetic potential of ancestors that determines breeding success, any cat you are thinking of breeding should possess outstanding qualities worthy of being passed on to offspring. The breeder should possess a knowledge of the virtues and faults, including the health, of all cats in the pedigree for at least three generations. They should have the judgment and experience to pick the best kittens and the willingness to eliminate from their breeding program all cats who do not have the potential to improve the breed. Breeders should also be willing and able to take back any kittens they breed, even if it is 10 years later, if their families are no longer able to keep them.

Feline Genetics

The domestic cat has 38 chromosomes, and each chromosome contains more than 25,000 *genes*. Although this permits a vast array of potential combinations, only a small number are actually concerned with the physical features that together define a breed or variety. The great majority are responsible for the smooth functioning of the many aspects of every cat's physiology.

Heredity is the random combination of countless genes. The smallest combination of genes that can determine an inherited trait is a pair. A pair of genes is called an allele. One gene in the pair is inherited from each parent. When they combine to form the allele, the dominant gene is the one that determines the expression of the trait. The other gene is recessive. For example, if a kitten inherits a dominant gene for a black coat and a recessive gene for blue, the coat will be black. Recessive genes can determine a trait too, but only when paired together. A kitten inheriting two recessive genes for a blue coat will be blue. When both genes in an allele are identical, the cat is said to be homozygous for the physical trait the allele determines. When they are different, the cat is heterozygous.

Body structure and conformation, as on this slender Burmese, are the result of a complex interaction of multiple genes.

Still other genes are additive, which means the trait will be expressed by the combined effects of two or more alleles. An example of the additive effect of multiple genes is seen in the range of eye colors typical of many cats. Orange, yellow, hazel, and green eye colors are determined by additive genes. In the Siamese and white breeds, however, eye color is determined by single genes. Body structure and conformation is another multiple-gene effect. In various combinations, multiple genes influence the rate of bone growth, the development of muscle, and the deposition of fat.

Dominant and Recessive Genes

The male and the female are equally responsible for determining the inheritance of their kittens. When both parents have identical homozygous alleles, either dominant or recessive, it does not matter how the genes are sorted because all the kittens will inherit the same allele, and all will express the same physical traits as their parents. In essence, this is the strategy behind most planned breeding programs.

Desirable and undesirable traits, as well as neutral traits, can be caused by both dominant and recessive genes. A dominant gene that may be associated with deleterious side effects is the gene for the completely white coat. This gene also predisposes cats to a form of deafness that affects one or both ears. Although deafness is more common in white cats with blue eyes, it also occurs in white cats with orange eyes. Not all white cats with blue eyes will be deaf, however, because it is pigment in the ear that is important (see *Deafness*, page 217).

In the typical shorthaired cat, the length of the guard hair is about five centimeters. In contrast, the silky, abundant coat of a longhaired show cat may exceed twice that length. This difference is caused by a recessive gene that appears to prolong the period of growth in hair follicles, so the hair reaches a greater length before entering the resting phase. Selective breeding over many generations for this longhaired homozygous recessive coat trait has resulted in the fuller and silkier coat of Persians and other longhaired breeds.

Genetic Mutations

A number of different breeds and varieties of the domestic cat have developed through the accidental or spontaneous appearance of genetic *mutations*. Genetic mutations are rare and occur in perhaps one in one million offspring. When mutations do occur, they are passed along like any others and follow the same rules. Most, but not all, are recessive.

Among the most important genetic mutations for breeders are those producing distinctive coat colors and patterns. There are only 12 of these, but in various combinations they are responsible for a wide range of cat breeds and varieties. The length and texture of the coat is another essential feature of

Long, silky hair, as on this Persian, is the result of a recessive gene.

many breeds. There are at least five such coat-determining mutations that have been identified and put to use.

A few breeds have arisen as the result of a physical characteristic caused by a single mutated gene. The Manx breed is one example; a single dominant gene causes the tail of this cat to be shortened or absent. Taillessness can occur as a genetic mutation in any cat. The Manx breed was developed from a cat who spontaneously showed this mutation.

The Scottish Fold is another example. His distinctive look is caused by the expression of a single dominant mutated gene that causes the tip of the ear to bend forward. However, if a cat is homozygous for the gene that causes the ear fold, serious skeletal deformities also occur.

Screening for Health Problems

The cat world has lagged behind the dog world in developing ways to screen breeding animals for health problems, but that is changing. The discovery of screening methods for cats with heart problems, hip dysplasia, and kidney disease is opening up new challenges for cat breeders. The ideal tests are DNA tests that indicate if a cat is normal for the defect, a carrier who could pass on the defect, or an affected animal who will eventually suffer from the problem. Such tests are not available for all diseases, partly because many health problems, such as hip dysplasia, involve multiple genes and environmental interactions. In the case of hip dysplasia, X-rays can be used to evaluate the hips and predict future problems.

To further complicate matters, the gene that causes a specific problem in one breed may not be the same gene that causes that problem in another breed. So genetic tests must be specific for each breed. Still, progress is being made, spurred on by the efforts of pedigreed cat breeders.

The institutions doing the screening will generally provide certifications and results that are available to the public, at least for normal cats and often for all cats screened.

Screening Tests for Health Problems

Health Problem	Screening Method	Institution
Hip dysplasia	X-ray	OFA, PennHIP
Elbow dysplasia	X-ray	OFA
Patella luxation	Palpation	OFA
Cardiac abnormalities	Auscultation/ Echocardiography	OFA
	DNA for Maine Coon Cats and Ragdolls	Veterinary Cardiac Genetic Laboratory, Washington State University
Polycystic kidney disease	DNA	VetGen
Metabolic defects	DNA	PennGen
Spinal muscular atrophy	DNA for Maine Coon Cats	Laboratory of Comparative Medical Genetics, Michigan State University

Breeds with Health Screening Tests

OFA

American Shorthair	Cardiac abnormalities
Bengal	Cardiac abnormalities, patella luxation
British Shorthair	Hip dysplasia
Maine Coon Cat	Hip dysplasia, cardiac abnormalities, elbow dysplasia, patella luxation
Persian	Cardiac abnormalities, hip dysplasia
Ragdoll	Cardiac abnormalities
Siamese	Hip dysplasia
Somali	Elbow dysplasia, hip dysplasia
Sphynx	Cardiac abnormalities
Turkish Angora	Cardiac abnormalities

VetGen

Persian, Persian crosses	Polycystic kidney disease

PennGen

Norwegian Forest Cat	Glycogenolysis Type IV
Persian, Domestic Shorthair	Mannosidosis
Siamese, Domestic Shorthair	Mucopolysaccharidosis VI
Domestic Shorthair	Mucopolysaccharidosis VII
Abyssinian, Somali, Domestic Shorthair	Pyruvate kinase

Veterinary Cardiac Genetics Laboratory at Washington State University

Maine Coon Cat, Ragdoll	Cardiac abnormalities

Laboratory of Comparative Medical Genetics, Michigan State University

Maine Coon Cat	Spinal muscular atrophy

Blood typing may also be recommended (see page 314), depending on your cat's breed and the prevalence of different blood types in that breed. Incompatible blood types can lead to neonatal isoerythrolysis (see page 469). Typing can be done using blood samples or DNA testing.

The Queen

The *queen* is the breeding female. If you are planning to breed pedigreed cats, it is best to get a good female kitten with an outstanding pedigree. It is not a good idea to start with the tom. The management of a tom requires considerable experience and expertise. It is equally unwise to buy male and female kittens, hoping that when they mature they will be suitable breeding partners.

Before making the decision to breed your female, give careful thought to the effort and expense of producing a litter of healthy and well-socialized kittens. It can be both time-consuming and expensive. Many pedigreed kittens cannot be sold locally. This means advertising, and the effort and cost of finding just the right home for them.

Genetic screening for known health problems should be done before any breeding is contemplated. If your queen is not of the quality to be bred—not just in terms of health, but also in her conformation to the breed standard—she should be spayed. Also, no cat should be bred unless you have quality homes already lined up for most of the kittens. The feline overpopulation problem is serious, and you would not want any kittens you produce to become shelter cats or end up on the street. Breeding a litter is a serious responsibility. You are responsible for the kittens you create, and all breeders should be willing to take back cats even years after they were sold, rather than see them homeless.

A cat does not need to have a litter to "feel fulfilled" or to "settle down" emotionally or behaviorally. A spayed female kept as a family companion will be a content and happy cat. By spaying your female before her first *heat*, you reduce her chances of developing mammary cancer later in life, eliminate the chance of uterine infections or cancers, and won't have stray *tom cats* coming around your house yowling and spraying urine. You and your cat will also be spared the extreme behavior that accompanies the feline heat cycle—which includes constant howling and posturing, as well as urine marking.

Cats usually have their first heat when they are at about 75 or 80 percent of their adult size. At that point they usually weigh at least 5 pounds (2.25 kg). Exposure to a long photoperiod is also important to stimulate the hormonal cycle. Cats should not be bred at their first heat, because they are still physically immature. Longhaired cats often come into their first heat later than shorthaired cats—possibly not until 18 months of age.

It is safe to breed a queen at her second heat, *after* she is at least 12 to 18 months old. At this age, she is physically and emotionally mature enough to nurture kittens.

How often a queen can be mated depends on the size of her litters, her general health and nutrition, and the adequacy of her care. Cats average four to six kittens per litter and are capable of producing up to three litters a year, although that would be extremely physically draining. Overweight queens and those who are depleted by improper diet, excessive breeding, or unsanitary living conditions are unsuitable brood matrons. Often, they do not come into season regularly, are difficult to breed, experience problems during delivery, and are unable to properly care for their kittens.

PRE-BREEDING CHECKUP

Once you decide to mate your queen, take her to your veterinarian for a physical checkup. She should be examined to check that her vaginal opening is of normal size and that there are no obstructions to successful mating. Be sure to have her checked for periodontitis and dental infections. Bacteria from the queen's mouth can be transmitted to newborn kittens when she bites the umbilical cord. This is one cause of serious navel infections in kittens.

A brood queen, if not vaccinated within the previous three years, should be given a feline panleukopenia, feline viral rhinotracheitis, and feline calicivirus booster shot *before* being bred. Her rabies vaccination should be current. If she has not been tested for feline leukemia (FeLV), feline immunodeficiency virus, and possibly feline coronavirus, you should have these tests performed. Indications to test for and vaccinate against these diseases are discussed in chapter 3.

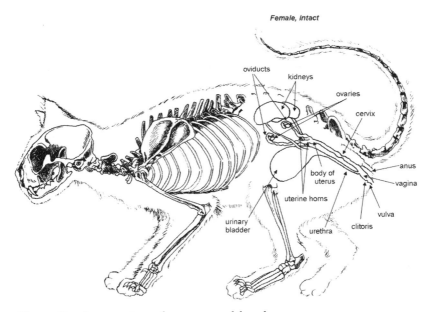

The genitourinary system of an unspayed female.

A stool test will show whether she has intestinal parasites. If found, they should be treated until they are completely eradicated before the queen is bred. A queen with active worm infestation will pass on the parasites to her kittens and possibly contribute to *zoonotic* problems, such as visceral larval migrans (see page 61). Genetic testing and screens for any health problems in your cat's breed should also be done before breeding.

SELECTING THE TOM

Part of the preparation for breeding is to choose the tom well in advance. The show record of a prospective tom may include a Championship or a Grand Championship. If he is a proven producer, his offspring's quality becomes a matter of considerable importance. If he has sired outstanding kittens, particularly out of several different queens, you have strong evidence of his quality. There can be a lapse of several years between a mating and a championship, so some of the best producers are often not recognized until well after they have stopped producing.

More important than the show records are the physical characteristics of the cat himself. If his faults are the same as your queen's, it does not make sense to double up on them. Also remember that many of the kittens will end up in pet homes, so health and temperament are equally important.

If your queen came from a breeder, it is a good idea to talk to that breeder, who should be familiar with the strengths and weaknesses of your queen and her bloodline before making a final selection. This knowledge can be vitally important in choosing a compatible mate. Some breeding catteries offer stud services. If you have an outstanding queen from that bloodline, you may give serious thought to using a tom from that same strain to reinforce the best qualities of your queen. However, you also need to avoid doubling up on any faults in the line.

It is the responsibility of the breeder (the owner of the queen) to come to a clear understanding with the tom's owner concerning breeding terms. Usually, a stud fee is paid at the time of mating, or the tom's owner may take the pick of the litter—a kitten of his or her own choosing. The age of the kitten should be agreed on. If the queen does not conceive, the tom's owner may offer a return service at no extra charge. However, this is not obligatory. Terms vary with the circumstances and the policies of the tom's owner. If these are in writing, there will be no misunderstandings later.

The Tom

The tom, or stud, is the breeding male. The age at which a male cat reaches sexual maturity and begins to produce sperm varies from 6 to 18 months, with the average at about 9 months. Two months later, sperm is present in the collecting tubules, so the male has reached sexual maturity and can now fertilize a queen.

Ordinarily, a tom should not be bred before he is a year old; ideally 18 months. If he is going to be shown, it may be two years before he is available.

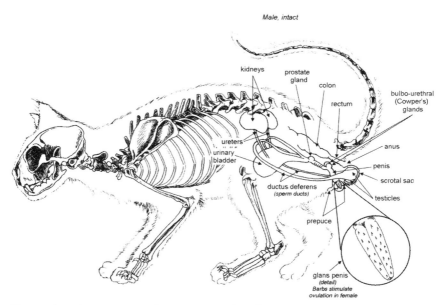

Male, intact

The genitourinary system of an unneutered male.

Genetic health screenings should be done *before* any breedings, and he should also be tested for FIP, feline leukemia, and feline immunodeficiency virus. The temperament of the tom is important, as well.

An active tom has a natural instinct to spray his surroundings with strong-smelling urine year-round. Toms are therefore usually kept in separate quarters. A tom should be maintained in top physical condition with regular exercise, routine health checkups, and a sound diet. All tests and vaccinations, as described for the queen (see Pre-Breeding Checkup, page 404), should be up-to-date for the tom.

A tom can be bred for three consecutive days or three times in one week. The first mating should be with an experienced queen who has already had a litter. The mating of two inexperienced animals can be fraught with difficulty and frustration.

If you own a male cat who is not of breeding quality, he should be neutered. This includes cats with incorrect conformation, structural faults, poor temperament, or health problems.

The Estrus (Heat) Cycle

Queens vary in the age at which they first go into *heat*. Some breeds (such as the Siamese) may have their first heat as early as 5 months. Others, particularly the longhaired breeds such as Persians, are not sexually mature until 10 months or older.

Cats are seasonally polyestrous. This means they will have repeated heat cycles over a year unless they are bred, and the heat cycles are influenced by the seasons. The mating season in cats is determined by a number of factors, including the length of daylight, environmental temperature, and the presence of other cats.

When there are 12 hours of daylight and other conditions are optimal, the hormonal system is activated, and the queen begins the *estrus cycle*. The mating season of cats in the northern hemisphere is from March to September. Cats in the southern hemisphere cycle from October to March.

Throughout the breeding season, queens go into and out of heat several times but do not always display estrous behavior at regular intervals. Often they exhibit continuous heat cycles in early spring (averaging 14 to 21 days from the beginning of one cycle to the beginning of the next), followed in late spring by cycles that are further apart. Each queen establishes her own normal rhythm.

Since cats are considered to be primarily induced ovulators (the physical act of mating causes them to ovulate), a cat will continue to cycle unless she is bred or the daylight factor takes over. Abnormal heat cycles are discussed in *Infertility*, page 416.

Stages of the Estrus Cycle

The estrous cycle of cats has four distinct stages. Signs of one cycle may overlap those of the next. Furthermore, there is individual variation in length of stages from one queen to another. Accordingly, it is not always possible to ascertain when a queen is most likely to conceive. *Vaginal cytology*, analyzed by those experienced in the technique, is helpful in predicting the moment of peak *fertility* in the difficult queen (see *Reluctant Breeders,* page 413). The following are the four stages of the estrus cycle.

Proestrus

This stage of heat is the first, lasting from one to two days. You may notice that the *vulva* enlarges slightly and appears somewhat moist, but this usually is not apparent. The queen shows increased appetite and restlessness, utters short low calls, and displays more than usual affection for her owners.

At this time, she begins to attract toms—but refuses to mate. She may urine mark around the house. *Proestrus* has been described as a period of courtship during which exposure to the male acts as a hormonal stimulus that brings on full heat. This belief stems from the observation that in feral cat colonies, where male companionship is common, the conception rate is higher than in catteries, where courtship is less spontaneous.

If you do not want your queen to become pregnant, take steps at the first sign of proestrus to prevent unwanted pregnancy (see *Unwanted Pregnancy,* page 425).

Estrus

The second stage is the period of sexual receptivity. It is what breeders refer to as heat and lasts four to six days. The queen begins to make more noise and her meows are louder and more frequent—eventually becoming almost constant. There is an obvious change in her behavior: She becomes much more affectionate toward people, weaves in and out of their legs, rubs against them, shakes her pelvis, and rolls about on the floor. If picked up when rolling, she may grab at your arm or even bite.

As the urge to mate becomes pronounced, her cries become alarming—sounding like those of an animal in pain. This call attracts toms from near and far.

Young cats having their first heat have been described by unknowing owners as "rabid," due to the dramatic changes in behavior. It is at this time that many families decide spaying is a good option.

To determine if your queen is receptive to mating, hold her by the scruff of the neck and stroke her down the back toward the base of her tail. If she is in estrus, she will raise her hindquarters, move her tail to the side, and tread up and down with her hind feet.

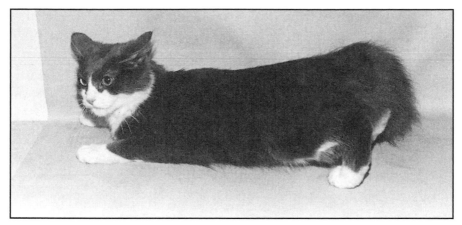

The characteristic stance of a queen in estrus.

This estrus period generally lasts 4 to 10 days. If they are not bred, some cats will continue in a prolonged estrus. This is seen most commonly in Siamese and similar breeds, and seems to be caused by high estrogen levels. Ideally, ovulation should be induced (see page 410).

Interestrus

The third stage lasts 7 to 14 days. During this stage, the queen refuses to mate and aggressively rejects the male if mating is attempted.

What happens during interestrus depends on what happened during estrus: If a mating did not occur, the queen will remain in interestrus for 7 to 14 days and then start a new cycle beginning with proestrus and proceeding to estrus. If sexual intercourse induced ovulation but the queen did not conceive, she will enter a period of pseudopregnancy lasting approximately 36 days. See *Pseudocyesis* (page 425). If sexual intercourse resulted in a pregnancy, her kittens will be delivered in about 63 days.

Anestrus

The fourth stage of the estrus cycle is reproductive rest. In the northern hemisphere, this is a 90-day period from November through January. This term may also be used for older female cats who no longer cycle.

HORMONAL INFLUENCES DURING THE ESTRUS CYCLE

Proestrus begins when the hypothalamus signals the pituitary gland to release follicle-stimulating hormone (*FSH*), which causes the ovaries to produce the egg follicles that begin to make estrogen.

Physical stimulation of the queen's vagina by the male's penis during mating triggers another signal to the pituitary gland, causing it to release luteinizing hormone (*LH*). LH stimulates the ovaries to release the eggs (ovulation).

Before ovulation, the ovarian follicles produce the female hormone estrogen, which prepares the eggs to be released, and also the queen's reproductive tract for mating and fertilization. Estrogen accounts for the physical and behavioral changes of the queen in heat.

After ovulation, the egg follicles become *corpus luteum* cysts and produce the pregnancy hormone *progesterone*. An important function of progesterone is to prepare the lining of the uterus to receive and support embryos. Removal of the ovaries during the first 50 days of pregnancy or inadequate output of progesterone from the ovaries during this period will result in abortion (see *Fetal Loss*, page 418).

OVULATION

Cats are primarily induced ovulators. This means that unlike most other mammals, they usually do not ovulate spontaneously. Instead, ovulation is induced by the act (or more accurately, the multiple acts) of sexual intercourse, during which the queen's vagina is stimulated by barblike projections on the male's penis. Three breedings a day during the first three days of her heat has been shown in one study to produce ovulation in 90 percent of cats.

Although it is uncommon, some cats may spontaneously ovulate—perhaps stimulated by the smells of a tom or being mounted but not bred. This could lead to a false pregnancy.

Ovulation takes place 24 to 30 hours after intercourse, although the time can vary. Some queens ovulate as early as 12 hours after intercourse. In most cases, four eggs are released from the ovaries, but this, too, varies. Up to 18 kittens have been reported in a single litter. After the queen ovulates, she loses interest in sex and refuses to mate.

It is possible to artificially induce ovulation by stimulating the queen's vagina with a plastic rod or a similar tool. This simulates a mating and induces

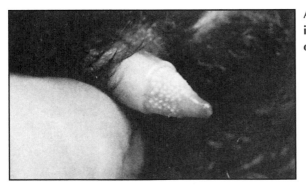

A protruded penis, showing the characteristic barbs of an intact male.

a false pregnancy lasting 36 days. It is one method of bringing the queen out of heat (see *Birth Control*, page 426). Ask your veterinarian to show you this technique, if needed.

FERTILIZATION

Fertilization occurs in the fallopian tubes that lead from the ovaries to the uterus. The embryos implant in the wall of the uterus about 14 days after mating. While only one sperm can fertilize each egg, a queen who has mated with a number of different toms could produce a litter of kittens having different fathers. This phenomenon is called superfecundity.

Mating

Once the signs of estrus are confirmed, the owner of the tom should be notified. He or she may want the queen at once. This has the advantage of letting the queen settle into her new surroundings before the mating. If possible, take the queen to the tom yourself. If the distance is great, you may have to ship her by air. However, an airplane trip can be nerve-wracking and may upset the queen, putting her out of heat.

A current rabies vaccination and a health certificate are required to ship a cat across state lines. The tom's owner may require a certificate showing that the queen has tested free of feline leukemia, feline immunodeficiency virus, and possibly coronavirus—as well as some hereditary diseases. All vaccinations, dewormings, and health screenings should be done ahead of time.

NORMAL MATING

The method of introducing the cats can be modified to suit the circumstances. Ideally, the queen's carrier is placed in a pen close to the tom's. The door of her carrier is opened to allow her to come out as she chooses and explore her surroundings. Once the queen approaches and begins to show interest in the tom, a gate is opened between the two pens to allow the two to greet each other.

A sexually receptive queen will allow the tom to approach her, touch noses, lick her face, and investigate her genital area. This necessary ceremony of greeting and foreplay helps initiate sexual arousal. In most cases, it provides sufficient stimulus for a mature queen to adopt a characteristic position in which she crouches down, raises her pelvis, and moves her tail to the side.

It is important that an experienced breeder be present during the mating. Even when both cats are experienced, their courtship and mating can become quite violent. However, some cats refuse to mate when a person is present. The

The mating sequence. The male mounts the queen and bites her on the nape of the neck. At the moment of ejaculation, the queen screams. The cats separate, and the queen may strike out with her claws.

breeder then should stay out of sight but in a position where he or she can observe the mating and step in quickly if it seems the pair is having a problem.

If the queen is not sufficiently aroused or not far enough along in estrus to be willing to breed, she will growl at the male and attempt to bite. The tom may become quite aggressive if he is unable to get the queen into position for mounting. In either case, the pair should be separated. A traumatic experience can be a serious setback to future breeding attempts. Be aware that either or both cats may bite or scratch when handled at this time. Wear protective gloves and use blankets or thick towels to pick up the cats. Ideally, let the queen finish her rolling and self-grooming behaviors before you try to pick her up.

Once the female assumes the receptive position, the tom will approach from the rear and mount, clasping her sides with his front legs. He then seizes her neck with his teeth and treads up and down with his back feet. Insertion of the penis is accomplished with a few deep thrusts. Ejaculation takes place in 5 to 15 seconds. At the moment of ejaculation, the male utters a low growl and the queen screams piercingly. This dramatic sequence is followed by an almost explosive separation, in which the queen may turn and strike out at the tom with her teeth and claws as he jumps back and to the side. The aggressive behavior of the queen at the end of ejaculation may be caused by the withdrawal of the penis. There are numerous barblike projections on the penis that produce an intense and possibly painful stimulation of the queen's vagina. The stimulation appears necessary to trigger the mechanism that causes ovulation to occur 24 hours later (see *Ovulation*, page 410).

After the first mating, subsequent matings may occur. The second usually occurs within a few minutes. Others follow at more extended intervals. Because ovulation usually does not occur with the first mating, it is recommended that the pair be left together under observation and allowed to mate freely for one to two hours a day, for three consecutive days. Most breeders agree that two to three mating sessions are necessary to ensure ovulation and conception. (Among free-roaming cats, this pattern of courtship and mating might be repeated many times over several hours for up to three days.) After each mating episode, the queen will roll and lick or groom extensively, paying special attention to her genital area.

After the mating session, the queen should be returned to her container or placed in a separate pen, but not until she has passed through the rolling over and self-grooming stage. If disturbed too soon, she may inflict a painful scratch or bite. At this time, you should check the tom to be sure his penis has returned to its sheath (see *Paraphimosis*, page 420).

Reluctant Breeders

The most common reason cats refuse to mate is breeding at the wrong time in the estrous cycle (usually during proestrus). If mating is attempted too early in the cycle, the queen will growl and attempt to bite the male. This is normal proestrus behavior, but some breeders might see it as a sign that the queen is reluctant. If the queen is sent to the tom too soon, the resulting stress may also send her off her heat. Most queens come into heat again in one to two days, but some may take longer.

If the queen is in the correct stage of her breeding cycle, yet refuses to mate, the problem is most likely one of preference. A pampered female raised as a house pet may be a reluctant breeder because of inadequate prior social contact with members of her own species. Mate preference, too, can be a determining factor. Some females will not mate with a timid tom; others prefer toms of a certain breed or even a specific coat color.

Sexual aggression in the male fluctuates at different times of the year, usually in association with the breeding season of the female. Male cats are territorial and mark their territory with the scent of urine. A male cat in unfamiliar surroundings may feel less dominant and show more interest in establishing territory and less interest in sex. Similarly, a gentle and friendly tom may lack the sexual aggressiveness to mate a dominant queen. Less commonly, a tom with a low libido may be suffering from impotence or a hormone deficiency. Obesity, whether caused by hormone disease or overfeeding, may be associated with reduced sex drive and may also interfere with the mechanics of mating. These subjects are discussed in *Diseases of the Male Genital Tract* (page 419).

Unsuccessful attempts to introduce the penis into the vagina can be associated with incompatible body lengths. The male's body is normally shorter than the female's. If this discrepancy is too great, the tom, while grasping the nape of the queen's neck with his teeth, may not be able to align his penis with her *vulva* and vagina. Occasionally, an inexperienced tom will grasp a female too far back (not at the nape of her neck) and thus will be too far away to accomplish intercourse. Similarly, a cat with dental disease or a sore mouth may be unable to take firm hold of the queen's neck.

If a tom appears unwilling to mate a receptive queen, examine his penis. It must be capable of fully protruding from its sheath to enter the vagina. Protrusion of the penis can be restricted by a ring of hair caught in the barbs and wrapped around the shaft of the penis (see *Paraphimosis*, page 420).

Treatment: When the queen refuses to accept the tom, she should not be tried again until 24 hours have passed. A successful mating may then take place. If not, there may be a hormonal problem or there may be preference issues. Hormone problems are discussed in *Fertility Problems in the Queen* (page 416).

Vaginal cytology can be used to determine if the heat cycle is normal. The process of taking the smear may induce ovulation, but only if the queen is in estrus. If the result is positive (showing estrus, the correct stage for mating), the pair should be mated at once. If intercourse occurs, a pregnancy should result. However, if the queen still won't mate, a preference issue can be inferred. Then, a decision is needed about whether to proceed with artificial insemination (see page 424) or abandon the breeding plans. Matings accomplished by artificial insemination must be timed to coincide with the estrous phase. Vaginal cytology is essential.

Infertility

When the queen fails to conceive kittens after a successful mating, either the tom or the queen, or both, may be responsible.

FERTILITY PROBLEMS IN THE TOM

A common cause of reduced *fertility* in the male is excessive use. Most virile toms can be bred three times in a single week. They should then be rested for at least a week. A tom used at regular intervals should receive a high-protein balanced diet.

When a tom is much in demand, a single mating and low sperm count may be the reasons why the queen fails to become pregnant. Sperm count tends to be inherited. Some lines produce toms that, for generations, are known to sire large healthy litters. However, litter size is actually a result of the number of eggs ovulated by the female, because there are almost always more sperm than needed unless the male is infertile. Toms who have not been used at stud for some time may have a low sperm count due to sexual inactivity. During a second mating, 48 hours after the first, the quality of semen is often much better. It is better to use a tom at regular intervals. Infrequent matings, instead of saving up sperm, often lead to decreased fertility due to the aging of the sperm in the male's genital tract. If a tom is known to have a low sperm count, it may be better to use him at least twice a week on the queen.

A male whose testicles failed to descend into the *scrotum* or in whom descent was delayed will have an absent or reduced sperm count (see *Cryptorchidism*, page 421). Cryptorchidism is inherited, and crytporchid males should therefore not be bred. As a tom grows older (beyond 8 years), his fertility may diminish because of a reduction in sperm number and quality. This may result in smaller litters, but the quality of the kittens will not be affected. After 12 years of age, testicular atrophy with an absence of sperm is common.

The prolonged elevation of body temperature depresses sperm production. A tom recovering from a serious illness with a fever may take several months to regain his normal sperm count. Some cats are less fertile in summer, especially when the weather is hot. An excess or deficiency of vitamin A can induce sterility. Signs of deficiency are weight loss, loss of hair, and night blindness. Vitamin A excess occurs among cats who are fed large amounts of raw liver. Feline leukemia has also been associated with *infertility*.

Hypothyroidism is a treatable condition that causes lack of vitality and sex drive; it can also lower a cat's sperm count. It is managed by thyroid replacement therapy. Naturally occurring hypothyroidism is rare in cats.

Other causes of reduced fertility are close confinement, boredom, improper diet, and lack of exercise. These factors are associated with stress and assume importance in the marginally fertile individual.

Genetic and chromosomal abnormalities are infrequent causes of infertility. Male tortoiseshell cats (a rare color pattern) are almost always sterile, as are male calico cats. Other chromosome abnormalities are difficult to diagnose. Genetic analysis must be carried out at a school of veterinary medicine. Infertility caused by diseases of the male genital tract are discussed beginning on page 419.

Treatment: A *semen* analysis will determine if sperm are of normal number and quality. The procedure for collecting the sample is described in *Artificial Insemination* (page 424). Absence of sperm may be *congenital* or acquired. When some sperm are present, the tom's potency can often be improved by treating the underlying problem.

Impotence

In most cases, impotence, or lack of the male sex drive or libido, is caused by behavioral factors (see *Reluctant Breeders*, page 413).

The male sex drive is under the influence of *testosterone*, which is produced by the testicles. Rarely, impotence is caused by failure of the testicles to produce this hormone. One explanation is that just before or after birth the male kitten receives a surge of testosterone that conditions or masculinizes his brain. If this surge does not occur, the male kitten develops a female behavior pattern and responds to the female hormone (estrogen) instead of the male one.

Serum testosterone levels can be measured to determine whether impotence is caused by a deficiency of testosterone. A semen analysis will only indicate if the testicles are sexually developed and able to produce sperm. Cells that make the sperm are not the same ones that make testosterone. Therefore, a fertile male can be impotent, and a sterile male can be quite willing and able to mate with a queen.

Treatment: Impotency due to hormonal rather than behavioral causes may improve when testosterone is given before breeding. Unfortunately, the dose that activates the male libido also depresses sperm production. It should be used with caution.

Catnip may increase the sexual aggressiveness of some males. Reproductive behaviors are somewhat heritable, and males with poor libido should not be bred unless they have other outstanding qualities.

FERTILITY PROBLEMS IN THE QUEEN
Abnormal Heat Cycles

The heat cycles of queens can vary a great deal. In general, each queen establishes her own normal rhythm. As a queen grows older, her heat periods become less regular and in some cases will not be accompanied by ovulation. Other factors that adversely affect a queen's estrous cycle are improper diet, environmental stress, and poor health.

Anestrus

If a queen remains in *anestrus* and does not cycle during the breeding season, consider one of the following:

- **Lack of photostimulation.** The length of daylight hours triggers the beginning of the estrous cycle. Less than 12 hours of light per day is often insufficient to initiate the cycle. Insufficient photostimulation is more likely to be a problem with indoor cats.
- **Silent estrus.** Many cases thought to be a lack of heat are really a normal heat in which the queen does not exhibit estrous behavior. A queen who is low in the social hierarchy of a group of cats, for example, may fail to exhibit estrous behavior until or unless she is removed from the group. Silent heat is confirmed by vaginal cytology and blood estrogen levels.
- **Hypothyroidism.** This is an uncommon cause of anestrus in cats. When present, other indications of thyroid deficiency may or may not be observed. The diagnosis is established by a blood test. It is treated by giving thyroid hormone. Since this is a health problem, many veterinarians recommend that hypothyroid cats not be bred.

- **Absence of ovaries.** An ovariohysterectomy is a possibility when the prior medical history of a cat is not known. An uncommon cause of estrogen deficiency is ovarian dysgenesis, in which the ovaries do not develop to sexual maturity. The vulva and vagina remain small and undeveloped. Heat does not occur because of low estrogen levels.

Cystic Ovarian Follicles

This condition is caused by an excess output of estrogen from the ovaries. A queen who cycles repeatedly but is never mated can, after several heat cycles, develop cysts on her ovaries. These cysts produce an abnormally high estrogen level that suppresses ovulation and also produces cystic endometrial hyperplasia, which prevents implantation. The queen may enter a continuous or prolonged heat. She becomes irritable, inclined to fight other cats (both male and female), and refuses to mate—or conversely, will mate frequently but be unable to conceive.

Ovarian cysts may be diagnosed by ultrasound. Inducing ovulation and medical hormonal manipulations may clear the condition. If not, ovarian cysts are treated by removing the ovaries or the cysts. When kittens are desired, removing the cysts may be sufficient to correct the problem. This can be delicate surgery. The queen may subsequently become pregnant. If breeding is not desired, both ovaries and the uterus should be removed (see *Ovariohysterectomy*, page 426). A queen with this problem may pass it on, so unless she is of otherwise outstanding quality, she should be spayed.

Administering preparations that contain progesterone—used to treat some skin diseases—can produce the same effects as cystic ovaries.

Treating Abnormal Heat Cycles

A female slow to come into heat may do so if she is exposed to light for 14 hours a day or is placed with another queen in estrus. Their heat cycles may even become synchronized. This can happen throughout a cattery. Exposure to the male through a period of socialization and foreplay is an important initiator of estrus.

Failure to come into heat can sometimes be treated successfully by giving follicle stimulating hormone (FSH) for four to five days. If there is follicle development and the queen goes into heat and accepts the male, ovulation will usually occur. The queen should be bred several times during the induced estrus. Human chorionic gonadotropin (HCG) is sometimes used after mating to ensure the likelihood of ovulation.

Further treatment depends on identifying the cause. A complete workup includes physical examination, vaginal cytology, hormone assays, and possible exploratory surgery. A feline leukemia virus test is essential in all cases of feline infertility. Infertility problems may be heritable, and if a queen has problems getting pregnant, it might be best to spay her and look elsewhere for a breeding animal.

Failure to Ovulate

A common cause of failure to ovulate is breeding too late in the estrous cycle. As a rule, a queen should be bred no later than the middle of her estrus: that is, by day four of her period of receptivity to the male. It is equally important to breed the queen several times during this time of receptivity since a single mating is rarely sufficient to induce ovulation.

Ovulation is followed by a rise in the serum progesterone level. Canine test kits may be used to check this. This test is positive seven days after estrus and remains so until day 40. If the rise did not occur, ovulation did not take place.

Cats may also spontaneously ovulate, thereby confusing the breeder and putting themselves into a pseudopregnancy.

FETAL LOSS

If the queen is found to be pregnant and subsequently does not deliver kittens, one of two things must have happened: She either miscarried (aborted) or reabsorbed her kittens.

Fetal loss may take place even before the embryos implant in the wall of the uterus because of unfavorable conditions in the lining of the uterus or defects in the fertilized eggs. Early embryonic death is most commonly associated with the feline leukemia virus, feline immunodeficiency virus, feline panleukopenia, or toxoplasmosis. Cystic endometrial hyperplasia (a condition where the lining of the uterus is overgrown) can cause early embryonic deaths and poor conception rates.

Taurine and copper deficiencies cause abortions and the delivery of kittens with low birth weigh. Inadequate progesterone can lead to fetal reabsorption or abortion. Many medications can cause developmental defects in the kitten embryos and subsequent loss.

Signs of abortion are vaginal bleeding and the passage of tissue. These signs may not be observed if the queen is fastidious about keeping herself clean. You will not be immediately aware that she has lost her litter.

Fetal reabsorption occurs before the seventh week of *gestation*. The developing kittens are absorbed back into the mother's body and are no longer felt in the abdomen. Occasionally, you may notice a slight pinkish vaginal discharge.

The death of kittens *in utero* can be due to an inadequate output of progesterone. During the first half of pregnancy, a uterine environment suitable for developing kittens is supported by progesterone made in the ovaries. At about day 40 of gestation, this function is taken over by the placenta. If this transition fails to occur, there is insufficient progesterone to support the pregnancy. Placental insufficiency tends to occur with subsequent pregnancies and becomes a consideration when a queen repeatedly loses her litters. Queens with this problem should be removed from the breeding colony and spayed.

A well recognized cause of habitual fetal loss is the feline leukemia virus. This is particularly important when an entire breeding colony is affected. Reproductive failure in a cattery may be the first indication of such infection. Most tom owners will not accept a queen for breeding unless she has a certificate showing she has been tested and found free of feline leukemia.

The coronavirus has been implicated as a cause of an entire spectrum of reproductive failures that include repeated abortions, fetal reabsorption, *stillbirths*, and kittens who sicken and die shortly after birth. Feline rhinotracheitis, feline immunodeficiency virus, feline calicivirus, feline panleukopenia, and chlamydiosis may all contribute to infertility.

Causes of sporadic miscarriages include emotional upsets, violent exercise (such as jumping from heights), a blow to the abdomen, and improper feeding and prenatal care. Care and feeding of the pregnant queen is discussed in chapter 16.

Treatment: The loss of kittens during pregnancy is an indication that a thorough medical evaluation is required. The queen should be screened for feline leukemia virus, feline immunodeficiency virus, and possibly coronavirus—if these tests results are not current. Other causes of habitual abortion should be investigated, including those related to diseases of the female genital tract. Queens with progesterone insufficiency can be treated during the next pregnancy by giving a weekly injection of long-acting progesterone, beginning a week before the anticipated transition to placental progesterone. This may be an inherited trait, however, and it is questionable whether this cat should continue to be bred.

Diseases of the Male Genital Tract

There are several disorders of the male genital tract that can lead to mating problems and, in some cases, cause infertility. Even if fertility is not an issue, these conditions should be treated for the general health of the cat.

If it is necessary to examine the penis for health reasons, this is best done by raising the tail to expose the perineum below the anus. A cat's penis points backward. The glans or head of the penis can be exposed by retracting the sheath that covers it. Grasp the sheath between your thumb and forefinger and slide it forward (toward the cat's head). The tip will protrude. Reverse the process to cover the glans.

In a fully mature tom, the shaft of the penis has barblike projections that slant toward the base. After ejaculation, as the tom begins to withdraw his penis, these barbs cause intense stimulation of the queen's vagina. This initiates the release of a hormone, causing the queen to ovulate. In the young tom and the neutered male, the penis is smooth.

Balanoposthitis (Infection of the Prepuce and Head of the Penis)

Irritation of the foreskin and head of the penis can be caused by hair caught in the barbs during mating. Frequent sexual activity can irritate the penis and foreskin. Any kind of small debris may become caught beneath the sheath. The irritation may be complicated by infection and abscess of the sheath. This makes intercourse painful or impossible. All of these problems are quite rare in the cat.

Treatment: First, clip away the hair near the foreskin. Push back the foreskin to expose the tip of the penis. Cleanse the area with dilute hydrogen peroxide solution or dilute Betadine solution and apply an antibiotic ointment. Slide the foreskin back over the tip of the penis. Repeat until all signs of discharge and inflammation are gone. If the infection persists, seek veterinary attention. Antibiotics or surgical cleansing under anesthesia may be required.

Cats with balanoposthitis should not be bred until the infection is cleared. The infection can be transmitted to the female during mating.

Phimosis (Strictured Foreskin)

In this condition, the opening in the foreskin is too small to let the penis extend. It may be so small that urine can escape only in small drops. Some cases are due to infection; others due to a birth defect.

Treatment: When the problem is related to infection of the sheath, treating the infection may correct the phimosis. If not, surgery is necessary. If this appears to be a birth defect, this may be heritable and this cat may not be a good prospect for breeding.

Paraphimosis (Penis Can't Retract)

In this condition, the penis is unable to return to its former position inside the sheath. Long hair on the skin around the sheath may cause the foreskin to roll under so that it cannot slide. The barbs on the glans penis may collect hair from the queen during the mating process, forming a ring of hair that prevents the penis from retracting and also inhibits mating.

Paraphimosis can be prevented by cutting long hair around the prepuce before mating. A tom usually licks the tip of his penis after intercourse and removes any attached hair. A persistent ring of hair should be removed. Check the male after mating to be sure the penis has returned to its sheath.

Treatment: The penis should be returned to its normal position as quickly as possible to prevent permanent damage. Push the prepuce back on the shaft of the penis toward the cat's head, while rolling it out so the hairs are not caught. Lubricate the surface of the penis with mineral oil or olive oil. With

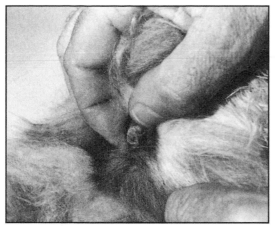

A ring of hair around the penis may prevent it from retracting into the sheath.

one hand, gently draw the head of the penis toward you. With the other hand, slide the prepuce forward. If these measures are not immediately successful, notify your veterinarian. In most cases, it will be necessary to medicate the sheath twice a day, as described for balanoposthitis (page 420).

CRYPTORCHIDISM (UNDESCENDED TESTICLES)

The testicles in kittens are thought to be descended into the scrotum at birth. Usually, they can be felt by 6 weeks of age. Testicles that do not descend are called *cryptorchid*. A male with one cryptorchid testicle may be fertile. If both testicles are cryptorchid, the cat is sterile.

The testicles should be of similar size and feel rather firm. Since much of the testicle's size is due to sperm-producing tissue, soft or small testicles in the sexually mature cat may be deficient in sperm. Even though a tom with one undescended testicle may be capable of fertilizing a queen, he should not be bred because the trait is hereditary.

Testicular hypoplasia is the absence of sexual development of the testicles. If both testicles fail to develop, the cat is sterile and does not exhibit sexual behavior.

Treatment: Cryptorchid cats should be neutered. Abdominal surgery may be necessary to find and remove the testicles.

ORCHITIS (TESTICULAR INFECTION)

The most frequent cause of orchitis is an infected bite wound of the scrotum. Infections can also be caused by penetrating wounds, frostbite, chemical and thermal burns, feline infectious peritonitis, and infections involving the bladder, *urethra*, and sheath of the penis.

Signs of orchitis are swelling and pain in the testicle. The testicle becomes enlarged, hard, and tender to touch. The cat assumes a spread-legged stance with his belly tucked. Later, the diseased testicle shrinks and becomes small and firm.

Treatment: Since most cat bites and other puncture wounds are quite likely to become infected, even injuries that appear to be minor should be examined and treated by a veterinarian.

Diseases of the Female Genital Tract
VAGINAL INFECTION

Inflammation and infection of the vagina are rare in queens. Signs of vaginitis include licking the *vulva* and discomfort when the vagina is examined. There may or may not be a vaginal discharge. Toms are sometimes attracted to queens with vaginitis, thereby giving the impression that the queen is in heat.

Bacterial infection of the vagina may spread to the bladder or uterus. Veterinary examination is necessary to confirm the diagnosis and determine the cause.

Treatment: An appropriate antibiotic is selected on the basis of culture and sensitivity tests. A queen with vaginitis should not be bred until her infection has been successfully treated.

UTERINE INFECTION

Uterine infection in cats begins with a disease called cystic endometrial hyperplasia. The disease changes conditions inside the uterus and creates the potential for secondary bacterial infection—either endometritis or pyometra.

Cystic Endometrial Hyperplasia

In cats with this condition, the endometrium, a layer of tissue lining the wall of the uterus, becomes thickened and bubblelike cysts form. These alterations are caused by the prolonged stimulatory effect of estrogen, produced by the ovarian follicles during estrus (see *Hormonal Influences During the Estrus Cycle*, page 409).

Queens who are allowed to cycle repeatedly during one or more breeding seasons but in whom ovulation is not induced by mating or artificial stimulation of the vagina are at increased risk. So are queens over 5 years old who have never been pregnant. This condition may also be associated with cats who spontaneously ovulate and put themselves into a state of false pregnancy.

Uncomplicated cystic endometrial hyperplasia causes few signs, although some queens may exhibit a bloody vaginal discharge.

Treatment: Pregnancy protects against cystic endometrial hyperplasia. When breeding is no longer desired, the treatment of choice is spaying. The estrous cycle can also be suppressed using drugs (see *Birth Control*, page 426).

Endometritis

Most cases follow cystic endometrial hyperplasia. A bacterial infection is limited to the lining of the uterus. Little pus is produced, but the endometrium becomes inflamed and infected. Endometritis occurs in an acute or chronic form.

A queen with acute endometritis exhibits listlessness, loss of appetite, fever, and a bloody or puslike vaginal discharge. A severe infection may be life threatening. If she has given birth, she may neglect her kittens.

A queen with chronic endometritis often appears in excellent health, has a normal heat period, and is mated successfully—yet fails to conceive or loses her kittens during pregnancy because the chronic infection creates unsuitable conditions for embryo implantation and growth. Suspect this condition when the queen is bred at the right time but fails to conceive on two or more cycles and when pregnancy is confirmed but she fails to deliver healthy kittens.

Treatment: The preferred treatment is ovariohysterectomy. If this is a valuable queen and you want to retain her bloodlines if at all possible, you can try treatment. The vaginal discharge of acute endometritis can be cultured and antibiotics prescribed based on sensitivity tests. They should be continued for three to four weeks. Chronic endometritis is difficult to diagnose and requires smears and cultures taken from the cervix. A uterine biopsy may be required. Antibiotics are prescribed on the basis of sensitivity tests.

Pyometra

Like endometritis, pyometra usually develops from an underlying cystic endometrial hyperplasia, complicated by bacterial infection. Pyometra differs from endometritis in that there is less inflammation of the wall of the uterus, but far more pus in the cavity of the uterus. An additional factor in the development of pyometra is the stimulatory effect of progesterone. This is why pyometra is more likely to occur in queens with cystic endometrial hyperplasia who subsequently ovulate and go on to develop *corpus luteum* cysts. These cysts produce high levels of progesterone (see *Hormonal Influences During the Estrus Cycle*, page 409).

Pyometra is a life-threatening infection that occurs most often in queens over 5 years old; the average is 7 or 8 years old. Signs appear four to six weeks after the queen goes out of heat. A queen with pyometra refuses to eat, appears dull and lethargic, loses weight, runs a fever (although her temperature may be normal), drinks a great deal of water, and urinates frequently. The abdomen is usually quite markedly distended and firm. This may suggest the possibility of either pregnancy or feline infectious peritonitis (the wet form of FIP), but the combination of a severe illness with a distended abdomen after a heat period will indicate the diagnosis of pyometra.

An enlarged uterus can usually be detected by abdominal palpation. In the unusual case of abdominal enlargement without signs of illness, X-rays and abdominal ultrasound will usually confirm the presence of an enlarged uterus and distinguish between pyometra and pregnancy.

Two types of pyometra occur: open and closed. In the open type, the cervix relaxes, releasing a large amount of pus that is often cream, pink, or brown. In the closed type, there is very little vaginal discharge. As pus collects in the uterus, the cat becomes more toxic, vomits, runs a high fever, and quickly dehydrates.

A disease similar to pyometra, acute metritis (page 445), occurs in the *postpartum* queen.

Treatment: *This is an emergency.* Call the veterinarian immediately. Ovariohysterectomy is the treatment of choice. It is much safer to do this surgery before the cat becomes toxic.

Artificial Insemination

Artificial insemination (AI) is a technique in which semen is collected from the male and artificially introduced into the female's reproductive tract. The procedures for AI are now well standardized. All of the criteria for health and screening that apply to a natural breeding also apply here. For example, feline immunodeficiency virus can be transmitted via semen alone.

In the matter of selecting equipment, collecting semen, and inseminating the queen, a strict protocol is important to ensure a successful pregnancy. For this reason, veterinary supervision, at least initially, is recommended. You may need to work with a veterinary reproductive specialist; very few veterinarians have done AI work with cats. When performed by experienced personnel, the conception rate is 75 percent. AI has its widest application when natural mating is contraindicated or impossible. Usually this is for behavioral reasons, anatomical reasons, or fear of transmitting a disease.

The queen's behavior will indicate when she is in estrus and receptive to successful fertilization. When, for behavioral reasons, she does not display signs of sexual receptivity, *vaginal cytology* must be used to stage the heat cycle.

Semen can be collected from the male by using an artificial vagina. Many toms can be trained to use this device. A teaser female in estrus is needed to stimulate the male. As an alternative, semen can be collected from an anesthetized tom by using an electroejaculator.

Once collected, the semen is diluted with special nutritional solutions and introduced into the queen's vagina. The queen must be hormonally prepared to ovulate in conjunction with the insemination. The best results with AI will be obtained by inseminating the queen two to four times over 24 hours. Additionally, good results can be obtained by putting the semen directly into the uterus via surgical intervention.

After AI, the queen should be confined until she goes out of heat. If she mates with another male, a mixed litter may result. DNA testing can determine parentage but is expensive.

Frozen semen has been used successfully. However, conception rates are not as high as they are when *fresh semen* is used. Advanced reproductive techniques using embryo transfer have a low success rate at this time.

Pseudocyesis (False Pregnancy)

When ovulation occurs but the eggs remain unfertilized, a pseudocyesis results. The condition is caused by progesterone, which is manufactured by the corpus luteum cysts in the ovaries following ovulation (see *Hormonal Influences During the Estrus Cycle*, page 409). A false-pregnant queen seldom shows signs of a true pregnancy. Occasionally, the queen will have an increased appetite, gain weight, or exhibit nesting behavior. Milk production is rare. False pregnancy can be easily confused with true pregnancy in which kittens have been aborted or reabsorbed (see *Fetal Loss*, page 418).

Treatment: No treatment is necessary. Signs disappear in 35 to 40 days after estrus.

A false-pregnant queen is likely to have other false pregnancies. This tendency may be inherited, so unless this queen has other outstanding qualities, it may be best to spay her. When breeding is no longer desired, the queen should definitely be spayed. This is best done after the false pregnancy is over.

Unwanted Pregnancy

The best way to prevent unwanted pregnancy is to spay your female cat. The best way to avoid causing an unwanted pregnancy is to neuter your male cat. A queen in heat will go to great lengths to get to a tom. Her vocal call and the potent pheromones in her urine attract toms from miles around. If the queen is left outdoors for just a few minutes, an unwanted pregnancy can occur. *When your queen is in heat, keep her indoors. Do not let her out of your sight.* Queens must be isolated throughout the entire estrous cycle, which begins with the signs of *proestrus* and continues for 10 to 14 days.

If a valuable breeding queen has been mismated, it may be best to let her go through with the pregnancy. She will be perfectly able to breed again during a subsequent heat cycle. If you do not have the time and facilities to care for a litter of kittens, or if the queen is not of breeding quality, consider the alternatives.

One option is spaying. This surgery can be performed during the first half of pregnancy without added risk to the female. During the second half of pregnancy, it becomes more difficult.

Another alternative is to induce abortion with the prostaglandin PGF2a. This requires hospitalization. It is given by injection for two or more days, after 30 days of gestation. PGF2a currently is not approved in the United States for use in cats. And its use is not without risk. Many cats will drool, vomit, and have diarrhea within an hour of the injections. Prolactin inhibitors (such as cabergoline) given for four to nine days between 36 and 40 days of pregnancy can also be used to induce abortion.

Birth Control
FOR THE FEMALE

The best way to prevent conception is to spay your female cat. Tubal ligation has almost the same risks as spaying and is only slightly less expensive in most veterinary clinics. It won't stop the queen from going into heat and attracting males. It does not have the health benefits of ovariohysterectomy. Most veterinarians recommend ovariohysterectomy as the surgery of choice for sterilization.

If it is important to preserve the fertility of the queen for future breeding, artificial stimulation of the vagina and birth control drugs can be used to postpone pregnancy.

Ovariohysterectomy (Spaying)

In this surgery, the uterus, fallopian tubes, and ovaries are removed. Spaying prevents the queen from coming into estrus and eliminates the problems of cystic ovaries, false pregnancies, uterine infection, irregular heat cycles, and confinement during the mating season. Spaying also reduces the frequency of breast tumors.

A queen does not need to have a litter of kittens to be psychologically fulfilled or to "settle down" behaviorally. The operation will not change her basic personality, except perhaps to make her less irritable at certain times of the year. Nor will it affect her hunting instincts. You have less chance of heat-related urine marking and none of the wild behaviors associated with heat cycles. A spayed female makes an outstanding pet. She is able to devote herself exclusively to her human family.

By spaying a cat before her first heat, you reduce the chances of her developing mammary tumors by 90 percent. You also eliminate the chance of her developing uterine cancers and infections.

Spaying does not make a cat fat and lazy. There is some evidence that spaying slows the metabolism of female cats, but obesity is caused by lack of exercise and feeding a cat more than she needs. By coincidence, a queen is usually spayed as she enters adulthood, at which time she requires less food. If she continues to eat high-calorie kitten food and puts on weight, the tendency is to blame the surgery.

The best time to spay a female is at 5 to 7 months of age, before she goes into her first heat. The operation is easy to do at this time, and there is less chance of complications. Many veterinarians and animal shelters are now doing spays and neuters on kittens as young as 7 weeks of age in an effort to combat pet overpopulation. So far, the results show the cats may end up a bit taller as bone closure rates are delayed, but no health problems ensue. Studies have so far shown no long-term behavioral effects from early spay and neuter surgery.

Having made arrangements to have your female spayed, be sure to withhold all food starting the evening before surgery (pediatric patients should only be fasted for three to four hours before surgery). The operation is done under general anesthesia, and a full stomach may result in vomiting and aspiration during induction of anesthesia. Check with your veterinarian concerning other special instructions or precautions to be observed before and after the operation. And make sure your cat receives adequate pain medication after the surgery.

Artificial Stimulation of the Vagina

A queen can be brought out of heat by artificially stimulating her vagina. The reasons for this are discussed in *Hormonal Influences During the Estrus Cycle* (page 409). Ovulation lengthens the interval between heat cycles from 7 to 14 days to 30 to 40 days. This method is best used to postpone breeding for several weeks.

With an assistant holding the cat by the scruff of her neck, raise her tail and insert a smooth, blunt-ended plastic rod or cotton-tipped swab half an inch (13 mm) into her vagina and rotate it gently. The queen should exhibit all the signs of actual mating, including crying out and postcoital rolling-over behavior. If the queen does not exhibit these signs, the procedure may not have been effective and should be repeated. However, there is a risk of injury to the vagina with repeated manipulations to induce ovulation. It may be best to enlist the help of your veterinarian.

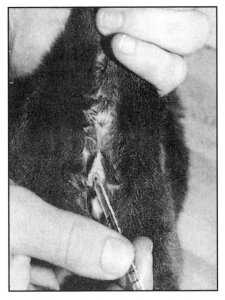

After successful artificial stimulation of the vagina, the queen will go out of heat in three to four days. She should not be allowed outdoors while still in heat. If she should mate a tom, pregnancy will almost certainly result. Many queens will go back into heat in about 44 days, when the ovaries stop manufacturing progesterone.

Artificial stimulation of the vagina is one way of bringing the queen out of heat.

Birth Control Drugs

Megestrol acetate (Ovaban), a long-acting progesterone, is effective in inhibiting the estrous cycle and in preventing estrus when given daily. It is not approved in the United States for use in cats. It should be prescribed under veterinary supervision. Adverse side effects can be very serious, and commonly include pyometra, mammary gland hypertrophy, breast tumors, diabetes mellitus, and suppression of adrenal gland activity.

Mibolerone (cheque drops) should *not* be used in cats due to the possibility of severe or fatal liver disease.

Delmadinone acetate (DMA), currently not available in the United States, shows promise as a safe and effective drug for estrous prevention. It can be given orally once a week or by subcutaneous injection every six months.

Chlorophyll tablets, which you can buy from your veterinarian or at pet supply stores, may help to mask the odor of a female in heat but are not effective for birth control.

Work is currently under way to test a contraceptive vaccine for use in cats. The goal is to block a cat's LH so that ovulation won't occur. In the study, cats resumed normal heat cycles about 500 days after vaccination. Long-term effects are not known, and this vaccine is still experimental.

Gonazon (azagly-nafarelin) has been approved for use in Europe in dogs. This is a reversible contraceptive that lasts for about a year and is given by injection or an implant. This product uses GNRH from salmonid fish, and may be used in cats in the future.

For the Male

The best way to avoid causing an unwanted pregnancy is to neuter your male cat. Two operations to sterilize the male are castration and vasectomy. However, *neutering* only the male is not an effective population control measure, because another male will always come along to fertilize a queen in heat.

Orchidectomy (Neutering)

Neutering is an operation in which both testicles are removed. The operation is not difficult or invasive, and the cat can often go home the same day.

Neutering does not change a male cat's personality, except to reduce or eliminate his desire to roam, his sexual impulses, and the aggressive behavior that accompanies them. His hunting instincts are not affected. He often becomes more affectionate and more oriented to the company of people. A neutered male is less likely to wander and become involved in cat fights. Spraying, with its accompanying unpleasant smell of cat urine, is often eliminated.

Most veterinarians believe that the best time to neuter a male is when he is 6 or 7 months old. At this time, he is mature enough that his growth and bone structure are not adversely affected, but sexual behavior, if present at all, has not yet become ingrained. If the male is castrated before 6 months of age, or more specifically, before the development of secondary sexual characteristics, his penis may remain small.

Many veterinarians and animal shelters are now doing spays and neuters on kittens as young as 7 weeks of age in an effort to combat pet overpopulation. So far, the primary differences seen with early neutering include slightly taller size

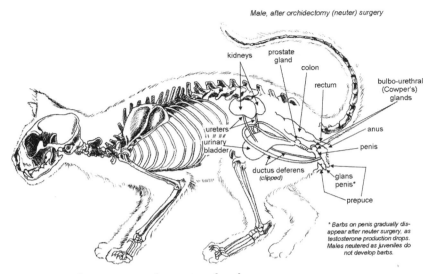

Male, after orchidectomy (neuter) surgery

kidneys
prostate gland
colon
rectum
bulbo-urethral (Cowper's) glands
ureters
urinary bladder
anus
penis
ductus deferens (clipped)
glans penis*
prepuce

* Barbs on penis gradually disappear after neuter surgery, as testosterone production drops. Males neutered as juveniles do not develop barbs.

The genitourinary system of a neutered male.

due to delayed bone growth plate closure and the inability to extrude the penis. At this time, there seems to be no increase in the incidence of urinary tract problems, and actual urethral diameter seems to be the same. Studies at this time have shown no long-term behavioral effects from early spay and neuter surgery. If an older male is neutered after he has mated queens, he may retain his sex drive. This is not common.

The precautions to take before surgery are the same as those described for spaying (see page 427).

Neutersol is a preparation of zinc gluconate that is injected directly into the testicle to sterilize pet dogs chemically rather than surgically. It has been used *off-label* in cats as well. This product is currently in limbo due to production problems. Neutersol will prevent sperm production but does not totally eliminate testosterone production, so undesirable behaviors may continue.

Vasectomy

Bilateral vasectomy is the treatment of choice when sterilization alone is desired. In this operation, a segment of the right and left vas deferens is removed. These tubes transport the sperm from the testicles to the urethra. A vasectomized tom is able and willing to mate with a queen but is unable to get her pregnant.

Vasectomy does not disturb the hormone function of the testes and does not influence the mating urge or territorial aggressiveness of toms. Nor does it reduce spraying.

Breeders who house a number of queens may keep a vasectomized tom. By mating with a queen, he takes her out of heat without the risk of pregnancy. The effects are similar to those described in *Artificial Stimulation of the Vagina* (page 427). Otherwise, there is no reason to keep a vasectomized male.

16

PREGNANCY AND KITTENING

Gestation is the period from conception to birth. From the first day of a successful mating, it averages 65 days. Kittens born from day 63 to day 69 fall within the normal range. Siamese cats may carry their kittens 71 days. However, if the kittens are born before day 60, they usually will be too immature to survive.

The uterus of a cat has two horns that are connected to the central uterine cavity. The cervix is the outlet to the vaginal birth canal. Developing kittens, encircled by their placentas, lie within the uterine horns.

Determining Pregnancy

At present, there is no early pregnancy detection test available for cats the way there is for people. During the first few weeks of gestation, few signs are detectable except for a slight gain in weight. Abdominal ultrasound done by an experienced evaluator may detect pregnancy as early as day 15. Fetal heartbeats, detectable at day 20, provide absolute indications of life.

The cat's uterus is Y-shaped with a horn on each side. The kittens grow and develop in the uterine horns. Twenty days after conception, the growing embryos can be felt by abdominal palpation as evenly spaced swellings about the size of unshelled peanuts. Palpating the queen's abdomen requires experience and gentleness, and should only be done by a veterinarian or an experienced breeder. There are also other structures in the abdomen that may feel lumpy. Excessive poking and prodding can damage the fetal-placental units and cause a miscarriage.

Cats occasionally suffer from morning sickness. This usually happens during the third to fourth week of pregnancy and is due to hormonal changes and the stretching and distention of the uterus. You may notice that your queen appears apathetic. She may be off her food and vomit from time to time. Morning sickness lasts only a few days. Unless you are particularly attentive, you may not even notice it. If your cat goes more than two days without eating or is not drinking, you should have her evaluated by your veterinarian.

The Witness Pregnancy Detection Kit, which was designed to detect the hormone relaxin in dogs, can also be used for cats to detect pregnancy after about 30 days.

By 35 days, the nipples become pink and obvious, and the size of belly is increasing. The fetuses are floating in capsules of fluid and can no longer be detected by palpation. As the time of birth approaches, the breasts enlarge and a milky fluid may be expressed from the nipples. However, many queens have breast enlargement after a normal heat, so this alone should not lead to a pregnancy diagnosis.

Ultrasounds are noted for being very accurate fairly early on in detecting pregnancy, but they are not as valuable as X-rays for determining the exact number of fetuses. Ultrasound can indicate viability, though, showing fetal heartbeats. An abdominal X-ray will show fetal bone structure past day 43. X-rays are also used as an alternative to ultrasonography when it is necessary to distinguish among pregnancy, false pregnancy, and pyometra. They should be avoided in early pregnancy.

By day 49, the kittens are sausage-shaped and their heads are large enough to be felt as separate structures. Late signs of pregnancy are an obvious

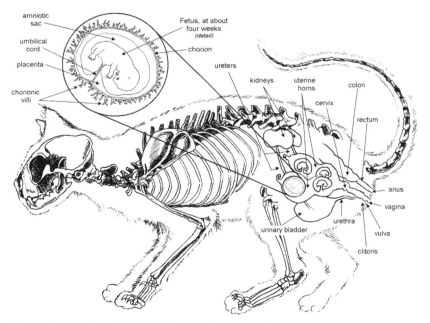

The anatomy of a cat who is four weeks pregnant.

pear-shaped abdomen and fetal movements, easily detectable during the last two weeks.

Care and Feeding During Pregnancy

A pregnant queen needs little special care. It is not usually necessary to restrict her activity, but she should definitely be kept indoors. Moderate exercise is beneficial, helping to prevent undue weight gain and poor muscle tone. Climbing can be dangerous in late pregnancy because the weight of the uterus alters the queen's center of gravity and affects her balance. If she is fond of climbing, jumping from high places, and roughhousing with children and other pets, you will need to prevent such activity.

During the first four weeks of pregnancy, feed the normal premium quality food. (See chapter 18 for more information on feline nutrition.) Avoid supplementing the diet with treats and table food, because the queen may not eat enough of her balanced diet to get all the nutrients she and her kittens need for a successful and healthy pregnancy. Vitamin and mineral supplements are not needed and may even be harmful. The only exception is the queen who may be below par from an earlier pregnancy or recovering from an acute illness. Discuss this with your veterinarian.

Protein requirements begin to increase during the second half of pregnancy. At this point, the cat should be gradually switched over to a premium kitten food, so that by delivery she is eating nothing but kitten food. While the queen must be well-nourished, obesity should be avoided at all costs. Overnourished queens are quite likely to carry fat kittens, which can complicate labor.

A queen may lose her appetite a week or two before kittening. Her abdomen is crowded and she may have difficulty eating a normal-size meal. Feed her several smaller meals spaced throughout the day.

PRENATAL CHECKUPS

Preparations to be done before breeding are described in *Pre-Breeding Checkup* (see page 404). The first prenatal visit should be scheduled two to three weeks after mating. Any further tests your veterinarian believes are necessary can be scheduled at this time. Your veterinarian will discuss any diet changes or supplements that might be indicated. Intestinal parasites, if present, should be treated by your veterinarian.

Vaccinations, most medications, and many deworming products are not recommended once pregnancy is established. This includes some of the flea and insecticide preparations, dewormers, and certain hormones and antibiotics. Tapeworm medications, in particular, can be quite toxic. Droncit is a tapeworm preparation safe for use in pregnant queens. Revolution is a flea control product approved for use in pregnant and lactating cats. Live virus vaccines (for example, feline panleukopenia and feline respiratory virus) should not be given to pregnant females. Check with your veterinarian before starting a pregnant queen on any drug, supplement, or medication.

One week before the expected kittening date, make an appointment to have the queen checked again. Your veterinarian will want to discuss with you the normal delivery procedures, alert you to signs of potential problems, and give you instructions for care of the newborns. Be sure to ask where you can get 24-hour emergency service, if needed.

Kittening Preparations

Queens should deliver at home, where they feel secure. They are easily upset by unfamiliar people and surroundings. This can delay or interrupt labor. The best place to deliver and care for newborn kittens is in a kittening box. It should be located in a warm, dry, out-of-the-way spot, preferably not in a bright area, and free from distracting noises.

A suitable box can be quickly made from a strong cardboard container. It should be large enough for the queen to move about. A rectangular box 24 inches (60 cm) long, 20 inches (50 cm) wide, and 20 inches high is ample. The box should have a removable lid, so you can clean it easily and open it to see the kittens. At one end, cut out a doorway about chest-high for the queen, so she can step in and out without jumping.

A sturdier box can be made of wood. This has the advantage that inside ledges (2 inches, 5 cm, high and 2 inches wide) can be nailed around all four sides. Kittens will instinctively crawl under these ledges, where they are protected from being rolled on by their mother. A wooden box should be coated with a nontoxic, washable preparation so that it is easy to clean and disinfect. A large plastic storage container is another possibility—just make sure one side is low enough for the queen to get in and out; you may have to cut down one side. Commercial kittening boxes are also available.

Lay several sheets of newspaper in the bottom of the box to absorb moisture. Newsprint without ink is best; you can ask at the local newspaper for rolls of paper that have not been printed. This also gives the queen something to dig and scratch, which she will do instinctively as she is making her nest. Do not use loose bedding such as straw or wood chips. These materials can be inhaled by the kittens and block their nostrils. Artificial fleece blankets may be suitable and are easy to keep clean. Tight-weave towels (not terry cloth) are also a good choice.

Cold, damp, dirty quarters are a leading cause of early kitten mortality. The kittening room should be draft-free and kept at a temperature of 85°F (29°C) for the first seven days following delivery. Thereafter, it should be kept at around 80°F (27°C) for the next three to four weeks. At that time, the temperature can gradually be lowered to about 70°F (21°C). Ideal humidity is 55 to 65 percent. Keep a constant check on the temperature by using a thermometer placed on the floor of the box. Additional heat can be supplied using 250-watt infrared heat bulbs, either suspended above the floor of the open-topped box or mounted in photographer's floodlight reflectors. Leave an area of the nest that is out of the direct source of heat so the mother can rest in a cooler area and the kittens can crawl away if they get overheated.

If the kittens are too warm they will spread out across the box. Also, kittens go toward the warmest area to nurse, so do not have the heat set up in such a way that it draws the kittens away from the mother.

Here is a list of other kittening supplies you should have available in case they are needed:

- Small separate box in which to place newborn kittens as the queen is giving birth
- Warm water bottle, heat lamp, or another way to keep kittens warm while in the small box
- Sterile surgical gloves
- Eyedropper or small syringe to aspirate mouth and nose secretions
- Dental floss or cotton thread to tie off the umbilical cords
- Scissors
- Artery forceps or hemostat to clamp a bleeding cord
- Antiseptic to apply to the umbilical stumps
- Clean towels
- Plenty of fresh newspapers, ideally without newsprint
- Postage scale to weigh the kittens daily

Signs of Imminent Delivery

One week before a queen is due to give birth, she begins to spend a lot more time grooming, paying special attention to her abdomen and genital areas. If you have a longhaired cat, it can be a good idea to carefully clip away the hair around the nipples to make it easier for the kittens to nurse. Be very careful not to damage a nipple and do not trim right down to the skin. Some hair around the nipples will protect against scratches when the kittens nurse.

The queen may be restless or irritable and begin to search for a place to have her kittens. Queens often rummage in closets, rearrange clothes in an open drawer, scratch up the owners' bed, and go about in a flurry of activity that is the ritual of making their nests.

Now is a good time to introduce your queen to the kittening box and encourage her to sleep in it. A queen who has had kittens will usually take to it without difficulty. But if the queen decides to have her kittens in some other spot, move the entire family to the kittening box as soon as she finishes delivering. Alternatively, move the box to the area she prefers.

Kittening

After day 61 of gestation, it is a good idea to take the queen's rectal temperature each morning. Twelve to 24 hours before she is due to deliver, the rectal temperature may drop from a normal of 101.5°F (38.6°C) to 99.5°F (37.5°C) or below. This 2°F drop may not occur, and if it does, it can be easily missed. Therefore, do not assume that if her temperature is normal, she won't be delivering soon. Some cats will pass a mucous-type "plug" right before delivery.

LABOR AND DELIVERY

There are three stages of labor. In the first stage the cervix dilates, opening the birth canal. In the second stage, the kittens are delivered. In the third stage, the placenta is delivered. The entire birthing process is seldom difficult and usually proceeds without human intervention.

The first stage, which may last 12 hours or more, begins with panting and rhythmic purring, which increases as the moment of birth approaches. Some cats will pace and perhaps even vomit. The queen becomes noticeably more

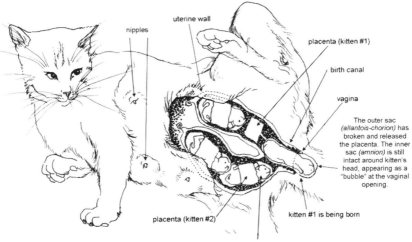

The birth of kittens.

active, digs at the floor, turns her head as if to snap at her rear, strains as if to pass stool, and may cry out. As her uterus contracts, she tightens her abdominal muscles and concentrates on bearing down.

At this point a novice queen may become extremely anxious, seek out her owner, and cry pitifully. Take her back to her kittening box and sit beside her. Speak soothingly and continue to comfort and pet her. Many queens, however, do not need or want the presence of their owner and may hiss and spit if disturbed.

The second stage begins with the onset of true labor, when one uterine horn contracts and pushes the presenting part of the kitten down into the central cavity. Generally, the delivery sequence alternates between the uterine horns, but not always. Pressure against the cervix causes it to dilate. At complete dilatation, the kitten slides into the vagina. The water bag around the kitten may rupture before the kitten is born. If so, yellow or straw-colored fluid is passed. A kitten should then be delivered within 30 minutes.

Most kittens are born in the "diving" position with feet and nose first. After the head is delivered, the rest of the kitten slides out easily. The mother instinctively licks and removes the fetal membranes with her rough tongue and severs the umbilical cord. The mother now vigorously licks the kitten's face to clear the nose and mouth. As the kitten gasps, the lungs inflate and breathing begins.

No attempt should be made to interfere with this normal maternal activity that is an important part of the mother-kitten bond. This is her kitten and she must learn to take care of it. If she appears rough, it is only because she is trying to stimulate breathing and blood circulation. However, if the queen is occupied with another kitten and fails to remove the amniotic sac, you should step in and strip away the fetal membranes so the kitten can breathe (see *Helping a Kitten to Breathe*, page 443).

The third stage, shortly after the birth of each kitten, is when the placenta is expelled. The queen may consume some or all of the placenta. This is an instinctive behavior and may stem from the days when it was important to remove the evidence of birthing to avoid attracting predators. However, it is not essential that she do so. Many veterinarians recommend letting the queen only consume one placenta; ingesting several can produce diarrhea. You may wish to remove some or all of the placentas from the nest. Count them, and make sure you have as many as you have kittens, since a retained placenta can cause a serious postnatal infection (see *Acute Postpartum Metritis*, page 445).

If the cord is severed too cleanly or too close to the kitten's navel, it may continue to bleed. Be prepared to clamp or pinch off the cord and tie a thread around the stump. The stump should be disinfected with iodine or some other suitable antiseptic.

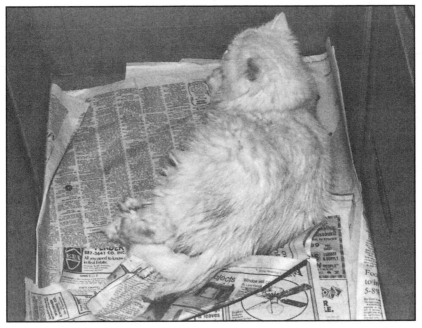

The queen is in her kittening box, beginning to strain.

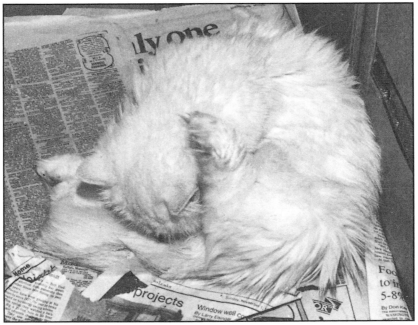

The queen is getting ready to deliver a kitten.

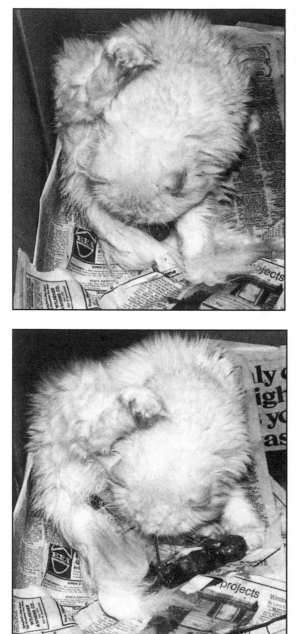

The water bag around the kitten can be seen bulging through the vulva at the bottom of the photo.

The mother licks and removes the fetal membranes and severs the umbilical cord.

As soon as some or all of her kittens are born, the mother will curl up on her side and draw the kittens to her nipples with her paws. Their sucking action stimulates uterine contractions by causing the release of oxytocin. It also helps bring on the colostrum, or first milk of the queen, which contains the all-important maternal antibodies.

Most kittens are born 15 to 30 minutes apart, but this can vary quite a bit. Although most deliveries are complete in two to six hours, it occasionally happens that a queen goes out of labor, appears at ease and cares for her kittens, then goes back into labor 12 to 24 hours later and delivers the rest of the litter. It is important to be aware that this can happen. Abnormal causes of arrested labor are discussed below.

ASSISTING THE NORMAL DELIVERY

When labor is going well, it is best not to interfere. But, on occasion, a large kitten may get stuck at the vaginal opening. The head or presenting part appears during a forceful contraction and then slips back when the queen relaxes. This situation can usually be corrected by lubricating the birth canal liberally with K-Y Jelly. If the queen does not deliver the kitten within 15 minutes, proceed as follows:

1. As the presenting part appears at the vaginal opening, place your thumb and index finger on each side of the perineum just below the anus and push down gently to keep the kitten from slipping back into the mother.
2. Next, grip the kitten in the birth canal and slide the lips of the vulva over the kitten's head. Once this is done, the lips will hold the kitten in place, giving you a chance to get another grip.
3. Now grip the skin of the kitten with a clean piece of cloth behind the neck or along the back and draw the kitten out. Apply forceful traction only to the skin, not to the legs or head. It may be helpful to gently rotate the kitten first one way and then the other, especially when something seems stuck, because the birth canal is usually wider in one direction.

If these measures are not successful, proceed as described under *Feline Obstetrics* (page 442).

Dystocia (Difficult Labor)

Queens can voluntarily prolong, delay, and even interrupt the normal birthing process for up to 24 hours. Domestic cats apparently retain this wild cat attribute—the ability to quickly move a nest if danger threatens during the birthing. Accordingly, excessive disturbances, interruptions, the arrival and departure of unfamiliar people, other pets, and any perceived threats can easily induce voluntary cessation of labor.

Nonbehavioral causes of prolonged and difficult labor include mechanical blockage—that is, the diameter of the kitten is too wide in relation to the birth canal diameter—and uterine inertia, in which the uterus becomes too

Persians, with their large round heads, are more likely to have difficulty delivering kittens.

exhausted to contract. These two are often related: fatigue follows unrelieved blockage.

Dystocia is rarely a problem in a healthy, well-conditioned queen. It is more likely to occur with small litters in which individual kittens are relatively large, with older queens, and with queens who are allowed to become too fat. It can be more common in breeds with large heads and flattened faces, such as Persians. When present, it usually involves the first kitten or the last.

MECHANICAL BLOCKAGE

The two common causes of mechanical blockage are an oversized kitten and a malpositioned kitten in the birth canal. Most kittens come down the birth canal nose and feet first (the diving position) with their backs along the top of the vagina. When a kitten comes down backward, the hind feet or tail and rump show first. The hind foot (posterior) presentation occurs about 20 percent of the time, and it seldom causes a problem. However, when the tail or rump presents first (breech position), this can cause a problem—particularly if it occurs with the first kitten. One other presentation that can complicate labor is a head bent forward or to the side (deviated head).

A queen with a history of a fractured pelvis is likely to have problems. X-rays before pregnancy may disclose a narrowed pelvis. A queen who has suffered a pelvic fracture should not be bred. If a cat with this condition accidentally does get bred, be prepared for a cesarean section.

UTERINE INERTIA

Uterine inertia is an important cause of ineffective labor. As the uterine muscle fatigues, the uterus becomes incapable of producing forceful and effective contractions. Mechanical factors that can lead to uterine fatigue include a single large kitten in a small uterus, a very large litter, twisting (torsion) of the uterus, and hydrops amnion, a condition in which there is an excess of amniotic fluid.

Some primary inertia is caused by a deficiency of oxytocin (produced by the pituitary gland) or calcium, or both. The uterus may respond to injections of oxytocin and calcium gluconate, which stimulate stronger contractions. However, if there is a mechanical blockage, giving oxytocin can lead to rupture of the uterus. The decision to use oxytocin and/or calcium should only be made by a veterinarian.

If labor is prolonged and a kitten cannot be seen or felt in the birth canal, it is best to X-ray the queen to determine the kittens' positions and relative sizes.

WHEN TO CALL THE VETERINARIAN

It is better to call your veterinarian on a "false alarm," if only to gain reassurance, than to delay in the hope that the problem will be corrected without help. Often the situation can be dealt with rather simply if it is attended to at once. However, the same problem, when neglected, becomes complicated—often leading to emergency procedures and possibly dead kittens and even a dead queen.

Call the veterinarian if you see any of these signs:

- 60 minutes of intense straining without the birth of a kitten
- 10 minutes of intense labor with a kitten visible in the birth canal
- 10 minutes of fresh bleeding during or after kittening
- Sudden apathy and weakness, with a rectal temperature above 104°F (40°C) or below 97°F (36°C), suggesting infection in the queen
- Labor stops and there are signs of restlessness, anxiety, weakness, or fatigue. Kittens come approximately 15 minutes to two hours apart; more than three hours between kittens is a sign of trouble. This need not apply, however, if the queen is resting happily and nursing kittens without signs of distress.

The passage of yellow fluid means rupture of the water bag (amniotic sac) surrounding the kitten. When this happens, the kitten should be born within 30 minutes. A dark green vaginal discharge indicates that the placenta is separating from the wall of the uterus. When this happens, the first kitten should be born within a few minutes. After the first kitten, however, passage of dark green fluid is not a concern, even if it is not followed by the birth of a kitten.

Feline Obstetrics

If it is impossible to get prompt veterinary help and labor cannot proceed because of an abnormal presentation, the following should be attempted, assuming you have fairly small hands and fingers. It is possible to badly damage the queen and/or kill the kittens if you are not careful, which is why veterinary help at an emergency clinic is best. Have help to gently restrain the queen so you are not bitten or scratched.

1. Clean the outside of the queen's vulva with soap and water. Put on a pair of sterile Latex gloves and lubricate your finger with Betadine solution, K-Y Jelly, or Vaseline. Before inserting your finger into the vagina, be careful not to contaminate your gloves with stool from the anus.

2. Place one hand under the queen's abdomen in front of the pelvis and feel for the kitten. Raise the kitten into a position aligned with the birth canal. With your other hand, slip a finger into the vagina and feel for a kitten's head, tail, or leg. If the head is turned and will not pass through the outlet of the pelvis, insert a finger into the kitten's mouth and gently turn the head, guiding it into the birth canal. Now apply pressure on the perineum just below the anus (a maneuver called feathering). This induces the queen to strain and holds the kitten in the correct position so his head won't slip back into the original position.

3. When the kitten is coming as a breech (rump first), hold the kitten at the pelvic outlet as described just above. With the finger that is in the vagina, hook first one leg and then the other, slipping them down over the narrow place until the pelvis and legs appear at the vulva.

4. If the mother is unable to deliver a large kitten coming normally, the problem is caused by a shoulder locking in the birth canal. You will see the head protruding through the vulva. Insert a gloved finger into the vagina alongside the kitten until you can feel the front legs at the elbow. Rotate the kitten first one way and then another so the legs can be brought forward. Hook them and pull them through individually.

5. Once a kitten is in the lower part of the birth canal, he should be delivered without delay. To stimulate a forceful push by the mother, gently stretch the vaginal opening. If you can see the kitten at the mouth of the vagina appearing and disappearing with straining, grip the kitten with a clean piece of cloth and pull out as described under *Assisting the Normal Delivery* (page 439). Time is of the essence—particularly when the kitten is breech. It is better to take hold and pull out the kitten, even at the risk of injury or death, since this kitten and perhaps all the others will die if something is not done.

6. Occasionally, the blockage is caused by a retained placenta. Hook it with your fingers and grasp it with a clean piece of cloth. Maintain slow and steady traction until it passes out of the vagina.

When the uterus becomes exhausted and stops contracting, it is difficult to correct an arrested labor. A cesarean section may be indicated. It is better to err and do a cesarean section early than wait too long and deliver dead kittens.

HELPING A KITTEN TO BREATHE

The amniotic sac that surrounds each newborn kitten should be removed within 30 seconds to allow the kitten to breathe. If the queen fails to do this, you should tear open the sac and remove it, starting at the mouth and working backward over the body. Aspirate the secretions from the mouth and nose with an eyedropper or a small syringe. Rub the kitten briskly with a soft towel.

Another method of clearing the secretions is to hold the kitten in your hands while supporting the head. Then swing the kitten gently in a downward arc. This helps to expel water from the nostrils. Present the kitten to the mother to lick, clean, and cuddle.

After a difficult delivery, kittens may be too weak or too flaccid to breathe on their own. Squeeze the kitten's chest gently from side to side and then from front to back. If the kitten still will not breathe, place your mouth over the nose and blow gently until you see the chest expand. *Do not blow forcefully* because this can rupture the lungs. Leaving the kitten's mouth uncovered helps to prevent this complication. Be sure to remove your mouth to allow the kitten to exhale. Repeat this several times until the kitten breathes easily. (Also see *CPR*, page 12.)

Cesarean Section

Cesarean section is the procedure of choice for any type of birthing problem that cannot be relieved by drugs or obstetrical manipulation. *The decision rests with the veterinarian.* Consideration is given to the condition of the queen, the length of labor, results of X-rays, the size of the kittens in relation to the pelvic outlet, failure of the queen to respond to oxytocin, and a dry vaginal canal.

The operation is done under general anesthesia in the veterinary hospital. The risk to a young, healthy queen is not great. However, when labor has been unduly prolonged, toxicity is present, the kittens are dead and beginning to decompose, or the uterus has ruptured, the risks are significant.

Usually a queen is awake, stable, and able to nurse her kittens within three hours of the surgery. A queen who has a cesarean section may or may not require a cesarean section with her next litter. This depends on the reasons for the first surgery.

Postpartum Care of the Queen

Twelve to 24 hours after the queen delivers, ask your veterinarian to do a postpartum checkup. Palpation of the uterus rules out a retained kitten or placenta. Many veterinarians prescribe an injection of oxytocin to aid emptying of the uterus. This reduces the likelihood of postpartum infection.

The veterinarian will want to check the color, consistency, and quality of the queen's milk. Milk that is thick, stringy, yellowish, or discolored may be infected. Take the mother's temperature at least once a day for the first week. A temperature of 103°F (39.4°C) or higher indicates a problem (retained placenta, or uterine or breast infection).

Some reddish-tinged or dark greenish discharge is normal for the first seven to ten days and may persist for up to three weeks. A foul-smelling, brownish, *purulent* discharge is abnormal and suggests a retained placenta or a uterine infection (see *Acute Postpartum Metritis,* page 445). An infected cat is often depressed, runs a fever, and may appear pale due to anemia. Be sure to consult your veterinarian if the vaginal discharge becomes purulent, contains blood, or persists for more than three weeks.

A nursing queen should be kept indoors. Also remember that during this period she could go into heat. If mated, she may conceive another litter. Breeding should not be allowed at this time, as it is too difficult, physically, for the queen.

FEEDING DURING LACTATION

Depending on the size of the litter, a lactating queen needs two to three times more calories than she did before pregnancy. If she does not get these needed calories, she will not be able to produce enough milk to nourish her kittens.

Feed the queen a high-quality food designed for the growth of kittens. Diets or foods formulated for growth contain all the essential nutrients required to support lactation. The daily caloric requirements of nursing queens and recommended amounts to feed are shown in chapter 18, page 492. This chapter should be consulted for general information on making informed choices about cat foods.

A nursing queen should be given all the food she can eat. There is no possibility for weight gain in a queen nursing four or more kittens. Dry food can be fed free choice. Canned food should be offered three or four times a day. The greatest nutrient drain will come at two to four weeks postpartum. By the second or third week, a nursing queen should be eating three times her normal daily maintenance diet, or the equivalent of three full meals a day.

If you are feeding a high-quality kitten growth food, vitamin and mineral supplements will not be necessary and could even be dangerous. They should be avoided unless the queen refuses to eat the kitten food or has a preexisting nutritional deficiency or a chronic illness. In these circumstances, consult with your veterinarian.

Postpartum Problems
POSTPARTUM HEMORRHAGE

Vaginal bleeding after an easy delivery is not common and is usually caused by a vaginal tear associated with a mechanical blockage and difficult labor. A retained kitten or placenta is another possibility. Occasionally, the uterus does not return to normal condition. Most of these problems will be evident on a postpartum veterinary examination.

Excessive loss of blood may produce shock and death. If you see bright fresh or clotted blood that persists for 10 minutes or longer, notify your veterinarian at once. Fresh bleeding should not be confused with the normal passage of a variable amount of reddish to dark greenish vaginal discharge that persists for several days (up to three weeks) following delivery. If you are unsure, always contact your veterinarian.

You can also check the color of your cat's gums by pressing on them and noting how fast the color returns (this is called *capillary refill time*). Normally, it should be under two seconds. Any longer suggests anemia due to loss of blood.

Treatment: Depending on the exact cause, surgery or medical management may be required.

ACUTE POSTPARTUM METRITIS

Acute metritis is a bacterial infection of the lining of the uterus that spreads upward through the birth canal during the birthing process or immediately thereafter. Unsanitary kittening quarters can cause it. Placentas provide an ideal medium for bacterial growth. Immediately after each delivery, change the bedding of the kittening box and remove all remaining products of delivery.

Acute metritis is likely to occur when part of a placenta has been retained in the uterus. Always count the placentas during delivery to be sure you have one placenta for each kitten. Some cases are caused by a retained fetus that has become mummified. Other cases are caused by contamination of the birth canal by unsterile fingers during a difficult or prolonged labor. Vaginitis (see page 422) is a less common cause. Vaginitis should be treated as soon as it is diagnosed, preferably before heat and certainly before labor and delivery.

A queen with acute metritis is lethargic, hangs her head, refuses to eat, and has a rectal temperature of 103°F to 105°F (39.4°C to 40.5°C). She may not keep the nest clean or care for her kittens. The kittens appear unkempt, cry excessively, and may die suddenly. This could be the first indication that the queen is ill.

There is a heavy, dark, bloody, greenish, or tomato-souplike discharge that appears two to seven days after delivery. It should not be confused with the normal greenish discharge present for the first 12 to 24 hours after delivery or the light reddish, serosanguineous discharge that can last up to three weeks but decreases in volume with time. A normal discharge is not accompanied by high fever, excessive thirst, or other signs of toxicity, such as vomiting and diarrhea.

Most cases of acute metritis can be anticipated and prevented by a postpartum checkup. The veterinarian often will want to clear the uterus with an injection of oxytocin. Preventive antibiotics are indicated if labor was difficult and the birth canal was contaminated during delivery.

Acute endometritis and pyometra are other uterine infections that may be confused with acute postpartum metritis. They are discussed in *Diseases of the Female Genital Tract* (page 422).

Treatment: Acute metritis is a life-threatening illness. A veterinarian should be consulted immediately to save the queen's life. The kittens will usually be taken off the mother and raised by hand if the queen is extremely ill, or put on a lactating foster mother (see *Raising Kittens by Hand*, page 460). If the queen is toxic, her milk may also be toxic and should be checked.

MASTITIS

The cat normally has four pairs of mammary glands, or eight individual breasts. The mammary glands should be checked daily on a nursing queen. Look for redness, hardness, and unusual discharges. Fluid expressed from the breast will look like ordinary milk.

Galactosis (Caked Breasts)

An accumulation of milk in the mammary glands is normal during late pregnancy and lactation. However, milk accumulation may increase to the point that the breasts become painful and warm. There is no infection and the queen does not appear ill. However, if the queen is uncomfortable and is licking at her breasts, treatment may be necessary.

Treatment: Apply warm, moist packs twice a day and express the gland to draw out some of the coagulated and caked milk. Your veterinarian may prescribe a diuretic to relieve swelling and have you reduce the queen's food intake. If the queen has no kittens, the breasts are dried up as described under *Weaning* (page 478).

Severely or persistently caked breasts may become infected, leading to an acute mastitis. This can be treated by administering an antibiotic such as amoxicillin. However, consult your veterinarian before administering any antibiotic, especially if the kittens are still nursing.

Acute Septic Mastitis

Acute mastitis is an infection of one or more of the mammary glands caused by bacteria that get into the nursing breast, often from a scratch or a puncture wound. It can occur from 24 hours to six weeks postpartum. Some cases are blood-borne and are associated with acute metritis (see page 445). The milk from an infected breast is toxic and often contains bacteria that can cause kitten septicemia and sudden death. In all such cases, be sure to check the vagina for a purulent discharge and each breast for signs of infection.

Mothers with acute mastitis refuse to eat, appear listless, and run a high fever (which suggests that an abscess has formed). They may neglect their kittens.

A mammary gland with acute mastitis is swollen, extremely painful, and usually reddish-blue. Milk may be blood tinged, thick, yellow, or stringlike. In some cases the milk will look normal, but an acidity test will reveal an abnormality. Litmus paper may be used to test the acidity of the milk. Normal feline breast milk should have a pH of 6.0 to 6.5. If the pH is 7.0, suspect acute septic mastitis.

Some cases of acute mastitis can be prevented by trimming the nails of kittens when they are two to three weeks old. Although some longhaired queens may need to be trimmed around the nipples to provide easier access for kittens to nurse, the hair around the queen's nipples is protective and should not be clipped to the skin unless it is matted.

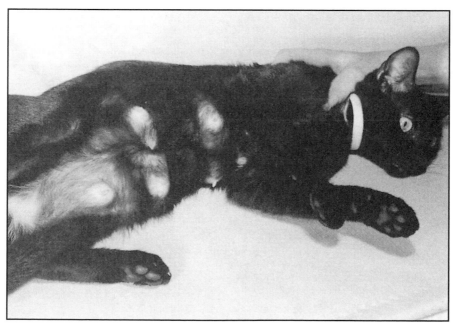

Breast caking is caused by an excessive buildup of thick, coagulated milk.

Treatment: *Remove all kittens immediately if you suspect mastitis and contact your veterinarian.* This disease must be treated by a professional. Routine measures include bacterial culture of the infected milk and prescribing appropriate antibiotics selected on the basis of sensitivity tests. Gently massage the glands three or four times a day and apply moist warm packs.

When only one breast is involved, it may be possible to tape the nipple of the infected gland and allow the kittens to nurse at the others. If more than one gland is involved or if the queen is toxic, the kittens should be raised by hand or placed with a foster mother, as described in *Raising Kittens by Hand*, page 460. If the kittens are three weeks old, they can be weaned. The procedure for drying up the breasts is explained in *Weaning* (see page 478).

When milk from an infected breast returns to normal appearance and tests to a pH of less than 7.0, the kittens may be able to nurse at that breast again.

AGALACTIA (INADEQUATE MILK SUPPLY)

The suckling action of the newborn kittens is an important stimulus to let down the queen's milk, because it releases oxytocin. When kittens do not suckle for 24 hours, the milk supply begins to dry up.

Experienced queens will encourage their kittens to suckle soon after delivery. A nervous, upset, insecure, or frightened queen may not exhibit this normal maternal behavior. Speak to her in a calm, soothing voice. Lay the queen on her side and put the kittens to her nipples. Continue this process until she learns to accept them.

A deformed nipple may cause difficulty in suckling. Examine all nipples to be sure they are open, fully formed, and erect. A recessed nipple can be improved by massaging it to stimulate the flow of milk and then putting a vigorous suckler directly on that nipple.

Occasionally, it becomes apparent that a queen is not producing enough milk to satisfy all her kittens. This is most likely to occur with novice queens and those with large litters. Rarely, it will occur after a cesarean section. It is most important that a nursing mother receive adequate nutritional support. The most common cause of inadequate milk production is failure to supply enough daily calories to the queen, especially after the second week, when nursing demands are greatest. This cause is correctable (see *Feeding During Lactation*, page 444). When the litter is large or the mother is constitutionally unable to produce enough milk, supplemental feedings using kitten milk replacer may be required (see *Raising Kittens by Hand*, page 460).

ECLAMPSIA (MILK FEVER)

Eclampsia is a muscular spasm associated with a low serum calcium level. It is sometimes called milk fever because it usually occurs several days to several weeks postpartum, when there is a steady drain on the body's calcium stores because of nursing. Even more rarely, it may show up in late pregnancy. It is more likely to occur in queens with large litters. It is much less common in cats than it is in dogs.

The first signs of eclampsia are restlessness, anxiety, rapid breathing, and pale mucous membranes. A queen frequently leaves her kittens and begins to pace up and down. Her gait is stiff-legged, uncoordinated, and jerky. Tightening of the face muscles exposes the teeth and gives the face a pinched look. As the condition worsens, she falls on her side and has spasms and seizurelike activity in which she kicks all four legs and salivates profusely. Her heart rate increases.

Her temperature is often elevated to as high as 106°F (41°C). This causes more panting, raises the pH of the blood, and lowers the serum calcium even further. *If there is no treatment within 12 hours, the queen will die.*

Treatment: Milk fever is an emergency. Notify your veterinarian at once. Intravenous calcium gluconate is a specific antidote indicated at the first signs of eclampsia. Your veterinarian will need to carefully monitor the cat's heart rate and rhythm while the calcium is being injected.

If the rectal temperature is over 104°F (40°C), treat as you would for heatstroke (see page 24).

Take the kittens off the queen for 24 hours and feed them by hand with kitten milk replacer. If they are at least three weeks of age, they can be weaned. Younger kittens may be returned to the queen when she has recovered completely, if you limit nursing to no more than 30 minutes at a time, two or three times a day, and if the queen is now on an appropriate supplement. If there are no adverse effects, these restrictions can be gradually relaxed over the next 48 hours until a normal routine is established. Mothers who must continue nursing should be supplemented with calcium, phosphorus, and vitamin D. Consult your veterinarian for the correct dosages.

Certain queens seem to be predisposed to milk fever. If your queen has had milk fever in the past, ask your veterinarian about supplementing her diet with calcium after she has delivered the kittens, or consider spaying her.

MOTHERS WHO NEGLECT OR INJURE THEIR KITTENS

The mother-kitten bond begins during and shortly after birth. The mother recognizes each kitten by a distinctive odor. During the process of licking, cleaning, and nursing the kitten, she establishes a relationship that will sustain that kitten in her care throughout the first few weeks of life. This bond may be less secure initially when kittens are born by cesarean section, although it is stronger when at least some of the kittens are born before the surgery or when the kittens are put to her nipples before she wakes from the anesthesia.

A novice mother may have difficulty coping with a litter of squirming kittens for the first few hours. With a little help, she can be shown how to nurse her kittens and to keep from stepping on them. Exceedingly dependent cats who are very people-oriented may neglect or abandon their kittens to be with their owners.

Stress caused by excessive noise or too much handling of her kittens by children or unfamiliar people can adversely influence a queen's normal maternal behavior. It is important not to allow visitors for the first few weeks, especially if the queen is high-strung and not well socialized to people. This includes keeping other pets away.

Occasionally, a queen's milk does not come down for the first 24 hours. During this time she may reject her kittens. Milk flow can be helped by oxytocin. Once the milk comes in, the kittens are usually accepted.

Postpartum problems that can depress the queen and interfere with mothering behavior include eclampsia, mastitis, and uterine infection. Depending on the severity of the infection, the kittens may need to be removed from the queen and raised by hand.

A fading kitten whose body temperature has dropped below normal due to sickness or constitutional weakness may be pushed out of the nest. The mother may also reject a kitten with a severe deformity, including cleft palate. This is nature's way of culling.

A queen often attempts to relocate her nest when the kittens are about four days old. This behavior may stem from a natural instinct, when it was necessary to move from a soiled nest to one less likely to attract predators. If the nest she chooses is not a satisfactory substitute for the kittening box, you should return the entire family to the kittening box and stay with the queen, talking softly and stroking her often until she settles in comfortably. Do not allow her to become agitated or frightened while carrying kittens, because she could accidentally injure them by biting too hard. Nest seeking can be prevented by introducing the queen to her kittening box two weeks before delivery and encouraging her to sleep there.

Cannibalism is a form of abnormal maternal behavior in which the queen consumes her young, particularly the firstborn. It does sometimes occur in cats, primarily in catteries.

Queens routinely consume stillborn kittens along with the products of delivery. While consuming a placenta, a queen could accidentally consume a kitten. A queen might damage the kitten while attempting to sever an umbilical cord, especially if the kitten has a large umbilical hernia. In some cases, cannibalism may involve the intentional destruction of a constitutionally inferior or malformed kitten. Other cases of maternal aggression may be activated by fear, anxiety, anger, overcrowding, or a perceived threat to the queen's survival.

Treatment: Provide a quiet kittening location away from all distractions, where the queen will feel least threatened and most secure. Be sure to distinguish real aggression from the natural culling a mother will do of a dead or seriously ill kitten.

If the cannibalism occurs with the firstborn kitten, remove the kittens as each is born, placing all of them in a warm accessory kitten box. Leave them in the accessory box until the queen has completed the birthing process. If the queen continues to exhibit aggression and you cannot persuade her to accept the kittens, they may need to be raised by hand or placed with another queen (see *Raising Kittens by Hand,* page 460). If possible, ensure that the kittens nurse for the first 24 hours to receive the all-important colostrum.

Maternal behavior is at least partly heritable. Queens who are not nurturing toward their kittens or show outright aggression should not be bred again, and their offspring should be spayed or neutered.

Cloning

Cloning of companion animals has appeared dramatically in the news but is not practical for many reasons. The cost is currently about $32,000. Cells are taken from the adult donor cat and put into an egg from another donor after the nucleus is removed from that egg cell. The resulting embryo is then implanted into the uterus of a donor mother.

Much was made of the fact that the first cloned cat did not turn out to be a calico like her mother. This is due to the fact that a female kitten will only have one effective X chromosome, but the calico coloring requires multiple genetic interactions. This same process is involved in health, which may explain why some cloned animals age rapidly, and also in imprinted genes, which might explain the overdevelopment of some clones.

Health concerns aside, a cloned animal will not be identical to the original cat no matter what, since the environment and outside influences always play a part in every animal's development. The company most actively involved in cloning is currently in financial difficulties. Some research facilities may continue with the work.

17

PEDIATRICS

During the neonatal period from birth to 4 weeks of age, a healthy kitten is the picture of contentment, sleeping much of the time and awakening only to eat. Kittens even shift directly from being awake to REM sleep (the rapid-eye movement sleep that is associated with dreaming). Newborns spend long hours nursing—often eight hours a day—with sessions lasting up to 45 minutes. Most neonatal kittens quickly develop a preference for nursing at a particular breast, which they locate by smell. Breasts not suckled will stop producing milk in three days.

A good mother instinctively keeps her nest and her kittens clean. By licking the belly and rectum of each kitten, she stimulates the elimination reflex. The suckling reflex kicks in fully at 1 to 2 days of age and starts to fade at about 20 days of age.

Kittens are born with their eyes closed. The eyes begin to open at 8 days and are completely open by 14 days. The eyes of shorthaired cats open sooner than those of longhairs. All kittens are born with blue eyes. Adult colors do not appear before 3 weeks and may take 9 to 12 weeks to reach the eye color required by the breed standard. Although kittens can see once their eyes open, the retina is not fully mature until they are about 5 weeks of age.

The ear canals, which are closed at birth, begin to open at 5 to 8 days. They are normally fully open by 14 days of age. The tiny, folded-down ears become erect by 3 weeks.

The sex of kittens can be determined shortly after birth, although it may be easier to do this when they are older (see *Sexing a Kitten*, page 454).

Kittens are born without any teeth. The baby teeth start to erupt from the gums at about 2 weeks of age, with a full set of deciduous (baby) teeth present by 8 weeks of age. It is important to check the queen's mammary area from about 11 days on for injury from sharp baby teeth.

Soon after, they begin to walk and can eat from a bowl. Kittens can orient themselves to sights and sounds at 25 days. They usually begin to crawl by 18 days and can stand at 21 days and exhibit a fairly normal gait. Kittens should have a good surface to walk on with adequate traction. At about 4 weeks of

The eyes begin to open at 8 days.

age, kittens are following each other and playing. By 5 weeks of age, they are perfecting the stalk and pounce of adult cats and will start grooming behaviors. By 3 months of age, the spinal cord and neurological reflexes are at adult levels of responsiveness.

They can eliminate on their own at 4 weeks (before that, their mother must stimulate urination and defecation by licking the anal region). At this time, they prefer to use a separate area for elimination, rather than soiling the nest. By 5 to 6 weeks of age, they can begin using a litter box and will have a lifelong preference for the litter substrate introduced at that time.

Kittens need to learn to identify with and relate to their mother and littermates. These species interactions are necessary in establishing the kitten's self-awareness as a cat. When these early social interactions do not take place, a kitten may exhibit aggression, shyness, an eating disorder, or some other behavior problem later in life. Hand-raised kittens and singletons may miss out on some of this socialization.

Most queens display anxiety when their very young kittens are constantly handled by unknown people or if unfamiliar pets or other household animals they are not comfortable with are allowed near the kittens. After 6 weeks, social interaction with unknown human beings and exposure to new and nonthreatening situations are important for proper development of a happy, well-adjusted pet. Crucial socialization takes place between 3 to 9 weeks of age and kittens need to be handled by humans by 7 weeks of age at the latest. Daily weighing can be a safe and easy way to offer early human exposure.

Kittens begin to crawl at 18 days. The folded-down ears become erect at 3 weeks.

Sexing a Kitten

The sex of kittens can be determined shortly after birth. Kittens' genitalia are more difficult to see than adults'. However, there should be no problem if you look carefully.

With the kitten facing away from, you lift the tail to expose the anal area. In both sexes, you will see two openings. The first opening just below the base of the tail is the anus.

In the female kitten, the vulva is a vertical slit seen immediately below the anus. In the adult female the space between the anus and vulva measures about half an inch (13 mm)—but it is closer than that in the kitten.

In the male, the opening for the penis is directed backward. The tip of the penis is hidden in a small, round opening located half an inch (13 mm) below the anus. These two openings are separated by the scrotal sacs, which appear as raised, darkish areas. The testicles may not be easily felt until the kitten is 6 weeks old. In the adult tom or neutered male, the anus and the opening for the penis are more than 1 inch (25 mm) apart.

Caring for Newborns

Newborn kittens are born with a limited capacity for adapting to environmental stress. With proper care and attention to the special needs of these infants, many neonatal deaths can be avoided. The two crucial factors to watch closely are the kitten's body temperature and weight. Also, the kitten's appearance, breathing rate, crying sounds, and general behavior can provide useful information about the animal's overall health and vitality.

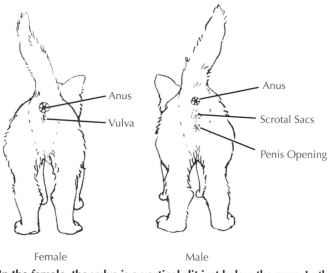

Female   Male

In the female, the vulva is a vertical slit just below the anus. In the male, the opening for the penis is found below the scrotal sacs.

GENERAL APPEARANCE AND VITALITY

Healthy kittens are round and firm. They nurse vigorously. Their mouths and tongues are wet. When you insert a finger into their mouths, they have a strong, vigorous suckle. When disturbed, they burrow down next to their mother or littermates for warmth.

For the first 48 hours, kittens sleep with their heads curled under their chests. While sleeping, they jerk, kick, and sometimes whimper. This is called activated sleep (REM sleep) and is normal. It is the newborn kitten's only way of exercising at this stage and helps to develop muscle tone. The umbilical cord dries up and should fall off two to three days after birth.

A newborn's skin is warm and pink. When pinched, it springs back resiliently. A kitten stretches and wiggles energetically in your hand when picked up. When removed from the mother, the kitten crawls back to her.

A sick kitten presents a dramatically different picture. These kittens are limp, cold, and hang like a dishcloth. Sick kittens show little interest in nursing and tire easily.

Healthy newborn kittens seldom cry. Crying indicates that a kitten is cold, hungry, sick, or in pain. As kittens become weaker and colder, the crying will fade out. Distressed kittens crawl about looking for help and fall asleep away from the life-sustaining warmth of their mother and littermates. Kittens may also crawl away from their littermates if the kittening box is too hot, but they are healthy in appearance otherwise.

Later, sickly kittens move slowly and with great effort. They sleep with their legs splayed apart and their necks bent to the side. Their mew is plaintive and may continue for 20 minutes or longer. Such a kitten is often rejected by the queen, who senses that the kitten is not going to survive and pushes him out of the nest rather than waste her energies caring for him. This situation can be reversed if the kitten is treated and his body temperature is brought back to normal (see *Warming a Chilled Kitten*, below)—unless the kitten truly has congenital problems that make survival unlikely.

BODY TEMPERATURE

When a kitten is born, his body temperature is the same as his mother's. Immediately thereafter, his core temperature drops several degrees (how much depends upon the temperature of the room). Within 30 minutes, if the kitten is dry and snuggles close to his mother, his temperature begins to climb and reaches about 95°F to 99°F (35°C to 37°C). Over the next three weeks, the body temperature remains between 96°F and 100°F (35.5°C and 37.8°C).

A healthy kitten in the nest can maintain his body temperature at 10 to 12 degrees above room temperature. But when the mother is away for 30 minutes and room temperature is 70°F (21°C—well below the recommended level), the kitten's temperature can fall. The kitten quickly becomes chilled, a condition that gravely reduces metabolism.

Most neonatal kittens have little subcutaneous fat. Nor do they have the capacity to constrict the blood vessels at the surface of their skin to retain heat. The heart rate of neonatal kittens is also increased, using up more energy. Energy is supplied from the kitten's meals. As there are few reserves, a kitten who does not eat *frequently*, for whatever reason, is likely to become chilled.

Chilling is the single greatest danger to infant kittens. The temperature of the kittening box and the surrounding area should be kept at 85°F to 90°F (29.4°C to 32.2°C) for the first few weeks. Thereafter, it should be lowered a few degrees each week until it reaches 70°F (21°C) at about 6 weeks of age. (Remember that the kittens still get heat from the mother cat, each other, blankets, and, often, a heat lamp over one corner of the box.) Keep a constant check on the temperature using a thermometer placed on the floor of the kittening box. Humidity should be kept around 55 to 65 percent. A suitable kittening box is described in *Kittening Preparations* (page 433).

WARMING A CHILLED KITTEN

Any kitten whose body temperature is below normal for his age is a chilled kitten and must be *gradually* warmed. Rapid warming (for example, using a heating pad) dilates the blood vessels in the skin, increasing the loss of heat, which creates a greater need for oxygen and forces the kitten to expend more calories.

The best way to warm a kitten is to tuck him down next to your skin beneath a sweater or jacket, letting your own warmth seep into the kitten. If his body temperature is below 94°F (34.4°C) and the kitten is weak, warming will take two to three hours. Afterward, the kitten may have to be placed in a homemade incubator and raised by hand.

Chilled kittens quickly become hypoglycemic. *Never feed cold formula or allow a cold kitten to nurse.* When chilled, the stomach and small intestines stop working and formula will not be digested. The kitten will bloat and perhaps vomit. A chilled kitten can be fed a *warmed* 5 percent to 10 percent glucose and water solution or Pedialyte solution (both can be bought at drugstores). Give 1cc per ounce (28 g) body weight every hour and warm slowly until the kitten is warm and wiggling. If one of these solutions is not available, use honey and water, or as a last resort, you can substitute a solution of 1 teaspoon (8 g) of granulated sugar to 1 ounce (30 ml) of water.

NURSING AND IMMUNITY

During the first 36 hours after kittening, mothers produce a special type of milk that is high in vitamins, minerals, and protein. This is the *colostrum*, or first milk of the dam. Colostrum also contains antibodies and other immune substances (primarily IgG) that provide protection against infectious diseases.

Kittens receive about 25 percent of the needed serum antibodies for temporary immunity via the placenta before birth. This only happens if the queen is a healthy cat and has a solid immune system herself.

It has long been felt that kittens needed to ingest colostrum within the first 24 hours of birth. It now appears that any feline milk in the first 24 hours will provide some protection against infections, so even a foster mother's milk will be helpful. If the kittens don't nurse from a cat during those first 24 hours, you need to consider giving them some *serum* from any healthy, well-vaccinated adult cat, injected under the skin. About 1 ml per pound (454 g) of kitten body weight is standard. This will help provide immunity for about six weeks.

THE IMPORTANCE OF WEIGHT GAIN

A healthy kitten weighs about 3 to 4 ounces at birth (110 to 125 g) and should double this birth weight by 2 weeks of age. Kittens with a birth weight of 3 ounces (90 g) or less have a higher risk of early death. Weight at 5 weeks should be about 1 pound (454 g); at 10 weeks, it should be about 2 pounds (907 g). Kittens should be weighed on a gram scale at birth, daily or even twice daily for the first two weeks of life, and thereafter every three days until they are 1 month old. A steady weight gain is the best indicator that a kitten is doing well. Failure to gain weight is a cause for concern. Ideally, healthy kittens who are nursing well will gain 7 to 10 grams every day.

Healthy newborn kittens nurse vigorously and compete for nipples.

When several kittens in the litter are not gaining weight, you should check maternal factors, especially inadequate milk supply (see page 448). If the mother is not getting enough calories, her milk supply will be inadequate to support her litter. A nursing queen needs two to three times more food than does a normal adult cat. In addition, the diet must be balanced to meet the needs of lactation (see *Feeding During Lactation*, page 444). The quantity and quality of the mother's milk is of utmost importance. Inadequate milk is a common cause of death in kittens. While size of litter and genetic influences may play a role, in most cases a diet low in calories and essential nutrients is the principal cause of this problem. Other maternal factors to be considered include toxic milk and acute metritis (see chapter 16).

When to Supplement

Kittens who gain weight steadily during the first seven days are in no danger. Kittens who lose weight, not exceeding 10 percent of their birth weight for the first 48 hours, and then begin to gain should be watched closely. Kittens who lose 10 percent or more of their birth weight in the first 48 hours and do not gain by 72 hours are poor survival prospects. Start supplemental feeding immediately (see *Raising Kittens by Hand*, page 460).

If, at birth, a kitten is 25 percent under the weight of his littermates, the likelihood that he will survive is low. Place this kitten in an incubator to be raised by hand. Many immature kittens can be saved if their condition is not complicated by diseases or congenital defects. Be sure to check for defects such as cleft palate and imperforate anus.

DEHYDRATION

Kidney function in the newborn kitten is 25 percent of what it will be later. Because immature kidneys are unable to concentrate urine, kittens must excrete large amounts of dilute urine. When kittens stop nursing, they dehydrate quickly. Therefore, consider dehydration whenever a kitten fails to thrive, loses weight, becomes chilled, or is too weak to nurse. This obligatory kidney water loss must be offset by sufficient intake of milk, or, in kittens raised by hand, by a formula containing adequate amounts of water. A sudden drop in weight with diarrhea is due to insufficient fluid—dehydration.

Signs of dehydration include lack of moisture in the mouth, a bright pink tongue and mucous membranes of the mouth, loss of muscle tone, and weakness. When dehydrated skin is pinched, it stays up in a fold instead of springing back into shape.

Dehydration is treated as described for diarrhea in *Common Feeding Problems* (page 466). When giving replacement fluids, either orally or by subcutaneous injection, remember that they must be warm so the kitten is not chilled by the fluids.

FADING KITTEN SYNDROME

The first two weeks of life present the greatest risk to newborn kittens. During this period, diseases acquired in utero and birth injuries acquired during labor and delivery begin to take their toll. Some deaths are undoubtedly due to lack of advance preparation—especially failure to provide adequate heat in the kittening quarters, failure to vaccinate the queen, and failure to get her onto a high-quality feeding program that provides adequate calories and essential nutrients, including taurine.

The developmentally immature kitten is at a distinct disadvantage because of low birth weight and lack of muscle mass and subcutaneous fat. Such a kitten may be unable to breathe deeply, nurse effectively, and maintain body warmth. Birth weight may be 25 percent below that of littermates. Such a kitten is likely to be crowded out by brothers and sisters and forced to nurse at the least productive nipples.

With chilling, failure to nurse, and dehydration, the kitten develops a shocklike state due to circulatory failure. This causes a drop in temperature, heart rate, and breathing. As the body temperature drops below 94°F (34.4°C), vital functions are further depressed. The crawling and righting ability is gradually lost, and these kittens lie on their sides. Later, poor circulation affects the brain, causing continuous muscle tremors or spasms, progressing to coma, accompanied by breathless periods lasting up to a minute. At this point the condition is irreversible.

A common cause of subnormal birth weight is inadequate nourishment during growth and development while in the uterus. When all the kittens are undersized, a poorly nourished queen is the likely reason. Poor nourishment can be the result of parasites, poor diet, or inadequate amounts of food. When one or two kittens are below par, most likely the cause is placental insufficiency, perhaps due to overcrowding or a disadvantageous placement of a placenta in the wall of the uterus. These kittens are immature by development rather than by age. If they are to survive, they must be separated from the queen and raised by hand.

If the queen is infected with toxoplasmosis, feline leukemia, feline panleukopenia, or feline infectious peritonitis, she may transmit the infection to her kittens *in utero*. Affected kittens are small and weak at birth. They sicken and die within the first few days.

Mothering attributes are also important determinants of kitten survival. Novice queens with first litters and obese queens experience higher kitten mortality than do experienced and well-conditioned queens. Cannibalism and maternal neglect are occasional causes of kitten death.

Congenital defects do occur and can be lethal. Cleft palate, often associated with harelip, prevents effective nursing. Large navel hernias allow prolapse of abdominal organs. Heart defects can be severe enough to produce circulatory failure. Other developmental disorders that may be responsible for the occasional mysterious or unexplained death include esophageal closure (*atresia*), pyloric stenosis, anal atresia, and malformations affecting the eyes and skeletal system (see *Congenital Defects*, page 474).

Other causes of early kitten mortality, which may present as failure to thrive, are discussed in *Kitten Diseases* (page 468).

Raising Kittens by Hand

A queen may be incapable of raising a litter because of uterine or breast infection, toxic milk, eclampsia, inadequate milk supply, or a behavioral reason. Or, for whatever reason, the mother may not be present. In such cases, the kittens have to be hand-fed.

If the mother is present and the kitten is able to nurse, the decision to hand-feed a kitten is based on general appearance and vitality, weight at birth, and progress in comparison to his littermates. As a rule, it is better to intervene early and start hand-feeding in borderline cases and not wait until the kitten is in obvious distress. Depending on the overall condition of the kitten and his response to supplemental feeding, it may be possible to feed him two or three times a day and let the kitten remain with the mother. Other kittens must be raised entirely as orphans.

It is ideal if you can find a female cat who has a small litter or who is about to wean her kittens and can be convinced to assist with the rearing of any orphans. A good queen with strong maternal instincts is better than any human substitute, because she will provide behavioral and social stimulation as well as feeding and cleaning the kittens. Even if you do not have a nursing queen, orphan kittens will benefit behaviorally from the presence of adult cats—as long as they are not aggressive with the kittens.

If your kitten needs supplemental feeding, calculate his total daily requirement (the method is given in *Calculating How Much Formula*, page 464) and assume that a nursing kitten eats four to six times a day. Smaller and weaker kittens should be fed at least six times a day. Space the feedings as evenly as possible over 24 hours.

Accurate record keeping is important at all times, but is absolutely essential when kittens are raised by hand. Weigh them on a gram scale at birth, at eight-hour intervals for four days, daily for the next two weeks, and then every three days until they reach 1 month of age.

Three areas of critical importance are furnishing the right environment, preparing and feeding the right formula, and providing the right management. Feeding equipment should be thoroughly cleaned and boiled. Visitors should not be allowed in the nursery. Everyone who comes in contact with the kittens should wash their hands before handling them—especially if they have handled other cats. Many diseases, including feline viral respiratory infections, can be transmitted to kittens by someone who has recently handled an infective cat.

Whenever possible, kittens should nurse for the first two days of their lives. If this is not possible, you can try to find a foster mother for them to nurse from during the first 24 hours of life. If that is not possible, consider serum from a healthy adult cat to be injected under the skin. This will provide some immunity protection for about six weeks.

THE INCUBATOR

Since chilling is another serious danger to the newborn kitten's survival, you will need an incubator or other means of keeping the kittens warm. You can make a satisfactory incubator in a few minutes by dividing a cardboard box into separate compartments, so each kitten has his own compartment. These pens are especially important if kittens are orphaned because, having no nipples to suckle, they suckle one another's ears, tails, and genitalia. This suckling behavior occurs for the first three weeks, after which they should be put together to establish normal socialization and behavior patterns.

The incubator temperature is of critical importance, because the kittens will not have a mother or other kittens to snuggle against when they are chilled. The incubator temperature should be the same as the room temperature (see page 456 for room temperature guidelines), provided there are no drafts. You can insulate the floor beneath the incubator with heavy padding. If the room temperature cannot be maintained with the existing heating system, you can provide additional heat by using overhead heating fixtures with thermostatic controls. (Use fixtures that emit heat but not light, because so much light is not good for the kittens at this early age.) These heating units should be placed so that kittens can move to a cooler area out of direct heat, if necessary.

Heating pads are not as safe as overhead fixtures. Kittens can become severely dehydrated or burned by continuous exposure to heating pads. If used, they should be heavily padded and should cover only half of the bottom of the box, so the kittens can crawl off them if they become overheated.

On the floor of each pen place a cloth diaper that can be changed as it becomes soiled. This also provides a method for checking the appearance of each kitten's stool, which is an excellent indicator of overfeeding and an early warning sign of infection.

A thermometer should be placed in the incubator to monitor the surface temperature. Keep the temperature between 80°F and 90°F (26.6°C and 32.2°C) for the first week. During the second week, reduce it to 80°F to 85°F (26.6°C to 29.4°C). Thereafter, gradually decrease the temperature to 75°F (23.9°C) by the end of the fourth week. Maintain constant warmth and avoid chilling drafts.

Maintain the room humidity at about 55 percent. This helps prevent skin drying and dehydration.

ELIMINATION

Keep the kittens clean with a warm, damp cloth. Be sure to cleanse the anal area and the abdominal skin. Change the bedding often to prevent urine scalds. When present, they can be helped by applying baby powder. If inflamed, apply a topical antibiotic ointment (such as Neosporin or triple-antibiotic ointment) or aloe ointment.

For the first three weeks, gently swab the kitten's anal and genital areas after each feeding to stimulate elimination. This is something the mother would do. At this age, kittens cannot urinate and defecate on their own, so this is a vital step. The kittens will not survive without it. A wad of cotton or tissue soaked in warm water works well. You may need to rub the stomach gently, too. Dry and massage the kitten gently.

HAND FEEDING

Commercially available milk formulas made specifically for kittens, such as KMR, Kittylac, Nurturall, Just Born, Kitten Gro, and others, are the best formulas for infant kittens because they most closely approximate the composition of the queen's milk. These milk replacers are available through veterinarians and many pet supply stores.

The composition of various milk sources is shown in the table below. As you can see, cow's milk is not suitable for raising kittens. Dogs also cannot be substitute mothers.

Composition of Maternal Milk and Substitutes

	% Solids	Calories per 100 cc	% Protein	% Fat	% Carbohydrates
Cat	18	90	42	25	26
Cow	12	70	25	35	38
Dog	24	150	33	33	16
Feline milk replacer	18	100	42	25	26

Kitten milk replacers can be purchased as premixed liquids or powders. The powdered forms are reconstituted by adding water. Unused formula should be refrigerated but not frozen. Preparation and feeding instructions vary with the product. Follow the directions of the manufacturer. Always warm formula before feeding but do not feed hot.

Although commercial milk replacers are the most desirable substitutes for queen's milk, home formulas can be used in *emergency* situations, as a *temporary* expedient. Mix well and warm before using. Refrigerate the unused portions.

Emergency Formula #1

(Provides 120 calories per 100 cc)

8 ounces (237 ml) homogenized whole milk

2 egg yolks

1 teaspoon (5 ml) vegetable oil

1 drop liquid pediatric vitamins

Emergency Formula #2

(Provides 100 calories per 100 cc)

1 part boiled water to 5 parts evaporated milk (reconstituted to 20 percent solids)

1 teaspoon (2.3 g) bone meal per quart (947 ml) of formula

Calculating How Much Formula

The best way to determine how much formula each kitten needs is to weigh the kitten and use a table of caloric requirements. Daily requirements according to the weight and age of a kitten are given in the table below.

		Formula Requirements for Kittens			
Age (in weeks)	Average weight that week	Calories needed per day (estimated)	cc of commercial milk replacer per day*	cc of emergency formula per day	Suggested number of feedings per day
1	4 oz. (113 g)	24	32 cc	48 cc	6
2	7 oz. (198 g)	44	56 cc	77 cc	4
3	10 oz. (283 g)	77	80 cc	90 cc	3
4	13 oz. (368 g)	107	104 cc	104 cc	3

*The composition of various commercial milk replacers is similar. However, the exact amount to feed may vary with the specific product. Read the label carefully.

To calculate the amount of formula for each feeding, weigh the kitten to determine how much formula to give *per day* and divide by the number of feedings. For example, a 4-ounce kitten requires 32 cc of milk replacer per day during the first week. Divide by the number of feedings (6), which gives 5 cc to 6 cc per feeding. Remember, all feeding recommendations are guidelines; you may need to adjust the amount for an individual kitten.

Small, weak kittens at birth are often dehydrated and chilled (see *Dehydration*, page 459). Before feeding formula, they should be rehydrated by feeding a *warmed* glucose and water solution (5 percent to 10 percent glucose) or Pedialyte solution at the rate of 4 cc per feeding every one to two hours until they are warm and well hydrated. Then begin using the calculated formula and feed every four hours. Older, larger kittens can manage on three meals a day. However, if a kitten cannot take the required amount at each feeding, then the number of feedings should be increased so the kitten gets all the recommended calories per day.

When fed adequately, a kitten's abdomen will feel full, but not tense or distended. Milk may bubble out around the lips, especially when using a nursing bottle. *Avoid overfeeding, because this produces diarrhea.*

As long as the kitten does not cry excessively, gains weight, feels firm to the touch, and has a light brown stool four to five times a day, you can be almost certain the diet is meeting his nutritional needs. Gradually increase the amount you are feeding, using the table above as a guide.

At 3 weeks old, most kittens can learn to lap milk from a dish. At 4 weeks, you can mix the formula with a commercial kitten food. Weaning to solids can begin at this time (see *Weaning,* page 478).

HOW TO GIVE THE FORMULA

Kittens may be fed using a special pet nursing bottle, or via a stomach tube. With either, it is important to keep the kitten upright so formula won't be aspirated into the lungs. Always be sure to feed formulas warmed to avoid chilling the kitten.

Bottle Feeding

The bottle has the advantage of satisfying the suckling urge but requires that the kitten be strong enough to suck. When using a small doll's bottle or a commercial kitten nurser with a soft nipple, you will usually have to enlarge the hole in the nipple with a hot needle so the milk will drip slowly when the bottle is turned over. Otherwise, the kitten will tire after a few minutes and will not get enough nourishment. However, the hole in the nipple should be small enough to prevent the milk from coming out too fast because this will cause the kitten to choke or possibly inhale formula, leading to pneumonia.

The correct position for bottle-feeding is to hold the kitten upright on his stomach and chest. Do not cradle him on his back like a human baby, because the formula will run into the kitten's trachea. Open the kitten's mouth with the tip of your finger, insert the nipple, and hold the bottle at a 45-degree angle. The angle of the bottle should be such that air does not get into the kitten's stomach. Keep a slight pull on the bottle to encourage suckling. When a kitten has had enough formula, you will see bubbles come out around the mouth. With a slow drip, feeding takes five minutes or more.

Tube Feeding

Tube feeding takes about two minutes to complete each feeding and little air is swallowed. This ensures that a proper amount of formula is administered to each kitten. It is the only satisfactory method of feeding immature or sick kittens who are too weak to nurse. However, if too much formula is ingested or if it is ingested too rapidly, it will be regurgitated. This may cause aspiration. The problem can be avoided if you take care to monitor the weight of the kitten, compute the correct amount of formula, and administer it slowly. Kittens fed by tube must be kept in separate incubator compartments to avoid suckling damage to littermates.

Tube feeding is not difficult and can be mastered in a few minutes. It's best to have someone experienced in the technique demonstrate for you the first time. You'll need a soft rubber catheter (size 5 French for smaller kittens—size 8 or 10 for larger kittens), a 10-cc or 20-cc plastic syringe, and a gram scale to calculate each kitten's weight and monitor his progress. These items can be bought at drugstores or from your veterinarian.

A kitten's stomach is located at the level of the last rib. Measure the tube on the outside of the kitten's body from the mouth to the last rib and mark the

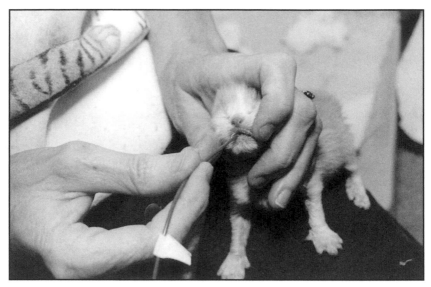

Tube feeding is the best way to feed an immature or sick kitten who is too weak to nurse.

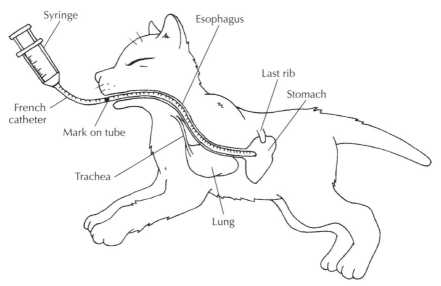

Syringe

Esophagus

Last rib

Stomach

French catheter

Mark on tube

Trachea

Lung

Slowly pass the tube over the tongue, down the throat and into the stomach, to the level of the tape mark you made.

tube with a piece of tape. Connect the tube to the syringe and draw the formula up through the tube into the syringe, taking care to expel all air from the system. Warm the formula to body temperature by immersing the syringe in hot water. Check the temperature on your wrist before feeding.

Arouse and place the kitten on his chest and stomach in a horizontal position. Moisten the tip of the tube with formula and allow the kitten to suckle it briefly. Then slowly pass the tube over the kitten's tongue and into his throat. With steady pressure, the kitten will begin to swallow the tube. Pass it to the level of the tape mark. *Slowly* inject the formula down the tube and into the kitten's stomach. Then gently remove the tube, raise the kitten to a vertical position, and allow a burp. Then swab the anal and genital areas to stimulate urination and defecation.

At about 14 days old, the trachea of many kittens will become large enough to accommodate the smaller tube. If the tube goes down the trachea rather than the esophagus, the kitten will begin to cough and choke. Change to a larger tube (size 8 or 10 French). By now the kitten may be strong enough to suckle from a bottle.

COMMON FEEDING PROBLEMS

The two most common feeding problems are overfeeding and underfeeding. Overfeeding causes diarrhea. Underfeeding causes dehydration and failure to gain weight. A steady weight gain of 10 grams a day and a normal stool (firm, light brown) are good indications that you are feeding the right amount. Experience indicates that cat owners are much more likely to overfeed than underfeed. The best way to tell is to monitor the stools. If a kitten is fed four times a day, you can expect four to five stools, or about one stool after each feeding.

Overfeeding

The first sign of overfeeding is loose stool. A loose yellow stool indicates a mild degree of overfeeding. Reduce the strength of formula by diluting it one-third with water. As the stool returns to normal you can gradually restore the formula to its full strength.

With moderate overfeeding, there is a more rapid movement of food through the intestinal tract, indicated by greenish stool. The green color is due to unabsorbed bile. Dilute the strength of the formula by one-half (using either Pedialyte or water). You can add two or three drops of a generic kaolin and pectin suspension to the formula. Make sure it does not contain salicyclates! Administer every four hours until the stools become formed. Gradually return the formula to full strength as the kitten recovers.

Unchecked overfeeding leads to a depletion of digestive enzymes and causes a grayish diarrhea. Eventually, when there is little or no digestion of formula due to rapid transit, the stool looks like curdled milk. At this point, the kitten is getting no nutrition and is rapidly becoming dehydrated. As a temporary expedient in this urgent situation, discontinue the formula and administer a balanced pediatric electrolyte solution, 1 cc per 2 ounces (57 g) of body weight per hour, by bottle or stomach tube. Balanced pediatric electrolyte solutions, such as Pedialyte, are preferable to water in this situation and are available at drugstores. Add 3 drops per ounce (28 g) of body weight of a kaolin and pectin solution (make sure it does not contain salicyclates) every three hours while awaiting the arrival of your veterinarian. Other supportive measures, such as warming a chilled kitten, are also called for. Your veterinarian may choose to administer additional electrolyte solution subcutaneously. Kittens with grayish diarrhea may be suffering from neonatal infection. Using a lactobacillus complex (probiotic), such as BeneBac, is helpful to keep intestinal flora normalized.

Underfeeding

Kittens who are being underfed cry continuously, appear listless and apathetic, frequently attempt to suckle littermates, gain little or no weight from one feeding to the next, and begin to chill. Kittens dehydrate quickly when they are not getting enough formula. Review your feeding procedure, and check the temperature of the incubator.

Constipation

Some kittens have fewer bowel movements than others do. This is not a cause for concern unless the stools are quite firm and the kitten appears to have difficulty passing them. This is most likely to show up when a kitten has been on solid food (not formula or nursing) for at least a couple of days. The kitten's abdomen may feel firm and appear bloated. If the kitten is constipated, a warm water enema can be given by eyedropper to an older kitten (two or three full droppers after each feeding). Alternately, you can give up to 1 to 3 cc of mineral oil by enema. Milk of Magnesia (3 drops per ounce, 28 g of body weight) can be given by mouth.

Keep in mind that hand-fed kittens must have their anal and genital areas massaged with a wad of cotton soaked in warm water after each feeding to stimulate the elimination reflex. Once they are on solid food, most kittens will eliminate on their own. A kitten who has never passed any stool may have a congenital defect, such as an imperforate anus.

Kitten Diseases
KITTEN MORTALITY COMPLEX

The kitten mortality complex, once thought to be caused by the same virus that causes feline infectious peritonitis, is best viewed as a spectrum of illnesses that can affect young kittens during the first weeks of life. Some kittens are predetermined to fail the test of survival because of low birth weight and influences that affect growth and development in the uterus.

During the first two weeks of life, kittens are at risk for neonatal illnesses, including kitten septicemia, umbilical infection, toxic milk syndrome, isoerythrolysis, feline infectious peritonitis, and panleukopenia. Although these diseases can cause neonatal kitten mortality, statistically, they cause fewer deaths than low birth weight, birth trauma, and inadequate milk supply.

From 3 to 6 weeks of life, parasites (both internal and external), hypoglycemia (low blood sugar), diarrhea, and dehydration are the greatest dangers. From 5 to 12 weeks of age, kittens are most susceptible to infections—in particular, viral pneumonia. This susceptibility is caused by a decline in passive immunity when active immunity (by vaccination) is not yet well established.

NEWBORN ANEMIAS
Neonatal Isoerythrolysis

Neonatal isoerythrolysis, also called *hemolytic anemia*, is the most common cause of kitten anemia. It affects pedigreed kittens most often and is more common among British Shorthairs, Exotics, and the Rex breeds. The disease occurs when the queen's blood is type B and the tom's is type A (see *Blood Types*, page 314). Even if they have never been exposed to type A blood, all type B cats will have antibodies against type A blood by about 3 or 4 months of age. This means that if a female cat with type B blood is bred to a type A male, the kittens born with type A blood may be affected by neonatal isoerythrolysis as a result of nursing, which exposes them to the type A antibodies in their mother's milk.

The disease process begins shortly after kittens ingest colostrum containing antibodies that destroy their own red blood cells. Symptoms appear within hours or days. Affected kittens become weak and jaundiced and pass dark reddish urine containing hemoglobin. Death can occur in 24 hours, or the kittens may simply "fade away" in a matter of days. In some cases, the only symptom is tissue death of the tip of the tail. By the time you notice signs of neonatal isoerythrolysis, it may be too late to save the kittens.

Treatment: The moment you suspect neonatal isoerythrolysis, stop all nursing. The kittens may require blood transfusions from the queen to restore their red cells, since she will not have antibodies against her own blood—but the blood must be "washed" to remove any anti-A antibodies. Many kittens will not survive despite all efforts, while others will show only temporary setbacks. Kittens from subsequent litters should not be allowed to receive colostrum from the queen. Determining the blood types of the queen and the tom before breeding, using either blood or DNA tests, can prevent these problems from occurring.

Iron Deficiency Anemia

Iron deficiency anemia affects the offspring of queens who are anemic. It is caused by a low iron content in the milk. This is not a common cause of kitten anemia. Intestinal parasites also can cause iron deficiency anemia because of chronic blood loss through the gastrointestinal tract. This is more common in older kittens and adults. External parasites, such as fleas, can cause a fatal anemia by feeding on the blood of young kittens.

Kittens with iron deficiency anemia are undersized, grow slowly, tire easily and have pale mucous membranes. They should be examined by a veterinarian so tests can be made to determine the cause.

Treatment: Early detection of iron deficiency anemia is important; this anemia is easily treatable by giving the queen and her kittens iron supplements and vitamins.

Feline Porphyria

Feline porphyria is a rare cause of anemia in kittens. It is due to a defect in the formation of red blood cells and can be recognized by seeing a peculiar brownish discoloration of the teeth, and a reddish brown urine.

Treatment: This is genetic defect and there is no treatment.

TOXIC MILK SYNDROME

A queen's milk can be toxic to kittens. The most common cause is acute septic mastitis (see page 446), a breast infection, or abscess. Acute metritis (a uterine infection, see page 445) also can lead to toxic milk. Kitten formulas that are not properly prepared or stored may become contaminated with bacteria and cause this problem.

Toxic milk syndrome usually affects kittens at 1 or 2 weeks of age. Kittens appear to be distressed and cry continuously. Diarrhea and bloating are especially common. The anus often is red and swollen from continual diarrhea. One complication of this syndrome is kitten septicemia (see page 471).

Treatment: The kittens should be removed from the queen and treated for diarrhea and dehydration, as described in *Common Feeding Problems* (page 466). Chilled kittens should be warmed, placed in an incubator, and handfed. The queen and the kittens need to see a veterinarian. Do not allow the kittens to return to the mother to nurse until your veterinarian approves.

UMBILICAL INFECTION

The navel (umbilicus) can be the site of infection. This is most likely to happen if an umbilical cord is severed too close to the abdominal wall. Normally, the cord stump dries up and falls off two to three days after birth. But when it is cut too close, there is no stump to wither and separate cleanly, and the navel can become infected. Predisposing causes are a queen with a dental infection who transmits bacteria to the umbilical cord when she severs it, and an unclean kittening box contaminated by stools.

An infected navel looks red and swollen and may drain pus or form an abscess. There is direct communication to the liver, which makes even a low-grade umbilical infection potentially dangerous. Untreated, signs of kitten septicemia are likely.

Treatment: If the cord has been clipped too close to the naval ring, cleanse the area with a surgical soap and apply warm compresses. Medicate with triple antibiotic ointment or Neosporin. Watch the queen carefully to be sure she does not repeatedly lick the area on her kitten, because this can aggravate the situation and increase the chance of infection. At the first sign of skin infection or abscess, contact your veterinarian. Injectable antibiotics should be started at once. This infection can also be present in other kittens in the litter. Iodine routinely applied to all navel stumps at birth may reduce the chance of this complication.

KITTEN SEPTICEMIA

Blood-borne infections in infant kittens are caused by bacteria that spread rapidly and cause signs mainly in the respiratory tract and abdomen. They occur in kittens under 2 weeks old. The portal of entry is usually an abscessed umbilical stump, although other sources of infection are possible. Bacteria from infected milk can also penetrate the lining of the intestinal wall and enter the bloodstream.

The initial signs are crying, straining to defecate, and bloating. They are like those of toxic milk syndrome. At first, they may be mistaken for simple constipation. But as the disease progresses, the abdomen becomes distended and takes on a dark red or bluish tint. These are signs of *peritonitis*. Other signs include refusal to nurse, chilling, weakness, dehydration, and weight loss. Many kittens simply appear to fade away and die in the first three to seven days of life.

Treatment: Septicemia must be managed by a veterinarian. The cause must be discovered at once; otherwise, the whole litter can be affected. Sick kittens should be treated for dehydration, diarrhea, and chilling, as described in *Caring for Newborns* (page 454). They should be treated aggressively with an injectable antibiotic, removed from the kittening box, and raised by hand.

VIRAL PNEUMONIA

Viral pneumonia is a leading cause of respiratory-induced death in kittens older than 2 weeks. It is caused by the same herpes and caliciviruses that produce the feline viral respiratory disease complex (see page 78). The severity of illness varies from kitten to kitten and from outbreak to outbreak, but overall, the mortality rate approaches 50 percent.

In kittens younger than 6 weeks old, the chance of infection is increased if the mother was not current on her vaccinations during pregnancy and did not pass protective antibodies to the kittens during the first two days of nursing.

The incubation period is one to six days. Regardless of which viral group is responsible, the signs are similar. Neonatal kittens abruptly stop nursing, cry pitifully, and weaken rapidly. At times, kittens may be found dead without apparent cause. Older kittens may show sneezing, nasal congestion, eye discharge, coughing, and fever. Ulcers of the tongue and palate and a conjunctivitis that may become complicated by ulcerations of the cornea can occur.

Treatment: Veterinary assistance is required. Weak, dehydrated kittens should be given intravenous fluids. Kittens with nasal congestion or mouth ulcers who may be unable to nurse should be tube fed. Steam vaporization helps keep mucous membranes from drying. The eyes should be swabbed gently with a cotton ball moistened in warm water or artificial tears at regular intervals, and then medicated as described in *Neonatal Conjunctivitis in Newborn Kittens* (page 473). Antiviral eyedrops may help kittens with corneal ulcers caused by the herpes virus.

Preventing viral respiratory disease is discussed in *Feline Viral Respiratory Disease Complex* (page 78).

Neonatal Feline Infectious Peritonitis

The FIP virus in the queen has been implicated as a cause of sudden neonatal death and fading kittens. Other related problems believed to be produced by this virus include reduced litter size (one or two kittens), repeated abortions, fetal reabsorptions, stillbirths, and deformed kittens.

In newborn kittens, signs of FIP include a low birth weight associated with weakness, emaciation, and ineffective nursing. In some cases, kittens appear healthy but then grow weak, lose weight, stop nursing, and die within a few days. Others experience sudden difficulty breathing, turn blue, and die within hours from circulatory collapse.

This condition is especially serious in catteries, where entire litters can be lost. Preventive measures are discussed in *Feline Infectious Peritonitis* (page 86). Treatment involves supportive measures, as discussed in *Caring for Newborns* (page 454). The prognosis is poor.

Neonatal Feline Panleukopenia

The virus of panleukopenia (see page 84) can be transmitted to unborn kittens and to kittens shortly after birth. Like FIP, it may be responsible for fading kittens and some cases of reproductive failure.

Kittens who recover from this infection may have a type of brain damage called cerebellar hypoplasia. These kittens develop a jerky, uncoordinated gait and tend to overshoot or undershoot when pouncing or reaching for objects. These signs are evident by 2 to 4 weeks of age. There is no treatment beyond supportive care.

This kitten has cerebellar hypoplasia following recovery from neonatal panleukopenia. Note his lack of coordination and difficulty in moving.

SKIN INFECTIONS OF THE NEWBORN

Scabs, blisters, and *purulent* crusts can develop on the skin of newborn kittens 1 to 2 weeks old. They usually appear on the abdomen. These sores sometimes contain *pus*. They are caused by poor sanitation in the kittening box and secondary bacterial infection.

Treatment: Quickly clean up any food, stools, and debris in the kittening box. Cleanse scabs with a dilute solution of hydrogen peroxide or chlorhexidine and wash with a surgical soap. Then apply an antibiotic ointment such as triple antibiotic ointment or Neomycin, or an aloe ointment. Kittens with severe infections may need oral or injectable antibiotics.

NEONATAL CONJUNCTIVITIS

Newborn kittens' eyes do not open fully until they are 10 to 12 days old. Before they open, there is a closed space behind the eyelids that can become infected if bacteria or other infectious agents gain entrance via the bloodstream or through small scratches around the eyes. The closed eyelids bulge out. A partially opened eye may develop a dry, crusty covering. *Any discharge from the eye of a kitten is abnormal.*

Feline herpesvirus can cause neonatal infectious conjunctivitis, as can chlamydophila. These are transmitted from the queen to her kittens at birth

The eyelids of kittens with neonatal conjunctivitis must be opened by a veterinarian to remove pus and to treat the infection.

or shortly thereafter. Neonatal conjunctivitis usually affects several kittens in the litter.

Treatment: The eyelids must be teased open by a veterinarian to allow the pus to drain out. Otherwise, there can be permanent damage to the forepart of the eye. Once the eyelids have been separated, pus will drain out in large drops. The eyes should be flushed with boric acid eyewash or a sterile ophthalmic irrigating solution. Crusted eyelids *must* be gently cleansed several times a day to prevent them from pasting shut.

Afterward, medicate with antibiotic drops (such as neomycin or erythromycin), as prescribed by your veterinarian. If herpesvirus is suspected, your veterinarian can prescribe antiviral medications. There is a vaccine for chlamydophila infections in cats, but while it reduces the severity of symptoms, it does not totally prevent the disease.

Congenital Defects

Congenital physical defects are not common in kittens. Some are obvious at birth; these include hernias, cleft palate, harelip, imperforate (absent) anus, polydactyly (extra toes), hydrocephalus (enlarged head), absent tail, kinked

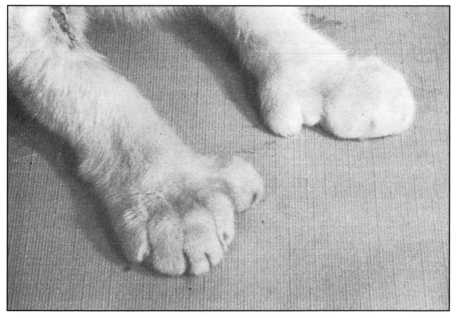

Polydactyly is a common congenital defect, but it generally does not cause health problems. Extra toes are found most often on the front feet.

tail, undescended testicle(s), strabismus (crossed eyes), entropion (eyelid rolled in), and developmental eye diseases.

Other defects require special tests to diagnose. These include malformations in the urogenital tract (including the kidneys and uterus), pyloric stenosis, sterility in male tortoiseshell cats, deafness in some white cats with blue eyes, and cerebellar hypoplasia (incomplete development of this part of the brain).

Birth defects can be inherited, such as deafness in some blue-eyed white cats and sterility in male tortoiseshells. Or they can be caused by something that affects the growth and development of the fetus *in utero*. In either case they are *congenital*—that is, they exist at birth. Malformations in the growing fetus can be caused by X-rays, viruses (such as FIP and panleukopenia), live virus vaccines, some flea and insecticide preparations, and certain antibiotics.

The antifungal agent Griseofulvin, used to treat ringworm infection, has been found to be associated with severe congenital defects, including hydrocephalus, spinal cord defects, missing eyes, cleft palate, imperforate anus, and fused toes. This drug should never be given to pregnant females. It is important to remember this, especially in a cattery where ringworm has been chronic and where several individuals might be under treatment.

Congenital defects that may respond to treatment are listed in this section.

Hernia

A hernia is a protrusion of the contents of the abdomen through an opening in the abdominal wall that would normally close during development. When a bulge can be pushed back into the abdomen, the hernia is said to be reducible. When it cannot, the hernia is incarcerated. An incarcerated hernia becomes strangulated if the blood supply to the tissues is pinched. Accordingly, a painful, hard swelling in a typical hernia location, such as the midline abdominal wall or the groin area, could be an incarcerated hernia—which is an emergency. Seek professional help.

Hernias are hereditary. There is a genetic predisposition for delayed closure of the abdominal ring, in most cases. Occasionally, a navel hernia may be caused by severing the umbilical cord too close to the abdominal wall.

Umbilical hernias are the most common. This hernia is often seen in kittens at about 2 weeks of age. It usually gets smaller and disappears before 6 months.

Inguinal hernias are not common. The bulge appears in the groin, usually in a female. It may not be seen until she is mature or bred. A pregnant or diseased uterus may be incarcerated in the sac.

Treatment: If an umbilical hernia does not resolve on its own, you can have it surgically repaired. The operation is not serious, and the kitten usually goes home the same day. If your kitten is female and you are planning to have her spayed, repair can usually be postponed until that time.

Inguinal hernias should be surgically repaired.

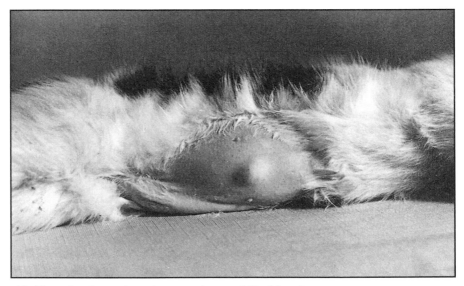

This kitten has been shaved to reveal an umbilical hernia.

CLEFT PALATE

This is a birth defect of the nasal and oral cavities commonly associated with a harelip. It is caused by failure of the palate bones to develop and fuse. This results in an opening from the oral to the nasal cavity. It is usually impossible for a kitten to nurse. Survival depends on tube feeding. A similar condition can occur in adult cats from a blow to the face associated with a fracture of the palate.

Harelip can occur without a cleft palate. It is due to abnormal development of the upper lip. This problem is primarily cosmetic.

Treatment: Cleft palate and harelip can be corrected by plastic surgery. This often requires a surgical specialist and aftercare may be extensive. The risk of complications, such as infection, is fairly high.

PYLORIC STENOSIS

Congenital pyloric stenosis is caused by a thickening of the ring of muscle at the outlet of the stomach. The narrowed pyloric canal prevents food from passing out of the stomach. This deformity tends to occur among related individuals (often among Siamese cats), suggesting a heritable basis.

The characteristic sign is vomiting of partially digested food without bile, usually several hours after eating. Vomiting may not appear until weaning, when the kitten begins to eat solid foods. The diagnosis is confirmed by upper gastrointestinal X-rays or ultrasound that shows the typical deformity.

Treatment: Pyloric stenosis can be treated with surgery that divides the enlarged muscular ring, allowing food to pass through the channel, or by dietary management. Treatment will be determined by your veterinarian.

ACHALASIA

This is a condition in which the lower esophageal ring enlarges and blocks the passage of food into the stomach. It is characterized by regurgitation of undigested food. For more information, see *The Esophagus* (page 261).

IMPERFORATE ANUS

This uncommon birth defect is caused by failure of the anal opening to develop. Examination of the perineum will show that the anus is either absent or sealed by skin, preventing passage of stool.

Treatment: Surgical correction may be possible in some cases.

Weaning

The best time to wean a kitten depends on several factors, including the size of the litter, the condition of the queen, and the availability of her milk. If a queen with a small litter is left to her own devices, she might continue to nurse for 6 to 10 weeks or even until the birth of her next litter. In general, though, kittens can be started on weaning when they are about 25 days old. If the queen is in good shape, she may continue to nurse the kittens even as they begin to eat solid foods.

Choose a premium commercial kitten food—one formulated to meet the needs of growing kittens. Read the label to be sure the product is suitable for feeding kittens 3 to 4 weeks of age and older. The daily caloric and nutritional requirements for kittens of different ages is discussed in *Feeding Kittens,* page 505.

To stimulate the kittens' appetite, remove the queen two hours before each feeding. After the meal, let her return to nurse. To promote socialization and avoid behavior problems, feed kittens together until they are at least 6 weeks of age.

To feed dry food, mix one part kibble to three parts water or kitten milk replacer. Soften to the consistency of gruel. Warm to room temperature. Feed in a somewhat shallow saucer. Dip your fingers into the mixture and let the kittens lick it off. Offer this three to four times a day. Gradually reduce the moisture content over several weeks until the kittens are eating the mixture dry. This usually occurs by 7 to 8 weeks of age.

To feed canned food, begin with two parts canned food to one part water or kitten milk replacer. Follow the same steps as described for feeding dry food.

Kittens who eat too much food may get diarrhea. This may be due to excessive food or some degree of intolerance to the food. Temporarily reduce the number of feedings and continue with breast feeding until the stools are normal.

Kittens have high water requirements and will dehydrate quickly if they do not get enough fluids. (Prior to weaning, these requirements were being supplied by the queen's milk.) Accordingly, it is of utmost importance to keep a bowl of clean, fresh water available at all times. Ideally, this should be set up so that kittens cannot get in it, get wet, and become chilled.

Vitamin and mineral supplements are not necessary or desirable when you are feeding a nutritionally balanced growth food.

As the kittens are weaned, there is less demand on the queen's milk supply. You should decrease her caloric intake, if you have not already started to do so. This initiates the drying-up process. If it becomes necessary to quickly dry up the queen's milk supply, withhold all food and water from the queen for 24 hours. The next day, feed her one-fourth the normal amount, the third day one-half the normal amount, and the fourth day three-fourths the normal amount. Thereafter, restore her to an adult maintenance food.

At 10 to 14 weeks of age, kittens become susceptible to respiratory and digestive tract infections because they have lost the protective immunity of the mother's milk. Ideally, they should be vaccinated before this time to stimulate immunity of their own. If they become ill, there is a marked reduction in food intake at a time when they should be gaining 6 or more ounces (170 g) a week. As a result, they stop growing and become weak and debilitated. This further impairs their resistance to illness. Such kittens should receive special attention. Every effort should be made to ensure adequate nutrition. Appropriate vaccinations during kittenhood will prevent most of these ailments (see chapter 3). Probiotics, such as BeneBac, can be helpful.

A healthy diet for fully weaned kittens is outlined in chapter 18.

Choosing a Healthy Kitten

The best time to acquire a kitten is when he is about 12 weeks old. At this age, kittens are well socialized and are starting to become self-reliant. Good sources for random-bred kittens are shelters, animal welfare organizations, and veterinary offices. For a pedigreed cat, it is best to go to an experienced breeder. Many of the leading cat publications carry classified ads for various breeds, or you can contact one of the registration organizations listed in appendix D for information on breeders. You can also meet breeders at cat shows.

After you find several breeders, contact each and explain whether you are interested in a male or female and whether you plan to breed or show. A sincere inquiry providing the breeder with some information about the prospective buyer is much more likely than a casual inquiry to elicit the type of information you are looking for.

If the kitten will be shipped sight unseen, you should insist on buying him on the approval of your veterinarian. The breeder should allow you to return the kitten for a refund if he is not healthy. However, no breeder should be expected to provide a guarantee that a kitten will win in the show ring. Picking a future champion at this age is extremely difficult, even for breeders with considerable experience. Then too, the training, feeding, medical care, and socialization of the kitten after the purchase are every bit as important to the outcome as the genetic background of his parents.

Whenever possible, visit the cattery and make your own selection. Although most kittens appear equally lovable at first glance, a closer examination may disclose attributes that make some individuals more desirable than others.

Before taking your kitten home, be sure to ask for and receive a diet sheet and a current vaccination record. If the kitten comes with a diet sheet, be sure to follow it at least at first, because abrupt changes in diet may cause digestive upsets and eating problems. First vaccinations should be given at 8 to 10 weeks.

If the kitten is pedigreed, you should also receive a pedigree with several generations of ancestors and registration papers. If the breeder has not yet received the registration papers from the cat registry, be sure to make arrangements to have them sent to you as soon as they arrive. These papers are essential if you plan to show and breed your cat. A pedigree is a document that is signed by the breeder. Any other conditions of the sale should be discussed and agreed on *before* the check is signed.

What to Look for in a Healthy Kitten

Whether you're buying a show prospect or adopting a kitten at a shelter, healthy kittens all have the same attributes. First, examine the kitten head-on. The nose should be cool and damp, the eyes bright and clear. Nasal or eye discharge may indicate respiratory infection. A prominent third eyelid indicates a chronic eye ailment or poor health.

The eyes should look straight ahead. A cross-eyed look is undesirable. This occurs most often in the Siamese breed. A kitten with a blue iris and a white coat has the potential for congenital deafness (although not all white, blue-eyed cats are deaf).

The ears should be clean and sweet smelling. A dark brown, waxy discharge in the ear canals indicates ear mites. Their presence does not necessarily disqualify a kitten, but it does tell you something about the way the kittens are being kept.

A swollen stomach indicates poor feeding or possibly worms. A bulge at the navel is most likely an umbilical hernia. The skin around the anus and vulva should be clean and healthy looking. Redness, discharge, and hair loss indicate infection, chronic diarrhea, or worms.

The coat should be fluffy, glossy, and free of mats. Moth-eaten bare areas are characteristic of ringworm and mange.

Next, examine the kitten for structure and soundness. The legs should be straight and well formed, the feet cupped, and the toes well arched. The kitten should be able to jump and pounce with ease. It is abnormal for a kitten to limp, stumble, sway, or exhibit uncoordinated movement when reaching with his front paws.

Kittens at 10 weeks should weigh about 2 pounds (907 g). A thin, bony, underweight kitten is not desirable; nor is one who is overly fat.

Personality and Disposition

The most important consideration in selecting a kitten for a family pet is personality and disposition. Kittens who remain with their littermates and mothers until 10 to 12 weeks learn to relate well to other cats and to people by watching and taking cues from their mothers and from one another. Once a pattern of socialization has been established, it is not easy to change.

These 4-week-old kittens are learning to interact successfully with members of their own species. Kittens removed from their mother and littermates too early lack crucial social skills.

Heredity also influences a kitten's disposition. For these reasons, you can tell a lot about a kitten's confidence and personality by observing his mother and how well she interacts with strangers.

Well-socialized kittens appear eager for attention. When picked up, they relax. When stroked, they purr. See if the kitten follows you around. Dangle a piece of ribbon or throw a wad of crumpled paper and see if he wants to play. Clap your hands or stamp your feet. After a brief startle, does the kitten recover?

A tense, withdrawn kitten who interacts poorly with littermates and shies away when picked up may be timid or in poor health. A shy kitten is unlikely to make a good family pet if you have children, but may be fine for adults who are willing to be patient at first.

Because good health and good disposition often go hand in hand, it is perhaps wise in making the final selection to pick the sturdy individual with bright eyes who is full of life and bursting with self-confidence.

EARLY HANDLING

Kittens should be groomed daily and their nails trimmed weekly. It is easy to establish a routine at this young age. The process of grooming and handling is a good socializing experience, particularly if you plan to show the cat later. It is more difficult to groom a cat who has not had this early training.

Daily handling also gives you the opportunity to check your kitten's eyes, ears, teeth, and skin. Fleas and other parasites should be treated under the guidance of a veterinarian. Check the bite to be sure the adult teeth are coming in properly. Now is the time to start a program of good home dental care, as described in *Taking Care of Your Cat's Teeth* (page 244).

Training

Cats learn quickly if we account for certain aspects of feline behavior and understand that cats are not dogs. Although cats live in social groups, they do not form a strictly structured hierarchy the way dogs do. Following an authority figure is not part of feline culture. Accordingly, training strategies that rely on the pet to defer to his master will not be successful in gaining the cooperation of cats.

Administer a stern rebuke and many cats will hiss in a defensive display. Striking a cat will teach the cat to distrust and avoid you but will not teach him anything else. Cats are quite likely to associate punishment with the person doing the punishing, rather than whatever they were doing when they were interrupted. They also very quickly learn that when you are not around, they can do whatever they want.

That doesn't mean you can never correct a cat. But it does mean corrections work best when they come from the environment. For example, if your cat jumps up on the kitchen counter and finds it is covered with bubble wrap (which most cats hate to walk on), the unpleasant experience will often be enough to teach him not to jump up again.

If—and only if—you catch the cat in the act of doing something you want to discourage, you may deter him by startling the cat with a sound behind him or by spraying some compressed air (*not* directly at the cat). Many cats learn to associate the correction with you being present, however, and they definitely will if you speak. It makes no sense at all to attempt any correction after the damage has been done. The cat will not associate the correction with the previous action, but he will associate it with you.

Clicker training is also very effective with many cats. There are excellent resources available (see appendix D).

Cats generally do not respond to commands unless it is convenient, fun, or profitable for them. A system of rewards involving praise and tasty tidbits is more likely to hold the cat's attention. Cats respond extremely well to clicker training, for example. However, many behavior problems are best managed by removing the cause. For example, if the cat is eating your houseplants, moving them to an inaccessible location solves the problem.

It is much easier to train a kitten than it is to change the behavior of an adult. If you will not be home very much during the kitten's early life, set up a special kitten room with a litter box, toys, a scratching post, snuggle beds, and a window perch. That way, bad habits such as counter surfing and plant chewing will not develop. An alternative is to use a large dog crate for short periods of time (just a few hours—not all day) when the kitten would be left home alone. Provide the same comforts in the crate as the kitten would have out of it, including food and water, litter box, toys, and a soft sleeping spot.

The best results are achieved with patience, steady praise, love, and consistent rewards for accomplishments well done.

COMING WHEN CALLED

It is not difficult teach your cat to come when called. Because cats normally respond to commands only when it is to their advantage, get your cat's cooperation by rewarding him with tasty treats, play time, and affection. At mealtimes, call your cat by name and follow up with the word "come." Repeat this exercise when the cat comes to you for stroking. With repetition, the cat will learn to associate the word "come" and his name with a pleasurable experience.

The cat who refuses to come when called can often be enticed by throwing a toy nearby. Many cats will come to the sound of a treat container being shaken. Be sure to reward your cat every time he complies. Sometimes the reward can be a cuddle or play time—but it must always be something the cat values. Do not expect obedience for something your cat does not enjoy. And *never* call the cat to you for something he does not like; that will just teach him not to come when you call. For example, do not call your cat and then give him a bath!

Behavior Problems

Although behavior is strongly influenced by genetics and early socialization, each cat also has an individual disposition and temperament. A cat's natural personality may or may not harmonize with what you expected when you got a cat and the kind of household you wish to maintain. If the cat is not what you expected, it's important to remember that this is not a behavior problem. The cat is being who he is and you are having a difficult time adapting to his personality. Some breeds have a tendency to show certain temperaments and behaviors. You should research these traits before acquiring your kitten. For example, Siamese are known for "talking." If you do not want a very vocal cat, it might be best to avoid this breed.

Normal, natural feline behaviors, such as climbing and scratching and meowing, are not behavior problems. You cannot stop a cat from doing the things all cats do. The key is to find acceptable outlets for those behaviors.

To change an undesirable habit, it is nearly always necessary to find a substitute activity and rechannel the cat's behavior from an activity you find unacceptable to one that is acceptable. Remember, too, that unacceptable behavior often stems from boredom. Cats are fun-loving and playful and should be given suitable toys and activities with which to amuse themselves. Choose toys that are sturdy and cannot be torn or chewed apart. They should be large enough so they can't be swallowed. Indoor cats, in particular, need ways to release their energy.

Cats are creatures of habit. They resent intrusions and changes in their routine. Stress often stems from a change in the living pattern or the inability to express normal behaviors such as hunting and play. Cats under stress may eliminate inappropriately; this behavior is sometimes misinterpreted as spite or jealousy, when it is really stress caused by separation or change or overcrowding (too many cats).

Behavior also is rooted in the state of health, age, and sex of the individual. Some cases of inappropriate behavior are caused by physical ailments; for example, a cat with FLUTD may urinate outside the litter box. Inappropriate elimination is discussed on page 393.

In all cases, if simple changes do not address the problem, it is wise to seek the advice of a qualified feline behavior expert.

SCRATCHING

Cats *must* scratch. Cats groom their claws as part of their normal grooming routine. In this process, the claw's worn-down outer sheath is caught and removed, exposing a new inner claw beneath. Cats also scratch to get a good stretch, anchoring their claws high above them and pulling down to stretch out the spine. Because scratching also serves the purpose of marking territory, the placement of the scratching post is also important.

To prevent damage to upholstery and furnishings, the best alternative is to provide your cat with suitable and appropriate scratching materials, and to place them in areas where your cat likes to be. You can buy a scratching post or make one at home. Whatever you decide, keep a few points in mind. First, the post must be tall enough for the cat to reach up his full length and anchor his claws. Many commercially sold scratching posts are therefore too short to interest a cat. The base must be wide and heavy, so when the cat leans on the post it does not wobble or tip. If you are shopping for a post, test the stability yourself.

Cats prefer a variety of rough surfaces to scratch on. Wound sisal rope, the back side of carpeting (not the upholstered side), and a tree limb with rough bark are all attractive surfaces. Some cats also prefer to scratch horizontally as well as vertically, so a scratching station that offers a variety of surfaces and angles will be most likely to attract a cat. Multi-tier cat trees serve this purpose very well.

The scratching post should be ready when your cat arrives. Set it up in a place the cat is likely to spend a lot of time, such as near a sunny window or at the entrance to the family room. A scratching post that is hidden away in an area the cat seldom frequents will never get much use. To entice your cat to use the post, play with the cat right next to the post using an interactive toy, and praise him (and offer a treat) whenever he touches the post. Take advantage of a cat's natural tendency to stretch when he wakes up by luring the cat to the post (using a toy or treat) right after a nap. You can also rub catnip on the post, or stick small bits of dry food between coils of wound sisal, to attract a cat to the scratching post.

Trimming your cat's claws every week or so will greatly limit any unwanted scratching damage, and most cats tolerate this well. Start with your kitten and do just one foot or even one toe at a time to accustom the cat to the handling. Gradually work up to trimming a whole paw, then two, then four. End each trimming session with a treat and some happy playtime. There are also soft gel caps that can be applied over the claws to minimize scratching damage. These are temporary and need to be replaced periodically. Your veterinarian or a professional groomer can show you how to apply them.

A good way to keep a cat from scratching at a favorite spot is to cover it with something the cat does not like to touch. This could be a shower curtain or a piece of carpet runner or a car mat with the nubby side up. You can also use double-sided tape. A product called Sticky Paws is made for this purpose—it is low-tack and will not damage furniture. Place the scratching post right next to the furniture you are covering and lure the cat to it using the methods just described. Praise the cat every time he uses the post. Eventually, as the new habit is established, you can uncover the furniture.

EATING HOUSEPLANTS

Wild cats eat a small amount of plant matter as part of their diet, as do domestic cats who go outdoors. When indoor cats cannot find the plant matter they crave, they turn to houseplants—some of which may be poisonous. (See page 42 for a list of dangerous indoor plants.) Eating plants is a natural and normal feline behavior.

The best course of action is to remove all dangerous houseplants from your home and move the others to inaccessible locations. Then, grow a pot of something the cat can eat and enjoy, and place that one pot in a spot that is easy for the cat to get to. Possibilities for the cat include lawn grass, "cat grass" (usually oat grass), parsley, and clover. (Do not pick grass from along roadsides, where toxic chemicals and fumes may have accumulated.) Some cats also enjoy eating a little finely chopped lettuce, offered in a dish.

Cats may also disturb the soil in houseplants or even eliminate in it. This is part of their natural urge to dig and bury their wastes. Keep cats out of your potted plants by covering the exposed soil with rocks, aluminum foil, or strips of double-sided tape (Sticky Paws makes a product for plants).

ENERGY RELEASE ACTIVITIES

Cats have natural drives that include hunting, bringing home prey, eating plants, and engaging in play-pouncing. When outlets for their energy are not provided, cats may engage in activities that become problems for their owner. The solution to all these behaviors is to manage the environment so the cat cannot get into trouble, and to increase the amount of stimulation and interactive play the cats gets every day.

Compulsive Grooming

This problem, known as neurodermatitis or psychogenic *alopecia*, is an energy-displacement phenomenon that occurs in cats who are inordinately stressed. Siamese, Burmese, Himalayans, and Abyssinians may have a predisposition. It occurs in cats who are hospitalized, boarded, stressed, deprived of their freedom, or subjected to long periods of boredom.

Before considering this to be a behavior problem, medical issues need to be ruled out. Cats will lick an area that is painful and may lick in response to skin conditions and external parasites. It is interesting to note that a large portion of cats presented to veterinary behavior clinics for compulsive grooming turn out to have allergies and other skin conditions.

A prominent sign of compulsive grooming is thinning of the hair in a stripe down the back or a bare abdomen. The skin does not appear inflamed in most cases, but compulsive self-licking and chewing may progress to involve the abdomen, flanks, and legs. Unless you see this behavior, it may not be obvious that the cat is doing it.

Diagnosis is made by excluding other causes of hair loss and areas that may be painful. Modifying the cat's routine to include a more active and varied lifestyle, along with a reduction in stress, is the best approach to treatment. There are medications that can be used to decrease this behavior (see *Drug Treatment of Behavior Disorders,* page 551), but they should only be used in conjunction with behavior and environmental modifications.

Bringing Home Prey

The hunting instinct is deeply ingrained in cats, especially females. Well-fed cats will hunt even when they do not need to eat. If they choose not to eat their prey, they may deposit a variety of dead or near-dead things at your feet. This may be related to the female's natural role in teaching her kittens how to hunt—she brings disabled prey to the nest to teach them how to dispatch it. It may also simply be a gift. You must regard it as the expression of love the cat intends it to be.

Cats are carnivores, and you cannot stop them from hunting. If you attach a bell to the cat's collar, it will be more difficult for the cat to surprise mice and birds. However, this does not always work. In fact, most cats learn to stalk without ever ringing the bell. If you do not want the cat to hunt and kill small animals, confine him indoors. Cats will learn to stalk and "kill" toys that you provide for them, especially if you play along too, moving the toys to stimulate a pounce. You will find that some indoor cats, especially females, present you with their toys as if they were bringing a prey item.

Play Pouncing

This energy-releasing mechanism includes biting at the ankles or attacking imaginary objects. It is not aggression. The answer is to provide your cat with more interactive exercise—at least 10 minutes, at least twice a day. You can also distract him by throwing a toy across the room when he crouches in preparation for a play pounce. Yelling at or chasing the cat only makes the game more fun. The best way to discourage this activity is to completely withdraw your attention.

Cats are hardwired to be hunters, and you cannot stop them from stalking and killing prey—including insects. Accept the prey items your cat brings you as gifts of love.

These high-energy cats often enjoy having another cat as a playmate. Many of these cats will also learn to retrieve. This is an excellent way to wear out an active cat!

SEPARATION ANXIETY

Although separation anxiety is a well-known behavior problem in dogs, it can also occur in cats. This may be related to being orphaned or early weaning. Cats will show separation anxiety in many different ways. They may eliminate outside the litter box, often on items that hold their owner's scent. They may be destructive, digging up plants, tipping things over, counter surfing, and scratching at furniture and walls. Cats may overgroom, vocalize for hours, or even become aggressive. Some cats start out by being very clingy and possessive of their chosen person.

It is important to make arrivals and departures low key as part of the behavior and environmental modifications. The suggestions for entertaining a cat are important here. The environment needs to provide stimulation and the cat may need more exercise. There are medications that can help to modify the behavior (see *Drug Treatment of Behavior Disorders*, page 551), but they should only be used in conjunction with behavior and environmental modifications.

NOCTURNAL ACTIVITY

Cats can bring new meaning to the phrase "midnight madness." They are nocturnal animals and many cats will sleep up to 16 hours or more during the day, especially if the household is quiet and then comes to life in the evening. Nighttime feline activities may consist of vocalizing, running throughout the house, or pouncing on the person they want to interact with—who is trying to sleep.

Behavior modification is key here. A cat's natural activity cycle is to hunt, kill, eat, groom, and then nap. You can tap into this cycle to help the cat sleep at night. If the cat is free fed, pick up the food in the early evening so he will be ready for a meal before bed. Exercise the cat with interactive games in the evening, and gradually wind down the game so there is a "calm down" period at the end that simulates the prey being killed and becoming still. Then feed the cat. A grooming session and a long nap should follow.

Do not feed the cat first thing when you get up in the morning or alternately, leave a small snack for midnight munchies. Do not respond to the cat's "wake-up" demands. Giving in, even once, will reinforce the behavior.

AGGRESSION

Aggression in cats is usually defensive and is related to self-protection. This is not offensive aggression (although some cats will attack offensively, this is not common). When cornered, a frightened cat will nearly always take aggressive action.

During socialization, a kitten learns to relate to and trust humans. This trust must be strong enough to overcome the natural fear and avoidance behavior seen in cats who grow up in the wild. Cats who miss the period of primary socialization at 3 to 9 weeks of age may never make a good adjustment and will always retain some anxiety when confronted by unfamiliar people.

Many cases of unexplained aggression are brought on by environmental stress, leading to heightened fear. A distressed cat may suddenly attack another cat or a person who is nearby, even though that person played no part in causing the upset. A cat who has just been in a fight may accept handling by one person, yet scratch and bite another who approaches too closely. This is known as displaced aggression.

Some cats, when they are rubbed anywhere on the belly or along the back near the tail, will turn suddenly and scratch or bite. These cats are saying "no" to petting. Some cats like to be petted; others do not. (Also see *Feline Hyperesthesia Syndrome*, page 348). Some cats will accept petting for a while, and then decide they have had enough. An outright display of aggression is almost always preceded by a signal—such as ears back, lashing tail, twitching skin, whiskers coming forward, or a vocalization—that gives you enough time to stop petting before the cat strikes.

Cats who develop a thyroid problem often become aggressive. Hunger and physical stresses may induce irritable behavior. Pain can also cause aggression. A cat with hip dysplasia may lash out if the hip area is petted. Always have a thorough physical examination and blood work done on an aggressive cat, especially if the aggression represents a change in behavior.

Use startle techniques, such as a whistle, a puff of compressed air, or a small, soft object thrown across the cat's field of vision (not at the cat), to interrupt aggressive behavior.

A poorly socialized cat should be allowed to retreat from threatening situations and not forced to confront the causes of his anxiety. These cats are often "one person" cats. They make excellent companions but must be watched carefully around strangers, particularly children.

A frightened cat who resists handling should be left alone until he is relaxed. Minimize all stimuli that impose stress and elicit fear. One way is to feed the cat. Sit alongside as the cat eats and speak soothingly. Soon, the cat will come to you for petting. However, if the cat is too frightened to eat with you nearby, leave him alone for meals, because not eating can lead to serious health problems.

Cats who like to be petted or handled on their own terms should be respected as individuals and treated accordingly. Do not encourage aggressive play as it may easily escalate. And never, ever play with any cat, no matter how relaxed, using your hands or any part of your body as a toy. The cat cannot be expected to know when body parts are fair game and when they are not.

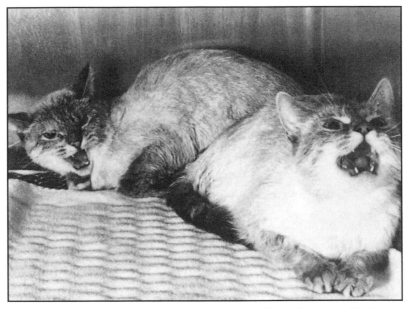

When cornered in unfamiliar surroundings, a frightened cat may hiss in an exhibit of defensive aggression.

It is important in cases of aggression to seek the advice of a qualified feline behavior expert. Try to identify the exact type of aggression, as this will aid a behaviorist in setting up a modification program. To determine the cause of aggressive behavior, consider how and when it started, the circumstances under which it occurred, and what the various attacks may have in common. True aggression should be distinguished from play pouncing (see page 487).

A truly aggressive cat may need behavior-modifying drugs and you should consult a behaviorist or veterinary behaviorist (see *Drug Treatment of Behavior Disorders*, page 551), but they should only be used in conjunction with behavior and environmental modifications.

NUTRITION

18

Compared to humans, the cat's sense of taste is far less refined. We have 9,000 taste buds, while cats have only 473. These special mushroom-shaped papillae are present at the tip and sides of the tongue. A set of cup-shaped papillae are located at the back of the tongue.

Cats are responsive to the basic tastes of sour, bitter, and salty. Recent studies have shown that cats cannot taste sweet things at all. As strict carnivores, there really is no need for them to respond to sweet tastes.

The rough, prickly feline tongue is covered with tiny hooklike barbs. Cats use their tongues to remove feathers or fur from their prey and to lick meat from the bones. They also use them to groom. A cat's tongue mimics a spoon when drinking, enabling her to lap up liquids in quantity, swallowing after every third or fourth lap.

Cats make up for their poor sense of taste with a superior sense of smell. In fact, both senses are registered in the same area of the feline brain. That is why heating food to intensify the aroma may tempt a cat who is not eating well. Food straight from the refrigerator doesn't appeal to cats, whose wild ancestors ate freshly killed prey while it was still warm.

Basic Nutritional Requirements

Cats are obligate carnivores, which means that in the wild, they subsist on a diet that consists only of meat. The ideal natural cat diet, the mouse, is 40 percent protein, 50 percent fat, and only 3 percent carbohydrates. In fact, cats require considerably more protein than dogs do—about two to three times as much. *Never* feed dog food to a cat! The diet will be deficient in many nutrients.

Due to their natural diet and certain enzyme deficiencies, cats are somewhat uniquely adapted to metabolize protein and fat as energy, in preference to carbohydrates. Even when a cat is on a limited protein diet, her body will try to use up all protein first. For this reason, it is easy for a sick cat who is not eating well to quickly become protein deficient. The diet of an adult cat must be at least 26 percent protein. Cats also need adequate fat in their diet. Fat is used for energy but also for a healthy nervous system, skin, and many metabolic processes. Ideally, a cat's diet should be at least 9 percent fat.

Cats lack many of the amylases, which are enzymes that aid in carbohydrate digestion. Large amounts of carbohydrates may decrease the efficiency of protein digestion as well as cause high levels of blood glucose.

The basic nutritional requirements for cats are listed in the table below. In this table, minimal requirements are the bare minimum amount an average cat needs to stay healthy; adequate intake is the amount that will keep a cat in a healthy state; recommended allowance is the amount suggested to be sure the cat receives adequate nutrients; safe upper limit is the amount not to be exceeded for nutrients (exceeding this amount can cause problems). Not every column has a number because values have not been determined for every nutrient in every category.

The table also refers to metabolizable energy (ME). The ME of a food is the amount of energy available to the cat after the energy required for digestion and absorption is subtracted. If there is a loss of energy because some parts of the food are indigestible, that is also subtracted. So this is the "net" energy available to your cat after she eats the food.

Nutrient Requirements of Adult Cats for Maintenance

Nutrient (amount per kilogram of dry matter food[1])	Minimal Requirement	Adequate Intake	Recommended Allowance	Safe Upper Limit
Crude Protein	160		200	
Amino Acids				
Arginine (g)[2]		7.7	7.7	
Histidine (g)		2.6	2.6	
Isoleucine (g)		4.3	4.3	
Methionine (g)[3]	1.35		1.7	
Methionine & Cystine (g)	2.7		3.4	
Leucine (g)		10.2	10.2	
Lysine (g)	2.7		3.4	
Phenylalanine (g)		4.0	4.0	
Phenylalanine & Tyrosine (g)[4]		15.3	15.3	
Threonine (g)		5.2	5.2	
Tryptophan (g)		1.3	1.3	
Valine (g)		5.1	5.1	
Taurine (g)[5]	0.32		0.40	

Nutrient (amount per kilogram of dry matter food[1])	Minimal Requirement	Adequate Intake	Recommended Allowance	Safe Upper Limit
Total Fat (g)		90	90	330
Fatty Acids				
Linoleic Acid (g)		5.5	5.5	55
Alpha-Linolenic Acid (g)				
Arachidonic Acid (g)		0.02	0.06	2
Eicosapentaenoic & Docosahexaenoic Acid (g)[6]		0.1	0.1	
Minerals				
Calcium (g)	1.6		2.9	
Phosphorus (g)	1.4		2.6	
Magnesium (mg)	200		400	
Sodium (mg)	650		680	>15
Potassium (g)		5.2	5.2	
Chloride (mg)		960	960	
Iron (mg)[7]		80	80	
Copper (mg)[7]		5.0	5.0	
Zinc (mg)		74	74	>600
Manganese (mg)		4.8	4.8	
Selenium (µg)		300	300	
Iodine (µg)	1,300		1,400	
Vitamins				
Vitamin A (µg retinol)[8]		800	1,000	100,000[8]
Cholecalciferol (µg)[9]		5.6	7	750
Vitamin E (Alpha-tocopherol) (mg)		30	38	
Vitamin K (Menadione) (mg)[10]		1.0	1.0	
Thiamin (mg) (Vitamin B1)		4.4	5.6	
Riboflavin (mg) (Vitamin B2)		3.2	4.0	
Pyridoxine (mg) (Vitamin B6)	2.0		2.5	

continued

Nutrient Requirements of Adult Cats for Maintenance (continued)

Nutrient (amount per kilogram of dry matter food[1])	Minimal Requirement	Adequate Intake	Recommended Allowance	Safe Upper Limit
Niacin (mg) (Vitamin B complex)		32	40	
Pantothenic Acid (mg) (Vitamin B–Coenzyme A)	4.6		5.75	
Cobalamin (µg) (Vitamin B12)		18	22.5	
Folic Acid (µg) (Vitamin B complex)	600		750	
Biotin (µg)[11] (Vitamin B complex)		60	75	
Choline (mg)	2,040		2,550	

Adapted from National Research Council's Nutrient Requirements for Cats. Reprinted with permission from the National Academies Press, Copyright 2007, National Academy of Sciences.

[1] The values for amount per kilogram of dry matter have been calculated assuming a dietary energy density of 4,000 calories ME per kilogram of food. If the energy density of the diet is not 4,000 calories ME per kilogram, then to calculate the per kilogram of dry matter for each nutrient, multiply the value for the nutrient by the energy density of the pet food (in calories ME per kilogram) and divide by 4,000.

[2] 0.02 g arginine should be added for every gram of crude protein above 200 g for the Recommended Allowance of arginine.

[3] Methionine is presumed to be half the sum of the requirement for methionine and cystine combined.

[4] To maximize black hair color, an equal quantity or greater of tyrosine to that of phenylalanine is required.

[5] The recommended allowance of taurine for highly digestible purified diets is 0.4g/kg diet, whereas the allowances for dry expanded and canned diets are 1.0 and 1.7 g/kg diet, respectively.

[6] Includes docosahexaenoic acid only; no information is available on eicosapentaenoic acid. It is advised that eicosapentaenoic acid is included but not to exceed 20 percent of the total eicosapentaenoic plus docosahexaenoic amount.

[7] Some oxides of iron and copper should not be used because of low bioavailability.

[8] One IU of vitamin A is equal to 0.3 µg of all-trans retinol or 1 µg retinol =3.333 IU of vitamin A. Safe upper limits values expressed as µg retinol.

[9] 1 µg cholecalciferol = 40 IU vitamin D3.

[10] Cats have a metabolic requirement, but a dietary requirement has not been demonstrated when natural diets (except fish-based diets) are fed. Under most conditions, adequate vitamin K is probably synthesized by intestinal microbes. The vitamin K allowance is expressed in terms of the commercially used precursor menadione that requires alkylation to the active vitamin K.

[11] For normal diets that do not contain raw egg white, adequate biotin is probably provided by microbial synthesis in the intestine. Diets containing antibiotics may need supplementation.

AMINO ACIDS

A cat's diet must contain more than 20 amino acids to be complete. Amino acids are the building blocks of proteins. They must be present in adequate amounts and in just the right balance. Many amino acids can be synthesized in the cat's body. Others, known as the essential amino acids, must be present in the diet.

Cats have 11 essential amino acid requirements: histidine, isoleucine, arginine, methionine, phenylalanine, threonine, tyrptophan, valine, leucine, lysine, and taurine. Although many mammals can convert other amino acids to taurine, cats cannot. Without adequate taurine, cats develop retinal changes leading to blindness and the serious heart condition cardiomyopathy (see page 318). A deficiency of taurine may also cause reproductive problems, including infertility, death of unborn kittens, and birth of fading kittens. Taurine is found in highest concentration in certain seafoods and also in organ meats. Cat foods should contain at least 0.02 percent taurine on a dry matter basis (see page 501 for an explanation of dry matter basis).

Arginine is used in large amounts by cats to process urea. Without adequate arginine, cats show neurological signs from high levels of ammonia in the blood, including tetany or tremors, salivation, vomiting, and coma, often leading to death. Arginine supplements may be needed for cats with hepatic lipidosis.

Cats have high requirements for methionine and cysteine, as these amino acids are converted to glucose and then used to provide energy. Cysteine is also important for hair growth and to provide felinine, which is excreted in urine and may be important for scent marking.

Tyrosine is an amino acid that is conditionally essential for cats; many cats can manufacture enough, but some cats will need to get it from their diet. Tyrosine is important in the production of melanin. A deficiency is primarily noted in black cats, who develop a reddish brown tinge to their hair.

Carnitine is another amino acid that is felt to be conditionally essential in cats. It is synthesized in feline kidneys (not in the liver, as in dogs and humans). It is important for weight loss in cats and also in the treatment of hepatic lipidosis.

VITAMINS AND MINERALS

Cats cannot convert tryptophan to niacin efficiently and may need added pyridoxine (B6) and cobalamin (B12), especially when they are ill or not eating well.

Cats are unable to convert beta-carotene to retinol, which is the active form of vitamin A. They must get vitamin A in the diet—another plus for feeding animal tissues. Vitamin D (calcitriol) is another essential dietary component for cats because they cannot synthesize it (humans synthesize vitamin

D in the skin through exposure to sunlight). Neither of these vitamins should be supplemented without veterinary consultation as overdosing is common and can be toxic.

Calcium deficiency is the most frequent nutritional disorder in cats. It should not occur if the cat is eating a nutritionally balanced diet. It may be brought on by feeding meats exclusively or by lactation that puts an extreme drain on a queen's calcium reserves (see *Eclampsia,* page 448).

Phosphorus is another mineral that must be kept in correct balance with calcium to prevent bone and kidney disorders. The ideal ratio is about 1.2 parts calcium to 1 part phosphorus for adult cats; that's about 0.9 percent calcium to 0.8 percent phosphorus. This ratio changes from kittenhood to adulthood. Growing kittens need about 1.8 percent calcium to 1.6 percent phosphorus in their diet. Cats rarely show a phosphorus deficiency, but excess phosphorus can be related to kidney disease.

Commercial Cat Foods

The commercial importance of cat foods has made the industry a multi-billion-dollar business. Accordingly, cat food manufacturers have conducted extensive research and feeding trials to establish nutritious and highly palatable diets that do not require supplements.

Your cat's overall condition—haircoat, weight, activity level, and so on—are all influenced by her diet. If any of these seems less than optimum, a poor diet may be the culprit. You can also gauge the effectiveness of a product by observing its effect on your cat's stool. Poor quality protein passes through a cat's intestinal tract unused, resulting in loose or mushy stool, or diarrhea. Very large stools, or large amounts of stool, on the other hand, indicate excessive amounts of fiber and other indigestibles that are not being used by your cat's body.

Commercial foods contain instructions on the label about how much to feed based on the weight of the cat. The manufacturer's recommended serving size is often greater than many cats require. Follow the directions at first, but monitor your cat's weight. Feed more if the cat starts to lose weight and less if she gains weight or leaves food in the dish. Each cat really needs a customized diet based on her size, health, age, and activity.

Types of Cat Food

There are three types of cat food: dry, semimoist, and canned. To make meaningful comparisons, all must be compared on a dry matter basis (see page 501). When the water content is factored out and the products compared this way, you'll find that most canned foods contain more all-important protein than dry or semimoist foods. Another way to compare products is by energy content (calories). Again, factoring out the moisture content, dry food provides far more calories per ounce (28 g) than canned food, which means you would have to feed three to four times more canned food than dry food to provide the same amount of energy.

The value of a cat food depends not only on the form but on the quality of the ingredients used to produce it. Good quality and inferior quality products are available in canned and dry foods. Each has advantages and disadvantages.

Dry Cat Food

All dry foods contain some sort of carbohydrate product that is used to form the kibbles. Often, it's a grain such as wheat, corn, or rice. Grain-free dry foods are also available, but they contain an alternate carbohydrate source, such as potatoes. During processing, dry foods are cooked to 150°F (65.5°C), which breaks down the starch in the cereals, increasing their digestibility. The temperature flash also sterilizes the product and removes most of the moisture.

Dry foods are the least expensive. They can also be left out at all times, enabling the cat to eat at will. This is a more natural way for cats to eat, but may contribute to obesity.

Dry foods are abrasive and help keep the teeth clean and sharp. However, the shearing forces generated when a cat chews dry kibble may also be implicated in feline oral resorptive lesions (see page 243).

A disadvantage of dry food is that palatability may be less than other types. However, most cats accept it well. Dry foods often have 20 percent to 50 percent carbohydrates, so they have less animal tissues. The protein content in some dry foods may not be ideal for cats. It's important to read the labels carefully.

A potential disadvantage of dry food is that the high carbohydrate content has been suggested as a possible predisposing factor in the development of diabetes. Also, because of its lower moisture content, it may predispose a cat to FLUTD. Due to their desert origins, cats drink little water and may not drink until they are 3 percent to 5 percent dehydrated. Cats who eat only dry food are not taking in nearly the amount of fluid that cats eating canned food are. Some cats may need to be encouraged to drink more if they are fed only dry food.

Dry foods tend to lose their nutritional value over time and should not be used after six months of storage.

Semimoist Cat Food

Semimoist foods have more eye and taste appeal to humans, but these come at a price. They are usually loaded with artificial colors and preservatives. They also usually have a high sugar content—which cats do not need and cannot even taste.

Canned Cat Food

It is tempting to think of canned cat foods as being full of cooked meat with some nutritional supplements added in. But the fact is that inexpensive canned foods may have almost as many nonmeat items as dry foods. Not all canned products are complete and balanced foods, either. It's important to read the labels and compare foods on a dry matter basis to choose a good canned food for your cat.

Canned foods contain more water, which may be an important factor in your cat's diet. The premium brands also contain very few or no carbohydrates. They usually contain more fat and therefore more energy. They may be preferred for the energetic cat who will not eat other foods because of taste preference. Canned foods do not reduce dental tartar.

They are not suitable for free-feeding. Once opened, they quickly develop an unpleasant smell that is even more unpleasant for the cat. Canned food should not be left out for more than about 20 minutes. Opened cans of food should be covered and stored in the refrigerator. It will have to be warmed at least to room temperature to be fed.

It is suggested that cats fed from pop-top cans have a five times greater risk of hyperthyroidism. The tops contain bisphenol, a diglycidyl ether, which may be the contributing factor. Cats fed a diet of 50 percent canned food have a 3.5 percent increased risk of hyperthyroidism.

CAT FOOD BRANDS

Commercial cat foods can be classified as generic, popular, and premium. Generic foods are less expensive than popular ones, and premium foods are the most expensive. Generally, you get what you pay for. The premium foods tend to have higher quality proteins and fewer fillers. Cats also need to eat less of these foods, which means they are not as expensive as they first appear. And because they are more nutrient-dense, less ends up in the litter box.

A common misconception is that the protein in dry foods is primarily from grain sources, while the protein in canned foods is all from meat sources. In fact, all varieties contain protein from meats and grains, although canned food usually has the most meat protein. Although nonmeat protein is the least expensive, it is also the least desirable. The cost of the food thus becomes an index of protein quality, with the more expensive cat foods having a greater percentage of their proteins derived from meat products.

Pet food manufacturers sometimes add ingredients to increase palatability—but this may be at the expense of nutritional value. Gourmet foods, in particular, usually contain meat from one specific source, such as tuna, shrimp, chicken, liver, or kidneys. They have excellent palatability and a high protein and fat content, but being from a single source they may not be nutritionally balanced. Usually, these foods must contain other ingredients to be labeled as completed and balanced.

Generic and Private-Label Brands

Generic cat foods do not have a brand name. Private-label pet foods carry the names of the stores in which they are sold. These foods provide a list of ingredients as required by law, but most cannot make claims that the food is nutritionally balanced or complete.

Generic products are less expensive than popular and premium brands, because the food is manufactured using low-cost ingredients. Furthermore, the ingredients vary from package lot to package lot, depending on which nutrient sources were available at the time the food was manufactured. In tests, many of the generic products were found to have lower digestibility, due to the addition of indigestible fibers.

Popular Brands

Popular cat foods are the recognizable brands from major food manufacturers. They are available at most supermarkets and grocery stores. These companies spend a good deal of time and energy testing and advertising their products. However, to keep costs low, they do not contain as much meat as the premium brands. In dry foods, a look at the ingredient lists often reveals a grain source as the first ingredient. If the first ingredient is a meat source, the next several ingredients may all be grains.

Premium Brands

Premium foods are available through veterinarians, specialty pet supply stores, feed stores, and online. In general, the ingredients used in these products are highly digestible and have good to excellent nutrient availability. In contrast to popular brands, premium foods are produced by using fixed formulas. The ingredients used do not fluctuate in response to availability or market price. Manufacturers of these foods validate their claims through AAFCO feeding studies (see page 501).

Because these products contain high-quality food sources that are easily digested, smaller amounts can be fed. Therefore, even though they cost more, the cost per serving may be comparable to many popular brands.

READING THE LABELS

When choosing a cat food, it is important to determine whether it has been formulated to meet all the daily protein, fat, vitamin, and mineral requirements of your cat. The Food and Drug Administration has established very specific guidelines for pet food labeling. All cat food manufacturers provide a list of ingredients in their foods. Ingredients are listed according to amount: the ingredient provided in the greatest amount first, the least amount last. However, the required labels do not contain enough information for you to determine the exact nutrient content of the product. The nutrients must be converted to dry weight (adjusted for the amount of liquid, see page 501). Also, the true quality of the ingredients is not indicated on the label.

Rules About Names

An ingredient list gives only a rough idea of the quality of the food. For example, protein in cat food is derived from meat, poultry, fish, the by-products and meal of these meat sources, soybean meal, and cereal grains such as corn, wheat, and rice. These various protein sources are not all of the same quality and digestibility. The mere fact that beef or some other protein is mentioned on the label is no guarantee of quality—it may indicate levels as low as 3 percent.

If the product's name contains the words "beef," "chicken," "lamb," "fish," and so on, 95 percent of the dry matter of the product must be derived from that protein source. An example might be "Beef for Cats." In this case, at least 95 percent of the product must be beef, not counting the water added for processing and "condiments." Counting the added water, the food must still be 70 percent beef. Since ingredient lists must be declared in the order of predominance by weight, the beef ingredient is listed first. If the name includes a combination of ingredients, the two together must make up 95 percent of the total weight.

If the product's name contains the word "dinner" (as in "Beef Dinner for Cats"), beef must compose at least 25 percent of the product (not counting the water for processing). Many other words also apply under the "dinner" rule, including "platter," "entree," "nuggets," and "formula." Because, in this example, only one-quarter of the product must be beef, it would most likely be found third or fourth on the ingredient list.

If the product's name contains the word "with," only 3 percent of the product (not counting the water for processing) contains that ingredient. So "Cat Food with Beef" has just 3 percent beef. Under the "flavor" rule, a specific percentage is not required, but a product must contain an amount sufficient to be able to be detected.

Guaranteed Minimums

At minimum, a pet food label must state guarantees for the minimum percentages of crude protein and crude fat, and the maximum percentages of crude fiber and moisture. Some manufacturers include guarantees for other nutrients, as well. The maximum percentage of ash (the mineral component) is often guaranteed on cat foods. Cat foods usually list guarantees for taurine and magnesium as well.

"Crude" refers to the specific method of testing the product, not to the quality of the nutrient itself. So, in fact, these guarantees tell you nothing about the digestibility of the ingredients.

Guarantees are listed on an "as fed" or "as is" basis, which means the amounts present in the product as it is found in the can or bag. This doesn't have much bearing when you are comparing two products with a similar moisture content. But if you want to compare the guaranteed analyses of dry and canned foods, moisture content matters. Canned foods typically contain 75 percent to 78 percent water, while dry foods contain 10 percent to 12 percent water.

Dry Matter Basis

To make meaningful comparisons of nutrient levels between a canned and dry product, you'll need to convert the guarantees for both products to a dry matter basis. The percentage of dry matter of the product is 100 percent minus the percentage of moisture guaranteed on the label. So if a dry food is 10 percent water, it's 90 percent dry matter (100 minus 10).

To convert a nutrient guarantee to a dry matter basis, divide the percent guarantee by the percentage of the dry matter, then multiply by 100. For example, if a particular canned food is 75 percent moisture, that means it is 25 percent dry matter. If it guarantees 8 percent crude protein, you divide the 8 percent by the 25 percent dry matter to get .32. Multiply that by 100 to get 32 percent dry matter protein.

Complete and Balanced

An important indicator of quality is a statement on the label that says the diet meets the standards set by the Association of American Feed Control Officials (AAFCO), a nonprofit association of federal and state officials that develops guidelines for the production, labeling, and sale of animal foods.

There are two ways a food can meet AAFCO guidelines, and which one the manufacturer uses must be stated on the label. One standard requires that the food meet an AAFCO profile that is based on a calculation of all the nutrients cats are theoretically known to require to maintain health and fitness. The other standard involves feeding tests that show actual cats can live and thrive on the product.

The calculation approach is limited in its usefulness because current knowledge is not complete for all nutrients cats require. In addition, there is no guarantee that the cat can digest and absorb all the nutrients in a specific food. Feeding trials are superior because they show that the product actually works and delivers the desired results. The drawbacks are that only a six-month feeding trial and a small number of test cats are required for a manufacturer to make the claim.

Also look for a statement on the label that describes the product as "complete and balanced." If it does not so state, you can assume it is not a complete diet and you should choose another product. If a food has been formulate to support the growth of kittens (also used for pregnant and nursing queens), the product will be labeled as one that supports growth, is suitable for young kittens, or is suitable for the first year of your kitten's life. To make such a claim on the label, the product must conform to one of the AAFCO profiles for that stage of life. Any food marketed as "for all life stages" must have the extra protein and calories needed to support growing young kittens as well as maintain older cats.

Diets for Health Problems

Great progress has been made in developing diets that are helpful in treating and/or controlling health problems in cats. Many of these are available only by prescription or through your veterinarian. These diets are customized to be ideal for certain health problems, such as allergies and food intolerance, kidney problems, diabetes, and certain types of urinary stones. Do not start your cat on one of these diets without veterinary supervision, as they may cause problems for a cat with normal health.

Raw Diets

Raw diets have become popular recently. These diets stress feeding primarily raw meat along with meaty bones, with some vegetables and supplements mixed in. There are numerous serious problems that can be associated with feeding a diet like this. Getting a correct nutritional balance can be tricky. Raw meats must be handled very carefully to prevent bacterial diseases such as *Salmonella*—which can affect people as well as cats. Careful storage, thawing, and superb hygiene in handling are essential to prevent health problems. Parasites can be a serious problem in raw meat. And muscle meat alone will not be sufficient—cats must also eat organ meats.

Chewing bones could lead to splinters if the cat isn't observed carefully, and most cats cannot ingest the types of meat bones that are available for purchase (remember, in the wild they would eat mice and very small birds). However, a diet without bones is not nutritionally complete.

The average cat owner does not have the time or nutritional background to feed a diet like this successfully and safely. If you choose to go with a raw diet, you need to consult a veterinary nutritionist for guidance. The same rules and need for guidance apply if you choose to cook homemade meals for your cat. You can get balanced diets from a veterinary nutritionist if you wish to cook for your cat.

Feeding Your Cat
FOOD PREFERENCES

Many owners assume a cat will naturally eat a nutritionally balanced diet if given a variety of foods from which to choose, and will stop eating when she has had enough. This is incorrect. Many cats will starve rather than eat a food they find unappetizing. And many cats will eat out of boredom or enthusiasm until they are dangerously obese.

In general, cats prefer meat—whether cooked or raw makes no difference. They prefer food at body temperature, rather than hot or cold. In the wild, mice are the primary food of cats. Meat alone is not a complete diet, though. If you feed it exclusively, your cat will probably develop a preference for meat and stop eating anything else. These cats will eventually show calcium deficiencies.

Cats may become addicted to single-ingredient foods (such as liver or tuna) if that is all they are fed. These single-source foods are not nutritionally balanced and should not be fed as the only food. However, there is no reason a cat should not develop a preference for a particular product as long as it is nutritionally complete. The problem arises when a cat develops a preference for a food that is not a complete cat food. Canned specialty or gourmet foods, in particular, are highly addictive. At the very least, the cat should be fed a variety of flavors of a single brand.

Another type of food preference occurs when an owner oversupplements an already complete diet with a highly palatable item such as liver, kidneys, milk, eggs, or chicken. The cat then develops a preference for that item and refuses to eat the complete diet. More tidbits are then required and eventually the diet becomes unbalanced.

Many cats develop a liking for liver. Large amounts should not be given because of high concentration of vitamin A, which could produce vitamin A toxicity. Similarly, raw fish and raw eggs should not be given in excess. Both contain antivitamin factors, which bind with vitamins or interfere with vitamin metabolism and could produce a lethal deficiency.

Many cats enjoy milk. How much they can consume without experiencing diarrhea varies greatly with the individual. Some adult cats do not have adequate lactase to digest dairy products without problems. Milk should not sit out for more than two hours—nor should canned food—because of the risk of spoilage.

FEEDING ADULT CATS

The actual amount of food a cat needs varies among cats of equal weight because of differences in metabolic rate and activity level. Labels only provide guidelines—the actual amount to feed must be customized to the individual cat. Spayed and neutered cats have a much lower metabolism than intact cats.

Generally, an active adult cat will need about 30 to 35 calories per pound (.45 kg) of body weight per day, and some will do well with about 25 calories per pound per day. An inactive cat will need about 18 calories per pound (.45 kg) of body weight per day. Even if they are active, many spayed and neutered cats do very well on the lower calorie estimate.

Pregnant and nursing cats have much higher requirements—figure about 45 calories per pound of body weight per day during the last trimester of pregnancy and as high as 140 calories per pound during the peak of lactation.

Body type, activity level, coat, individual metabolism, and a host of other factors affect how much food a cats needs. This lithe, active Abyssinian will need more calories per day than a sedentary, heavy-bodied cat.

The bottom line on feeding requirements is that each cat is an individual. You need to look at your cat objectively and determine the correct amount of food based on her activity level and metabolic rate, as well as the nutrient density of the food you feed her.

Cats vary widely in the amount of food required to maintain normal body weight and should be fed whatever is necessary to maintain the ideal body condition. This means the ribs cannot be seen but are easily felt, and the abdomen is trim but not flabby. Older, sedentary cats require fewer calories than the amounts indicated in the table, while active cats require more. Considerably more food is required for nonmaintenance activities, such as pregnancy and lactation.

Select several nutritionally complete cat foods and offer them one at a time to your cat for several days in succession. Note which ones your cat seems to like best. Having found two or three products acceptable to your cat, use them interchangeably to provide variety and appetite appeal. This is also a good idea in case of food recalls so that your cat will eat another food.

Cats may be fed free choice, where dry food is available at all times, if the cat is active and maintains good body condition. (Canned products should be fed twice a day, at the same time each day, and left out for just 20 minutes. After that, throw away what hasn't been eaten in the cat's dish.) If your cat tends toward obesity, however, food should not be left down free choice. Even dry food can be put out for just 10 or 15 minutes two or three times a day. Here it becomes important to consult page 503 to determine caloric requirements—with a view to keeping the cat healthy and trim.

There are advantages to feeding meals. You will know how much your cat is eating and whether your cat is eating at all. Regular meals give the cat something to look forward to. For a cat on medication, feeding meals makes it easier to sneak in pills in treats. Cats with health problems such as diabetes may need to be on regimented feeding schedules. Regular meals in a multicat household enable you to monitor and make sure timid cats are not being bullied away from their food. (Of course, each cat must have her own dish.)

Remember to keep a bowl of clean, fresh water available at all times.

FEEDING KITTENS

When they're first born, kittens basically eat and sleep—and grow. From birth to about 7 weeks old, kittens grow from about a quarter of a pound (113 g) to about 2 pounds (907 g). That means they're gaining half an ounce (14 g) a day. This amazing growth is fueled by their mother's milk.

After that, kitten food takes over as fuel. Kittens need a growth formula food for a simple reason: By the time a cat is 9 months old, she is basically full-grown and sexually mature. It takes humans about 13 years to reach the same level of growth. And it takes a lot of nutrition to make that fast growth possible.

Ten-week-old kittens require about twice as much protein and 50 percent more calories per pound (.45 kg) than do adult cats. At 12 weeks of age, a kitten's energy needs are three times those of an adult cat. The growth rate slows

Fast-growing, energetic kittens need much more protein and fat in their diet than adults need.

by the time the kitten is 6 months old, but she still needs 25 percent more nutrition than an adult cat. High protein and high calories are really important, and kittens who don't get a good start may have health and development problems all their lives. Accordingly, it is important to feed a nutritionally complete diet specifically formulated to support the growth of kittens.

A kitten's body uses protein to build muscles–including heart muscle. Protein also plays an important role in circulation and coat growth. Rapid growth, along with the bursts of energy kittens display, uses up a lot of calories, and that's where the fat comes in—fat is the most concentrated source of calories. Vitamins and minerals are important as well, especially vitamin A, which is critical for growth and metabolism. And water is vital for the health of cells and skin.

If you have purchased a pedigreed cat, the breeder should supply diet guidelines with a new kitten. This should be followed, at least for the first few days, since an abrupt change in diet can cause indigestion.

Labels on cat food packages provide recommended daily feeding amounts. They are useful guidelines but are not applicable to every kitten. As a rule, young kittens should be fed as much as they will eat. They burn calories and absorb nutrients so quickly that it's almost impossible to overfeed them.

Kittens can be fed free choice—which may be preferable when feeding a litter—or they can be fed at specific meal times. Spread their food out over at least three meals a day, because little stomachs can only hold so much at one meal. If you're using canned food, feed three times a day until kittens are 7 months old. Leave some dry kitten food out for snacking, too. However, with the trend toward early neutering, it's important to realize that neutering decreases metabolism by at least 25 percent. This means that standard feeding recommendations may not be correct for a kitten neutered before 6 months of age. You need to check with your veterinarian about correct feeding practices for your kitten.

Kittens tend to gain about 1 pound (.45 kg) a month until they reach 8 to 10 months of age. They should stay on kitten food until about 1 year. Growth slows down a bit at 6 months and levels off at about 9 months of age, but a cat is not fully an adult until about 1 year. And some cats, especially larger breeds such as Maine Coon Cats and Ragdolls, continue to grow, especially their muscles and bones, until they are 1½ or even 2 years old.

Food preferences are generally established before a kitten is 6 months old. Therefore, it is important to accustom your kitten to eating a nutritionally complete diet at an early age. You should choose two or three products in different forms (dry and canned) that fulfill these requirements and then use them interchangeably.

Vitamin and mineral supplements are not necessary if you are feeding a nutritionally balanced diet. In fact, they may even be harmful. If your kitten is a poor eater and you think these supplements may be needed, discuss this with your veterinarian.

FEEDING GERIATRIC CATS

Preventing obesity is the single most important thing you can do to prolong the life of an older cat. Geriatric cats are less active and may require up to 30 percent fewer calories than do younger cats. If the cat's diet is not adjusted accordingly, overfeeding will result in weight gain.

If you are feeding canned cat food, divide the daily ration into two or three equal parts and feed them at regular intervals throughout the day. Although canned foods need to be stored in the refrigerator once opened, many geriatric cats will eat better if the food is slightly warmed before feeding. Underweight cats may be better off with three or four meals a day.

Counting Calories

Unless maintaining a good body weight is a problem, senior cats should be on a reduced-calorie diet. In general, an older cat who is neither too fat nor too thin needs about 20 calories per pound (.45 kg) of body weight per day—and sometimes even less—to meet her caloric needs. These are guidelines, and the exact amount needed to keep your cat at an ideal weight may vary. Various health conditions may also dictate that your cat needs more or fewer calories.

If the cat's diet is not lower in calories, feeding the adult maintenance food in the same amount the cat has had all her life may result in weight gain. However, you do not need to switch your cat to a senior food if she is doing well on her current adult maintenance diet; you may simply need to feed her a little less. The actual amount to feed your senior cat will depend on the individual cat and her activity level, health, and metabolism. The cat food label will tell you how many calories are in a serving of cat food, and the serving size. Weigh your cat and compute the daily calories required, then determine how much to feed her each day, based on the caloric content of the food. Adjust the amount depending on whether the cat is above or below her ideal weight and whether she is active or sedentary. Cats who lose weight on a calorie-adjusted feeding program may have a medical problem and should be seen by a veterinarian.

Overweight cats should be placed on a weight-loss diet, as described in *Obesity* (page 510). Before doing so, consult your veterinarian to be sure there are no medical reasons for the obesity and that it is safe to cut back the number of calories. Your veterinarian will provide you with diet instructions.

Older cats should lose weight gradually—no more than 1.5 percent of their initial body weight per week. It is important not to feed table scraps and snacks between meals, as the additional calories can unbalance the cat's diet. If you offer treats during the day, you need to adjust the daily meal amounts.

When feeding geriatric cats, it is a good idea to divide the daily ration into several meals spread throughout the day. If your geriatric cat is on a set feeding schedule due to health problems, consult your veterinarian before changing anything.

And remember that older cats are less tolerant of changes in diet, and even of changes in drinking water. When changes are necessary, make them gradually (see *Switching Diets*, page 509).

Protein Requirements

Since you are feeding your older cat less, it is most important that the food be highly digestible to make sure the cat gets all the nutrients she needs. Protein *quality* is of particular importance. Information on how to assess the quality and nutritional value of various cat foods is found beginning on page 496. To ensure that the protein is of the highest quality, look for meat sources of protein in the first ingredients printed on the label.

Although protein is important, a diet too rich in meat produces an increase in nitrogen that must be eliminated by the liver and kidneys. Old cats tend to have reduced kidney function. When given protein in excess of their capacity to excrete it, the blood urea nitrogen level (BUN) rises, and the cat develops *uremia* or kidney failure. This can happen from adding meat products to an already balanced diet in excess of 10 percent of the total daily ration.

Phosphorus, too, has been shown to accelerate the progress of kidney failure. For cats with kidney failure, a special prescription diet may be recommended.

Since taste and smell diminish with age, the palatability of food becomes increasingly important in encouraging appetite and acceptance. The maintenance food should be supplemented if the cat will not eat enough to maintain body weight. High-quality supplements suitable for the digestive tract of older cats can be supplied by adding small amounts of white meat chicken, white fish meat, boiled egg, cooked and drained ground beef, and, if the cat does not have lactose intolerance problems, low-fat plain yogurt or cottage cheese. If the cat does not maintain weight on this diet, add small amounts of fat to increase palatability and supply extra calories. Plain olive or vegetable oil, or fish oils, are good fat supplements. Always consult your veterinarian before adding any supplements to your cat's diet.

Vitamins and Minerals

Older cats need more vitamins and minerals, because their ability to absorb vitamins through the intestinal tract diminishes as they age. In addition, B vitamins are lost in the urine of cats with reduced kidney function. Calcium and phosphorus in correct balance (1.2:1) help prevent softening of the bones. Most high-quality commercial foods for geriatric cats contain added B vitamins and balanced minerals. If you are feeding one of these products, you should not need to add vitamin and mineral supplements. If the cat has an eating problem, however, discuss supplements with your veterinarian.

A food that's low in magnesium (less than 0.1 percent on a dry-weight basis) is an important consideration for cats suffering from FLUTD. However, low-magnesium diets are not necessarily recommended for all cats.

Despite the iconic image of a cat licking up cream, not all cats can eat dairy products. Diarrhea is a common sign of lactose intolerance.

Antioxidants slow down or prevent the damage done to cells by free radicals. Free radicals are the result of oxidation processes that occur in normal and damaged tissue. A free radical is a molecule that is missing an electron. This molecule basically "steals" an electron from a protein or a piece of DNA, causing damage to that cell. Antioxidants donate a molecule to the free radical, which neutralizes its effects. This also ends the usefulness of the antioxidant, so these substances need to be replaced.

There is some evidence that the accumulation of free radicals accelerates the aging process, and it may even lead to degenerative diseases such as osteoarthritis. Although specific proof is lacking, many veterinarians believe antioxidants can benefit older cats. The antioxidants used most often are vitamin E, vitamin C, and co-enzyme Q. You can safely supplement your cat's diet using an antioxidant product prescribed by your veterinarian.

Special Diets

Prescription diets may be required for cats with heart disease, kidney disease, gastrointestinal disease, or obesity. They are available through your veterinarian.

Switching Diets

It may become necessary to adjust a cat's diet and switch to a new food because of a health problem. This is yet another reason to get your cat accustomed to eating several different foods early on. If the cat refuses to eat the new diet, you can switch the food gradually.

Mix together 80 percent of the original food and 20 percent of the new food, and feed the mixture until the cat accepts it. When she does, gradually increase the amount of new food while reducing the original food until the switch is complete. This could take several weeks.

If a cat will not eat a new food, don't assume she will eventually eat rather than starve herself. Some cats will starve themselves rather than eat a food they find unacceptable.

Obesity

Overfeeding leads to obesity. This is a big problem in cats, with estimates of 40 percent of all cats being obese. If you think your cat may be overweight, ask your veterinarian to help you determine the ideal weight in proportion to the cat's height and bones. There should be a layer of subcutaneous fat over the ribs, thick enough to provide some padding and insulation, but not too thick. You should be able to feel the ribs as individual structures but not see them. From above, you should see a well-defined narrowing or waistlike effect below the rib cage and above the hips. If you are unable to feel the individual ribs and the cat has lost her waist, she is carrying too much fat. Many cats, even at a good weight, will have a small "pouch" by the hind legs, but the overall body condition should be fit and trim.

Don't box your cat in by letting her get too fat.

Obesity contributes to arthritis, a fourfold increase in type 2 diabetes, poor haircoat, and hepatic lipidosis—a potentially life-threatening problem.

Food preferences may present problems in redirecting the cat's eating habits. Remember, many cats simply turn carbohydrates directly into fat. They are better off with a diet that is higher in protein and fat and lower in carbohydrates. Review your feeding practices and take the following steps:

- Feed a restricted-calorie reducing diet. Current studies suggest that a high-protein, low-carbohydrate diet may be just as effective or even more so than a low-calorie, high-fiber diet. The high-protein diet is closer to a cat's ideal natural diet, as well.

- Feed regular, measured meals two or three times a day. When your cat has finished what's in her bowl, she must wait for her next meal.

- Do not feed gourmet cat foods, table scraps, or treats. Set aside a few bits of your cat's food from her regular meals for treats during the day.

- Monitor the cat's activity to be sure food is not being found elsewhere.

- Chart the cat's weight weekly. The cat should lose about 1 percent of her body weight per week. Rapid weight loss can lead to hepatic lipidosis.

- Provide daily exercise and human companionship. Many indoor cats need more exercise. Toys, games, and even making the cat work for her food will help—moving food dishes, putting food into interactive toys, and so on.

- L-carnitine as a supplement may be helpful in getting your cat's weight down, as it may increase lean body mass. Discuss with your veterinarian the possibility of feeding 250 to 500 mg per day.

- After four to eight weeks, or when the ideal weight is obtained, feed the cat a high-quality balanced food in the proper amount to maintain her new weight.

Common Feeding Errors

A frequent error is feeding dog food. Never feed dog food to a cat! Cats require twice as much protein and B vitamins as do dogs. Cats, unlike dogs, cannot convert certain dietary precursors into necessary amino acids and water soluble vitamins. A cat given dog food over a long period can develop taurine deficiency, vitamin A deficiency (night blindness), niacin deficiency, retinal degeneration, and other serious or fatal illnesses.

Another common error is to overdose a cat with vitamins A and D or calcium and phosphorus, either by giving the vitamins directly or by supplementing the diet with products that are high in them (such as raw liver or fish oils). Excess vitamin A causes sterility and loss of hair. Excess calcium, phosphorus, and vitamin D cause metabolic bone and kidney disease.

Raw fish should not be fed to cats. Raw fish contains an enzyme that destroys vitamin B1 (thiamin). A deficiency of this vitamin results in brain damage. Fish is also deficient in vitamin E and has the potential to transmit diseases.

SOME GUIDELINES FOR FEEDING CATS

- Never feed dog food. It is deficient in essential nutrients cats require.
- Specialty foods and even table scraps can be given as treats once or twice a week—but only after the regular diet is eaten. Cooked meats (including organ meats such as liver or kidney), cottage cheese, cooked vegetables, cooked fish, milk, and yogurt are foods with strong taste appeal that cats seem to enjoy. Only give them in small amounts and do not offer dairy products if your cat appears to be lactose intolerant (usually evidenced by diarrhea).
- Never feed meats exclusively.
- Treats should never exceed 20 percent of a cat's total daily food.
- Uncooked meat and raw fish should not be given because of the dangers of vitamin deficiency and transmitting diseases.
- Vitamin and mineral supplements are not necessary or desirable if you are feeding a balanced cat food.
- Cats have highly selective eating habits. The location of the food dish, noise, the presence of other animals, and other threats or distractions can adversely affect how much they are willing to eat. A cat in a boarding facility may go an entire week without eating (which can be dangerous).
- Cats prefer to have their food served at room temperature.
- Many cats will not eat if the food dish is located near the litter box.
- Water is a very important nutrient for cats. Always have plenty of fresh water available. Canned food diets are more likely to provide an adequate amount of water than are other types of food.

TUMORS AND CANCERS

19

A *tumor* is any sort of lump, bump, growth, or swelling. That description includes everything from an abscess to a cancer. Tumors that are true growths are called *neoplasms*. Benign neoplasms are tumors that grow slowly and are surrounded by a capsule, do not invade and destroy surrounding tissue, and do not spread to other areas. They are generally not life threatening but may also be called cancers. They are often cured by surgical removal, provided that all of the tumor is removed.

Malignant neoplasms are often referred to simply as cancers (also called carcinomas, lymphomas, or sarcomas, depending on the cell type). Cancers tend to enlarge rapidly. They are not usually encapsulated. They infiltrate into or invade the surrounding tissue. When they are on the surface of the body, they often ulcerate and bleed. At some point, cancers spread via the bloodstream or lymphatic system to remote body parts (metastasis).

Cancer in the Cat

Cats have higher rates of cancer than do dogs and other domestic animals. Most feline cancers occur in middle-aged and older individuals 10 to 15 years of age. Lymphoma is an exception, occurring most often in young cats. The majority of feline cancers are not visible by outward inspection, except for skin and breast tumors. These neoplasms can be detected by inspection and palpation.

The high cancer rate in cats is felt to be at least partly related to the feline leukemia virus and the feline immunodeficiency virus. Common sites of involvement are lymph nodes (lymphoma) and circulating blood cells (leukemia), but any organ or tissue in the cat's body can be affected. Taken together, the feline leukemia virus accounts for perhaps half of all internal

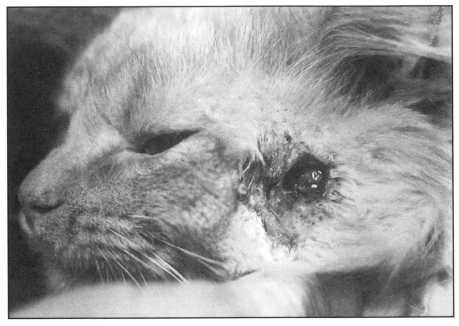

This ulcerating tumor may be an abscess or a neoplasm.

cancers, the majority of which are lymphomas. It is also associated with other serious cat diseases, including anemia, feline infectious peritonitis, glomerulonephritis, spinal cord cancers, and toxoplasmosis. The depressed immunity level associated with feline leukemia virus disease complex undoubtedly contributes to the high incidence of such secondary diseases.

Skin tumors are common in cats. Many skin tumors are not malignant; however, the incidence of skin cancer is still high and accounts for 25 percent of feline cancers. Next in frequency is the breast (17 percent).

Cancer is a condition in which rapid cell division and tissue growth occur at the expense of organ-specific function. For example, a cancer from a cat's kidney is biopsied and found to be a mass of tissue that bears only slight resemblance to normal kidney cells under the microscope. The mass on the kidney does not function as kidney tissue, nor does it help the kidney to make urine. If the cancer goes untreated, it eventually replaces the kidney while simultaneously metastasizing to other parts of the body. In time, through a number of possible events, it causes the cat's death.

Cancer is graded or staged according to the degree of malignancy. Low-grade cancers continue to grow locally and reach a large size. They spread to distant organs late in the course of the illness. High-grade cancers spread early, when the primary tumor is still quite small or barely detectable.

Growths of the mouth account for up to 10 percent of feline cancers. Nearly all of them are malignant (squamous cell cancers). Signs include drooling, difficulty eating, and the appearance of a lump or ulcerated growth involving the tongue or gums. A mouth cancer should be distinguished from an infected mass produced by an imbedded foreign body or string cutting into the underside of the tongue.

Other cancer sites include the digestive and female reproductive tracts. Such cancers may grow large before they are detected—usually by the presence of a palpable mass or by signs of intestinal blockage. Early detection of these cancers rests on a suspicion that a symptom caused by some internal disorder could be due to a cancer. You should consider the possibility of cancer when your cat has difficulty eating or digesting food or when there is an unexplained bowel disturbance such as constipation or passing blood. Cancers of the reproductive tract in females cause few signs, but you should look for vaginal discharge and bleeding.

Primary lung cancer (the cancer originates in the lungs) is rare among cats. Virtually all primary lung cancers in cats are related to exposure to secondhand cigarette smoke. The lungs, however, are often a site for metastases. The same applies to the liver.

Bone cancer also is rare (3 percent of cancers). The first sign may be swelling of the leg or a limp in a mature cat without a history of injury. Pressure over the swelling causes varying degrees of pain. Bone cancer spreads early and to the lungs.

The bone marrow may be involved by a group of diseases called myeloproliferative disorders. In these diseases, the marrow stops making red or white blood cells, or else makes them in excessive amounts. These disorders are rare and are difficult to detect. Diagnosis is made by bone marrow biopsy. These problems may be associated with feline leukemia virus infection.

Signs and symptoms of common tumors affecting the internal organs are discussed in the chapters dealing with these organs.

SOME FELINE CANCER FACTS

- 32 percent of all cats over 10 years of age will die from some type of cancer.
- 25 percent of all feline cancers are skin cancers, with 50 to 65 percent of them being malignant.
- About 25 out of every 100,000 female cats will develop mammary cancer; 17 percent of all feline cancers are mammary related.
- Feline lymphoma will strike 200 out of every 100,000 cats, with cats who are FeLV positive being at 60 percent higher risk.
- 10 percent of all feline tumors are found in the mouth.
- Vaccine-associated sarcomas occur in 1 in 1,000 to 1 in 10,000 cats.

Looking at these facts, we see that 52 percent, or just over half of all feline cancers, occur in areas that can be examined—the skin, the mammary glands, and the mouth. Frequent at-home examinations can lead to early cancer detection in many cases.

What Causes Cancer?

Cancer is influenced by both genetic and environmental factors. Some genes, if present at certain locations on chromosomes, cause cells to become cancers. Other genes suppress cancer genes at these sites; still other genes inhibit the suppressors. Throughout life, some genes are changing due to aging. Thus cancer is a multifactor, largely unpredictable phenomenon involving the interaction of many genes and chromosomes—all subject to familial and environmental influences. With cats living longer lives, we can expect to see more cancer in the years to come.

Carcinogens are environmental influences known to increase the likelihood of cancer in proportion to the length and intensity of exposure to them. Carcinogens gain access to tissue cells, cause alterations in genes and chromosomes, and disrupt the orderly system of checks and balances that controls cellular growth and tissue repair. Examples of carcinogens known to increase the risk of cancer in people are ultraviolet rays (skin cancer), X-rays (thyroid cancer), nuclear radiation (leukemia), chemicals (aniline dyes cause bladder cancer), cigarettes and coal tars (lung and skin cancer), viruses (sarcoma in AIDS patients), and parasites (bladder cancer).

The feline leukemia virus causes several types of cancer. Exposure to secondhand cigarette smoke will increase the risk of primary lung cancer in cats. Some herbicides are associated with increased bladder cancer in dogs. The adjuvants in some vaccines have been associated with the development of fibrosarcomas.

A prior injury or blow is sometimes thought to be the cause of cancer. Trauma can be a cause of certain benign swellings. However, it is rarely the cause of a cancer. An injury to a breast, for example, may cause the breast to be carefully examined, resulting in the incidental finding of a preexisting breast cancer.

Some benign tumors, such as warts and papillomas, are clearly due to a virus. Other benign tumors, such as lipomas, simply grow for reasons unknown.

Diagnosing Cancers

Clearly, one of the first diagnostic steps for any cat suspected of having cancer is to run a combination FeLV and FIV blood test. A cancer associated with an immune-suppressing virus presents special challenges in treatment. A blood panel might show an increase in calcium—which is seen in some cancers. A urinalysis might indicate protein loss. Those are relatively easy tests to do, require no anesthesia, and can be done at most veterinary clinics.

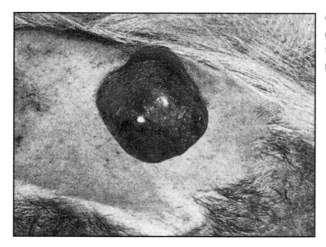

Only a biopsy can determine if this skin tumor is benign or malignant.

X-rays are often the next step. An X-ray may show changes in bones or the spread of a cancer. Ultrasound is helpful for identifying soft tissue growths. *MRI* (magnetic resonance imaging) and *CAT* (computerized axial tomography) scans are imaging techniques that will only be found at large veterinary referral centers.

A *fine needle aspirate* or *biopsy* may be done to take a sample of the growth for analysis. This may not only identify a cancer but also give an idea of the stage and prognosis. Once the type of cancer is known, a treatment plan can be developed. Genetic markers are a hope for the future identification of cancer-causing genes.

Here is an example of how a diagnosis of cancer might be made: Suppose a female cat has a lump in her breast. Since it is solid, it is probably a neoplasm. It could be benign or malignant. A decision is made to biopsy the lump. During this surgery, the lump or part of the lump is removed and sent to a pathologist—a doctor with advanced training to make a diagnosis by inspecting the tissue under a microscope. The pathologist can tell whether a growth is a cancer and can often provide additional information about the degree of malignancy. The pathologist's report gives the rationale for the best type of treatment. This report also includes information about the prevalence of this type of cancer in cats, an idea of the prognosis, and whether further diagnostics should be done before starting any treatment.

Treating Tumors and Cancers

A summary of the types of cancer treatment currently available can be found on page 519. The effectiveness of any form of treatment depends on early recognition. Early-stage cancers have a higher cure rate than do late-stage cancers. This holds true for all types of cancer.

The best possible treatment option is surgical removal of a cancer that has not spread. To prevent recurrence, a surrounding margin of normal tissue should also be removed. An initial approach that removes the tumor with an adequate margin of normal tissue may be the most important factor in controlling cancer. When a cancer recurs locally because of incomplete excision, the opportunity for cure is often lost. That's why surgeons speak of "clean margins," meaning no cancer cells are found on the edges of the surgical excision.

A cancer that spreads only to local lymph nodes may still be cured if all the involved nodes can be removed along with the primary tumor. Even when a cancer is widespread, removing a bleeding or infected mass, or simply a large one that is interfering with a normal physical function, can provide relief and temporarily improve the quality of life.

Electrocautery and cryosurgery are two techniques by which tumors on the surface of the body can be removed. Electrocautery means burning off the tumor using electricity; cryosurgery involves freezing the tumor to remove it. These methods provide an alternative to surgical removal and are suitable for benign tumors. New surgery techniques may use lasers or hyperthermy—heat treatment.

Radiation therapy is useful in managing some surface tumors and deeply situated tumors that cannot be controlled by surgery. Cures are possible. A potential disadvantage of radiation therapy is that it requires special equipment and must be done at a medical center. Radiation therapy can also be done to relieve pain, especially with very painful cancers such as osteosarcoma (bone cancer).

Chemotherapy uses anticancer drugs given at prescribed intervals. These drugs, even when tightly controlled, have major side effects. Still, they are useful in managing some widely spread cancers. The development of new chemotherapy agents will lead to higher success with less side effects. In humans, chemotherapy is aimed at achieving a cure. In cats, chemotherapy is aimed at controlling the disease and giving the cat a period of remission. Lower dosages are generally used and many cats do not have the severe reactions to chemotherapy that people do.

Photodynamic therapy uses special chemotherapy compounds that are sensitive to certain light waves. The substances are injected along with an attractant to cancer cells. Light, using a laser with infrared wavelengths, is then shone on the area of the cancer.

Hormone therapy has been successful in managing some tumors.

Immunotherapy can use two types of compounds. One is a general stimulant for the entire immune system, such as interferon. The other is the use of specific cancer vaccines—a vaccine made from a cat's own cancer cells in an attempt to stimulate an immune reaction against the cancer.

A combination of the treatment methods (for example, surgical excision followed by radiation or chemotherapy) is often more effective than surgery alone. Only those treatments known to be effective against a particular cancer should be considered for combination therapy.

Pain medications and nutritional management are now also important parts of cancer therapy. Nutritionally, cancerous cells seem to do well on carbohydrates and not so well on fat. Adding omega-3 fatty acids (think fish oils) to the diet may be helpful, as may adding the amino acid arginine. Although much of this work has been done primarily with dogs, it should apply to cats as well. The use of additional antioxidants is under discussion at this time. Some veterinarians believe this is absolutely beneficial. Others believe extra antioxidants might interfere with the actions of chemotherapy drugs.

Cancer Treatments	
Surgery	Surgery can completely remove a cancer or make it smaller so that chemotherapy and radiation are more effective. Risks include anesthesia, bleeding problems, and postoperative pain. Cures are possible with certain cancers and early intervention.
Chemotherapy	Chemotherapy uses drugs to try to kill the cancer cells with the least amount of damage to normal cells. Side effects can include nausea, lowered immunity, and bleeding problems. Cats don't usually experience major hair loss. Not all cancers are susceptible to chemotherapy.
Radiation	Radiation uses specially calibrated X-rays to damage cancer tissues with the least amount of damage possible to normal tissues. Side effects include tissue sloughing, lowered immunity, and damage to normal tissue. Anesthesia is required. This treatment is only available at veterinary referral centers. Not all cancers are susceptible to radiation and the location of the cancer may make this impossible.
Cryotherapy	Cryotherapy uses probes to freeze cancerous tissues. The goal is to destroy the cancer with the least damage to surrounding normal tissues. This is only available at veterinary referral centers. Not all cancers are susceptible to cryotherapy, and the location of the cancer may make this therapy impossible.
Hyperthermy	Hyperthermy uses heat probes or radiation to destroy cancerous tissues by overheating them. The goal is to destroy the cancer with the least damage to surrounding normal tissues. This is only available at veterinary referral centers. Not all cancers are susceptible to heat damage. The location of the cancer may make this therapy impossible.
Diet	Diet has been shown to be helpful in controlling cancer. The goal is a diet with limited simple sugars, moderate amounts of complex sugars such as carbohydrates, highly digestible protein in moderate amounts, and set amounts of certain types of fats. These dietary guidelines tend to "starve" the cancer cells and help the normal cells stay healthy.
Immunotherapy	Immunotherapy uses immune reactions to fight off the cancer cells. This method may use a nonspecific immune modifier such as interferon, or vaccines specifically tailored to the cancer of the individual. Much of this work is experimental but shows great promise.

Finding Treatment

It makes sense if your cat has cancer to seek out a referral center that routinely deals with cancer cases. But that is sometimes easier said than done. Most veterinary schools and other referral centers have a veterinary oncologist on staff. These veterinarians may offer treatments at their facility or confer with your veterinarian on treatments such as chemotherapy regimens.

Most of these referral centers are also conducting research and may be looking for patients with a specific disease to be involved in clinical trials. Being included in a cancer study can help with expenses, give you access to the latest techniques, and possibly help other cats in the future.

Common Surface Tumors

Surface tumors are common in cats. It is often impossible to determine whether a surface tumor is benign or malignant by appearance alone. The only conclusive way to make a diagnosis is by *biopsy*, a procedure in which tissue or cells are removed by your veterinarian and examined under a microscope by a veterinary pathologist.

For small tumors, it is best for your veterinarian to remove the growth and present the entire specimen to the pathologist. For tumors larger than 1 inch (25 mm) across, it may be advisable for your veterinarian to obtain a tissue sample by fine needle aspiration. In this procedure, a needle connected to a syringe is inserted into the tumor and cells are obtained by pulling back on the plunger. Alternatively, the vet can use a cutting needle to obtain a core sample. An open biopsy, in which an incision is made, is preferred for suspected sarcomas and tumors that present diagnostic problems for the pathologist.

Epidermal Inclusion Cysts (Sebaceous Cysts)

Epidermal inclusion cysts, also called sebaceous cysts, are benign tumors that arise from glands found beneath the skin. They can occur anywhere on the body. Although less common in cats than in dogs, they are still the most common surface tumor in cats.

A sebaceous cyst is made of a thick capsule that surrounds a lump of cheesy material called sebum. It may grow to 1 inch (25 mm) or more. Eventually, it is likely to become infected and will have to be drained. This sometimes leads to a cure.

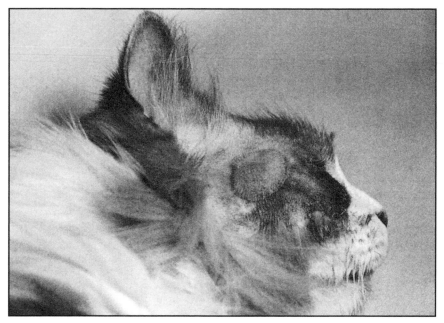

This cat has a sebaceous cyst on the side of his head.

Treatment: Most cysts should be removed. Cysts can often be removed by electrocautery or cryotherapy. At the very least, sedation and a local anesthetic will be required, and many cats may need general anesthesia.

WARTS AND PAPILLOMAS

These growths are not nearly as common in cats as they are in people. They tend to occur on the skin of older cats. Some are on a stalk, while others look like a piece of chewing gum stuck to the skin.

Treatment: If they become irritated or start to bleed, they should be removed. In general, they are not a threat to the health of the cat.

LIPOMAS

A lipoma is a growth made of mature fat cells surrounded by a fibrous capsule that sets it apart from the surrounding body fat. It can be recognized by a round, smooth appearance and soft, fatlike consistency. Lipomas grow slowly and may get to be several inches in diameter. They are not common in cats and are not painful.

Treatment: Surgical removal is indicated only for cosmetic reasons or to rule out a malignant growth.

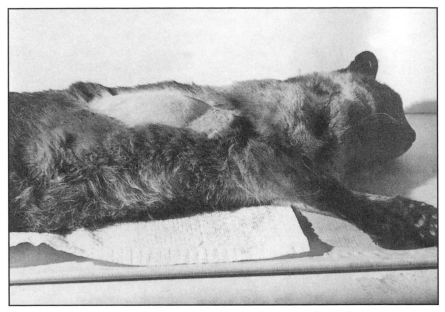

This cat has been shaved to reveal a lipoma on the side of his abdomen.

HEMATOMAS

A hematoma is a collection of blood beneath the skin, caused by a blow or a contusion. The area will be swollen, somewhat painful, and usually a reddish-purple color.

Treatment: Small hematomas may resolve spontaneously. Large ones may need to be opened and drained. Ear flap hematomas require special care (see *Swollen Pinna*, page 209).

TENDER KNOTS

A small knot may be present at the site of an injection and is often present for a few days in kittens who have been given their vaccinations. It seldom requires treatment. If a firm area remains where an injection was given or develops afterward, you need to contact your veterinarian immediately. This could be a vaccine-associated sarcoma (see page 530).

A painful swelling beneath the skin may be an abscess. You can usually move and compress them, and they feel warm to the touch. Abscesses are discussed on page 49.

Common Skin Cancers

Several types of skin cancer can affect cats. It is important to distinguish a cancer from a benign neoplasm. Signs that a growth might be a cancer are visible enlargement, ulceration of the skin with bleeding, and a sore that does not heal. Physical appearance alone is not always a reliable indicator. Surgical removal or biopsy is necessary to establish an exact diagnosis. The following are the most common malignant skin tumors in the cat.

Basal Cell Carcinoma

This is the most common type of skin cancer in cats. It tends to show up in older cats, often as a single growth on the head. Basal cell carcinomas occur as small nodular growths beneath the skin, often next to each other, producing solid sheets of bumps. They also tend to occur on the back and upper chest. Basal cell tumors enlarge locally and spread by direct extension. They do not usually metastasize.

Basal cell tumors are most commonly seen in Siamese and domestic longhair cats. Rarely, basal cell tumors become malignant. This occurs in Persians cats primarily, so any lumps on a Persian's head should be checked out right away.

Treatment: Wide surgical removal prevents recurrence.

Squamous Cell Carcinoma

This neoplasm, also called an epidermoid carcinoma, appears as a cauliflower-like growth or a hard, flat, grayish ulcer that does not heal. Size varies. These cancers tend to occur around body openings and in areas of chronic skin irritation. Hair may be lost because of constant licking.

A peculiar form of squamous cell carcinoma involves the upper and lower lips of cats who suffer from a condition called indolent ulcer (see *Eosinophilic Granuloma Complex*, page 166). Another type involves the ear tips and nose of cats with white hair in these areas who are exposed to ultraviolet sunlight.

Oral squamous cell carcinomas tend to occur in older cats, often near the base of the tongue. It is suggested that while grooming, cats may lick off carcinogens that then lodge near the tissues of the mouth. Your cat may have loose teeth or go to his food and water bowls but not eat or drink. Drooling and bad mouth odor are common. This cancer has been associated with exposure to secondhand cigarette smoke, possibly a canned food diet, and possibly the use of flea collars.

Treatment: Early detection and treatment of squamous cell carcinoma is important. This neoplasm is capable of spreading to other locations. Treatment may involve a combination of surgery and radiation, with chemotherapy included in some protocols.

Mast Cell Tumors

Mast cell tumors are single or multinodular growths, usually less than 1 inch (25 mm) long. The skin overlying the tumor may be ulcerated. Look for these neoplasms on the hind legs, scrotum, and lower abdomen. About one out of three is malignant. Malignancy is more likely when growth is rapid and the neoplasm is larger than 1 inch. Malignant mast cell tumors spread to distant organs.

In another version of mast cell tumors in cats, the spleen is the organ of choice for the cancer. An enlarged spleen may be palpable and many cats with this form of cancer show up with complaints of vomiting. Surgery is recommended.

Treatment: Cortisone may be given to temporarily decrease the size of mast cell tumors. The treatment of choice is wide surgical removal. Siamese cats may have a predisposition to these cancers.

Melanomas

A melanoma is a malignant neoplasm that takes its name from the brown or black pigment usually associated with it. Some melanomas lack in the gene for pigmentation and are called amelanotic melanomas.

Some melanomas develop in preexisting moles. You should suspect melanoma when a pigmented spot starts to enlarge or spread, becomes raised above the surface of the skin, or starts to bleed. Melanomas may be found anywhere on the skin and may also occur in the mouth.

Treatment: Any suspicious pigmented spot on the skin should be removed. Melanoma spreads widely, often at an early stage.

Uveal Melanomas

These are slow-growing malignant tumors seen in the eyes of older cats. This is the primary tumor found in cats' eyes. The pigment in the eye will change and there might be redness or pain as well. Usually just one eye is affected. Older orange cats tend to get pigment changes in their irises, as well, but this is a benign change. Have your veterinarian examine the eye.

Ultrasound, MRI, and CAT scans all are helpful in detecting any metastasis of this cancer around the eye.

Treatment: The ideal treatment is removal of the eye early on before any spread, but most of these cancers have spread before detection. The prognosis is not good, but chemotherapy and radiation may prolong good quality of life. Persians have a predisposition to this type of cancer.

Breast Swellings and Tumors

The cat normally has four pairs of mammary glands. The upper two pairs have a common lymphatic channel and drain into the axillary (armpit) lymph nodes. The lower pairs also have a common channel and drain into the inguinal (groin) lymph nodes. Infections and tumors of the breasts may cause enlargement of the corresponding lymph nodes.

MAMMARY HYPERPLASIA

This condition is most commonly seen in young cats. Unspayed female cats can experience an enlargement of one or more breast glands that begins one to two weeks after their first heat cycle. This condition, called mammary hyperplasia or mammary hypertrophy, is caused by high levels of progesterone (see *Hormonal Influence During the Estrus Cycle*, page 409). Pregnant queens also may experience mammary hypertrophy that begins during the first two weeks of pregnancy. In a pregnant cat, this needs to be distinguished from mastitis and mammary cancer. The condition has also been reported in neutered females and males receiving progesterone therapy for another condition, and will appear two to six weeks after the therapy.

The breast enlargement may or may not be painful. In severe cases, characterized by rapid increase in breast size, there is reddish-blue discoloration, warmth, pain, and ulceration of the skin overlying the swollen breast. The hind legs may become swollen.

One very severe complication of mammary hyperplasia is clotting of the veins in the breast. This occurs in a small number of cases. The clotting process extends centrally. If the clots break free and are carried to the lungs, these cats may die suddenly from pulmonary thromboembolism. Secondary infections can lead to septic shock.

Painful, swollen breasts in lactating queens is discussed in *Postpartum Problems* (see page 446).

Treatment: The best treatment for mammary hyperplasia is spaying the cat. When the condition is related to pregnancy or progesterone therapy, consider either allowing the queen to deliver or discontinuing the progesterone. The risks must be balanced against the benefits. Breast *biopsy* is indicated only when breast swelling or enlargement occurs in a cat who is neither pregnant nor experiencing her first *estrous*, or when the swelling does not disappear after the source of the progesterone has been removed.

A new medication, aglepristone, is a progesterone blocker and removes the hormonal stimulus for the problem. It has been used experimentally with good success, but at this time it is not approved for use in the United States; it may become available in the future.

BREAST TUMORS

Breast tumors occur frequently in unspayed cats. Eighty percent are malignant (adenocarcinoma). The rest are benign adenomas. Breast cancer is the third most common cancer in cats. Most affected cats are unspayed females over

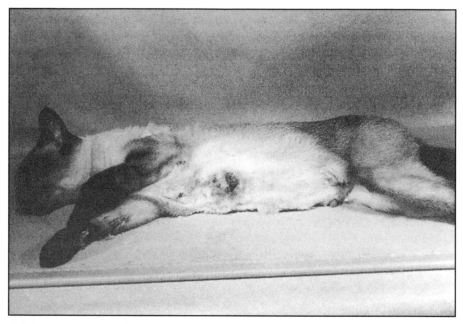

This is a severe case of mammary hyperplasia with skin ulceration. This breast swelling is caused by high levels of progesterone.

6 years old. Siamese have an increased risk for mammary cancer, as do cats with the calico pattern. Breast cancer is rare among spayed females, especially those neutered before their first heat cycle. Early spaying reduces the risk factors sevenfold.

Feline breast cancer is a rapidly progressing neoplasm that has a high rate of local recurrence following treatment. It tends to spread widely, with the lungs being the favored site for metastases, as well as local lymph nodes. The typical presentation is a painless, firm, nodular mass in one or more breasts, most commonly involving the first and fourth nipples in line. The skin ulcerates as the tumor advances. A chest X-ray is advisable to rule out lung involvement before embarking on radical surgery.

Progesterone therapy may also increase the risk of breast tumors, including cancers. Avoid the use of progestins to treat skin or behavior problems.

Treatment: Surgical removal is the treatment of choice for all breast tumors. Surgery may appear quite radical, with a very large incision to increase the likelihood of removing all the cancerous tissue. Close follow-up to detect local recurrence after surgery is advisable. Chemotherapy may help to improve quality of life. Secondary infections are common, so most cats end up on postoperative antibiotics.

The success of the operation depends on the stage of the tumor at the time of surgery. The earlier the cancer is discovered and treated, the better the outlook. Prognosis is closely related to the size of the tumor at the time of surgery,

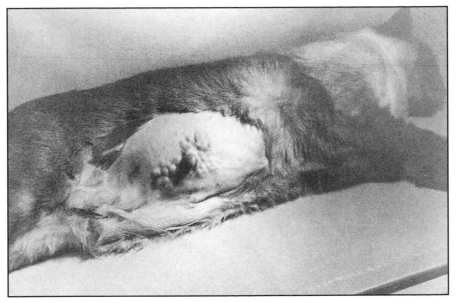

This cat shows a rapidly growing multinodular neoplasm that is typical of feline breast cancer.

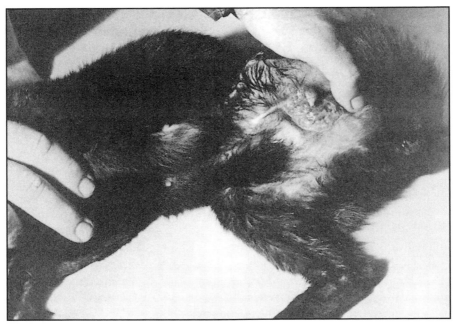

The ulcerating form of breast cancer causes growths like this one.

with smaller tumors offering the best prognosis. Therefore, when your unspayed female is 3 or 4 years old, begin examining her breasts at least once a month. If you detect a suspicious swelling or a firm lump, ask your veterinarian to examine it.

Feline Leukemia Virus

Feline leukemia virus (FeLV) is a retrovirus, so named because of the way it behaves within infected cells. All retroviruses produce an enzyme that enables them to insert copies of their own genetic material into the cells they have infected. Although FeLV is not a cancer, it can cause many health problems directly and also indirectly by lowering immunity, and is the most common cause of cancer in cats. FeLV is directly associated with two types of cancer of the blood (leukemia): acute nonlymphoid leukemia and acute lymphoid leukemia. (Also see *Feline Leukemia Virus*, page 89.)

Although not all cats who test positive for FeLV or are exposed to the feline leukemia virus will become ill, it is best to test young cats, isolate any who test positive, and vaccinate all cats who might be exposed.

To diagnose these cancers, blood tests are done, including checking the cat's FeLV status, but a bone marrow *aspirate* may be necessary for the definitive diagnosis. Cats tend to become inactive, not eat well, and may have a fever. With acute lymphoid leukemia, there may be swollen and reactive lymph nodes that you can feel.

Treatment: Cats with acute lymphoid leukemia may do well for a period of time with corticosteroids and immune stimulants. The acute nonlymphoid type has a very grave prognosis, with many cats dying within two weeks of being diagnosed.

Feline Lymphoma

Lymphoma (cancer that originates in the lymphocytes, a type of white blood cell) is one of the more common cancers in cats. Male cats, and cats in the Northeast in general, have an increased risk—probably related to an increased risk of feline leukemia virus. Cats who test positive for FeLV have a 60-fold increased risk of developing lymphoma, while cats who are positive for feline immunodeficiency virus (FIV) have a 5-fold increased risk for developing this type of cancer. Cats who are positive for both viruses have an 80-fold increase in their risk of developing lymphoma. Whether these viruses have a direct effect in causing the cancer or act primarily by interfering with the cat's normal immunity is not known for certain.

The most common lymphoma sites in cats are the gastrointestinal system, the spine, and the chest cavity. The gastrointestinal type is the most common

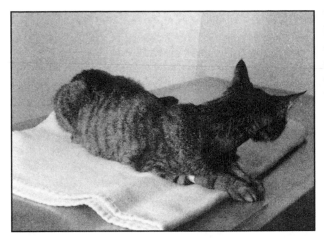

This young cat has lymphoma. The rough coat and emaciated appearance are the only outward signs of this cancer.

of the three forms of lymphoma and is not as closely associated with FeLV as are the other two. This type appears in older cats as weight loss and a drop in appetite. Some cats will vomit and/or have diarrhea, depending on the exact location of the cancer. Stomach cancers tend to cause vomiting and intestinal cancers are more likely to cause diarrhea. Siamese and domestic shorthairs seem to have an increased risk of developing this type of lymphoma.

Mediastinal lymphoma occurs in the lymph nodes inside the chest cavity. Cats under 5 years of age who are FeLV positive are at risk for developing this type of cancer, especially if they are Siamese or one of the Oriental breeds. Fluid will build up and leads to difficulty breathing, along with regurgitation and loss of appetite.

Spinal lymphoma tends to show up in 3- to 4-year-old male cats, especially if they are FeLV positive. The first signs may be problems with their hind legs.

Diagnosing lymphoma usually requires blood tests, including tests for FeLV and FIV. Chest X-rays help with mediastinal masses and ultrasound can be helpful for abdominal growths. Spinal growths may require special dye studies, combined with X-rays or a spinal tap (removing spinal fluid for analysis).

Treatment: Surgery, radiation, and chemotherapy have all been used to treat lymphomas, depending on the exact location and whether the cancer has spread. The prognosis is best for a cat with a single intestinal nodule and worst for a cat with a spinal growth.

Hyperthyroidism (Thyroid Cancer)

Hyperthyroidism in cats is almost always associated with a cancer—a benign adenoma (more common) or a malignant adenocarcinoma. These cancers tend to occur in older cats and the major effect is the increased thyroid hormone production they stimulate. Exposure to secondhand cigarette smoke may be a factor. Himalayans and Siamese have a lower risk for this problem.

The first signs may be dramatic. The increase in thyroid hormones tends to cause an increase in appetite—the finicky eater now wolfs everything down and may even open cupboards looking for more—and an increase in activity. The sedate older cat who used to spend his days soaking in the sun on his window seat is now flying around the house like a wild kitten. Weight loss, vomiting, and panting may all be noted. Careful palpation of the area under the chin when the head is lifted may reveal a small lump. Thyroid tumors may appear only on one side, but they can be bilateral.

Blood work is important to see if thyroid hormone levels are truly elevated. It is important to check kidney function, because the increased metabolic rate may hide kidney failure. It is also important to thoroughly evaluate the heart, which can be damaged from the increased metabolic rate. High blood pressure or hypertension is often seen in hyperthyroid cats.

Treatment: Treatment tends to start with an oral medication called methimazole, which lowers hormone production. This must be given daily and manufacturers are working on palatable and easy-to-administer forms for cats, including a compounded version that is applied to the ear and absorbed through the skin. Medical treatment enables your veterinarian to evaluate the cat's kidney and cardiac status prior to the more definitive treatment of surgery or radioactive iodine.

Surgery is another option, with the cancerous gland removed. Care must be taken not to damage or remove the parathyroid glands that regulate calcium metabolism. If both thyroid glands are removed, the cat will need supplemental thyroid for the rest of his life.

A third and popular option is to use radioactive iodine to destroy the cancerous tissue. Cats who undergo this therapy must stay at a treatment center for 7 to 25 days while the radioactivity shed in the cat's urine and feces decreases to a safe level. These cats may need supplemental thyroid for the rest of their lives.

Caught early, before any residual damage is done to the heart or the kidneys, this can be a very treatable disease. If the heart and kidneys are already damaged, they will still need treatment after the cancer is removed. For the rare cats who get an adenocarcinoma, as opposed to simply an adenoma, the cancer has often metastasized by the time it is diagnosed and the prognosis is very poor.

Vaccine-Associated Feline Sarcoma

A sarcoma is a cancer of the connective and soft tissues. Sarcomas are not a new form of cancer in cats. But in 1991, veterinarians began to notice a higher than expected number of sarcomas occurring in places where vaccines are

commonly injected. Subsequently, an association between vaccine administration and sarcoma development has been established. FeLV and rabies virus
vaccines have more frequently been implicated in sarcoma development than
have other vaccines. Both subcutaneous and intramuscular sites have been
affected. Injections other than vaccines may also be implicated.

The increased appearance of these sarcomas roughly coincided with the
change from using a modified-live rabies virus vaccine to an adjuvanted killed
virus vaccine. At about the same time, an aluminum-adjuvanted FeLV vaccine
was introduced. Adjuvants are added to vaccines to increase the immune
response—especially in vaccines that use killed versions of a virus. Adjuvants
in general, and aluminum adjuvants in particular, were therefore thought to
be the culprit. However, researchers are no longer certain this is the case. It is
believed that these vaccines cause some kind of inflammation at the vaccination site that, in some cases, is associated with sarcoma development, but an
exact link has not been proven.

Nonetheless, vaccine manufacturers are developing recombinant vaccines
that do not use adjuvant and that cause less inflammation at the vaccination
site. Many modified-live virus vaccines are available for other viral diseases
and some of them do not contain adjuvant. New vaccination guidelines (see
page 111) try to minimize the number of injections given over a cat's lifetime,
as well, and also recommend specific sites on the body for injections to
be given.

It's important to remember that vaccine-associated sarcoma is still a very
rare form of cancer. The occurrence rate varies from 1 in 1,000 to 1 in 10,000.
The wide range seems to be associated with a genetic predisposition to this
problem in certain cats and lines of cats. For instance, some geographic areas
show an increased rate.

These cancers may show up months or even years after a vaccination.
Although a fair number of cats have a small lump after getting a vaccination,
the lump should be gone within a month. If it is not, have the cat examined
by a veterinarian.

Because so much is still unknown, the Vaccine-Associated Feline Sarcoma
Task Force was formed as a joint effort of the American Association of Feline
Practitioners, American Animal Hospital Association, American Veterinary
Medical Association, and Veterinary Cancer Society. This group is working to
determine the true scope of the problem, the cause, and the most effective
treatment for vaccine-associated sarcomas.

Treatment: This is an aggressive cancer that tends to spread in and
between muscle layers, making it very difficult to remove all of the cancerous
cells surgically. Surgery, with radiation done either before or after the surgery,
seems to be the most successful treatment plan, but most of these cancers
recur, nonetheless.

20

GERIATRICS

Indoor cats now live an average of 15 years, and it is not uncommon to see cats 18 to 20 years of age. The domestic cat in the wild (sometimes called a feral cat) has a short life expectancy—about 6 years. Accidents, diseases, parasites, the trials of securing food, and the stresses of multiple and frequent pregnancies all contribute to this shortened life. The city cat fares somewhat better, but still contends with infectious diseases, accidents, fights, and sometimes malicious behavior on the part of humans. The indoor pet, being well nourished, vaccinated against infectious diseases, and protected from accidents, fares the best.

Of greatest importance is the care the cat has received throughout her life. Well-cared-for pets suffer fewer infirmities as they grow older. But when sickness, illness, or injury is neglected, the aging process is accelerated.

The Geriatric Checkup

Caring for an older cat is directed at preventing premature aging, minimizing physical and emotional stress, and meeting the special needs of the elderly. Cats older than 7 should have a complete veterinary examination *at least* once a year—often, twice a year is preferred. If the health of the cat is questionable, she should be seen by a veterinarian more often. If symptoms appear, she should be seen at once.

The annual geriatric checkup should include a physical examination, complete blood count, blood chemistries, stool exam, and urinalysis. Depending on the results, special liver and kidney function tests, a chest X-ray, and an *electrocardiogram* may also be needed. Some veterinary clinics include checking blood pressure as part of the geriatric exam for cats. Thyroid hormone levels, such as T4, are also important in older cats.

Kidney disease is relatively common in older cats, and a new, simple urine test called Early Renal Disease Healthscreen (ERD) checks for protein leakage into the urine—specifically, albumin. This test may pick up kidney failure very early on so you can take steps to slow its progression.

Routine dental care, including scaling the teeth, may be needed more frequently than once a year.

TEMPERATURE, PULSE, AND RESPIRATION

The rectal temperature is an important indicator of health. How to take the cat's temperature is described in appendix A. A temperature over 103°F (39.4°C) indicates inflammation or infection. In older cats, the most common sites are the lungs and the urinary tract.

A rapid heart rate is often a sign of anemia, infection, or heart disease. Anemia is suggested by paleness of the mucous membranes, especially the tongue. Possible causes of anemia include liver disease, kidney failure, and cancer.

A rapid breathing rate (more than 30 breaths per minute at rest) suggests lung disease. Rarely, it is related to heart disease. Chronic cough suggests bronchitis or airway disease. A new-onset cough suggests cancer.

It is even more important with an elderly cat to know what is normal for her— including eating habits, behavior, elimination, and vital signs.

DANGER SIGNS IN THE GERIATRIC CAT

If you see any of the following signs, take your cat to the veterinarian as soon as possible.

- Loss of appetite or weight
- Coughing, shortness of breath, or rapid, labored breathing
- Weakness or difficultly moving about
- Increased thirst and/or frequency of urination
- Change in bowel function with constipation or diarrhea
- Bloody or purulent discharge from a body opening
- An increase in temperature, pulse, or breathing rate
- A growth or lump anywhere on the body
- Any unexplained change in behavior

Physical Changes

The cat's life cycle can be divided into three stages—kittenhood, adulthood, and old age. The periods marked by youth and old age are relatively short when compared with the length of adulthood. After puberty, an adult cat's physique changes very little until quite close to the end of life with the exception of changes in weight. (For a relative comparison of human and feline ages, see appendix B.)

A periodic examination done at home may reveal an age-related condition that can be improved by modifying the cat's care or routine. Although aging is inevitable and irreversible, some infirmities attributed to old age may in fact be due to disease, and thus are correctable or at least treatable by your veterinarian. Understand that many old cat problems are not curable, but they can be controlled or, at the very least, the rate of progression slowed.

MUSCULOSKELETAL PROBLEMS

To examine your cat's musculoskeletal system, *gently* flex the front and rear legs, noting any stiffness or limitations on movement. Compare one side with the other. Look for swollen, painful joints.

An early sign of aging is loss of muscle tone and strength, especially in the legs. The muscles may begin to shake when the cat stands. The cat becomes less agile and perhaps incapable of jumping up to a favorite spot. Degenerative changes in the joints and muscles lead to stiffness and intermittent lameness, most apparent when the cat gets up from a nap. Stiffness in the joints is made worse by drafts and by sleeping on cold, damp, hard surfaces such as tile or cement. Make a comfortable bed for the cat indoors on a well-padded surface. The cat may need to be covered at night. Many cats like to burrow into a pile of warm blankets or a "hidey hole" cat house or tunnel.

Moderate exercise helps keep joints supple and should be encouraged. However, older cats should not be forced to exert themselves beyond their comfort level—best judged by themselves. A specific condition (such as heart disease) may require that exercise be restricted.

Older cats who have trouble getting up to favorite spots, such as the bed or the windowsill, will appreciate having steps or a ramp to help them up. Ramps should have a nonslip covering.

Some pain medications are now available for cats and can be used for arthritic pain. Acupuncture and even hydrotherapy (if your cat will accept swimming!) have also been found to be effective. Do not give any medications without consulting your veterinarian, because some common pain medications used for dogs and people are very toxic to cats.

Nutraceuticals that protect joint cartilage, such as polysulfated glycosaminoglycan and chondroitin sulfate, are available through your veterinarian and from health food stores, and may also help to keep a geriatric cat active and pain-free. For more information on the treatment of osteoarthritis, see page 362.

Massage and TTouch (developed by Linda Tellington-Jones) techniques can make an old, stiff cat much more comfortable.

COAT AND SKIN PROBLEMS

Skin disorders are more frequent in aging cats. The skin is thinner in old cats, and so it is more susceptible to damage.

Older cats will especially appreciate soft, warm places to rest and sleep.

One skin problem that tends to occur more frequently in aging cats is maggots. A cat's fur that has become matted and soiled becomes a target for flies. Then, too, the debilitated individual is less capable of keeping flies away. This problem is mainly seen in geriatric cats with access to the outdoors.

Any chronic illness can be reflected in poor coat quality or even loss of hair. Hair loss may be associated with compulsive self-grooming, a condition that has a psychological cause. Overgrooming may also be associated with an area that is painful. A debilitated or depressed cat may lose interest in grooming. A stiff, older cat may be unable to flex enough to groom. An overweight cat may not be able to reach all parts of her body to groom. Geriatric cats should be combed or brushed every day. Grooming may need to be done in several short sessions if the cat quickly becomes uncomfortable. Frequent grooming and cleaning with a damp cloth will keep the coat free of parasites and the skin healthy. A comb may be needed to gently work through matts. Look closely at your cat's coat and skin as you groom. Examination of the hair and skin may reveal tumors, parasites, or other skin disorders that require prompt veterinary attention.

Cats enjoy the stroking and attention that accompanies these sessions. As self-esteem is restored, the cat may once again begin to take pride in her appearance and begin self-grooming again.

Occasionally, it may be necessary to bathe a cat whose coat has become matted or especially dirty. The procedure for giving a bath is described on page 124. Old cats chill easily. They should be towel dried and kept in a warm room. Badly matted longhaired cats may need to be clipped or shaved.

Claws may need to be trimmed more often. They are less likely to be worn down by activity and will overgrow and become brittle.

Some older cats enjoy having a sweater or jacket to wear, especially in chilly or damp weather. Other cats would never consider wearing clothing. Find out what your cat prefers.

THE SENSES

Gradual hearing loss occurs as cats grow older but may not be apparent until the cat has lost a significant portion of her hearing. That's because a cat with impaired hearing compensates by relying on other senses. Accordingly, it is often difficult to tell if a cat is going deaf. Techniques to test your cat's hearing are described in *Deafness* (see page 217). Senile deafness has no treatment. However, a hearing problem could be exacerbated by a wax blockage in the ear canal or some other problem, such as ear mites or a tumor, *all of which can be treated*. Do not assume a hearing problem is caused by aging alone. Veterinary evaluation is important.

Always loudly say the cat's name or stamp your foot when you approach an older cat who is asleep and is hard of hearing. That way, the cat will not startle when you touch her and accidentally bite or strike out.

Loss of eyesight is also difficult to assess in the cat—again, because the other senses become more acute. Old age cataracts are not common in cats. In fact, loss of vision in geriatric cats is more likely to be caused by retinal diseases (often secondary to hypertension) or by uveitis or glaucoma. How to test your cat's vision is discussed on page 172.

Cats adjust well to the loss of eyesight if they retain their hearing. Even when both senses are impaired, cats can still adjust to familiar surroundings and get around nicely by using their whiskers, the carpal hair on the backs of their front legs, and the pressure receptors in their feet. It is important to avoid moving furniture and household belongings if you have a blind cat, because the cat will have a mental map of where everything is and will move with confidence around the house as long as nothing is changed.

Loss of smell is a serious handicap. The cat's odor-sensing mechanism is a powerful stimulant to appetite. If cats cannot smell, they may lose interest in food. You may be able to test the cat's sense of smell by passing an alcohol swab under her nose. A cat with an intact sense of smell will draw back away from the swab. A cat with an impaired sense of smell should be fed highly aromatic and palatable foods. Gently warming foods can increase the intensity of their aroma. Homemade diets may be the answer for a finicky older cat. Always check with your veterinarian to be sure the diet is balanced and complete.

MOUTH, TEETH, AND GUMS

Periodontal disease and tooth decay are more common in older cats. Periodontal disease is a gradual process that begins in early adulthood. If it goes unchecked, it culminates in advanced gum disease and tooth decay in geriatric cats. But this need not happen. Periodontal disease is preventable by routine dental care, as described in *Taking Care of Your Cat's Teeth*, page 244. Medicated oral gels may be gently applied to your cat's gums if she doesn't tolerate tooth brushing.

Cats with infected gums and teeth experience mouth pain, often accompanied by halitosis and drooling. A cat with a painful mouth eats poorly and loses weight rapidly. Dental treatment relieves suffering and improves health and nutrition. Loose teeth should be removed. If the cat is unable to chew dry cat food, switch to canned food. Geriatric cats may need more frequent dental care, including scaling the teeth at least twice a year.

Behavior Changes

In general, older cats are more sedentary, less energetic, often less curious, and more restricted in their scope of activity. They adjust slowly to changes in diet, activity, and routine. They are less tolerant of extremes of heat and cold. They seek out warm spots and sleep longer. When disturbed, they are cranky

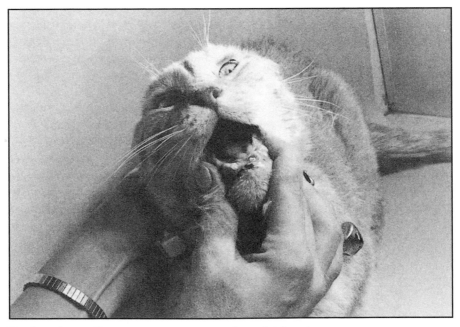

Tooth and gum disease are more common in geriatric cats.

and irritable. Most of these behavior changes are because of physical ailments—diminished hearing and smell, stiffness, and muscular weakness—that restrict a cat's activity and ability to participate in family life. A cat so deprived may withdraw, engage in compulsive self-grooming, or eliminate in places other than the litter box.

Encourage your cat to participate more actively by finding a warm nesting spot for her near the center of family activity. Provide a low window seat so she can soak up the sun and watch the birds. Sitting quietly with her will be good for you too! Some cats enjoy regularly going outside for a comfortable walk on leash in the yard or the neighborhood. A geriatric cat may prefer being carried or riding in a stroller, and will not enjoy outings in the cold weather. Activities that provide human companionship will be deeply appreciated and will give the cat a sense of being valued and loved.

Boarding and hospitalization are poorly tolerated in old age. Often, cats left in these situations eat poorly or not at all, become overly anxious or withdrawn, and sleep poorly. If possible, care for them at home under the guidance of your veterinarian. If you are going away, instead of boarding the cat, ask a friend to drop by once or twice a day to attend to the cat's needs. Some communities offer cat-sitting services.

Behavior changes caused by physical infirmities may improve with treatment. If they do not, abnormal behavior can sometimes be modified or improved through the use of behavioral modification medications.

COGNITIVE DYSFUNCTION SYNDROME

Cognitive dysfunction syndrome has become a well-known syndrome in geriatric dogs. A similar condition is seen in some older cats. Just as in some older people, the older cat may have memory problems, forget behaviors such as how to use the litter box, and lose some awareness of her surroundings. Some cats will pace, sleep less at night, or walk around crying as if they are lost. Disorientation may be evident in up to 40 percent of cats from 16 to 20 years of age.

First, any medical problems that could cause these changes need to be eliminated. If medical causes can be ruled out, the diagnosis is cognitive dysfunction syndrome.

A drug called L-deprenyl (Anipryl) is approved for use in dogs with this condition, but not for cats at this time. L-deprenyl has been used off label in some cats and seems to be beneficial. A release must be signed to use a drug off label. Research is ongoing into other drugs that will increase the action of neurotransmitters such as dopamine and serotonin, in the hope that they will help older cats with cognitive dysfunction.

Functional Changes

Changes in eating and drinking patterns, voiding habits, and bowel function occur frequently in older cats. If you are not especially alert to such changes, you may overlook an important clue to a developing health problem. Make sure that water and food bowls are easily accessible, and note any changes in eating and drinking habits. Elimination habits can be difficult to observe. Some cats dislike using their litter box in front of their owners. Some effort will be required to see if the cat is having problems defecating or voiding—particularly if the cat spends time outdoors.

INCREASED THIRST AND FREQUENT URINATION

Most very old cats develop some degree of kidney failure. The kidneys of cats appear to wear out sooner than do other organs, and as cats live longer lives, their kidneys sometimes appear to be unable to keep up. Early signs of kidney failure include increased frequency of urination and a compensatory increased frequency of drinking.

Increased thirst (polydypsia) and urination (polyuria) are also signs of diabetes, a condition more common in older cats. Hyperthyroidism may also cause increased thirst and urination.

HOUSE SOILING

Older cats who stop using their litter boxes and begin urinating in the house may be suffering from urinary tract disease or some other treatable condition, discussed in *Urinary Incontinence* (page 390). The conditions described in the previous section, which produce increased urination and thirst, may also lead to house soiling. Enlarged prostate is not a major cause of urinary symptoms in the cat.

Some cases of house soiling are due to musculoskeletal problems, such as arthritis, that restrict activity. Cats with difficulty getting about may be unwilling or unable to go to the litter box. If the box is on another floor of the house, the cat may feel too uncomfortable to climb the stairs. If the sides of the box are too high or the cat must climb into or onto another piece of furniture to get to the box, she also may stop using it. An older cat may need several low-sided litters boxes placed all around the home. Sometimes, an ordinary cafeteria-type tray with litter in it may be all an old cat can manage. A cat who goes outdoors and had been in the habit of eliminating outside may also decide that is no longer comfortable, and will need low, indoor litter boxes.

House soiling may also be due to failing memory and a decline in learned behavior associated with cognitive dysfunction syndrome (see page 538).

Another possible cause of house soiling is hormone-responsive incontinence. This is rare in cats but is sometimes seen in older spayed females. Hormone-responsive incontinence is much like bed wetting. The cat urinates normally but wets when relaxed or asleep. Treatment is discussed in *Urinary Incontinence*, page 390. Inappropriate defecation may be due to loss of sphincter control.

In all cases of house soiling, it is important to thoroughly clean the soiled areas with an enzymatic cleaner to prevent odors that might attract the cat to return to the area. *Do not punish the cat.* Most likely, the cat is unable to control herself. Scolding and punishment only produces fear and anxiety, which makes the problem worse.

CONSTIPATION

Constipation is one of the most common problems in older cats. Contributing factors include lack of exercise, voluntary fecal retention, improper diet, reduced bowel activity, and weakness of the abdominal wall muscles. Along with a tendency to drink less water that is seen in some older cats, this produces hard, dry stools that are difficult to pass. Hairballs, which produce constipation in cats of all ages, are particularly troublesome in the older individual.

It is important not to mistake straining to urinate with straining to defecate. The obstructed bladder is an emergency that requires immediate veterinary attention to relieve the cause of the blockage (see *Feline Lower Urinary Tract Disease*, page 380).

Treating constipation is discussed on page 276; preventing hairballs is discussed on page 128.

DIARRHEA

Cats with chronic diarrhea exhibit skin irritation around the anus, dehydration, weight loss, and a poor coat. Chronic diarrhea in the geriatric cat can be a sign of cancer, pancreatic disease, or malabsorption syndrome. When due strictly to old age, diarrhea can be controlled through diet and medication. Diarrhea may go unnoticed in cats who eliminate outdoors. See *Diarrhea* on page 278 for more information.

ABNORMAL DISCHARGES

Abnormal discharges are those that contain pus or blood. Often, they are accompanied by an offensive odor. Discharges from the eyes, ears, nose, mouth, penis, or vagina suggest infection. In the geriatric cat, cancer is a consideration.

Pyometra (abscess of the uterus) typically occurs in older, barren, intact females. It does not occur in spayed female cats. Signs include lethargy and depression, loss of appetite, increased thirst, and excessive drinking. These signs may at first suggest kidney failure, but the abdomen of the cat becomes quite markedly distended and firm. Purulent vaginal discharge makes the diagnosis obvious, but in some cases, a discharge is absent. Pyometra is a true surgical emergency requiring immediate veterinary attention (see *Uterine Infection*, page 422).

Weight Changes

Weight loss is serious in the aging cat. Many cases are caused by kidney disease; others by cancers, periodontal disease, and loss of smell. Weigh your cat once a month. Weight loss is an indication for a veterinary checkup.

Excessive weight gain is an important but largely preventable problem that must be corrected in the geriatric cat. Obesity is a complicating factor in arthritis and heart disease. Overweight cats are less likely to exercise and maintain their overall strength and vitality.

A large pot belly may appear to be a fat problem when in reality a heart, liver, or kidney disease with *ascites* (fluid buildup in the abdomen) is the cause. Thus, a change in physique with a swollen abdomen is an indication for veterinary examination.

The specific nutritional needs of geriatric cats are addressed in *Feeding Geriatric Cats*, page 507.

HYPERTHYROIDISM

The diagnosis of hyperthyroidism may not be suspected in a geriatric cat for many months because of other illnesses of aging that may obscure the symptoms. A cat may lose a surprising amount of weight while eating well and appearing to be bright and alert. Thyroid blood tests establish the diagnosis.

Treatment: Treatment is directed at returning the cat to a normal thyroid status. This can be accomplished with antithyroid drugs, surgery to remove the thyroid gland, or administering radioactive iodine at a referral center equipped to handle radioactive materials. Your veterinarian will advise you about the best treatment for your cat. For more information, see *Hyperthyroidism*, page 529.

Adding a New Kitten

Adding a kitten to the household can be a rejuvenating experience for a geriatric cat, or it can make her remaining time a nightmare. Some older cats delight in the companionship. Through renewed interest and added exercise, they seem to recapture their youth. Others—in fact, most older cats—do not appreciate the addition of a kitten. This is especially true if the older cat has been a single cat for most of her life. It is best to start with a few temporary kitten visits, to see if your older cat is interested and to be sure both cats are compatible.

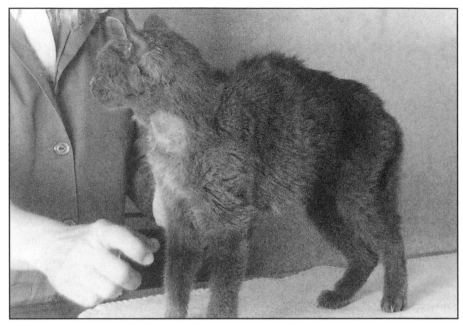

This hyperthyroid cat is seriously underweight. She underwent a thyroidectomy to remove a toxic nodular goiter.

Prevent jealousy by giving attention to the older cat first. Always affirm the older cat's senior privileges. It is also important to have an area where the older cat can go to be alone when she needs a break from a rowdy kitten. Make sure the geriatric cat gets special one-on-one attention every day.

Hospice Care

Hospice care for cats has come to the forefront in recent years. Hospice care can be chosen when your cat has a terminal illness and you don't want to pursue more extensive medical care, but would like to provide comfort care for as long as possible. The goals of hospice are to control pain, keep the cat comfortable and provide a decent quality of life for as long as possible.

Hospice care is a big commitment. Although your veterinarian will draw up a care plan for the cat, you will be administering virtually all of the care. Some training may be required to enable you to safely give medications and to detect signs of problems. Some hospice programs involve occasional home visits by a veterinarian or a veterinary technician to assist with care and evaluations. A few hospitals provide hospice care on-site with owners visiting or staying for the duration.

Talk to your veterinarian about home care that will ease this final transition for your cat.

Euthanasia

The time may come when you are faced with the prospect of having to end your pet's life. This is a difficult decision to make—both for you and for your veterinarian. Many old and infirm cats can be made quite comfortable with just a little more thoughtfulness and tender loving care than the average healthy cat needs. Old cats can still enjoy months or years of happiness in the company of loved ones.

But when life ceases to be a joy and a pleasure, when the cat suffers from a painful and progressive condition for which there is no hope of betterment, then perhaps at this time we owe the cat the final kindness of helping her to die easily and painlessly. Quality of life issues are always difficult, but questions to ask yourself include the following:

- Is she having more good days than bad days?
- Can she still do the things she loves to do best?
- Is she in pain or discomfort that can't be relieved?
- Is she eating and drinking?

When it is clear that comfort is no longer possible, it is time for euthanasia. This is accomplished by an intravenous injection of an anesthetic agent in a sufficient amount to cause immediate loss of consciousness and cardiac arrest. Some cats will vocalize at the last instant or appear to take a deep breath after death; this is normal, as is the loss of urine and/or stool. Although adults must make the final decisions, children often handle all of this better than adults suspect, and should be involved in the decisions following the death of the cat.

How involved children will be in this process will depend on their age and emotional maturity. Euthanasia should not be referred to as "putting to sleep," as this may frighten children at bedtime and/or lead to expectations that the cat will "wake up" and return.

Grieving for a cat may involve different stages. These include denial, bargaining, anger, sadness, and acceptance. Not everyone will go through all these stages, and the length of time and order for each stage is individual. There are pet loss hotlines available and grief counselors are now better equipped to deal with pet loss.

Pet loss hotlines include these:

- University of California–Davis Veterinary Students; (530) 752-3602 or (800) 565-1526; www.vetmed.ucdavis.edu/petloss/index.htm
- Colorado State University–Argus Institute; (970) 491-4143; www.argus institute.colostate.edu/grief.htm
- Cornell University Veterinary Students; (607) 253-3932; web.vet.cornell .edu/public/petloss/

- University of Illinois College of Veterinary Medicine; (217) 244-2273 or (877) 394-2273; www.cvm.uiuc.edu/CARE/
- Washington State University College of Veterinary Medicine; (509) 335-5704; www.vetmed.wsu.edu/plhl/index.htm

Almost all veterinary colleges offer some grief counseling. Your veterinarian can guide you to local groups and resources such as helpful books.

A FINAL MEMORIAL

Ideally, you need to think about how to handle the body before your cat has died. Burial is the choice of many families. Local laws may prohibit burying pets in your yard, but most communities have a pet cemetery close by. There will be a fee for this—particularly if perpetual care is included.

Cremation is ideal for many people who don't have a burial site. Costs vary dramatically, especially if you want a private cremation so that you can receive all of your own cat's ashes back. The ashes can then be spread in your cat's favorite places, buried in a small area, or kept by you in an urn.

There are many ways to memorialize your cat. A lock of hair enclosed in a locket can be comforting. Having ashes sealed in a locket is another possibility. Many families decide to make a donation in their cat's memory to a local humane society, a rescue group, or a feline health research fund. All of these are worthy causes and keep your cat's memory alive in a very positive way.

21

MEDICATIONS

Before discussing the specifics of the most common medications used in veterinary medicine, it's important to review some basic rules that apply to all medications you give your cat.

- The label should list the name of the drug, its strength, how much there is in the container, the expiration date, and how to give it.
- Be sure you understand the dose. For example, is it two pills once a day or one pill twice a day?
- Make sure you know how the medication is to be given. For example, are the drops to go in the mouth or in the ears?
- Make sure you know whether the medication can be given with food.
- Ask your veterinarian about side effects.
- Make sure you know how the medication is to be stored and if it needs to be refrigerated or shaken.
- Always be sure your veterinarian is aware of all supplements and other medications your cat is taking.

Anesthesia

Anesthetics are drugs used to block the sensation of pain. They are divided into two categories: local anesthesia and general anesthesia.

Local anesthesia is used for surgery on the surface of the body, where it is injected into tissues and around regional nerves. It may be applied topically to mucous membranes. Local anesthetics (such as xylocaine) have the fewest risks and side effects but are not suitable for most major surgeries.

General anesthesia renders the cat unconscious. It can be given by injection or inhalation. Light anesthesia sedates or relaxes the cat and may be suitable for short procedures, such as removing a foreign body from the mouth.

Inhaled gases (such as halothane, sevoflurane, and isoflurane) are administered through a tube placed in the trachea.

Combinations of anesthesia often are used to lessen potential side effects. For example, ketamine and xylazine (Rompun) are common injectable anesthetics used together for short procedures. The guideline dose of an injectable anesthetic is computed by the cat's weight. Since cats are unusually sensitive to ordinary doses of a drug such as barbiturates, veterinarians often administer the anesthetic in repeated small doses until the desired affect is obtained, rather than giving it all at once.

For gas anesthesia, the mixture of oxygen and anesthetic is balanced and the dose adjusted according to the breathing of the cat. Many factors require that the exact dosage be customized to the individual cat. Certain breeds have an increased sensitivity to barbiturates and other anesthesia, and that must also be taken into account. This may be related to structure, such as cats with short faces, or conformation, such as thin cats without extra weight or fat.

Anesthesia is removed from the cat's system by the lungs, liver, and kidneys. Impaired function of these organs can cause dose-related complications. If your cat has a history of lung, liver, kidney, or heart disease, the risk from anesthesia and surgery is increased. Cats with those problems may require less anesthetic to attain the needed depth of anesthesia or may take longer to become fully aware after anesthesia. Presurgery bloodwork is recommended to

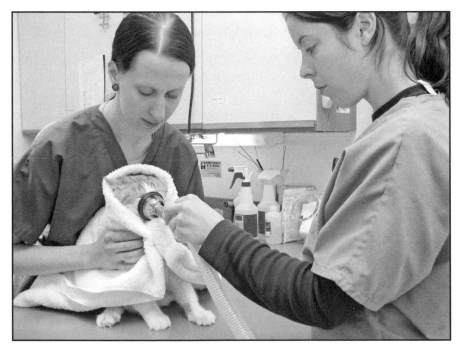

This cat is being put under using an inhaled anesthesia, in preparation for a dental procedure.

detect any such problems. Some clinics may also suggest chest X-rays, an EKG, and blood pressure evaluations, especially if your cat is geriatric.

A major risk of a general anesthetic is the cat vomiting when going to sleep or waking up. The vomitus refluxes into the trachea and causes asphyxiation. This can be avoided by keeping the stomach empty for 12 hours before scheduled surgery. If you know your cat is going to have surgery, *do not give anything to eat or drink the night before*. This means picking up the water dish and keeping the cat away from the toilet bowl and other sources of water, as well. If your cat has liver or kidney problems, your veterinarian may suggest leaving water available. Diabetic cats may need adjustments in their feeding schedule and insulin injections.

Your cat will also have an endotracheal tube placed into his trachea. This has a small balloon cuff to prevent any fluids from leaking into the lungs. This tube is attached to the gas anesthetic machine.

Analgesics

Analgesics are drugs used to relieve pain. There are many classes of painkillers. All must be used with caution in cats. Even though human analgesics are common household items, they should not be given to cats.

Demerol, morphine, codeine, and other narcotics are subject to federal regulation and cannot be bought without a prescription. The effect of these drugs on cats is highly unpredictable. Morphine, in a dose appropriate for a small dog, produces apprehension, excitability, and drooling in the cat. When this minimum dose is exceeded, the cat may convulse and die. Fentanyl, usually incorporated into a patch placed on the skin, is a pain medication used in cats. Again, never use this without veterinary guidance, as there can be severe side effects.

NSAIDS

Aspirin (acetylsalicylic acid) is one of a class of drugs called nonsteroidal anti-inflammatory drugs (NSAIDs). Buffered or enteric-coated aspirin is a safe analgesic for home veterinary use in dogs, but it must be administered with extreme care to cats. Small doses of aspirin given to cats can produce loss of appetite, depression, and vomiting. One aspirin tablet a day for three or four days is sufficient to cause salivation, dehydration, vomiting, and a staggering gait. Severe disturbances in the acid-base balance may ensue. The bone marrow and liver may show signs of toxicity. Gastrointestinal bleeding is common.

Be aware of this potential toxicity and use aspirin only under veterinary supervision. The recommended dosage for cats is 5 mg per pound (.45 kg) of body weight every 48 to 72 hours. One adult aspirin tablet (324 mg) is eight times the recommended dosage for an 8-pound (3.6 kg) cat. A baby aspirin given every three days is a typical safe cat dose. It should only be given with food and not on an empty stomach. At the first signs of toxicity, the drug should be withdrawn.

Meloxicam is a relatively safe NSAID for use in cats, but is currently approved in the United States only for injectable use. This should also be used only after consultation with your veterinarian.

TOXIC ANALGESICS

Other NSAIDs, such as ibuprofen (Motrin, Advil), naproxen (Aleve), and other aspirin substitutes, used for treating aches and pains in humans, are toxic to cats. Furthermore, these drugs are not as well tolerated as aspirin. Their absorption patterns are highly unpredictable in small animals. This makes these drugs unsuitable for use in cats.

Acetaminophen (Tylenol) is another analgesic that must never be given to cats. A cat given even a child's dose of Tylenol can develop fatal hemolytic anemia and liver failure.

Butazolidin (phenylbutazone) is an analgesic prescribed for horses, dogs, and other animals. When used as recommended in these animals, it may be safe and effective. When used in cats, it produces toxicity much like that of aspirin and acetaminophen. In addition, phenylbutazone causes kidney failure. It is therefore not recommended for use in cats.

Antibiotics

Antibiotics are used to fight bacteria and fungus in and on the body. Bacteria are classified according to their ability to cause disease. Pathogenic bacteria are capable of producing a particular illness or infection. Nonpathogenic bacteria live on or within the host but do not cause illness under normal conditions. These bacteria are called normal flora. Some actually produce substances necessary to the well-being of the host. For example, bacteria in the bowel synthesize vitamin K, which is necessary for blood clotting. Rarely, nonpathogenic bacteria will overgrow and cause symptoms due to their sheer numbers.

Antibiotics fall into two categories: Bacteriostatic and fungistatic drugs inhibit the growth of microorganisms but don't kill them; bactericidal and fungicidal drugs destroy the microorganisms outright.

POTENTIAL PROBLEMS

Antibiotics are specific for certain bacteria. So, one antibiotic will not be effective against all infections. The large number of antibiotics now available brings with it new possibilities for cats to develop sensitivities and allergies to specific drugs and multiplies the potential hazards of administration.

Antibiotics alter the normal flora that serves as a protective barrier against pathogens. When these normal, beneficial organisms are killed off, harmful bacteria are free to multiply and cause disease. The best example is severe diarrhea that follows the use of certain antibiotics, which change the normal flora of the bowel.

Certain antibiotics can affect the growth and development of unborn or newborn kittens. Tetracycline and griseofulvin are two examples. They should not be used in pregnant queens.

ANTIBIOTICS AND STEROIDS

Steroids are often combined with antibiotics, particularly in topical preparations for the eyes and ears, and on the skin. Corticosteroids have anti-inflammatory effects. By reducing swelling, redness, and tenderness, they often give the impression that the cat is getting better when actually, he is not.

Steroids have one other side effect that is undesirable: They depress the normal immune response. This can impair the cat's ability to fight the infection. Antibiotic medications that contain steroids should be used only under the guidance of a veterinarian. This is particularly true for eye preparations.

WHY ANTIBIOTICS FAIL

Antibiotics may not always be effective, for a number of reasons.

Inadequate Wound Care

Antibiotics enter the bloodstream and are carried to the source of the infection. Abscesses, wounds that contain devitalized tissue, and wounds with foreign bodies (dirt or splinters, for example) are resistant areas. Under such circumstances, antibiotics can't penetrate the wound completely. Accordingly, it is essential to drain abscesses, clean dirty wounds, and remove foreign bodies.

Inappropriate Selection

An antibiotic chosen to treat an infection must be effective against the specific bacteria that is infecting the body. The best way to determine susceptibility is to sample the organism, grow it on a culture plate, and identify it by the way its colony appears and by microscopic characteristics. Antibiotic discs are then applied to the culture plate to see which discs inhibit the growth of bacteria colonies. The results are graded according to whether the bacteria is sensitive, indifferent, or insensitive to the effects of the antibiotic. Laboratory findings, however, do not always coincide with results in the patient. Nonetheless, sensitivity testing is the best way to select the most effective antibiotic.

Route of Administration

An important medical decision is choosing the best route for administration. In a cat with a severe infection, antibiotics may be given intravenously or by intramuscular or subcutaneous injection. Some oral antibiotics should be

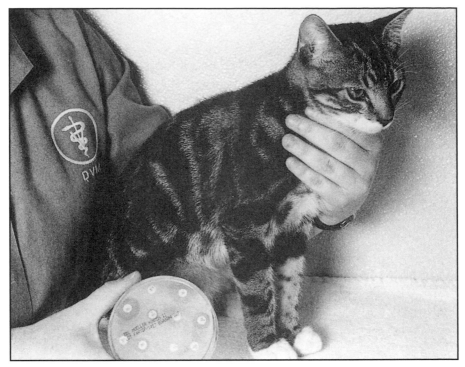

Discs containing various antibiotics on a culture plate show which antibiotics inhibit the growth of the specific bacteria that has infected the cat. This test is called a culture and sensitivity test.

given on an empty stomach; others with a meal. Incomplete absorption is one cause of inadequate levels of antibiotics in the blood. If the cat is vomiting, oral medications may not be absorbed.

Dose and Frequency of Administration

The dose is computed by weighing the cat, then dividing the total daily dose into equal parts and giving them at prescribed intervals. Other factors that must be accounted for when computing the daily dose are the severity of the infection, the age of the cat, his overall health and stamina, and whether the cat is taking another antibiotic. When the total dose is too low or the antibiotic is not given often enough, the drug may not be effective.

Resistant Strains

Antibiotics can destroy the normal flora in the body that crowds out pathogens. This allows harmful bacteria to multiply and cause disease. Furthermore, strains of bacteria may develop that are resistant to antibiotics and thus cannot be effectively controlled. This is particularly likely to occur when antibiotics are used

- For too short a time
- In too low a dosage
- When the antibiotic is not bactericidal

Microorganisms that are resistant to one antibiotic are usually resistant to other antibiotics of the same class. The development of antibiotic-resistant bacteria is one of the main reasons why antibiotics should be used exactly as prescribed and only in situations in which they will clearly benefit the cat. Antimicrobial resistance is becoming a serious health problem for both pets and people.

Antibiotics should only be used when necessary and always used appropriately. Most upper respiratory infections in cats are caused by viruses that are not affected by antibiotics. Also, most bladder problems in cats are not accompanied by bacterial infections and will not benefit from treatment with antibiotics.

Drug Treatment of Behavior Disorders

The best approach in treating a cat with a behavior disorder is to identify the underlying cause of the abnormal behavior and treat that cause using environmental and behavioral modification. In general, it is best to use drugs only when other methods have failed. The drug should be withdrawn from time to time to see if the problem behavior recurs.

Because of the potential for dangerous side effects, behavior drugs should only be prescribed and monitored by a veterinarian. *The use of these drugs should also be part of a comprehensive behavior and environmental modification program.* Many of these medications are not approved for use in cats and may also require compounding to get an appropriate dosage.

Before any medication is administered, the cat should have a complete physical examination and blood workup to identify any underlying medical problems.

TRANQUILIZERS

Tranquilizers are useful for calming an injured or frightened cat and for relieving anxiety attacks caused by moving, shipping, mating, or other traumatic experiences. A side effect of tranquilizers is that they block cortical inhibitory impulses. That means a tranquilized cat may stop using the litter box or may bite and scratch at the slightest provocation. It can be difficult to do behavior modification with a tranquilized cat.

Acepromazine (Promace) has a general depressive effect. It acts on the pain center and relieves anxiety. It is difficult to do any behavior modification with a cat who is tranquilized, though, so this drug should only be used very short-term. It should not be the first drug of choice and many behaviorists avoid it.

Diazepam (Valium) is less depressive and much preferred for most behavior problems requiring a tranquilizer. However, diazepam has been shown to cause serious liver problems in some cats and should not be used routinely. Cats taking diazepam need frequent liver enzyme evaluations. This drug is successful for 55 to 75 percent of cats with inappropriate elimination problems, but the behavior resumes when the medication is stopped. Since diazepam is not an appropriate drug for long-term use, it is therefore not the best choice for cats with inappropriate elimination problems.

PROGESTERONES

Medroxyprogesterone (Provera), megestrol (Megace), and other progestins have a calming effect and depress the pain center. They are useful in modifying aggressive behavior, particularly behavior with a sexual component. Effects are similar to those of castration.

Progesterones also are effective in treating urine marking and spraying, destructive scratching, compulsive self-grooming, and cannibalism. Side effects include cystic endometrial hyperplasia, mammary hyperplasia, pyometra, adrenal gland disease, weight gain, excessive drinking and urination, and diabetes.

Because the side effects are serious, these drugs have fallen out of favor for use in behavior problems with cats. When needed, they should be used only as short-term adjuncts to behavior modification.

OTHER DRUGS

Buspirone (Buspar) affects the brain chemical serotonin, a neurotransmittor. This medication is about 75 percent effective in stopping inappropriate elimination problems. It may take one to two weeks to truly see an improvement in the behavior, with the full effect often not apparent until four weeks or more. It must be given for about eight weeks and then the cat can be gradually weaned off in many cases—particularly if administration is accompanied by behavioral and environmental modification.

Amitriptyline (Elavil) is a neurotransmitter blocker. This drug can also help with inappropriate urination and possibly separation anxiety. Cardiac side effects may be seen, so cats on this medication should get an initial EKG and periodic follow-up EKGs.

Clomipramine (Anafranil) is a tricyclic antidepressant and helps with separation anxiety and urine marking behavior.

Fluoxetine (Prozac) is a selective serotonin reuptake inhibitor (SSRI). This drug may be recommended for elimination disorders in cats.

Drug Complications

Cats are unusually sensitive to drugs and medications. Cats are deficient in a liver enzyme called glucuronidase transferase that is very important in the metabolism of many drugs and medications. Because of this deficiency, many drugs and medications that are safe for humans and dogs when used according to the manufacturer's recommendations are not safe for cats. People and dog medications, even supplements, should never be given to your cat without first consulting a veterinarian.

Drugs are primarily dosed by patient weight. Since the margin of safety is often quite small, the body weight of the cat becomes important. Estimating the weight can lead to significant under- or overdosing.

It is also important to consider any concurrent illnesses in the cat when determining a drug dosage. For example, a cat with kidney or liver disease should receive a lower than standard dose of many medications.

It is important to realize that there are fewer drugs and medications approved for cats than there are for humans and dogs. This is partly due to the financial incentive, or lack thereof, for companies to go through FDA approval for cats. Many of the standard cat medications are routinely used *off-label*, meaning they are not approved for use in cats. Still, these can be effective and safe medications and, in some cases, life saving. Always work with your veterinarian regarding medications for your cat.

TOXICITY

There is a margin of safety, often rather small in cats, between a therapeutic dose and a toxic dose. Toxicity is caused by overdose or by impaired routes of elimination from the body. Either condition produces toxic drug levels. In older cats and cats with advanced liver or kidney disease, these organs fail to break down and excrete the drug. Similarly, kittens require a lower dose by weight than adult cats because their kidneys are immature. Accordingly, drug toxicity is more common in the very young and the very old. Another cause of overdose is giving a drug for a prolonged time.

Signs of toxicity are difficult to recognize in the cat. Thus, they may be far advanced before they come to your attention. Drug toxicity can affect one or more organs and systems.

- **Hearing.** Damage to the otic nerves leads to ringing in the ears, hearing loss, and deafness. The loss can be permanent.
- **Liver.** Toxicity can lead to jaundice and liver failure.
- **Kidneys.** Toxicity causes nitrogen retention, uremia, and kidney failure.
- **Bone marrow.** Toxicity depresses the production of red blood cells, white cells, and platelets. The effects can be irreversible. The antibiotic

chloramphenicol (Chloromycetin) is especially prone to cause bone marrow depression.

- **Gastrointestinal system.** Vomiting and/or diarrhea, nausea, or loss of appetite can result from drug toxicity.
- **Nervous system.** Signs of neurological problems include disorientation, *ataxia*, and coma.

ANAPHYLACTIC SHOCK

One danger of giving any foreign substance by injection is that of producing a sudden allergic or anaphylactic reaction in which the cat goes into severe or fatal shock through circulatory collapse. This is a type of hypersensitivity reaction. The most common agent producing anaphylactic shock is penicillin. Some cats have reactions to vaccines. As a precaution, do not administer a drug by injection to a cat who has any sort of past history of allergic reaction to that drug.

Treatment: Anaphylactic shock is an emergency and must be treated by a veterinarian. Treatment involves intravenous adrenaline (epinephrine) and oxygen. This is one reason why it is best to have your veterinarian give your cat most injections.

How to Give Medications

Don't give your cat any medication until you have spoken to your veterinarian to make sure it is the right medicine for the cat and the circumstances. You should also ask for instructions on how to give the drug and the correct dosage for your cat.

PILLS, CAPSULES, AND POWDERS

By far, the best way to give your cat a pill is to use one of the commercial treats made specifically for this purpose. Although a cat can delicately extract a pill from an entire dish of canned cat food, these treats are sticky enough to make removing the pill almost impossible. They are also soft, so they mold easily around the pill. Pill Pockets and Flavor Doh are two examples.

Administering pills this way avoids the daily struggle with your cat to give him his medicine—which can cause anxiety for you both. It also avoids the medical problems associated with pushing a pill down a cat's throat (see page 556).

You can also try making up tiny "meatballs" of canned cat food or tasty bits of meat. Give the cat one or two undoctored meatballs, then one with the pill. Follow up with an undoctored one so the cat will continue to take the treats even if he gets a small taste of the medicine.

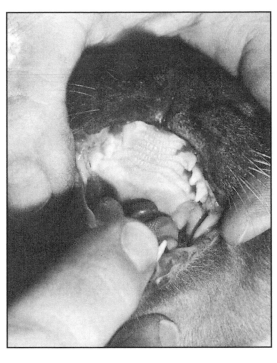

The correct way to give a pill—in the middle of the throat at the back of the tongue.

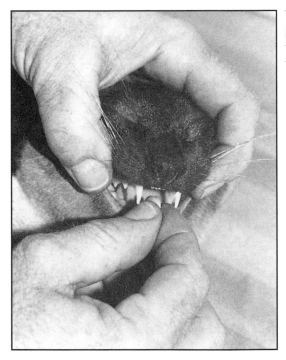

The incorrect way to give a pill—too far forward, where the cat can easily push it out with his tongue.

Of course, these two techniques will only work if it is acceptable to give your cat his medication with food. Always check with your veterinarian on this point. If the pills cannot be given with food, you will have to restrain the cat and give him his pill directly.

Unless the cat is used to taking pills, it may be helpful to wrap his body and legs in a towel. If you're working alone, you can cradle the cat in one arm. However, it is much more convenient to have an assistant who can hold the cat while you administer the pill.

Place one thumb and forefinger on either side of the cat's face from above and behind the whiskers. Apply gentle pressure at the space between the teeth. As the cat's mouth opens, press down on the lower jaw and deposit the pill well to the back of the tongue. Close the mouth and massage or rub the throat until the cat swallows. Blowing softly into the cat's nose or face will also cause many cats to gulp or swallow. If the cat licks his nose, it's likely the pill has been swallowed. Always follow up the pill by giving the cat at least 1 teaspoon (5 ml) of water from a syringe or an eyedropper. (For the correct technique, see *Liquids*, below.) This helps the pill enter the stomach, where it can take effect, rather then remaining in the esophagus, where it has no effect and can actually cause damage. Pills that sit in the esophagus may cause vomiting or even irritation to the tissues lining the esophagus. If medications routinely sit in the esophagus, stricture or ulcers may develop. This is true for capsules as well as pills. That is why pills given without food must *always* be followed by water.

Avoid breaking up pills. Pills broken into powder may have an unpleasant taste that is poorly accepted. Many pills have a protective coating that is important for delayed release in the intestinal tract.

Capsules can usually be opened and the medication inside sprinkled over the cat's wet food. Confirm this with your veterinarian. Other powdered medication can also be administered this way. Powders can also be diluted in water and administered as a liquid—if approved by your veterinarian.

LIQUIDS

Liquid medicines, including electrolytes and water solutions, are administered into the cheek pouch between the molars and the cheek. A medicine bottle, eyedropper, or plastic syringe without the needle can be used to dispense the liquid.

Adult cats can be given up to 3 teaspoons (15 ml) of liquid medicine as a single dose. Measure the required amount into the bottle, syringe, or medicine dropper. (Use a plastic dropper in case the cat bites it.) Secure the cat as described for administering pills (above). Insert the end of the dispenser into the cheek pouch and, while tilting the chin upward, slowly dispense the medication. The cat will swallow automatically.

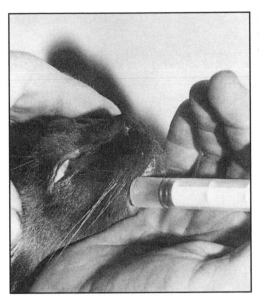

Liquids are administered into the cheek pouch between the molars and the cheek. Be sure to give the cat time to swallow between gulps.

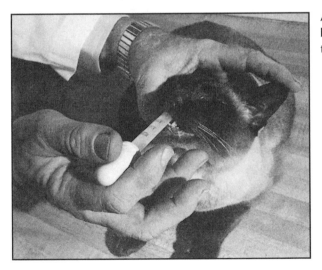

A medicine dropper can be inserted straight into the cat's mouth.

INJECTIONS

Injecting any foreign substance into the body always carries with it the danger of causing an acute allergic or anaphylactic reaction, as described on page 15. Treating anaphylactic shock requires immediate intravenous adrenaline (epinephrine) and oxygen. This is one reason why it is best to have your veterinarian give injections. As a precaution, do not administer a drug by injection to a cat who has had any sort of past history of an allergic reaction to that drug.

If it becomes necessary to give injections at home (for example, if the cat is diabetic), have your veterinarian demonstrate the procedure. Some injections are given under the skin (subcutaneous) and others into the muscle (intramuscular). Directions that come with the product will indicate the correct route of injection.

The injection itself usually is not painful, although intramuscular injections may hurt somewhat as the medicine is injected. Cats should be restrained as described in *Handling and Restraint* (page 2). Having an assistant is helpful.

Begin by drawing the medicine up into the syringe. If there is an air bubble inside, flick the syringe to get the bubble to the top. Then, point the needle toward the ceiling or into a sink and press the plunger to expel all air from the syringe and needle. Make sure the correct amount remains in the syringe after the air bubble is expelled. Do not spray out any of the injectable medication into the air.

Select the injection site, part the hair, and cleanse the cat's skin with a cotton ball soaked in alcohol.

Subcutaneous Injections

The back of the cat's neck or shoulder is used for subcutaneous injections because the skin here is loose and readily forms a fold when pinched. Grasp a fold of skin to form a ridge. Firmly push the point of the needle through the skin into the subcutaneous fat at an angle somewhat parallel to the surface of the body.

Before giving the injection, pull back a bit on the plunger and look for blood. If blood appears, the medicine might be injected into a vein or artery. Withdraw the syringe and start again. When you see no blood, push in the plunger. Withdraw the needle and rub the skin for a few seconds to disperse the medicine.

Insulin injections are usually given subcutaneously. They use special syringes and very tiny needles for the small amounts you need. Most cats do not even notice that they got an injection.

Intramuscular Injections

You would rarely need to give an intramuscular injection at home. Most intramuscular injections will be given by your veterinarian or a veterinary technician. Intramuscular injections are generally given in the back of the thigh, halfway between the knee and the hip. Use a ¾-inch-long (1.8-cm) needle. Note the location of the bone and plan to place the injection into muscle well away from the bone. You must angle the tip of the needle to be sure to enter muscle while avoiding the bone. Injections into bones, nerves, and joints can be avoided by giving the shots in the location described.

Repeat the same procedure as described for subcutaneous injections. Remember to withdraw the plunger and check for blood in the syringe before giving the injection.

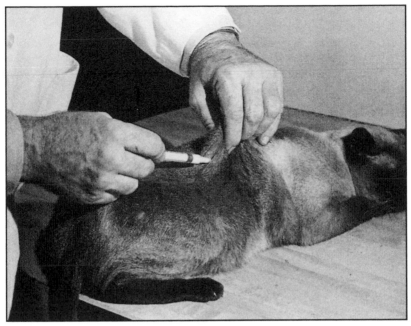

Subcutaneous injections are given beneath the loose skin in back of the shoulder.

SUPPOSITORIES

When the oral route is not satisfactory (for example, when a cat is vomiting), medications can be given by suppository. Your veterinarian may prescribe a suppository to treat a bout of severe constipation.

The suppository is lubricated with Vaseline and slipped all the way into the rectum, where it dissolves. Suppositories for constipation contain a mild irritant that draws water into the rectum and stimulates a bowel movement. Dulcolax is good for this purpose. You can buy it at any drugstore. The dose for an adult cat is one-quarter to one-half suppository.

Do not give suppositories to cats who are dehydrated or who might have an intestinal obstruction. A painful abdomen is another contraindication to the use of suppositories.

COMPOUNDED MEDICINES

Compounding uses new ways of combining or formulating medications to make them easier to give to your cat. This could mean mixing the medication into a flavored treat or liquid. Some medications can also be transferred to gels, which can then be rubbed onto an ear. Fentanyl patches are an example of a medication that is absorbed through the skin. Methimazole is a medication

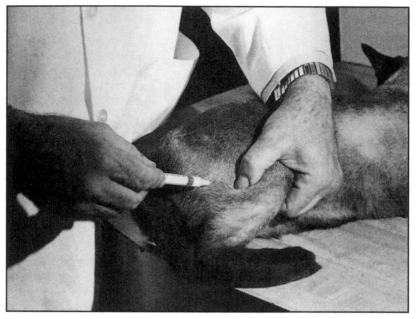

Give intramuscular injections into the back of the thigh.

given for hyperthyroidism that is sometimes successfully compounded as a gel applied to the ears instead of a pill.

Occasionally, compounding is used to combine medications that can be mixed together safely so fewer pills need to be given. Compounding may be used for medications that are not commercially available or are not available in dosages for cats. More research is needed to determine if the dosage in compounded drugs is appropriate and consistent for most medications.

OTHER MEDICATIONS

The proper way to medicate the eyes is discussed in *How to Apply Eye Medicines*, page 173. Medicating the ears is discussed in *How to Apply Ear Medicines*, page 207. Enemas are discussed in *Fecal Impactions*, page 277. Fleet phosphate enemas should never be given to cats because of the danger of causing a fatal phosphate overdose.

Over-the-Counter Drugs for Home Veterinary Use

Note that these medications are not labeled for use in cats and should only be used under the guidance of your veterinarian. Do not give your cat any drug without first consulting your veterinarian. The doses given here will need to be adjusted if your cat has other health problems, such as liver or kidney disease. Always check ingredients carefully—many over-the-counter medications include acetaminophen or salycilates.

1 teaspoon = 5 ml; 1 pound = .45 kg

Drug	Action	Dosage	Method of administration	Frequency of administration
Afrin Children's Strength Nose Drops (.025 percent)	Nasal decongestant	1 drop in 1 nostril; alternate nostrils each day	Intranasal	Once daily; do not use for more than 5 days
Aspirin (buffered; enteric coated)	Analgesic, anti-inflammatory	81 mg (dose varies with the purpose of the medication)	With food	Every third day
Betadine solution (povidone-iodine)	Topical antiseptic	Dilute to 0.2 percent (2 ml to 2 quarts, 1.9 l, tap water)	Topically	As prescribed for cleaning the wound
Charcoal (compressed activated charcoal)	Binds stomach poisons	5 g per 10 pounds of body weight	Orally	Keep at least 30 tablets available; give once, and only under the direction of a veterinarian
Chlorhexidine solution (Nolvasan and others)	Topical antiseptic	Dilute to 0.05 percent (25 ml to 2 quarts, 1.9 l, tap water)	Topically	As prescribed for cleaning the wound
Dramamine (dimenhydrinate)	For motion sickness	12.5 mg	Orally	Every 8 hours
Dulcolax (bisacodyl)	Stimulant laxative	5 mg (half of a suppository)	Rectally	Once daily
Flatulex (simethicone and activated charcoal)	For flatulence	25 mg	Orally	As needed, up to 3 times a day

continued

Over-the-Counter Drugs for Home Veterinary Use (continued)

Drug	Action	Dosage	Method of administration	Frequency of administration
Hydrogen peroxide (3%)	Induce vomiting	1 teaspoon per 10 pounds of body weight	Orally	May repeat every 15 to 30 minutes (3 times only)
Kaolin and pectin (beware: some formulations contain salicylates)	For persistent diarrhea	½ to 1 ml per pound of body weight (or 1 to 2 teaspoons per 10 pounds)	Orally	Every 6 hours
Loperamide (Immodium)	For diarrhea	1 mg per 10 pounds of body weight	Orally	Every other day, and no more than 3 times total
Metamucil (psyllium)	For constipation or to add fiber to the diet	1 teaspoon	Add to food	Once daily; for short-term use, unless otherwise directed
Milk of Magnesia, Mylanta, Maalox (magnesium hydroxide)	Antacid, laxative	½ teaspoon per 5 pounds of body weight	Orally	Every 12 to 24 hours
Mineral oil	Lubricant laxative	1 teaspoon per 5 pounds of body weight	Add to food; do not give separately due to aspiration risk	Once or twice a week; only for 2 to 3 days
Pepcid (famotidine)	Histamine blocker for antacid effect	.25 to .5 mg	Orally	Once a day
Robitussin (guaifenesin)	Expectorant	½ teaspoon per 10 pounds of body weight	Orally	Every 4 hours
Robitussin-DM, Benylin Expectorant (dextromethorphan and guaifenesin)	Cough suppressant and expectorant	0.5 to 1 mg per pound of body weight (or ½ teaspoon per 10 pounds)	Orally	Every 6 hours

Normal

Physiological

Data

Body Temperature

Adult cat: 100°F to 103°F (37.7°C to 39.4°C)

Average: 101.5°F (38.6°C)

Newborn kitten: 95°F to 99°F (35°C to 37.2°C); 100°F (37.8°C) or above after 2 weeks of age

How to Take Your Cat's Temperature

The only effective way to take your cat's temperature is to use a rectal thermometer. Bulb and digital rectal thermometers are equally acceptable, but the digital thermometer is more convenient and records the temperature faster.

If you're using a bulb thermometer, shake it down until the bulb registers 96°F (35.5°C). Lubricate the bulb with petroleum or K-Y jelly. With the cat standing, raise the tail and hold firmly to prevent the cat from sitting down. Using a slight twisting motion, gently insert the bulb into the anal canal 1 to 1.5 inches (25 to 38 mm).

Hold the thermometer in place for three minutes. (Placing a hand under the cat's tummy will help her remain standing.) Then remove it, wipe it clean, and read the temperature by the height of the silver column of mercury

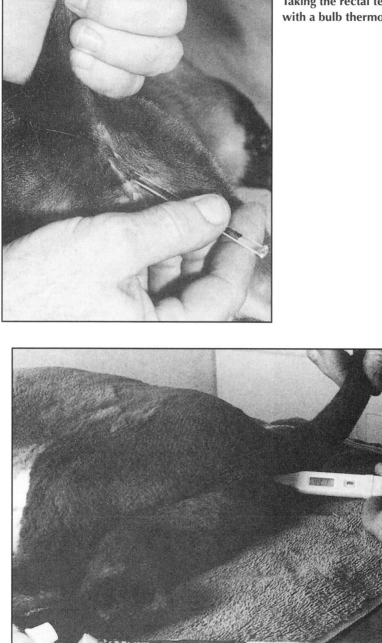

Taking the rectal temperature with a bulb thermometer.

Using a digital thermometer. In this case, the cat is lying on her side—another acceptable position for taking the temperature.

on the thermometer scale. Clean the thermometer with alcohol to prevent the transfer of diseases.

If you're using a digital thermometer, insert it the same way and follow the manufacturer's directions.

If the thermometer breaks off—this usually happens because the cat sits down—do not attempt to find and extract the broken end. Instead, notify your veterinarian immediately.

Heart Rate

Adult cat: 140 to 240 beats per minute (the mean is 195)

Newborn kitten: 200 to 300 beats per minute at birth; approximately 200 beats per minute at 2 weeks of age

To learn how to take your cat's pulse, see *Pulse*, page 312.

Respiratory Rate

Adult cat: 20 to 24 breaths per minute

Average: 22 breaths per minute at rest

Newborn kitten: 15 to 35 breaths per minute, up to 2 weeks of age

Gestation

Averages 63 to 65 days from the day of ovulation. (The normal range is 60 to 67 days.)

COMPARATIVE AGE OF CATS AND HUMANS

An old general rule is that one cat year is equivalent to seven human years, but this is not accurate. Cats age at different rates than humans do. Some cat years are equivalent to more than seven years, and some are equivalent to fewer. For example, it takes kittens about a year to grow into their adult bodies, while it takes children a lot longer. Thus, the first year of a cat's life is perhaps equivalent to about 16 years of a child's.

In addition, not all cats age at the same rate. A cat's biological age depends on genetic inheritance, nutrition, overall health, and the lifetime sum of environmental and behavioral stresses. Siamese are noted for being long-lived, while Persians tend not to survive quite as long. However, being a pure-bred or mixed breed does not alone influence the aging process.

The chart below indicates average figures for all cats. The numbers in bold indicate that the cat is considered senior; the numbers in italics indicate that the cat is considered geriatric.

Age of Cat	Equivalent Age of Human
1	16
2	21
3	25
4	29
5	33
6	37
7	41
8	45
9	49
10	**53**
11	**54**
12	**59**
13	**63**
14	**67**
15	**71**
16	*75*
17	*79*
18	*83*
19	*87*
20	*91*

C

LABORATORY TESTS

At some time in your cat's life, it is highly likely that laboratory tests will be performed. These tests can range from very simple tests, such as fecal checks for parasites or heartworm tests looking for antigens, to sophisticated blood work checking out various organs and their functioning. The most common tests done to the blood and urine are discussed here. Blood samples are normally taken from your cat's vein— either a leg or, more commonly, the jugular vein in the neck. Fasting is recommended before most blood tests.

Complete Blood Count (CBC) or Hemogram

A complete blood count (CBC) is done on blood taken directly from your cat's vein. The goal is to count the different types of cells present in your cat's blood. At the same time, an evaluation is made about the types of cells and their health and life stages. Blood counts may be lowered overall in cats with bone marrow disorders and those undergoing certain types of chemotherapy.

HEMATOCRIT OR PCV

A hematocrit test checks to see approximately how many red blood cells your cat has. Blood in a tiny tube is spun in a centrifuge and the number of red blood cells is given as a percent of the total blood volume. Normal cats run about 30 to 45 percent. A low packed cell volume (PCV) indicates anemia, which could have a number of causes, from hemorrhage to liver disease. A high PCV is often present in cats who are dehydrated.

RBC DATA

With the red blood cells (RBC), an actual count is made by estimating from the number of cells spread on a slide and examined under a microscope. The amount of hemoglobin present and the age and size of the red blood cells are also measured. MCV is mean corpuscular volume, which is the average size of the red blood cells. MCH is mean corpuscular hemoglobin (the substance in the red blood cells that transports oxygen), which is the average amount of hemoglobin inside a red blood cell. MCHC is mean corpuscular hemoglobin concentration, which is the average concentration of hemoglobin in the red blood cells, expressed as a percentage. Your veterinarian or the laboratory technician will also examine cells for maturity and for any blood-borne parasites.

WBC DATA

An estimate will also be made of the total number of white blood cells (WBC) in the sample. White blood cells include *eosinophils* (cells that fight parasite infestations and are involved in allergies) and cells that fight infections or cellular invaders, including *neutrophils, lymphocytes*, basophils, macrophages, and monocytes. The number of white blood cells, such as lymphocytes, may be elevated in cats with certain cancers, as well. Normally, white blood cell counts rise with infections, but if the infection is winning the battle, counts may be lower than expected.

PLATELETS

Platelets are cells that assist in clotting and coagulation. An estimate of their numbers is also made from a blood sample on a slide examined under a microscope. Platelets can be low in number in cats with certain immune disorders, some cancers, and bleeding disorders.

Blood Chemistry Panel

A blood chemistry panel evaluates the enzymes that are important to many organ functions, and also looks at certain proteins and minerals that are important for normal body functions. Important tests include these:

> **Albumin.** This is an important protein made by the liver. It decreases in cats with certain types of liver and kidney damage and can increase in dehydrated cats.
>
> **ALP.** Alkaline phosphatase is an enzyme that may increase in cats with liver or bone disease. It could also indicate bile problems.

Phenobarbital, used to control seizures, may also increase the levels of this enzyme.

ALT. Alanine aminotransferase is a liver enzyme that can increase in cats with virtually any type of liver damage.

Amylase. This is an enzyme manufactured primarily by the pancreas and released into the digestive tract to help digest starch and glycogen. It may be elevated in cats with pancreatitis (although not reliably so), kidney disease, or steroid use.

AST. Aspartate aminotransferase is an enzyme normally found in red blood cells, the liver, the heart, muscle tissue, the pancreas, and the kidneys. The test is used primarily as a measure of liver function. AST levels may also increase in cats with heart damage.

Bile acids. These tests are important for evaluating liver function. In this case, two blood samples are needed: one taken before eating and one taken two hours after eating.

Bilirubin. This is made in the liver from old red blood cells. This value may increase in cats with liver or gallbladder disease, or with diseases that destroy red blood cells. Accumulation of this pigment in the body may cause a yellow coloring or jaundice.

BUN. Blood urea nitrogen is protein waste material made by the liver and eliminated via the kidneys. A low BUN may indicate liver disease and a high BUN may indicate kidney disease.

Calcium. This mineral is very important for muscle and nerve action as well as bone development. High calcium levels can be seen in cats with certain cancers, kidney failure, certain rodenticide poisonings, and parathyroid problems. Low calcium can be seen in cats after whelping and nursing large litters and with some parathyroid problems.

Creatinine. This is a waste product of muscles and is normally removed by the kidneys. An increase can indicate kidney disease.

CPK or CK. Creatinine phosphokinase and creatinine kinase are different names for a muscle enzyme that increases with muscle damage, including damage to the heart muscle.

Glucose. This is blood sugar. Levels are increased in cats with diabetes mellitus or Cushing's disease, and with steroid use. Healthy cats who are stressed may show high blood glucose levels. Low blood sugar may be due to certain cancers, insulin overdose, liver problems, or infection.

Phosphorus. Abnormal levels of this mineral indicate parathyroid problems, kidney problems, and possible dietary inadequacies.

Potassium. This mineral is very important for muscle and nerve functions and for proper regulation of the heart. Kidney failure, an obstructed bladder, and antifreeze poisoning can all increase potassium levels.

Sodium. This mineral is important for normal muscle and nerve function. Levels can be affected by vomiting and diarrhea, and by Addison's disease.

Total protein. This is a measure of the proteins in the blood, including albumin and globulins (which are associated with infections and inflammations). High levels can occur in cats with dehydration or immune stimulation. Low levels may indicate liver problems.

Urinalysis

Urinalysis involves looking at a urine specimen. Urine samples may be collected as a "free catch" when the cat is voiding, by collecting urine from a clean litter box filled with Styrofoam pieces, or by using a catheter or a needle inserted directly into the bladder. The last two methods are much better if an infection is suspected, because the sample collected will be sterile and any bacteria cultured from it is likely to be the culprit.

The urine is checked for certain components, such as glucose and pH. Urine concentration and the presence of any cells are also evaluated. Some of this is done with a specially coated test strip that gives a range for results, and some is done with special instruments.

Dilute urine may indicate kidney problems or increased drinking. Concentrated urine could indicate dehydration or kidney problems. The urine is checked for glucose, suggesting diabetes mellitus, and for protein, suggesting kidney damage. The pH will tell if the urine is acidic or alkaline, which can be influenced by diet and may cause bladder crystals or stones to form.

The urine is also spun in a centrifuge and the cells collected and examined. The presence of red blood cells or white blood cells may indicate infections or damage to the urinary tract. Crystals suggest stone formation. Bacteria can indicate infection, in which case the sample may also be cultured to look for bacterial infections.

D

USEFUL RESOURCES

American Animal Hospital Association
12515 W. Bayaud Ave.
Lakewood, CO 80228
(303) 986-2800
www.aahanet.org
www.healthypet.com

American Association of Feline Practitioners
203 Towne Centre Dr.
Hillsborough, NJ 08844-4693
(800) 874-0498
(908) 359-9351
www.aafponline.org

American Holistic Veterinary Medical Association
2218 Old Emmorton Rd.
Bel Air, MD 21015
(410) 569-0795
www.ahvma.org

American Veterinary Medical Association
1931 North Meacham Rd., Suite 100
Schaumburg, IL 60173
(847) 925-8070
www.avma.org

ASPCA Animal Poison Control Center
424 East 92 St.
New York, NY 10128
(888) 426-4435
www.aspca.org/apcc

Center for Veterinary Medicine
Food and Drug Administration
Communications Staff
7519 Standish Place, HFV-12
Rockville, MD 20855
(240) 276-9300
www.fda.gov/cvm

Cornell Feline Health Center
College of Veterinary Medicine
Cornell University
Box 13
Ithaca, NY 14853
(607) 253-3414
Consults: (800) 548-8987 (M, W, F: 9 a.m.–noon, 2–4 p.m., EST)
www.vet.cornell.edu/fhc/hinformation.htm

Delta Society
875 124th Ave. NE, Suite 101
Bellevue, WA 98005
(425) 226-7357
www.deltasociety.org

International Veterinary Acupuncture Society
P.O. Box 271395
Ft. Collins, CO 80527-1395
(970) 266-0666
www.ivas.org

Laboratory of Comparative Medical Genetics
Michigan State University College of Veterinary Medicine
2209 Biomedical Physical Sciences
East Lansing, MI 48824
fyfe@cvm.msu.edu

Minnesota Urolith Center
University of Minnesota College of Veterinary Medicine
1352 Boyd Ave.
Saint Paul, MN 55108
(612) 625-4221
www.cvm.umn.edu/depts/
minnesotaurolithcenter/home.html

Morris Animal Foundation
45 Inverness Drive East
Englewood, CO 80112
(800) 243-2345
www.morrisanimalfoundation.org

National Association of Professional Pet Sitters
15000 Commerce Pkwy., Suite C
Mt. Laurel, NJ 08054
(856) 439-0324
www.petsitters.org

Ohio State University Nutrition Support Service
Ohio State University Veterinary Teaching Hospital
601 Vernon L. Tharp St.
Columbus, OH 43210
(614) 292-3551
http://vet.osu.edu/index.php?id=1846

Orthopedic Foundation for Animals (OFA)
2301 East Nifong Blvd.
Columbia, MO 65201
(573) 442-0418
www.offa.org

PennGen
Veterinary Hospital 4006
University of Pennsylvania
3900 Delancey St.
Philadelphia, PA 19104-6010
(215) 898-3375
PennGen@vet.upenn.edu
http://w3.vet.upenn.edu/research/
centers/penngen/

PennHIP
University of Pennsylvania School of Veterinary Medicine
3800 Spruce St.
Philadelphia, PA 19104
(215) 573-3176
www.pennhip.org

Pet Sitters International
201 East King St.
King, NC 27021-9161
(336) 983-9222
www.petsit.com

University of California, Davis, Veterinary Genetics Laboratory
One Shields Ave.
Davis, CA 95616-8744
(530) 752-2211
www.vgl.ucdavis.edu

Veterinary Cardiac Genetics Laboratory
Washington State University College of Veterinary Medicine
P.O. Box 647010
Pullman, WA 99164
(509) 335-9515
www.vetmed.wsu.edu/deptsVCGL/

VetGen
3728 Plaza Dr., Suite 1
Ann Arbor, MI 48108
(800) 483-8436
www.vetgen.com

Winn Feline Foundation
1805 Atlantic Ave.
P.O. Box 1005
Manasquan, NJ 08736-0805
(732) 528-9797
www.winnfelinehealth.org

Cat Registries

American Cat Fanciers Association
P.O. Box 1949
Nixa, MO 65714-1949
(417) 725-1530
www.acfacats.com

Canadian Cat Association/Association Félin Canadienne
289 Rutherford Rd., S #18
Brampton, ON
L6W 3R9, Canada
(905) 459-1481
www.cca-afc.com

Cat Fanciers' Association
P.O. Box 1005
Manasquan, NJ 08736-0805.
(732) 528-9797
www.cfa.org

The International Cat Association
P.O. Box 2684
Harlingen, TX 78551
(956) 428-8046
www.tica.org

Traditional Cat Association
P.O. Box 178
Heisson, WA 98622-0178
www.traditionalcats.com

Web Resources

HEALTH INFORMATION

Drs. Foster and Smith
www.peteducation.com

Dr. Jean Hofve
www.littlebigcat.com

Manhattan Cat Specialists
www.manhattancats.com

Vaccine-Associated Feline Sarcoma Task Force
www.avma.org/vafstf/

Veterinary Partner
www.veterinarypartner.com

BEHAVIOR INFORMATION

Cats International
www.catsintenational.org

Feline Advisory Bureau
www.fabcats.org

Karen Pryor Clicker Training
www.clickertraining.com/cattraining

Indoor Cat Initiative
www.vet.ohio-state.edu/indoorcat.htm

International Association of Animal Behavior Consultants
www.iaabc.org

Cat Food and Nutrition Information

Eukanuba
www.eukanuba.com

Iams
www.iams.com

Max's House
http://maxshouse.com/feline_nutrition.htm

Pet Diets
www.petdiets.com

Purina
www.purina.com

Royal Canin
www.royalcanin.us

Therapeutic Diets
www.prescriptiondiets.com

GLOSSARY

Words in italics are defined elsewhere in the Glossary.

Abortion   Death of a fetus after organ development (28 days), followed by expulsion of the products of conception.

Abscess   A collection of pus in a cavity. It may be beneath the skin, in an organ, or in a body space.

Accommodate   The process by which the lens of the eye changes shape to focus light on the retina.

Acidosis   A buildup of acids in the blood, resulting in a lower pH than normal.

ACTH   Adrenocorticotropic hormone, the pituitary hormone that stimulates the adrenal cortex to produce corticosteroids.

Acute   Occurring suddenly. Often indicates the early stage of a disease, when symptoms are most pronounced. Acute symptoms are usually short term.

Afebrile   Without fever.

Allergen   Any substance that is capable of causing an allergic reaction. Drugs, insect toxins, pollens, molds, dust mites, foods, and vaccinations are common allergens for cats.

Alopecia   Loss of hair or failure to regrow hair, resulting in an area of thinning or baldness.

Analgesia   Pain relief.

Anestrus   The fourth phase of the estrous cycle in which there is little, if any, ovarian activity. In cats in the northern hemisphere, this is usually from November through January.

Anomaly   Out of the ordinary; a condition that departs from the normal.

Anorectal   Anatomically, the area encompassed by the anus, anal canal, and rectum.

Anorexia   Loss of appetite and failure to eat.

Anthelmintic   A medication that acts to dispel or destroy parasitic intestinal worms.

Antibody   A protein substance produced by the immune system to neutralize the effects of an *antigen*.

Antigen   A substance recognized by the immune system as foreign to the body. The immune system develops antibodies that bind the antigen and prevent it from harming the animal or causing disease.

Arrhythmia   An abnormal heart rhythm. It may be inconsequential, or serious enough to cause cardiac arrest.

Ascarids   Roundworms.

Ascites   An abnormal accumulation of fluid in the *peritoneal (abdominal) cavity*. Congestive heart failure and liver failure are the most common causes.

Assay   Testing the *serum* to determine the relative proportion of a substance, such as the concentration of an *antigen* or *antibody*.

Ataxia   Incoordination; an inability to coordinate voluntary muscle movements that is symptomatic of some central nervous system disorders and injuries and is not due to muscle weakness. The adjective is ataxic.

Atresia   Failure of a channel or passage to open in the course of fetal development.

Atrophy   Shrinkage in the size of an organ or tissue due to disuse or death of cells.

Auto-antibodies   Antibodies that a host makes against its own tissues. Auto-antibodies cause destruction of the targeted cells.

Autoimmune disease   A disease resulting from *auto-antibodies* targeting host tissue.

Autosomal   All chromosomes that are not the X and Y sex chromosomes.

Bactericidal   Capable of killing bacteria, as opposed to just inhibiting their growth.

Benign   An abnormal growth that is not a malignant cancer. Benign growths are usually not life threatening and do not spread to other areas of the body.

Bezoars   Foreign bodies in the stomach, including hairballs, composed of hair and other ingested materials that form hard concretions too large to pass out of the stomach.

Bilateral   On both sides.

Biopsy   The removal of tissue for microscopic examination and diagnosis.

Bleb   A skin blister filled with *serum* or blood.

Blocked   A cat with a urinary tract blockage that prevents urination. This is an emergency.

Boil   A small skin *abscess*, usually at the site of a hair follicle.

Breeder   The owner of the queen when the cat was bred.

Bronchoscopy   A procedure in which an *endoscope* is passed into the trachea and bronchi to directly visualize the interior of the respiratory tract.

Bulla   A large skin blister filled with clear fluid. Or, in the case of the lungs, air sacs filled with air. May also refer to the tympanic bulla, a part of the inner ear.

Calico   A female cat with black and red coloring, and usually with white as well. Also see *tortoiseshell*.

Calculus   Dental calculus (also called tartar) is a plaquelike material composed of calcium salts, food particles, and bacteria.

Cancer   A tumor on the surface of the body or within an organ that has the potential to destroy tissue and kill the animal through local growth and/or spread to distant parts.

Capillary refill time   The time it takes for the gums to pink up after being firmly pressed with a finger—normally one to two seconds or less. A measure of the quality of the circulation.

Cardiac massage   Compression of the heart, resulting in temporary support of the circulation.

Castrate   To remove the testicles of a male cat.

Cellulitis   Infection of all layers of the skin along with inflammation of the connective tissue, characterized by redness, swelling, tenderness, and increased warmth. Usually very painful.

Cerebral edema   Swelling of the brain following injury or a period of oxygen deprivation.

Chemotherapy   The use of drugs that are cellular poisons to attack and kill cancer cells, or to suppress the immune system in the treatment of *autoimmune disease*.

Chondroprotective   Compounds that protect joint cartilage from the destructive effects of degenerative joint disease.

Chromosomes   The collection of DNA proteins that are organized into genes and aligned to provide genetic information to the body. Cats have 38 chromosomes—arranged in 19 pairs.

Chronic   Present for a long period. Often indicates that stage of a disease in which symptoms persist in a milder form.

Cilia   Hairlike projections on cells in the respiratory tract.

Colonoscopy   A procedure that uses an *endoscope* to view the interior of the colon and rectum.

Colostrum   The first milk of the dam, containing the all-important maternal antibodies that protect kittens from common diseases for the first three months of life.

Conceptus   The products resulting from the union between egg and sperm.

Condition (of the body)   A subjective term that refers to overall health as shown by the coat, general appearance, body weight, and musculature.

Conformation   How the various angles, shapes, and parts of the cat's body conform to the breed standard. At cat shows, cats are judged by how well they conform to the standard for their breed.

Congenital   A condition that exists at birth, although it is not always clinically evident until later in life. Congenital conditions can be either genetically determined or acquired before or during delivery.

Corpus luteum   A growth that forms in the ovary at the site of ovulation. The corpus luteum manufactures progesterone, essential to the support of pregnancy. The plural is corpora lutea.

CPK   Creatine phosphokinase, an enzyme found in muscle tissue that is released when there is muscle injury or disease.

CPR   Cardiopulmonary resuscitation; the combination of mouth-to-mouth resuscitation and cardiac massage.

Cryopreservation   Freezing and storing tissue for later use.

Cryotherapy   A procedure in which tissue is destroyed by freezing it with liquid nitrogen.

Cryptorchid   A male cat with one or both testicles retained in the abdomen or the inguinal area instead of in the scrotum.

CT scan   Computerized tomography, a diagnostic X-ray procedure that produces cross-sectional views of a body structure. CT scans may be available only at veterinary referral centers. Sometimes called CAT scan, an acronym for computer-assisted tomography.

Cyanosis   A bluish discoloration of the gums and tongue due to inadequate oxygen in the blood.

Cytology   The microscopic examination of cells to determine the cause of a disease.

Dam   The mother of a kitten.

Declaw   To surgically remove the last joint of the toe and the claw.

Dementia   Loss of memory and reasoning power characterized by varying degrees of confusion, disorientation, apathy, and stupor.

Depigmentation   Loss of dark color in the skin caused by destruction of *melanin*-producing cells. Depigmented areas are shades of white.

Depression   A marked decrease in activity in which the cat withdraws, spends most of her time lying down, is disinterested in her surroundings, and exhibits little or no interest in eating.

Dermis   The sensitive connective tissue layer of the skin located below the epidermis.

Dewclaws   Vestigial toes; the equivalent of a fifth digit high on the inside of each foot. Normally present on the front feet, unless they are removed.

Diestrus   The third stage in the *estrous cycle*, also called the *luteal phase* or *metestrus*, which begins when the female refuses to stand for mating. It lasts, on average, 7 to 14 days. What happens next depends on whether the queen was bred or induced to ovulate She will either have a false pregnancy, be pregnant, or resume the heat cycle.

Dominant   A gene is dominant if it alone is capable of determining the expression of a particular trait.

Duodenum   The first part of the small intestines, after the stomach.

Dysfunction   Abnormal performance of an organ or system.

Dysphagia   Painful and/or difficult swallowing.

Dysplastic   Developmentally malformed.

Dysuria   Painful and/or difficult urination.

Early embryonic loss   Loss of the productions of conception before 28 days gestation, often by internal resorption so that no external evidence of the loss is found.

ECG   Electrocardiogram; the readings from an electrocardiograph, which measures the changes in electrical currents associated with heart activity. An ECG is used to measure heart function and detect abnormalities. Sometimes called EKG.

Echocardiogram   A test that uses plain and doppler ultrasound (high-frequency sound waves) to create a computerized image of structures within the heart and a detail of blood flow. The procedure that uses an echocardiogram to diagnose heart disease is called echocardiography.

Edema   The accumulation of fluid beneath the skin.

EEG   Electroencephalography; a procedure that records the electrical activity of the cerebral cortex. It is used to diagnose epilepsy, *tumors*, and brain diseases. It is only available at some veterinary referral centers.

Ejaculate   The total volume of semen emitted by the tom cat during breeding.

Electrocautery   The use of an electric probe to destroy tissue using heat.

Electrolytes   Sodium, chloride, potassium, bicarbonate, calcium, phosphorus, and other minerals required for organ functioning.

ELISA   Enzyme-Linked Immunosorbent Assay, a *serologic* test used to detect antibodies to a protein, such as those associated with a bacteria or virus.

Embolus   A blood clot that develops at another site and travels through the circulatory system to a smaller vessel, where it becomes lodged and interrupts blood flow.

Embryo A *conceptus* younger than 28 days gestation, before the stage of organ development.

Encapsulated Surrounded by a capsule that creates a distinct boundary between two tissue planes.

Encephalitis Inflammation and/or infection of the brain.

Endemic Dwelling in or native to a particular population or region.

Endometrium A layer of glandular tissue lining the cavity of the uterus.

Endoscope An instrument that uses lights and fiber optics or a miniaturized video camera to view the interior of a body cavity. The procedure of using an endoscope to visualize the interior of a body cavity is called endoscopy.

Enteritis Inflammation of the lining of the intestines, caused by bacterial, parasitic, or viral infection as well as *immune-mediated* diseases.

Eosinophil A type of white blood cell that is often associated with diseases that have an allergic component or with parasites.

Epididymis The coiled tube on top of the testicle that stores the sperm.

Epithelium A layer of nonliving cells that forms the surface of the skin, mucous membranes, and cornea.

Erosion An area where a body surface has been destroyed by trauma or inflammation.

Erythrocytes Red blood cells; the cells that carry oxygen and carbon dioxide.

Estrous cycle The entire reproductive cycle, as determined from one ovulation to the next. Cats are seasonally polyestrous, with multiple heats over about a nine-month period each year. The number of heat cycles are influenced by induced or sometimes spontaneous ovulation.

Estrus Same as *heat*. The second phase of the *estrous cycle*, during which the *queen* is receptive to the *tom*; lasts an average of four to six days.

Etiology Cause of the disease.

Euthanasia The humane process of giving an animal a fatal, painless injection to end suffering.

Excision The surgical removal of a *tumor* or a *lesion*.

Excoriation A deep scratch or abrasion of the skin.

Exudate A liquid discharge that contains pus and bacteria.

FDA Food and Drug Administration; licenses the use of human and veterinary drugs.

Felid Referring to felines or cats. The Felidae family includes both domestic cats and large wild cats.

Fertility In tom cats, the ability to impregnate the queen. In queens, the ability to conceive and carry a litter.

Fetus   A *conceptus* older than 28 days' gestation, generally after the stage of organ development.

Fibrosis   The replacement of normal tissue by scar tissue.

Flatus   Breaking wind; passing gas from the rectum.

Follicle   A growth within the ovary that contains an egg. Also, the cells in the skin from which hairs grow.

Fresh semen   *Semen* that is artificially inseminated into the queen within a few hours of collection.

FSH   Follicle-stimulating hormone; produced by the pituitary gland. It causes the ovaries to produce egg *follicles*.

Furuncle   A small skin *boil*, about 2 to 3 millimeters in size.

Gastroesophageal junction   The anatomical area formed by the junction of the esophagus and the stomach.

Gastroscopy   A procedure that uses an *endoscope* to view the interior of the esophagus, stomach, and duodenum.

Gene   The basic unit of heredity. Each gene contains the code that produces a specific protein or molecule.

Genome   The map that gives the locus (chromosome and site) of all the genes that control the makeup of an animal; the complete set of hereditary factors.

Genotype   The combination of genes that determine a physical characteristic.

Gestation   Length of pregnancy; the period from conception to birth. It averages 65 days from the day of ovulation, with a normal range of 61 to 70 days.

GI   An abbreviation for gastrointestinal. GIT is sometimes used to denote the gastrointestinal tract.

Gn-RH   Gonadotrophin-releasing hormone; triggers the release of *FSH* and *LH* from the pituitary gland.

Gonadotropins   Hormones released from the pituitary gland or placenta, acting on the ovaries or testicles to cause them to manufacture and release the sex hormones.

Grand mal   A type of seizure that is typical of epilepsy. It usually involves loss of consciousness and falling down.

Head-pressing   Pressing the head against the wall or furniture without apparent purpose.

Heat   See *estrus*.

Hematocrit   The percentage of red blood cells in whole blood.

Hematoma   A collection of clotted blood beneath the skin at the site of an injury.

Hematuria The passage of blood in the urine, recognized by red-colored urine or blood clots in the urine. Microscopic hematuria is the presence of red cells on microscopic exam.

Hemolytic anemia The disease that results when red blood cells are destroyed in the cat's circulation.

Hepatic Referring to the liver.

Histiocyte A cell that is part of the immune system, found in the connective tissue, that kills foreign cells such as bacteria.

Histology The microscopic study of the structure of tissue to determine the cause of disease.

Hives Small, raised, red, pruritic areas, generally caused by an allergic reaction.

Hydrotherapy Cold water delivered to the site of injury using a showerhead or nozzle. This may also involve warm water pools and underwater treadmills.

Hyperpigmentation A darkening of the skin due to the deposition of *melanin* in the *dermis*. Associated with chronic inflammation of the skin.

Hypertrophy Enlargement of an organ or tissue; an increase in size and volume.

Hypoxia Lack of oxygen in the blood and tissues. If untreated, it results in coma and death.

Iatrogenic An unintended disease that results from a medical treatment or procedure.

Idiopathic A disease or condition for which no cause is known.

IFA Immunofluorescent antibody test; a *serologic* test used to detect antibodies to bacteria and viruses.

Ileocecal valve A flap of *mucosa* at the junction of the small bowel and the colon that acts like a valve.

IM Abbreviation for intramuscular; an injection given into the muscle.

Immune-mediated A process in the body in which proteins in the immune system lead the body to destroy its own cells. This can happen for unknown reasons (*idiopathic*) or due to a secondary cause such as infection, parasites, cancer, or a drug reaction.

Immunosuppressants Medications that suppress the immune response—a desirable effect in *autoimmune* diseases.

Incarceration Trapping an organ or part of an organ within a closed space. Most commonly refers to intestine trapped in a hernia.

Intubation Placing a breathing tube into the trachea to establish an airway for assisted breathing.

In utero Occurring in the uterus.

Infarction   Death of tissue as a consequence of an interruption in the blood supply.

Infection   Disease caused by a bacteria or a virus.

Infertility   Absence of *fertility*. A queen who can't conceive or a tom who can't sire a litter.

Infestation   The presence of parasites in numbers that may be sufficient to cause disease.

Intact   An animal who has not been *spayed* or *neutered*.

Intersex   The condition in which an animal has sex organs that have characteristics of both sexes and/or has chromosomes containing both male and female genetic material. Such animals are usually relatively or absolutely infertile.

Intromission   The introduction of the penis into the vagina during breeding.

Involution   The process by which the uterus empties and returns to normal size after *kittening*.

IV   Abbreviation for intravenous; an injection given into a vein.

IVP   Intravenous pyelogram; an X-ray of the kidneys taken after injecting a dye into a vein. This test provides an assessment of the renal circulation, ureters, bladder, and urethra.

Jaundice   A yellow discoloration in the whites of the eyes and mucous membranes of the mouth, caused by an accumulation of bile in the *serum* and tissues. Usually associated with liver disease or the destruction of red blood cells.

Karyotype   A "picture" of all the chromosomes in a cell.

Karyotyping   Analysis of the number, size, and shape of the paired chromosomes of a specific cat. Can be used to determine a cat's sex.

Killed vaccine   A vaccine made from killed virus or bacteria particles. Killed vaccines are generally safe, but may not be as effective as *modified live vaccines* (MLV).

Kittening   Giving birth. Also known as queening.

Laparoscopy   A surgical procedure in which an *endoscope* and surgical instruments are inserted into the abdomen through one or more small incisions.

Lavage   Flushing out a wound or cavity with large amounts of irrigating solution.

Lesion   Damaged tissue caused by an injury or a specific disease.

LH   Luteinizing hormone, produced by the pituitary gland. It causes ovarian *follicles* to mature and ovulate.

Ligation   Tying off a vessel.

Lobulated   Having the appearance of several lobes or swellings.

Luteal activity   The influence of the *corpora lutea,* particularly the effects of *progesterone.*

Luteal phase   See *diestrus.*

Luteolysis   The process that results in the regression and disappearance of the *corpora lutea.* Accompanied by a fall in *serum progesterone.*

Luxation   The displacement of a bone from its normal position within a joint.

Lymphadenopathy   The enlargement of one or more lymph nodes as the result of inflammation or cancer.

Lymphocytes   White blood cells that fight infection and disease.

Macule   A spot on the skin that is a different color (such as red or whitish) but is not elevated.

Malignant   A growth that is a cancer that is likely to spread throughout the body and may be life threatening.

Megaesophagus   An enlarged esophagus that does not contract well and interferes with normal swallowing.

Melanin   Naturally occurring dark pigment.

Melena   The dark or tarry black stools associated with upper gastrointestinal bleeding (bleeding in the stomach, duodenum, or small intestines).

Meniscus   A cushioning pad of cartilage interposed between two bones.

Metastasize   The spread of a cancer from its site of origin to another part of the body.

MLV   Modified live virus; a vaccine made from live bacteria or viruses that have been treated so that they cannot cause disease.

Monorchid   A cat who truly has only one testicle. True monorchids are unusual. See also *cryptorchid.*

MRI   Magnetic resonance imaging, a diagnostic procedure that uses a nuclear magnetic spectrometer to produce computerized images of body structures. Usually available only at veterinary referral centers.

Mucociliary blanket   The mucosal lining of the upper respiratory tract that contains cells with *cilia* that are capable of propelling inhaled irritants into the back of the throat.

Mucopurulent   A discharge containing mucus and pus.

Mucosa   The inner layer of mucus-producing cells that lines the respiratory, gastrointestinal, and genitourinary tracts.

Mucus   The slippery substance that is secreted as a protective coating by cells and glands of the mucosa. The adjective is mucoid.

Multinodular   A growth composed of *nodules*, giving it an irregular, bumpy surface.

Mutation   An alteration in a gene causing a change in some bodily function that is perpetuated in all the cells that descend from the original mutant cell.

Myelitis   An infection or inflammation of the spinal cord.

Myelogram   An X-ray study in which a contrast material is injected into the fluid around the spinal cord to show whether a disc or tumor is impinging on the spinal cord.

Myopathy   A disease of muscle or muscle tissue.

Necrosis   The death of a cell or group of cells that are in contact with living tissue.

Nephron   The basic working unit of the kidney, composed of a glomerulus that filters urine and a system of tubules that concentrates the urine and reabsorbs water and *electrolytes*.

Neutering   Removing both testicles in the male. Also known as castration or orchiectomy.

Neutrophil   A type of white blood cell that is filled with tiny sacs of enzymes that help the cell kill and digest invading microorganisms. It is the primary component of *pus*.

Nictitating membrane   The third eyelid; a membrane at the inner corner of the eye that comes out across the eye in response to eye pain and other conditions.

NSAID   Nonsteroidal anti-inflammatory drug.

Nutraceutical   A nutritional supplement that can have disease-modifying effects.

Nystagmus   A rhythmic movement of the eyeballs in which the eyes slowly wander a few degrees in one direction and then jerk back. Seen in cats with diseases of the inner ear and brain.

Occlusion   An obstruction or closure of a passageway or vessel. Also refers to how the teeth of the upper jaw contact those of the lower jaw.

Occult   Not evident by clinical signs.

OFA   Orthopedic Foundation for Animals, a group that certifies cats and dogs who are screened for certain inheritable health problems, such as hip dysplasia.

Off-label   Using a medication in a cat that is not approved by the FDA for use in cats. This may be a drug that is in common use for another species and it simply is not financially viable for a company to go through FDA testing.

Opacity   Loss of transparency of the cornea or lens of the eye.

Organisms   Living members of the animal or plant kingdom; usually refers to bacteria, viruses, and other small one-celled beings.

OTC   Over-the-counter; refers to drugs.

Ovariohysterectomy   Removal of the uterus and ovaries of a female cat. Also called spaying or OVH.

Oviduct   The tube that carries the egg from the ovary to the uterus.

Ovulation   The process during which the egg *follicle* releases the egg into the *oviduct*.

Palliation   Treatment that affords relief but not a cure. The adjective is palliative.

Palpation   Feeling, pressing on, and examining the body with the hands.

Papule   A small bump on the surface of the skin, varying in size from a pin-point to a split pea.

Paresis   Partial or complete impairment of movement; paralysis.

Parturition   Giving birth; the period covered by labor and delivery.

Pathogenic   Having the potential to cause disease.

Pathogens   Agents such as bacteria, viruses, and fungi that are capable of causing disease.

Pedigree   The written record of a cat's genealogy, covering three generations or more.

Perianal   The glands and skin structures surrounding the anal opening.

Perineum   The area extending from the anus to the bottom of the vulva in the female, and to the scrotum in the male.

Peristalsis   Rhythmic contractions that propel ingested foods and liquids from the mouth to the anus.

Peritoneal cavity   The abdominal cavity, containing organs of the intestinal, urinary, and reproductive tracts.

Peritonitis   Inflammation or infection of the peritoneal or abdominal cavity.

Placentitis   Infection of the placenta, usually caused by bacteria that ascend into the uterus through the cervix.

Plaque   A soft, yellow-brown material deposited on teeth that hardens into *calculus*.

Pleural effusion   An accumulation of fluid in the chest cavity caused by right-side heart failure, infection, or *tumor*.

PMN   Polymorphonuclear leukocyte; inflammatory cells that make up *pus*. Also called a *neutrophil*.

Pneumothorax   Air in the chest caused by a tear in the lung or a wound in the chest wall. The lung collapses, resulting in respiratory distress.

Polydactyl   A cat with extra toes.

Polygenic traits   Heritable traits that are controlled by the effects of multiple *genes*.

Polyuria   The passage of large amounts of urine, usually recognized by more frequent voiding.

Postmaturity   The condition in which the kittens are mature and ready to be born but the *dam* does not go into labor, especially after 70 days' *gestation*.

Postpartum   After giving birth; the period after *kittening* that lasts four to six weeks.

Premature kitten   A kitten born alive before 61 days' gestation.

Prodromal   The period in a disease just before the onset of symptoms.

Productive cough   One that brings up a quantity of phlegm. Also known as a moist cough.

Proestrus   The initial stage of the estrous cycle, lasting, on average, one to two days. The first signs are behavior changes.

Progeny   Descendents or offspring.

Progesterone   The pregnancy hormone, produced by the ovaries (*corpora lutea*).

Prognosis   A forecast based on the probable outcome of the disease.

Prolapse   The *protrusion* or falling out of a body part; generally referring to the gland of the third eyelid, the intestines, or the uterus.

Prophylactic   A medication or a procedure used as a preventive.

Protrusion   Extending beyond the normal location, such as a protruding eyeball.

Pruritic   Itchy.

Psychogenic   Caused by emotional or psychological factors, as opposed to a specific disease.

Pulmonary edema   The accumulation of fluid in the lungs, usually caused by congestive heart failure.

Purulent   Puslike; a discharge containing *pus*.

Pus   A discharge that contains *serum*, inflammatory cells, and sometimes bacteria and dead tissue.

Pustule   A small bump on the surface of the skin that contains *pus*.

Pylorus   The part of the stomach that forms a channel between the stomach and the *duodenum*.

Pyoderma   A *purulent* skin infection including *pustules*, boils, *abscesses*, *cellulitis*, and infected scabs.

Queen   An intact female cat; usually, one used for breeding.

Radiograph   The use of X-rays to take an image of the inside of the body; commonly referred to as X-ray.

Recessive   A *gene* that expresses a trait only when it is combined with another recessive gene.

Recombinant vaccine   A vaccine made by splicing gene-sized fragments of DNA from one organism (a virus or bacteria) and transferring them to another organism, where they produce antigen in large amounts for use in vaccines.

Reflux   A reversal in the normal direction of flow.

Regurgitation   The passive expulsion of esophageal contents without conscious effort.

Reinfestation   An *infestation* of parasites that occurs after the original group was eliminated.

Remission   The period during which the cat remains free of symptoms. Usually used in the context of cancer.

Renal   Referring to the kidneys.

Renal pelvis   The funnel that collects the urine excreted by the kidney. It tapers and becomes the ureter.

Resection   Removing *malignant*, dead, or unwanted tissue by surgically cutting it out.

Retrobulbar space   A space between the back of the eyeball and the bony socket, occupied by fat and blood vessels.

Sarcoma   A cancer that arises from muscle, bone, or other connective tissue.

Scaly   Shedding flakes of skin.

Sclera   The white membrane surrounding the cornea of the eye.

Scrotum   The bag of skin and connective tissue that surrounds and supports the testicles.

Semen   The contents of the *ejaculate*, containing sperm cells, gel, and the secretions of the accessory sex glands.

Senile   An age-related decline in physical and mental faculties.

Sepsis   The presence of infection, often accompanied by fever and other signs of illness, such as vomiting and diarrhea. The adjective is septic.

Septicemia   The stage of *sepsis* in which microorganisms and/or their toxins are found in the blood.

Serosanguinous   A discharge, generally pink or red, that contains *serum* and blood.

Serum   The clear fluid component of the blood. The adjective is *serous*. *Serologic* refers to blood tests that evaluate or measure antibody responses.

Sire   The father of a kitten.

Soundness   Mental and physical health when all the organs and systems are functioning as intended.

Spay   Neutering a *queen* by removing the ovaries and uterus.

Spermatogenesis   The production of sperm by the testicles.

Spinal tap   A procedure in which a needle is inserted into the spinal canal to remove cerebrospinal fluid for laboratory analysis.

Sporadic   Isolated, occasional, or infrequent.

SQ   Abbreviation for subcutaneous; an injection given beneath the skin. Also sometimes called sub-Q or SC.

Staging   A system developed to determine the extent and *prognosis* of a cancer, as well as its treatment.

Stenosis   Constriction or narrowing, especially of a channel or passage. The adjective is stenotic.

Stillbirth   A full-term kitten who is born dead.

Strangulated   The compression or pinching off of the blood supply to an abdominal organ, such as a segment of bowel. Leads to death of tissue.

Stridor   A high-pitched, raspy sound caused by air passing through a narrowed larynx.

Subclinical   A stage of illness in which infection occurs without apparent signs.

Subfertility   Less than normal *fertility*.

Subluxation   A partial dislocation, in which the bone is partly out of the joint.

Superinfection   The development of a second infection on top of (or following) the first infection.

Synovial fluid analysis   A procedure in which a needle is inserted into a joint to remove fluid for chemical and microscopic examination.

Systemic   Into the system; used in reference to widespread dissemination of infection or cancer, or a drug given orally, intramuscularly, intravenously, or subcutaneously.

Tartar   See *calculus*.

Teratogenic   That which causes developmental malformations in the fetus.

Testosterone   The male hormone, produced by the testicles.

Thromboembolism   The process by which a blood clot forms in a vein or artery and then moves up or down in the circulatory system, where it causes further clotting.

Titer   The concentration of a measured substance in the *serum*.

Tom cat   An intact (not neutered) male cat.

Torsion   The twisting of an organ and its blood supply, resulting in insufficient blood flow and death of that organ.

Tortoiseshell   A cat with red and black patches, usually female, since the genes for red and black are carried on the X chromosomes.

Toxemia   A state of shock induced by the absorption of bacterial toxins from an infected area in the body.

Tracheobronchitis   A viral or bacterial infection of the cells lining the trachea and bronchi.

Tracheostomy   Surgery in which an opening is made through the skin into the trachea to establish a new airway.

Transtracheal washings   Cells obtained by flushing the trachea with saline; used to diagnose the causes of upper respiratory infections.

Tucked up   A tightening of the muscles of the abdominal wall, creating a narrow waist and a hunched-up back.

Tumor   Any growth or swelling (such as an *abscess*). A cancerous growth is called a *neoplasm*.

Ulcer   A defect on the surface of an organ or tissue. A skin ulcer is an open sore with an inflamed base, involving the outer layer of the skin and often the *dermis*. A gastrointestinal ulcer is an open sore in the lining of the stomach or intestines. A corneal ulcer is on the clear surface of the eye.

Ultrasonography   A diagnostic procedure that uses high-frequency sound waves to map a picture of an organ or structure inside the body.

Unilateral   On one side only (as opposed to bilateral—on both sides).

Urethra   The tube that conveys urine from the bladder to outside the body.

Uterine inertia   Failure of the uterus to contract to start labor or to continue to contract during labor.

Vaginal cytology   A procedure in which cells are obtained from the vaginal lining and examined microscopically to determine the stage of the *estrous cycle*.

Ventricle   A cavity or chamber. Ventricles within the brain contain cerebrospinal fluid. Within the heart, the ventricles are the larger chambers on both sides.

Vesicle   A small skin blister filled with clear fluid.

Viremia   The presence of a virus in the blood.

Vulva   The labia (lips) of the vagina.

Wheal   An intensely itchy, raised patch of skin with a white center and a red rim. Varies in size from a pinhead to several inches. Often transient.

Zoonosis   A disease that is communicable from humans to animals and vice versa under natural conditions. The adjective is zoonotic.

ABOUT THE AUTHORS

Debra M. Eldredge, DVM

Debra Eldredge graduated from the New York State College of Veterinary Medicine at Cornell and was the first recipient of Cornell's Gentle Doctor Award, given for patient care. She has been in private practice, primarily small animal, since 1980, with two years as the staff veterinarian for the Humane Society of Huron Valley in Michigan. Dr. Eldredge is a member of the American Veterinary Medical Association and the New York State Veterinary Medical Association, and received the public service award from the Central New York Veterinary Medical Association.

Dr. Eldredge is a professional member of the Dog Writers' Association of America and the Cat Writers' Association. She has been a finalist in their writing contests many times and is the recipient of Muse Medallions and Maxwell Awards. Her previous books include the award-winning *Pills for Pets*; *Everything Guide to Dog Health* with Kim Thornton; the award-winning *Cancer and Your Pet* with Margaret Bonham; and the award-winning *Head of the Class*, a dog training book, with her daughter, Kate Eldredge. She is also the coauthor of *Dog Owner's Home Veterinary Handbook*.

Dr. Eldredge currently lives in upstate New York with six dogs, one cat, two donkeys, twelve sheep, one goat, five horses, one miniature horse, twelve ducks, and three primates: her husband, Chuck, her daughter, Kate, and her son, Tom. Her dogs are well trained; her cat is not.

Delbert G. Carlson, DVM

Del Carlson received his veterinary medical degree from the University of Minnesota Veterinary School in 1954 and interned at the Rawley Memorial Hospital in Springfield, Massachusetts.

He was a member of the Missouri Veterinary Medical Association and a past president of the Greene County Human Society.

Dr. Carlson is also the coauthor of *Dog Owner's Home Veterinary Handbook*.

Until his death, "Doc" could be found on his farm, caring for his horses, cats, and dogs. He consulted at the Carlson Pet Hospital, often volunteering to spend the night with a sick dog or cat.

Liisa D. Carlson, DVM

Liisa Carlson received her veterinary medical degree from the University of Missouri College of Veterinary Medicine and was a member of the Veterinary Honor Society, Phi Zeta. In 1988, Dr. Carlson returned to Springfield, Missouri, to join her father, Dr. Delbert Carlson, at the Carlson Pet Hospital.

She is a member of the American Veterinary Medical Society and the Southwestern Veterinary Medical Association, and is a founding member of the Emergency Clinics of Southwest Missouri. Dr. Carlson is also the coauthor of *Dog Owner's Home Veterinary Handbook*.

In 1994, Dr. Carlson was honored as Humanitarian of the Year by the Southwest Humane Society of Springfield. She says, "I was fortunate to work with my father and mentor before he retired in 1993. His knowledge, compassion, and love of animals are truly inspiring. I hope to follow with the same dedication and commitment that he has given for over 35 years."

James M. Giffin, MD

Jim Giffin graduated from Amherst College and received his medical degree from Yale University School of Medicine. After years of private surgery practice in Missouri and Colorado, Dr. Giffin was called to active duty during Operation Desert Storm, serving as chief of surgery at military hospitals in Alabama, Korea, and Texas.

Dr. Giffin had lifelong experience with cats, dogs, and horses. In 1969, he established a Great Pyrenees kennel and became active in breeding, showing, and judging dogs. He finished several champions, campaigned a Best-in-Show winner, and served on the board of directors of the Great Pyrenees Club of America. He is the coauthor of the award-winning books *The Complete Great Pyrenees*, *Dog Owner's Home Veterinary Handbook*, *Horse Owner's Veterinary Handbook*, and *Veterinary Guide to Horse Breeding*, and was a professional member of the Dog Writers' Association of America and the Cat Writers' Association.

Until his death in 2000, he made his home in western Colorado.

TECHNICAL REVIEWER

Lorraine Kogut Jarboe, DVM, DABVP, is a leading expert in companion animal medicine. She is a Diplomate of the American Board of Veterinary Practitioners (ABVP), certified in both the Feline Practice and the Canine/Feline Practice specialties. She has held many national leadership positions. In the ABVP, she is a past president and currently is a vice chair of the Examination Committee. In the American Association of Feline Practitioners (AAFP), she has been a member and chair of several committees, including the Practice Guidelines Committee and the Leadership Development Committee. She is also a member of the American Veterinary Medical Association (and represents the AAFP on its Clinical Practitioners Advisory Committee), the American Animal Hospital Association, the American Heartworm Society, and the Veterinary Information Network.

Now retired from the U.S. Army Reserve, she maintains a strong interest in regulatory medicine and zoonotic disease. She is a coauthor of *Feline Zoonoses Guidelines from the American Association of Feline Practitioners*. Her professional goal is to use her extensive training, knowledge, and experience to help shape the future of the practice of veterinary medicine.

LIST OF TABLES

GENERAL INDEX

NOTE: *Page numbers shown in boldface contain detailed coverage of the item.*

Skin diseases, **129–167**
  allergies, **151–156**
  with hair loss, 131
  hormonal, **160–162**
  immune-related, **156–157**
  infections
    fungal, **157–160**
    in newborn kittens, **473**
  itchy, 130–131
  with pus drainage, 132
Skin papilloma, 132
Skull fractures, 19, **331**
Slipping kneecap, **360–361**
Small intestine, 258, 259, 270
Smell, sense of, 221, 491, **536**
  loss of, in older cats, 536
Smoke inhalation, 23
Snake bites, **44–47**
Sneezing, **223–224**
Socialization, 453, 489
Sodium, levels of, 571
Sodium bicarbonate, 378
Sodium fluoroacetate, **34–35**
Sodium nitroprusside, 380
Solar dermatosis, **162**
Somalis, 314, 325
Sores, sunburn and, 211
Sore throat (pharyngitis), **253**
Soundness, musculoskeletal, 351
Spaying, 398, 422–425, **426–427**
Sperm, absence of, 415
Sperm count, 414–415
Sphingomyelinosis (Niemann-Pick), 338
Spiders, **43**
Spina bifida, **346**
Spinal arthritis (spondylitis), **345**
Spinal cord, 329, **342–346**
  infections, 345
  injuries, 278, **343–344,** 354, 390
  spina bifida, **346**
  tumors, **345–346**
Spinal lymphoma, 529
Spinal muscular atrophy in Maine Coon Cats, **345**
Spirometra mansonoides, 65
Splints, 17–19, 53
Spondylitis (spinal arthritis), **345, 364**
Spongiform degeneration, 338
Sporotrichosis, **99–100,** 132
Sprains, 354, **355**

Spraying. *See* Urine marking and spraying
Squamous cell cancers (carcinomas), 240, **523**
  of the eyelids, 183
Squamous cell skin, 212
Squinting, severe (blepharospasm), **178**
Staples, 51
Steroids, antibiotics and, **549**
Sticky Paws, 485
Stings, insect, **43–44**
Stomach, **264–267.** *See also* Abdomen; *and entries starting with "abdominal"*
  cancers, 529
  gastritis, **264–265**
  ulcers, **266–267,** 291
  worms, **66–67**
Stomatitis, **250–251**
Stones
  bladder (uroliths), 382–384, 386–388, **388–389**
  gallstones, 116, 288
Stools. *See* Feces (stools)
Strabismus (cross-eyed gaze), **177**
Strains, 354, **356**
Stress (stressful events), 57, 58, 297, 315
  FLUTD (feline lower urinary tract disease) and, 383, 386–388
  grooming as a response to, 161, 227
  immunity and, 83, 87, 89, 105
  inappropriate urination and litter box issues, **395–397**
  kittens and, 484, **488–490**
  queen's maternal behavior and, 450
Stricture, esophageal, **263**
String around the tongue, **249**
Stroke
  cerebral hemorrhage, **335**
  heat, **24–26,** 341
Strongyloides, 65–66
Struvite crystals (uroliths or stones), 382, 384, 387–389
Strychnine, **34**
Stud tail, 131, **164**
Submandibular abscesses, 256
Suckling reflex, 452
Sucralfate, 267
Suffocation, **22–24**
Sugar diabetes, **291–294**
Sulfa drugs, 72, 288
Sulfonamides, 70, 187

ART CREDITS

Unless otherwise noted here, photographs have been provided by the authors and by Krist Carlson, Dr. James Clawson, and Nancy Wallis.

Courtesy of BiteNot Products: 8

Courtesy of Delbert Carlson, DVM: 593 (top)

Krist Carlson: 125, 126

Courtesy of Liisa Carlson, MD: 593 (bottom)

J. Clawson: 2, 3, 5, 8, 9 (top and bottom right), *11, 12, 13, 18, 53, 54, 55, 174, 177, 184, 209, 232, 243, 299, 303, 313* (middle and bottom), *344, 555, 557, 559, 560, 564*

Courtesy of Cornell University: vii

Courtesy of James Giffin, MD: 594

Courtesy of KNOW Heartworms (American Heartworm Society, American Association of Feline Practitioners, and Pfizer Animal Health): 327

Courtesy of Brian Poteet, DVM, Diplomate ACVR: 360

Courtesy of Virbac Animal Health: 247 (top)

Wendy Christensen: 114, 122, 170, 204, 231, 241, 259, 297, 301, 311, 319, 330, 371, 405, 406, 429, 431, 435

Tom Eldredge: 592

Rose Floyd: 45, 284 (top)

Sue Giffin: 510

Weems Hutto: 4, 12 (bottom left)

Dusty Rainbolt: 7, 120, 466

Tammy Rao: 246, 546

Valerie Toukatly: 60, 64, 136, 145, 467

Sydney Wiley: v, 117, 118, 119, 129, 205, 221, 274, 350, 369, 399, 401, 412, 487, 504, 505, 509, 535

NOTES

NOTES